# TEXAS

## Real Estate
## LAW
### 10e

## CHARLES J. JACOBUS
### DREI, CREI

CENGAGE
Learning™

Australia • Brazil • Japan • Korea • Mexico • Singapore • Spain • United Kingdom • United States

**CENGAGE**
Learning™

**Texas Real Estate Law, 10e**
Charles J. Jacobus

Vice President/Editor-in-Chief: Dave Shaut

Executive Editor: Scott Person

Acquisitions Editor: Sara Glassmeyer

Developmental Editor: Arlin Kauffman

Senior Marketing Manager: Mark Linton

Frontlist Buyer, Manufacturing: Kevin Kluck

Art Director: Bethany Casey

Content Project Manager: Corey Geissler

Production Service: Newgen–Austin

Cover Designer: Chris Miller, Cmiller Design

Cover Image: iStockphoto/David Gilder

For product information and technology assistance, contact us at **Cengage Learning Customer & Sales Support, 1-800-354-9706**

For permission to use material from this text or product, submit all requests online at **www.cengage.com/permissions**

Further permissions questions can be emailed to **permissionrequest@cengage.com.**

Library of Congress Control Number: 2008926382
ISBN-13: 978-0-324-59248-1
ISBN-10: 0-324-59248-5

**Cengage Learning**
5191 Natorp Boulevard
Mason, OH 45040
USA

Cengage Learning products are represented in Canada by Nelson Education, Ltd.

For your course and learning solutions, visit **academic.cengage.com**

Purchase any of our products at your local college store or at our preferred online store **www.ichapters.com**

Printed in the United States of America
1 2 3 4 5 6 7 12 11 10 09 08

# Contents

## CHAPTER 9

## Contracts for the Sale of Real Estate 162

## CHAPTER 10

## Voluntary Conveyances 201

## CHAPTER 11

## Involuntary Conveyances 216

**APPENDIX**   **Subchapter E. Deceptive
Trade Practices and Consumer Protection
446**

# Preface

It's been over 25 years since this book was first published. Hopefully it reflects the benefit of the author's teaching during the entire time, with the tolerance of the school that will put up with the antics of the author. The book has grown more complex over the years, reflecting changing rules, statutes, and commonly accepted practice in the ever-changing real estate business. The first edition looks almost like *Ned in the First Reader*. It's a compliment to the Texas Real Estate Commission and our overall education system that we have been able to progress so far.

This new edition reflects a number of changes, including Texas Homestead Law (Chapter 3), reverse mortgages (Chapter 3), business organizations (Chapter 4), updates on the Texas Real Estate License Act (Chapter 7), revisions of deed forms (Chapter 10), changes in Notary Public legislation (Chapter 12), changes in mortgage forms (Chapter 13), closing procedures (Chapter 16), EPA rule changes (Chapter 20), and ad valorem tax law changes (Chapter 21).

As always, I am open to and appreciate constructive criticism of this textbook. Please direct all comments to the undersigned at JacobusBellaire@aol.com.

## Acknowledgments

I would like to acknowledge with a special thanks the following people for their assistance in preparing this edition of the textbook: Jim Howze, Bob Hale, Joe Irwin, Joe Goeters, Jack Wiedemer, Dorothy Lewis, Rita Santamaria,  Ken and Drue Combs, Gene Campbell, Mary Milford, Wade Whilden, Jr., Carol Cantrell, Rick Melamed, Kimberly Possert, Alex Binkley, Pat Streeter, and Justin Markel.

**Charles J. Jacobus**

## CHAPTER 1

# Introduction to the Basic Processes of Real Estate Law

## The Role of Real Estate Law

Brokers and lawyers will surely agree on one thing—that the real estate business is becoming more and more complex. The common-law doctrines that have controlled real estate law for centuries are eroding as a result of innumerable statutes, both at the federal and state level, which often seem to create more problems than they solve. However, this erosion is yielding some benefits in that it requires both brokers and lawyers to become more proficient and more sophisticated in keeping up with these areas of the law, and this could well force both brokers and lawyers to a more conscientious attitude in representing their various clients' interests. It has also drawn much more attention to the fact that real estate is a constantly changing subject and one that is rapidly becoming a field for true professionals.

Real estate laws have become so diversified that one can no longer think of real estate law as only one subject. Real estate law used to consist basically of brokerage, contract negotiation, drawing legal instruments, and establishing and litigating various property rights. Only a few years ago, real estate law was just a small segment of every lawyer's practice. Today, real estate involves a much broader scope of law as a result of constantly changing aspects of mortgage law, Texas homestead protection, governmental "takings" of real property, and modifications in agency theory. There are always interesting developments in contract law, securities law, and land-use planning law. In addition, there are frequent changes and supplements to landlord and tenant laws; mechanics' and materialmen's liens; and the probate, estate, and community property laws that are unique to this state. Then to this list, one must add the expanding role of federal legislation and the never-ending anathema of federal regulations.

The State Bar of Texas took a giant stride in recognizing the complications of real estate law when it began to board-certify three areas of real estate law specialization. After an attorney has had five years' practice and the requisite percentage of his practice is devoted to real estate law, he may take a series of examinations to qualify himself as a specialist in one or more of the three areas of real estate law: residential, commercial, and farm and ranch. This will now give consumers, real estate brokers, and out-of-state investors an additional indication of a lawyer's area of specialization when they are attempting to hire a qualified real estate lawyer.

As we accept this premise, there is yet a deeper problem that is much more intrinsic to the real estate business; that is, a client often has two representatives, his real estate agent and his attorney. Now, couple this with the fact that there are at least two clients in most transactions (making a total of at least six interested parties—all of whom are striving to "protect" someone), and the result is that the problems, stories, and third-hand information (and misinformation) contribute mistrust and confusion to what is already the overregulated field of real estate law. This results in brokers versus lawyers, brokers versus brokers, lawyers versus lawyers, clients versus clients, and every other permutation and combination that can logically result from the proverbial "can of worms."

# The Various Laws

It is interesting to note the various priorities of the laws and how they have come to interact with each other over their years of development. There are two basic sources of statutory law—one state, the other federal. In the area of real estate, state law has generally been considered controlling because of the uniqueness of the backgrounds and doctrines that various states have developed over the years. However, we are finding in more recent times that the federal government is now taking a vital interest in passing voluminous amounts of federal legislation to regulate the real estate business.

## Constitutions

The basic sources of law are found in our state and federal constitutions. The **U.S. Constitution** is the primary source and vests in all citizens of the United States certain inalienable rights that are considered inviolate and so basic to our system of government that no statute, ordinance, or any contractual right can waive its obligations or privileges. It is from this document that our individual freedoms and prohibition from abridging these individual freedoms are derived. For instance, discrimination on the grounds of race, color, or creed is considered patently unconstitutional, as is the denial of one's property rights without **"due process of law."** No statute, contract, or restriction upholding same will ever be enforced. Constitutional rights are, of course, the most fundamental legal rights that one can have, and these rights can only be altered by constitutional amendment.

It must also be remembered that this same Constitution gives the federal government extraordinary powers of enforcement when it comes to federal laws or federal issues that are considered within the parameters and scope of the Constitution. In the field of real estate, one of the more important areas comes under the interstate commerce clause. For example, Congress is finding more and more ways to regulate **intrastate** real estate activities because of the far-reaching effects these have on other states by virtue of the use of the U.S. mail, telephone, or other means of **interstate** commerce. This will be discussed in greater detail in a later chapter.

Texas also has a constitution, and the **Texas Constitution** contains certain inalienable rights that apply to residents of Texas. These rights basically come from the codification and derivation of the heritage of this state and embrace a myriad of subjects, including the Texas homestead laws, certain mechanics' and materialmen's lien laws, and the community property rights. One must remember that these rights are constitutional and cannot be waived by private contract or by subsequent statute or ordinance. The individual rights embraced by the Texas Constitution are far-reaching and are specified in much greater detail than those of the U.S. Constitution. However, if there is a conflict between the U.S. Constitution and the Texas Constitution, one can generally consider that the U.S. Constitution would control if the issues involve a federal issue (i.e., an issue over which power has been delegated to the federal government by the Constitution) rather than a substantive state question. If the issues involved are purely state issues and do not involve powers granted to the federal government or rights reserved to individuals, the U.S. Constitution would not be involved because of the Tenth Amendment, which reserves all powers not granted to the federal government to the states. If the court determines that a federal issue exists, the U.S. Constitution would control over the Texas Constitution.

## Statutes

The sources of law that affect property rights in greater detail (than what is contained in the federal or state constitutions) are those created by our legislatures, both state and federal, in their infinite wisdom. A law or a statute can be declared unconstitutional and its enforcement prohibited, which was what happened to laws on racial discrimination in the South for many years. The conflict between statutes and constitutions is often a very technical and complicated legal problem and need not be delved into at this point. However, it is clearly understood that all statutes have the force of law until declared unconstitutional by the courts. Texas state laws are codified and bound in volumes called *Vernon's Annotated Texas Statutes*, and the federal laws are likewise codified and bound in volumes called the *United States Code* and the *United States Code Annotated*. In case of a conflict between federal and state laws, federal law would control if there were a federal question involved. However, as in constitutional matters, if the issue is a particularly unique state matter of substantive law, the state statute would control, the theory being that under the Tenth Amendment to the U.S. Constitution and the derivation of local laws, the local statute is probably more pertinent to conditions as they exist in that state. In more current times, however, federal statutes seem to be getting more consideration because of the more liberal interpretation of the federal powers given by the courts.

## Ordinances and Regulations

Beyond the statutes at the state level, we generally encounter the various categories of municipal and county ordinances. City and county ordinances must, of course, undergo the same constitutional scrutiny that state statutes are subject to. The local ordinances are inferior to state statutes where there is a conflict in the two laws.

Beyond the statutes at the federal or state level, one also encounters the far more extensive rulings and **regulations** of state and federal agencies. The decisions made by those agencies that have **quasi-judicial power** (i.e., the agency can make binding decisions pursuant to the scope and powers under which that agency was created) are generally considered to have the force of law unless there is a clear abuse of discretion on the part of that agency.

The large number of regulations is a result of the fact that the various laws are often very broad, often vague, and always confusing. The particular agency whose duty it is to enforce the law, therefore, passes its own regulations that serve as guidelines on how that agency is going to interpret and enforce the law passed by the legislature. These regulations can be changed at the whim of the regulatory agency. For instance, the Internal Revenue Service can change its position on particular tax exemptions or how it will interpret a certain portion of the Internal Revenue Code. This same type of change in position can occur in all agencies, and each agency regularly publishes rules and regulations that can even expand that agency's scope of jurisdiction; a rule or regulation can be issued to clarify a stand that the agency may have taken previously, even though the effect on the taxpayer may be entirely different. These rules and regulations issued by the agencies have, of course, the effect of law, subject to review by the courts. It is in this area that the federal government is gaining more and more power, which may or may not have been the purpose of the original congressional acts enacting the legislation.

## Judicial Interpretation

Too often the interplay of people's emotions and interpretations of laws results in decisions being made by the final arbiter, the court system. Although sometimes unpredictable, this system is probably the best in the world. It is the basis from which precedents are set and priorities are maintained, and the courts often expose additional questions and interpretations that then become the foundation for new laws and statutes.

# Historical Background of the Courts

## Courts of Law

Our present court system arose from a centuries-old system of an objective third party making a fair and just decision to solve a problem between two adversaries. As our structure of the law developed through basic legal principles and doctrines of equity, the written aspects of a transaction were carefully and rigorously adhered to, as being important for an orderly society. Since the principles of law were fairly well settled back in the seventeenth century, when one might consider disorder as being a little more commonplace, this rigorous interpretation of law was probably a logical approach to setting up a civilized and ordered society. As a result, we fell into the situation where, if a man breached his agreement by being a day late for his mortgage payment, the mortgagee thereunder could foreclose, having the agreement strictly upheld in the courts of law. The mortgagor (who under Texas law is generally the purchaser), then, could lose his property because he was a day late in making his mortgage payment, or for some other minor breach of the contract between the parties, even though the circumstances surrounding this breach may have been beyond his control.

## Courts of Equity

As our system of justice evolved, however, **courts of equity** were established to soften the impact of these strict legal principles. These equity courts had particular significance in the area of real estate since real estate is considered unique and money damages could not compensate for its loss. The equity courts had **concurrent jurisdiction** with the courts of law, which were still in existence, and would impose their jurisdiction when fairness or **equity** dictated that the rules in some circumstances were too strict, sometimes changing the result. For instance, if a farmer could not make his mortgage payment on the day it was due because of matters beyond his control, the court of equity could impose its jurisdiction to do what was fair and would allow him to redeem by making his payment a day late, a month late, or whatever was "reasonable" to see that equity and justice were done.

The **courts of equity** imposed certain equitable principles. These principles, such as "**unjust enrichment**," "**unconscionable bargain**," and "irreparable harm," were used as reasons to find an equitable conclusion. They were created and construed ad infinitum (or ad nauseam, depending on your point of view) and resulted in literally hundreds of clichés, often called **equitable maxims**, which were ultimately used as **precedents** to control later decisions. Although having no true legal effect, these maxims could also be used as grounds for the defendant and were easy to roll off the lips, so that silver-tongued orators could constantly remind the court that "he who seeks equity must do equity"; "equity does that which ought to be done"; and the all-time favorite, "he who seeks equity must have clean hands."

It was in these courts that equitable remedies, such as specific performance, rescission and restitution, quantum meruit, and quasi-contractual recovery (to name a few), were imposed. These remedies differ from damages and actions in tort or contract, which arise under the law (and for which the damaged party can get money damages or recovery of his property). **Specific performance**, for instance, is generally granted where damages are not shown to be an adequate and just remedy and can only be enforced when there is not an adequate remedy at law. **Rescission** and **restitution** generally arise when the breach of the contract constitutes a failure of the consideration bargained for and the nonbreaching party prefers to rescind the contract and sue for complete restitution of whatever benefits have accrued to date. *Rescission* is the voiding of the contract or agreement. *Restitution* is the restoration of the parties' original rights. In this particular equitable remedy, the parties are put back in the same condition that they were in prior to execution of the contract. **Quasi-contractual principles** generally arise when there has been something material omitted in the original contract and the court imposes its own contractual principles as if these had been bargained for and written in the contract itself. This is also the principle behind **quantum meruit**, where one party performs his part of the obligation and the breaching party refuses to pay (or perform). In this situation, the court can impose quasi-contractual remedies in order that the party performing the duties be paid the reasonable value of the performance rendered. It is interesting to note that these remedies, which are not by any means all of the equitable remedies available, are not conferred by statute or by any other type of codified jurisprudential consideration. They are remedies that have evolved over the years through the courts seeking fair and just results.

# The Current Civil Court Systems

The Texas court system as it exists today, as well as the federal court system, has both legal and equitable jurisdiction merged into the same court. The distinction between the state courts, although their legal and equitable jurisdictions are similar, is not quite so simple. The jurisdictions of these courts are statutory and are maintained separate and distinct for the purposes of expediting the judicial process and facilitating access to the court system. To help simplify this explanation, we will discuss only the civil (and not the criminal) court systems. These civil court systems, for the purposes of this discussion, will be divided into two distinct and separate systems. The first is the state court system, which, in order of ascending importance, includes the justice of the peace courts and municipal courts, county courts, district courts, courts of civil appeals, and the Supreme Court of the State of Texas. The second system is the federal system, which, in order of ascending importance, includes the federal district courts, circuit courts of appeals, and the Supreme Court of the United States.

## State Courts

All courts have specific jurisdictional requirements, although some may overlap and some may vary from county to county. In general terms, however, the **justice of the peace courts**, small claims courts, and **municipal courts** have **original jurisdiction** for the first judicial proceeding for claims of not more than $10,000, *V.T.C.A., Government Code, §28.003, §27.031(a)(1)*. More important to real estate law, the justice of the peace courts have original jurisdiction in causes of action for forcible entry and detainer actions (eviction proceedings). These courts also have jurisdiction for suits relating to enforcement of deed restrictions in residential subdivisions that do not concern a structural change to the dwelling *§27.034(a)*. A losing party in the lower courts can appeal his cause of action to the county court if the judgment is in excess of $250, or in other cases as provided for by statute. In most counties, the **county courts** have no particular jurisdiction as it pertains to real estate except that of appellate jurisdiction for forcible entry and detainer cases (and probate in the less populous counties). In counties of two million or more, however, their jurisdiction is expanded. They have concurrent jurisdiction with **district courts** on deciding matters pertaining to title to real estate and other civil matters not to exceed $100,000, *V.T.C.A., Government Code, §25.1032(b)*. The **state district courts** are probably the more important courts in the area of real estate law. The district courts by statute have original jurisdiction in civil cases of suits for the trials of title to land and for the enforcement of liens thereon, and suits for the trial of right to property levied on by virtue of any writ of execution, sequestration, or attachment. Decisions made in these courts, subject to statutory regulation for appeals, are appealed to the **Texas Courts of Appeals** and the **Texas Supreme Court**. The significance of the appellate process will be discussed later.

## Federal Courts

The federal court system differs primarily in jurisdiction. Its jurisdiction basically depends either on a conflict of jurisdiction between individuals or states and an amount in excess of $10,000 in controversy, or on a question of controversy over federal law. There is only one level of trial courts, the **federal district court**. These cases can only be appealed to one of the **circuit courts of appeals** (there are currently 13). Texas is in the jurisdiction of the Fifth Circuit Court of Appeals, located in New Orleans, Louisiana. Beyond the Fifth Circuit Court of Appeals, the only avenue of appeal is to the **Supreme Court of the United States**. This is, of course, the highest court to which any case can be appealed.

## Court Procedure

Cases can bounce from the state system to the federal system and sometimes back, depending on jurisdictional problems, amounts in controversy, and what is termed **federal questions**. It is at this point that you may very often find the demarcation between an attorney who deals primarily in real estate law and one who deals primarily in trial practice. An attorney may have a particular expertise in the area of real estate law but may want a "trial attorney" or an attorney who specializes in trial practice, whether it is in federal jurisdictions or state jurisdictions, to handle the case because of the technicalities involved in trial and appellate procedure. In this age of specialization for attorneys, an increase in specialization in the field of real estate law or trial practice of this type is to be expected.

Interesting points about the trial procedure itself can give you some insight as to why these complexities exist and why the details of the law are often elusive to an individual reading the statutes, a text, or reported case law. First, there are two deciding bodies, the **judge** and the **jury**. In state courts, judges are elected to their positions, must be members of the bar in courts above the justice of the peace level, and are paid a salary according to state statute. In federal courts, the judges are appointed by the President of the United States, with the advice and consent of the Senate, and must pass very strict scrutiny prior to their appointment. The judge's role in the trial proceedings is to interpret the law. The jury's role is to decide the facts. There is no set rule as to when you can or cannot have a jury. The presence of a jury depends on the request of either of the parties involved.

The trial process works by putting the burden on the **plaintiff** (the party filing the suit) to present the evidence. After the plaintiff's attorney presents the case, the defendant's attorney responds and presents the defendant's case. After the defense has rested, there may be further examination of witnesses by either attorney. After the case is presented and arguments are given, the judge may render a decision. If there is a jury, the judge gives **charges** to the jury. These charges are generally prepared by the counsel for both sides under the direction of the judge. The charges that the judge reads are directions to the jury and explanations of what the Texas law is concerning the particular matter in controversy. It is the jury's job, then, to take the law and the facts as presented and to render a decision as to which party should prevail. It puts the burden on the jury to determine which of the witnesses was telling the truth, which of the witnesses may have been stretching the truth a bit, and, ultimately, what the facts actually were. If the jury comes back with a verdict for a party that is contrary to law, then the judge can overrule the jury and enter his own ruling.

Beyond the trial stage, the only question is whether or not there is a point of law in controversy. Since the jury has decided the facts, only points of law can be appealed to the appellate court. An appeal is made only to settle a question of law or incorrect ruling that a trial court may have made. There is no jury present beyond the trial court level. The appeal might be based on a rule of evidence, procedure, substantive law, jury charge, or other more technical legal points.

The process of appeals can be a relatively complicated process in regard to exactly what it takes to appeal to which court. In the state court system, there are proceedings in which you can appeal certain matters directly to the Texas Supreme Court, but most appeals go to the courts of civil appeals first. There are other rules for appeals from the courts of civil appeals to the Texas Supreme Court. The federal courts have similar, but not the same, rules. It is not pertinent to our discussion to go into detail over these matters, but it should be emphasized that the appellate process and the infinite amount of detail that arises during litigation make any litigation very complicated and difficult to predict. It has been said that when a case goes to court, no one wins. Considering the attorney's fees that are paid, the emotions that are dealt with, the time consumed, and the overloaded dockets that litigation promotes, the amount in controversy generally has to be fairly high before litigation is worthwhile.

Keeping in mind the foregoing basic substantive and procedural aspects of the law, one can appreciate the complexities that may arise in any given legal situation, particularly if any litigation should take place. It should also be kept in mind that the impact of the law is often flexible and most rules of law are general rules, subject to exceptions and equitable interpretation. These are the major reasons why, when asking your attorney a question, it is so difficult to get a simple answer in response. All of these alternatives, both procedural and substantive, must stay ever-present in the practitioner's "areas of concern" so that he can competently represent and advise his client.

## Alternative Dispute Resolution

An alternative to the court system, generally referred to as **alternative dispute resolution**, is rapidly gaining momentum. Courts have experienced congested dockets, infinite delays, and lengthy appeals following trial. Often, the litigants discover that victory leaves a plaintiff broke, although a winner. Alternative dispute resolution has arisen as an alternative where both parties may lose a little, but may soon make up their losses in the time that is saved with the elimination of lengthy trial procedures and legal bills. The most common alternative dispute resolution procedures are **mediation** and **arbitration**.

**Mediation.** Mediation is a process by which a neutral third party assists parties in the conflict situation, hopefully arriving at a mutually acceptable solution. The mediator facilitates communication between the parties in an effort to promote settlement but does not impose a decision. The mediator interacts between the parties in a confidential matter in an effort to promote a resolution to the dispute. A mediator is usually a person who is knowledgeable about the subject matter that is in dispute. Although the mediator will not make the decision, he will encourage the parties to reach a mutually acceptable solution, and to execute a settlement agreement at the end of the mediation. The agreement is an enforceable contract, with a lot of witnesses. A decision doesn't have to be reached. If the negotiations during the mediation result in an impasse (agreement not to agree), the dispute proceeds to court.

**Arbitration.** In an arbitration, a third party acts as judge and jury over the dispute. Under Texas law, arbitration is a binding procedure resembling a decision made by a trial judge. However, unlike a trial judge, an arbitrator need not support his award with an opinion. In arbitration, pretrial discovery is usually rapid and is conducted on a less formal basis and under less formal rules of civil procedure than at trial. Arbitration tends to achieve speedy resolution, at a much lower cost than a trial; under Texas law, arbitration is not an appealable decision, except in egregious circumstances involving the arbiter's fraud or conflict of interest.

Alternative dispute resolution has already had a positive result. Note that the Texas Real Estate Commission's promulgated real estate contracts provide for mediation, and the National Association of REALTORS® has published a Home Sellers/Home Buyers Dispute Resolution System program. There is little doubt that this will gain much wider acceptance over the next few years as courts become more familiar with enforcing mediation and arbitration procedures. It saves the courts a lot of time and allows them to concentrate on more complicated subject matter, and it creates significantly less expense in resolving disputes.

## Legal Research

One might wonder how the details of all the foregoing information become available to the attorney. It is basically through the efforts of research in a law library. Unlike any other type of library, a law library has an almost never-ending supply of legal treatises, articles, statutes, opinions, and case law reports. Every case above the district court level in the United States is written and bound in volumes called **Reporters**, which, along with statutes, digests, and current treaties, must constantly be updated.

Texas cases are reported in the **Southwestern Reporter**. Each volume is given a separate number as it is bound (more recent cases are reported in paperback volumes). Therefore, when searching for a case, one may find it cited as:

> *Case v. Case, 376 S.W.2d 941 (Tex. App.—Waco, 1936)*

if it is a Texas civil appeals court decision, or

> *Case v. Case, 376 S.W.2d 941 (Tex. 1936)*

if it is a Texas Supreme Court decision. Each of the foregoing examples indicates that the case is found in volume 376, page 941, of the *Southwestern Reporter*, second series. The material in parentheses refers to the court and year of decision. Statutes are normally cited as:

> *Tex. Rev. Civ. Stat. Ann., Art. 6573a, or V.T.C.A., Property Code, §5.001*

which indicates that the statute is located in the Texas civil statutes, Article 6573a, or the Property Code, Section 5.001. The statutes are updated with "pocket parts" located in the back of each volume. A plethora of sources are now also available on computer.

As the student reads the following chapters, he will find a number of citations as authority for a particular point of law. These are not intended to dazzle or baffle the reader but only to give him additional sources of information for more in-depth study.

After this cursory introduction, one will find the following chapters are more detailed and concern the more substantive aspects of real property law. For the layman, it is important to recognize these problem areas and understand them as such, always keeping in mind that they should be avoided at all costs. Any advice, litigation, or negotiation of a client's rights should be left for the attorneys who are trained to handle such problems. It is the attorney's job to relieve real estate agents and other laypersons from shouldering this type of burden.

## ■ SUMMARY

Real estate is rapidly becoming a field for true professionals. Similarly, real estate law is becoming more and more specialized.

There are two sources of law: federal and state. Both sources have constitutional foundations. The source of law that affects property rights in greater detail is the statutes that are created by the state and federal legislatures. The city ordinances and federal regulations may apply the respective laws in even greater detail.

The modern court system is a blend of courts of law and equity. The state civil court system consists of justice of the peace courts, county courts, district courts, courts of civil appeals, and the Texas Supreme Court. The federal court system consists of the federal district courts, the circuit courts of appeals, and the U. S. Supreme Court. The rules and procedures regarding jurisdiction are defined by the various statutes and consist of substantive as well as procedural laws concerning jurisdiction, trial, and appellate procedure. Basically, the jury decides all questions of facts, whereas the court (the judge) decides questions of law.

Texas has adopted a policy of encouraging alternative dispute resolution as a less expensive alternative to judicial proceedings. They include arbitration and mediation.

## CHAPTER 2

# Estates in Land—
# Freehold Estates

An **estate in land** has been defined as the degree, quantity, nature, and extent of interest that a person has in real property. *Pan Amer. Petroleum Corp. v. Cain*, 355 S.W.2d 506 (Tex. 1962). The estates in land that will be discussed in this chapter are **freehold estates**. Freehold estates are estates that manifest some title to real property. They include estates in fee simple, life estates, fee on conditional limitation, fee on condition subsequent, and fee on condition precedent. The laterally severed estates of mineral rights and air rights will also be discussed as freehold estates. The title to freehold estates is created in the deed or will and is not to be confused with, and should be distinguished from, statutory estates and leasehold estates. **Statutory estates** are created by statute and vest in the person rather than in the land itself. These statutory estates will be discussed in the next chapter and consist of homestead rights, community property rights, cemetery lots, and Texas water rights. **Leasehold estates** will be discussed in Chapter 18, Landlord and Tenant Relationships.

# Introduction

As an introduction to the concept of freehold estates in land, there are two basic theories that need to be explained to help establish guidelines for further discussion.

## Rule against Perpetuities

The first basic restriction on ownership of real property is provided Rule against for in the Texas Constitution under Article I, Section 26, and is commonly called the **Rule against Perpetuities**. This provision reads as follows:

> **§26. Perpetuities and Monopolies; Primogeniture or Entailments**
> Perpetuities and monopolies are contrary to the genius of a free government, and shall never be allowed, nor shall the law of primogeniture or entailments ever be in force in this State.

The reasoning behind the Rule against Perpetuities is the idea that land, by its nature, is unique and cannot be held forever by any one interest. This theory has not always been accepted. For example, there is an opposing theory in common law whereby a person could be the grantee of certain property, along with the "heirs of his body." This would enable the property to literally stay in a man's family so long as there were descendants. During this time in history, **primogeniture** (the right of the first male child to become legal title holder to the property upon the death of the father) and **entailments** (only heirs of the individual's body could get fee title to the property) were the common practice for real property owners, and wealthy families could effectively monopolize real estate holdings. This is not the case today. According to Article I, Section 26, of the state constitution, such conditions simply cannot exist in this state because they are "contrary to the genius of a free government." The Rule against Perpetuities, then, encourages the free transferability and conveyance of property and prohibits the monopolizing and perpetual control of certain real estate interests. The Rule is interpreted to prohibit unreasonable restraints on a person's ability to sell. Any vested interest in real estate must vest in some grantee no later than 21 years after some life in being plus the normal period of gestation. *Forderhouse* v. *Cherokee Water Co.*, 623 S.W.2d 435 (Tex. Civ. App.—Texarkana, 1981); *Peveto* v. *Starkey*, 645 S.W.2d 770 (Tex. 1982). For instance, one can't convey title to a grandson when there are no children, as there is no named person who can accept title within the time period prescribed by the Rule. If it is possible that the ownership interest created could not vest within the time prescribed by the Rule against Perpetuities, it is void. *Garza* v. *Sun Oil Company*, 727 S.W.2d 115 (Tex. Civ. App.—San Antonio, 1986). It is important to remember that as we discuss real estate in Texas, this constitutional doctrine underlies all theories of ownership of real property, whether it deals with estates in land or ownership control. Subsequent statutes have been passed that further reinforce this constitutional provision, and it continues to be one of the basic underlying theories in Texas real estate law.

## Title Theory Versus Lien Theory

A second basic theory in Texas is that once title is conveyed, the grantee (subsequent owner) gets a true legal title. In some states it is felt that if the grantee's property is mortgaged, the owner has only an equitable title, and the lender (mortgagee) has true legal title. In those states, the borrower (mortgagor), or owner, only has an equitable ownership in the property until the mortgage is paid in full. In Texas, the theory is reversed. The homeowner, although his or her home is not fully paid for, has legal title to the property; the lender has a lien on the property. Therefore, Texas is called a **lien theory** state. Those states that recognize the mortgagee as legal title holder to the property are called **title theory** states.

Since Texas is a lien theory state, the owner of the property has full **legal title** to the property. Those who have any interest in the property that is subordinate or inferior to the owner's full legal title of the property have what is commonly referred to as an **equity interest**, or **equitable title**, to that property. Those who have an equity interest in the property (there could be quite a large number) will therefore have certain rights under equitable principles in addition to whatever perfected rights they might have in law to try to enforce their rights in that property.

# Freehold Estates

With the foregoing fundamentals in mind, the topic of freehold estates will be somewhat easier to understand. We will explore virtually every type of freehold estate recognized in this state to give some insight into just how complicated legal titles and equity interests can become. The primary concepts to remember are that all freehold estates are (1) interests in real estate, (2) of indefinite duration, and (3) *inheritable* by the heirs of the owner. Let's look at each type separately.

## Types of Freehold Estates

**Fee Simple Estates.** A **fee simple estate** is one entitling the owner to:

1. The entire property
2. Unconditional powers of disposition during his life.
3. Title that descends to heirs and legal representatives upon his death.
4. Includes both legal and equitable title. *Field* v. *Rudes*, 204 S.W.2d 1 (Tex. Civ. App.—El Paso, 1947).

This is the type of estate that most people consider when they think of a clear, unencumbered title. The four criteria referred to above indicate virtually everything that makes a title "good" for the landowner. The vast majority of real estate conveyed in this state is conveyed with fee simple title. Statutorily, an estate in fee simple in Texas is presumed unless otherwise specified in the conveyancing instrument, *V.T.C.A., Property Code, §5.001.*

It is important to remember that a fee simple title can be encumbered, however, in that there could be other equitable or legal interests as exceptions or reservations to the title. Although encumbered, the estate being conveyed would still be termed a fee simple estate because it had the four criteria set out above. Easements, liens, and other encumbrances on real estate do not mean that the quality of the estate one gets is less than fee simple, but they can limit the owner's use of that estate. Specific encumbrances will be discussed in detail in later chapters.

**Life Estates.** Estates that are less than fee simple limit the grantee's title and rights to varying degrees. Texas recognizes three types of life estates: (1) a *regular life* estate; (2) a life estate *pur autre vie*; and (3) a *homestead* life estate (discussed in Chapter 3). A **life estate**, generally defined, is an estate for the life of some person, along with a second estate that is termed a **remainder interest**. No particular form of words is necessary to create a life estate. It is created by a deed or a will where the grantor manifests an intention to convey to some person the right to possess, use, or enjoy the property during the period of some person's life. In a regular life estate, the property is generally conveyed to a grantee for the term of the grantee's life. The remainder interest, which entitles the remainderman to possession of the property at a future date, is another separate estate. It vests fee simple in the remainderman upon the grantee's death. *Collins* v. *New*, 558 S.W.2d 108 (Tex. Civ. App.—Corpus Christi, 1977). For instance, I could specify in a deed that I convey my house to my brother for his life; then upon his death it would pass to my wife. This conveyance would create a life estate in my brother and a remainder interest in my wife. Thus, it becomes clear that two estates are created: One is the life estate; the other is the remainder interest.

It is important to understand that you can also convey the life estate interest to someone for the life of someone else. Life estates for the life of another person are called life estates **pur autre vie**. Assuming the same situation, I could convey the life estate to my brother for the life of my great-great-grandfather. The life estate then would pass upon the death of my great-great-grandfather, and the remainder interest would go to my wife.

The life estate may be conveyed separate and apart from the remainder interest. *Arensberg* v. *Drake*, 693 S.W.2d 588 (Tex. Civ. App.—Houston, 1985). When a life estate is conveyed, whoever purchases and takes possession of the estate under those rights does so subject to the life of the life estate grantee and the rights of the remainder interest. The interest of the life estate holder may be worth a very small amount of money, and the remainder interest may be worth a large amount of money, or vice versa. Remember that in this situation, the life estate holder has a limited legal and equitable interest, subject to the rights of the holder of the remainder interest. Neither party may encumber the property if it results in waste, deterioration, or alienation of the other's rights. For instance, the life tenant, although he may have the right to possession of the property for his life, cannot unreasonably encumber, waste, or allow the property to deteriorate during his occupancy if it adversely affects the right of the person holding the remainder interest. Conversely, the life estate owner can maximize the economic benefits (oil and gas leases, leasing it to tenants, or developing it), but must also bear the expense of maintenance (taxes, expenses, and insurance). See *V.A.T.S., Property Code*, §5.009. The **remainderman** (the owner of the future interest) likewise cannot do anything that would affect the rights of the life tenant. Since the remainderman is a nonoccupant and a nontenant, he has less opportunity to create waste and deterioration in the property. However, both parties have the right to hypothecate, encumber, or convey their particular interests in the real estate as long as this does not result in waste, deterioration, or alienation of any of the other's interest.

**Fee on Conditional Limitation.** A **fee on conditional limitation** exists where the estate is limited to the happening of a certain event, and when such event happens, the estate is terminated and reverts to the grantor by what is called an *eo instanti* reversion; that is, the estate automatically goes back to the grantor. This estate is also referred to as a **determinable fee**, or **fee simple defeasible**.

An example of this type of estate would be one where the estate is created by the use of a deed saying that the property will be conveyed to the grantee "so long as" intoxicating beverages are never served on the premises. The reversionary and remainder interests here are truly contingent because none of the parties know if the condition will ever be breached. Deeds creating a fee on conditional limitation generally use the words "so long as," "until," or "during," which intend to limit the type of estate that is going to be created. Upon the happening of that certain stated event, the estate automatically transfers, by operation of law, to either the grantor, by reversion, or to some third party, by executory remainder. The important thing to remember in this type of estate is that the estate is transferred automatically upon the happening of that certain stated conditional event. *Bagby* v. *Bredthauer*, 627 S.W.2d 190 (Tex. Civ. App.—Austin, 1981).

**Fee on Condition Subsequent.** A **fee on condition subsequent** is very similar to a fee on conditional limitation. In fact, these two estates are so similar that many judicial opinions demonstrate confusion as to what is the actual difference between the two types of estates. However, authorities generally seem to agree that the basic distinction between a fee on condition subsequent and a fee on conditional limitation lies in the fact that the fee on conditional limitation has an *automatic* reversion upon the happening of that event, but the fee on condition subsequent gives the grantor the *right* to terminate the estate by reversion, rather than the automatic reversion provided for by the fee on conditional limitation. *Field* v. *Shaw*, 535 S.W.2d 3 (Tex. Civ. App.—Amarillo, 1976). This right of reversion of the fee on condition subsequent is properly called the **right of reentry**.

An example of this type of conveyance would be one with the use of a deed that would convey the property to the grantee "on the condition that" or "provided however," or "if" the property would never be used for the sale or service of alcohol or intoxicating beverages. This type of language used in the fee on condition subsequent implies that the grantor, his heirs, or assigns would have the right to reenter the property and take it back. However, they can only get title back if they take the initiative to reenter the property within a reasonable time. It is not an automatic reversion. Isn't this fun?

**Fee on Condition Precedent.** A **fee on condition precedent** is a title passed by a deed such that the title will not take effect in the named grantee until a condition is performed. For instance, a conveyance may be made to a grantee with the condition being that full fee title will not vest until the grantee has built a house on the property within two years from the date of the conveyance. This would indicate a fee on condition precedent. In this case, the grantee gets a conditional title that will only be fully vested upon the construction of the home as provided for in the deed. This specifically applies when there is no other consideration shown in the deed, or no other value has changed hands except this particular condition. One generally finds this type of title when the grantor is attempting to increase the value of his property by encouraging development of the adjacent property. Using this time limitation, the grantor forces the purchaser to build something on the adjacent property to enhance the value of his own property. This type of conveyance might be used by developers to encourage home building in a subdivision. Texas does not favor the fee on condition precedent. Where other conditions have to be performed or have been performed, especially when a full value has been paid, the fee on condition precedent is generally considered by courts to be a fee on condition subsequent. In the more accepted common-law usage, this type of estate is referred to as a **springing executory use**. The case law in Texas, however, does not utilize this term very freely.

After reviewing these types of estates, it becomes apparent that remainder interests can be of two types: (1) a vested remainder or (2) a contingent remainder. A **vested remainder** exists if, at any moment during the continuance of the previous estate (in this case, the life estate), the remainderman is ready to come into possession whenever that life estate terminates. For instance, a vested remainder would exist if I conveyed a regular life estate in property, with no additional qualifications. The remainderman knows my estate will definitely terminate at some time in the future, and he or his heirs will ultimately take title to the real estate. A **contingent remainder**, on the other hand, requires some sort of fulfillment of a condition before it may vest. An example of a contingent remainder interest would be a life estate to my brother with a remainder interest to go to my wife upon his death, if she is not married at that time. If she is married at that time, the **future interest** would not vest in her upon my brother's death but would create a **reversionary interest** that would revert to my legal heirs or to another party whose remainder interest may not be contingent. In the life estate, however, the grantor generally keeps no reversionary interest. If there is no remainder interest, there can be no life estate, and the law may presume a fee simple in the life estate grantee. *Benson* v. *Greenville*

*Nat. Exchange Bank*, 253 S.W.2d 918 (Tex. Civ. App.—Texarkana, 1953). In common-law states, there is often a careful discrimination between a contingent remainder and what is termed a **shifting executory use** in the future interest. Texas case law appears to consider the terms basically the same. See *Deviney* v. *Nationsbank*, 993 S.W.2d 443 (Tex. App.—Waco 1999).

Table 2.1 may be helpful in identifying the possible estates that can be created in freehold estates other than fee simple, as well as serving as an introduction for the following explanations of other types of estates. It's getting more fun!

Since Texas courts tend to presume fee simple, they look with disfavor on any type of deed that creates an estate that is less than fee simple. Courts have frequently interpreted a deed whose conditions are not very clear to create nothing more than a covenant (contractual promise) between the original grantor and the grantee. If the court construes these conditions as mere covenants, the remedies are injunctive relief and damages. In those cases, forfeiture of title would not occur. *Humphrey* v. *C G. Jung Education Center of Houston*, 714 F.2d 477 (5th Cir.—1983).

## Subsurface Estates

**Mineral interests**, of course, have been a primary concern for a state like Texas where the **subsurface rights** have proved to be of enormous value. Subsurface rights are, by all means, a freehold estate and an interest in land; and the owner of a fee title may separate his estate on the surface from the minerals underneath and sell one type of estate (the subsurface), while reserving the other (the surface) for his own use and benefit. Even when the subsurface is leased, it is really a conveyance, giving the grantee a **determinable fee** (see "Fee on Conditional Limitation"). *Cherokee Water Co.* v. *Forderhouse*, 641 S.W.2d 522 (Tex. 1982). The severance of minerals in an "oil, gas, and other minerals" clause in an instrument of conveyance includes all substances within the ordinary and natural meaning of "oil, gas, and other minerals," whether or not their presence or value is known at the time of extraction. That is, "oil, gas, and other minerals" includes virtually everything a person anticipates as a valuable mineral. *Moser* v. *United States Steel Corp.*, 676 S.W.2d 99 (Tex. 1984). Some minerals, however, are not considered valuable enough to be minerals. As a matter of law in Texas, those substances that have been held not to be minerals have been building stone, limestone, caliche, and surface shale.

**Lateral Severance.** It is important to understand that estates in land are generally considered to go to the center of the earth. Therefore, a separation of the mineral estate results in a **lateral severance** (separation) of the surface estate from the mineral estate. *Bagby* v. *Bredthauer*, supra. The grantor will own the surface estate, whereas a grantee of the mineral interest will own or lease the subsurface estate.

| Table 2.1 | Possible estates created in freehold estates. | |
|---|---|---|
| **Reversionary Interest** | **Current Estate** | **Future Interest** |
| None | Life estate | Remainderman (vested or contingent remainder) |
| Automatic | Fee on conditional limitation | Contingent remainder ("so long as," "until," "during") |
| Right of reentry | Fee on condition subsequent | Contingent remainder ("on the condition that," "provided however," "if") |
| | Possible possession | Fee on condition precedent (ripens to fee simple) |

Lateral severance generally provides that the grantee or lessee of the mineral estate may acquire rights to drill for oil and gas or to mine certain minerals on the grantor's property, but that the grantor still owns the surface estate, subject to the rights of the mineral owner. They are estates of equal dignity, so neither is greater than the other so far as title is concerned, and they remain separate estates in land. If the owner of the surface estate reacquires the subsurface estate, the laterally severed estates still retain their separate identity and do not "merge" into one title again. *Gibson Drilling Co.* v. *B&N Petroleum, Inc.*, 703 S.W.2d 822 (Tex. Civ. App.—Tyler, 1986).

An interesting legal precedent has created some recent conflict in determining whether or not there is a lateral severance. In confirming a prior Texas Supreme Court case, the Texas Supreme Court in *Reed* v. *Wylie*, 554 S.W.2d 169 (Tex. 1977) upheld the Texas rule that "a grant or reservation of 'minerals' or 'mineral rights' should not be construed to include a substance that must be removed by methods that will, in effect, consume or deplete the surface estate." The court further stated that a substance is not a mineral if substantial quantities of that substance lie so near the surface that the production will entail the stripping away and substantial destruction of the surface. This ruling has extreme importance in strip-mining coal, iron ore, and other substances that may have been presumed to be passed along with the mineral estate. If these substances are so near the surface that extraction depletes the land surface, there is no lateral severance, and the substances belong to the surface estate and the compensation paid must include compensation to the surface owner for surface destruction. The "surface" is defined, as a matter of Texas law, to be on the surface of the real estate, or within 200 feet of the surface. *Reed* v. *Wylie*, 597 S.W.2d 743 (Tex. 1980).

In certain circumstances the mineral owner has the statutory duty to reclaim the surface after surface mining under the **Texas Uranium Surface Mining and Reclamation Act**, *V.T.C.A., Nat. Res. Code Ann., §1 through 1.001 et seq.*, and the **Surface Mining Control and Reclamation Act of 1977**, 30 *U.S.C., §12.01.* These obligations may include the mineral owner's submitting and effecting a reclamation plan, or the surface owner's having the land classified as unsuitable for surface mining if he believes the land cannot be reclaimed. *Moser* v. *United States Steel Corp.*, supra.

**Dominant Estates.** The concept of lateral severance creates a conflict of estates—between the surface owner's right to use the surface and the mineral owner's right to enter upon that surface to extract the minerals. Under Texas law, the mineral owner has what is termed the **dominant estate**. This means that he has the right to use the surface, reasonably, to exercise his rights to extract the minerals from the subsurface. *Humble Oil and Refining Co.* v. *Williams*, 420 S.W.2d 133 (Tex. 1967). This applies even to an owner of a portion of the subsurface interests. *Byrom* v. *Pendley*, 717 S.W.2d 602 (Tex. 1986). There has been case law that indicates that this concept of the dominant estate has been eroded somewhat and must be exercised reasonably. *Getty Oil Co.* v. *Jones*, 470 S.W.2d 618 (Tex. 1971). However, this case law has not yet been expanded so as to curtail severely the long-standing superior rights of the mineral owner (the dominant estate).

Any subsequent purchaser of the **surface rights** of the property, then, would get a fee title to that property, subject to the rights of the mineral owner. This may seem at first to be a disadvantage to the surface owner. However, practically speaking, the surface owner often leases the subsurface and will receive benefits from the mining of those minerals in terms of a percentage of the payments or of the production of these minerals (called "**royalties**"), and perhaps even a cash "bonus" payment, in addition to the lease payments for allowing the mineral owner to mine the subsurface minerals. These payments or "royalty interests" are not real estate, and the owner relinquishes his right to explore for minerals himself. *Martin* v. *Schneider*, 622 S.W.2d 620 (Tex. Civ. App.—Corpus Christi, 1981); *Bagby* v. *Bredthauer*, supra.

It is generally anticipated that the surface will be diminished somewhat during extraction, and the surface owner calculates the value of this diminution into the compensation he receives. *Moser* v. *United States Steel Corp.*, supra.

**Waiver of Surface Rights.** In the event the surface owner does not wish to have the mineral owner on his property mining or extracting the minerals, he may reserve the sole rights to the surface estate, which may force the mineral estate owner to enter upon some adjacent property to extract the minerals through various underground drilling and excavation methods. Over many years, however, this has created a number of problems for developers who have purchased property that never had surface control reserved. Legislation now provides that in counties of population greater than 400,000 (or counties of population greater than 140,000 that border counties with population greater than 400,000) subdivisions can apply to the Railroad Commission to designate drill sites and eliminate some of these conflicts, *V.T.C.A., Natural Resources Code, §92.001.*

## Realty Versus Personality

An interesting area of mineral estates has involved the concept of **realty** versus **personalty**. In the ownership of mineral estates, it is easy to understand that all the oil, gas, and other minerals that may be in a mineral estate are, of course, considered to be real property. Once those minerals are extracted, or the oil and gas reach the wellhead, the oil, gas, and other minerals are considered personalty rather than real property. Recently, developments that further complicate this concept have arisen from the use of underground storage of oil and gas in salt domes along the Gulf Coast area. These domes, being large underground caverns, have proved to be an effective method of storing large amounts of oil and gas beneath the surface for future use. The Texas Supreme Court has made it clear that it considers that the minerals that are put back into the subsurface remain personalty rather than reverting back to real estate. *Humble Oil and Refining Co.* v. *West*, 508 S.W.2d 812 (Tex. 1974).

Beyond the lateral severance and surface rights concepts, one steps into a deep chasm of very technical and heavily litigated oil and gas law. For the purposes of real estate law, it is most important to understand that if one acquires any property that does not include the subsurface estate and use of the surface estate has not been reserved, the owner of the surface estate may, at some future date, be surprised to find an oil company moving in its drilling equipment. This would obviously alter the rights of the person using the surface estate.

## Air Rights

There is another area of lateral severance, one that involves the ownership of **air rights**. Although the concept of air rights is self-explanatory to some extent, air rights tend to be nebulous and difficult to describe. One can sell his air rights, mortgage them, and treat them as any other right in real estate. Generally, however, the concept of air rights means that the surface owner has control over his own air rights. They may, however, be subject to certain limitations.

The initial question of air rights came from owners of property that was adjacent to airports. It was understood that between the two private property owners (the private owner of the airport and the private owner of the property abutting that airport) there had to be a conflict of rights over the noise, pollution, and litter that accompanied the airplanes taking off and landing, conditions that adversely affected the adjacent property owners. This type of law found its origin in the law of nuisance, where one property owner would sue the other property owner because of the nuisance value and discomfort caused by the other property owner.

In more current times, and with municipal ownership of airports, we have found that there is a more severe problem between the concepts of private ownership and the public welfare. In the airport situation, we find that for the good of the public there are certain ordinances that are passed prohibiting the building of structures adjacent to an airport because of both the danger to air traffic and the discomfort of the people adjacent to the airport. The municipality generally exercises its power of eminent domain to acquire adjacent property or to restrict use of the adjacent property to uses that would be nondetrimental to the public airport purposes.

**Overhead Structures.** Other air rights concepts have involved the construction of overhead walkways, office buildings, and similar structures across streets. Such structures may create pollution hazards, carbon monoxide buildup, and other unhealthy conditions if the structure is not built properly. In these cases, of course, we have the conflict of the private ownership of the building versus the public welfare of people who have to live adjacent to or pass through the type of environment this building might create.

**Solar Rights.** Another concept of air rights is the right of adjacent property owners to the sun. Although this is a very old concept, one that generally was predicated on creating "tunnels" in downtown areas, a new type of legal problem could arise because of the use of solar energy.

## ■ SUMMARY

An estate in land has been defined as the degree, quantity, nature, and extent of interest that a person has in real property. Freehold estates consist primarily of fee simple estates, life estates, fee on conditional limitations, fee on condition subsequent, and fee on condition precedent. Mineral estates are freehold estates resulting primarily from lateral severance, a separation of the surface and subsurface estates. Texas considers the mineral estate to be the dominant estate, allowing the subsurface mineral owner the right to cross the surface estate to extract the minerals. Air rights are another severable estate, which concerns air traffic, overhead structures, and solar rights.

## ■ CASE STUDIES FOR DISCUSSION

1. Mr. and Mrs. Richard Carl Crawford were owners of royalty interests in oil and gas produced from their property. The natural reservoir of gas contained under their property had been substantially depleted by the oil company. The oil company then proceeded to inject gas reserves into the existing reservoir for storage purposes. The oil company maintained that all gas extracted from this reservoir in the future was their personalty. The landowners maintained that at least part of the gas still in the ground was a real property right on which they deserved payment for their royalty interest. What legal ramifications do you see?

## CHAPTER 3

# Estates in Land— Statutory Estates

**Statutory estates** are also estates that have been created by statute or constitution that also typify the degree, quantity, nature, and extent of an individual's interest in his real estate. These are estates created by the Texas Constitution or by Texas statute that attach to the real property as a result of the rights of the individual's ownership of that real property. These statutory estates exist concurrently with the estates discussed in Chapter 2. The particular statutory estates to be considered in this chapter are homesteads, community property rights, water rights, and cemetery lots.

## Homesteads

The change in Texas homestead laws over the last few years have been dramatic. At one time, Texas had the most significant homestead protection in the United States. New people moving into Texas and perhaps, more importantly, new lenders moving into Texas have effected a significant change in Texas homestead protection and the rights of Texas citizens. Through the advent of interstate banking and mortgage lending procedures, a lot of pressure was put on the Texas legislature to conform to lending practices which are common in other states. We have not repealed homestead protection so far, but one can see even more changes looming on the horizon. We will discuss traditional homestead theory and its historical significance, then talk about the new changes.

The **homestead** in Texas is a place used as a home or as a place to exercise the calling or business for a family or a single adult person; it provides a secure place of which the family cannot be deprived. The homestead laws accomplish this protection by providing certain exemptions for the Texas homeowner against his creditors. Therefore, only specific, allowed liens are enforceable against homesteads, and one cannot encumber the homestead for any other purpose (we call this protection against forced sales). Since a homestead is a statutory estate, it may not be assigned or conveyed in such a manner as to vest one's homestead rights in someone else, as this estate vests solely in the claimant. Even the U.S. Supreme Court has acknowledged the significance of the Texas homestead as an estate in land, describing it as giving "each spouse in a marriage a separate and undivided possessory interest . . . which is only lost by death or abandonment and which may not be compromised either by the other spouse or by his or her heirs" along with remainder interests that vest in each spouse, similar to a life estate with a future interest. *United States* v. *Rodgers*, 103 S. Ct. 2132, 2138 (1983). Creditors cannot force the sale of the subject property of either spouse as claiming a homestead interest, even though the other spouse may have abandoned it or conveyed it away. *Taylor* v. *Mosty Brothers Nursery, Inc.*, 777 S.W.2d 568 (Tex. App.—San Antonio, 1989). The Texas homestead laws have been so consistently upheld and liberally construed that it is important to understand some of the history behind these homestead laws (keep the Alamo in the back of your mind).

## History

The earliest homestead exemption law was passed as a statute on January 26, 1839. It had three basic purposes:

1. To preserve the integrity of the family as a basic element of social organization and to encourage colonization.
2. To provide the debtor with a home for his or her family and some means of support and to recoup economic losses so that the family would not become a burden upon the public.
3. To retain and pioneer the feeling of freedom and a sense of independence deemed necessary to the continued existence of democratic institutions.

As a statute, the homestead exemption was subject to change by the legislature, which is not the most predictable group of lawmakers. This made the security provided by the homestead law somewhat questionable. Therefore, the homestead exemption laws first became constitutionally incorporated in 1845 to put them beyond the reach of the state legislators. Therefore, in order to change any of the homestead laws, it is now a requirement that this be done by amendment to the Texas Constitution, which requires a vote of the people of the state. The legislature, by its own acts, cannot repeal, change, or modify the Texas homestead law except by passing statutes in furtherance of the basic purposes as set forth in the Texas Constitution.

As stated in Chapter 1, it is important to remember that constitutional rights cannot be waived by mere contractual interest or by an intent of the parties. As a constitutional right, the homestead exemption is an exemption that vests in every single Texas resident regardless of whatever he or she may have signed or agreed to after those homestead rights have been properly vested.

## Who Can Claim?

It should be noted that homestead rights have traditionally been interpreted to vest in individuals, not in companies or business entities such as trusts or partnerships. *Bradley* v. *Pacific Southwest Bank, F.S.B.* 960 F.2d 502 (5th Cir.—1992). Remember, it is to protect the borrower from overreaching creditors. As a result, it limits the type of liens that a person can have on homestead property. Therefore, this "protection" limits a homeowner's rights to encumber their property, and always has.

From time to time, people have attempted to create corporations or trusts to own real estate in an effort to get around the homestead protection (i.e., so they could encumber their property and use it as collateral for a mortgage). In general terms, courts have held that you cannot do that. It was nothing more than a contractual effort to get around the constitutional homestead protection, *In Re Rubarts*, 896 F.2d 107 (5th Cir.—1990).

The 1993 legislature amended the Tax Code to allow for a residence homestead held in a qualifying trust to make the trust available for homestead exemptions for ad valorem tax purposes. So, at least for property tax purposes, a trust may have homestead exemptions, *V.T.C.A., Tax Code, §11.13(j)*. This was apparently passed in an effort to allow homestead owners to take advantage of tax and probate benefits, which are available to trust so that one could use their homestead property as a part of the trust assets, but not lose the ad valorem tax exemption that is available in some jurisdictions. The general rule, though, is still very simple. You cannot contract around your homestead protections. Our most recent change in the amendments to the Constitution, however, has greatly expanded the number of liens that one can put on their homestead.

## Constitutional Criteria

At one time the only liens that were enforceable against homestead were purchase money mortgages, taxes due thereon and home improvements (and then only when properly contracted for by both husband and wife). The amended Article 16 Section 50 of the Texas Constitution, now very complicated, has added to these basic liens, and is set forth in its entirety below (it used to be a few lines long, now look at it!):

> **§50. Homestead; protection from forced sale; mortgages, trust deeds and liens**
> Sec. 50 (a) The homestead of a family, or of a single adult person, shall be, and is hereby protected from forced sale, for the payment of all debts except for:
>
> (1) the **purchase money** thereof, or a part of such purchase money;
>
> (2) the **taxes** due thereon;
>
> (3) an **owelty of partition** imposed against the entirety of the property by a court order or by a written agreement of the parties to the partition, including a debt of one spouse in favor of the other spouse resulting from a division or an award of a family homestead in a divorce proceeding;
>
> (4) the **refinance of a lien** against a homestead, including a federal tax lien resulting from the tax debt of both spouses, if the homestead is a family homestead, or from the tax debt of the owner;
>
> (5) work and material used in **constructing** new improvements thereon, if contracted for in writing, or work and material used to repair or renovate existing improvements thereon if:
>
>> (A) the work and material are contracted for in writing, with the consent of both spouses, in the case of a family homestead, given in the same manner as is required in making a sale and conveyance of the homestead;
>>
>> (B) the contract for the work and material is not executed by the owner or the owner's spouse before the fifth day after the owner makes written application for any extension of credit for the work and material, unless the work and material are necessary to complete immediate repairs to conditions on the homestead property that materially affect the health or safety of the owner or person residing in the homestead and the owner of the homestead acknowledges such in writing;
>>
>> (C) the contract for the work and material expressly provides that the owner may rescind the contract without penalty or charge within three days after the execution of the contract by all parties, unless the work and material are necessary to complete immediate repairs to conditions on the homestead property that materially affect the health or safety of the owner or person

residing in the homestead and the owner of the homestead acknowledges such in writing; and

(D) the contract for the work and material is executed by the owner and the owner's spouse only at the office of a third-party lender making an extension of credit for the work and material, an attorney at law, or a title company;

(6) an **extension of credit** that:

(A) is secured by a voluntary lien on the homestead created under a written agreement with the consent of each owner and each owner's spouse;

(B) is of a principal amount that when added to the aggregate total of the outstanding principal balances of all other indebtedness secured by valid encumbrances of record against the homestead does not exceed 80 percent of the fair market value of the homestead on the date the extension of credit is made;

(C) is without recourse for personal liability against each owner and the spouse of each owner, unless the owner or spouse obtained the extension of credit by actual fraud;

(D) is secured by a lien that may be foreclosed upon only by a court order;

(E) does not require the owner or the owner's spouse to pay, in addition to any interest, fees to any person that are necessary to originate, evaluate, maintain, record, insure, or service the extension of credit that exceed, in the aggregate, three percent of the original principal amount of the extension of credit;

(F) is not a form of open-end account that may be debited from time to time or under which credit may be extended from time to time unless the open-end account is a home equity line of credit;

(G) is payable in advance without penalty or other charge;

(H) is not secured by any additional real or personal property other than the homestead;

(I) is not secured by homestead property designated for agricultural use as provided by statutes governing property tax, unless such homestead property is used primarily for the production of milk;

(J) may not be accelerated because of a decrease in the market value of the homestead or because of the owner's default under other indebtedness not secured by a prior valid encumbrance against the homestead;

(K) is the only debt secured by the homestead at the time the extension of credit is made unless the other debt was made for a purpose described by Subsections (a)(1)-(a)(5) or Subsection (a)(8) of this section;

(L) is scheduled to be repaid:

(i) in substantially equal successive periodic installments, not more often than every 14 days and not less often than monthly, beginning no later than two months from the date the extension of credit is made, each of which equals or exceeds the amount of accrued interest as of the date of the scheduled installment; or

(ii) if the extension of credit is a home equity line of credit, in periodic payments described under Subsection (t)(8) of this section;

(M) is closed not before:

(i) the 12th day after the later of the date that the owner of the homestead submits an application to the lender for the extension of credit or the date that the lender provides the owner a copy of the notice prescribed by Subsection (g) of this section;

(ii) one business day after the date that the owner of the homestead receives a final itemized disclosure of the actual fees, points, interest, costs, and charges that will be charged at closing. If a bona fide emergency or another good cause exists and the lender obtains the written consent of the owner, the lender may provide the documentation to the owner or the lender may modify previously provided documentation on the date of closing; and

(iii) the first anniversary of the closing date of any other extension of credit described by Subsection (a)(6) of this section secured by the same homestead property, except a refinance described by Paragraph (Q)(x)(f) of this subdivision, unless the owner on oath requests an earlier closing due to a state of emergency that:

(a) has been declared by the president of the United States or the governor as provided by law; and

(b) applies to the area where the homestead is located;

(N) is closed only at the office of the lender, an attorney at law, or a title company;

(O) permits a lender to contract for and receive any fixed or variable rate of interest authorized under statute;

(P) is made by one of the following that has not been found by a federal regulatory agency to have engaged in the practice of refusing to make loans because the applicants for the loans reside or the property proposed to secure the loans is located in a certain area:

(i) a bank, savings and loan association, savings bank, or credit union doing business under the laws of this state or the United States;

(ii) a federally chartered lending instrumentality or a person approved as a mortgagee by the United States government to make federally insured loans;

(iii) a person licensed to make regulated loans, as provided by statute of this state;

(iv) a person who sold the homestead property to the current owner and who provided all or part of the financing for the purchase;

(v) a person who is related to the homestead property owner within the second degree of affinity or consanguinity; or

(vi) a person regulated by this state as a mortgage broker; and

(Q) is made on the condition that:

(i) the owner of the homestead is not required to apply the proceeds of the extension of credit to repay another debt except debt secured by the homestead or debt to another lender;

(ii) the owner of the homestead not assign wages as security for the extension of credit;

(iii) the owner of the homestead not sign any instrument in which blanks are left to be filled in;

(iv) the owner of the homestead not sign a confession of judgment or power of attorney to the lender or to a third person to confess judgment or to appear for the owner in a judicial proceeding;

(v) the lender, at the time the extension of credit is made, provide the owner of the homestead a copy of all documents signed by the owner related to the extension of credit;

(vi) the security instruments securing the extension of credit contain a disclosure that the extension of credit is the type of credit defined by Section 50(a)(6), Article XVI, Texas Constitution;

(vii) within a reasonable time after termination and full payment of the extension of credit, the lender cancel and return the promissory note to the owner of the homestead and give the owner, in recordable form, a release of the lien securing the extension of credit or a copy of an endorsement and assignment of the lien to a lender that is refinancing the extension of credit;

(viii) the owner of the homestead and any spouse of the owner may, within three days after the extension of credit is made, rescind the extension of credit without penalty or charge;

(ix) the owner of the homestead and the lender sign a written acknowledgment as to the fair market value of the homestead property on the date the extension of credit is made;

(x) except as provided by Subparagraph (xi) of this paragraph, the lender or any holder of the note for the extension of credit shall forfeit all principal and interest of the extension of credit if the lender or holder fails to comply with the lender's or holder's obligations under the extension of credit and fails to correct the failure to comply not later than the 60th day after the date the lender or holder is notified by the borrower of the lender's failure to comply by:

(a) paying to the owner an amount equal to any overcharge paid by the owner under or related to the extension of credit if the owner has paid an amount that exceeds an amount stated in the applicable Paragraph (E), (G), or (O) of this subdivision;

(b) sending the owner a written acknowledgement that the lien is valid only in the amount that the extension of credit does not exceed the percentage described by Paragraph (B) of this subdivision, if applicable, or is not secured by property described under Paragraph (H) or (I) of this subdivision, if applicable;

(c) sending the owner a written notice modifying any other amount, percentage, term, or other provision prohibited by this section to a permitted amount, percentage, term, or other provision and adjusting the account of the borrower to ensure that the borrower is not required to pay more than an amount permitted by this section and is not subject to any other term or provision prohibited by this section;

(d) delivering the required documents to the borrower if the lender fails to comply with Subparagraph (v) of this paragraph or obtaining the appropriate signatures if the lender fails to comply with Subparagraph (ix) of this paragraph;

(e) sending the owner a written acknowledgement, if the failure to comply is prohibited by Paragraph (K) of this subdivision, that the accrual of interest and all of the owner's obligations under the extension of credit are abated while any prior lien prohibited under Paragraph (K) remains secured by the homestead; or

(f) if the failure to comply cannot be cured under Subparagraphs (x)(a)-(e) of this paragraph, curing the failure to comply by a refund or credit to the owner of $1,000 and offering the owner the right to refinance the extension of credit with the lender or holder for the remaining term of the loan at no cost to the owner on the same terms, including interest, as the original extension of credit with any modifications necessary to comply with this section or on terms on which the owner and the lender or holder otherwise agree that comply with this section; and

(xi) the lender or any holder of the note for the extension of credit shall forfeit all principal and interest of the extension of credit if the extension of credit is made by a person other than a person described under Paragraph (P) of this subdivision or if the lien was not created under a written agreement with the consent of each owner and each owner's spouse, unless each owner and each owner's spouse who did not initially consent subsequently consents;

(7) a **reverse mortgage**; or

(8) the conversion and refinance of a personal property lien secured by a **manufactured home** to a lien on real property, including the refinance of the purchase price of the manufactured home, the cost of installing the manufactured home on the real property, and the refinance of the purchase price of the real property.

(b) An owner or claimant of the property claimed as homestead may not sell or abandon the homestead without the consent of each owner and the spouse of each owner, given in such manner as may be prescribed by law.

(c) No mortgage, trust deed, or other lien on the homestead shall ever be valid unless it secures a debt described by this section, whether such mortgage, trust deed, or other lien shall have been created by the owner alone, or together with his or her spouse, in case the owner is married. All pretended sales of the homestead involving any condition of defeasance shall be void.

(d) A purchaser or lender for value without actual knowledge may conclusively rely on an affidavit that designates other property as the homestead of the affiant and that states that the property to be conveyed or encumbered is not the homestead of the affiant.

(e) A refinance of debt secured by a homestead and described by any subsection under Subsections (a)(1)–(a)(5) that includes the advance of additional funds may not be secured by a valid lien against the homestead unless:

(1) the refinance of the debt is an extension of credit described by Subsection (a)(6) of this section; or

(2) the advance of all the additional funds is for reasonable costs necessary to refinance such debt or for a purpose described by Subsection (a)(2), (a)(3), or (a)(5) of this section.

(f) A refinance of debt secured by the homestead, any portion of which is an extension of credit described by Subsection (a)(6) of this section, may not be secured by a valid lien against the homestead unless the refinance of the debt is an extension of credit described by Subsection (a)(6) or (a)(7) of this section. SECTION 3. Subsection (g), Section 50, Article XVI, Texas Constitution, is amended to read as follows:

(g) An extension of credit described by Subsection (a)(6) of this section may be secured by a valid lien against homestead property if the extension of credit is not closed before the 12th day after the lender provides the owner with the following written notice on a separate instrument:

"NOTICE CONCERNING EXTENSIONS OF CREDIT DEFINED BY SECTION 50(a)(6), ARTICLE XVI, TEXAS CONSTITUTION:

"SECTION 50(a)(6), ARTICLE XVI, OF THE TEXAS CONSTITUTION ALLOWS CERTAIN LOANS TO BE SECURED AGAINST THE EQUITY IN YOUR HOME. SUCH LOANS ARE COMMONLY KNOWN AS EQUITY LOANS. IF YOU DO NOT REPAY THE LOAN OR IF YOU FAIL TO MEET THE TERMS OF THE LOAN, THE LENDER MAY FORECLOSE AND SELL YOUR HOME. THE CONSTITUTION PROVIDES THAT:

"(A) THE LOAN MUST BE VOLUNTARILY CREATED WITH THE CONSENT OF EACH OWNER OF YOUR HOME AND EACH OWNER'S SPOUSE;

"(B) THE PRINCIPAL LOAN AMOUNT AT THE TIME THE LOAN IS MADE MUST NOT EXCEED AN AMOUNT THAT, WHEN ADDED

TO THE PRINCIPAL BALANCES OF ALL OTHER LIENS AGAINST YOUR HOME, IS MORE THAN 80 PERCENT OF THE FAIR MARKET VALUE OF YOUR HOME;

"(C) THE LOAN MUST BE WITHOUT RECOURSE FOR PERSONAL LIABILITY AGAINST YOU AND YOUR SPOUSE UNLESS YOU OR YOUR SPOUSE OBTAINED THIS EXTENSION OF CREDIT BY ACTUAL FRAUD;

"(D) THE LIEN SECURING THE LOAN MAY BE FORECLOSED UPON ONLY WITH A COURT ORDER;

"(E) FEES AND CHARGES TO MAKE THE LOAN MAY NOT EXCEED 3 PERCENT OF THE LOAN AMOUNT;

"(F) THE LOAN MAY NOT BE AN OPEN-END ACCOUNT THAT MAY BE DEBITED FROM TIME TO TIME OR UNDER WHICH CREDIT MAY BE EXTENDED FROM TIME TO TIME UNLESS IT IS A HOME EQUITY LINE OF CREDIT;

"(G) YOU MAY PREPAY THE LOAN WITHOUT PENALTY OR CHARGE;

"(H) NO ADDITIONAL COLLATERAL MAY BE SECURITY FOR THE LOAN;

"(I) THE LOAN MAY NOT BE SECURED BY AGRICULTURAL HOMESTEAD PROPERTY THAT IS DESIGNATED FOR AGRICULTURAL USE AS OF THE DATE OF CLOSING, UNLESS THE AGRICULTURAL HOMESTEAD PROPERTY IS USED PRIMARILY FOR THE PRODUCTION OF MILK;

"(J) YOU ARE NOT REQUIRED TO REPAY THE LOAN EARLIER THAN AGREED SOLELY BECAUSE THE FAIR MARKET VALUE OF YOUR HOME DECREASES OR BECAUSE YOU DEFAULT ON ANOTHER LOAN THAT IS NOT SECURED BY YOUR HOME;

"(K) ONLY ONE LOAN DESCRIBED BY SECTION 50(a)(6), ARTICLE XVI, OF THE TEXAS CONSTITUTION MAY BE SECURED WITH YOUR HOME AT ANY GIVEN TIME;

"(L) THE LOAN MUST BE SCHEDULED TO BE REPAID IN PAYMENTS THAT EQUAL OR EXCEED THE AMOUNT OF ACCRUED INTEREST FOR EACH PAYMENT PERIOD;

"(M) THE LOAN MAY NOT CLOSE BEFORE 12 DAYS AFTER YOU SUBMIT A LOAN APPLICATION TO THE LENDER OR BEFORE 12 DAYS AFTER YOU RECEIVE THIS NOTICE, WHICHEVER IS LATER; AND MAY NOT WITHOUT YOUR CONSENT CLOSE BEFORE ONE BUSINESS DAY AFTER THE DATE ON WHICH YOU RECEIVE A COPY OF YOUR LOAN APPLICATION IF NOT PREVIOUSLY PROVIDED AND A FINAL ITEMIZED DISCLOSURE OF THE ACTUAL FEES, POINTS, INTEREST, COSTS, AND CHARGES THAT WILL BE CHARGED AT CLOSING; AND IF YOUR HOME WAS SECURITY FOR THE SAME TYPE OF LOAN WITHIN THE PAST YEAR, A NEW LOAN SECURED BY THE SAME PROPERTY MAY NOT CLOSE BEFORE ONE YEAR HAS PASSED FROM THE CLOSING DATE OF THE OTHER LOAN, UNLESS ON OATH YOU REQUEST AN EARLIER CLOSING DUE TO A DECLARED STATE OF EMERGENCY;

"(N) THE LOAN MAY CLOSE ONLY AT THE OFFICE OF THE LENDER, TITLE COMPANY, OR AN ATTORNEY AT LAW;

"(O) THE LENDER MAY CHARGE ANY FIXED OR VARIABLE RATE OF INTEREST AUTHORIZED BY STATUTE;

"(P) ONLY A LAWFULLY AUTHORIZED LENDER MAY MAKE LOANS DESCRIBED BY SECTION 50(a)(6), ARTICLE XVI, OF THE TEXAS CONSTITUTION;

"(Q) LOANS DESCRIBED BY SECTION 50(a)(6), ARTICLE XVI, OF THE TEXAS CONSTITUTION MUST:

"(1) NOT REQUIRE YOU TO APPLY THE PROCEEDS TO ANOTHER DEBT EXCEPT A DEBT THAT IS SECURED BY YOUR HOME OR OWED TO ANOTHER LENDER;

"(2) NOT REQUIRE THAT YOU ASSIGN WAGES AS SECURITY;

"(3) NOT REQUIRE THAT YOU EXECUTE INSTRUMENTS WHICH HAVE BLANKS FOR SUBSTANTIVE TERMS OF AGREEMENT LEFT TO BE FILLED IN;

"(4) NOT REQUIRE THAT YOU SIGN A CONFESSION OF JUDG-MENT OR POWER OF ATTORNEY TO ANOTHER PERSON TO CONFESS JUDGMENT OR APPEAR IN A LEGAL PROCEEDING ON YOUR BEHALF;

"(5) PROVIDE THAT YOU RECEIVE A COPY OF YOUR FINAL LOAN APPLICATION AND ALL DOCUMENTS YOU SIGN AT CLOSING;

"(6) PROVIDE THAT THE SECURITY INSTRUMENTS CONTAIN A DISCLOSURE THAT THIS LOAN IS A LOAN DEFINED BY SEC-TION 50(a)(6), ARTICLE XVI, OF THE TEXAS CONSTITUTION;

"(7) PROVIDE THAT WHEN THE LOAN IS PAID IN FULL, THE LENDER WILL SIGN AND GIVE YOU A RELEASE OF LIEN OR AN ASSIGNMENT OF THE LIEN, WHICHEVER IS APPROPRIATE;

"(8) PROVIDE THAT YOU MAY, WITHIN 3 DAYS AFTER CLOS-ING, RESCIND THE LOAN WITHOUT PENALTY OR CHARGE;

"(9) PROVIDE THAT YOU AND THE LENDER ACKNOWLEDGE THE FAIR MARKET VALUE OF YOUR HOME ON THE DATE THE LOAN CLOSES; AND

"(10) PROVIDE THAT THE LENDER WILL FORFEIT ALL PRINCI-PAL AND INTEREST IF THE LENDER FAILS TO COMPLY WITH THE LENDER'S OBLIGATIONS UNLESS THE LENDER CURES THE FAILURE TO COMPLY AS PROVIDED BY SECTION 50(a)(6)(Q) (x), ARTICLE XVI, OF THE TEXAS CONSTITUTION; AND

"(R) IF THE LOAN IS A HOME EQUITY LINE OF CREDIT:
"(1) YOU MAY REQUEST ADVANCES, REPAY MONEY, AND REBORROW MONEY UNDER THE LINE OF CREDIT;
"(2) EACH ADVANCE UNDER THE LINE OF CREDIT MUST BE IN AN AMOUNT OF AT LEAST $4,000;
"(3) YOU MAY NOT USE A CREDIT CARD, DEBIT CARD, SIMI-LAR DEVICE, OR PREPRINTED CHECK YOU DID NOT SOLICIT, TO OBTAIN ADVANCES UNDER THE LINE OF CREDIT;
"(4) ANY FEES THE LENDER CHARGES MAY BE CHARGED AND COLLECTED ONLY AT THE TIME THE LINE OF CREDIT IS ESTABLISHED AND THE LENDER MAY NOT CHARGE A FEE IN CONNECTION WITH ANY ADVANCE;
"(5) THE MAXIMUM PRINCIPAL AMOUNT THAT MAY BE EX-TENDED, WHEN ADDED TO ALL OTHER DEBTS SECURED BY YOUR HOME, MAY NOT EXCEED 80 PERCENT OF THE FAIR MARKET VALUE OF YOUR HOME ON THE DATE THE LINE OF CREDIT IS ESTABLISHED;

"(6) IF THE PRINCIPAL BALANCE UNDER THE LINE OF CREDIT AT ANY TIME EXCEEDS 50 PERCENT OF THE FAIR MARKET VALUE OF YOUR HOME, AS DETERMINED ON THE DATE THE LINE OF CREDIT IS ESTABLISHED, YOU MAY NOT CONTINUE TO REQUEST ADVANCES UNDER THE LINE OF CREDIT UNTIL THE BALANCE IS LESS THAN 50 PERCENT OF THE FAIR MARKET VALUE; AND
"(7) THE LENDER MAY NOT UNILATERALLY AMEND THE TERMS OF THE LINE OF CREDIT. "THIS NOTICE IS ONLY A SUMMARY OF YOUR RIGHTS UNDER THE TEXAS CONSTITUTION. YOUR RIGHTS ARE GOVERNED BY SECTION 50, ARTICLE XVI, OF THE TEXAS CONSTITUTION, AND NOT BY THIS NOTICE."

If the discussions with the borrower are conducted primarily in a language other than English, the lender shall, before closing, provide an additional copy of the notice translated into the written language in which the discussions were conducted.

(h) A lender or assignee for value may conclusively rely on the written acknowledgment as to the fair market value of the homestead property made in accordance with Subsection (a)(6)(Q)(ix) of this section if:

(1) the value acknowledged to is the value estimate in an appraisal or evaluation prepared in accordance with a state or federal requirement applicable to an extension of credit under Subsection (a)(6); and

(2) the lender or assignee does not have actual knowledge at the time of the payment of value or advance of funds by the lender or assignee that the fair market value stated in the written acknowledgment was incorrect.

(i) This subsection shall not affect or impair any right of the borrower to recover damages from the lender or assignee under applicable law for wrongful foreclosure. A purchaser for value without actual knowledge may conclusively presume that a lien securing an extension of credit described by Subsection (a)(6) of this section was a valid lien securing the extension of credit with homestead property if:

(1) the security instruments securing the extension of credit contain disclosure that the extension of credit secured by the lien was the type of credit defined by Section 50(a)(6), Article XVI, Texas Constitution;

(2) the purchaser acquires the title to the property pursuant to or after the foreclosure of the voluntary lien; and

(3) the purchaser is not the lender or assignee under the extension of credit.

(j) Subsection (a)(6) and Subsections (e)–(i) of this section are not severable, and none of those provisions would have been enacted without the others. If any of those provisions are held to be preempted by the laws of the United States, all of those provisions are invalid. This subsection shall not apply to any lien or extension of credit made after January 1, 1998, and before the date any provision under Subsection (a)(6) or Subsections (e)–(i) is held to be preempted.

(k) "Reverse mortgage" means an extension of credit:

(1) that is secured by a voluntary lien on homestead property created by a written agreement with the consent of each owner and each owner's spouse;

(2) that is made to a person who is or whose spouse is 62 years or older;

(3) that is made without recourse for personal liability against each owner and the spouse of each owner;

(4) under which advances are provided to a borrower based on the equity in a borrower's homestead;

(5) that does not permit the lender to reduce the amount or number of advances because of an adjustment in the interest rate if periodic advances are to be made;

(6) that requires no payment of principal or interest until:

(A) all borrowers have died;

(B) the homestead property securing the loan is sold or otherwise transferred;

(C) all borrowers cease occupying the homestead property for a period of longer than 12 consecutive months without prior written approval from the lender; or

(D) the borrower:

(i) defaults on an obligation specified in the loan documents to repair and maintain, pay taxes and assessments on, or insure the homestead property;

(ii) commits actual fraud in connection with the loan; or

(iii) fails to maintain the priority of the lender's lien on the homestead property, after the lender gives notice to the borrower, by promptly discharging any lien that has priority or may obtain priority over the lender's lien within 10 days after the date the borrower receives the notice, unless the borrower:

(a) agrees in writing to the payment of the obligation secured by the lien in a manner acceptable to the lender;

(b) contests in good faith the lien by, or defends against enforcement of the lien in, legal proceedings so as to prevent the enforcement of the lien or forfeiture of any part of the homestead property; or

(c) secures from the holder of the lien an agreement satisfactory to the lender subordinating the lien to all amounts secured by the lender's lien on the homestead property;

(7) that provides that if the lender fails to make loan advances as required in the loan documents and if the lender fails to cure the default as required in the loan documents after notice from the borrower, the lender forfeits all principal and interest of the reverse mortgage, provided, however, that this subdivision does not apply when a governmental agency or instrumentality takes an assignment of the loan in order to cure the default;

(8) that is not made unless the owner of the homestead attests in writing that the owner received counseling regarding the advisability and availability of reverse mortgages and other financial alternatives;

(9) that requires the lender, at the time the loan is made, to disclose to the borrower by written notice the specific provisions contained in Subdivision (6) of this subsection under which the borrower is required to repay the loan;

(10) that does not permit the lender to commence foreclosure until the lender gives notice to the borrower, in the manner provided for a notice by mail related to the foreclosure of liens under Subsection (a)(6) of this section, that a ground for foreclosure exists and gives the borrower at least 30 days, or at least 20 days in the event of a default under Subdivision (6)(D)(iii) of this subsection, to:

(A) remedy the condition creating the ground for foreclosure;

(B) pay the debt secured by the homestead property from proceeds of the sale of the homestead property by the borrower or from any other sources; or

(C) convey the homestead property to the lender by a deed in lieu of foreclosure; and

(11) that is secured by a lien that may be foreclosed upon only by a court order, if the foreclosure is for a ground other than a ground stated by Subdivision (6)(A) or (B) of this subsection.

(l) Advances made under a reverse mortgage and interest on those advances have priority over a lien filed for record in the real property records in the county where the homestead property is located after the reverse mortgage is filed for record in the real property records of that county.

(m) A reverse mortgage may provide for an interest rate that is fixed or adjustable and may also provide for interest that is contingent on appreciation in the fair market value of the homestead property. Although payment of principal or interest shall not be required under a reverse mortgage until the entire loan becomes due and payable, interest may accrue and be compounded during the term of the loan as provided by the reverse mortgage loan agreement.

(n) A reverse mortgage that is secured by a valid lien against homestead property may be made or acquired without regard to the following provisions of any other law of this state:

(1) a limitation on the purpose and use of future advances or other mortgage proceeds;

(2) a limitation on future advances to a term of years or a limitation on the term of open-end account advances;

(3) a limitation on the term during which future advances take priority over intervening advances;

(4) a requirement that a maximum loan amount be stated in the reverse mortgage loan documents;

(5) a prohibition on balloon payments;

(6) a prohibition on compound interest and interest on interest;

(7) a prohibition on contracting for, charging, or receiving any rate of interest authorized by any law of this state authorizing a lender to contract for a rate of interest; and

(8) a requirement that a percentage of the reverse mortgage proceeds be advanced before the assignment of the reverse mortgage.

(o) For the purposes of determining eligibility under any statute relating to payments, allowances, benefits, or services provided on a means-tested basis by this state, including supplemental security income, low-income energy assistance, property tax relief, medical assistance, and general assistance:

(1) reverse mortgage loan advances made to a borrower are considered proceeds from a loan and not income; and

(2) undisbursed funds under a reverse mortgage loan are considered equity in a borrower's home and not proceeds from a loan.

(p) The advances made on a reverse mortgage loan under which more than one advance is made must be made according to the terms established by the loan documents by one or more of the following methods:

(1) at regular intervals;

(2) at regular intervals in which the amounts advanced may be reduced, for one or more advances, at the request of the borrower; or

(3) at any time by the lender, on behalf of the borrower, if the borrower fails to timely pay any of the following that the borrower is obligated to pay under the loan documents to the extent necessary to protect the lender's interest in or the value of the homestead property:

(A) taxes;

(B) insurance;

(C) costs of repairs or maintenance performed by a person or company that is not an employee of the lender or a person or company that directly or indirectly controls, is controlled by, or is under common control with the lender;

(D) assessments levied against the homestead property; and

(E) any lien that has, or may obtain, priority over the lender's lien as it is established in the loan documents.

(q) To the extent that any statutes of this state, including without limitation, Section 41.001 of the Texas Property Code, purport to limit encumbrances that may properly be fixed on homestead property in a manner that does not permit encumbrances for extensions of credit described in Subsection (a)(6) or (a)(7) of this section, the same shall be superseded to the extent that such encumbrances shall be permitted to be fixed upon homestead property in the manner provided for by this amendment.

(r) The supreme court shall promulgate rules of civil procedure for expedited foreclosure proceedings related to the foreclosure of liens under Subsection (a)(6) of this section.

(s) The Finance Commission of Texas shall appoint a director to conduct research on availability, quality, and prices of financial services and research the practices of business entities in the state that provide financial services under this section. The director shall collect information and produce reports on lending activity of those making loans under this section. The director shall report his or her findings to the legislature not later than December 1 of each year.

(t) A home equity line of credit is a form of an open-end account that may be debited from time to time, under which credit may be extended from time to time and under which:

(1) the owner requests advances, repays money, and reborrows money;

(2) any single debit or advance is not less than $4,000;

(3) the owner does not use a credit card, debit card, preprinted solicitation check, or similar device to obtain an advance;

(4) any fees described by Subsection (a)(6)(E) of this section are charged and collected only at the time the extension of credit is established and no fee is charged or collected in connection with any debit or advance;

(5) the maximum principal amount that may be extended under the account, when added to the aggregate total of the outstanding principal balances of all indebtedness secured by the homestead on the date the extension of credit is established, does not exceed an amount described under Subsection (a)(6)(B) of this section;

(6) no additional debits or advances are made if the total principal amount outstanding exceeds an amount equal to 50 percent of the fair market value of the homestead as determined on the date the account is established;

(7) the lender or holder may not unilaterally amend the extension of credit; and

(8) repayment is to be made in regular periodic installments, not more often than every 14 days and not less often than monthly, beginning not later than two months from the date the extension of credit is established, and:

(A) during the period during which the owner may request advances, each installment equals or exceeds the amount of accrued interest; and

(B) after the period during which the owner may request advances, installments are substantially equal.

(u) The legislature may by statute delegate one or more state agencies the power to interpret Subsections (a)(5)-(a)(7), (e)-(p), and (t), of this section. An act or omission does not violate a provision included in those subsections if the act or omission conforms to an interpretation of the provision that is:

(1) in effect at the time of the act or omission; and

(2) made by a state agency to which the power of interpretation is delegated as provided by this subsection or by an appellate court of this state or the United States.

**In General.** This statute is long, so let's summarize some of the more important provisions. As amended, the provision of the Texas homestead laws now protects the homeowner from forced sale for payment of all debts except:

1. Purchase money, or part thereof, which must be coincident with the transfer of title.

2. Taxes due thereon (ad valorem taxes).

3. An owelty of partition, including a debt of one spouse in favor of the other spouse resulting from a division of an award of a family homestead in a divorce proceeding (owelty liens are discussed later in this chapter).

4. The refinance of a lien against a homestead, including a federal tax lien resulting from the tax debt of other spouses, if the homestead is a family homestead, or from the tax debt of the owner, *United States* v. *Rodgers*, supra; provided that the IRS files a lien and then gets the personal approval of the regional director of the Internal Revenue Service, *26 U.S.C.A., §6334(e)*, and *Crowder* v. *Benchmark Bank*, 919 S.W.2d 657 (Tex. 1996).

5. Work and material used in constructing new improvements thereon, if contracted for in writing; or work and material used to repair or renovate existing improvements thereon (provided the owner has a five-day cooling off period and a three-day right of recision).

    This new provision is somewhat confusing. How do you know if improvements are new, or simply repaired and renovated? There is very little guidance on this. Only one case, *Spradlin* v. *Jim Walter Homes, Inc.*, 34 S.W.3d 578 (Tex. 2000) seems to clearly indicate that totally new home construction does not have to have the requirements for a cooling off period or a right to rescind.

    The contract must also be recorded in the county clerk's office, *V.T.C.A., Property Code, §53.059(d)*. If an owner is single, only the single claimant needs to sign a construction contract, and the constitutional homestead lien is superior to the contractor's lien as contractor's constitutional lien for improvements. *Moray Corp.* v. *Griggs*, 713 S.W.2d 753 (Tex. Civ. App.—Houston, 1986).

6. Home equity loans (Sec. 50(a)(6))—look at all the requirements! For most consumers, the most significant criteria seem to be no personal liability, no prepayment penalty, and an 80% loan-to-value ratio. One must foreclose by judicial proceeding, under special rules established by the Texas Supreme Court. Note that if the lender doesn't comply with the statute, the lender forfeits all principal and interest. See *§50(a)6(Q)*. These can be very risky for lenders; they are *not* the standard home equity loan one finds in other states. Texas has a long history of strict enforcement of homestead protection. However, in interpreting the above provision (allowing the lender a reasonable time for failure to correct the defect within a reasonable time) the Texas Supreme Court was very liberal in allowing lenders to correct defects. *Doody* v. *Ameriquest Mortgage Company No. 01-0137* (Tex. 2001). See also *Doody* v. *Ameriquest Mortgage Corp.* 242 F.3d 286, at 289 (5th Cir.—2001).

    These mortgages will be discussed in greater detail in the chapter on mortgages.

7. A reverse mortgage loan. A reverse mortgage is now defined under Texas law as an exchange of credit:
    a. That is secured voluntarily on homestead property created by a written agreement with the consent of each owner and each owner's spouse.
    b. Is made to a person who is or whose spouse is 62 years of age or older.

    c. Is made without recourse for personal liability against each owner and the spouse of each owner.

    d. Under which advances are provided to a borrower or based on the equity of the borrower's homestead.

    e. That does not permit the lender to reduce the amount or number of advances because of an adjustment in the interest rate, if periodic advances are to be made.

    f. That requires no payment of principal or interest until: (a) the homestead property securing the loan is sold or otherwise transferred; or (b) all borrowers cease occupying the homestead property as a principal residence for more than 180 consecutive days, and the location of the homestead property owner is unknown to the lender.

    g. That provides if the lender fails to make loan advances as required in the loan documents, and if the lender fails to cure the default as required in the loan documents, the lender forfeits all principal and interest on the reverse mortgage.

    h. That is not made unless the owner of the homestead attests in writing that the owner received counseling regarding the advisability and availability of reverse mortgages and other financial alternatives.

A new loan product in Texas is the "Loan for Life." The lender, using actuarial tables, determines the borrower's life expectancy and sets up an amortizing loan for the life of the individual. Most people who plan on living in their present home for as long as they are able can reap significant benefits from these types of loans, which can mean the difference between a comfortable existence or living on a very tight budget. This creates a new, nontaxable income for older Americans and can be a very useful estate planning vehicle. When the borrower dies, the heirs can always pay off the loan. Recall, however, that you must take a seminar before getting one of these loans, as they can be very complicated and the technicalities of the loan need to be explained in depth to the borrower.

8. Loans for mobile homes, now that they can be real estate (discussed in Chapter 6).

**Exceptions.** Once the "sacred cow" of Texas, the homestead protection has been eroded. Note the following course cases holding that a homestead is subject to forced sales under certain circumstances:

1. The homestead is subject to forced sale for nonpayment of maintenance fund liens. This foreclosure is apparently limited to liens retained as vendor's liens in the deed restrictions and may require judicial foreclosure. *Inwood North Property Owners' Association* v. *Pamilar*, 736 S.W.2d. 632 (Tex. 1987).

2. A lien existed prior to the property's designation as homestead, since a subsequent homestead right cannot defeat the right to enforce a preexisting lien. *Day* v. *Day*, 610 S.W.2d 195 (Tex. Civ. App.—Tyler, 1980); *Minnehoma Financial Company* v. *Ditto*, 566 S.W.2d 354 (Tex. Civ. App.—Ft. Worth, 1978).

3. A conversion of property to homestead status with intent to defraud one's creditors, *Matter of Reed*, 700 F.2d 986 (5th Cir.—1983), or when wrongfully obtained money has been used to acquire a homestead. *Baucum* v. *Texas Oil Corp.*, 442 S.W.2d 434 (Tex. Civ. App.—El Paso, 1967).

4. Renouncing homestead rights to property at any time before the property is used as homestead. *Miles Homes of Texas, Inc.* v. *Brubaker*, 649 S.W.2d 791

(Tex. Civ. App.—San Antonio, 1983). This can also include waiving homestead protection pursuant to prenuptial agreements between a husband and wife, wherein either spouse agrees not to claim homestead protection as a part of their agreement to marry, *Williams* v. *Williams*, 569 S.W.2d 867 (Tex.—1978).

5. State law allows a homestead to be seized if the occupant violates drug laws. *Lot 39, Section C, Northern Hill Subdivision* v. *State*, 85 S.W.3d 429 (Tex. App.—Eastland 2002).

6. The homestead may not be a yacht, as that does not constitute real property, *Norris* v. *Thomas*, 215 S.W.3d 851 (Tex. 2007).

7. Homestead limits are limited to $125,000.00 if the homestead claimant files bankruptcy within 1,215 days after acquiring the homestead. The $125,000.00 cap also applies if the court finds that the debtor committed crimes involving a violation of federal securities laws, or any criminal act, intentional tort, or willful or reckless misconduct that caused serious physical injury or death to another individual in the preceding five years, *11 U.S.C., §522 (q) (1) (B)*; and *§522 (p) (1)*.

Once a homestead exemption has been vested in a homeowner's real property, however, it provides for total exemption from forced sale of the homestead. For instance, a man owning his homestead could incur $4 million in debt (even in bad faith), *Garrard* v. *Henderson*, 209 S.W.2d 225 (Tex. Civ. App.—Dallas, 1948), and default on said $4 million debt. Under the constitutional provision, his creditors could not force this man to sell his house in order to satisfy his indebtedness. This applies even if his house is owned in fee, with no encumbrances, and may be worth a substantial amount of money, so long as his homestead is within the allowable limits (discussed next). It has even been held that wrongfully obtained monies can be used to repair or remodel an existing homestead, and the home is still exempt from forced sale. *Curtis Sharp Custom Homes, Inc.* v. *Glover*, 701 S.W.2d 24 (Tex. Civ. App.—Dallas, 1985). Did the Enron executives qualify for protection? Were their funds acquired by fraud?

If married, neither spouse may sell or abandon the homestead without the consent of the other spouse given in such manner as may be prescribed by law. If one spouse contracts for or conveys homestead property, it is not void, however. It is merely inoperative while the property remains the nonsigning spouse's homestead. *Zable* v. *Henry*, 649 S.W.2d 136 (Tex. Civ. App.—Dallas, 1983).

Even the proceeds from the sale are exempt from creditors for six months after the sale of the homestead, *V.T.C.A., Property Code, §41.002(b)*; *Simmons and Newsome Co.* v. *Malin*, 196 S.W.2d 281 (Tex. Civ. App.—Amarillo, 1917); *Jones* v. *Maroney*, 619 S.W.2d 296 (Tex. Civ. App.—Houston, 1981).

The six-month exemption may be qualified, though. If the homestead claimant acquires another homestead, which costs less than his existing homestead, the excess proceeds cannot maintain the homestead exemptions. For instance, if proceeds from a homestead sale are $900,000.00, but only $400,000.00 is reinvested in the new homestead, the excess $500,000.00 can be seized by the homestead claimant's creditors. Otherwise, the homestead claimant would be allowed two homestead exemptions (new home plus the $500,000.00 proceeds). *In Re England*, 975 F.2d 1168 (5th Cir.—1992).

**Limitations.** However, as you may expect, there are limitations as to exactly what can be declared as one's homestead. Article 16, Section 51, of the Texas Constitution provides for the amount and value to which a homestead exemption may apply. This provision is set out in its entirety as follows:

### §51. Amount of Homestead; Uses

The homestead, not in a town or city, shall consist of not more than two hundred acres of land, which may be in one or more parcels, with the improvements thereon; the homestead in a city, town or village, shall consist of lot or contiguous lots amounting to not more than 10 acres of land, together with any improvements on the land; provided, that the homestead in a city, town or village shall be used for the purposes of a home, or as both an urban home and a place to exercise a calling or business, of the homestead claimant, whether a single adult person, or the head of a family; provided also, that any temporary renting of the homestead shall not change the character of the same, when no other homestead has been acquired; provided further that a release or refinance of an existing lien against a homestead as to a part of the homestead does not create an additional burden on the part of the homestead property that is unreleased or subject to the refinance, and a new lien is not invalid only for that purpose.

This provision can be explained most succinctly by defining the homestead in terms of rural and urban homesteads. A **rural homestead** cannot be greater than 200 acres and must include the portion of acreage with the claimant's home on it. If the tract of land contains more than 200 acres, the owner has the option of designating which 200 acres (as long as it includes the home) constitutes the homestead. It may include more than one parcel as long as these parcels are reasonably contiguous. There is no dollar limit put on the rural homestead. Therefore, it could be the 200 acres with the house and the oil well, as long as the one or more parcels are reasonably contiguous and, when combined, contain less than 200 acres. *In Re Moody*, 862 F.2d 1194 (5th Cir.—1989). However, it must be remembered that the minerals as they reach the wellhead are personalty and are possibly subject to forced sale as personal property, not constituting a part of the real property homestead exemption. The statute limits the homestead of a single adult person not in a city, town, or village to not more than 100 acres, *V.T.C.A., Property Code, §41.001(a)(1)*; *In Re Moody*, supra. The "head of the household" has been broadly interpreted to include almost any sort of family relationship so long as there is a legal or moral duty to support the defendants. *Zielinski* v. *Hill*, 972 F.2d 116 (5th Cir.—1992); *NCNB Texas National Bank* v. *Carpenter*, 849 S.W.2d 875 (Tex. App.—Ft. Worth, 1993).

In contrast, the **urban homestead** consists of contiguous tract size not greater than ten acres.

Legislature also defined urban homestead, again, as property:

1. located within the limits of a municipality or extraterritorial jurisdiction, or a plat in subdivision; and

2. served by police protection, paid or volunteer fire protection, and at least three of the following services provided by a municipality or under contract to a municipality:

   (A) electric.

   (B) natural gas.

   (C) sewer.

   (D) storm sewer.

   (E) water.

It is important to note that the homestead claimant can only claim one homestead, either urban or rural. How does one know if the homestead is urban or rural? The statute controls. *Bouchie* v. *Rush Truck Centers of Texas*, 324 F3d. 780 (5th Cir.—2003)

Another interesting point provided for in this constitutional provision is that the homestead may be rental property, *V.T.C.A., Property Code, §41.001(b)*. This applies to tenants who may occupy said rental property as well as to homeowners who subsequently may buy a new home but keep their old home as rental property. The subject of termination of homestead rights will be discussed later in this chapter.

## Lots in Excess of Exemption—Urban

Under the old urban homestead theories, the homestead was limited to a certain dollar amount, and a creditor was allowed to force the sale of the entire homestead that was in excess of that exemption. *Hoffman* v. *Love*, 494 S.W.2d 591 (Tex. 1973). The constitutional exemption criteria, however, were changed in 1983 to provide for a size exemption rather than a dollar limit exemption.

In construing the newer constitutional provision, the courts have recited the following purposes for the change of the urban homestead from the dollar limitation to the size limitation:

1. It increases the protections afforded all homestead claimants in this state as a result of the effects of inflation and increased demands (making it unnecessary to amend the Texas Constitution periodically).

2. The state's obligation to protect its people will be limited.

3. It reinforces the long-established policy of this state to apply exemption laws liberally and to resolve any doubts in favor of the homestead claimant.

4. It ends the different treatment of urban and rural homesteads by basing both exemptions on an acreage standard. *In Re Barnhart*, 47 B.R. 277 (Bkrptcy.—1985); *In Re Starnes*, 52 B.R. 405 (Dist. Ct.—1985).

Therefore, the creditor's ability to force the sale of the homestead in excess of the limitation has probably now been diminished, and the creditor's only right is to force the sale of that amount of land that exceeds the ten-acre homestead exemption. The homestead claimant can designate his ten acres by filing an instrument to that effect in the county deed records, and the creditor gets what is left, *V.T.C.A., Property Code, §41.005*. The creditor can force the sale of the excess, thereby creating a cotenancy between the creditor and the homestead claimant, *Niland* v. *Deason*, 825 F.2d 801 (5th Cir.—1987), although this may be difficult if the house is in a platted subdivision with prohibitions against further re-subdivision.

## Lots in Excess of Exemption—Rural

Since the Texas Constitution provides that the family homestead is not more than 200 acres, the head of the family may voluntarily designate not more than 200 acres of the property as homestead. If the execution is issued against an owner of a homestead that is eligible for voluntary designation but that has not been designated, the officer holding the execution may notify the claimant that if the claimant fails to designate the homestead before the 11th day after the date of notice is delivered, the officer has the legal right to make the designation, *V.T.C.A., Property Code, §41.023*.

There is additional protection built in, however, to land that exceeds the homestead exemption. Sale of the homestead cannot be made until there has been a full trial on the merits as to the value of the homestead, as well as to the amount of the excess subject to levy by execution. *Bank of Texas* v. *Laguarta*, 565 S.W.2d 363 (Tex. Civ. App.—Houston, 1978). This puts a major stumbling block in the path of most creditors who are trying to force the sale of a homestead. See also *Steenland* v. *Texas Commerce Bank National Assoc.*, 648 S.W.2d 387 (Tex. Civ. App.—Tyler, 1983).

## Creation

Contrary to popular opinion and belief, creation of the homestead is simple and requires no formal designation whatsoever. There are no documents to sign, no oath to take, and no magic dust to sprinkle. The possession of the real estate by the owner who, whether single or with his family, resides upon it makes it the homestead of the family, both in law and in fact. *Braden Steel Corp.* v. *McClure*, 603 S.W.2d 288 (Tex. Civ. App.—Amarillo, 1980). If the real property is raw land (i.e., a lot in a subdivision), it is only important that the claimant must have intended to reside there as his home, and that intention must be evidenced by some overt act of preparation. That is, there must be some other act (in addition to legal title) by the claimant that impresses the land with the intention of establishing a home. This act can be having plans drawn, having the lot cleared, buying construction materials, or whatever other fact may be proven to indicate that the family intended to occupy same as its homestead. *Clark* v. *Salinas*, 626 S.W.2d 118 (Tex. Civ. App.—Corpus Christi, 1981); *Farrington* v. *First National Bank of Bellville*, 753 S.W.2d 248 (Tex. App.—Houston [1st Dist.], 1988). Mere intent of occupying the property, by itself, is not enough to render the lot exempt pursuant to the homestead law. *Cheswick* v. *Freeman*, 287 S.W.2d 171 (Tex. 1956).

## Termination

The nature of the homestead exemption and the strength with which it has been applied and upheld in the State of Texas may indicate the strength to which Texas law resists termination of any homestead rights. It has been judicially determined that the only way for property to lose its homestead character is by death, alienation, or abandonment.

**Death.** of the head of the household or homestead claimant, although terminating the claimant's homestead rights, does not necessarily terminate homestead rights altogether. The right to occupy the homestead passes to surviving spouses and adult, unmarried children upon the death of the husband or wife, or both, so long as the survivor elects to occupy the property as a homestead, *Vern. Ann. Tex. Const., Art. 16, §52*. It therefore creates a life estate in the survivors, with rights and duties similar to that of a life tenant. *Hill* v. *Hill*, 623 S.W.2d 779 (Tex. Civ. App.—Amarillo, 1981). The right even passes to minor children, although the right must be asserted by a guardian or other representative. In this situation, there is no requirement that the minor child reside with the decedent for the purposes of asserting the homestead claim. *National Union Fire Insurance Company of Pittsburgh* v. *Olson*, 920 S.W.2d. 458 (Tex. App.—Austin, 1996). A family cemetery is also exempt. Property Code, *§41.001(a)*. This right to occupy the homestead apparently stops here, though. The survivor of the survivor (i.e., second spouse) does not succeed to these rights. *Marino* v. *Lombardo*, 277 S.W.2d 749 (Tex. Civ. App.—Beaumont, 1955). Regardless of the amount of indebtedness or obligations incurred on the part of the homestead claimant, the house cannot be sold for any of his nonhomestead debts. *Cornerstone Bank, N.A.* v. *Randle* (Tex. App.—Dallas, 1993). In addition, the homestead rights cannot be partitioned between surviving spouse and minor children. It is in this type of situation that the homestead exemption clearly protects the family from a forced sale by creditors. It should be noted that the homestead claimant must be deceased before survivorship benefits can be maintained. Insanity, by itself, is not enough to maintain the survivorship benefits. *Hunter* v. *NCNB Texas National Bank*, 857 S.W.2d 722 (Tex. App.—Houston [14th Dist.], 1993).

**Alienation.** involves the sale of the house. In the event the family sells the house and buys a new home, the homestead character is terminated in the old homestead and manifests itself in the new homestead. If the family buys a new home and the old homestead is not sold, this does not necessarily terminate the old homestead, even if the old home is converted to rental property. In such a case, the creditors would have to prove abandonment of the old homestead if they were trying to force the sale of that home to satisfy the obligations. The Texas Constitution (Art. 16, §50) provides that any pretended sale of the homestead is void.

Therefore, the alienation of the property must be legitimate and cannot be merely "pretended." *McGahey* v. *Ford*, 563 S.W.2d 857 (Tex. Civ. App.—Ft. Worth, 1978); *In Re Rubarts*, supra. For instance, if the homeowner sells his homestead to his brother, who then borrows money against it as nonhomestead property and later conveys the property back to the previous homeowner with the increased debt (in effect, attempting to use the equity of his house to secure new financing) by use of the pretended conveyance, the entire transaction would be void. So the lender has the duty to inquire as to the nature of the sale, and not to rely blindly on statements by the pretended purchaser. The sale of a homestead by a debtor to a relative who signs a note and lien is in itself a circumstance that ought to excite the suspicion of a prudent lender. *Fuller* v. *Preston State Bank*, 667 S.W.2d 214 (Tex. Civ. App.—Dallas, 1983). The same may also be true if the original homeowner maintained possession of the premises after the pretended sale, or if an affluent homeowner moved to a very inexpensive house and attempted to borrow money using his previous residence (to which he still has title) as security for the loan. The Texas legislature finally passed a new statute in 1987 that specifically addresses many of these sham sales, characterizing the transaction as a mortgage only, *V.T.C.A., Property Code, §41.006.*

**Abandonment.** of a homestead has been a heavily litigated area, even in recent years. It is sufficient to say that it is not very easy to abandon a homestead. It is a question of fact for the jury to decide rather than one of law. If a homestead claimant is married, the homestead cannot be abandoned without the spouse's consent, *V.T.C.A., Property Code, §41.004.* It has been held that the acquisition of the new home is not necessarily an acquisition of a new homestead and that an individual does not necessarily abandon a homestead by merely moving his home. *Coury* v. *Prot*, 85 F.3d 244 (5th Cir.—1996); *In Re Leonard* 194 B.R. 807 (N.D. Tex. 1996). Abandonment of homestead property cannot be accomplished by mere intention. There must be a discontinuance of use, coupled with an intention *not again to use the property as a home*, to constitute abandonment. Any abandonment or waiver of the homestead requires clear and convincing evidence of *informed* consent, *V.T.C.A., Family Code, §5.101.* The courts put the burden of proving abandonment on the creditors, not on the homestead claimant. Business homesteads create a different issue, however. If a homestead claimant conveys more than 50% of the business to another, it may result in the loss of the homestead claim. *In Re Finkel*, 151 B.R. 779 (Bkrptcy. W.D. Tex. 1993).

## Other Issues

There are a number of other issues concerning homestead rights that people continue to question. One of these issues is whether or not the homestead claimant has the right to waive his homestead rights. The courts in Texas have consistently held that you cannot waive your homestead rights since they are constitutionally vested. *Englander* v. *Kennedy*, 424 S.W.2d 305 (Tex. Civ. App.—Dallas, 1968). This has been a common issue for lenders. Many lenders attempt to make loans secured by homestead property by having the homestead claimant sign a "homestead waiver" or "nonhomestead" affidavits. Lenders have a very high duty of care of investigating the homestead nature of the property before making a loan. A homestead claimant can sign anything he wants to, but if the property is in fact a homestead, the lien is void on its face. *Niland* v. *Deason*, supra. It is also important to note that if the lien is void, it stays void and cannot be resurrected into existence by later signing disclaimers or additional waivers. *Hruska* v. *First State Bank of Deanville*, 747 S.W.2d 783 (Tex. 1988). A claimant can even change his mind (for instance, claim 10 acres of his rural homestead when making the loan, but later claim all 200 acres prior to foreclosure). *In Re Skinner*, 74 B.R. 571 (Bkrptcy. N.D. Tex. 1987). There-fore, most prudent lenders never rely on waivers or affidavits unless they have inves-tigated the property and have satisfied themselves that the waivers are consistent with the facts of their specific case. In those cases the lien will be considered valid. *In Re Lane*, 103 B.R. 816 (Bkrptcy. N.D. Tex. 1989).

**Refinancing.** One of the most important issues concerning homestead rights is that they effectively preclude the homeowner's ability to refinance his home. Since a lender can only foreclose for liens securing purchase money, taxes, and home improvements, very few lenders are willing to use the home as security for a loan knowing they could not force the sale of the property to satisfy their debt. In times when we are recognizing renegotiable mortgages and people anticipate refi-nancing their home when interest rates decline, it must be remembered that the note can be renegotiated to provide for an interest rate, but the amount of the prin-cipal balance may never exceed the then-current principal balance of the note. Any renewal or extension of the existing note in excess of the current principal balance creates an advance of money, which is not purchase money, and the lender would forfeit the right to foreclose on the property to secure the payment of that debt even though part of the note is purchase money. *Lewis* v. *Investor's Savings Associ-ation*, 411 S.W.2d 794 (Tex. Civ. App.—Ft. Worth, 1967).

**Earnest Money Contracts.** There have also been questions concerning the homestead exemption as it pertains to earnest money contracts. At one time, it was felt that a remedy of specific performance in an earnest money contract would not be available to a purchaser because it would be, in effect, forcing the sale of the constitutionally protected homestead. *Jones* v. *Goff*, 63 Tex. 248 (1855). This deci-sion was based primarily on the interpretation of the then-existing statutes govern-ing the joinder of the spouse on conveyance. These statutes have since been repealed, and the Texas Supreme Court has now removed this antiquated burden and allows such a specific performance suit to be recognized. *Allen* v. *Monk*, 505 S.W.2d 523 (Tex. 1974).

Another complicated question that has arisen in homestead laws in recent years is whether or not the homestead is urban or rural. It is basically a question of fact rather than one of law, since there is no statutory or constitutional guide to deter-mine to what extent a property may be "urban" or "rural." The 1989 legislature gave some guidance on this issue. A homestead is now considered to be rural if, at the time the designation is made, the property is not served by municipal utilities and fire and police protection, *V.T.C.A., Property Code, §41.002(c)*. At least one Texas court decision has indicated that the facts will be liberally construed to give effect of the purpose and intent of the constitution to protect the family. *Connelly* v. *Johnson*, 259 S.W.2d 634 (Tex. Civ. App.—San Antonio, 1924).

**New Home Construction.** As Texas sees a better economic future, new home-stead issues have emerged concerning new construction. For instance, if you own a house and decide to build a new one, which house is your homestead—the first or the second home? This is an important matter. If the second home is the home-stead, homestead lien requirements would have to be followed on the second home. Some have felt that since the first home has not been sold or abandoned, it is still the homestead. The cases seem to indicate that intent to create a homestead can be very influential in creating homestead rights. Therefore, in all situations, it is prudent to assume that the homestead construction lien statutes should be complied with because of the strength of the intent issue in creating homestead rights. *Farrington* v. *First National Bank of Bellville*, supra. This also applies to new construction for business homesteads. *Moore* v. *Bank of Commerce*, 110 B.R. 255 (Bkrptcy. N.D. Tex. 1990).

**Judgment Liens.** The traditional rule is that judgment liens do not attach to homesteads. *Gill* v. *Quinn*, 613 S.W.2d 324 (Tex. Civ. App.—Eastland, 1981, no writ). The title companies, however, have difficulty determining whether or not property is homestead, particularly if the claimant owns more than a parcel of real estate. In most cases, the title company would require a declaratory judgment from a district court confirming the homestead character of the property. This causes problems and delays in closing when the homeowner may not be aware that the judgment liens were of record against the house, or the homeowner may have assumed that the judgment liens wouldn't be reflected in the title report because of the homestead nature of the property.

Recent cases, however, have clarified the issue to the benefit of the homestead claimant. In *Tarrant Bank* v. *Miller*, 833 S.W.2d 666 (Tex. App.—Eastland, 1992, writ den.), a bank refused to grant a partial release of judgment lien, even though the bank knew that the property was the claimant's homestead. The title company refused to issue an owner's title policy, and the claimants were unable to complete the sale of their home. The homestead claimants then sued the bank for slander of title. The court held that even though the lien was unenforceable, it did constitute a cloud on the defendant's title. A similar result was reached in *In Re Henderson*, 18 F.3d 1305 (5th Cir.—1994). When there is no question as to the homestead character of the property, the lender may be best advised to partially release their judgment liens (as it relates to the homestead only) to protect themselves against a slander of title claim.

The 1997 Legislature made significant strides in codifying this area of the law. Section 52.0012 was added to the Texas Property Code, which provides that a judgment debtor may, at any time, file an affidavit in the real property records in the county in which the judgment debtor's homestead is located, and it serves as a release of record of the judgment lien. A bona fide purchaser or mortgagee (or any other successors or assigns) may rely on this affidavit, provided it contains confirmation that the judgment debtor was sent a letter and a copy of the affidavit, and that the judgment creditor had not filed a contravening affidavit within 30 days after their receipt of that affidavit. Hopefully, this will clear up a lot of judgment lien issues without going to the expense of court proceedings.

**Ad Valorem Tax Issues.** Texas homesteads also have a protected interest for homestead occupants at least 65 years of age. These occupants are not required to pay their ad valorem taxes, nor will penalties accrue because of nonpayment of those taxes during their period of occupancy (although interest will accrue). The taxes are deferred until the occupant dies, or the homestead is ultimately sold. This will be discussed in greater detail in Chapter 21 on taxation.

## Owelty Issues

**Owelty.** is the difference that is paid or secured by one co-parcener or co-tenant to another for the purpose of equalizing a partition. This has had unusual application in Texas because of the nature of our homestead laws, because of the inability to perfect liens on homestead property for any purpose other than purchase money, home improvements, and taxes.

A primary complication arises because the co-tenants of the property acquire title at a given date (say, 1953), and at such time, as tenants in common, they are deemed to have possession of the property. A subsequent partition (say, 1969) creating a lien securing the acquisition of a co-tenant's separate parcel cannot, then, technically be purchase money if a lien is perfected on the remainder of the partitioned property. Logically, the lien for the parcel financed could only encumber the 50% interest acquired.

The seminal case on owelty is *Sayers* v. *Pyland*, 161 S.W.2d 769 (Tex. 1942). *Sayers* involved a suit to foreclose a lien on a homestead. It involved two lots, roughly lot 4 and lot 5, with lot 5 being the improved property, while lot 4 was an adjacent unimproved parcel. A partition deed was executed wherein Williams acquired the vacant portion of lot 4, and Pyland retained the ownership to the improved lot 5. Williams, however, assumed a portion of the debt encumbering *both* lots 4 and 5. The partition deed indicated that the property was to be secured by purchase money lien and vendor's lien against the entire property. It was a rather complicated financial transaction, but the net result of the partition was that Williams owed debts secured by the entire property, also encumbering the more expensive lot 5. The primary questions in *Sayers* involve the fact that the tract 5 was Pyland's homestead, and could the lien be a valid lien as purchase money. The *Sayers* court held that the lien was valid, noting that the parties were tenants in common, and that their interests extend to every part thereof. The court further noted that each party had the right to defend partition upon the property as co-tenants. The court went on to give Texas's classic definition of owelty:

> In partition proceedings the court may, if necessary, divide the property into shares of unequal value, and fix a lien on the larger share in favor of the party receiving the smaller share, for the difference. This difference is referred to as owelty. In such cases, the owelty so assessed in adjusting the equities is recognized as being in the nature of purchase money secured by a vendor's lien on the larger tract.

One co-tenant cannot defeat this right in the other by moving onto the property and asserting a homestead right therein.

*Sayers* was cited in a companion case by the Court of Civil Appeals. *Travelers' Insurance Company* v. *Nauert*, 200 S.W.2d 661 (Tex. Civ. App.—El Paso, 1941, no writ). Both of these cases are considered to be the standard and landmark cases on owelties in Texas. Both of these cases involved a true partition of real estate where co-parceners divided their interests and secured that acquisition by liens on the entire property. A presumption that has been made for years in Texas, relying on *Sayers* and *Travelers'*, is that the reverse seems to be logically true. If you have two co-tenants who choose to (instead of separating the parcels) convey one parcel to the other co-owner, so that title to the large parcel will be held entirely by one party, they should logically be allowed the same treatment if: (1) there is an agreement between co-tenants to equalize their portions, in the second instance for cash rather than partition of ownership interests; (2) it is agreed to by the parties and is "in the nature of" purchase money; (3) the net effect, in both circumstances, is nothing more than creating a lien on both parcels with a cross default provision (i.e., it's the same), creating a lien on the whole parcel for the purpose of purchase money reflecting the sharing of equity interests between the co-parceners. This has been useful in acquiring separated interests of property from heirs who choose to "take their money and run" while the remaining co-tenant acquires the entire interest in the property.

The lien, if the remaining co-tenant chooses to borrow money, allows the lender to lien the entire property rather than just the selling tenant's one-half interest. This is in theory no different than the *Sayers* decision of allowing a lien on the entire property for the partition. Utilizing the owelty theory for the acquisition of the co-tenant's interest is also logically supported in divorce cases wherein the wife may want to acquire the husband's proportional interest in the property awarded during the divorce. This would result in a ratification of the existing purchase money mortgage. A second mortgage is executed for the acquisition of the one-half interest, which is "in the nature of purchase money." Instead of cross-categorizing the loans, both of which are theoretically legal, we simply roll both liens into one loan, and it stands to reason that that lien would be valid and enforceable, even on homestead property under the *Sayers* doctrine. This preserves the homestead claim, rather than destroying it, which has always been the ultimate aim of homestead protection.

## Additional Homestead Rights

There are frequent questions about the extent to which homestead rights provide exemptions for your property other than your home. Texas statutes provide for a number of other exemptions including one or more lots held for uses of sepulcher, *V.T.C.A., Property Code, §41.00(a)*, and personal property owned by a family that has an aggregate fair market value of not more than $60,000, or for a single adult who is not a member of a family for an aggregate fair market value of not more than $30,000. These exemptions are provided only if the personal property is eligible for exemption. The following personal property is eligible for the exemption:

### §42.002. Personal Property

(a) The following personal property is exempt under Section 42.001(a):

(1) home furnishings, including family heirlooms;

(2) provisions for consumption;

(3) farming or ranching vehicles and implements;

(4) tools, equipment, books, and apparatus, including boats and motor vehicles used in a trade or profession;

(5) wearing apparel;

(6) jewelry not to exceed 25 percent of the aggregate limitations prescribed by Section 42.001(a);

(7) two firearms;

(8) athletic and sporting equipment, including bicycles;

(9) a two-wheeled, three-wheeled, or four-wheeled motor vehicle for each member of a family or single adult who holds a driver's license or who does not hold a driver's license but who relies on another person to operate the vehicle for the benefit of the nonlicensed person;

(10) the following animals and forage on hand for their consumption:

(A) two horses, mules, or donkeys and a saddle, blanket, and bridle for each;

(B) 12 head of cattle;

(C) 60 head of other types of livestock; and

(D) 120 fowl;

(11) household pets.

The homestead claim is proceeds of the sale of a homestead are not subject to seizure for creditor's claim for six months after the date of the date of the sale; *Texas Property Code §41.001(c)*.

# Community Property Rights

The State of Texas has a very deeply ingrained Spanish heritage, which includes a very firm belief in the home and family unit concept. This is reflected in our homestead laws and is also reflected in certain marital property rights, which we term **community property**. Texas is one of eight states that recognize community property rights. The law in Texas basically presumes that, subject to some exceptions, every parcel of real property acquired after marriage becomes community property, which means the property of both husband and wife. This is true even if the property is acquired by the spouses at another time in another jurisdiction, so long as the division of the property (by marriage or death) occurs in Texas. Community property rights also vest certain rights in the children in the event of the intestate death of one of the spouses. The laws were passed with the specific purpose in mind of maintaining and keeping the cohesiveness of the family unit. The community property laws become operative upon the marriage of the parties. See Richard R. Powell and Patrick J. Rohan, *Powell on Real Property* (New York: Matthew Bender & Company, Inc., updated annually), ¶624.3[1].

In contrast to community property is **separate property**. Separate property is specifically designated by Texas law to cover exceptions to the community property law, and those exceptions are as follows:

1.  Property owned by a spouse prior to marriage.
2.  Property acquired by gift, devise, or descent during marriage, *Vernon's Ann. Tex. Const., Art. 16, §15.*
3.  Recovery for personal injuries, except for loss of earning capacity, *V.T.C.A., Family Code, §3.001(3)*.
4.  Military nondisability retirement benefits, if the spouses have been married less than 10 years, *10 U.S.C., §1408(c)(1)*.

However, any income from separate property or any offspring of said community property (i.e., cattle or other additional property that comes into being) is community property. This does not include the increase in value of separate property after marriage. For instance, if a spouse owns a home worth $60,000 at the time of the marriage and the home is worth $90,000 after the marriage, that increase in value is not community property. However, if community efforts or community credit is used to secure a loan for the house, or community funds are used to maintain or improve the house, certain community property rights may accrue, and one spouse may be entitled to reimbursement, which is measured by the enhancement in value to the benefitted estate. *Anderson* v. *Gilliland*, 684 S.W.2d 673 (Tex. 1985); *Jensen* v. *Jensen*, 665 S.W.2d 107 (Tex. 1984). There is even a theory that property may be partially separate and partially community! See *Gleich* v. *Bongio*, 99 S.W.2d 881 (Tex. Comm. App.—1937). A professional education acquired during marriage is not a property right and therefore is not divisible upon divorce. *Frausto* v. *Frausto*, 611 S.W.2d 656 (Tex. Civ. App.—San Antonio, 1980).

# Contractual Separate Property

The difference between community and separate property tends to be "gray" in certain areas of income, increase in value, and certain obligations of the community for extensions of credit. This problem is further complicated by amendments to the constitution that were voted in by referendum on November 4, 1980, and November 3, 1987. The current provision is as follows:

**§15. Separate and Community Property of Husband and Wife**
All property, both real and personal, of a spouse owned or claimed before marriage, and that acquired afterward by gift, devise or descent, shall be the separate property of that spouse; and laws shall be passed more clearly defining the rights of the spouses, in relation to separate and community property; provided that persons about to marry and spouses, without the intention to defraud pre-existing creditors, may by written instrument from time to time partition between themselves all or part of their property, then existing or to be acquired, or exchange between themselves the community interest of one spouse or future spouse in any property for the community interest of the other spouse or future spouse in other community property then existing or to be acquired, whereupon the portion or interest set aside to each spouse shall be and constitute a part of the separate property and estate of such spouse or future spouse; spouses also may from time to time, by written instrument, agree between themselves that the income or property from all or part of the separate property then owned or which thereafter might be acquired by only one of them, shall be the separate property of that spouse; if one spouse makes a gift of property to the other that gift is presumed to include all the income or property which might arise from that gift of property; spouses may agree in writing that all or part of their community property becomes the property of the surviving spouse on the death of a spouse; and spouses may agree in writing that all or part of the separate property owned by either or both of them shall be the spouses community property.

The Constitution now provides that, in addition to the old rules, agreements prior to marriage (**prenuptial agreements**) and agreements after marriage, in writing, may:

1. Effectively partition the spouse's property then existing or to be acquired to create separate property of such spouse or future spouse.
2. Establish income or property from separate property as separate property of that spouse (where this has formerly been presumed to be community).
3. Establish that if a gift is made to one spouse, the gift is presumed to include all the income or property that may arise from the gift of that property (a gift being separate property; the income, however, was also formerly presumed to be community).
4. Create a right of survivorship in the spouse's community property.

A Texas Supreme Court case has recently held that these agreements are "impliedly retroactive." So, if a prenuptial agreement was signed prior to 1980, it was validated by the 1980 constitutional amendment. *Beck* v. *Beck*, 814 S.W.2d 745 (Tex. 1991).

**Contractual Community Property.** The 1999 change provides that spouses may agree to all or part of their separate property owned by either or both spouses, can be converted to community property. The agreement is enforceable without consideration, but must be in writing and (1) signed by both spouses, (2) identify the property being converted and (3) specify that the property is being converted to the spouse's community property. The mere transfer of a spouse's separate property to the name of the other spouse or to the name of both spouses is **not sufficient** to convert the property to community property.

The community property agreement is not enforceable if the spouse against whom enforcement is sought proves that the spouse did not: (1) execute the agreement voluntarily or (2) receive a fair and reasonable disclosure of the legal effect of converting the property to community property. The agreement must contain a statement and is rebuttably presumed to provide a fair and reasonable disclosure if it contains the specified statements, prominently displayed in boldfaced type, capital letters, or underlined. Note Tex. Const. Art. XVI, Sec. 15, on page 52.

## New Community Property Rules

**Equitable Interests of Community Property.** Another 1999 legislature created a major change in community property. You may recall that separate property is property that is acquired prior to marriage, or after marriage by gift, devise or descent, or as contractually agreed to between the parties.

This new statutory change creates an equitable interest in a spouse's separate property if there is (1) an enhancement in value during the marriage of the separate property due to financial contribution made with community property funds or (2) if community property funds are used to discharge all or part of the debt on the separate property owned by the spouse during the marriage.

The equitable interest created is a proportional value determined by the amount of payments made the community versus the amount of payments made by the separate property contributions. On termination of the marriage, the court is required to impose an equitable lien on community or separate property to secure a claim arising by reason of this equitable interest. *V.T.C.A., Family Code, §3.406.*

## Management and Control of Community Property

No one spouse can claim all the community property because all real property that is community property is generally considered to be of joint control and cannot be conveyed without the joinder of the other spouse. Statutory provisions have been enacted, however, that allow for a **sole control community property**, where a spouse may have the sole management, control, and disposition of real estate as if he or she were single, if the property is held in that spouse's name, *V.T.C.A., Family Code, §3.102.* This sole control community property includes, but is not limited to, revenue from separate property, personal earnings, recoveries for personal injuries, and the increase in value and revenue from all property subject to sole control and management, *V.T.C.A., Family Code, §3.102.*

## Liabilities

There are different liabilities for community property depending on whether or not it is jointly controlled community property, sole control community property, or separate property of either spouse. The liabilities also change depending on whether or not the liabilities incurred are **tortious** (actions for money damages) or **contractual** (either written or oral), or whether the contract was for necessary or nonnecessary items. This text will not attempt to go into depth on the subject of marital property rights because the complex nature of those rights goes far beyond the realm of real estate law. It is more important to remember that in the marital community, any interest in real estate may be subject to joint control, and both spouses should be aware of any real estate transaction affecting presumed community property. The old rule was simply that either spouse could bind the community assets for debts, and all property acquired during marriage other than by gift, devise, or descent was community. The new constitutional provision now provides for written agreements to the contrary. Since separate property is not liable for the debts and obligations of the other spouse, this puts creditors, brokers, and third parties in the awkward position of not being able to presume community property assets or liabilities in any given situation.

To help this problem, statutes provide some answers and general requirements of the new written instrument rule for separate property. The agreement must further be in writing and subscribed by all parties and recorded in the county in which the real property is located, *V.T.C.A., Family Code, §3.004(a)*. As another protection for creditors and third parties, an agreement, partition, or exchange agreement made to change otherwise community real property to separate real property is not constructive notice to a good faith purchaser for value or a creditor without actual notice, unless the instrument is acknowledged and recorded in the county in which the real property is located, *V.T.C.A., Family Code, §3.004(b)*.

As an interesting sidelight, in order to prevent the abusive use of palimony suits (resulting from unmarried couples living together), a new (1989) amendment now provides that any agreement between nonmarried couples must be in writing and signed by the parties to be charged in order to comply with Section 26.01 of the Texas Business and Commerce Code (the Statute of Frauds).

## Common-Law Marriage

Since the marital community is the determining factor for the subject of community property, it is interesting to note what can constitute marriage in the State of Texas. A formal or ceremonial marriage, of course, presumes a legal marriage as long as the ceremonial marriage is not illegal or invalid. Texas, however, is one of the two community property states that recognize the validity of **common-law marriage**, *Powell*, supra, ¶624.3[3]. It has long been upheld by statute and case law that a common-law marriage can exist if the following elements are present:

1. There is an agreement, express or implied, presently to be husband and wife.
2. The couple are living together in cohabitation as man and wife.
3. The parties hold each other out to the public as husband and wife. *Reilly* v. *Jacobs*, 536 S.W.2d 406 (Tex. Civ. App.—Dallas, 1976). See *Family Code*, §2.401.

There is no authority establishing the time limit as to how long cohabitation would have to exist; presumably it could be for a very short period of time, as long as the other two elements exist. Direct evidence of an agreement to be married is not required to establish a common-law marriage. It can be proved by circumstantial evidence. *Russell* v. *Russell*, 865 S.W.2d 929 (Tex. 1993). A "mere sexual relationship" is not enough to create the marriage. *Bolash* v. *Heid*, 733 S.W.2d 698 (Tex. App.—San Antonio, 1987). This becomes a very complex matter in the event of an untimely death, where certain heirs may have a right to community property interests. The rights of a common-law heir and common-law spouse are in all respects the same as though the marriage had been duly solemnized under more formal marriage proceedings.

This matter is complicated because once the common-law marriage is formed, Texas law resists dissolving that marriage without formal proceedings. Once the marriage exists, the spouses' subsequent denials of the marriage, if disbelieved, do not undo the marriage. Common-law divorce is unknown to Texas law. *Claveria* v. *Claveria*, 615 S.W.2d 164 (Tex. 1981). Will contests and heirship rights, as well as rights of the common-law spouse, can prove to have disastrous consequences to unsuspecting family members. The most recent marriage is preserved valid, *V.T.C.A., Family Code, §1.102.*

The legislature gave some protection for allegations of common-law marriage. If one of the parties to the marriage is going to allege common-law marriage, any proceedings to assert that marriage must be commenced not later than the second anniversary after the date on which the relationship ended, *V.T.C.A., Family Code, §2.401.* Apparently, common-law marriages will automatically terminate one year after the relationship ends. This statute, though, creates an interesting question: When does "the relationship" end? What is the "relationship"? Now that is fertile ground for discussion!

This creates a peculiar problem for real estate licensees. If it is apparent that an unmarried couple is living in a home, do one or both parties need to sign the listing? If there is a common-law marriage, it may require the joinder of both spouses for conveyance even if the property was originally separate property. It may also be important for the real estate broker's interest to be sure that both parties sign the listing agreement. There is very little guidance in these matters, except that when in doubt the broker should secure both signatures!

# Water Rights

The concept of water rights has undergone dramatic changes over the past few years. The Texas National Resources and Conservation Commission (TNRCC), in one way or another, regulates every drop of water in the State. In many parts of the State, the water has almost become a third estate in land. Similar to oil and gas rights, water rights are now transferred from one landowner to another and may be a significant part of the negotiation of the purchase price of real property. This 2003 Legislature even enacted laws to provide for value to be attributed to water rights in condemnation proceedings. Particularly in large acreage transactions, the water rights are negotiated as aggressively as oil and gas rights. In general terms, water rights fall into two categories, ground water and surface water. There is a long involved history of Texas water rights. A few of these historical factors deserve to be discussed to put these rights in perspective. Recent legislation has made current applications of water rights so important that we will expand on those that are currently in effect.

**Surface Water Rights** There have been common-law theories of water rights, basically classified in three categories: **riparian rights** of land bordering a stream, **littoral rights** of land adjoining a large body of water, and a governmental-controlled use of water through **prior appropriation**. Texas falls basically into this third category, since Texas has specific statutory guidelines for the use, enjoyment, and appropriation of its water resources. The Texas Water Rights Adjudication Act provides the exclusive means by which water rights may be recognized. *In Re Adjudication of Water Rights of the Brazos III Segment of the Brazos River Basin*, 746 S.W.2d 207 (Tex. 1988). These laws with respect to water rights are contained in the state Water Code, which basically gives all water rights to the state. It does not recognize any riparian rights in the owner of any land the title to which passed out of the State of Texas after July 1, 1895, *V.T.C.A., Water Code, §11.001(b)*, although current owners who can trace their riparian rights to a date prior to that date may still claim them.

The Texas Supreme Court has held, however, that the vested right to that water is only a **usufructuary** use of what the state owns. A usufruct has been defined as the right to use, enjoy, and receive the profits of property that belongs to another. *In Re The Adjudication of the Water Rights of the Upper Guadalupe Segment of the Guadalupe River Basin*, 642 S.W.2d 438 (Tex. 1983).

***Ownership of Waterways.*** In establishing the ownership of waterways, the Texas Water Code specifies that the water of the ordinary flow, underflow, and tides of every flowing river, natural stream, and lake, and of every bay or arm of the Gulf of Mexico; and the storm water, flood water, and rainwater of every river, natural stream, canyon, ravine, depression, and watershed in the state are the property of the state. In addition, all water imported from any source outside the boundaries of the state for use in the state, and which is transported through the beds and banks of any applicable stream within the state or by utilizing any facilities owned or operated by the state, is also the property of the state, *V.T.C.A., Water Code, §11.021* (Supp. 1982–1983). Texas holds the title to the waters in a navigable stream in trust for the public. *In Re Upper Guadalupe*, supra.

The state may authorize the use of state water, which may be acquired by the process of appropriation from the Department of Water Resources in the manner and in the preference provided for by statute. Once the permit has been obtained from the Department of Water Resources, the right to use the state water under that permit is limited not only to the amount specifically appropriated, but also to the priority of purposes specified in the appropriation. One should always try to use this appropriation, since all water not used within the specified limits is not considered as having been appropriated and the owner may lose his right to that appropriation. Therefore, if one doesn't use his appropriation in the current year, it may be limited or prohibited in future years. This theory encourages the beneficial use of water as a conservation measure. The nonuse of appropriated water is equivalent to waste, since the water would then run unused into the sea.

***Conflicting Claims.*** All persons having an appropriation by the state must file by March 1 of each and every year a written report to the Department of Water Resources on forms prescribed by the department or be subject to a statutory penalty. If the appropriation has been given to two conflicting claimants, the first in time is first in right, *V.T.C.A., Water Code, §11.027*. The only exception to the doctrine of appropriation is that any city or town can make further appropriations of the water for domestic or municipal use without paying for the water.

One can acquire an appropriation through a process similar to adverse possession, however. When a person uses water under the terms of a certified filing or permit for a period of three years, he acquires title to his appropriation against any other claimant of the water. Conversely, if any lawful appropriation or use of state water is willfully abandoned during a three-year period, the right to use the water is forfeited and the water is again subject to appropriation, *V.T.C.A., Water Code, §11.029*.

**Ground Water.** The majority of water in Texas is ground water. It includes percolating water, underground flow, artesian water and well water. Ground water is owned by the owner of the property with two exceptions: (1) the landowner only has the right to pump the water and (2) regulatory programs of underground water conservation districts that have the legislative right to regulate the use of ground water. The historical right to use the ground water by the landowner is designated as the **Rule of Capture**, which means that the owner of the land can pump unlimited quantities of water from under the land. The ground water, however, is subject to state regulations. *Cipriano v. Great Spring Waters of America, Inc.*, 1 S.W.3d 75 (Tex. 1999). The TNRCC has established a number of local water conservation districts to regulate the use of ground water. To date, they have mostly regulated the use of ground water pumping where it has caused land subsidence. However, the legislature has given the local conservation districts expanded powers to regulate any number of different ways. This area of water law will be constantly expanding because of our legislative power to regulate in the public interest. *Barshop* v. *Medina County Underground Water Conservation District*, 925 S.W.2d 618 (Tex. 1996).

## Texas Natural Resources Conservation Commission

The agency of the state given primary responsibility for implementing the provisions of the constitution and laws of the State of Texas is the Texas Natural Resources Conservation Commission, *V.T.C.A., Water Code, §5.011.* This agency is responsible for carrying out executive and judicial functions provided under the Texas Water Code, delegated to it by the constitution and other laws of the State of Texas. The Texas Natural Resources Conservation Commission was created for the purpose of assigning and coordinating the duties, responsibilities, and functions of the previously existing state agencies and has jurisdiction over 15 wide-ranging functions as specified by law, *V.T.C.A., Water Code, §5.013.*

The Texas Natural Resources Conservation Commission also exercises the judicial function of the department and holds hearings to authorize the issuing of permits and judicial review. Any person affected by a ruling, order, decision, or other act of the department may file a petition to review, set aside, modify, or suspend the act of the department.

## Water Development Board

The functions of the Texas Natural Resources Conservation Commission for developing statewide water plans and administration of the various state's water-assistance and -financing programs are vested in the Texas Water Development Board. It is composed of six members who are appointed by the governor with the advice and consent of the state senate. The members of the board hold office for staggered terms of six years, with the terms of two members expiring every two years. The board establishes and approves all general policies of the Department of Water Resources.

## State Water Agencies

There are other state agencies concerned with specific requirements for water use and water development. They include Water Control and Improvement Districts, Underground Water Conservation Districts, Fresh Water Supply Districts, Municipal Utility Districts, Water Improvement Districts, Drainage Districts, Levee Improvement Districts, and Navigation Districts. Recently, Subsidence Districts have been established that effect control and permit procedures for development along Texas coastal areas. There is a very good chance that if any development is to take place, one or several of the preceding districts or agencies will significantly affect the proposed project.

# Cemetery Lots

One of the more unique types of estates in Texas is a **cemetery lot**. Since 1945, Texas state law requires that all cemeteries have a perpetual care fund for the administration and maintenance of the cemetery. **Perpetual care funds** are established as charitable trusts, which are specifically exempt from the Rule against Perpetuities. *Foshee* v. *Republic National Bank*, 617 S.W.2d 675 (Tex. 1981). The cemetery association responsible for the perpetual care has the authority to sell and convey the "exclusive right to sepulture" in the burial plots to prospective purchasers. These sales are specifically exempt from the Real Estate License Act, and all of the plots are, of course, indivisible, except with the consent of the cemetery association or as provided for by law. All burial space in which the exclusive right to sepulture has been conveyed is presumed to be the separate property of the person named as grantee rather than community property. The spouse has a vested right of interment in any burial plot in which the exclusive right of sepulture has been conveyed to the other spouse.

State statutes are very specific as to how cemeteries are to be administered, how perpetual care funds are to be invested, how records are to be kept, locations of cemeteries, removals from said cemeteries, and almost every other conceivable area of property or business concerns applicable to cemeteries. After interment, the cemetery association, along with certain specified relatives, is given the power to remove any remains of the deceased person located in the cemetery.

# Nonoperational Estates

There are certain estates that existed at common law, and still exist in some states, but are considered to be **nonoperational estates** (having no effect) in the State of Texas. Even though they are not applicable, a speaking knowledge of the subject matter always helps to broaden the scope of understanding of real estate law.

**Curtesy** rights are rights a husband has in his spouse's estate upon her demise. Conversely, **dower** rights are rights that a wife has in her husband's estate when he dies. Dower and curtesy rights have varying degrees of application, depending upon jurisdiction. However, the Texas concept of community property rights (discussed earlier in this chapter) as well as the laws of heirship (*Prob. Code*, §38, discussed in Chapter 11) preclude any rights of dower and curtesy in Texas.

The **Rule in Shelley's Case** is a grant of title to the grantee and his "heirs" or "the heirs of his body," in an attempt to limit the chain of title to a parcel of real estate to a particular ancestry. Although this rule is recognized in Texas, it is not looked upon with favor. Only if no other intention can be implied, and the grant is so specific that no other conclusion can be reached, will the court uphold it. The Rule in Shelley's Case (along with two other outmoded doctrines) was statutorily abolished on January 1, 1964, *Tex. Rev. Civ. Stat. Ann.*, Art. 1291a. Curiously, Section 3 of the act, as passed, provides that the new statute does not apply to conveyances that took place prior to the effective date of the law. So it is presumed that the complications of the Rule in Shelley's Case will continue to arise for some time to come. This is neat stuff, huh?

There have been a number of estates in land and interests in real estate discussed in this chapter, some of which may be confusing and some of which may be difficult to discriminate from each other. To help isolate these various types of estates and interests, please note Figure 3.1, which shows these various estates and their interrelationships with other interests in real estate. Please note that all of these interests coexist as part of the bundle of rights concept of interest and ownership.

**FIGURE 3.1   INTERESTS IN REAL ESTATE.**

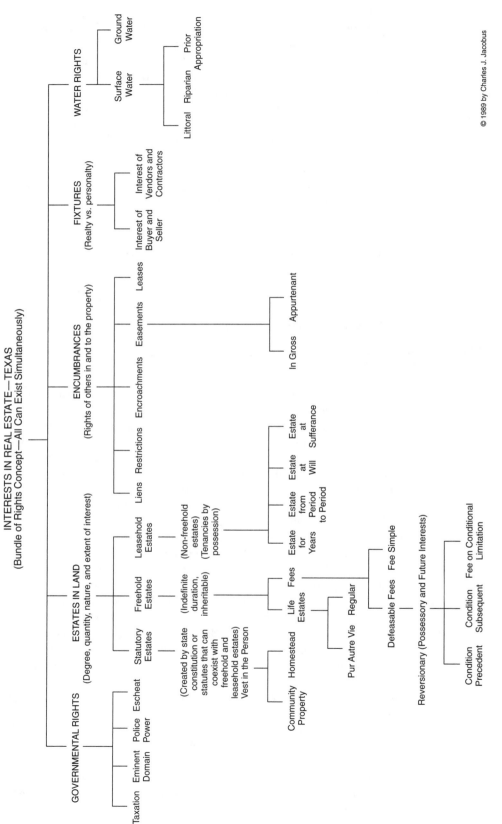

## ■ SUMMARY

Statutory estates are rights vested in the individual by statute or constitutional provision. Homesteads are a very important legal estate in Texas and vest on the individual upon his occupancy of the property. Homestead rights provide an exemption from forced sale of the owner's principal residence except in very specific circumstances. Urban and rural homestead rights exist in Texas, and each homestead is either urban or rural, but not both. A person may claim only one homestead at a time, although he may concurrently claim a business and residential urban homestead. Homesteads may only be terminated by death, abandonment, or alienation. Community property rights exist because of the marital status of the owners. There is a presumption that all property acquired during marriage is community property and subject to the joint management and control of both the husband and the wife. A concern with community property rights is the concept of common-law marriage, since parties may be legally married but not know it.

Cemetery lots are technically considered to be an exclusive right of sepulture.

## CASE STUDIES FOR DISCUSSION

1. Mr. Arnold P. North executed a general warranty deed to Mr. and Mrs. Holly P. Field. Sometime later, Holly P. Field and his wife executed a deed to Holly P. Field, Inc., a Texas corporation. Shortly thereafter, Holly P. Field, Inc., executed a deed of trust in favor of Friendly Lender Savings and Loan Association to borrow money, using their property as security for the debt. Three months later there was a default in the mortgage, and the lender attempted to foreclose on the property. What legal ramifications do you see?

2. Mr. and Mrs. Niland owned a large single-family residence on a 1.5-acre lot in Dallas, Texas. They also owned a condominium in the same general area of town. They went to Lender No. 1 and claimed that their single-family residence was their homestead and used the condominium as security for a loan. They signed a non-homestead affidavit and a designation of homestead for their single-family residence. They then went to Lender No. 2 and claimed the condominium was their homestead and borrowed money using the single-family residence as security for the loan. They used part of the proceeds to pay off Lender No. 1 and then defaulted to Lender No. 2. Upon Lender No. 2's foreclosure, the Nilands alleged that the house was their homestead, the loan was invalid, and the lender could not foreclose. What result, and legal ramifications, do you foresee?

## CHAPTER 4

# Legal Descriptions

To the extent one has determined the degree, quantity, nature, and interest that one has in real estate, the next step is determining how to describe precisely this real estate so that it can properly be conveyed, encumbered, and contracted for. In determining the requirements for a sufficient **legal description**, there are a few general rules and many, many, many exceptions. The general rule in Texas seems to be that the **"nucleus of description" theory** is followed. It is generally stated that to comply with the Statutes of Conveyance and the Statute of Frauds, the description of the land in deeds and contracts is that the writing must furnish within itself, or by reference to some other existing writing, the means or data by which the particular land to be conveyed may be identified with reasonable certainty. *Broaddus* v. *Grout*, 258 S.W.2d 308 (Tex. 1953); *Greer* v. *Greer*, 191 S.W.2d 848, 849 (Tex. 1946). Reasonable certainty is all that the law requires. Conviction beyond all reasonable doubt is unnecessary. *Mansel* v. *Catles*, 55 S.W. 559, 560 (Tex. 1900). The term "reasonable certainty" may be open to interpretation but was cited in one case as:

> Upon such certainty we act in all the highest concerns of life, and it is sufficient for the purposes of the law. *Gates* v. *Asher*, 280 S.W.2d 247, 249 (Tex. 1955).

How can one deny such an eloquent determination?

Generally, absent specific reservation in a deed, buildings and other improvements used in connection with realty in such a way as to constitute appurtenances or fixtures pass as a matter of course by the conveyance. *Olmos* v. *Pecan Grove Utility District*, 857 S.W.2d 734, 738 (Tex. App.—Houston [14th Dist.], 1993).

In real life, however, it's never that simple, but the general rules follow.

## Metes and Bounds

One of the most commonly utilized methods for describing real property in Texas is the metes-and-bounds description. The **metes-and-bounds** description is one that identifies a parcel by specifying the shapes and boundaries of the perimeter of the property. At one time this was determined by natural or synthetic monuments involving tree stumps, riverbeds, creeks, or piles of rocks. In more current times, however, surveyors are using much more sophisticated equipment to minimize error and establish more precise measuring techniques.

In beginning the description, the surveyor typically starts with a **permanent reference mark** (also called a **benchmark**) to begin the description of the property. Benchmarks are normally established by government survey teams such as the United States Geological Survey (USGS) or the United States Coast and Geodetic Survey (USCGS). This creates a point from which the survey description can begin and is a permanent, well-established location, which can easily be found.

Once this benchmark has been determined and the permanent reference mark is ascertained, the surveyor can establish a bearing by which he can start the description of the subject property. Once the bearing and distance to the subject property has been determined, he can start the description of that property and reference it as the **place of beginning** to describe the subject parcel.

Once the surveyor has reached the place of beginning, he begins the description by using the plane coordinate system to determine the **bearings** and **calls** to describe the perimeter of the property. Direction is shown in degrees, minutes, and seconds. There are 360 degrees in a circle, 60 minutes in each degree, and 60 seconds in each minute. Therefore, one would find a description as North 29 degrees, 14 minutes, and 52 seconds East to determine the bearing (direction) the surveyor used in describing the first perimeter line of the description of the subject property. This would indicate that the surveyor measured North 29 degrees, 14 minutes, and 52 seconds East to determine the first direction of the descriptive call. An example of simple bearing directions is shown in Figure 4.1.

The description for the first bearing would be complete by giving it a proper distance measurement to determine the point from which bearing the next call would be made. Each time a direction and measurement is changed, a similar bearing and distance is determined to find the point at which the next measurement is

**FIGURE 4.1  NAMING DIRECTIONS FOR A METES-AND-BOUNDS SURVEY.**

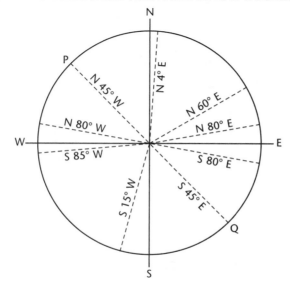

Moving in a clockwise direction from the point of beginning, set the center of a circle compass (like the one shown here) on each corner of the parcel to find the direction of travel to the next corner. (Note: Minutes and seconds have been omitted here for clarity.)

to be made. Figure 4.2 shows how the direction of travel along each side of a parcel can be determined.

More sophisticated measurement techniques are used to describe a curve. These measurements usually are made in terms of the radius of the circle necessary to make the required arc of the curve, the angle necessary to make the arc, and the length of the arc. In addition, there is often a "**long chord**" measurement showing the tangent points of both sides of the arc for a verification by more conventional measuring techniques.

## Rules of Construction

With the foregoing information in mind, it is understandable that the metes-and-bounds descriptions are not always simple to interpret and understand. Conflicts are common, and even the best surveyors make mistakes, which may go undetected for years. When there are conflicts, there are generally acceptable rules of interpretation as to which legal description will control.

Generally, the respective priority of calls made by a surveyor is as follows:

1. Natural objects (rivers, creeks, streams, mountains, nature of soil, and similar objects that occur naturally on the ground).

2. Artificial objects (objects placed by the surveyor including calls for adjoining property lines, stakes, lines marked, or marks made on trees).

3. Courses (the direction of a line as it varies from north or south).

4. Distances.

5. Quantities.

Even these general rules have exceptions, and a few specific areas of litigation deserve more discussion. The location of highways, streets, and watercourses as boundaries has created conflicts between joint lot owners as well as governmental entities. The general rule is that land adjoining highways and streets vests title to the center of that street. *Pebsworth* v. *Behringer*, 551 S.W.2d 501 (Tex. Civ. App.—Waco, 1977). This same general rule is also true of watercourses. When a

**FIGURE 4.2  DESCRIBING LAND BY METES AND BOUNDS.**

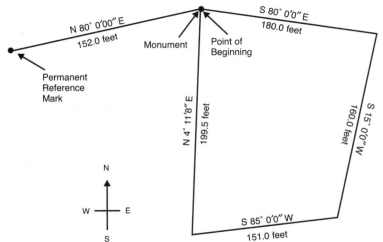

party conveys property bordering a stream, whether navigable or nonnavigable, the conveyance passes title to one-half of the streambed, subject, of course, to the rights of the state in and to that streambed. *Selkirk Island Corp.* v. *Stanley*, 683 S.W.2d 793 (Tex. Civ. App.—Corpus Christi, 1984). More serious questions are presented when those watercourses or roads change. When the road changes, the general rule to the center of the street controls. When a streambed or watercourse changes, the rules are much more complicated, and title can either be gained or lost. This is discussed in greater detail in Chapter 11, Involuntary Conveyances.

Whereas there is a certain amount of expertise required by surveyors in creating this exacting type of legal description, both brokers and lawyers must be familiar with the methods of measurement as well as the terms and descriptions used so that they can adequately determine the description of the property. It requires patience and practice to become proficient in using this method of legal description, but it is necessary to develop this skill to be more proficient in the real estate business.

# Rectangular Survey System

The **rectangular survey system** was established by Congress in 1785 to provide a faster and simpler method than metes and bounds for describing land and newly annexed territories. Rather than using physical monuments, the rectangular survey system is based on imaginary latitude and longitude lines. In determining descriptions across the vast area of the United States (only 18 states, including Texas, do not use the rectangular survey system) along longitudinal lines, **principal meridians** were established. Along the latitude lines, **base lines** were established. Every 24 miles north and south of the base lines **standard parallels** were established; every 24 miles east and west of the principal meridians, **guide meridians** were established. Guide meridians changed because of the curvature of the earth and had to be adjusted each 24 miles by a slight shift in the guide meridians known as **checks**. An example of how these measurements are taken is shown in Figure 4.3. In each 24-mile square area are 16 townships of 6 miles each. These are described north and south of the base line as **townships** and east and west of a meridian as **ranges**. An example of this type of description is shown in Figure 4.4. Each township is further divided into 36 sections, numbered as shown in Figure 4.5. Each section consists of 1 square mile.

Legal descriptions are then further divided into fractional areas of each section. An example of this further subdivision is shown in Figure 4.6.

Since Texas has never adopted the rectangular survey system, an exhaustive discussion of this subject is not necessary. It is important to understand the system of measurement, however, when dealing in other states and in understanding the basic definitions required to utilize this method of land description.

# Recorded Plat

One of the most convenient methods of describing land is by **recorded plat**. This is usually accomplished by a developer ascertaining a proper metes-and-bounds description of a large tract of property, dividing it into identifiable parcels, and

**FIGURE 4.3  SELECTED LATITUDE AND LONGITUDE LINES SERVE AS BASE LINES AND MERIDIANS.**

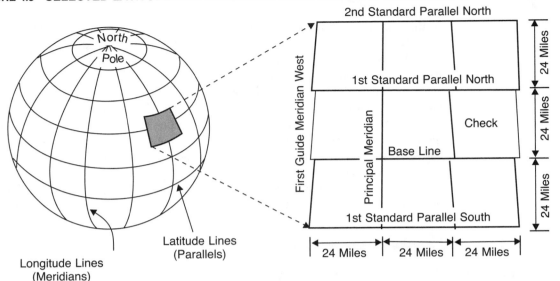

**FIGURE 4.4  IDENTIFYING TOWNSHIPS.**

recording the subdivision in the county clerk's office in the county in which the land is located. When recorded, it is recorded in the map records of the county. After this recordation the description in the subdivision plat will prevail over a competing metes-and-bounds description in the event of a conflict. *Ross* v. *Houston Oil Fields Associates*, 88 S.W.2d 586 (Tex. Civ. App.—Galveston, 1935).

**FIGURE 4.5 TOWNSHIP DIVIDED INTO SECTIONS.**

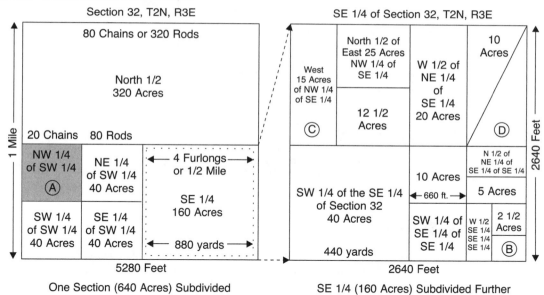

**FIGURE 4.6 SUBDIVIDING A SECTION.**

A proper identification of the property, then, could be made by referring to the description of the subdivided parcel in referencing the recordation information for the subdivision plat. The most common methods of description indicated by a recorded plat would be those of lot, block, section, and subdivision, as in Figure 4.7.

A legal description by recorded plat is not the same as a description by a tax assessor's parcel number. The description of property by tax assessor's parcel number is for the convenience of the tax assessor and cannot be relied upon as being legally accurate. *Meek* v. *Bower*, 333 S.W.2d 175 (Tex. Civ. App.—Houston, 1960).

**FIGURE 4.7  LAND DESCRIPTION BY RECORDED PLAT.**

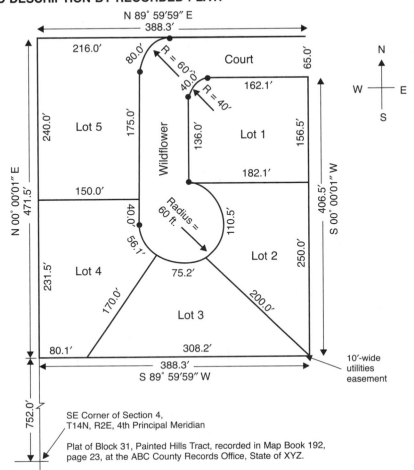

## ■ SUMMARY

In general, Texas requires that the description of the land in any written document describes the land with reasonable certainty. Texas uses two basic theories of legal descriptions: the metes-and-bounds method and the lot and block method. Texas has never adopted the rectangular survey method.

Even though the land may be sufficiently described, there can be a conflict in priorities if there are calls to natural monuments. Even man-made monuments can move to some degree. References to streets typically go to the center of the street, as do references to streams.

The rectangular survey system was established by Congress in 1785. It is based on imaginary latitude and longitude lines. While it is consistent and easy to use for very large parcels of real estate, it is not precise enough to be very accurate.

The recorded plat system is used for all recorded subdivisions. The perimeter of the subdivision is defined by metes and bounds; then the subdivision is divided into a recorded series of lots and blocks that, when recorded in the county courthouse, creates a much more simplified method of legal description.

# CHAPTER 5

# How Ownership Is Held

Ownership of real estate must be vested in a specific, identifiable legal entity. Some person, company, or organization maintains legal control over real estate and is held to be responsible for activities and obligations arising as a result of that ownership and control. So it is important to know that a party acting in any capacity has the authority to engage in the transaction.

On the other hand, a group of people, or an individual, contemplating a purchase of real estate will want to give serious consideration as to how the ownership to that real estate should be held. This normally requires sound legal advice because the means of ownership dictates tax consequences, scope of control, and liabilities of ownership—liabilities that may have far-reaching, and sometimes unexpected, legal complications.

The entities of ownership discussed in this chapter will include ownership in severalty, tenancy in common, joint tenancy, partnerships, limited partnerships, corporations, limited liability companies, and trusts. Each type of ownership will be discussed in its purest, most basic form to simplify its unique characteristics.

## Ownership in Severalty

Ownership in **severalty** is the easiest to understand, simply being **individual ownership**. One person is the owner. He has sole control over the use and possession of the property and also has unlimited liability for all causes of action arising as a result of his ownership of that property.

## Tenancy in Common

The ownership of real estate by multiple entities is generally for a specific purpose, or to achieve a specific, desired result. However, when there are no special circumstances to compel a different conclusion, multiple ownership in Texas is presumed to be a **tenancy in common**.

Tenancy in common can best be defined as an *ownership of real estate by more than one, in undivided interests*. This means there is no requirement that the fractional undivided interests be equal. The main characteristic of tenancy in common is the unity of possession (i.e., all of the co-tenants have the right to possession of the real estate since each interest is undivided). All of the co-tenants do not have to occupy the real estate at one time, however. A possession of one co-owner is deemed a possession by all co-owners. Upon the death of a co-owner, their respective interest passes to their heirs.

## Rights of Parties

Since there is a multiple ownership, there are certain obligations among the co-owners to each other. When only one of the co-owners is in possession, the relationship of the possessor and the other co-owners is generally construed to be one of landlord and tenant. However, if a co-owner receives more than his proportionate share of rights (for instance, if the property is income-producing), he owes a duty to pay the other co-owners their proportionate benefits and to give them full accounting thereof. *Perez* v. *Hernandez*, 658 S.W.2d 697 (Tex. App.—Corpus Christi, 1983). The same is true of expenses. If one of the co-tenants incurs necessary expenses, he is entitled to reimbursement from the other co-tenant or co-tenants. *Smith* v. *Smith*, 777 S.W.2d 798 (Tex. App.—Beaumont, 1989, no writ). On the other hand, if the one co-owner's possession is clearly in disavowal of the rights of the other co-owners, this co-owner may be construed to be an adverse possessor.

## Liabilities

There is no prohibition from a co-owner encumbering, selling, or leasing his respective interest as long as it does not adversely affect the rights of the other co-owners in his financial affairs; his obligation to third-party creditors extends only to his proportionate, undivided interest in the real property. *Barstow* v. *State*, 744 S.W.2d 495 (Tex. App.—Austin, 1988). If a co-owner loses his share, the creditor becomes a tenant (owner) in common with the other co-owners. If the property is encumbered by a single mortgage or other obligation incurred by all the co-owners, however, the creditors can seek collection from one or all of the co-owners, jointly or severally. In such a case, the co-owner who ultimately pays the debt has the right to reimbursement from the other co-owners. *Dutcher* v. *Owens*, 647 S.W.2d 948 (Tex. 1983). This apparently applies to legitimate debts only. If the expenses are voluntarily paid for the development of the property without the consent of the other co-tenants, the expenses are not reimbursable. *Perez* v. *Hernandez*, supra; *Pendley* v. *Byrom*, 703 S.W.2d 405 (Tex. Civ. App.—Eastland, 1986).

To simplify this concept, one may want to think of ownership by tenants in common as more than one undivided ownership in severalty. Conflicts among the co-tenants (co-owners) may be resolved through a suit for **partition**, in kind or value, of the property. Such partitioning may be a voluntary agreement or may be judicially imposed.

# Joint Tenancy

Ownership by joint tenancy is often confused with ownership by tenancy in common, and an effort should be made to distinguish between the two types of ownership. **Joint tenancy** is generally defined as ownership of real estate by two or more, with the parties having a **right of survivorship**. Right of survivorship means that upon the death of one of the joint tenants, the other joint tenant(s) automatically succeeds to the decedent's interest. Normally, as tenants in common, the decedent's interest would go to her heirs or the beneficiaries of her will. This is not so if the decedent held title to her real estate as a joint tenant.

At common law, the primary characteristic of tenancy in common is unity of possession. Joint tenancy requires **four unities**: **time**, **title**, **interest**, and **possession**. All of these unities must vest simultaneously, almost necessitating the use of a single conveying instrument for all grantees. That is the only sure way all four unities can vest at one time.

## Creation

Texas, long steeped in the heritage of homesteads and community property rights, does not look favorably on joint tenancies because joint tenancies normally leave the joint tenants' families with no rights to the real estate. In fact, Texas even goes one step further by statutorily abolishing joint tenancies except where created by an agreement in writing of the joint owners, *V.A.T.S., Probate Code, §46[a], §46[b]; V.T.C.A., See Family Code, §4.102*. However, in no event is such an agreement assumed from the mere fact that the property is held in joint ownership.

Since this statutory reference is the only authority for the establishment of joint tenancies in Texas, it leads one to assume that the four-unities theory is not a requirement in Texas. However, this has not been judicially determined to date.

There is a form of ownership in other states between a husband and wife called **tenancy by the entireties**. It creates a life estate in each spouse, with a right of survivorship, such that the surviving spouse has a predetermined future interest in the other spouse's estate. This means of ownership, the subject of several landmark Texas Supreme Court decisions, is not recognized in Texas. Texas allows the spouses to accomplish the same effect by using a right of survivorship in community property, discussed in Chapter 3.

It would seem that a well-written will would accomplish the same end result without most of the complications and adverse case law of joint tenancies in Texas. However, creating a joint tenancy vests title to the surviving joint tenant immediately upon the death of the other joint tenant by operation of law. It may provide the appropriate avenue to avoid will contests and lengthy probate proceedings.

## Liabilities

Both joint tenancy and tenancy in common share the mutual obligations of co-ownership. That is, each of the joint tenants owes the duty of care to the other(s) not to commit waste or arbitrarily withhold economic benefits of the other(s). Each joint tenant has a liability of his fractional interest for debts. When a joint tenant conveys or loses his interest, the new owner becomes a tenant in common rather than a joint tenant, although the other joint tenants maintain their existing status.

Note that the unity of time requirement, needed for the creation of a joint tenancy at common law, is not satisfied when a new co-owner receives an interest in the ownership. One owner may also partition his interest in the event of a conflict, similar to that right of a tenant in common.

# Community Property Right of Survivorship

As previously discussed in Chapter 3, the Texas Probate Code now specifically enables spouses to agree between themselves that all or part of their community property, then existing or to be acquired, can create a **community property right of survivorship**, *V.T.C.A., Probate Code, §452.* The agreement shall be sufficient to create a right of survivorship in community property if it includes any of the following phrases:

1. "With right of survivorship."
2. "Will become the property of the survivor."
3. "Will vest in and belong to the surviving spouse."
4. "Shall pass to the surviving spouse."

If the agreement "otherwise meets" with requirements of this part, however, the agreement shall become effective without including any of those phrases. The statute, therefore, gives broad authority as to what the actual verbiage could be and should be liberally construed. Except for the right of survivorship, the ownership, management, and operation of the community property during the marriage remain the same.

An interesting portion of the statute (Section 454) indicates that the transfer at death resulting from an agreement involving the community property with right of survivorship is *not* a testamentary transfer. It is, therefore, not subject to the other statute applicable to testamentary transfers under the Probate Code. It is enforced purely as an agreement between the parties to effect a vesting of title into the surviving spouse. Apparently, a mere revocation terminates the title and does not require a reconveyance by deed.

The agreement may be revoked in accordance with its terms. If the agreement does not specify the method for revocation, the agreement *may* be revoked by written instrument signed by both spouses or by written instrument signed by one spouse and delivered to the other spouse. The agreement may also be revoked with respect to specific property upon disposition of that property by one or both of the spouses, if that disposition is not inconsistent with the right of survivorship agreement. The difficult portion of this statute is that it consistently uses the term "may," and not the term "will" or "shall." So in all circumstances it will require some form of proof to show that the agreement to revoke was effective. This form of ownership creates so many complications on death (due to creditor's rights, etc.) that it is seldom used.

## Business Organizations

In 2003, the Texas Legislature established a whole new series of statutes for business organizations called the Business Organizations Code. This was done in order to make the law of business organizations more accessible and understandable while rearranging the statutes into a more logical order, accommodate future expansion of this area of the law, and eliminate duplicitous and ineffective provisions of the current law. Most other statutes relating to business organizations have been repealed and replaced by this new Code. The statute provides a massive amount of definitions which are applicable to virtually all of the business organizations and then develops "spokes" of areas of the law that are specific or unique to certain types of business organization. For our purposes we will discuss the basics of organization first, then discuss each entity separately, and discuss only those entities which are most common to real estate ownership.

**Powers and Authority.** The code gives all domestic entities the powers to take action as necessary or convenient to carry out its business and affairs including the power to: (1) sue, (2) sue and be sued, (3) make contracts, (4) lend money, (5) incur indebtedness and a myriad of other powers, not specifically excluded by the Code. *V.T.C.A., Business Organizations Code, §2.101.* Not-for profit entities can acquire, own, hold mortgage and dispose of and invest its funds in property for the use and benefit of its members.

**Formation.** All business entities must file a certification of formation described under the Code and comes into existence when the filing of the certificate takes affect. A domestic entity exists perpetually unless otherwise provided in the governing documents to the entity. A certificate of formation must include (1) the name of the filing entity being formed, (2) the type of filing entity being performed, (3) for filing entities other than limited partnerships, the purpose or purposes for which the filing entity is formed, which may be stated to be or include any lawful purpose for that type of entity, (4) for filing entities other than limited partnerships the period of duration, if the entity is not performed to exist perpetually, (5) the street address as to the initial registered office of the filing entity and the name of the initial registered agent or the filing entity of that office, (6) the name and address of each (a) organizer for the filing entity unless the entity is formed under a plan of conversion or merger, (b) general partner, if the filing entity is a limited partnership, or (c) trust manager, if the filing entity is a real estate investment trust; (7) if the filing entity is formed under a plan of conversion or merger, a statement to that effect; and (8) any other information required by the Business Organizations Code. See generally §3.001 of the Code.

# Partnerships

A **partnership** is statutorily defined as:

> an association of two or more persons to carry on as co-owners a business for profit.

There are three basic partnership entities that will be discussed: (1) general partnerships, (2) joint ventures, and (3) limited partnerships.

## General Partnerships

For **general partnerships**, Texas has enacted Chapter 152 of the **Texas Business Organization Code**, which contains a large number of statutes and sets out most of the basic guidelines within which partnership law is determined. These laws can, as in most other areas of the law, become very complicated because of the technicalities to which the statutes address themselves. Therefore, only the major components of partnerships as they pertain to real estate ownership will be discussed.

**Creation.** There are no specific statutory guidelines necessary for the creation of a partnership; a written or oral agreement is not necessarily essential. A partnership is normally inferred when there is a clear intention to create a partnership, and when the partners in fact have a co-ownership with the intention of sharing profits or losses on a particular business venture. Any estate in real property may be acquired in the partnership name or the names of individual partners, and any property bought by the partnership or acquired by the partnership by purchase or otherwise is considered partnership property. Once so acquired, the estate can be conveyed only in the partnership name. As a matter of form, the purchase or conveyance of partnership property generally includes the name of the partnership and then lists each of the partners individually, so that there is no mistake as to who is liable on the partnership debts or obligations.

Once it has been determined that a partnership has been created, the law tends to support the maintenance and continuity of that partnership. It is important to understand that each partner actually gets three distinct rights:

1. The partner's rights in *specific partnership property*.
2. The partner's *interest in the partnership*.
3. The partner's *right to participate in the management* of that partnership.

Of these three rights, the only one that may be considered community property (and therefore subject to a spouse's interest) is the partner's interest in the partnership. A partner's rights to specific partnership property and his right to management in the partnership are partnership property and cannot be conveyed or assigned without the consent of all the members of the partnership. Similarly, a person cannot become a partner in a partnership without the consent of all the other partners, unless their partnership agreement provides otherwise.

Partnership law creates a very high duty of care and trust that each partner owes to the other partners. This relationship of trust and confidence is termed a **fiduciary** relationship. Each partner is an agent for the whole partnership and can bind the partnership to any obligations incurred in the usual course of business. For instance, where title to real property is in the partnership name, any single partner may convey title to such property by conveyance executed in the partnership name. Similarly, a single partner can incur a partnership debt or other contractual obligation without the joinder of the other partners.

Although some of these conditions may seem rather onerous, the basic reason for this regulation and total obligation of the partners revolves around the obligations and liabilities to which the partners are bound, pursuant to the provisions of the Texas Uniform Partnership Act. Since every act of the partner for carrying on, in the usual way, the business of the partnership binds the partnership totally, each of the partners is liable jointly and severally; that is, the partnership is liable and each of the partners is liable individually for the entire obligation of the partnership. The partnership is bound by the partners' acts, even if they are wrongful, and even if one of the partner's acts amounts to a breach of trust between the partners.

**Advantages.** The advantages of a partnership are basically the pooling of resources (one firm of partners may have many experts to share ideas) and liabilities so that, at least theoretically, no one partner bears the brunt of all the losses. Another advantage is that all losses to the partnership, as well as all profits, are passed through directly to each of the partners individually. Although the partnership itself is required to file a federal tax return, the payment of all taxes or deduction of all losses is proportionately applicable to the individual partner's tax return. This is in contrast to corporate or trust ownership where there are less advantageous elements of taxation. Since real estate has tax benefits to owners (depreciation allowances, capital gains tax treatment, tax-free exchange, and installment sale benefits), it is sometimes very important for tax purposes that these losses and deductions be able to pass to the individual purchasers rather than to an ownership entity, which provides no direct benefits to the individual's tax return.

**Disadvantages.** The disadvantages of a general partnership are self-explanatory. Since there is joint and several liability, one partner may be required to meet all the obligations of the partnership if the other partners choose not to fund the partnership obligations. Even though the paying partner could seek recovery from the other partners, the risk is often too high for the benefits obtained.

## Joint Ventures

A **joint venture** is a partnership, sometimes more appropriately called a **joint adventure**. This is a particular type of partnership where two or more partners jointly pursue a specified project. They are not simply in business for a profit, as is the typical definition of partnerships as a whole. Rather, they are in business for profit from a particular project. Legally, a joint venture is governed by the same rules as partnerships generally. Texas courts have traditionally held that the establishment of a joint venture requires four basic elements: (1) community of interest in the venture; (2) agreement to share profits; (3) agreement to share losses, costs, or expenses; and (4) mutual right of control or management in the venture of the enterprise. Failure by parties to agree to share losses precludes the existence of a joint venture. *Gutierrez* v. *Yancey*, 650 S.W.2d 169 (Tex. Civ. App.—San Antonio, 1983).

The more typical joint venture situations involve two partners, one of whom is a financial partner and the other of whom is a managing partner. The financial partner is generally a lending institution, insurance company, or other financially strong investment group. The managing partner is generally a very experienced developer who has had a long track record of building certain types of projects. The financial partner (company or institution) normally visualizes a chance for more profits than simply the return on its investment capital if it owns half of the project. The developer visualizes no financing worries or funding problems while the project proceeds to final completion. Both partners, of course, have mutual dependencies on each other by sharing risks, but they also have those certain areas of expertise that make those risks less. Joint ventures are usually very sophisticated transactions, although they can be as small as two brokers agreeing to work together and share a commission on a particular sale. As in all general partnerships, there is a high fiduciary duty to the other joint venturers. *Sanchez* v. *Matthews*, 636 S.W.2d 455 (Tex. Civ. App.—San Antonio, 1982).

## Limited Liability Partnerships

The Texas Business Organizations Code also provides for the creation of limited liability partnerships. A partner in a registered **limited liability partnership** is not individually liable for debts and obligations of the partnership arising from errors, omissions, negligence, incompetence, or malfeasance committed in the course of partnership business by another partner, or a representative of the partnership, not working under the supervision or direction of the first partner at the time the errors, omissions, negligence, incompetence, or malfeasance occurred, unless the first partner directly involved had knowledge of the misconduct at the time of the occurrence.

To register a limited liability partnership, the partnership must file with the Secretary of State an application stating the name of the partnership, the address of the principal place of business, the number of partners, and a brief statement of the business in which the partnership engages. The registered limited liability partnership's name must contain words "registered limited liability partnership" or the abbreviation "L.L.P." as the last words or letters of its name. The registered limited liability partnership must carry, if reasonably available, at least $100,000 of liability insurance of the kind that is designated to cover the kinds of errors, omissions, negligence, incompetence, or malfeasance for which liability is limited.

## Limited Partnerships

**Limited partnerships** have been a very effective tool for real estate ownership and investment. These partnerships are sometimes considered the standard form of investment ownership to achieve maximum benefits for private investors. Limited partnerships have been of such long-standing acceptance that this method is considered by many professionals to be one of the more stable means of ownership, as well as one of the most beneficial. The law in this area is reasonably well settled and is generally understood by most investors. This form of ownership has been effectively utilized in small to very large investments, some of which have been syndicated using large numbers of investors, and which have been offered for sale by large stock brokerage firms.

A limited partnership is statutorily defined as a partnership formed by two or more persons under the provisions of the act and having as members one or more **general partners** and one or more **limited partners**. The limited partners, as such, are a separate class of partners and are not bound by the obligations of the partnership to third parties, so long as the formalities of the limited partnership agreement and applicable statutes are complied with.

**Creation.** The creation of a Texas limited partnership involves a certain amount of formality and structure. Two of the instruments needed to properly create a limited partnership are the **certificate of limited partnership** and the **limited partnership agreement**.

The limited partnership agreement can be written or oral. The certificate of limited partnership, however, must be in writing, and an original and one copy of the certificate must be filed with the **Secretary of State** of the State of Texas. The certificate must conform with the filing requirements of the code, but must also contain the address of the principal office in the United States where records are kept. The name of the limited partnership must contain the word "limited," "limited partnership" or an abbreviation of that word or phrase.

The certificate must be signed by all general partners when filed and be accompanied by the statutory filing fee.

**Liabilities.** One of the more attractive aspects of ownership by limited partnership is the limited liability it provides for the limited partners. The general partner in a limited partnership has all the liabilities of the partner in a general partnership, that is, joint, several, and total. The limited partners, however, are not bound by any of the obligations of the partnership, and none of the limited partners' assets are considered liable for partnership debts or liabilities. In theory, the only risk the limited partner takes is the loss of his contribution. However, it should not be overlooked that the limited partner does have the statutory liability to the partnership for the difference between his contribution as made and for any unpaid contribution that he agreed to make in the future. So where a limited partner may not be liable to third-party creditors, he may be personally liable (both by statute and by the terms of the limited partnership agreement) to his other partners for his contributions to the partnership. Limited partners, because of the nature of their contribution, are sometimes given preferential returns on their contribution. However, they cannot get a return on their investment until all of the obligations of the partnership have been met. The limited partnership's interest is generally assignable, subject to the restrictions in the limited partnership agreement and the certificate of limited partnership.

**Advantages.** The advantages of limited partnership are self-explanatory once the basic provisions of the law concerning limited partnerships are understood. The main advantage is the limited liability of the limited partners as far as business obligations of the partnership to third parties are concerned. As stated previously, the limited partner's liability to a third party is limited to his contribution to the partnership and the obligations for additional contribution, but he may also have a personal liability to the other partners for his contributions.

Tax benefits are an additional advantage to limited partnerships. Partnerships, as stated previously, are taxed as a partnership; but the profits are normally passed through to the individual partners, who get the benefits of whatever tax savings, investment credit, or depreciation benefits accrue to the partnership. Therefore, at least in theory, the limited partner gets all the benefits of tax-sheltered real estate investments with virtually no liability except for his contribution to the partnership.

**Disadvantages.** The primary disadvantage to a limited partnership is that there is total reliance by the limited partners on the expertise and management capabilities of the general partner. Although the general partner enjoys joint, several, and total liability, one normally expects that the general partner selected will be one of prudent and capable past experience. There have been recent attempts to make the general partner a corporation, thereby limiting the liability of the general partner as well as that of the limited partners. Although this is not in itself illegal, it should be understood that there are certain tax consequences that may arise as a result of this type of organization. The Internal Revenue Service sometimes feels that if the general partner is a corporation, the limited partners are, in effect, shareholders rather than limited partners. The Internal Revenue Service, then, would look on the partnership as a corporation that would be taxed as a corporation rather than as a limited partnership. The guidelines and criteria for the Internal Revenue Service can sometimes be very technical, and one's accountant should always be consulted when considering this type of investment.

A second disadvantage revolves around the Securities and Exchange Commission. Limited partnerships, being investments, can be considered to be securities, and, if so, must be filed either with the Texas State Securities Board or with the federal Securities and Exchange Commission. This requirement to file is always a requirement unless the limited partnership falls under one of two basic exemptions provided by the Securities and Exchange Act or under the one single exemption provided by the Texas State Securities Board. The scope of these exemptions will be discussed in Chapter 20, Regulation of Real Estate.

A third disadvantage is that in filing a certificate of limited partnership, there is a certain amount of disclosure. Upon examining the required limited partnership records, there may be a disclosure of personal business that an individual may not want the public to know. There are times when a private investor may prefer not to have his interest known to the public when making real estate investments. If this is the case, limited partnerships may not be the most effective tool of investment.

The last disadvantage to be discussed is one important to all investors and brokers anticipating this type of investment. This disadvantage is one of control. It is statutorily provided that only general partners are allowed to take part in the control of the business. If any limited partner assumes the position of taking control of the business or taking part in any significant management of the partnership, he will become a general partner and be liable as a general partner. This principle applies even though the limited partner may assume such control in good faith and in the best interest of the partnership. Therefore, when a client or investor is interested in taking part in the business of the limited partnership, he may be well advised to keep his involvement to a minimum or he may be construed as a general partner.

Some changes to the Texas Revised Limited Partnership Act provide for additional authority that a limited partner may exercise and not be held liable as a general partner. The new statute specifies that a limited partner shall not become liable as a general partner unless he takes part in control of the business, and even then he is liable only to a person who transacts business with a partnership, reasonably believing that the limited partner is a general partner. The new change in the statute specifically provides that a limited partner can consult with and advise general partners; transact business with the partnership (having the same rights as a third-party creditor); and act as a contractor, agent, or employee of the partnership without assuming the responsibilities of a general partner.

# Corporations

**Corporations** as an ownership entity are probably affected by more statutory provisions than any other type of ownership entity in Texas. Corporations are rather complicated in nature, and it is important that the basics of the corporate structure be understood before further legal aspects of corporation ownership and control of real estate are discussed.

## Organization

Three basic classes of individuals are involved in the organization of all corporations: shareholders, directors, and officers.

**Shareholders** are, in fact, the owners of the corporation. A corporation normally raises its money for capital and initial ownership costs by selling shares to the shareholders. The shareholders, after advancing the money for the corporation's initial costs, ultimately control the corporation through the corporation's bylaws, and by voting their shares at the annual shareholders' meeting. At the annual shareholders' meeting, the shareholders elect the board of directors. The business and affairs of the corporation are managed by the **board of directors**, who are not required by law to be residents of the state, or even shareholders of the corporation. The **officers** of the corporation are elected by the board of directors. The officers and agents of the corporation (including employees) have the authority to perform the duties of the management of the corporation on a day-to-day basis and as may be determined by the board of directors. The corporation may then return the shareholders' investments through payment of dividends, normally paid quarterly. Figure 5.1 may serve to diagram these functions more clearly.

The same basic organization is involved whether it is a small, closely held corporation (this can even be a single person) or a major, publicly held corporation. In the closely held corporation, directors' and shareholders' meetings can be held over the family breakfast table instead of the more formal surroundings of a publicly held corporation. The key factor is that these meetings *must be held* to maintain the corporate formality and take advantage of the benefits of the corporation's existence.

## Creation

A Texas corporation is created upon filing of the charter with the office of the Secretary of State. The name of the corporation must contain the word "company," "corporation," "incorporated," "limited," or an abbreviation of one of those words. The **corporate charter**, though fairly general, requires certain disclosures similar to those of a limited partnership certificate. The charter also requires disclosure of the incorporators and of the first directors, as well as of the number of shares authorized to be distributed. After the corporation has been formed, the only requirement to maintain the corporate entity is to pay its corporate franchise tax each year.

If a corporation is formed in another state, it is deemed to be a **"foreign" corporation**. A foreign corporation may qualify to do business in Texas by registering with the Secretary of State, designating a resident agent for service of process, and paying the applicable annual franchise fees similar to the ones that domestic corporations pay. This provides a means by which a corporation organized in another state (the vast majority of major corporations are organized under the laws of the State of Delaware) can do business in Texas and not necessarily have to be organized under the laws of this state.

Although creation of a corporation may appear to be deceptively simple, it is important to realize that this normally requires the services of an attorney who is experienced in corporate law. There are additional statutory requirements for shareholders' and directors' meetings, minutes to be kept, bylaws, and other ancillary

**FIGURE 5.1 CORPORATE ORGANIZATION.**

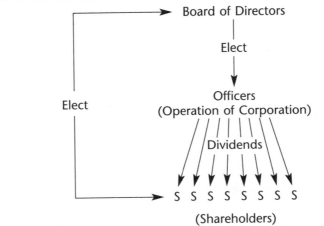

documents and functions required by law but which are not part of the simple filing of the corporate charter. These additional requirements, along with others involving corporate ownership (particularly in the field of real estate), require the expertise of individuals well versed in the area of corporate law as well as real estate law.

## Corporate Real Estate

Since all aspects of corporations are so carefully controlled by statute, it is only logical that the ownership and management of corporate real estate are also controlled by statute. Corporations are given the specific power to purchase and acquire real property, as well as the specific power to sell same. However, there is a significant difference between selling property and assets of a corporation in the regular course of business and the sale of all, or substantially all, of the corporation's assets. Sales in the regular course of business (a real estate developer, for instance) can effect the conveyance of real estate simply by the signature of the president, vice president, or attorney-in-fact of the corporation. A deed conveying a corporation's real property must be authorized by a resolution of the board of directors authorizing said sale. If the sale of the real estate consists of substantially all of the assets of said corporation, however, a resolution by the shareholders is required before such conveyance can be made.

## Corporate Liability

The primary purpose for which any group of people incorporates is for the protection and insulation from any liability of the shareholders and individuals organizing the corporation. The liability of the assets of the corporation is the only exposure. There is absolutely no personal liability whatsoever to third parties dealing with the corporation. Individuals can guarantee a corporate note or a corporate liability, or an officer can sign individually for the corporation and be personally liable, however. This is true even if the corporation has subsequently been dissolved, *V.T.C.A., Business Organizations Code, §21.223.*

The Business Organization Code has specific provisions that provide that any officer of a corporation acting in good faith and ordinary care has the right to rely on information, opinions, reports, and statements (including financial statements and other financial data) concerning the corporation or another person that will be prepared or presented by:

1. One or more officers or employees of the corporation, including members of the board of directors.
2. Legal counsel, public accountants, investment bankers, or other persons as to matters the officer reasonably believes are within the person's professional or expert competence.

This may prevent imputing absolute knowledge of all facts to officers and directors of corporations. Similar provisions are enacted for directors of corporations.

## Advantages of Corporate Ownership

The primary advantage of corporate ownership consists of the insulation from liabilities of all individuals concerned. As long as all the corporate debts, liabilities, and obligations are incurred through the corporate name, and without fraud or material misrepresentation, there is no personal liability on the part of the shareholders, offi-cers, or directors of the corporation.

There are times, however, when the courts will impose personal liability on individuals within the corporation. When this is done, it is referred to as "**piercing the corporate veil.**" In Texas, this is relatively difficult to achieve because the courts tend to uphold the corporate entity. However, if a person fraudulently induces a creditor to give a loan to the corporation, or if a corporation is created to perpetrate a fraud, there is adequate authority to pierce the veil and the indi-viduals will be held personally liable. *Castleberry* v. *Branscum*, 721 S.W.2d 270 (Tex. 1986). This is particularly true in small, closely held corporations.

The same theory applies to large corporations and their subsidiaries when a cred-itor has been misled into reliance on a parent corporation for a subsidiary's debt. This is simply another form of fraud. *Edwards Company, Inc.* v. *Monogram Industries, Inc.*, 700 F.2d 994 (5th Cir.—1983). This is true for liabilities under tort and contract if it appears that the subsidiary corporation is nothing more than a mere "alter ego" of the parent. This potential liability depends on such facts as whether or not: (1) the corporations are independently financed units; (2) the daily operations of the two cor-porations are separate; (3) management is different; and (4) third parties are ade-quately aware of the separate identities of the two corporations. *Miles* v. *American Telephone and Telegraph Co.*, 703 F.2d 193 (5th Cir.—1983).

Another distinct advantage to corporate ownership, and a major reason for the use of family corporations, is for estate planning purposes. The U.S. Congress and the Internal Revenue Service have constantly provided for better pension and re-tirement plans for those utilizing the corporate entity of ownership. As in other tax benefits, this has proved to be an incentive for many unincorporated entities to in-corporate to effect a greater tax savings.

## Disadvantages of Corporate Ownership

It has often been stated that the corporate ownership of real estate is not a desirable form of ownership because of the technical problems that result through the corpo-rate tax laws and the structures of organization within the corporation itself.

One of the biggest drawbacks of corporate ownership is the problem of dou-ble taxation. Income from real estate, profits from tax-free exchanges, capital gains benefits, and depreciation benefits—all normally considered attributable to real estate tax shelter techniques—are benefits accrued on behalf of the corporation, not on behalf of the shareholders. Therefore, the corporation gets the extra tax benefits and tax shelter, not the shareholders. To further complicate matters, all income of the corporation is taxed twice if it is distributed to the shareholders. To explain, the corporation is taxed once on its real estate income. Then, if there are any excess profits to be distributed to the shareholders, these profits are dis-tributed in the form of dividends, which are taxed a second time and are reflected on the shareholders' individual income tax returns. Therefore, as a tax shelter, cor-porations are generally not considered the best form of ownership for real estate purposes.

Further problems in corporate ownership result from the technical require-ments of state law pertaining to corporate ownership, to distribution of securities, and to disclosure to shareholders, as well as the requirements of other statutes per-taining to shareholders' and directors' obligations that are peculiar to corporate law.

A third difficulty of corporate ownership, particularly if the corporation is a large one, involves the infrastructure of the corporation itself. For example, it is not always clear to outsiders as to who has the authority to negotiate contracts, attend closings, and sign papers on behalf of the corporation. There has been further concern over the fact that it takes too much time for a corporation to operate from the initial negotiations between parties to the final ratification by shareholders and directors, plus the never-ending complications that "committees" create in the corporate process. A number of theories contend that corporations *per se*, as owners and managers of real estate, can never operate as fast as individuals or partnerships, and, therefore, they are not one of the better methods of owning, acquiring, and developing real estate. These theories are based on the assumption that decisions cannot be made quickly enough to satisfy the real estate market. It should be pointed out, however, that a number of extremely large corporations own, operate, and develop real estate very profitably because of the corporations' strength and stability, qualities that generally are not affected by the cyclical tendencies normally incident to the real estate industry as a whole.

## S Corporations

For many years the Internal Revenue Code has recognized an ownership called an S corporation. Basically, an **S corporation** is a recognized corporation under state statutes, but for income tax purposes it is treated similarly to a partnership (a regular corporation that does not elect this tax treatment is called a C corporation). The income and losses for the S corporation in any given year pass directly through to the shareholders, and therefore there is no "double taxation" disadvantage that the law recognizes in regular corporations.

Federal legislation passed in November 1982 significantly expanded a person's eligibility to utilize the S corporation status, so that these corporations may become a popular vehicle for real estate investment. In general, a small business corporation can elect S status under Section 1362(a)(1) of the Internal Revenue Code by unanimous vote of all of its shareholders. It may have only one class of stock, however, although the law does provide that you can have differences in voting rights. Therefore, that one class of nonvoting stock could provide a situation similar to that of limited partnerships, where all partners are entitled to a share of the profits but their ability to manage the business entity is limited. If a person becomes a shareholder after the election is filed, his consent is not required unless he owns more than 50 percent of the corporation's stock.

In 1996 Congress passed the Small Business Job Protection Act. It made S corporations even easier to use for real estate and other businesses. The number of allowable shareholders has been increased to 75 (it used to be 35). Married couples are treated as one shareholder. Under the same statute, S corporations are allowed to have active corporate subsidiaries to further insulate shareholders' liability. There were also more lenient rules passed in 1996 allowing subdivided land to be treated as capital gains property under certain conditions.

In short, the S corporation appears to create the best of both worlds, and an investor can insulate himself from liability as a corporate shareholder but can take advantage of the tax benefits, which are similar to those of a partnership, as long as the corporation remains reasonably active and does not concentrate its income on passive sources. If one is anticipating this method of holding property, however, it is imperative to seek competent legal and tax advice to help the corporation avoid some of the peculiar pitfalls of the application of corporate statutes as well as to help it cope with the unique requirements of the Internal Revenue Service as they apply to S corporations.

# Limited Liability Companies

There has been legitimate, and probably justified, concern over liabilities of defendants in a business environment. One understands that if a person is harmed, there should be an ability to recover from the wrongdoer, yet many juries are awarding significant sums of money, and plaintiffs are attempting to pursue personal liability for officers and directors of corporations because of their roles in the business entity.

Limited Liability Companies are now in Chapter 101 of the Texas Business Organizations Code. It is a lengthy, complicated statute, and only the most general descriptions can be explained at this time. There will be a lot of case law and perhaps amendments to the statutes forthcoming in the next few years.

## Creation

Any natural person of 18 years of age or older can act as an organizer of a **limited liability company** by signing the articles of organization of such limited liability company and giving the original and a copy of the articles to the Secretary of State. In additional to general filing requirements, the articles of organization must include:

1. Whether the limited liability company will or will not have managers.
2. If the limited liability company will have managers, the name and address of each initial manager of the limited liability company.
3. If the limited liability will not have managers, the name and address of each additional member of the limited liability company.

The Secretary of State then issues a certificate of organization, and the existence of the limited liability company begins at that time.

In general terms, a member or manager of a limited liability company is not liable for debts, obligations, or liabilities of a limited liability company. A membership interest is considered to be personal property, and the member has no interest in specific limited liability company property.

## Operations of a Limited Liability Company

The limited liability company name must include the word "limited" or the abbreviation "Ltd." or "L.C." It must maintain the registered office and registered agent (similar to a corporation), and all real or personal property owned or purchased by the limited liability company shall be held and owned, and the conveyance shall be made, in the name of the limited liability company. All instruments and documents providing for the acquisition, mortgage, or disposition of the limited liability company shall be valid and binding upon the company if they are executed by one or more persons acting as manager or member.

# Ownership by Trusts

In Texas, there are three major types of **trust** ownership. These include: (1) testamentary or inter vivos trusts, (2) land trusts, and (3) real estate investment trusts.

## Organization

As in corporation ownership, it is fairly important that we understand the basics of how a trust form of ownership operates before going into each of the individual types of trusts. Trusts generally have a **trustor**, sometimes called a **settlor**, who establishes the trust. Ownership and control of the trust are held by the **trustee**, who holds the trust in name only for the true owners, the **beneficiaries** of the trust. Normally, once a trust has been established by the trustor, it is usually irrevocable (and if irrevocable, it must be set out in the trust instrument) and title stays in the name of the trustee until the assets of the trust (called the **corpus**) are ultimately distributed to the beneficiaries. The income from the trust can be distributed to the beneficiaries at varying intervals, depending on the trust instrument. Trusts per se do not pay taxes if the income is distributed to the beneficiaries. The income is taxed as it is distributed to the beneficiaries. When the corpus of the trust and other undistributed income vest in the beneficiaries, however, it should be understood that the entire amount is taxed at that time, and this tax can be quite substantial. Figure 5.2 may help explain how the trust form of ownership generally operates.

According to the **Texas Trust Code**, the trustee individually is not liable for debts or obligations of the trust. The only liability is to the assets of the trust. The trustee has a fiduciary obligation to administer the trust properly. The trustee can be held personally liable to the beneficiaries for not protecting the beneficiaries' respective interests. There are certain statutory provisions restricting certain conveyances by the trustee to relations and affiliates, although this restriction can be waived for a noncorporate trustee, *V.T.C.A., Trust Code, §113.053, 113.059*. As in corporate ownership, however, when a third party deals with a person who operates as a trustee, such party is bound by law to understand that the trust is not individually liable under most circumstances.

## Testamentary and Inter Vivos Trusts

**Testamentary** and **inter vivos** trusts are normally trusts set up for the benefit of the beneficiaries for estate purposes of the trustor. The Rule against Perpetuities dictates that the period that the trust may exist is limited to approximately 21 years after the death of the trustor at the time the trust was created, plus any actual period of gestation (this period of time is typically 21 years, plus 9 months after the death of the trustor). If the beneficiaries are children or grandchildren of the trustor, it is generally very functional for the trustor to set up the estate in a trust so that it will not be taxed, and the income and benefits of that trust will be managed professionally by a bank trust department or by some other responsible entity. The

**FIGURE 5.2  TRUST ORGANIZATION.**

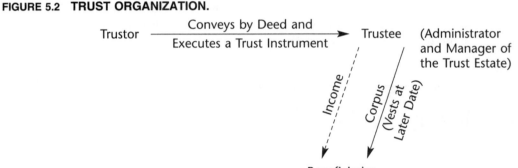

corpus of the estate may then vest in the beneficiaries (probably at a lower tax rate, depending on their incomes when it vests) and may also provide for their well-being, expenses, and usual standard of living.

As previously stated, real estate held by a trustee in this capacity is subject to very high fiduciary obligations between the trustee and beneficiaries. The only personal liability involved is that of the trustee to the beneficiaries, and not to third-party creditors. If a trustee has mismanaged the assets or acted in bad faith, the beneficiaries have a cause of action against the trustee. Real estate conveyed, sold, mortgaged, or encumbered on the part of the trustee, therefore, must be done only in good faith and in the exercise of sound business judgment. The trustee binds the assets of the trust for whatever obligations may be incurred. The Texas Trust Code creates a presumption that anyone signing as "trustee" has the authority to act as such, *V.A.T.S., Trust Code, §114.082.*

## Land Trusts

A second type of trust that has been emerging in Texas in recent years is what we are now calling the **land trust**. This type of trust has been called an Illinois Land Trust, and sometimes a Massachusetts Business Trust. Texas is now developing its own brand of this trust, which is becoming a common means of ownership in Texas. This type of ownership is normally created by an individual or promoter who buys land for a venture as a "trustee" for management or speculative holding purposes for a group of individual investors. The theory behind this is that the management, handling, and ownership will vest in only one person, who will be the trustee, for the benefit of the investors, who are the beneficiaries. A new Texas Trust Code was passed in 1983, but the legal requirements for this entity are still a little hazy in Texas. *Neeley* v. *Intercity Management Corporation*, 623 S.W.2d 942 (Tex. Civ. App.—Houston, 1981). It is generally presumed that the same fiduciary capacity exists between the trustee and beneficiaries, and the trustee generally recognizes having a duty of full disclosure for aspects of the transaction and in keeping the beneficiaries fully informed. The trustee's duties to third parties are still puzzling. There has been some litigation in this area, which has left the issue unresolved and basically found the trustee personally liable, rather than looking to the assets of the trust. Just calling a person "trustee" does not create a trust. *Nolana Development Association* v. *Corsi*, 682 S.W.2d 246 (Tex. 1984). A recent amendment to the Property Code gives the trustee absolute power to deal with real property, however, and gives rise to a better presumption of authority for trustees of undisclosed trusts, *V.T.C.A., Property Code, §101.001.*

This type of trust has often been used as a very functional, expedient, and simple way of owning and controlling real estate, but it must be understood that the laws affecting the liabilities of the parties are not well settled and may be subject to a wide variety of interpretations by the Texas courts. This type of ownership does maintain the secrecy of all the beneficiaries (often called beneficial owners), it requires no initial cost to form this kind of entity, and it has been used countless times without any adverse consequences. However, before this type of ownership is utilized, it is very important to get very competent legal counsel to ensure the maximum protection for everyone's interest.

## Real Estate Investment Trusts

The **real estate investment trust** was specifically provided for by federal statute in the form of an amendment to the Internal Revenue Code. The new provision enables the ownership and development of large real estate interests by a trust for the benefit of large numbers of investors while maintaining the tax benefits of real estate ownership for each investor. In these cases, the promoter or developer is the trustor, and the assets of the trust are the investors' cash. The trust is generally administered by a board of trustees (who are professional real estate consultants), and the beneficiaries are, of course, the investors.

Real estate investment trusts for a number of years prospered greatly on the real estate investment market and sold shares as over-the-counter stocks or were registered on the New York Stock Exchange or the American Stock Exchange. This form of real estate ownership encouraged the small investor to invest small amounts of money in very large projects; but unlike other investments on the stock market, the small investor could enjoy all the tax shelter benefits of real estate ownership in addition to the income from the project. In theory, this turned out to be one of the true booms in the real estate industry because it provided a large amount of capital and equity dollars to buy and develop projects from private sources (i.e., small individual investors). However, in the early to middle 1970s, there were a number of mismanagement, overextension, and negligence problems that arose as a result of this boom in real estate investment. This caused a decline in real estate investment trusts. Other reasons for the decline are unusually complicated because they involve not only the technicalities of real estate law, but technicalities pursuant to stock exchange registration, disclosures required by the Securities and Exchange Commission, and certain theories of economics and finance. However, the basic premises under which real estate investment trusts were originally formed are still good, and these trusts will probably become strong once again, perhaps under a slightly stricter federal regulation. Any real estate investment trust formed in Texas must additionally comply with Chapter 200 of the Texas Business Organizations Code, with regard to the formation and managing of said trust. These requirements, coupled with the additional requirements of the Internal Revenue Service and the Securities and Exchange Commission, make this a relatively complicated method of real estate ownership. However, its effectiveness should not be underestimated.

# Unincorporated Associations

The 1995 legislature recently adopted the Texas Uniform Unincorporated Non-Profit Association Act. A non-profit association is defined under the statute as "an unincorporated organization, other than one created by a trust, consisting of three or more persons joined by mutual consent for a common, non-profit purpose." The statute provides that a nonprofit association may hold title to real estate in its own name, and can transfer and encumber real estate, or be beneficiary of a trust, contract, or will. The statute, in effect, gives nonprofit associations, regardless of their lack of organization, separate status as an entity under Texas law. One of the more important provisions of the statute is that the nonprofit association is a separate legal entity from its members for the purposes of determining and enforcing rights, duties, and liabilities in contract and in tort. Under this statute, a person is not liable for a breach of a nonprofit association's contract, tortious act, or omission merely because that person is a member. *V.A.T.S., art. 1396-70.01; V.T.C.A., Business Organization Code, §252.001 et seq.*

A chart showing the various methods of ownership is shown on the following page as Figure 5.3.

**FIGURE 5.3 REAL ESTATE OWNERSHIP.**

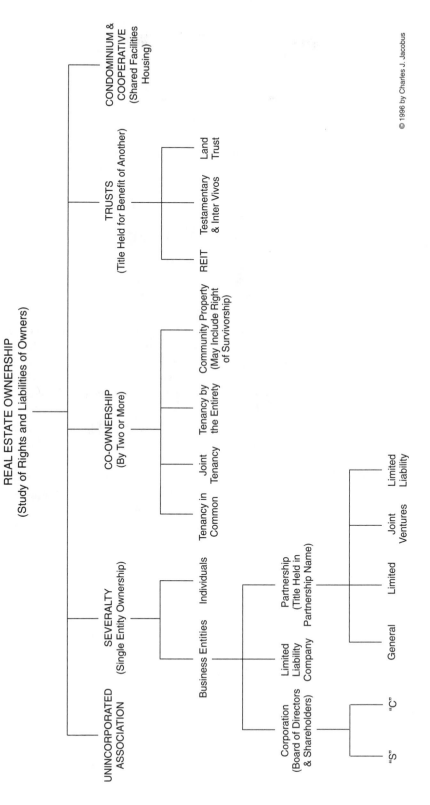

© 1996 by Charles J. Jacobus

## ■ SUMMARY

Anyone contemplating the purchase of real estate will want to give serious consideration to how the ownership of the real estate should be held. Ownership in severalty is individual ownership. Ownership by more than one person normally involves a tenancy in common, joint tenancy, and partnerships. Partnerships are classified further as general partnerships, joint ventures, or limited partnerships.

Ownership in severalty can also include two other forms of ownership: corporate and trust. Ownership in these is controlled and regulated by both state and federal statutes.

Each type of ownership has its own advantages and disadvantages. Determination of an owner's rights and considerations of any ownership entity require sound legal advice.

## CASE STUDIES FOR DISCUSSION

1. A husband and a wife opened three bank accounts, depositing $10,000 of community funds in each account. They signed an agreement with the bank indicating that in the event of the death of either party, the money in the account would go to the survivor. What legal ramifications do you see?

2. A husband and a wife opened three bank accounts, depositing $10,000 in each account, which were separate funds of the wife and separate funds of the husband. They signed an agreement with the bank indicating that in the event of the death of either party, the money in the account would go to the survivor. What legal ramifications do you see? Did a constitutional amendment eliminate the distinction between questions 1 and 2?

3. Arthur Tucker bought a tract and held title to the property as Arthur Tucker, Trustee. There was no executed trust instrument. The trustee subsequently borrowed money, using the property as security without informing the beneficiaries of the trust. Upon default of the note, the bank sued to foreclose on the property. The beneficiaries sued the trustee because of breach of fiduciary capacity. What legal ramifications do you see?

## CHAPTER 6

# Fixtures and Easements

Fixtures and easements share a common characteristic that enables them to be discussed in the same chapter: They both involve rights that a third party may have in an owner's real estate. Fixtures involve the rights that a materialman, supplier, seller, or purchaser may have in certain appliances or appurtenances to one's real estate. Easements, on the other hand, involve the rights of a third party to the use of an access across another individual's real estate.

## Fixtures

There are a large number of different laws applicable to the concept of fixtures, making the exact meaning of the term "fixture," as used in every case, difficult to define. A **fixture** has been defined by case law as an article or personalty that has been attached to the real estate so that it becomes real estate. *Ruby* v. *Cambridge Mutual Fire Ins. Co.*, 358 S.W.2d 945 (Tex. Civ. App.—Dallas, 1962). Statutorily, it has been determined that goods are "fixtures" when they become so related to particular real estate that an interest in them arises under the real property law of the state in which the real estate is situated, *Texas Business and Commerce Code, §9.102(a)(41)*.

### Realty to Personalty—Personalty to Realty

The difficulty in the determination of fixtures results from the change in the nature of articles that are to become fixtures. For instance, a light fixture is very clearly an item of personalty (properly called **chattel**) that one may buy at a store that sells lights. However, once the fixture has been bolted into the ceiling and has been established as a part of the particular decor of a dining room, one might expect that it will become part of the real estate. Similar problems occur with drapes, certain types of shelving, carpeting, and many other objects that can be affixed to real estate in one form or another. On the other hand, there is an equal difficulty in determining the characteristics of items that are real estate and then become personalty. There are interesting applications of this concept in the oil and gas law, where the minerals are considered part of the real estate, but once they reach the wellhead or are extracted from the ground, they are considered personalty, to be sold by the owners as a non–real estate item. Similarly, it is easy to envision a house being destroyed and several items of realty being converted for personal use and sold at auctions, garage sales, and even lumber- and brickyards.

This problem can be further complicated by the fact that the conveyancing instruments utilized for realty and personalty are entirely different. Real estate is normally conveyed by the use of a deed, will, or other conveyancing instrument; items of personalty are normally transferred by an instrument called a bill of sale. A copy of a **bill of sale** is shown in Figure 6.1.

**FIGURE 6.1  BILL OF SALE.**

BILL OF SALE

THE STATE OF TEXAS      §

                                     §         KNOW ALL MEN BY THESE PRESENTS

COUNTY OF _____ §

THAT the undersigned _____, ("Seller") for the sum of Ten and No/100 ($10.00), and other good and valuable consideration, the receipt and sufficiency of which is hereby acknowledged, and for the execution and delivery by Buyer of its one certain promissory note in the original principal sum of _____ payable to the order of _____ as therein provided does hereby GRANT, BARGAIN, SELL and TRANSFER to ("Buyer"), its successors and assign the following described personal property located in _____ County, Texas, to-wit:

    All the furniture, equipment, fixtures, goodwill, inventory, and other tangible assets being further described as Exhibit "A" attached hereto.

TO HAVE AND TO HOLD, all the singular, the said personal property to Buyer, to their own use forever.

The Seller hereby binds itself, its successors and assigns, to warrant and defend the title to all of the herein described property unto Buyer, its successors and assigns forever against every person whomsoever lawfully claiming or to claim such herein described property or any part thereof.

EXECUTED this the _____ day of _____, 20 _____.

SELLER

_____

To add more confusion, it should also be mentioned that additional complications can arise in fixtures depending on who is claiming an interest in those fixtures. Once it has been determined that an item is a fixture, real estate law applies, along with certain mechanics' and materialmen's liens, statutes, and certain laws relating to mortgages. If an item is not a fixture, the **Uniform Commercial Code** applies to rights of parties, and the real estate law does not. A party may also qualify to claim an interest in the item both as an item of realty and as an item of personalty. Therefore, the law of fixtures must include certain applications of mortgage law, real estate liens, and fixture filing provisions of the Texas Business and Commerce Code. It is through the interrelationships of these three areas of the law that one can determine who has the right to a particular item, after it has been determined whether or not that item is a fixture.

Now that total confusion has set in, it is important to discuss the determination of a fixture and then attempt to untangle the problem of priorities once the concept of fixture is fully understood.

## Determination of a Fixture

In most real estate sales, the key concern in the determination of a fixture generally involves a fact situation where a prospective purchaser is buying real estate, normally a home, and this purchaser expects certain items to remain with the real estate because he considers them to be fixtures. To make the situation more interesting, however, we may also have a homeowner who, having installed a fixture, fully expects to remove it and take it with him to his new residence. It is at this point that we set the stage (a stage found in many home sales) to determine whether an item is a fixture. Inevitably, the criteria revolve around the situations as they occur, and the facts seem to differ in every case. Generally, however, three criteria are consistently applied: annexation, adaptation, and intent. *Logan* v. *Mullis*, 686 S.W.2d 605 (Tex. 1985).

**Annexation.** The first method of determining whether or not an item is a fixture is by the manner in which the article is attached to the real estate. *First National Bank of Dallas* v. *Whirlpool Corp.*, 517 S.W.2d 262 (Tex. 1974). It is easy to see that wallpaper, for instance, is attached to the real estate in such a manner that it is certainly meant to stay with the property as the property is sold. The same is generally true of shelves that have been built into the wall of the house. At the opposite end of the spectrum, however, we have pictures, hanging plants, swag lamps, and furniture. The questionable areas, of course, in this particular method can be quite large. Lightbulbs, for instance, are certainly attached to the real estate but are easily removable, as are drapes, light switch plates, carpeting, and light fixtures that have been attached to the ceiling.

**Adaptation.** A second method for determining whether or not an article is a fixture depends on the character of the article and its **adaptation** to the real estate. It is certainly easy to determine that a lamp and freestanding stove would not have to be used in just one place; they could readily be removed and be used in another residence. However, these examples should be contrasted with custom-made drapes, custom-built bookcases, and even movable, matching kitchen counters, which have been made for a particular home. All of these items can easily be seen to be movable but probably would not have an equally effective use in another home.

Therefore, adaptation, combined with the mode of annexation of the article, forms the basis for the third method, which is the intention of the parties.

**Intention.** The **intention** of the parties is, of course, the ultimate fact situation—What did each of the parties, the home purchaser and the homeowner, really intend to transfer when their earnest money contract was signed? The question of intention is inferable from the acts of the parties and the nature of the article, and it incorporates the first two methods—the mode of annexation and the adaptation to real estate—because all of these particular factors come into the minds of the purchaser and seller as they enter into their negotiations. *McConnell* v. *Frost*, 45 S.W.2d 777 (Tex. Civ. App.—Waco, 1932).

In utilizing the above three criteria, preference is given to the question of intention in deciding what constitutes a fixture. The question is not a question of law but of fact, as created by the conduct of the parties. The intent should be clearly expressed in the earnest money contract. One should note that Paragraph 2 of the promulgated Texas Real Estate Commission earnest money contracts specifies that certain "items" are considered part of the "property" to be conveyed. These "items" may or may not be fixtures. Frequently, parties' ideas differ, and a good real estate agent should encourage the parties to read and understand the significance of this paragraph. There can never be enough emphasis given to the care a real estate agent must utilize in representing either party in a contractual negotiation.

## Other Determinations

When one steps out of the realm of the real estate purchaser and homeowner negotiating a contract, the determination of fixtures becomes very important to **vendors** (sellers of the merchandise), **mechanics and materialmen** (sellers and installers of the merchandise), and the holder of the mortgage on the house to which that item has become attached. These people are not interested in the subsequent purchase of a house but have a very important interest in those fixtures as they are installed in the house if the fixtures are not paid for. For example, take the situation of a homeowner purchasing a central air-conditioning unit. The seller of the air-conditioning unit has an interest in the chattel even before it becomes attached to the real estate, and he maintains his interest after it becomes attached as a fixture (until it has been paid for). The man who installs it may have an interest in that fixture if his labor was performed in installing it (and he has not been paid), and the mortgage company is interested in that fixture because it materially affects the value of the lender's lien interest in the real estate.

Therefore, it is important to realize that another determinative test is frequently employed in the event of conflicting interests in a fixture, that is, whether or not the fixture may be removed from the real estate without **material injury** to the building. *First National Bank of Dallas* v. *Whirlpool Corp.*, supra; *Texas Business and Commerce Code, §9.313(a)*. If it can be so removed, it will not ordinarily be considered a fixture and may be subject to prior claims of materialmen, suppliers, and vendors of that particular fixture. If there is a claim between the vendor and the contractor, Texas law favors the contractor. This is discussed in greater detail in Chapter 17, Liens. Therefore, even if the home purchaser and homeowner fully agree on an item being a fixture, the purchaser may be subsequently surprised when a prior existing security interest in that fixture may have priority interest in his new home.

## Security Interests

To help explain the conflict in the fixture that may be created, it must be understood that when personalty (**chattel**) is purchased on credit, the seller of that item may protect his interest in it by recording his lien interest in that chattel pursuant to the statutes contained in the Texas Business Commerce Code. These liens are commonly called UCC liens (named after the Uniform Commercial Code) and "**chattel mortgage**" liens. For instance, if a homeowner purchased a new central air-conditioning unit and did not pay cash for same, the seller of that unit may wish to reflect that he still has an interest in the air-conditioning unit because it has not been fully paid for. As the item is purchased, the lender would prepare a **promissory note** for payment (Figure 6.2), a **security agreement** (a document that provides for repossession in the event of nonpayment), and two **financing statements** (the financing statements are commonly called **UCC-1 forms**). The seller would record his interest in that chattel by filing the financing statements or security agreement in two places: (1) in the real property records in the county clerk's office in the county of the purchaser's residence, and (2) in the office of the Secretary of State. When a UCC lien has been properly recorded, it is considered to be "perfected," and the public is legally on notice of that vendor's interest in the air-conditioning unit. A copy of a UCC-1 financing statement is shown in Figure 6.3. A subsequent purchaser, for his own protection, is supposed to search the records of the county and determine that no such liens exist against the real estate he is about to purchase.

When it is anticipated that the collateral will be affixed to real estate, there are additional provisions for filing the UCC liens in the real property records of the county in which the real estate is located, as well as in the office of the Secretary of State of the State of Texas. This type of lien is also referred to as a **UCC lien**, and its recordation is termed a **fixture filing**. It has long been determined in Texas law that a perfected security interest in fixtures has a priority over the conflicting interest of an encumbrance or owner of the real estate where the security interest is:

1. A purchase money interest.
2. The fixture filing is perfected before the interest of the encumbrance or owner is of record.
3. The fixture is readily removable factory or office machines.
4. The lien is prior in time to any other conflicting security interest.

The legal ramifications of chattel mortgages and fixture filings can be rather far-reaching. However, it is very important that all real estate agents understand the complications and conflicts that can arise if a UCC lien is of record in the county courthouse affecting a property that the agent may be attempting to sell or list.

Once a chattel mortgage is perfected, it is released by the use of a **UCC-3 form** for termination of a security agreement. A copy of a UCC-3 form is shown in Figure 6.4.

The conflicts of mechanics' and materialmen's liens and mortgagees' liens have special applications to other areas of real estate law and will be discussed in greater detail in later chapters.

# Trade Fixtures

There is a special class of fixtures, termed **trade fixtures**, which includes articles that enable a tenant to carry on his business for trade. One normally finds the concept of trade fixtures in landlord–tenant situations where the tenant installs certain fixtures for his own use and benefit and for his own specific business purposes.

**FIGURE 6.2 PROMISSORY NOTE.**

2422
Prepared by the State Bar of Texas for use by lawyers only
Revised 11/82; 8/84; 10/85; 12/87.
©1987 by the State Bar of Texas

NOTE
(Secured by Security Agreement)

Date: February 23, 1999

Maker: Buyer Beware

Maker's Mailing Address (including county):   1234 A Street, Houston, Harris Co.,
Texas

Payee: Caveat Vendor, Inc.

Place for Payment (including county): 1234 B Street, Houston, Harris Co., Texas

Principal Amount: 9,400.00

Annual Interest Rate on Unpaid Principal from Date: 9%

Annual Interest Rate on Matured, Unpaid Amounts: 10%

Terms of Payment (principal and interest):   On or before the 23rd day of
February, 2000

Security for Payment
    A Security Interest Created and Granted in the following Security Agreement:

    Date: February 23, 1999

    Debtor: Buyer Beware

    Secured Party: Payee

    County Where Collateral Located: Harris County

    Collateral:   1) One High Performance Air Conditioning Unit, Model No.
                        694, Serial No. SE3469R739

                  2) Deluxe Woodburner One Freestanding Stove, Model No. 3.
                        Serial No. QR586543.

    Other Security for Payment:

        NONE

*(continued)*

**FIGURE 6.2 CONTINUED.**

Maker promises to pay to the order of Payee at the place for payment and according to the terms of payment the principal amount plus interest at the rates stated above. All unpaid amounts shall be due by the final scheduled payment date.

If Maker defaults in the payment of this note or in the performance of any obligation in any instrument securing or collateral to it, and the default continues after Payee gives Maker notice of the default and the time within which it must be cured, as may be required by law or by written agreement, then Payee may declare the unpaid principal balance and earned interest on this note immediately due. Maker and each surety, endorser, and guarantor waive all demands for payment, presentations for payment, notices of intention to accelerate maturity, notices of acceleration of maturity, protests, and notices of protest, to the extent permitted by law.

If this note or any instrument securing or collateral to it is given to an attorney for collection or enforcement, or if suit is brought for collection or enforcement, or if it is collected or enforced through probate, bankruptcy, or other judicial proceeding, then Maker shall pay Payee all costs of collection and enforcement, including reasonable attorney's fees and court costs, in addition to other amounts due. Reasonable attorney's fees shall be 10% of all amounts due unless either party pleads otherwise.

Interest on the debt evidenced by this note shall not exceed the maximum amount of nonusurious interest that may be contracted for, taken, reserved, charged, or received under law; any interest in excess of that maximum amount shall be credited on the principal of the debt or, if that has been paid, refunded. On any acceleration or required or permitted prepayment, any such excess shall be canceled automatically as of the acceleration or prepayment or, if already paid, credited on the principal of the debt or, if the principal of the debt has been paid, refunded. This provision overrides other provisions in this and all other instruments concerning the debt.

Each Maker is responsible for all obligations represented by this note.

When the context requires, singular nouns and pronouns include the plural.

---

Buyer Beware

PREPAID IN THE LAW OFFICE OF:

**FIGURE 6.3 UCC-1 FINANCING STATEMENT.**

UNIFORM COMMERCIAL CODE — FINANCING STATEMENT — FORM UCC1 (REV. 7/29/98)

IMPORTANT — READ INSTRUCTIONS ON BACK BEFORE FILLING OUT FORM — **DO NOT DETACH STUB**

**UCC FINANCING STATEMENT**
FOLLOW INSTRUCTIONS (front and back) CAREFULLY

A. NAME & PHONE OF CONTACT AT FILER [optional]

B. SEND ACKNOWLEDGMENT TO: (Name and Address)

THE ABOVE SPACE IS FOR FILING OFFICE USE ONLY

1. DEBTOR'S EXACT FULL LEGAL NAME — insert only one debtor name (1a or 1b) — do not abbreviate or combine names

| 1a. ORGANIZATION'S NAME | | | |
|---|---|---|---|
| OR  1b. INDIVIDUAL'S LAST NAME  BEWARE | FIRST NAME  BUYER | MIDDLE NAME | SUFFIX |
| 1c. MAILING ADDRESS  4736 Madison | CITY  Houston | STATE TX   POSTAL CODE  USA | COUNTRY |

| 1d  TAX ID#: SSN OR EIN | Optional Add'l info re organizational debtor | 1e. TYPE OF ORGANIZATION | 1f. JURISDICTION OF ORGANIZATION | 1g. ORGANIZATIONAL ID#, if any   ☐ NONE |

2. ADDITIONAL DEBTOR'S EXACT FULL LEGAL NAME — insert only one debtor name (2a or 2b) — do not abbreviate or combine names

| 2a. ORGANIZATION'S NAME | | | |
|---|---|---|---|
| OR  2b. INDIVIDUAL'S LAST NAME | FIRST NAME | MIDDLE NAME | SUFFIX |
| 2c. MAILING ADDRESS | CITY | STATE   POSTAL CODE | COUNTRY |

| 2d  TAX ID#: SSN OR EIN | Optional Add'l info re organizational debtor | 2e. TYPE OF ORGANIZATION | 2f. JURISDICTION OF ORGANIZATION | 2g. ORGANIZATIONAL ID#, if any   ☐ NONE |

3. SECURED PARTY'S NAME (or NAME of TOTAL ASSIGNEE of ASSIGNOR S/P) insert only one secured party name (3a or 3b)

| 3a. ORGANIZATION'S NAME  CAVEAT VENDOR, INC. | | | |
|---|---|---|---|
| OR  3b. INDIVIDUAL'S LAST NAME | FIRST NAME | MIDDLE NAME | SUFFIX |
| 3c. MAILING ADDRESS  3737 Arnold | CITY  Houston | STATE TX   POSTAL CODE  USA | COUNTRY |

4. This FINANCING STATEMENT covers the following collateral:

One (1) Deluxe Woodburning Free Standing Stove, Model No. 3, Serial No. QRS86543.

5. ALTERNATIVE DESIGNATION (if applicable): ☐ Lessee/Lessor ☐ Consignee/Consignor ☐ Bailee/Bailor ☐ Seller/Buyer ☐ Ag. Lien ☐ Non-UCC

6. ☐ This FINANCING STATEMENT is to be filed (for record) (or recorded)   7. Check to REQUEST SEARCH REPORTS on Debtor(s)
in the REAL ESTATE RECORDS.  Attach Addendum  (if applicable)   [Additional Fee] [optional] ☐ All Debtors ☐ Debtor 1 ☐ Debtor 2

8. OPTIONAL FILER REFERENCE DATA

Rel. #9/2002          Form VI-131 (1 of 2 pages)          Page VI-205

With few exceptions, the concept of trade fixtures is well settled in Texas law. The parties' rights are usually set out in a lease or other contractual obligation between the parties. The general rule is that all trade fixtures are ordinarily removable during or at the expiration of the tenant's term of occupancy, provided they can be completely removed without material or permanent injury to the building. *Connelly v. Art & Gary, Inc.*, 630 S.W.2d 514 (Tex. Civ. App.—Corpus Christi, 1982); *Jim Walter Window Components* v. *Turnpike Distribution Center*, 642 S.W.2d 3 (Tex. Civ. App.—Dallas, 1982). Unless otherwise specified in the contract, the fixtures must be removed within a reasonable time after the termination of the tenant's occupancy. "Reasonable," as in other cases, is a question of fact for the jury to decide. In the event the tenant does fail to remove the trade fixtures within a reasonable

**FIGURE 6.4  RELEASE UCC-3.**

period of time, he forfeits his rights to those improvements, and they will become the property of the landlord.

Although this concept may seem to be simple and hardly worthy of explanation, one must remember that even when the rights are set up by terms of a written agreement between the parties, conflicts may arise and can create difficult situations. In at least one Texas case, "fixtures and floor coverings" were determined by the court to include permanent floor coverings and various built-in items that could not be removed without material damage to the premises. *Haverfield Company* v. *Siegel*, 366 S.W.2d 790 (Tex. Civ. App.—San Antonio, 1963). There are always exceptions!

# Manufactured Housing

## Definitions

There has been a rapid growth in Texas in HUD manufactured housing (previously known as **mobile homes**). This is not surprising, due to the fact that we can now put homestead liens on mobile homes (note Chapter 3). The cost is approximately half that of a regularly constructed home, and there are a number of areas in the state where building materials are almost non-existent. Manufactured housing provides a cheap and easy alternative to traditional construction methods in these areas. To help focus on these issues, let's first define the concept:

A "HUD-Code manufactured home" is a structure: (1) constructed on or after June 15, 1976, according to the Rules of the United States Department of Urban Development; (2) transported in one or more sections, which, in the traveling mode, is 8 body feet or more in width or 40 body feet or more in length or, when erected on site, it is 320 or more square feet, and (3) is built on a permanent chassis and designed to be used as a dwelling with or without a permanent foundation when connected to the required utilities, and includes the plumbing, heating, air-conditioning and electrical systems. *V.T.C.A. Art. 5221f §3(9)*. If the structure was constructed before June 15, 1976, it is defined as a "mobile home."

This is not the same as **industrialized housing**. Industrialized housing is a residential structure that is designed for the use and occupancy of one or more families, as constructed in one or more modules or constructed using one or more modular components built at a location other than the permanent residential site, and that is designed to be used as a permanent residential structure, when the modular components are transported to the permanent residential site and are erected or installed on a permanent foundation system. It does not include any residential structure that is in excess of 3 stories or 49 feet in height as measured from the finished grade elevation at the building entrance to the peak of the roof. *V.T.C.A. Art. 5221f-1 §1(1)*.

Apparently, if the home can be moved in a single unit, it will be a HUD manufactured home, but if it were built by components it would be industrialized housing. In transacting the sale of any of the foregoing units they are obviously sales of personal property and certificates of title are issued as personal property.

## Real Property Issues

The Property Code describes a manufactured home as personal property. If the home is placed:

1. On a lot, whether permanently or temporarily, that is not titled in the name of the consumer under a deed or contract of sale.

2. In a manufactured home rental community as defined in the Local Government Code V.T.C.A., *Property Code §2.001*.

Recent amendments to the Property Code and enactment's of the Texas Manufactured Housing Standards Act have established code and manufacturing standards. They also established a supervisory state agency that has adopted standards and requirements for the installation of manufactured housing throughout Texas. This has enabled a tremendous amount of new, inexpensive and affordable housing to be developed in Texas with controls on quality. This may be the fastest growing area of new homeownership in the state. The old "mobile home" just is not what it once was.

Are these fixtures? Good question. Probably not. Since they are not financed with traditional fixture documents (UCC-1's), they are probably just creatures created by a new law, and judicial interpretation will center around these statutory definitions, procedures and contractual agreements. Stay tuned, this area of the law is developing.

# Easements

An **easement** is generally defined as the right acquired by one person to the use of the land of another for a special purpose. If you would like to dazzle your friends with your brilliance, you may choose to describe easements as "**incorporeal hereditaments**" because they are, in fact, incorporeal (intangible) rights that may be inherited. Each easement carries with it the right to reasonable use, but only reasonable use, such that it is necessary, convenient, and as little burden to the owner of that real estate as possible. *Exxon Corp.* v. *Schutzmaier*, 537 S.W.2d 282 (Tex. Civ. App.—Beaumont, 1976). An easement right carries with it only user privilege and not any privilege of ownership. A mere easement can never be transposed into fee simple title or a feasible claim of title to the real estate. *Reiter* v. *Coastal States*, 382 S.W.2d 243 (Tex. 1964).

## Appurtenant Versus In Gross

Easements are generally categorized into two types: (1) an **easement appurtenant** and (2) an **easement in gross**. An easement appurtenant is an easement created for the benefit of another tract of land. There must be two different owners involved, one being the owner of the estate over which the easement crosses; this is called the **servient estate**. The other owner owns the property that the easement serves; this is called the **dominant estate**. Figure 6.5 illustrates how the appurtenant easement concept can be applied. Because of the nature of an appurtenant easement (it benefits a particular piece of property), an appurtenant easement is considered to be a covenant running with the land; that is, the right to use that easement passes along with the title to the dominant estate. *Hidalgo* v. *Maverick*, 349 S.W.2d 768 (Tex. Civ. App.—San Antonio, 1961); *McWhorter* v. *City of Jacksonville*, 694 S.W.2d 182 (Tex. Civ. App.—Tyler, 1985). It is important to note that an easement appurtenant is a benefit to the dominant estate and an encumbrance to the servient estate, and, once created, it stays in existence (along with title to the dominant estate) until title easement is terminated.

An **easement in gross**, on the other hand, is an easement that does not normally benefit any particular piece of property but benefits only the individual owner for his particular use. The holder of a commercial easement in gross (usually for specified, personal use) does not normally have the right to sell, assign, or devise it.

**FIGURE 6.5 ESTATES CREATED BY AN APPURTENANT EASEMENT.**

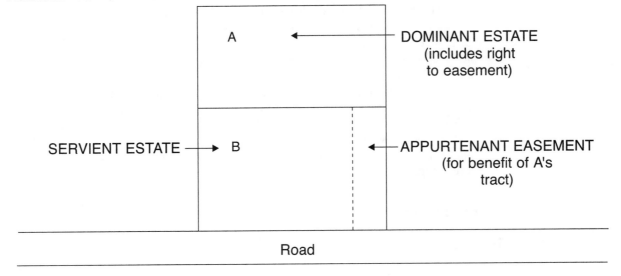

*Farmer's Marine Cooper Workers, Inc.* v. *City of Galveston,* 757 S.W.2d 148 (Tex. App.—Houston [1st Dist.], 1988). An easement in gross normally terminates with the dissolution of the entity that has the right to use that easement. *Sisco* v. *Hereford,* 694 S.W.2d 3 (Tex. Civ. App.—San Antonio, 1984). This type of easement is generally a right-of-way easement for power companies, gas transmission companies, flood-control authorities, and other governmental and quasi-governmental authorities. It should be emphasized that if the court is in the position of determining whether or not an easement is an easement in gross or an easement appurtenant, the court will generally attempt to find that it is an easement appurtenant since easements in gross are not favored under Texas law. An easement in gross is generally in writing and is agreed to by all parties; it is often acquired by eminent domain proceedings by some condemning authority.

## Creation

In Texas, easements are created in one of eight ways, four of which are in writing and four of which are oral. Those that are required to be in writing must comply with the Statute of Frauds (discussed later in Chapter 9) and define the location of the easement with reasonable clarity. *Pick* v. *Bartel,* 659 S.W.2d 636 (Tex. 1983). These include: (1) easements by express grant; (2) easements by express reservation; (3) easements by reference to a plat; and (4) easements by statute. The other four easements are created by conduct of the parties, are not normally in writing, and must be enforced by some judicial proceeding. They include easements created: (1) by implication; (2) by prescription; (3) by estoppel; and (4) by necessity. Let's discuss each of these methods of easement creation individually.

**Easement by Express Grant.** If an express easement is made by an agreement between the parties (**easement by express grant**), it has to follow the normal formalities of any real estate instrument and be in writing, be properly subscribed by the party to be charged, manifest the intent to grant the easement with adequate legal description, be acknowledged (if it is to be recorded), and be properly delivered. *Pick* v. *Bartel,* supra. This is, by all means, the simplest and most direct method of creating an easement: The intent of the parties is obviously clear, the use is properly set out, and it includes termination and other pertinent terms requested by the respective parties. If recorded, the instrument can meet all the requirements of constructive notice for the parties' own protection, as well as for the protection of third parties.

**Easement by Express Reservation.** An **easement created by express reservation** in a deed is also an express easement. However, the details and terms of an easement created in this manner are often left out because the use of an easement reserved in a conveyance by a deed is usually appurtenant and necessary either for the property being conveyed or for the real estate contiguous thereto. For instance, property owner A may be willing to sell his frontage to property owner B but will reserve an easement to himself for access to the remainder of his property. The property over which the easement crosses still vests fee title unto the grantee but reserves the right to reasonable use to the grantor. Note that this is usually not an exception to title, but rather a property right reserved out of the conveyance passed by the deed. A more detailed discussion of exceptions and reservations in deeds will be included in Chapters 10 and 11 on conveyancing.

**Easement by Reference to a Plat.** An **easement** can be created by reference to an existing **subdivision plat**. It is quite common for subdivision developers, when laying out a subdivision, to record that subdivision's plat in the county in which the subdivision is located. The legal descriptions to a given lot, block, and section can then be made by reference to the plat rather than by the more complicated metes-and-bounds system. It logically follows that as the developer changes the legal description to a piece of property by filing a subdivision plat, he may also create easements for water mains, gas distribution lines, road rights-of-way, and other types of easements that are similarly created by governmental and quasi-governmental authorities through the promulgation of official city, county, and state maps that delineate floodway areas, flood-control districts, power lines, and major utility distribution systems.

**Easement by Reference to a Statute.** The state legislature has passed a series of statutes that create an easement in the public pursuant to the Texas "**Open Beaches Act**," *V.T.C.A., Natural Resources Code, §61.001 et seq.* The statutes create a "right of use" or "easement" in the public over the beaches of the State of Texas from the mean low tide to the line of vegetation bordering on the Gulf of Mexico. If there is no marked vegetation line, the size of the easement may vary but cannot extend farther than 200 feet from the seaward line of mean low tide.

This has created a lot of controversy in recent years. After a hurricane in 1983, the natural vegetation line on Galveston Island moved landward about 125 to 150 feet and changed the boundary line of the property owners' land. This statute, then, creates a "migratory public easement," which prohibits homeowners from rebuilding when the vegetation line is forced inland. The statutes do not affect title, *V.T.C.A., Natural Resources Code, §61.023.* In addition to the statute, it has also been held that the public's right to easement arises from "custom" because of the public's right to use these beaches along the Texas coastline for hundreds of years. *Matcha v. Mattox*, 711 S.W.2d 95 (Tex. Civ. App.—Austin, 1986).

**Easement by Implication.** An **easement by implication** is one that is not in writing. It is imposed by a court in the form of an equitable remedy to provide access to a landlocked parcel of real estate. *Persons v. Russell*, 625 S.W.2d 387 (Tex. Civ. App.—Tyler, 1981). This is normally an easement that has been in continuous use for some time but was not created by any agreement in writing between the parties affected. However, before a court will impose such an easement by implication, certain criteria must be met to justify the court's intervention:

1. The prior use of the easement must be apparent and obvious by the party seeking to enforce his easement right at the time the dominant and servient estates are separated.

2. The prior use must also have been reasonably continuous. This does not mean that the party must have used it every day, but he must have used it often enough to establish a certain continuity of use.

3. The use of that easement must be reasonably necessary to a fair and enjoyable use of the dominant estate.

4. There must have originally been a unity of ownership of the dominant and servient estates immediately prior to the easement being created. *Westbrook* v. *Wright*, 477 S.W.2d 663 (Tex. Civ. App.—Houston, 1972); *Getz* v. *Boston Sea Party of Houston, Inc.*, 573 S.W.2d 836 (Tex. Civ. App.—Houston, 1978); *Koonce* v. *Brite*, 663 S.W.2d 451, 452 (Tex. 1984).

The typical fact situation surrounding an easement by implication is one in which two owners have an oral agreement for the use of an easement to a landlocked parcel of real estate that was originally owned by one of the two parties, or in which parties partition their property without mentioning a preexisting easement right. When the oral agreement is breached, the aggrieved party petitions the court for intervention. *Cotter* v. *Moore*, 634 S.W.2d 332 (Tex. Civ. App.—Corpus Christi, 1982). When an easement by implication is reserved by a grantor (rather than granted to a third party), the degree of necessity required to establish the implied easement must be a physical or economic necessity, not just a convenience or advantage. *Duff* v. *Matthews*, 311 S.W.2d 637 (Tex. 1958).

**Easement by Prescription.** An easement by **prescription** is one that has been obtained and is held by a claimant against the wishes of the landowner. It is very similar and analogous to obtaining title to property by adverse possession. However, one should remember that adverse possession and easement by prescription are entirely different concepts. An easement, as stated previously, never ripens into fee simple ownership, but adverse possession does. The requirements to create an easement by prescription are understandably a little more difficult than those required to create an easement by implication. A claimant's right to this easement is generally imposed by a court, as is the case in an easement by implication. The requirements for an easement by prescription are as follows:

1. The use of the easement must be adverse, open, notorious, and hostile to the interest of the landowner over which the easement passes. This does not mean that the claimant must have used the easement under artillery fire or carrying a sack of grenades, but the landowner must have been clearly against the creation and use of said easement. There must have been no permissive use. *Vrazel* v. *Skrabanek*, 725 S.W.2d 709 (Tex. 1987).

2. The use of the easement must be exclusive to the claimant and not to the public and not a joint use easement. *Brooks* v. *Jones*, 578 S.W.2d 669 (Tex. 1974).

3. The use of the easement must have been uninterrupted and continuous for a period of at least 10 years. *Davis* v. *Carriker*, 536 S.W.2d 246 (Tex. Civ. App.—Amarillo, 1976); *Exxon Corp.* v. *Schutzmaier*, supra.

**Easement by Estoppel.** "Estoppel" is a rather elusive legal concept that alludes to a claim made as an affirmative defense to a cause of action when the defendant has been induced into doing an act by the plaintiff. This concept is sometimes called

**promissory estoppel**. An **easement by estoppel** normally occurs when a party, by oral agreement, has granted a right to an easement in his land upon which the other party has relied in good faith and has expended money—money that would be lost if the right to use and enjoy that easement is revoked by the promisor. Since the owner of the dominant estate relied on the servient tenant's promise for using that easement, equity normally prohibits the owner of the servient estate from preventing the dominant owner's use of that easement. This theory also applies to subsequent owners after the easement right is established. *Vrazel* v. *Skrabanek*, supra. The only requirements for creating an easement by estoppel are that:

1. The representation must have been communicated to the promisee or owner of the dominant estate.

2. The representation must have been believed by that promisee.

3. There must have been a reliance on such promise to the detriment of the dominant estate owner. *Exxon Corp.* v. *Schutzmaier*, supra.

The nature of an easement by estoppel is one that is imposed by equity because of the bad faith evidenced by the promisor in granting an easement and then attempting to take it back after the promisee has relied on his promise. The strong equitable nature of this particular type of easement is such that the same strict and conclusive rules of law as an easement by implication, which has many of the same characteristics, do not apply. As in the case of all other easements, generally, the use of this easement can only be reasonable use that is necessary and convenient and of as little burden to the servient estate as possible.

**Easement by Necessity.** There has often been confusion between easements by implication and **easements by necessity**. They are not the same, and they need to be discussed in more detail to emphasize the differences. In order for an easement by necessity to exist, it must be shown that:

1. There was a unity of ownership with the alleged dominant and servient estates.

2. The roadway is a necessity, not a mere convenience.

3. The necessity existed at the time of the severance of the two estates. *Othen* v. *Rosier*, 226 S.W.2d 622 (Tex. 1950); *Koonce* v. *Brite*, supra; *Rushin* v. *Humphrey*, 778 S.W.2d 95 (Tex. App.—Houston [1st Dist.], 1989).

No one can have an easement by necessity over the land of a stranger. Therefore, there must be some conduct between the dominant and servient estates that creates the easement right. Being landlocked, by itself, does not create the necessity. The courts have further held that the necessity required must be a "strict" necessity, providing the only access to the dominant tenant's property. It cannot exist just because a road is impassable. *Duff* v. *Matthews*, supra. Note that in this type of easement there is no requirement that the easement be apparent or continuously used. An easement by necessity is a temporary right and ceases when the necessity terminates. *Bains* v. *Parker*, 182 S.W.2d 397 (Tex. 1944).

## Termination

If it has been determined that an **easement** has been properly created and is in existence, even if it is an oral easement created by implication, by estoppel, or by prescription, the termination of that easement, as in the termination of most other property rights, has certain requirements that must be met before that termination becomes effective. The methods of terminating an easement are release, merger, failure of purpose, and abandonment.

**Release.** As an easement can be created by an express reservation or express grant, it can also be released by **express agreement** of termination between the parties involved. The same care in drawing the instrument for creating the easement should also be taken in the termination of that easement. There may be rights created that could be overlooked when the release is drawn, and such an oversight may inadvertently create a cloud on the title.

**Merger. Merger** is accomplished when the owner of the dominant estate purchases the servient estate or vice versa and therefore owns fee simple title to the entire property and no longer has any use for the easement. Figure 6.6 will help to illustrate this matter more clearly. Note that property owner A has the dominant estate and property owner B has the servient estate that is encumbered by the easement. Recall that the easement is a right that vests in the dominant estate. Although property owner B still owns the land encumbered by the easement, it logically follows that when property owner A acquires property owner B's interest to the fee title to the property, the rights in the easement and his rights to the fee title of the real estate merge, and the easement terminates.

**Failure of Purpose.** If an easement is created for a particular purpose, whether express or implied, it is within this purpose that guidelines are established for reasonable use. When the **purpose** for an easement fails, so does the easement. An illustration of this would be a right of way that was created to cross property solely for train traffic when the trains are permanently re-routed. It may reasonably be assumed that the servient owner may terminate the easement for **failure of purpose** because the grant is conditioned on that purpose. *Kearney v. Fancher*, 401 S.W. 2d 897 (Tex. App.-Ft. Worth, 1966).

**Abandonment.** An easement can be terminated by **abandonment**. However, as in the terminations of all other real estate rights, abandonment is difficult to prove and is not an easy method of termination. There must be proof of an intent of the

FIGURE 6.6 **EASEMENT TERMINATION BY MERGER.**

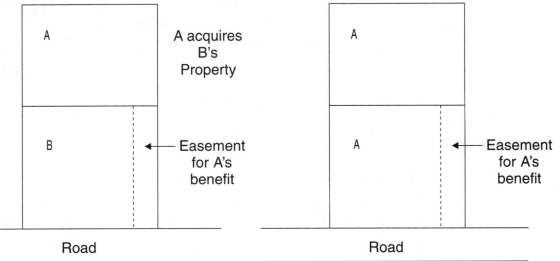

party using the easement to abandon that easement before it can be properly terminated. This abandonment must be proved by the person attempting to terminate the easement rights and must be established by clear and satisfactory evidence. Mere nonuse, by itself, does not constitute abandonment. *Peterson* v. *Greenway Parks*, 408 S.W.2d 261 (Tex. Civ. App.—Dallas, 1966). It is not difficult to see that the burden of proof in a situation constituting abandonment requires much more effort than the failure of purpose or merger doctrines that can be proved without such intent.

## ■ SUMMARY

The determination of the fixture is made by considering the mode of attachment, the adaptation of that fixture, and the intention of the parties to the agreement. Another determination involves the rights of the vendor or seller of the fixture and whether or not the fixture can be removed without material injury to the premises. This last determination is normally construed in accordance with the Texas Business and Commerce Code, which deals with security interests of the buyer versus those of the seller of the fixture. An exception to the general classification of fixtures is trade fixtures. An owner of a trade fixture normally retains title to that fixture, regardless of how it is attached to the realty.

An easement is the right acquired by the owner of one parcel of land to the use of someone else's land for a special purpose. An easement right carries with it only user privilege and not any privilege of ownership. Easements are further classified into appurtenant easements and easements in gross. An appurtenant easement is one that benefits an adjoining piece of property. An easement in gross does not normally benefit any particular piece of property. It benefits only the individual user for his particular use. An easement may be created in writing, verbally, or through the actions and conduct of the parties. Easements can be terminated by express release, merger, failure of purpose, or abandonment.

## CASE STUDIES FOR DISCUSSION

1. Mr. and Mrs. Louis Emerald moved into a home and installed carpeting was stretched over the floor and held in place by pressing the carpeting over tack boards. The carpeting was specially cut and used solely for the area in which it was placed. The house was subsequently destroyed, and the insurance company refused to pay for the carpeting since it was not a "part of the dwelling" and was not a fixture. What legal ramifications do you see?

2. Whitaker owned a block of land that he divided into eight lots for subsequent sale. There was a single sewer line that ran across three of the lots and that was designed to serve all eight lots on the block through stubs or connection points. The sewers were used for a period of years until a new party purchased lot 8. Because of deteriorating conditions, the owner installed a new sewer line across lot 8, but because of the elevation, the owner of lot 8 could not use the other connecting sewer lines. The owner of lot 8, upon his own initiative, built a box in the back of the lot to correct the elevation problem, but the remaining lot owners still would not allow him to connect. The owner of lot 8 attempted to obtain a new easement, parallel and close to the existing easement, to allow drainage of his newly constructed sanitary sewer across the other lots. Could he get an easement? By what method?

3. Mr. and Mrs. McGuffin owned a tract bordered on three sides by water. The only access to the McGuffin tract was by utilization of a road across a parcel of land owned by Mr. Wilson. The use of the road was never impeded until 1999, when Mr. Wilson's son posted notice that he planned to close the road. McGuffin alleged that he had created an easement by necessity, or an easement by prescription, or an easement by estoppel. Wilson alleged that it was not created by any of these ways. Under what theories could an easement be created? Was there an easement created in this situation?

4. A 300 lb. tomato-slicing machine was moved into a prison unit in Brazoria County, Texas. It was bolted to the floor and immediately put into service in the kitchen area. During its operation, a prisoner fell into the tomato slicing machine and suffered severe bodily injury. If the item is a fixture, it is part of the real estate and the prisoner needs to sue the State of Texas. If it is an item of personalty, it becomes a products liability case, and the defendant is the manufacturer of the machine. What legal ramifications do you foresee? Who is ultimately liable?

## CHAPTER 7

# Real Estate Brokerage

Real estate brokerage is an ever-changing, complicated subject. Real estate brokers and real estate brokerage have been regulated by law in Texas since 1939.

The **Texas Real Estate License Act** is a general law that applies to all persons who engage in the real estate business, which includes residential rental locators. It is now in the Texas Occupation Code, and all references to the license act will refer to the newly created sections of that Code. Its legislative intent is to avoid fraud on the public by requiring a license of anyone who deals in real estate. *Henry S. Miller* v. *Treo Enterprises*, 585 S.W.2d 674 (Tex. 1979). The licensee is not only responsible to the Texas Real Estate Commission, but also to the public. The public has the right to believe that all licensees are competent, honest, trustworthy, and of good character. It is reasonable to think that the public has the right to trust a licensee, to rely on his experience and training, and to presume him to be an honest and ethical person.

Certain provisions of the Texas Real Estate License Act will be reproduced in their entirety throughout this chapter. The most current version of the Texas Real Estate License Act is available at no charge on the Texas Real Estate Commission website: www.trec.state.tx.us. As an assignment for this chapter, print the act and read it. The act must be read thoroughly and be understood in detail since all brokers and salespersons are regulated by it. Ignorance of the law is no excuse for violations of it.

## The Texas Real Estate Commission

The Real Estate License Act is administered through the **Texas Real Estate Commission (TREC)**, which is a body composed of nine COMMISSION appointed by the governor with the advice and consent of two-thirds of the senate present. The governor appoints the chairperson.

Six members of the commissioners must have been engaged in the real estate brokerage business as licensed real estate brokers as their major occupation for at least five years directly preceding their appointment to the commission. The other three members must be representatives of the general public who are not licensed under the Texas Real Estate License Act and who do not have, other than as consumers, a financial interest in the practice of a real estate broker or real estate salesperson, and who are not acting for anyone holding such an interest. All appointments to the commission must be made without regard to the race, creed, sex, religion, or national origin of the appointee.

The commission creates administers and enforces all rules and regulations that govern the procedure for the institution, conduct, and determination of all causes and proceedings before the commission. The rules that the commission administers additionally promulgate the canons of professional ethics and conduct for real estate licensees, to which the commission expects all licensees to adhere. These rules and regulations are also available on the TREC website.

# Licensing Requirements

## Salesperson Licensure

To be eligible for a Texas real estate salesperson's license, the **salesperson** must be joined in his application by a sponsoring broker on a form prescribed by the commission. The individual must be a citizen of the United States or a lawfully admitted alien, be at least 18 years of age, and be a legal resident of Texas. Immediately preceding the filing of an application, he must also satisfy the commission as to his honesty, trustworthiness, integrity, and competency.

The commission then conducts a criminal history check of each applicant for license or renewal of a license. An applicant for a license or renewal of an unexpired license must submit a complete and legible set of fingerprints to the commission or the Department of Public Safety for the purpose of obtaining criminal history information from the Department of Public Safety and the Federal Bureau of Investigation. The commission will refuse to issue a license or a renewal license to a person who fails to submit the fingerprint information. A licensee is also required to notify the Texas Real Estate Commission within 30 days of the date of the final conviction of a felony or criminal offense involving fraud.

As additional requirements, the Real Estate License Act specifies that each applicant for salesperson's licensure must furnish the commission satisfactory evidence of having completed 14 semester hours of postsecondary education, 10 semester hours of which must be completed in core real estate courses (of which a minimum of 4 semester hours must be completed in principles of real estate, a minimum of 2 semester hours must be in the law of agency, a minimum of 2 semester hours must be in law of contracts, and a minimum of 2 hours of an additional core course). The remaining 4 semester hours must be completed in core real estate courses or related courses. "**Related courses**" are courses determined by the commission as satisfying the requirements of the act. "**Core real estate courses**" include principles of real estate, real estate appraisal, real estate law, real estate finance, real estate marketing, real estate mathematics, real estate brokerage, property management, real estate investments, law of agency, and law of contracts.

As a condition precedent for first annual certification, the applicant must furnish the commission satisfactory evidence of having completed the minimum 18 semester hours, 14 semester hours of which must be completed in core real estate courses. The requirements are cumulative, so it is not necessary to take additional course requirements each year. If the real estate salesperson applicant has completed the required 18 semester hours in her first year of licensure, she need not complete any additional education for her second annual through fourth annual certification years. See chart showing the minimum course requirements.

| | Related Courses | Core Real Estate Courses | Total Semester Hours | Equivalent Classroom Hours |
|---|---|---|---|---|
| For application | 4 | 10 | 14 | 210 |
| 1st annual certification | 4 | 14 | 18 | 270 |

## Broker Licensure

The requirements for broker licensure require both experience in the real estate business and education in real estate–related curriculum. Each applicant for broker licensure must furnish the commission satisfactory evidence that he has had not less than two years' active experience in this state as a licensed real estate salesperson during the 36-month period immediately preceding the filing of the application. The educational requirements are particularly strong—among the strongest in the United States. The broker must furnish the commission satisfactory evidence of having successfully completed 60 semester hours of core real estate courses or related courses, which must include 18 semester hours of core real estate courses, two semester hours of which must be a course in real estate brokerage.

In enforcing the rules and regulations, the commission inspects and credits educational programs and establishes standards for accreditation of such programs conducted in the state. In establishing equivalency standards for courses other than in accredited colleges and universities, the commission establishes acceptable classroom hour requirements, calculated as 15 hours of classroom instruction for each semester hour of an accredited college or university. After the foregoing requirements have been met, competency is then determined by the commission by an examination prepared by or contracted for by the commission. All licensees must take and pass the required examination, except for:

1.  An applicant for broker licensure who has, within one year previous to the filing of the application, been licensed in the state as a broker; and

2.  An applicant for salesperson licensure who has, within one year previous to the filing of the application, been licensed in the state as either a broker or a salesperson.

The commission may also provide a waiver of some or all of the requirements for a license under the Act for an applicant who was licensed under the Act within the six years preceding the date of filing the application.

**Mandatory Continuing Education.** Texas also requires continuing mandatory education to maintain real estate licensure. The commission now requires proof of attendance of at least 15 classroom hours of continuing education courses approved by the commission during the term of the current license. At least six hours of that instruction must be devoted to legal topics as set out in the Act, including fair housing laws, landlord–tenant law and other property code issues, agency laws, antitrust laws, the Deceptive Trade Practices–Consumer Protection Act, and other current topics. Core real estate courses can also be used for credit. The commission may not require examinations except for correspondence courses. Daily course segments must be at least one hour long but cannot last more than ten hours a day.

## Brokers and Salespersons

The Act requires licensure for a person to perform certain functions applicable to real estate transactions. It is specifically unlawful for a person to hold himself out or engage in the business of brokerage without being licensed by the Texas Real Estate Commission. It is also unlawful for any salesperson to conduct any acts or attempts to act as a real estate agent unless he is associated with a Texas real estate **broker**, and the **salesperson** cannot accept compensation from any person other than that broker. The definitions of **broker** and **salesperson** are the key to how closely the commission can regulate the industry. Any attempt to circumvent the act as a "consultant" or other similar sham will not be overlooked by the courts. *Anderson* v. *Republic National Life Insurance Co.*, 623 S.W.2d 162 (Tex. Civ. App.—Ft. Worth, 1981). Similarly, if a broker acts in two capacities (broker/executor of an estate), the broker is held to the duty of care of a broker when performing a brokerage function. *Texas Real Estate Commission* v. *Nagle*, 767 S.W.2d 691 (Tex. 1987). Section 1101.002 of the Act defines real estate broker and real estate salesperson as follows:

(2) "Real estate broker" means a person who, for another person and for a fee, commission, or other valuable consideration, or with the intention or in the expectation or on the promise of receiving or collecting a fee, commission, or other valuable consideration from another person:

(A) sells, exchanges, purchases, rents, or leases real estate;

(B) offers to sell, exchange, purchase, rent, or lease real estate;

(C) negotiates or attempts to negotiate the listing, sale, exchange, purchase, rental, or leasing of real estate;

(D) lists or offers or attempts or agrees to list real estate for sale, rental, lease, exchange, or trade;

(E) appraises or offers or attempts or agrees to appraise real estate;

(F) auctions, or offers or attempts or agrees to auction, real estate;

(G) buys or sells or offers to buy or sell or otherwise deals in options on real estate, including buying, selling, or offering to buy or sell options on real estate;

(H) aids, offers, or attempts to aid in locating or obtaining for purchase, rent, or lease any real estate;

(I) procures or assists in the procuring of prospects for the purpose of effecting the sale, exchange, lease, or rental of real estate; or

(J) procures or assists in procuring property for the purpose of effecting the sale, exchange, lease, or rental of real estate.

(3) "Broker" also includes a person employed by or on behalf of the owner or owners of lots or other parcels of real estate. It also includes a person who engages in the business of charging an advance fee or contracting for collection of a fee in connection with a contract whereby he undertakes primarily to promote the sale of real estate either through its listing in a publication issued primarily for such purpose, or for referral of information concerning the real estate to brokers, or both.

(4) "Real estate salesperson or salesman" means a person associated with a Texas-licensed real estate broker for the purposes of performing acts or transactions comprehended by the definition of "real estate broker" as defined in this Act.

No real estate salespersons can accept compensation for real estate sales and transactions from any person other than the broker under whom they are licensed at the time or under whom they were licensed when they earned the right to compensation.

**Real estate** is defined by the act as a leasehold, as well as any other interest or estate in land, whether corporeal, incorporeal, freehold, or nonfreehold, and whether the real estate is situated in this state or elsewhere.

A **person**, as defined by the act, means an individual, a partnership, a limited liability company, a limited liability partnership, or a corporation, foreign or domestic; this person may hold a broker's or salesperson's license. However, there is some indication under Section 1101.453 of the act that a limited liability company or corporation, while it must be licensed, must have an officer to act for it who must be qualified as a real estate broker.

Considering the foregoing definitions, the commission can actually regulate every phase of the real estate industry, unless the individual performing the functions of a licensee is exempt from the application of the act.

## Exemptions

Section 1101.005 of the Act provides for circumstances by which real estate transactions can be consummated by an unlicensed (exempt) person. These circumstances are very strictly construed, however, and include the following:

(a) an attorney at law licensed in this state or in any other state;

(b) an attorney in fact under a duly executed power of attorney authorizing the consummation of a real estate transaction;

(c) a public official in the conduct of his official duties;

(d) a person calling the sale of real estate by auction under the authority of a license issued by this state provided the person does not perform any other act of a real estate broker or salesperson as defined by the Act;

(e) a person acting under a court order or under the authority of a will or a written trust instrument;

(f) a salesperson employed by an owner in the sale of structures and land on which said structures are situated, provided such structures are erected by the owner in the due course of his business;

(g) an on-site manager of an apartment complex;

(h) transactions involving the sale, lease, or transfer of any mineral or mining interest in real property;

(i) an owner or his employees in renting or leasing his own real estate whether improved or unimproved;

(j) transactions involving the sale, lease, or transfer of cemetery lots;

(k) transactions involving the renting, leasing, or management of hotels or motels;

(l) a partnership or limited liability partnership acting as a broker or real estate salesperson through a partner who is a licensed broker; or

(m) a person registered under Section 9A of this Act who sells, buys, leases, or transfers an easement or right-of-way for use in connection with telecommunications, utility, railroad, or pipeline service;

(n) a transaction involving the sale, lease, or transfer of a mineral interest or mining interest in real property;

(o) the sale of real property under a power of sale conferred by a deed of trust or other contract.

Interestingly, since the foregoing are exempt from licensure, it is easier to sue for a commission, since they do not have to prove a written commission agreement, or any of the other requirements for real estate broker's commissions, generally. *Young* v. *Del Mar Homes, Inc.*, 608 S.W.2d 804 (Tex. Civ. App.—Houston, 1980). See also *Collins* v. *Beste*, 40 S.W.2d 788 (Tex. App.—Ft. Worth, 1992).

**Property Managers.** One of the confusing areas of licensure involves that of real property management. It appears that the person who is an on-site manager of an apartment complex is exempt from licensure regardless of the activity performed. Any other type of management function, however, would probably include some items that were specified under the definition of broker. If so, these managers would have to be licensed. *Shehab* v. *Xanadu, Inc.*, 698 S.W.2d 491 (Tex. Civ. App.—Corpus Christi, 1985). The reader may have noticed that property management is not considered to be a "brokerage" function as defined under Section 2 of the Real Estate License Act. It is common practice, though, for property managers to attempt to lease or solicit prospective tenants to lease space in the property they are managing. The Texas Real Estate Commission takes the predictable position that if the property manager, regardless of his title or job description, performs a brokerage function, he will be required to be licensed, *Rules of the Texas Real Estate Commission, §535.3(c)*. Additional authority for this may be assumed since the act considers real estate management as a core real estate course.

**Attorneys at Law.** A very controversial exemption has been the attorney at law exemption. It is common for lawyers to perform functions to solicit purchasers, listings, or to ultimately effect sales of real estate as a part of their law practice. Not exempting attorneys at law would mean that to perform this function would require a broker's license in addition to a license to practice law. The controversy occurs, however, when a lawyer demands a brokerage commission when he is representing one of the parties as a lawyer, and over whether or not that is performing a brokerage function requiring licensure. One case has held that attorneys are exempt from licensure for any reason. *Elin* v. *Neal*, 720 S.W.2d 224 (Tex. App.—Houston [14th Dist.], 1986, no writ). The 1989 legislature addressed this issue in two different sections of the license act: (1) Section 1101.651 of the Real Estate License Act now makes it unlawful for a seller to pay a commission for a brokerage function to anyone who is not a real estate licensee; (2) Section 1101.652(b)(11) now also makes it unlawful for a licensee to split a commission with anyone who is not a licensee (including attorneys). It should be understood, however, that nothing in the Real Estate License Act prevents a seller, buyer, or other party from paying an attorney an attorney's fee in any amount for any legal function.

There have been circumstances where attorneys have requested attorney's fees from the seller (requesting the listing broker to lower their commission) or situations where an attorney or other principal may be a purchaser and request the real estate licensee to split the commission with them. There has never been a restriction against a licensee splitting a commission with a *principal* (because the principal is not performing a brokerage function!). People requesting these commission splits, however, should be cautioned as to three items: (1) they will have to be provided with a 1099 form reporting the income to the Internal Revenue Service; (2) it will have to be reported to the lender because it may affect the definition of "sales price," and, as a result, the loan to value ratio and truth-in-lending statement; and (3) it should be agreed to by the seller, to prevent any insinuation that the licensee inadvertently became the buyer's agent.

## Penalties

The act provides that a nonexempt person acting as a real estate broker or salesperson without obtaining a license is guilty of a Class A misdemeanor. Violations are punishable by a fine not to exceed $5,000. Each day a violation continues or occurs may be considered a separate violation (that's $5,000 per day!) if the Real Estate Commission find that the person charged engaged in activity for which a real estate license is required and was not licensed by the Commission as a real estate broker licensed by the Commission at any time in the four years preceding the day of the violation. See Sec. 1101.702.

If the person received money, or the equivalent thereof, or profited by the consequence of his violation, he shall additionally be liable for damages. The amounts are limited to not less than the amount so received, and not more than three times the sum received, as may be determined by the court, Texas Occupations Code, §1101.754. Under new provisions of the License Act effective September 1, 2007, the Commission also has the authority to order a licensee to pay a refund to a consumer as provided in an agreement resulting from an information settlement conference or enforcement order. The refund cannot exceed the amount that the broker earned (see §1101.659). The Texas Real Estate Commission also has instituted informal proceedings to contest cases, and also has the authority to appoint a disciplinary panel to determine whether or not a person's license to practice real estate should be temporarily suspended. If the disciplinary panel determines that the licensee constitutes a threat to the public, or the licensee constitutes a continuing threat to the public welfare, the panel has the authority to temporarily suspend the license of that person (see §1101.660).

## Inactive Status

An inactive salesperson is a currently licensed salesperson who is not sponsored by a currently licensed broker. If, for any reason, a salesperson is no longer sponsored by a licensed broker, she is required to surrender her license to the commission. This inactive status, however, allows her to retain her license on inactive status until it expires or until she finds a new sponsoring broker. The inactive licensee is effectively unlicensed and cannot act as an agent or receive commissions during the inactive period. The legislature has also allowed a broker to elect inactive status. If the broker chooses to reactivate, he must make application, pay the required fee, and must take at least 15 hours of continuing education during the two-year period preceding the filing of the application. The broker must continue to pay the annual renewal fees. (See §1101.366; .377.)

# Licensee's Employment

The act specifically states under Section 1101.806 that an action may not be brought in a court in this state for the recovery of a commission for the sale or purchase of real estate unless the agreement on which the action is brought, *or some memorandum thereof*, is in writing and is signed by the party to be charged. As in all other real estate contracts, the listing agreement must be sufficient to enforce performance. This statutory provision brings listing agreements within the requirements of the Statute of Frauds. *Givens* v. *Dougherty*, 671 S.W.2d 877 (Tex. 1984). A **listing agreement**, or memorandum thereof, is normally considered to be specific enough when:

1. It is in writing and is signed by the person to be charged with the commission.
2. It promises that a definite commission will be paid or refers to a written commission schedule.
3. It specifies the name of the broker to whom the commission is to be paid.
4. It must, either itself or by reference to some other existing writing, identify with reasonable certainty the land to be conveyed.

If the employment agreement is for a buyer's broker, the real estate doesn't need to be identified, but the obligation to pay a commission must be set out. *LA+N Interests, Inc.* v. *Fish*, 864 S.W.2d 745 (Tex. App.—Houston [14th Dist.], 1993).

If the written agreement does not contain the required information, it must refer to an existing agreement or form from which the information can be obtained. If there is no listing agreement, or memorandum thereof, an obligation to pay the broker's commission contained in the earnest money contract may be specific enough to enforce payment. *Maloney* v. *Strain*, 410 S.W.2d 650 (Tex. Civ. App.—Eastland, 1966).

Generally, where an exclusive listing agreement is of indefinite duration, it may be terminated at the will of the principal. However, if the agent partially performs his duties under the agreement, the contract becomes binding and the agent must be given a reasonable opportunity to perform. *James* v. *Baron Industries, Inc.*, 605 S.W.2d 330 (Tex. Civ. App.—Houston, 1980). Although it is not a legal requirement of enforceability, any employment agreement (other than a contract to perform property management services) should also contain a definite termination date. Section 1101.652(b)(12) of the Real Estate License Act specifies that failure to specify a definite termination date in the employment contract provides grounds for license revocation or suspension. One court case has held that failure to specify the termination date makes the agreement unenforceable, *Perl* v. *Patrizi*, 20 S.W.3d 76 (Tex. App.—Texarkana, 2000), but the appellate courts are not in agreement on this issue. Another gray area of the law!

## Types of Listing Agreements

Most real estate brokers prefer to use standard-form listing agreements supplied by the local board of REALTORS® to keep their rights more clearly specified and defined. Standard listing agreements are generally considered to be of three types: (1) the exclusive right to sell, (2) the exclusive agency to sell, and (3) the open listing. The net listing and the multiple listing are variations of one of these types of listings. The Texas Association of REALTORS® updates and publishes listing forms regularly for their members. Their residential listing agreement form is shown in Figure 7.1.

**Exclusive Right to Sell.** In the **exclusive right to sell** listing, the property owner agrees to employ the real estate broker to sell the property, and, in addition, the property owner is prohibited from selling the property himself without paying the broker a commission. Thus, the broker is entitled to his commission if the owner or anybody else makes a sale of the real estate during the term of the listing agreement even though the broker may have had nothing to do with the sale. *Wade* v. *Austin*, 524 S.W.2d 79 (Tex. Civ. App.—Texarkana, 1975). It gives the broker complete protection against "backdoor" dealings by others in the profession, or by the owner himself.

Almost by definition, there cannot be two exclusive right to sell listing agreements at the same time because entering into the second one violates the first. *Browning* v. *Johnson*, 729 S.W.2d 331 (Tex. App.—Dallas, 1987, writ ref'd n.r.e.)

**FIGURE 7.1 EXCLUSIVE RIGHT TO SELL AGREEMENT.**

TEXAS ASSOCIATION OF REALTORS®

## RESIDENTIAL REAL ESTATE LISTING AGREEMENT
## EXCLUSIVE RIGHT TO SELL

USE OF THIS FORM BY PERSONS WHO ARE NOT MEMBERS OF THE TEXAS ASSOCIATION OF REALTORS® IS NOT AUTHORIZED.
©Texas Association of REALTORS®, Inc. 2003

1. **PARTIES:** The parties to this agreement (this Listing) are:

   Seller: _____
   _____
   Address: _____
   City, State, Zip: _____
   Phone:_____ Fax: _____
   E-Mail: _____

   Broker: _____
   Address: _____
   City, State, Zip: _____
   Phone:_____ Fax: _____
   E-Mail: _____

   Seller appoints Broker as Seller's sole and exclusive real estate agent and grants to Broker the exclusive right to sell the Property.

2. **PROPERTY:** "Property" means the land, improvements, and accessories described below, except for any described exclusions.

   A. <u>Land</u>: Lot_____, Block_____, _____
   _____ Addition, City of_____,
   in _____ County, Texas known as _____
   _____ (address/zip code),
   or as described on attached exhibit. *(If Property is a condominium, attach Condominium Addendum.)*

   B. <u>Improvements</u>: The house, garage and all other fixtures and improvements attached to the above-described real property, including without limitation, the following permanently installed and built-in items, if any: all equipment and appliances, valances, screens, shutters, awnings, wall-to-wall carpeting, mirrors, ceiling fans, attic fans, mail boxes, television antennas and satellite dish system and equipment, heating and air-conditioning units, security and fire detection equipment, wiring, plumbing and lighting fixtures, chandeliers, water softener system, kitchen equipment, garage door openers, cleaning equipment, shrubbery, landscaping, outdoor cooking equipment, and all other property owned by Seller and attached to the above-described real property.

   C. <u>Accessories</u>: The following described related accessories, if any: window air conditioning units, stove, fireplace screens, curtains and rods, blinds, window shades, draperies and rods, controls for satellite dish system, controls for garage door openers, entry gate controls, door keys, mailbox keys, above-ground pool, swimming pool equipment and maintenance accessories, and artificial fireplace logs.

   D. <u>Exclusions</u>: The following improvements and accessories will be retained by Seller and excluded: _____
   _____.

   E. <u>Owners' Association</u>: The property ❑ is ❑ is not subject to mandatory membership in an owners' association.

(TAR-1101) 10-16-03    Initialed for Identification by Broker/Associate _____ and Seller _____, _____    Page 1 of 8

**FIGURE 7.1 CONTINUED.**

Residential Listing concerning _____

3. **LISTING PRICE:** Seller instructs Broker to market the Property at the following price: $_____ (Listing Price). Seller agrees to sell the Property for the Listing Price or any other price acceptable to Seller. Seller will pay all typical closing costs charged to sellers of residential real estate in Texas (seller's typical closing costs are those set forth in the residential contract forms promulgated by the Texas Real Estate Commission).

4. **TERM:**

   A. This Listing begins on _____ and ends at 11:59 p.m. on _____.

   B. If Seller enters into a binding written contract to sell the Property before the date this Listing begins and the contract is binding on the date this Listing begins, this Listing will not commence and will be void.

5. **BROKER'S FEE:**

   A. <u>Fee</u>: When earned and payable, Seller will pay Broker a fee of:

   ❏ (1) _____ % of the sales price.

   ❏ (2) _____.

   B. <u>Earned</u>: Broker's fee is earned when any one of the following occurs during this Listing:
      (1) Seller sells, exchanges, options, agrees to sell, agrees to exchange, or agrees to option the Property to anyone at any price on any terms;
      (2) Broker individually or in cooperation with another broker procures a buyer ready, willing, and able to buy the Property at the Listing Price or at any other price acceptable to Seller; or
      (3) Seller breaches this Listing.

   C. <u>Payable</u>: Once earned, Broker's fee is payable either during this Listing or after it ends at the earlier of:
      (1) the closing and funding of any sale or exchange of all or part of the Property;
      (2) Seller's refusal to sell the Property after Broker's Fee has been earned;
      (3) Seller's breach of this Listing; or
      (4) at such time as otherwise set forth in this Listing.

      Broker's fee is <u>not</u> payable if a sale of the Property does not close or fund as a result of: (i) Seller's failure, without fault of Seller, to deliver to a buyer a deed or a title policy as required by the contract to sell; (ii) loss of ownership due to foreclosure or other legal proceeding; or (iii) Seller's failure to restore the Property, as a result of a casualty loss, to its previous condition by the closing date set forth in a contract for the sale of the Property.

   D. <u>Other Fees</u>:

      (1) <u>Breach by Buyer Under a Contract</u>: If Seller collects earnest money, the sales price, or damages by suit, compromise, settlement, or otherwise from a buyer who breaches a contract for the sale of the Property entered into during this Listing, Seller will pay Broker, after deducting attorney's fees and collection expenses, an amount equal to the lesser of one-half of the amount collected after deductions or the amount of the Broker's Fee stated in Paragraph 5A. Any amount paid under this Paragraph 5D(1) is in addition to any amount that Broker may be entitled to receive for subsequently selling the Property.

      (2) <u>Service Providers</u>: If Broker refers Seller or a prospective buyer to a service provider (for example, mover, cable company, telecommunications provider, utility, or contractor) Broker may receive a fee from the service provider for the referral. Any referral fee Broker receives under this Paragraph 5D(2) is in addition to any other compensation Broker may receive under this Listing.

**FIGURE 7.1  CONTINUED.**

Residential Listing concerning _____

(3) Transaction Fees or Reimbursable Expenses: _____

_____

_____.

E. Protection Period:

(1) "Protection period" means that time starting the day after this Listing ends and continuing for _____ days. "Sell" means any transfer of any interest in the Property whether by oral or written agreement or option.

(2) Not later than 10 days after this Listing ends, Broker may send Seller written notice specifying the names of persons whose attention was called to the Property during this Listing. If Seller agrees to sell the Property during the protection period to a person named in the notice or to a relative of a person named in the notice, Seller will pay Broker, upon the closing of the sale, the amount Broker would have been entitled to receive if this Listing were still in effect.

(3) This Paragraph 5E survives termination of this Listing. This Paragraph 5E will not apply if:
(a) Seller agrees to sell the Property during the protection period;
(b) the Property is exclusively listed with another broker who is a member of the Texas Association of REALTORS® at the time the sale is negotiated; and
(c) Seller is obligated to pay the other broker a fee for the sale.

F. County:  All amounts payable to Broker are to be paid in cash in _____

_____ County, Texas.

G. Escrow Authorization:  Seller authorizes, and Broker may so instruct, any escrow or closing agent authorized to close a transaction for the purchase or acquisition of the Property to collect and disburse to Broker all amounts payable to Broker under this Listing.

**6.  LISTING SERVICES:**

❑  A.  Broker will file this Listing with one or more Multiple Listing Services (MLS) by the earlier of the time required by MLS rules or 5 days after the date this Listing begins.  Seller authorizes Broker to submit information about this Listing and the sale of the Property to the MLS.

Notice:  MLS rules require Broker to accurately and timely submit all information the MLS requires for participation including sold data.  Subscribers to the MLS may use the information for market evaluation or appraisal purposes.  Subscribers are other brokers and other real estate professionals such as appraisers and may include the appraisal district.  Any information filed with the MLS becomes the property of the MLS for all purposes. **Submission of information to MLS ensures that persons who use and benefit from the MLS also contribute information.**

❑  B.  Broker will not file this Listing with a Multiple Listing Service (MLS) or any other listing service.

**7.  ACCESS TO THE PROPERTY:**

A. Authorizing Access:  Authorizing access to the Property means giving permission to another person to enter the Property, disclosing to the other person any security codes necessary to enter the Property, and lending a key to the other person to enter the Property, directly or through a keybox.  To facilitate the showing and sale of the Property, Seller instructs Broker to:
(1) access the Property at reasonable times
(2) authorize other brokers, their associates, inspectors, appraisers, and contractors to access the Property at reasonable times; and
(3) duplicate keys to facilitate convenient and efficient showings of the Property.

B. Scheduling Companies:  Broker may engage the following companies to schedule appointments and to authorize others to access the Property: _____.

**FIGURE 7.1 CONTINUED.**

Residential Listing concerning _____

C. <u>Keybox</u>: **A keybox is a locked container placed on the Property that holds a key to the Property. A keybox makes it more convenient for brokers, their associates, inspectors, appraisers, and contractors to show, inspect, or repair the Property. The keybox is opened by a special combination, key, or programmed device so that authorized persons may enter the Property, even in Seller's absence. Using a keybox will probably increase the number of showings, but involves risks (for example, unauthorized entry, theft, property damage, or personal injury). Neither the Association of REALTORS® nor MLS requires the use of a keybox.**

(1) Broker ❑ is ❑ is not   authorized to place a keybox on the Property.

(2) If a tenant occupies the Property at any time during this Listing, Seller will furnish Broker a written statement (for example, TAR No. 1411), signed by all tenants, authorizing the use of a keybox or Broker may remove the keybox from the Property.

D. <u>Liability and Indemnification</u>:  When authorizing access to the Property, Broker, other brokers, their associates, any keybox provider, or any scheduling company are not responsible for personal injury or property loss to Seller or any other person.  Seller assumes all risk of any loss, damage, or injury. **Except for a loss caused by Broker, Seller will indemnify and hold Broker harmless from any claim for personal injury, property damage, or other loss.**

8. **COOPERATION WITH OTHER BROKERS:** Broker will allow other brokers to show the Property to prospective buyers.  Broker will offer to pay the other broker a fee as described below if the other broker procures a buyer that purchases the Property.

A. <u>MLS Participants</u>: If the other broker is a participant in the MLS in which this Listing is filed, Broker will offer to pay the other broker:
(1) if the other broker represents the buyer: _____% of the sales price or $_____; and
(2) if the other broker is a subagent:        _____% of the sales price or $_____.

B. <u>Non-MLS Brokers</u>: If the other broker is not a participant in the MLS in which this Listing is filed, Broker will offer to pay the other broker:
(1) if the other broker represents the buyer: _____% of the sales price or $_____; and
(2) if the other broker is a subagent:        _____% of the sales price or $_____.

9. **INTERMEDIARY:** *(Check A or B only.)*

❑ A. <u>Intermediary Status</u>:  Broker may show the Property to interested prospective buyers who Broker represents.  If a prospective buyer who Broker represents offers to buy the Property, Seller authorizes Broker to act as an intermediary and Broker will notify Seller that Broker will service the parties in accordance with one of the following alternatives.

(1) If a prospective buyer who Broker represents is serviced by an associate other than the associate servicing Seller under this Listing, Broker may notify Seller that Broker will: (a) appoint the associate then servicing Seller to communicate with, carry out instructions of, and provide opinions and advice during negotiations to Seller; and (b) appoint the associate then servicing the prospective buyer to the prospective buyer for the same purpose.

(2) If a prospective buyer who Broker represents is serviced by the same associate who is servicing Seller, Broker may notify Seller that Broker will: (a) appoint another associate to communicate with, carry out instructions of, and provide opinions and advice during negotiations to the prospective buyer; and (b) appoint the associate servicing the Seller under this Listing to the Seller for the same purpose.

(3) Broker may notify Seller that Broker will make no appointments as described under this Paragraph 9A and, in such an event, the associate servicing the parties will act solely as Broker's intermediary representative, who may facilitate the transaction but will not render opinions or advice during negotiations to either party.

**FIGURE 7.1 CONTINUED.**

Residential Listing concerning _____

❑ B. <u>No Intermediary Status</u>: Seller agrees that Broker will not show the Property to prospective buyers who Broker represents.

**Notice:** **If Broker acts as an intermediary under Paragraph 9A, Broker and Broker's associates:**
- **may not disclose to the prospective buyer that Seller will accept a price less than the asking price unless otherwise instructed in a separate writing by Seller;**
- **may not disclose to Seller that the prospective buyer will pay a price greater than the price submitted in a written offer to Seller unless otherwise instructed in a separate writing by the prospective buyer;**
- **may not disclose any confidential information or any information Seller or the prospective buyer specifically instructs Broker in writing not to disclose unless otherwise instructed in a separate writing by the respective party or required to disclose the information by the Real Estate License Act or a court order or if the information materially relates to the condition of the property;**
- **may not treat a party to the transaction dishonestly; and**
- **may not violate the Real Estate License Act.**

10. **CONFIDENTIAL INFORMATION:** During this Listing or after it ends, Broker may not knowingly disclose information obtained in confidence from Seller except as authorized by Seller or required by law. Broker may not disclose to Seller any confidential information regarding any other person Broker represents or previously represented except as required by law.

11. **BROKER'S AUTHORITY:**

A. Broker will use reasonable efforts and act diligently to market the Property for sale, procure a buyer, and negotiate the sale of the Property.

B. In addition to other authority granted by this Listing, Broker may:
   (1) advertise the Property by means and methods as Broker determines, including but not limited to creating and placing advertisements with interior and exterior photographic and audio-visual images of the Property and related information in any media and the Internet;
   (2) place a "For Sale" sign on the Property and remove all other signs offering the Property for sale or lease;
   (3) furnish comparative marketing and sales information about other properties to prospective buyers;
   (4) disseminate information about the Property to other brokers and to prospective buyers, including applicable disclosures or notices that Seller is required to make under law or a contract;
   (5) obtain information from any holder of a note secured by a lien on the Property;
   (6) accept and deposit earnest money in trust in accordance with a contract for the sale of the Property;
   (7) disclose the sales price and terms of sale to other brokers, appraisers, or other real estate professionals;
   (8) in response to inquiries from prospective buyers and other brokers, disclose whether the Seller is considering more than one offer, provided that Broker will not disclose the terms of any competing offer unless specifically instructed by Seller;
   (9) advertise, during or after this Listing ends, that Broker "sold" the Property; and
   (10) place information about this Listing, the Property, and a transaction for the Property on an electronic transaction platform (typically an Internet-based system where professionals related to the transaction such as title companies, lenders, and others may receive, view, and input information).

C. Broker is not authorized to execute any document in the name of or on behalf of Seller concerning the Property.

**FIGURE 7.1 CONTINUED.**

Residential Listing concerning _____

12. **SELLER'S REPRESENTATIONS:** Except as provided by Paragraph 15, Seller represents that:
   A. Seller has fee simple title to and peaceable possession of the Property and all its improvements and fixtures, unless rented, and the legal capacity to convey the Property;
   B. Seller is not bound by a listing agreement with another broker for the sale, exchange, or lease of the Property that is or will be in effect during this Listing;
   C. any pool or spa and any required enclosures, fences, gates, and latches comply with all applicable laws and ordinances;
   D. no person or entity has any right to purchase, lease, or acquire the Property by an option, right of refusal, or other agreement;
   E. there are no delinquencies or defaults under any deed of trust, mortgage, or other encumbrance on the Property;
   F. the Property is not subject to the jurisdiction of any court;
   G. all information relating to the Property Seller provides to Broker is true and correct to the best of Seller's knowledge; and
   H. the name of any employer, relocation company, or other entity that provides benefits to Seller when selling the Property is: _____.

13. **SELLER'S ADDITIONAL PROMISES:** Seller agrees to:
   A. cooperate with Broker to facilitate the showing, marketing, and sale of the Property;
   B. not rent or lease the Property during this Listing without Broker's prior written approval;
   C. not negotiate with any prospective buyer who may contact Seller directly, but refer all prospective buyers to Broker;
   D. not enter into a listing agreement with another broker for the sale, exchange, or lease of the Property to become effective during this Listing;
   E. maintain any pool and all required enclosures in compliance with all applicable laws and ordinances;
   F. provide Broker with copies of any leases or rental agreements pertaining to the Property and advise Broker of tenants moving in or out of the Property;
   G. complete any disclosures or notices required by law or a contract to sell the Property; and
   H. amend any applicable notices and disclosures if any material change occurs during this Listing.

14. **LIMITATION OF LIABILITY:**

   A. If the Property is or becomes vacant during this Listing, Seller must notify Seller's casualty insurance company and request a "vacancy clause" to cover the Property. Broker is not responsible for the security of the Property nor for inspecting the Property on any periodic basis.

   B. **Broker is not responsible or liable in any manner for personal injury to any person or for loss or damage to any person's real or personal property resulting from any act or omission not caused by Broker's negligence, including but not limited to injuries or damages caused by:**
      **(1) other brokers, their associates, inspectors, appraisers, and contractors who are authorized to access the Property;**
      **(2) acts of third parties (for example, vandalism or theft);**
      **(3) freezing water pipes;**
      **(4) a dangerous condition on the Property; or**
      **(5) the Property's non-compliance with any law or ordinance.**

   C. **Seller agrees to protect, defend, indemnify, and hold Broker harmless from any damage, costs, attorney's fees, and expenses that:**
      **(1) are caused by Seller, negligently or otherwise;**
      **(2) arise from Seller's failure to disclose any material or relevant information about the Property; or**
      **(3) are caused by Seller giving incorrect information to any person.**

**FIGURE 7.1 CONTINUED.**

Residential Listing concerning _____

## 15. SPECIAL PROVISIONS:

16. **DEFAULT:** If Seller breaches this Listing, Seller is in default and will be liable to Broker for the amount of the Broker's fee specified in Paragraph 5A and any other fees Broker is entitled to receive under this Listing. If a sales price is not determinable in the event of an exchange or breach of this Listing, the Listing Price will be the sales price for purposes of computing Broker's fee. If Broker breaches this Listing, Broker is in default and Seller may exercise any remedy at law.

17. **MEDIATION:** The parties agree to negotiate in good faith in an effort to resolve any dispute related to this Listing that may arise between the parties. If the dispute cannot be resolved by negotiation, the dispute will be submitted to mediation. The parties to the dispute will choose a mutually acceptable mediator and will share the cost of mediation equally.

18. **ATTORNEY'S FEES:** If Seller or Broker is a prevailing party in any legal proceeding brought as a result of a dispute under this Listing or any transaction related to or contemplated by this Listing, such party will be entitled to recover from the non-prevailing party all costs of such proceeding and reasonable attorney's fees.

19. **ADDENDA AND OTHER DOCUMENTS:** Addenda that are part of this Listing and other documents that Seller may need to provide are:
- [X] A. Information About Brokerage Services;
- [ ] B. Seller Disclosure Notice (§5.008, Texas Property Code);
- [ ] C. Seller's Disclosure of Information on Lead-Based Paint and Lead-Based Paint Hazards (required if Property was built before 1978);
- [ ] D. MUD, Water District, or Statutory Tax District Disclosure Notice (Chapter 49, Texas Water Code);
- [ ] E. Request for Information from an Owners' Association;
- [ ] F. Request for Mortgage Information;
- [ ] G. Information about On-Site Sewer Facility;
- [ ] H. Information about Special Flood Hazard Areas;
- [ ] I. Condominium Addendum to Listing;
- [ ] J. Keybox Authorization by Tenant;
- [ ] K. Seller's Authorization to Release and Advertise Certain Information; and
- [ ] L. _____
  _____.

## 20. AGREEMENT OF PARTIES:

A. <u>Entire Agreement</u>: This Listing is the entire agreement of the parties and may not be changed except by written agreement.

B. <u>Assignability</u>: Neither party may assign this Listing without the written consent of the other party.

**FIGURE 7.1 CONTINUED.**

Residential Listing concerning _____

C. <u>Binding Effect</u>: Seller's obligation to pay Broker an earned fee is binding upon Seller and Seller's heirs, administrators, executors, successors, and permitted assignees.

D. <u>Joint and Several</u>: All Sellers executing this Listing are jointly and severally liable for the performance of all its terms.

E. <u>Governing Law</u>: Texas law governs the interpretation, validity, performance, and enforcement of this Listing.

F. <u>Severability</u>: If a court finds any clause in this Listing invalid or unenforceable, the remainder of this Listing will not be affected and all other provisions of this Listing will remain valid and enforceable.

G. <u>Notices</u>: Notices between the parties must be in writing and are effective when sent to the receiving party's address, fax, or e-mail address specified in Paragraph 1.

**21. ADDITIONAL NOTICES:**

A. **Broker's fees or the sharing of fees between brokers are not fixed, controlled, recommended, suggested, or maintained by the Association of REALTORS®, MLS, or any listing service.**

B. **Fair housing laws require the Property to be shown and made available to all persons without regard to race, color, religion, national origin, sex, disability, or familial status. Local ordinances may provide for additional protected classes (for example, creed, status as a student, marital status, sexual orientation, or age).**

C. **Seller may review the information Broker submits to an MLS or other listing service.**

D. **Broker advises Seller to remove or secure jewelry, prescription drugs, and other valuables.**

E. **Statutes or ordinances may regulate certain items on the Property (for example, swimming pools and septic systems). Non-compliance with the statutes or ordinances may delay a transaction and may result in fines, penalties, and liability to Seller.**

F. **If the Property was built before 1978, Federal law requires the Seller to: (1) provide the buyer with the federally approved pamphlet on lead poisoning prevention; (2) disclose the presence of any known lead-based paint or lead-based paint hazards in the Property; (3) deliver all records and reports to the buyer related to such paint or hazards; and (4) provide the buyer a period up to 10 days to have the Property inspected for such paint or hazards.**

G. **Broker cannot give legal advice. READ THIS LISTING CAREFULLY. If you do not understand the effect of this Listing, consult an attorney BEFORE signing.**

| | | | |
|---|---|---|---|
| _____ | _____ | _____ | _____ |
| Broker's Printed Name | License No. | Seller | Date |
| By:_____ | _____ | _____ | _____ |
| Broker's Associate's Signature | Date | Seller | Date |

**Exclusive Agency to Sell.** Under the **exclusive agency to sell** agreement, the owner employs the broker to sell the property, and if so sold, the broker is entitled to a commission. This is true even if the property is sold through another broker's efforts. However, in contrast to the exclusive right to sell agreement, in this situation the owner reserves the right to sell the house himself and does not have to pay the commission to the broker.

**Open Agency Listing.** An **open agency listing** merely gives the broker the right to sell the property, and if the broker sells the property, she is entitled to her commission. Such an agreement is effective in enforcing the payment of a commission, but serious conflicts may arise as to whether or not the broker under an open listing agreement is truly the "procuring cause" of finding the purchaser. The open agency listing agreement clearly allows the owner to give other open agency agreements to other brokers, and the facts surrounding any particular transaction can create quite a lengthy dispute between brokers. The widespread use of the multiple listing service by realtors normally precludes the use of open listings. The exposure to several brokers, although originally obtained for the owner's benefit, also protects the listing broker from potential conflicts.

**Net Listing.** A **net listing** agreement can technically be used in any listing agreement. The term "net listing" refers to the payment of commission rather than to the broker's authority to market the property. In a net listing agreement the commission is not specified but, rather, is referred to in terms of the owner's net profit to be made out of the sale of the real estate. For instance, an owner may require that a broker sell the property for whatever price will net $35,000 for the owner. The broker, then, is free to sell the property for whatever price the open market may bring, knowing that out of his sales price, the first $35,000 will go to the owner and the remaining monies will go to closing costs; if any additional monies are still available, the funds will go to the broker as his commission. Although a net listing can be lucrative, most brokers prefer to rely on a percentage of the sales price for the purposes of convenience and to avoid any conflicts of interest of the property owner. One can see that if a broker walks away from a closing with more money than the property owner, there may be some question as to how well the property owner was represented in the sale.

**Multiple Listing.** A **multiple listing** is a listing that is normally an exclusive right to sell taken by a broker who is a member of an association of brokers. The brokers use their association as a means of providing all member brokers a right to find an interested client. Usually the commissions earned on such listings are split by an agreement between cooperating brokers.

# Actions for Commissions

## Listing Brokers

In most written agreements, each party promises to perform an obligation. These are called **bilateral contracts**. A listing agreement, on the other hand, is a **unilateral contract** because only one party, the owner, promises to perform. The owner promises to pay the broker a commission to sell certain property, for a certain price, and within a certain period of time. The broker, in effect, makes no promises and incurs no obligations other than to use his best efforts to market the property. Therefore, the contract is considered completed and the contractual obligations fulfilled when the broker performs his part of the agreement and produces a ready, willing, and able buyer to purchase the property according to the terms of the listing agreement. The broker completes his half of the contract by performance rather than by satisfying promises contained in the listing agreement. This is discussed in greater detail in the chapter on Contracts.

A broker's right to a commission is conditioned on five factors. First, Section 1101.806 of the Texas Real Estate License Act specifically requires that any person bringing an action for a commission must be a duly licensed real estate broker or salesperson at the time the alleged services are commenced. *Terry* v. *Allied Bancshares, Inc.*, 760 S.W.2d 45 (Tex. App—Ft. Worth, 1988).

Second, Section 1101.806 of the act requires that the agreement for the payment of the commission must be in writing. *Texas Builders, et al.,* v. *Keller*, 928 S.W.2d 479 (Tex. 1996); *Trammel Crow Co. No. 60, et al.,* v. *William Jefferson Harkinson*, 944 S.W.2d 631 (Tex. 1997). This requirement is satisfied if there is a listing agreement or if the promise to pay the commission is set out in the earnest money contract. *Maloney* v. *Strain*, supra.

The third requirement is set out in Section 1101.555 and Section 1101.806 of the Real Estate License Act. The broker must advise the purchaser, in writing, that the purchaser should have the abstract covering the real estate examined by an attorney or obtain a policy of title insurance. *Jones* v. *Del Anderson and Associates*, 539 S.W.2d 348 (Tex. 1976).

The fourth requirement applies to the terms of the listing agreement. If the broker has an exclusive right to sell listing agreement and produces a **ready, willing, and able buyer**, he is entitled to his commission if the first three requirements are met, so long as the contract submitted is on substantially the same terms as those specified in the listing agreement. *Bayer* v. *McDade*, 610 S.W.2d 171 (Tex. Civ. App.—Houston, 1980).

The fifth requirement, occurring when using listing agreements other than the exclusive right to sell, requires the broker to be the **procuring cause** of the sale. If the broker has an exclusive right to sell, the owner is bound to pay the commission, pursuant to the terms of the listing agreement. In the exclusive agency listing agreement, if a purchaser deals with the owner directly, the seller would not be obligated to pay a commission. In the open listing, when a ready, willing, and able buyer is produced, there may also be some question as to who was the procuring cause of the sale. In addition, there may also be situations where the broker's exclusive right to sell listing agreement provides for a commission to be payable for certain sales after the listing agreement has expired. *White* v. *Larson*, 586 S.W.2d 212 (Tex. Civ. App.—El Paso, 1979). The same rule also applies when a seller interferes with a sale and miraculously "finds" a buyer (who had previously seen the property) on the day after a listing expires. *Boyles* v. *Thompson*, 585 S.W.2d 821 (Tex. Civ. App.—Ft. Worth, 1979); *Snoddy* v. *Wallace*, 625 S.W.2d 81 (Tex. Civ. App.—Tyler, 1981). It is in these situations that the procuring cause requirement becomes important.

## Buyer's Brokers

Buyer's brokers create a complicating issue involving procuring cause that has caused considerable unrest in the real estate brokerage community. There are times when a prospect may visit a property one or more times and spend a great deal of the listing broker's time asking questions and getting information. Before submitting an offer, however, the prospect goes to a buyer's broker and requests their assistance and advice in preparing a contract before presentation to the owner's agent. Who was the procuring cause? While the listing agent may feel that they were the procuring cause, the buyer is likely to support the buyer's broker's position, since the buyer chose to retain the services of that buyer's broker in presenting the offer. In the age of email, the internet, and highly informed consumers there is an argument that buyers want and need representation. Once a consumer has sought and obtained a buyer's broker's advice, conceptually, the buyer's broker may become the real procuring cause when the contract is signed and presented to the listing broker.

The buyer's broker may not even need a written agreement to obtain the commission. The license act provides that a broker can sue another broker (the listing broker) for an oral agreement to share commissions or for interference with business relationships (e.g., the listing broker encouraging the buyer to fire the broker). Under these circumstances, a written agreement to recover your commission is not required.

## Consummation of Sale?

Once all the foregoing requirements have been met, the broker is entitled to his commission. There have been a number of cases in which the seller has refused to pay the commission because the sale was not consummated. It must be emphasized that the closing of the sale, by itself, is not the determinative factor as to whether or not the broker is entitled to a commission. If the seller backs out, he clearly has breached the terms of the listing agreement, and the commission must be paid. If the sale has not been consummated through no fault of the broker, the broker is still entitled to his commission. Even if the commission is contingent upon the consummation of the sale, as provided in many earnest money contracts, the agent can successfully maintain an action for the commission if the seller chooses to back out, on the grounds that the production of a ready, willing, and able buyer consummated the terms of that listing agreement upon signing the earnest money contract. *Duckworth* v. *Field*, 516 F.2d 952 (5th Cir.—1975); *Cotton* v. *Deasey*, 766 S.W.2d 874 (Tex. App.—Dallas, 1989). There has been additional authority that even if the purchaser backs out of the agreement and the seller chooses not to enforce specific performance, the broker still may maintain a successful cause of action to obtain his commission. *Davidson* v. *Suber*, 553 S.W.2d 430 (Tex. Civ. App.—Austin, 1977). In most cases, if a broker is required to sue the seller, he is also entitled to the attorney's fees incurred.

A broker may have difficulty, however, in obtaining a commission for an option agreement. An option agreement is not an earnest money contract, but rather a contract executed by the optionor that gives the optionee the right (not the obligation) to purchase the property at a later date. This is discussed in greater detail in Chapter 9. The law is well settled in Texas that if a purchaser produced by the broker enters into a mere option agreement, the broker will not be entitled to a commission. *Moss & Raley* v. *Wren*, 120 S.W. 847 (Tex. 1909); *John Dull & Co.* v. *Life of Nebraska Insurance Co.*, 642 S.W.2d 1 (Tex. Civ. App.—Houston, 1982). In order to prevail for a commission under an option contract, there must be a closing. It is only at that point that a ready, willing, and able buyer has been procured in an option agreement.

Leasing commissions are payable in basically the same manner. It has already been determined in Texas that a lease is a "sale" within contemplation of the Real

Estate License Act, *Moser Company* v. *Awalt Industrial Properties, Inc.*, 584 S.W.2d 902 (Tex. Civ. App.—Amarillo, 1979) although another case holds differently, *Collins* v. *Beste*, supra. The only difficulty is when the leasing commission is paid over a long period of time. Lease commissions are not a covenant running with the land, and if the existing landlord sells the property, the new purchaser is not liable for the lease commission payments. *Dauley* v. *First National Bank of Ft. Worth*, 565 S.W.2d 346 (Tex. Civ. App.—Ft. Worth, 1978). Therefore, it is probably advisable that the broker should get a cash commission payment for obtaining a lessee's lease even if it has to be discounted.

Except for filing suit to recover commissions pursuant to the terms of the listing agreement, the broker is rather limited as to how else to protect his interest. There has been some question in the past as to whether or not a residential real estate agent may file a lien against the real estate while maintaining an action for his commission. It must be emphasized that the real estate agent has no interest in the real estate at all. He only has an interest in consummating the sale of that real estate. Therefore, he is not entitled to cloud the title to real estate, or attempt to put a lien on that real estate, or in any other way slander the title of an owner's parcel of real estate if he (the broker) is only maintaining an action for his brokerage commission. If title to an owner's real estate becomes clouded as a result of a broker's intentional act, the broker may be liable for significant damages. *Walker* v. *Ruggles*, 540 S.W.2d 470 (Tex. Civ. App.—Houston, 1976). There is a statutory right for commercial brokers and appraisers to put liens on property, however. This is discussed in detail in Chapter 17.

# Special Problem Areas

There are certain problem areas unique to the real estate brokerage business that deserve special discussion in order to make a real estate agent more aware of these problems and, hopefully, to help him avoid them.

## Securities

There has been a lot of emphasis on investment real estate in recent years. Real estate has special tax benefits that many other investment opportunities do not share. For example, the investments generally take the form of syndication interests (usually limited partnerships or land trusts) or ownership of rental housing such as resort condominiums (which can be readily rented by a project manager when not in use by the owner). In these cases, the broker may be selling real estate **interests**, from which the owner expects a **profit** through the **efforts of a third party**. This, by definition, *SEC* v. *Howey*, 328 U.S. 293 (1946), is considered to be a **security** rather than a parcel of real estate. In the event the interest sold is in fact deemed a security, the broker may find he cannot maintain an action for a commission on the sale unless he has a securities broker's license. *Sunshine* v. *Mid-South Construction Co.*, 496 S.W.2d 708 (Tex. Civ. App.—Dallas, 1973). After all, a stockbroker cannot maintain an action for a commission on a real estate sale unless he is licensed. The converse is true of a real estate broker.

## Truth-in-Lending

The Board of Governors of the Federal Reserve Board has passed a series of regulations known as **Regulation Z**, to implement enforcement of the federal **Truth-in-Lending Act** (T-i-L Act). The T-i-L Act, simply explained, requires the lending institution (in the business of loaning money) to make a full disclosure of all costs of a loan to a consumer. Although the first impression of the T-i-L Act makes very good sense, it does provide a pitfall for an unwary broker. In at least one case, *Eby* v. *Reb Realty*, 495 F.2d 646 (9th Cir.—1974), a broker who personally financed five real property sales (typical in many real estate sales situations) was found to be "in the business of making loans." The broker, never realizing he should make a full disclosure as required by Regulation Z, was found in violation of the T-i-L Act and was subjected to its penalties.

## Employees Versus Independent Contractors

When a real estate broker hires sales personnel to represent his brokerage company in seeking listings and negotiating real estate transactions, something that is far too often overlooked is whether or not that sales agent should be classified as an **independent contractor** or as an **employee**.

The broker normally assumes that the sales agent will be an independent contractor because there are a number of advantages, from the broker's point of view, favoring independent contractor status of the sales personnel. These advantages generally include a smaller amount of paperwork and fewer records to maintain on behalf of the broker; no office hours are required to be kept; and the sales personnel are more motivated to sell if they work on a commission basis only. These also are tax savings to the firm because there are no Social Security and unemployment taxes to be paid by the firm, and the system tends to promote more professionalism and advantages for more experienced sales agents. The independent contractor status basically provides for a more professional, harder-working, motivated sales agent because there is no limit to his potential income, and there are fewer controls on the individual's time and effort.

If classified as an employee, on the other hand, the individual salesperson may not be as well motivated since the basic check amount is the same every month regardless of whether or not any results are achieved. Furthermore, the employing broker's overhead remains relatively constant but quite high. Accounting and bookkeeping become more expensive because of the larger amount of paperwork and office records required. Added costs of Social Security taxes and unemployment benefits as well as other requirements by the federal government that apply to employees generally must also be considered.

This issue has been greatly simplified for the services of real estate agents. The **Tax Equity and Fiscal Responsibility Act of 1982** provides a "safe harbor" to eliminate the vast majority of conflicts that have existed for real estate agents. The new federal law is an addition to the Internal Revenue Code and provides that a qualified real estate agent shall not be treated as an employee nor shall the person for whom such services are performed be treated as an employer. The key to compliance with the statute revolves around the definition of "qualified real estate agents." It includes any individual who is a salesperson if: (1) such individual is a licensed real estate agent; (2) substantially all the remuneration is directly related to sales rather than to the number of hours worked; and (3) the services are performed pursuant to a written contract between such individual and the person for whom the services are performed and such contract provides that the individual will not be treated as an employee with respect to such services for federal tax purposes.

This has been held to apply to real estate appraisal services as well, *Internal Revenue Code, §3508.*

## Brokers Versus Lawyers

Saying that there is a conflict between brokers and lawyers in Texas has got to be the understatement of the century. Both represent clients. Furthermore, they often represent the same client, and conflicts in this type of situation are inevitable. Unfortunately, you may find brokers who attempt to give legal advice, and you may find lawyers who attempt to advise their clients on the fair market value of real estate. You may also find attorneys who attempt to split the commission on the sale of a piece of property. (A split commission is generally more than legal fees.)

You may also find that many brokers are more than happy to give their clients all types of legal advice concerning the interpretation of legal instruments, although this is specifically prohibited under the Texas Real Estate License Act. But it should also be pointed out that the broker's ability to "fill in the blanks" of an earnest money contract is specifically approved through the use of the Texas Real Estate Commission–promulgated contract forms, which are prescribed for brokers' use. Prior to the promulgation of the forms sanctioned by the commission, the use of any form by a real estate broker was considered suspect, and possibly in violation of the Texas Real Estate License Act (Attorney General's Opinion Number M-1256, November 1, 1972). In 1983, the legislature made the use of promulgated forms mandatory and exempted the use of these forms as a practicing law criterion. This will be discussed in greater detail in Chapter 9, Contracts for the Sale of Real Estate.

The relationship between a professional broker and a professional lawyer should be complementary, and neither profession should make even the slightest attempt to downgrade the other while working together, before working together, or after working together. Unfortunately, there will be lawyers and brokers who are "unprincipled." It will take the efforts of both parties, and the understanding of both parties, to help keep these conflicts at a minimum.

## Antitrust Laws

**Antitrust laws** may seem to have a limited impact on the individual licensee; however, they create an increasing concern for brokers, REALTOR® boards, and multiple listing services (MLS).

There are several common names for the antitrust statutes and their subsequent amendments. The two that have the most far-reaching impact on real estate are the **Sherman Antitrust Act**, *15 U.S.C.A., §1 et seq.*, and the **Clayton Antitrust Act**, *15 U.S.C.A., §12 et seq.* The provisions of these acts are enforced by the Federal Trade Commission and the Department of Justice. The basic theory of antitrust laws is that **monopolies** and dominance in any industry are against the public interest and free flow of goods and services through interstate commerce.

**Sherman Act.** Pertinent provisions of the Sherman Antitrust Act prohibit unreasonable restraint of trade and monopolies. This act was "specifically intended to prohibit independent businesses from becoming 'associates' in a common plan which is bound to reduce their competitor's opportunity. . . ." This has been interpreted by the Supreme Court of Pennsylvania as prohibiting a Board of REALTORS® from excluding a licensee from MLS membership, even for cause. *Collins* v. *Main Line*

*Board of Realtors*, 304 A.2d 493 (Sup. Ct. of Penn.—1973). While the Pennsylvania case is a complicated one, its primary holding is well reasoned, and the U.S. Supreme Court declined to hear an appeal.

**Clayton Act.** The Clayton Act is not as broad in scope as the Sherman Act and seeks to reach specified practices that have been held by courts to be outside the scope of the Sherman Act, but which Congress considered to adversely affect free competition. It specifically deals with price discrimination, acquisitions and mergers, and exclusive dealing arrangements. The Clayton Act was passed to complement the Sherman Act, although both can be violated at the same time.

One pertinent part of the Clayton Act that may affect real estate brokers is the aggressive acquisition of smaller brokerage offices by larger ones. If a very large brokerage office moves into a new area of the state and their acquisition of smaller real estate companies significantly lessens the competition in the area, it may be a merger or acquisition that results in the violation of Section 7 of the Clayton Antitrust Act.

**Price Fixing.** One of the key areas of concern for real estate licensees has been "**price fixing**," which is generally defined as the setting of prices by an industry at an artificial level. Price fixing, whether good or evil, express or implied, is **illegal per se**. In theory, prices must be set by competitors only, and not by any agreement between or among competitors.

Two decisions made in the area of antitrust law as it pertains to real estate brokers involved a conspiracy to set prices. In the first case, six corporate and three individual defendants were convicted of conspiracy to fix real estate commissions in Montgomery County, Maryland (commission rate at 7%) in violation of Section 1 of the Sherman Act. The facts in this case indicated that there was, in fact, a conspiracy. There was even testimony in the case that some brokers took a 6% listing and one of the "conspiring" brokers called the 6% broker to inform him of his "mistake." There was further testimony that the conspiring brokers called each other to be sure that they were "holding the line" for setting the new, higher commission rate. *United States* v. *Foley, et al.*, 598 F.2d 1323 (1979).

The second case was a U.S. Supreme Court case, which was decided on January 8, 1980. The more serious question was whether or not real estate brokerage constitutes interstate commerce. If real estate brokerage does involve interstate commerce, it automatically establishes federal jurisdiction and antitrust jurisdiction for the Federal Trade Commission. If it does not, it will mean that the regulation of real estate brokerage will remain primarily a state matter and therefore not be subject to federal antitrust jurisdiction.

The Supreme Court discussed the possibility that the courts may consider the broker's activities within the flow of interstate commerce because of the movement of their clients into and out of the state, and the broker's assistance in securing financing and title insurance. The Supreme Court remanded the case to the trial court to determine whether or not, by the facts of the case, the broker's activities were or were not within the flow of interstate commerce. This greatly emphasizes how critical the facts of each case are. If the jury can determine from this case that the broker's activities are substantially affected by interstate commerce or substantially affect interstate commerce, it could set a very important precedent for the federal government's regulation of brokerage activities. In many cases it could even supersede state law as it pertains to real estate brokerage. *McLain* v. *Real Estate Board of New Orleans*, 100 U.S. 512 (U.S. Sup. Ct.—1980).

As in all areas of the law, particularly those involving very sophisticated federal laws, arguments on both sides of the issues are very good. The public needs to be protected against restraints in trade and price fixing in order to increase competition and to prevent conspiracy. However, as all licensees know, there are very few businesses as competitive as the real estate business. It is probably fair to say, again, that the decisions yet to be made in this area will be determined largely by the facts of each case, and how the respective federal laws apply to those facts.

**Boycotting.** There has also been complex litigation in recent years over **boycotting** practices by Associations of REALTORS® and their subsidiary MLS systems in refusing to allow membership to real estate licensees. Rather than the *per se* rules of illegality, courts have tended to invoke the "**rule of reasonableness**" to determine whether or not the boycotting did, in fact, restrain trade. *United States* v. *Realty Multi-List, Inc.*, 629 F.2d 1351 (5th Cir.—1980). The rule-of-reasonableness standard acknowledges the anticompetitive effect of excluding members but also acknowledges the competitive effects of MLS, and the ability of its members to provide better service because of the existence of the MLS system.

In alleging a restraint of trade by boycotting, the complaining party must show that a concerted effort to boycott exists in an attempt to monopolize a segment of the market. This must be more than just refusing to deal with another licensee. Before a board of realtors can be boycotting, for instance, it must be proved to be the conduct of the board, rather than just a few of its members. *Park* v. *El Paso Board of Realtors*, 764 F.2d 1053 (5th Cir.—1985). Reasonable requirements for membership, then, are not necessarily anticompetitive. Requiring members to attend orientation courses, pay dues, and maintain a residency can provide a reasonable basis for allowing membership. However, arbitrary exclusions from the board or MLS systems because applicants are part-time brokers or can't pay an unreasonably high membership fee could be construed to be exclusionary conduct.

It should also be noted that the membership requirements of MLS and other realtor trade organizations can also be protected through copyright laws. These laws can help by refusing access to certain publications through nonmember brokers. *Supermarket of Homes, Inc.* v. *San Fernando Valley Board of Realtors*, 786 F.2d 1400 (9th Cir.—1986).

**Tying Claims.** A tying claim requires that a consumer be tied to a particular product. For instance, if a broker agrees to perform her services for no charge, on the condition that you are required to use her at some future date for another transaction, regardless of her quality of services, she has "tied" herself into the transaction. The tying arrangements can be analyzed under either the *per se* rule or the rule of reason but are generally analyzed under the rule of reason. The general criteria for tying arrangements are: (1) that there are two separate products, a "tying" product and a "tied" product; (2) that those products are in fact "tied" together—that is, the buyer was forced to buy the tied product to get the tying product; (3) that the seller possess a sufficient economic power and the tying product to coerce buyer acceptance of the tied product; and (4) the involvement of a "non-insubstantial" amount of interstate commerce in the market of the tied product.

Tying has surfaced in two separate issues. In *King City Realty, Inc.* v. *Sun Pace Corporation*, 633 P.2d 784 (Ore. 1981), a listing contract provided that the defendant would purchase seven lots but included a "list-back" under which the defendant agreed to list exclusively with the plaintiff realty company for resale of all of the lots purchased by the defendant under the agreement after construction of houses on such lot. In *Thompson* v. *Metropolitan Multi-List, Inc.*, 934 F.2d 1566

(11th Cir.—1991), the court held that tying the multiple listing service to a real estate board membership may also constitute an unfair competition, and therefore may be an antitrust violation.

# Deceptive Trade Practices—Consumer Protection Act

Two areas of broker liability are particularly important. The first is the law of agency, which will be discussed in more detail in Chapter 8. The second is the **Deceptive Trade Practices–Consumer Protection Act**, hereinafter referred to as the Deceptive Trade Practices Act (DTPA). Pertinent provisions of the DTPA are reproduced in their entirety in Appendix I for your reference. The DTPA was originally passed in 1973 and was made specifically applicable to real estate in 1975. Since that time there has been an extensive amount of litigation involving real estate as well as brokerage services. Under the provisions of the DTPA, anybody who receives "**goods**" or "**services**" can sue the provider of those goods or services if the consumer has been deceived or if the producer of those goods or services has engaged in false, misleading, or deceptive acts or practices. A Texas Supreme Court case defined a deceptive trade practice as one "which has the capacity to deceive an average, ordinary person, even though that person may have been ignorant, unthinking, or credulous." *Spradling* v. *Williams*, 566 S.W.2d 561 (Tex. 1978). It is interesting to note that the act defines who can sue but does not define who can be sued. This has resulted in extensive litigation even between consumers (who seem to end up suing each other).

To facilitate the study of the Deceptive Trade Practices Act as it applies to the real estate business, we will discuss the various portions of the act only as they apply to the real estate business and in the cases that have direct application to real estate. It is important to note that the Act is liberally construed in favor of the consumer. A consumer may waive the right to sue under the DTPA provided that: (1) the waiver is in writing and is signed by the consumer; (2) the consumer is not at a significantly disparate bargaining position; and (3) the consumer is represented by legal counsel in seeking or acquiring the goods or services. The waiver is not effective if the consumer's legal counsel is directly or indirectly identified, suggested, or selected by the defendant or an agent of the defendant.

To be effective, the waiver must be: (1) conspicuous and in boldface of at least 10 points in size; and (2) identified by the heading "Waiver of Consumer Rights," or words of similar meaning and in substantially the following form:

> I waive my rights under the Deceptive Trade Practices–Consumer Protection Act, Section 17.41 et seq., Business & Commerce Code, a law that gives consumers special rights and protections. After consultation with an attorney of my selection, I voluntarily consent to this waiver. See §17.42.

One seldom sees this waiver. It is doubtful that any consumer's lawyer would advise them to waive it.

## Causes of Action

Virtually every lawsuit brought against a real estate broker in Texas includes a cause of action under the Texas Deceptive Trade Practices Act. Any consumer can maintain a deceptive trade practices action for one of the following violations designated in Section 17.50 if it is a **producing cause** of **economic damages** or damages for mental anguish:

1.  The use or employment by any person of a false, misleading, or deceptive act or practice that is specifically enumerated in the subdivision of Subsection (b) of Section 17.46 of this subchapter [certain of these specific provisions will be discussed later].

2.  Breach of an express or implied warranty.

3.  Any unconscionable action or course of action by any person.

4.  The use or employment by any person of an act or practice in violation of Article 21.21, Texas Insurance Code, as amended.

**Producing cause** has been held to require proof of: (1) actual causation in fact, (2) that but for the defendant's conduct the plaintiff's injury would not have occurred, and (3) that the act or omission was such a substantial factor in bringing about injury that liability should be imposed. The plaintiff only has to show producing cause and does not have to show that the harm was foreseeable.

Section 17.50 provides for "**economic** damages" rather than "actual" damages, or damages for mental anguish. The amount of economic damages is found by the trier of fact (jury, or judge if there is no jury). If the trier of fact finds that the conduct of the defendant was committed **knowingly**, the consumer may also recover damages for mental anguish, as found by the trier of fact, and the trier of fact may award not more than three times the amount of economic damages, or if the trier of fact finds the conduct was committed "**intentionally**," the consumer may recover damages for mental anguish, as found by the trier of fact, and the trier of fact may award not more than three times the amount of damages for mental anguish and economic damages.

"Economic damages" means compensatory damages for pecuniary loss, including costs of repair and replacement. The term does not include exemplary damages or damages for physical pain and mental anguish, loss of consortium, disfigurement, physical impairment, or loss of companionship and society.

"Knowingly" means actual awareness of a falsity, deception, or unfairness of an act or practice giving rise to the consumer's claim or, in an action brought under a breach of an express or implied warranty as provided in Section 17.50, actual awareness of the act or practice constituting the breach of warranty, but actual awareness may be inferred where objective manifestations indicate the person acted with actual awareness.

"Intentionally" is actual awareness, or flagrant disregard of prudent and fair business practices.

**"The Laundry List"** Section 17.46 of the subchapter specifies a "laundry list" of 27 acts that would constitute a deceptive trade practice. Many of them are generally worded to encompass a wide scope of other acts. Some of these acts, which can be particularly applicable to real estate, include:

1.  Representing that goods are original or new, if they are deteriorated, reconditioned, reclaimed, used, or secondhand.

2.  Representing that goods or services are of a particular standard, quality, or grade or that goods are of a particular style or model if they are of another.

3.  Making false or misleading statements of fact concerning the reasons for, existence of, or amount of price reductions.

4.  Representing that an agreement confers or involves rights, remedies, or obligations that it does not have or involve, or which are prohibited by law.

5. Knowingly making false or misleading statements of fact concerning the need for parts, replacement, or repair service.

6. Representing the authority of a salesperson, representative, or agent to negotiate the final terms of the consumer transaction.

7. Representing that work or services have been performed on or parts replaced in goods when the work or services were not performed or the parts replaced.

8. Failing to disclose information concerning goods or services that was known at the time of the transaction if such failure to disclose such information was intended to induce the consumer into a transaction into which the consumer would not have entered had the information been disclosed.

It is important to note how all of these provisions can apply to the sale of an average residential house and can certainly apply to a more complicated commercial or residential transaction. The last provision referred to above goes hand in hand with Section 1101.652(b)(3); (b)(4) of the Real Estate License Act, which makes it grounds for suspension or revocation of licensure for failing to disclose a latent structural defect or other defects that would make a difference in the mind of the prudent purchaser.

**DTPA Breach of Warranties.** In determining the breach of an express or implied warranty as provided in the DTPA, the criteria for the breach appear to be circumstances existing where the knowledge of the seller, in conjunction with the buyer's relative ignorance, operates to make the slightest divergence from mere praise into representations of fact. *Chrysler-Plymouth City, Inc.* v. *Guerrero*, 620 S.W.2d 700 (Tex. Civ. App.—San Antonio, 1981). This is really nothing more than taking unfair advantage of a "consumer" who is "credulous, ignorant, and unthinking" (which may be easy to prove when a professional real estate licensee misrepresents something to a consumer).

While the services of a real estate broker have not yet been held to have an implied warranty, it may be on the horizon. Texas courts have held that there are implied warranties for homebuilders, *Humber* v. *Morton*, 426 S.W.2d 554, 556 (Tex. 1968); implied warranties for repair of residential structures, *Melody Home Manufacturing Company* v. *Barnes*, 741 S.W.2d 349 (Tex. 1987). Implied warranties with a good and workmanlike manner for developers have been specifically rejected by the Texas Supreme Court, *Parkway Co.* v. *Woodruff*, 901 S.W.2d 434 (Tex. 1995).

**Unconscionable Acts.** An unconscionable action or course of action is defined as follows: "taking advantage of a consumer's lack of knowledge to a grossly unfair degree, thus, requires a showing of intent, knowledge or conscious indifference" at the time the misrepresentation was made. *Chastain* v. *Koonce*, 700 S.W.2d 579 (Tex. 1985). A real estate agent has been held to be "an expert who has been tested and found to be such." *Holloman* v. *Denson*, 640 S.W.2d 417 (Tex. Civ. App.—Waco, 1982).

Therefore, it is very important that all brokers deal with consumers in a very, very careful manner and be sure that the consumer understands even the most obvious detail of what the consumer might interpret as a warranty, or which may be included in the "laundry list." A real estate broker makes representations in the normal course of business. It is clear now that making such representations can be very, very hazardous if they are not true since there is such a disparity between a professional real estate agent's knowledge of the business and that of a "consumer" purchaser or seller. Brokers are particularly ripe for litigation, and old-fashioned references to "mere puffing" are no longer applicable in Texas. What may be mere

**puffing** to a broker could be understood as absolute fact by an ignorant, unthinking, or credulous purchaser or seller. *Dowling* v. *NADW Marketing, Inc., et al.*, 631 S.W.2d 726 (Tex. 1982); *Ridco* v. *Sexton*, 623 S.W.2d 792 (Tex. Civ. App.—Ft. Worth, 1981).

One of the peculiar applications of the Deceptive Trade Practices Act runs contrary to what people normally think of in the real estate brokerage business. The broker normally represents the seller; however, it seems to be clear under interpretations of the Deceptive Trade Practices Act that the broker represents "goods" to the purchaser and also provides some "services" to the purchaser. *Manchac* v. *Pace*, 608 S.W.2d 314 (Tex. Civ. App.—Beaumont, 1980); *Cameron* v. *Terrell & Garrett, Inc.*, 618 S.W.2d 535 (Tex. 1981).

Property management has also been under attack by the Deceptive Trade Practices Act. If a broker is going to undertake property management, he is probably under the duty of care at least to inspect the property on a fairly frequent basis, send reports to the owner, and properly look after and protect the property entrusted to him by the "**consumer**" owner. *Lerma* v. *Brecheisen*, 602 S.W.2d 318 (Tex. Civ. App.—Waco, 1980). One of the more disturbing aspects of the Deceptive Trade Practices Act is that even an errors-and-omissions insurance policy (which most brokers can acquire to cover malpractice claims) may not cover violations of the Deceptive Trade Practices Act. *St. Paul Insurance Company* v. *Bonded Realty, Inc.*, 583 S.W.2d 619 (Tex. 1979).

## Remedies

The statutory damages recoverable under the Deceptive Trade Practices Act include:

1. The amount of **economic damages** found by the trier of fact. If the trier of the fact finds that the conduct of the defendant was committed **knowingly**, the customer may also recover damages for mental anguish, as found by the trier of fact may award not more than three times the amount of economic damages; if the trier of fact finds that the conduct was committed **intentionally**, the consumer may recover damages for mental anguish, as found by the trier of fact, and the trier of fact may award not more than three times the amount of damages for mental anguish and economic damages.

2. An order adjoining such acts or failure of act.

3. Orders necessary to restore to any part of the suit any money or property, real or personal, which may have been acquired in violation of this subchapter.

4. Any other relief that the court deems proper, including the appointment of a receiver or the revocation of a license or certificate authorizing the person who engages in business in this state if the judgment has not been satisfied within three months of the date of final judgment. *The court may not revoke or suspend a license to do business in the state or appoint a receiver to take over the affairs of the person who has failed to satisfy judgment if the person is a licensee of or regulated by a state agency that has the statutory authority to revoke or suspend a license or to appoint a receiver or trustee* [emphasis added].

It has further been held that the treble damages must be found by the trier of the fact and is not an automatic award. *Martin* v. *McKee Realtors, Inc.*, 663 S.W.2d 446 (Tex. 1984).

# Defenses: Statutory

There is some relief for the broker in Sections 17.505 and 17.506. Section 17.505 provides that the consumer must give written notice at least 60 days before filing suit and provides some rather severe limits for recovery in the event a settlement offer is made within 60 days after receipt of the notice from the consumer. A copy of some of the pertinent provisions of these sections are reproduced here:

**§17.505. Notice: Inspection**

(a) As a prerequisite to filing a suit seeking damages under Subdivision (1) of Subsection (b) of Section 17.50 of this subchapter against any person, a consumer shall give written notice to the person at least 60 days before filing the suit advising the person in reasonable detail of the consumer's specific complaint and the amount of actual damages and expenses, including attorneys' fees, if any, reasonably incurred by the consumer in asserting the claim against the defendant. During the 60-day period a written request to inspect, in a reasonable manner and at a reasonable time and place, the goods that are the subject of the consumer's action or claim may be presented to the consumer.

(b) If the giving of 60 days' written notice is rendered impracticable by reason of the necessity of filing suit in order to prevent the expiration of the statute of limitations or if the consumer's claim is asserted by way of counterclaim, the notice provided for in Subsection (a) of this section is not required, but the tender provided for by Subsection (d), Section 17.506 of this subchapter may be made within 60 days after the filing of the suit or counterclaim.

**§17.5051. Mediation**

(a) A party may, not later than the 90th day after the date of service of a pleading in which relief under this subchapter is sought, file a motion to compel mediation of the dispute in the manner provided by this section.

**§17.5052. Offers Of Settlement**

(a) A person who receives notice under Section 17.505 may tender an offer of settlement at any time during the period beginning on the date the notice is received and ending on the 60th day after that date.

(b) If a mediation under Section 17.5051 is not conducted, the person may tender an offer of settlement at any time during the period beginning on the date an original answer is filed and ending on the 90th day after that date.

(c) If a mediation under Section 17.5051 is conducted, a person against whom a claim under this subchapter is pending may tender an offer of settlement during the period beginning on the day after the date that the mediation ends and ending on the 20th day after that date.

(g) If the court finds that the amount tendered in the settlement offer for damages under Subsection (d)(1) is the same as, substantially the same as, or more than the damages found by the trier of fact, the consumer may not recover as damages any amount in excess of the lesser of:

   (1) the amount of damages tendered in the settlement offer; or

   (2) the amount of damages found by the trier of fact.

The offer to settle must include attorney's fees. *Cail* v. *Service Motors, Inc.*, 660 S.W.2d 814 (Tex. 1983). The 1995 changes to the DTPA also provide for compulsory mediation and offers of settlement through mediation. Under this new procedure, a party may, not later than the 90th day after the date of service of the pleading, file a motion to compel mediation in a dispute. After the motion is filed, the court must, not later than 30 days after the motion is filed, sign an order setting the time and place of the mediation. The mediation must be held within 30 days after the date the order is signed, unless the parties agree otherwise. A party, however, may not compel mediation if the amount of economic damages claimed is less than $15,000, unless the party seeking to compel the mediation agrees to pay the cost of the mediation. Offers made during the mediation are treated very similarly to those under §17.505. See, generally, §§17.5051 and 17.5052.

Section 17.506 provides some other significant changes in damages that may be recovered. A copy of this section is reproduced here with emphasis supplied in certain significant areas:

### §17.506. Damages: Defenses

(a) In an action brought under Section 17.50 of this subchapter, it is a defense to the award of any damages or attorneys' fees if the defendant proves that before consummation of the transaction he gave reasonable and timely written notice to the plaintiff of the defendant's reliance on:

> (1) written information relating to the particular goods or service in question obtained from official government records if the written information was false or inaccurate and the defendant did not know and could not reasonably have known of the falsity or inaccuracy of the information;

> (2) written information relating to the particular goods or service in question obtained from another source if the information was false or inaccurate and the defendant did not know and could not reasonably have known of the falsity or inaccuracy of the information; or

> (3) written information concerning a test required or prescribed by a government agency if the information from the test was false or inaccurate and the defendant did not know and could not reasonably have known of the falsity or inaccuracy of the information.

(b) In asserting a defense under Subdivision (1), (2), or (3) of Subsection (a) of Section 17.506 above, the defendant shall prove the written information was a producing cause of the alleged damage. A finding of one producing cause does not bar recovery if other conduct of the defendant not the subject of a defensive finding under Subdivision (1), (2), or (3) of Subsection (a) of Section 17.506 above was a producing cause of damages of the plaintiff.

(c) In a suit where a defense is asserted under Subdivision (2) of Subsection (a) of Section 17.506 above, suit may be asserted against the third party supplying the written information without regard to privity where the third party knew or should have reasonably foreseen that the information would be provided to a consumer, provided no double recovery may result.

(d) In an action brought under Section 17.50 of this subchapter, it is a defense to a cause of action if the defendant proves that he received notice from the consumer advising the defendant of the nature of the consumer's specific complaint and of the amount of economic damages, damages for mental anguish, and expenses, including attorneys' fees, if any, reasonably incurred by the consumer in asserting the claim against the defendant, and that within 30 days after the day on which the defendant received the notice the defendant tendered to the consumer:

> (1) the amount of economic damages and damages for mental anguish claimed; and

> (2) the expenses, including attorneys' fees, if any, reasonably incurred by the consumer in asserting the claim against the defendant.

One of the most significant defenses is that the broker can rely on written representations made by a governmental agency or the listing seller as a defense to award for any damages if he did not know or **could not reasonably have known**

**of** the falsity or inaccuracy of the information. Therefore, it would indicate that the broker would be protected if he were sure all of his representations were in writing from the seller or if he gave the purchaser enough time to inspect the property to satisfy himself as to the condition. In these cases, the broker could allude to the representations by third parties, whether they be seller, inspectors, or contractors, to relieve the broker of some liability. *Lone Star Machinery Corp.* v. *Frankel*, 564 S.W.2d 135 (Tex. Civ. App.—Beaumont, 1978); *Pfeiffer* v. *Ebby Halliday Real Estate*, 747 S.W.2d 887 (Tex. App.—Dallas, 1988).

### §17.555. Indemnity
A person against whom an action has been brought under this subchapter may seek contribution or indemnity from one who, under the statute law or at common law, may have liability for the damaging event of which the consumer complains. A person seeking indemnity as provided by this section may recover all sums that he is required to pay as a result of the action, his attorney's fees reasonable in relation to the amount of work performed in maintaining his action for indemnity, and his costs.

The statute provides that the defendant may seek contribution or indemnity from one who, under statutory law or at common law, may have liability for the damaging event of the consumer complaint. This allows the defendant to cross-file against the seller, property inspector, or other person who may be determined to have the ultimate liability for the misrepresentation. Note that the statute also provides for reimbursement for reasonable attorney's fees and court costs.

**New Exemptions.** Section 17.49 provides for exemptions for causes of action under the DTPA. One prohibits a claim for damages based on the rendering of a professional service, the essence of which is the providing of advice, judgment, opinion, or similar professional skill. Logically, this should apply to real estate brokers as a very broad exemption. The exemption does not apply, however, (1) to an express misrepresentation of the material fact; (2) to an unconscionable action or course of action, the failure to disclose information and violation of §17.46(b)(23); or (3) to breach of an express warranty that cannot be characterized as advice, judgment, or opinion.

This section also provides for an exemption under the DTPA for a claim arising out of a written contract, if the contract relates to a transaction involving total consideration by the consumer of more than $100,000 if the consumer is represented by legal counsel and the contract does not involve the consumer's residence. Similarly, the act also exempts any transaction involving total consideration by the consumer of more than $500,000 other than a cause of action involving a consumer's residence, even if the consumer is not represented by legal counsel.

## Defenses: Case Law

There have been a few cases that have been beneficial for real estate brokers in providing a defense to causes of action. It is a defense to a cause of action under the Deceptive Trade Practices Act if, in fact, the broker never made the representation. *Stagner* v. *Friendswood Development Company, Inc.*, 620 S.W.2d 103 (Tex. 1981). It also may be a defense if the broker did not know of any defect (although one can assume that this would have to be a genuine lack of information). *Robinson et ux* v. *Preston Chrysler-Plymouth, Inc.*, 633 S.W.2d 500 (Tex. 1982). There may also be a successful defense plead if the court can be convinced that the plaintiff relied on somebody else's representation other than the real estate broker. *Lone Star Machinery Corp.* v. *Frankel*, supra and *Pfeiffer* v. *Ebby Halliday Real Estate*, supra. One case has also held that if there was a defect disclosed to the seller and the seller bought the property anyway, aware of the defect, that he may not later turn around and sue the broker for failing to disclose. *Zak* v. *Parks*, 729 S.W.2d 875 (Tex. App.—Houston, 1987).

## Defenses: Contractual

There may be some other defenses contained in contracts. Note that in the TREC promulgated form, if a broker is sued as a result of that contract and ultimately wins the case, he can recover attorney's fees from the other party (note paragraph 17 of TREC Form 20-6). Similarly, the Texas Association of REALTORS® (TAR)[1] has published a seller disclosure form in which the seller makes representations about the condition of the premises. This is a very useful form and may provide a successful defense by saying that all representations concerning the condition of the property were made by the seller, not the broker.

Providing in a contract that the purchaser will buy and accept the house in "as is" condition might not be a defense to the DTPA and therefore should not be relied on with any comfort. *Wietzel* v. *Barnes*, 691 S.W.2d 598 (Tex. 1985); *Wyatt* v. *Petrila*, 752 S.W.2d 683 (Tex. App.—Corpus Christi, 1988, writ den.). The Texas Supreme Court has clearly held, though, that "as is" is a proper defense under certain circumstances. *Prudential Insurance Co. of America* v. *Jefferson Associates*, 896 S.W.2d 156 (Tex. 1995).

At least one court of appeals has held that the TREC Promulgated Form, Section 7.D. creates an "as is" defense. *Larsen* v. *Langford and Associates, Inc.*, 41 S.W.3d 245 (Tex. App.—Waco, 2001).

The Deceptive Trade Practices Act provides that all actions brought under the act must be commenced within two years after the date on which the deceptive act or practice occurred or within two years after the consumer discovered or should have discovered the false, misleading, or deceptive act or practice. When does it end?!!!

**Harassment.** There is a provision under the Texas Deceptive Trade Practices Act that if a suit is brought solely for the purposes of harassment, it will support a counterclaim from the defendant so the defendant can recover his attorney's fees and expenses in defending the lawsuit. While the statutory provision is there, Texas courts have been very hesitant to enforce this harassment provision. *Splettstosser* v. *Myer*, 779 S.W.2d 806 (Tex. 1989).

**Real Estate Inspectors.** One of the better defenses to causes of action under the Deceptive Trade Practices Act is provided by the broker having the property inspected by a licensed **real estate inspector** prior to the sale. Section 1102 was added to the Texas Occupations Code, providing a system by which a real estate agent could refer his customer to a bonded inspector to do the inspection and representation as to the condition of the home. Real estate inspectors have their own recovery fund, and a real estate inspector cannot be the real estate broker in the same transaction. The remedies for a consumer against a real estate inspector are similar to those against a real estate broker so that the "protection of the public" and "consumer protection" theories are as strong as they are against real estate licensees.

---

[1] TAR has published a variety of forms, prepared by their counsel for use by members, in their REALTOR® Reference notebook. It is kept current and is a valuable tool in one's real estate practice.

The statute also created a three-level system of licensing for real estate inspectors. The new categories are: (1) apprentice-inspector, (2) real estate inspector, and (3) professional inspector. Eligibility requirements increase with each level. Continuing education is required for inspectors. The inspector program is to continue to remain under the Texas Real Estate Commission, and an Inspector Advisory Committee will be required to recommend rules governing inspectors and the entry of final orders and disciplinary hearings involving inspectors.

# Broker's Recovery Fund

In an effort to protect the public against unscrupulous brokers, the Texas Real Estate License Act establishes a **recovery fund** that provides for a solvent fund from which an aggrieved party (a person who suffers actual damages) can recover cash in the event of the broker's failure to pay or inability to pay damages. The use of the fund is limited to recovery from an act that is a violation of Section 15(3) or (4) of the Real Estate License Act. An **aggrieved party** has even been held to include a sponsoring broker, who can recover for the wrongful acts of his agents. *Texas Real Estate Commission* v. *Century 21 Security Realty, Inc.*, 598 S.W.2d 920 (Tex. Civ. App.—El Paso, 1980). The statute provides that after the aggrieved party has recovered a valid judgment in the court of competent jurisdiction against a real estate broker or real estate salesperson, he may give 20 days' written notice to the commission and apply to the court for an order directing payment out of the real estate recovery fund for the amount unpaid on the judgment. The recovery fund is liable for attorney's fees also. *Texas Real Estate Commission* v. *Hood*, 617 S.W.2d 838 (Tex. Civ. App.—Eastland, 1981). This will result in a suspension of the broker's or salesperson's license, and no broker or salesperson is eligible to receive a new license until he has repaid the recovery fund in full plus interest at the current legal rate.

The Real Estate License Act requires the commission to furnish a list of remedies available to any complainant filing a complaint to the commission relating to a real estate broker or salesperson. After the complaint is filed with the commission, the commission must, at least quarterly, inform the complainant and the person against whom the complaint is filed as to the status of the complaint. This provides a strong remedy for a consumer to complain to the Real Estate Commission about the questionable acts of the licensee, and the commission must monitor the complaint, *Tex. Rev. Civ. Stat., Art 6573a, §18B*.

The Real Estate License Act provides that the broker must notify consumers of the availability of the Real Estate Recovery Fund established for reimbursing certain aggrieved persons. The notice must include the name, mailing address, and telephone number of the commission and any other information required by commission rule. This notice may be provided (1) in the written contract for the services and material or salesperson (presumably the listing agreement), (2) on a brochure distributed by the salesperson, (3) on a sign prominently displayed in the place of business of a salesperson or broker, or (4) in a bill of receipt for service provided by a broker or salesperson. The individual claims limit in judgments arising out of the recovery fund from any one transaction is $50,000, and the total amount of payments for claims against any one broker is $100,000.

## ■ SUMMARY

Revisions in the Texas Real Estate License Act have upgraded the educational requirements for brokers and salespersons. The Texas Real Estate Commission administers all rules and regulations that govern the procedure for institution, conduct, and determination of all causes and proceedings before the Real Estate Commission. Licensing requirements are specific and strictly adhered to. The definitions of "broker" and "salesperson" are very broad and meant to be all-inclusive in order to effect a more comprehensive regulation of the real estate industry.

Brokers and salespersons are employed through listing agreements, which must be in writing in order for the broker to maintain an action in court for a commission.

In addition to the specific statutory requirements that concern the duties and obligations of a real estate licensee, the laws of principal and agent apply to the broker in his normal employment relationship. As an agent, the real estate licensee has certain duties to the principal as well as to third parties. The laws of agency are of particular application in management responsibilities when a licensee may be transacting business on behalf of his principal.

There are special problem areas in real estate brokerage that have become increasingly important over the past few years. These include securities law, truth-in-lending laws, the employment status of sales personnel, relationships between brokers and lawyers, and application of federal antitrust laws.

## CHAPTER 8

# Agency

## Law of Agency

The changing provisions of the Texas Real Estate License Act, as well as generally accepted provisions for employment contracts, have underscored the technicalities of the law as they apply to real estate brokerage. The law of agency has long been considered by courts as the fundamental relationship between clients and brokers. The Texas Real Estate License Act now specifically states that a licensee who represents a party in a real estate transaction acts as that party's agent, *V.A.T.S., Art 6573a, §15C(c)*. Historically, the real estate agent was hired by the seller to assist in marketing and sales. The concepts of buyer brokerage, dual agency, and intermediary have added new dimensions to the traditional theories. To simplify the issues, let's first consider the traditional listing relationships. The parties necessary to agency relationship are the **principal** (the SELLER, also called the CLIENT and OWNER of the property); the **agent** (the BROKER); and **third parties** (the BUYER, CUSTOMER, or PURCHASER).

## Creation of the Agency Relationship

Recall the discussion in the previous chapter that, in order to maintain an action for a commission, a broker must have an employment agreement *in writing* to satisfy the requirements of the Texas Real Estate License Act. This is not generally true of agency relationships, however. One can be deemed to be an agent of a principal through written or verbal authority.

Brokers frequently think that the person who pays the commission is the principal. Who pays the commission is *not* determinative. The Texas Real Estate License Act even provides that a real estate agent can get a commission from both sides as long as all parties are aware of it. *LaGuardia* v. *Snoddy*, 690 S.W.2d 46 (Tex. Civ. App.—Dallas, 1985). The agency can even arise if the agency relationship is specifically rejected because a jury may make the ultimate decision. *Wilson* v. *Donze*, 692 S.W.2d 734 (Tex. Civ. App.—Ft. Worth, 1985).

Another factor also becomes important in creating the agency relationship, and that is determining *when* the agency relationship arises. There has been convincing authority in other states that the agency relationship can arise before any written agreements are signed because confidences can be exchanged in the earliest stages of negotiating the listing agreement! See *Lyle* v. *Moore*, 599 P.2d 336 (Mont. 1979).

## Types of Agency

Agency relationships are classified according to the authority given to the agent to represent the principal, or to the agent's authority represented by the principal to a third party. These types of agency include agency by actual authority, agency by ostensible authority, and agency by ratification.

**Agency by Actual Authority. Agency by actual authority** exists where the agent is employed by the principal by either an express or oral contract. This type of agency generally outlines in detail what authority the agent has to act on behalf of and to bind the principal. When this is specifically given to an agent either in writing or verbally, it is considered to be **express authority**. Along with express authority there is often created a certain amount of **implied authority**. Implied authority is the right to do certain acts on behalf of the principal even though the acts may not have been specified in the contract. This authority may arise from custom in the industry, common usage, or conduct of the parties (an inference or implication as to the agent's right to act). An example of implied agency would be a listing agreement that does not specify that the broker has a right to put a sign in the yard offering the house for sale. However, it is customarily recognized that the broker may erect a sign in the front of the house offered for sale. The same might also be true of hours for showing the house, or means of advertising the house for sale. These are not things usually set out in the listing agreement, but the authority to do these things arises as implied authority because of common custom and usage in the industry.

Historically, a real estate agent was usually employed to represent the seller. It was considered a marketing business. Times have changed. An agent is often employed to represent the buyer, however, creating the fiduciary duty to the purchaser rather than to the seller. *Tatum* v. *Preston Carter Co.*, 702 S.W.2d 186 (Tex. 1986). The duties are somewhat different, though. Buyer brokerage will be discussed in greater detail later in this chapter.

**Agency by Ostensible Authority. Agency by ostensible authority** is one that exists because the principal intentionally or negligently causes a third party to believe that another was his agent, even though that agent may not actually be employed by the principal. If the third party reasonably believes that the agent is employed by the principal, the principal is bound by the act of his agent. *Canada* v. *Kearns*, 624 S.W.2d 755 (Tex. Civ. App.—Beaumont, 1981).

It is important to remember that an agent possessing apparent authority has no actual authority at all. If, however, the principal cloaks the agent in the authority to act in his behalf, or negligently gives him the authority by failing to exercise proper control over him, the agency relationship arises. *Hall* v. *Halamicek Enterprises, Inc.*, 669 S.W.2d 368 (Tex. Civ. App.—Corpus Christi, 1984). It should be emphasized that declarations of the agent alone are not sufficient, and it must be **acts of the principal** that create the apparent authority. Creation of agency through this type of conduct has also been called an **agency by estoppel** or **agency by apparent authority**.

A cautious licensee should also note that, notwithstanding the existence of a listing agreement, an agency by ostensible authority can create an agency for a purchaser. *Little* v. *Rohauer*, 707 P.2d 1015 (Colo. App.—1985). This could create the classic "dual agency" situation, discussed later in this chapter.

**Agency by Ratification.** An **agency by ratification** is an agency that occurs **after the fact**. For instance, if an agent secures a contract on behalf of the principal and the principal subsequently agrees to the terms of the contract, the courts may hold that the agency was created as of the time the initial negotiation was transacted. The critical factor in determining whether a principal has ratified an unauthorized act by his agent is the principal's knowledge of the transaction and his actions in light of such knowledge. If the principal fails to repudiate the unauthorized transaction, it gives rise to an agency by ratification. *Land Title Company of Dallas, Inc.* v. *Stigler, Inc.*, 609 S.W.2d 754 (Tex. 1980).

## Agency Coupled with an Interest

An **agency coupled with an interest** is a particular type of agency relationship where the agent has an interest or estate in the property as part or all of his compensation. An agency coupled with an interest is generally considered to be irrevocable, although it may be terminated pursuant to an express agreement between the parties. It may not be terminated by unilateral act on behalf of the principal.

## Agency Liabilities

One of the significant factors in any agency relationship is the liability that the agent or the principal may impose on the other. (We will talk about the duties of these parties to each other for the remainder of this chapter.) If the duties are not met, however, it is important to know where the ultimate liability will lie between the principal and agent once the agency relationship has been created. Recent Texas court rulings seem to indicate a strong trend toward suing licensees, not only for deceptive trade practices but also for other liabilities as a result of their agency, such as misrepresentation as to encumbrances. *Stone* v. *Lawyers Title Ins. Corp.*, 554 S.W.2d 183 (Tex. 1977); *Ingalls* v. *Rice*, 511 S.W.2d 78 (Tex. Civ. App.—Houston, 1974); *Canada* v. *Kearns*, supra; terms of an agreement, *Newsom* v. *Starkey*, 541 S.W.2d 468 (Tex. Civ. App.—Dallas, 1976); slandering title, *Walker* v. *Ruggles*, supra; failure to disclose defects, *Smith* v. *National Resort Communities, Inc.*, 585 S.W.2d 655 (Tex. 1979); failing to inform the client as to appreciation in value of this property, *Ramsey* v. *Gordon*, 567 S.W.2d 868 (Tex. Civ. App.—Waco, 1978); engaging in conduct that constitutes real estate fraud, *McGaha* v. *Dishman*, 629 S.W.2d 220 (Tex. Civ. App.—Tyler, 1982); and even expressions of opinion, *Trenholm* v. *Ratcliff*, 646 S.W.2d 927 (Tex. 1983).

The legislature made an attempt to limit some of this liability through an amendment to the Texas Real Estate License Act. The act provides that a party is not liable for misrepresentation or concealment of material fact made by a license holder in a real estate transaction unless the party knew of the falsity of the misrepresentation or concealment and failed to disclose the party's knowledge of the falsity of the misrepresentation or concealment, *Tex. Occ. Code, §1101.805(d)*. Note, however, that the new provisions do not diminish the real estate broker's liability for the broker's own acts, nor the acts or admissions of the broker's salespersons.

**Special Agency.** There are two types of agency relationships—a special agency and a general agency. The relationship between a listing broker and the principal is normally deemed to be a **special agency**. In a special agency, the principal is not responsible for the acts of the agent. *Ingalls* v. *Rice*, supra. The broker's responsibility is limited to marketing the house. If a misrepresentation is made to the third party, it is probably made by the broker, since there is no relationship in contract or tort between the purchaser and seller prior to the earnest money contract being signed. In practice, the seller has little, if any, control over the conduct of the agent. Therefore, these misrepresentations will result in the broker being liable for them rather than the seller. So, in a special agency relationship, the principal is not responsible for the acts of her agent. This results in the agent being primarily liable in tort law (money damages for misrepresentation or negligence) to third parties, and to the principal in contract law (in the event he breaches any of his duties of care or misrepresents anything to the seller because of his fiduciary relationship).

**General Agency.** More difficult problems occur when there is a general agency relationship. In a **general agency** relationship the principal is always responsible for the acts of her agent as long as that agent is acting within the scope of his duties. In the typical listing situation, a general agency relationship exists between the salesperson and his sponsoring broker. The salesperson is the agent of the sponsoring broker, and a **subagent** of the principal. The general agency relationship creates a wide scope of authority for the salesperson, who signs contracts on behalf of his principal and binds the principal on matters within the scope of his duties on a daily basis. In the general agency situation, if the agent makes a misrepresentation to the purchaser, the sponsoring broker is responsible for the acts of his agent, and the third party sues the sponsoring broker rather than the sales agent. *Canada* v. *Kearns*, supra. This may be particularly harsh when an agency has been created by ostensible authority or ratification (the principal may have an agent and not know it!). Remember, the principal is responsible for those acts regardless of how the agency was created.

A disturbing trend is developing in Texas law that may be converting special agencies to general agencies under certain circumstances. If a seller benefits from the fraud, or the seller knew of the fraud and did not reject the benefits of that fraud, he may be jointly and severally liable for misrepresentations made by his real estate agent. *Century 21 Page One Realty* v. *Naghad*, 760 S.W.2d 305 (Tex. App.—Texarkana, 1988).

# Duties of the Agent to the Principal

The agent acts in the capacity of a **fiduciary**. That is, there is a duty of **trust, confidence**, and **honest business dealing** that is owed to his principal. There will probably be communications between the principal and agent that could not be disclosed to third parties without breaching that fiduciary relationship. An example of this would be a principal who chooses to list his house for a $100,000 sales price but informs the broker that he would probably take $80,000 from a qualified purchaser who offers good terms. The agent is, of course, under a fiduciary capacity not to disclose anything that would be adverse to the interest of his principal. There are issues, though, that may need to be discussed in detail with the seller.

## Specific Disclosure Issues

**Sales Information.** A particularly sensitive issue exists as to whether or not a licensee may disclose information about the real property sales price or terms of the sale. While in many cases this may be deemed to be confidential information, the Real Estate License Act provides that a licensee, or not-for-profit real estate board, may provide information about real property sales prices or terms of the sale for purposes of facilitating, selling, leasing, financing, or appraising real property. In such event, any entity providing this information shall not be held liable to any other person as a result of providing the information, unless this disclosure is specifically prohibited by statute or written contract.

**HIV Issues.** Similarly, there was a concern about whether or not AIDS or HIV-related viruses infecting occupants of real property should be disclosed. The more traditional theory, at least at this time, is that a person infected with AIDS or an HIV-related virus is considered to be handicapped and therefore belongs to a protected class of people such that the handicap need not be disclosed. It also provides a basis for discrimination under the Fair Housing Act. See also *Section 1101.804* of the License Act.

**Death.** There is a similar provision for death occurring on the property. A real estate licensee now has no duty to inquire about, disclose, or make representations concerning a death on the property that was a result of suicide, natural causes, or accidents unrelated to the condition of the property. Apparently, disclosures still have to be made if death occurred as a result of murder, condition of the premises, or unnatural causes. This is still a major concern, however. There are a lot of purchasers who will not buy a house in which a death has occurred, regardless of the reason. In many cases, their reluctance to purchase is based on cultural or religious factors. If a buyer has an inquiry concerning death on the premises, it is probably best to discuss it with the seller. A truthful disclosure may save the expense of litigation in the future, even with a successful outcome.

**Sex Offender Registration.** The Code of Criminal Procedure provides that a person's broker, sales person, or other agent or representative in a residential real estate transaction does not have a duty to make a disclosure to a perspective buyer or lessee about registrants under the statute. In real life, however, it is not that easy. If a potential buyer has children, and you know there is a sex offender next door, does this statute protect you when you can't sleep at night?

How does one handle this sensitive situation if asked? Some ideas:

When representing a seller, one may want to emphasize the issue of sexual offenders and show them information on the web site. It is probably better to address the problem during a listing meeting than it is to address it when a contract is submitted and the buyer asks the difficult questions. The seller will feel less threatened if this issue is discussed early.

If you are representing the buyer, it may be a good business practice to be sure the buyer is informed of a Texas web site for sex offenders. The database is available at: www.txdps.state.tx.us, click on "Sex Offender Search" under "Crime Records Service." It is probably prudent for licensees to be cautious, and disclose any information about sex offenders that is known to the buyer's agent, regardless of whether the licensee is an exclusive buyer's agent or an agent appointed to represent a buyer in an intermediary relationship.

Statistics are also available for murder, rapes, and burglaries in most jurisdictions. Agents have not traditionally worried about these kinds of issues in the past, unless the problem was obvious or ongoing. It may also be interesting to determine how many neighborhoods are "free" of sex offenders (there may be none). In addition, there is certainly no prohibition against a sex offender moving to the neighborhood at a later date. Fascinating issue, more and more questions.

Generally, it has been held by Texas courts that a real estate broker, as an agent, owes the duty to his principal of performance, loyalty, reasonable care, and an accounting for all monies received with regard to the transaction.

## Performance

**Performance** indicates that the broker will use his best efforts and diligence to market the property on behalf of his principal and to obey the principal's instructions as to asking price, condition of the property, and marketing practices. The duty means nothing more than doing his job, which is obtaining for his principal the highest price then obtainable and known to him. *Riley* v. *Powell*, 665 S.W.2d 578 (Tex. Civ. App.—Ft. Worth, 1984); *Ramsey* v. *Gordon*, supra. The Texas Real Estate License Act specifically speaks to these obligations of performance under Section 15, which provides for license **revocation** if it has been determined that the broker or salesperson has been guilty of:

(1) making a false promise of a character likely to influence, persuade, or induce any person to enter into a contract or agreement when the licensee could not or did not intend to keep such promise [Section 1101.652(b)(5)]; or

(2) soliciting, selling, or offering for sale real property under a scheme or program that constitutes a lottery or deceptive practice [Section 1101.652(b)(14), (15)]; or

(3) acting in the dual capacity of broker and undisclosed principal in a transaction [Section 1101.652(b)(16)]; or

(4) placing a sign on real property offering it for sale, lease, or rent without the written consent of the owner or his authorized agent [Section 1101.652(b)(18)]; or

(5) negotiating or attempting to negotiate the sale, exchange, lease, or rental of real property with an owner or lessor, knowing that the owner or lessor had a written outstanding contract, granting exclusive agency in connection with the property to another real estate broker [Section 1101.652(b)(22)]; or

(6) offering real property for sale or for lease without the knowledge and consent of the owner or his authorized agent, or on terms other than those authorized by the owner or his authorized agent [Section 1101.652(b)(19)]; or

(7) publishing, or causing to be published, an advertisement including, but not limited to, advertising by newspaper, radio, television, or display which is misleading, or which is likely to deceive the public, or which in any manner tends to create a misleading impression, or which fails to identify the person causing the advertisement to be published as a licensed real estate broker or agent [Section 1101.652(b)(23)]; or

(8) establishing an association, by employment or otherwise, with an unlicensed person who is expected or required to act as a real estate licensee, or aiding or abetting or conspiring with a person to circumvent the requirements of this Act [Section 1101.652(b)(26)]; or

(9) acting negligently or incompetently in performing an act for which a person is required to hold a real estate license [Section 1101.652(b)(1)].

# Loyalty

The duty of **loyalty** is a very touchy subject for real estate agents. It is common practice for a broker to feel that he acts on behalf of both the buyer and the seller in a transaction. There is even some case law that reflects that this may be done properly, but only with the full knowledge and consent of both principals (the buyer and the seller). In most circumstances, however, it is a near impossibility to represent both the buyer and the seller. This situation is analogous to a couple going to one lawyer for a divorce and asking that lawyer to represent both the husband and the wife. It simply cannot be done because no one can represent a client to the very best interest when he represents two opponents. For instance, how can a broker represent a seller to get the highest price for the house when he is also representing a purchaser trying to get the best buy for the same house?

Loyalty also implies the broker's duty **not to advance his own interest** in profit to the detriment of his principal and is the essence of the agent's fiduciary responsibility. The Texas Real Estate License Act has statutorily provided for license revocation for disloyalty under Section 15, if the licensee has been found guilty of any of the following actions:

(1) the licensee, when selling, trading, or renting real property in his own name, engaged in misrepresentation or dishonest or fraudulent action [Section 1101.652(a)(3)]; or

(2) making a false promise of a character likely to influence, persuade, or induce any person to enter into a contract or agreement when the licensee could not or did not intend to keep such promise [Section 1101.652(b)(5)]; or

(3) failing to make clear, to all parties to a transaction, which party he is acting for, or receiving compensation from more than one party except with the full knowledge and consent of all parties [Section 1101.652(b)(7), (8)]; or

(4) accepting, receiving, or charging an undisclosed commission, rebate, or direct profit on expenditures made for a principal [Section 1101.652(b)(13)]; or

(5) acting in the dual capacity of broker and undisclosed principal in a transaction [Section 1101.652(b)(16)]; or

(6) conduct which constitutes dishonest dealings, bad faith, or untrustworthiness [Section 1101.652(b)(2)]; or

(7) failing or refusing on demand to produce a document, book, or record in his possession concerning a real estate transaction conducted by him for inspection by the Real Estate Commission or its authorized personnel or representative [Section 1101.652(a)(5)]; or

(8) failing without just cause to surrender to the rightful owner, on demand, a document or instrument coming into his possession [Section 1101.652(a)(7)].

**Full Disclosure.** The duty of loyalty also includes the broker's duty of **full disclosure** to his principal. In addition to the obligations enumerated above under the Texas Real Estate License Act, the rules of the Texas Real Estate Commission further require that the licensee convey all known information that would affect the principal's decision to accept or reject offers, and to keep the principal informed of all applicable, significant information (TREC Rules and Regs. §535.156). The amount of information that needs to be disclosed appears to be total. *Janes* v. *CPR Corporation*, 623 S.W.2d 733 (Tex. Civ. App.—Houston, 1981); see also *Kinnard* v. *Homann*, discussed later in this chapter. There have been a number of cases, however, where the courts have determined that full disclosure was not made and held the agent liable for breach of his fiduciary capacity. For instance, if the real estate appreciates in value and the broker buys the property during the listing period himself while failing to disclose that appreciation in value, a liability has been created for the broker. *Ramsey* v. *Gordon*, supra. One of the most obvious forms of nondisclosure is the "flip" sale. In this transaction the broker may find himself liable if he acquires the property from his principal and sells it for a higher price to a prospective purchaser on the same day or soon thereafter. *Southern Cross Industries, Inc.* v. *Martin*, 604 S.W.2d 290 (Tex. Civ. App.—San Antonio, 1980). A broker must also disclose if the agent owns an interest in the purchaser. *Nix* v. *Born*, 890 S.W.2d 635 (Tex. App.—El Paso, 1993).

Frightening cases have come out of courts of other states, which might indicate a trend toward more disclosure than the broker might expect. In one case there was a disputed closing and the seller's broker dutifully "held his ground" to demand an interest payment from the purchaser that was said to be under protest. The purchaser ultimately sued to have his interest refunded and lost his claim. However, the seller sued the broker for his commission, plus the expenses of defending the lawsuit, on the grounds that the broker had breached his contractual and fiduciary duties in closing subject to the purchaser's protest. The court found that the broker had followed the *letter* of the instructions given to him by the principal but had violated the *spirit* of those instructions by failing to inform the seller of the dispute over the interest amount. *Owen* v. *Shelton*, 277 S.E. 189 (Va. 1981). A similar result was reached in a Montana case where the Montana Supreme Court held that the broker breached his fiduciary relationship with his client by failing to make a full disclosure to his client of the contract with the broker (the listing agreement). The court held that the fiduciary relationship between a broker and his client includes a full and understandable explanation to the client before having him sign a contract, particularly when the contract is with the broker himself. Basically, the court held that the broker had a fiduciary relationship with his client before he was an agent. *Lyle* v. *Moore*, supra. So it would be perhaps part of a broker's disclosure to reveal the nature and extent of his broker's fees to the client before he signs the client listing contract. In the *Lyle* case, the client alleged he did not understand the extent of an exclusive right to sell listing agreement when he ultimately sold his property to his sons.

This duty of disclosure has also been held to include submitting an offer to purchase, although it is limited to that. The broker has no control over the decisions as to who the property will be sold to. *Shore* v. *Thomas A. Sweeney & Associates*, 864 S.W.2d 182 (Tex. App.—Tyler, 1993). A broker should disclose, however, all facts within the agent's knowledge that could reasonably be calculated to influence the principal's actions. *Hercules* v. *Robedeaux, Inc.*, 329 N.W.2d 240 (Wis. Ct. App.—1982). The licensee's explanation of various aspects of the transaction must be commensurate with the education and understanding of the principal. *Mallory* v. *Watt*, 594 P.2d 629 (Id. 1979).

## Reasonable Care

The duty of **reasonable care** generally implies competence and expertise on the part of the broker. He has a duty to disclose knowledge and material facts concerning the property and cannot become a party to any fraud or misrepresentation likely to affect the sound judgment of the principal. In procuring a purchaser, the broker obviously has a duty to discover whether or not that purchaser is financially able to pursue the transaction. The broker should also disclose any material changes in property values so that his principal may stay fully informed at all times. The broker further has a duty to make sure that all material facts of a transaction are disclosed to his principal. However, the broker may not give legal interpretations of the documents involved in a transaction. To give legal interpretations of an instrument is practicing law without a license and is specifically prohibited under Section 16 of the Texas Real Estate License Act.

There are other provisions in the Texas Real Estate License Act that provide for license revocation if the duty of reasonable care has been breached, including the following:

(1) making a material misrepresentation, or failing to disclose to a potential purchaser any latent structural defect or any other defect known to the broker or salesman. Latent structural defects and other defects do not refer to trivial or insignificant defects but refer to those defects that would be a significant factor to a reasonable and prudent purchaser in making a decision to purchase [Section 1101.652(b)(3)]; or

(2) pursuing a continued and flagrant course of misrepresentation or making of false promises through agents, salesmen, advertising, or otherwise [Section 1101.652(b)(6)]; or

(3) having knowingly withheld from or inserted in a statement of account or invoice, a statement that made it inaccurate in a material particular [Section 1101.652(b)(24)]; or

(4) failing or refusing on demand to furnish copies of a document pertaining to a transaction dealing with real estate to a person whose signature is affixed to the document [Section 1101.652(b)(28)].

## Accounting

The duty of **accounting** is provided for generally in requiring that any money accepted as earnest money must be placed in a proper escrow account within a reasonable amount of time [Section 15a(6)(E)]. The Real Estate Commission has enforced this provision at least once and the agent's license was suspended. *Kilgore* v. *Texas Real Estate Commission*, 565 S.W.2d 114 (Tex. Civ. App.—Ft. Worth, 1978). This duty of accounting would also apply to failure to report undisclosed commissions or failure to disclose the true purchase price of the seller's property. This type of conduct, of course, represents the severest type of fraud and misrepresentation. These subjects are discussed in almost every provision of the Texas Real Estate License Act.

The areas that deal specifically with escrow and accounting for funds are set out in the following sections, which prohibit:

(1) accepting, receiving, or charging an undisclosed commission, rebate, or direct profit on expenditures made for a principal [Section 1101.652(b)(13)]; or

(2) failing within a reasonable time to deposit money received as escrow agent in a real estate transaction, either in trust with a title company authorized to do business in this state, or in a custodial, trust, or escrow account maintained for that purpose in a banking institution authorized to do business in this state [Section 1101.652(b)(30)]; or

(3) disbursing money deposited in a custodial, trust, or escrow account, as provided in Subsection (Y) before the transaction concerned has been consummated or finally otherwise terminated [Section 1101.652(b)(31)].

# Duties of the Principal to the Agent

Similar to the duties specified above, there are also certain duties that the principal owes to his agent. While these duties are not nearly as concrete and so distinctly spelled out by state statutes, the duties are important in determining the rights of the agent when the principal fails to live up to his obligations as created by the agency relationship. These duties are:

1. Performance.
2. Compensation.
3. Reimbursement.
4. Indemnification.

## Performance

**Performance** is normally considered to be an agent's obligation; however, the principal is expected to do whatever he reasonably can to help accomplish the purpose of the agency.

## Compensation

**Compensation** is normally specified in the listing agreement or in the employment contract. In most real estate situations, even if the contract is contingent on the closing of the sale, if the agent can produce a ready, willing, and able buyer, he is entitled to be paid.

## Reimbursement

**Reimbursement** implies that the principal must reimburse the agent for expenses made on the principal's behalf. This does not mean that the principal has to reimburse the agent for the costs of advertising, entertainment, and other costs of doing business. Those are clearly the agent's responsibility. However, in the event of an absentee landlord or seller, the agent is often required to perform minor repairs and incur other small expenses in order to keep the property in good condition. When these expenses are made in good faith and within the scope of the agent's authority, he is entitled to reimbursement from the principal for funds expended on the principal's behalf.

## Indemnification

**Indemnification**, in these days of consumer awareness, is becoming more and more important for the agent. This duty arises when the agent suffers a loss through no fault of his own while performing his duties on behalf of the principal, such as an innocent misrepresentation by the broker when he is performing acts on behalf of the principal. As previously discussed, the agent is almost always liable when he makes a misrepresentation to a third party. However, if this misrepresentation has in fact been represented to the broker who was carrying out his activities in good faith, relying on a representation made by the principal, the agent may be reimbursed for his losses if the principal has in fact misrepresented those items to his agent. This would often include concealed defects and representation as to the quality and condition of the property. The Deceptive Trade Practices Act has specific provisions for reliance in good faith and indemnification. (See Appendix I, §17.506, §17.555.)

# Duties to Third Parties

Even though the broker is supposed to act on his principal's behalf and only in the best interest of his principal, he does have an ever-expanding duty of care to third persons of utilizing fair and honest business practices. The agent cannot be a part of any fraud on behalf of his principal, and if a case arises where the principal asks the agent to lie or misrepresent certain material defects, the broker should refuse to engage in any such acts on behalf of his principal. A broker is liable to third parties for misrepresentations, and particularly for failure to disclose certain material defects that may affect the buyer's good judgment and sound business practice. The Texas Real Estate License Act specifically speaks to this, again under Section 1101.652, under the following prohibitions:

(1) making a material misrepresentation, or failing to disclose to a potential purchaser any latent structural defect or any other defect known to the broker or salesman. Latent structural defects and other defects do not refer to trivial or insignificant defects but refer to those defects that would be a significant factor to a reasonable and prudent purchaser in making a decision to purchase [Section 1101.652(b)(3)]; or

(2) making a false promise of a character likely to influence, persuade, or induce any person to enter into a contract or agreement when the licensee could not or did not intend to keep such promise [Section 1101.652(b)(5)]; or

(3) pursuing a continued and flagrant course of misrepresentation or making of false promises through agents, salespeople, advertising, or otherwise [Section 1101.652(b)(6)]; or

(4) failing to make clear, to all parties to a transaction, which party he is acting for, or receiving compensation from more than one party except with the full knowledge and consent of all parties [Section 1101.652(b)(7), (8)]; or

(5) soliciting, selling, or offering for sale real property under a scheme or program that constitutes a lottery or deceptive practice [Section 1101.652(b)(14), (15)]; or

(6) guaranteeing, authorizing, or permitting a person to guarantee that future profits will result from a resale of real property [Section 1101.652(b)(17)]; or

(7) negotiating or attempting to negotiate the sale, exchange, lease, or rental of real property with an owner or lessor, knowing that the owner had a written outstanding contract, granting exclusive agency in connection with the property to another real estate broker [Section 1101.652(b)(22)]; or

(8) publishing, or causing to be published, an advertisement including, but not limited to, advertising by newspaper, radio, television, or display which is misleading or which is likely to deceive the public, or which in any manner tends to create a misleading impression, or which fails to identify the person causing the advertisement to be published as a licensed real estate broker or agent [Section 1101.652(b)(23)]; or

(9) failing to advise a purchaser in writing before the closing of a transaction that the purchaser should either have the abstract covering the real estate which is the subject of the contract examined by an attorney of the purchaser's own selection, or be furnished with or obtain a policy of title insurance [Section 1101.652(b)(29)]; or

(10) failing or refusing on demand to produce a document, book, or record in his possession concerning a real estate transaction conducted by him for inspection by the Real Estate Commission or its authorized personnel or representative [Section 1101.652(a)(5)]; or

(11) failing without just cause to surrender to the rightful owner, on demand, a document or instrument coming into his possession [Section 1101.652(a)(7)].

Note that Section 1101.652 of the Texas Real Estate License Act requires at least four affirmative disclosures a broker must make to a third party under certain circumstances. These are **latent structural defects** under Section 1101.652(b)(3), advising a purchaser to have the abstract of title covering the real estate examined under Section 1101.652(b)(29), making clear to the parties of the transaction exactly which party he is working for under Section 1101.652(b)(7), and production of documents under Section 1101.652(b)(28). This is true even if the licensee is a principal. A licensee, when engaging in a real estate transaction in his own behalf, is obligated to inform any person with whom he deals that he is a licensed broker or salesperson and shall not use his expertise to the disadvantage of a person with whom he deals (TREC, Rules and Regs., §535.144).

A common difficulty has been determining how much information should be disclosed to the purchaser without disclosing the confidences of the seller. A simple rule is that a broker should disclose anything that would make a material difference to a prudent purchaser in her decision making; for instance, a licensee cannot conceal any confidential information that could cause potential harm to a prospective purchaser. The 1993 legislature amended the Property Code to make a **seller's disclosure statement**, shown in Figure 8.1, a requirement for all 1–4 family residential real estate transactions. Figure 8.1 is the form set out in the statute, but a licensee can use another form as long as it is substantially the same as this one. The form is signed by both parties to the transaction and, at least theoretically, enables the *seller* to make the disclosure to the purchaser rather than putting the burden on the real estate broker, *V.T.C.A., Property Code, §5.008*. The form *is* a representation, and liability can result if filled out incorrectly. *Kessler v. Fanning*, 953 S.W.2d 515 (Tex. App.—Ft. Worth, 1997).

# Cooperating Brokers

Other problems arise when we talk about the duties of care, liabilities, and obligations of the cooperating broker. Cooperating brokers are usually "subagents" and do not have a contractual relationship with the seller/principal and, in many cases, may *think* they represent the purchaser (and don't have a buyer/tenant representation agreement). There are a number of unanswered questions in Texas as "consumers" become more sophisticated and as more real estate transactions are "co-opped" between brokers. There are confusing issues as to whether or not one broker (the co-op) can make a misrepresentation that will create a liability for the listing broker. *Sullivan* v. *Jefferson*, 400 A.2d 836 (N.J. App.—1979). The Texas legislature, however, has attempted to eliminate this liability by providing that a party is not liable for a misrepresentation or a concealment of material fact made by the license holder unless the party knew of the misrepresentation or concealment and failed to disclose the party's knowledge of the falsity of the misrepresentation or concealment, *Tex. Occ. Code §1101.805(d)*. There are further theories of brokers "conspiring" to sell the property at a cheaper price so that they can get their commissions rather than actively represent the seller to try to achieve the highest price possible. *Lester* v. *Marshall*, 352 P.2d 786 (Col. 1960). There is also the ever-present problem of the couple who comes into the broker's office and says "help us find a house." It is difficult to explain to them (after showing them 467 houses) that you actually work for the seller and are trying to achieve the highest price the market will bear.

**FIGURE 8.1 SELLER'S DISCLOSURE STATEMENT.**

APPROVED BY THE TEXAS REAL ESTATE COMMISSION (TREC)

09-01-07

## SELLER'S DISCLOSURE OF PROPERTY CONDITION

(SECTION 5.008, TEXAS PROPERTY CODE)

CONCERNING THE PROPERTY AT_____

(Street Address and City)

THIS NOTICE IS A DISCLOSURE OF SELLER'S KNOWLEDGE OF THE CONDITION OF THE PROPERTY AS OF THE DATE SIGNED BY SELLER AND IS NOT A SUBSTITUTE FOR ANY INSPECTIONS OR WARRANTIES THE PURCHASER MAY WISH TO OBTAIN. IT IS NOT A WARRANTY OF ANY KIND BY SELLER OR SELLER'S AGENTS.

Seller ❑ is ❑ is not occupying the Property. If unoccupied, how long since Seller has occupied the Property?

1. The Property has the items checked below [Write Yes (Y), No (N), or Unknown (U)]:

| | | |
|---|---|---|
| __ Range | __ Oven | __ Microwave |
| __ Dishwasher | __ Trash Compactor | __ Disposal |
| __ Washer/Dryer Hookups | __ Window Screens | __ Rain Gutters |
| __ Security System | __ Fire Detection Equipment | __ Intercom System |
| __ TV Antenna | __ Smoke Detector | __ Satellite Dish |
| __ Ceiling Fan(s) | __ Smoke Detector-Hearing Impaired | __ Exhaust Fan(s) |
| __ Central A/C | __ Carbon Monoxide Alarm | __ Wall/Window Air Conditioning |
| __ Plumbing System | __ Emergency Escape Ladder(s) | __ Public Sewer System |
| __ Patio/Decking | __ Cable TV Wiring | __ Fences |
| __ Pool | __ Attic Fan(s) | __ Spa  __ Hot Tub |
| __ Pool Equipment | __ Central Heating | __ Automatic Lawn Sprinkler System |
| __ Fireplace(s) & Chimney (Woodburning) | __ Septic System | __ Fireplace(s) & Chimney (Mock) |
| __ Gas Lines (Nat./LP) | __ Outdoor Grill | __ Carport |
| __ Garage: __ Attached __ Not Attached | __ Sauna | __ Water Supply __ City __ Well __ MUD __ Co-op |
| __ Garage Door Opener(s): __ Electronic __ Controls | __ Pool Heater __ Water Heater: __ Gas __ Electric | |

Roof Type: _____ Age: _____ (approx)

Are you (Seller) aware of any of the above items that are not in working condition, that have known defects or that are in need of repair? ❑ Yes ❑ No ❑ Unknown If yes, then describe. (Attach additional sheets if necessary): _____

_____

2. Does the property have working smoke detectors installed in accordance with the smoke detector requirements of Chapter 766, Health and Safety Code? ❑ Yes ❑ No ❑ Unknown

If the answer to the question above is no or unknown, explain. (Attach additional sheets if necessary):

_____

_____

_____

TREC No. OP-H

**FIGURE 8.1  CONTINUED.**

Seller's Disclosure Notice Concerning the Property at_____ Page 2   09-01-07
(Street Address and City)

3. Are you (Seller) aware of any known defects/malfunctions in any of the following?

Write Yes (Y) if you are aware, write No (N) if you are not aware.

| | | |
|---|---|---|
| __ Interior Walls | __ Ceilings | __ Floors |
| __ Exterior Walls | __ Doors | __ Windows |
| __ Roof | __ Foundation/Slab(s) | __ Basement |
| __ Walls/Fences | __ Driveways | __ Sidewalks |
| __ Plumbing Sewers/Septics | __ Electrical Systems | __ Lighting Fixtures |

__ Other Structural Components (Describe) _____
_____
_____

4. Are you (Seller) aware of any of the following conditions?  Write Yes (Y) if you are aware, write No (N) if you are not aware.

| | | |
|---|---|---|
| __ Active Termites (includes wood destroying insects) | __ Termite or Wood Rot Damage Needing Repair | __ Previous Termite Damage |
| __ Previous Termite Treatment | __ Previous Flooding | __ Improper Drainage |
| __ Water Penetration | __ Located in 100-Year Floodplain | __ Present Flood Insurance Coverage |
| __ Previous Structural or Roof Repair | __ Hazardous or Toxic Waste | __ Asbestos Components |
| __ Urea-formaldehyde Insulation | __ Radon Gas | __ Lead Based Paint |
| __ Aluminum Wiring | __ Previous Fires | __ Unplatted Easements |
| __ Landfill, Settling, Soil Movement, Fault Lines | __ Subsurface Structure or Pits | |

__ Previous Use of Premises for Manufacture of Methamphetamine

5. Are you (Seller) aware of any item, equipment, or system in or on the Property that is in need of repair? ☐ Yes (iIf you are aware) ☐ No (if you are not aware). If yes, then describe. (Attach additional sheets if necessary)
_____
_____
_____

6. Are you (Seller) aware of any of the following? Write Yes (Y) if you are aware, write No (N) if you are not aware.

__ Room additions, structural modifications, or other alterations or repairs made without necessary permits or not in compliance with building codes in effect at that time.

__ Homeowners' Association or maintenance fees or assessments.

__ Any "common area" (facilities such as pools, tennis courts, walkways, or other areas) co-owned in undivided interest with others.

__ Any notices of violations of deed restrictions or governmental ordinances affecting the condition or use of the Property.

__ Any lawsuits directly or indirectly affecting the Property.

__ Any condition on the Property which materially affects the physical health or safety of an individual.

If the answer to any of the above is yes explain.  (Attach additional sheets if necessary):
_____
_____
_____

TREC No. OP-H

**FIGURE 8.1 CONTINUED.**

Seller's Disclosure Notice Concerning the Property at_____ Page 3  09-01-07
(Street Address and City)

7. If the property is located in a coastal area that is seaward of the Gulf Intracoastal Waterway or within 1,000 feet of the mean high tide bordering the Gulf of Mexico, the property may be subject to the Open Beaches Act or the Dune Protection Act (Chapter 61 or 63, Natural Resources Code, respectively) and a beachfront construction certificate or dune protection permit may be required for repairs or improvements. Contact the local government with ordinance authority over construction adjacent to public beaches for more information.

_____       _____
Date           Signature of Seller      Date           Signature of Seller

The undersigned purchaser hereby acknowledges receipt of the foregoing notice and acknowledges the property complies with the smoke detector requirements of Chapter 766, Health and Safety Code, or, if the property does not comply with the smoke detector requirements of Chapter 766, the buyer waives the buyer's rights to have smoke detectors installed in compliance with Chapter 766.

_____       _____
Date           Signature of Purchaser      Date           Signature of Purchaser

TREC No. OP-H

The high degree of fiduciary care that an agent owes to his principal coupled with the "real world" function of trying to facilitate a real estate transaction might seem to complicate the duties of care a broker would owe to the seller. One should recall that the fiduciary relationship developed between the listing broker and the owner of the property creates the fiduciary duty of **full and complete disclosure** of absolutely *everything* the agent knows, and this should include information that the buyer has chosen to divulge to the real estate broker. *Kinnard v. Homann*, 750 S.W.2d 30 (Tex. App.—Austin, 1988). This presumably would include all information given to him by the buyer. It should also be pointed out that even if the buyer gives *confidential* information to the broker, the broker still has the duty to disclose that to the seller or he runs the risk of breaching his fiduciary duty of loyalty.

Please remember that the broker has a duty of disclosure to the purchaser of anything that may materially affect the purchaser's decision, such as latent structural defects, but it is not a fiduciary duty to disclose everything the broker knows.

The difficulty arises, then, when a buyer voluntarily discloses confidential information to the cooperating broker because he is not aware of the broker's complete fiduciary duty to the seller. In many cases, the buyer thinks the real estate broker represents him while the buyer is in the process of looking for a house. This has created many conflicting and difficult situations. After all, shouldn't the buyer be assisted also?

# Buyer Brokerage

The alternative to traditional seller brokerage and the co-op confusion is the concept of **buyer brokerage**. In this situation the broker represents the purchaser through a buyer representation agreement, contrary to the typical listing situation. The buyer hires the broker to represent him, creating a single agency and fiduciary duty solely to the buyer. It should be noted that there are a number of concerns if you are going to undertake buyer brokerage. The first is the fiduciary duty is owed to the *buyer*, not the seller. The buyer brokerage employment is procured by utilizing a Buyer Representation Agreement (TAR® Form 039), which employs the broker.

## Duties of Care

One would presume that the agent's duties of care of a broker as a buyer's agent would probably be the same as those of a seller's agent (performance, accounting, reasonable care, and loyalty). It should be pointed out, however, that the functions are different. In representing a seller, the broker is supposed to try to get the highest price in the marketplace. *Riley v. Powell*, supra. In representing the buyer, it is arguable that the broker's duty should be to get the lowest price in the marketplace, or at least a reasonable price, not the highest price the market will bear. There may be additional duties concerning: (1) the market analysis for the benefit of the buyer, (2) diligently inquiring as to the potential use of the property for the buyer's benefit; (3) pursuing answers to buyer's questions about financing and school districts; (4) seeking out properties that may not be listed, and other duties of performance and obedience, may be different from those owed to the seller. For instance, if the buyer requests the toughest inspector in town, does the broker have the duty to recommend or seek out that inspector? What if the buyer discloses a particularly devastating negotiating strategy to "beat down" the seller? What if the buyer directs the broker to insert meaningless contingencies in the contract so the buyer can have an "easy out"?

There is at least some authority that indicates a buyer's broker has the duty to inquire as to zoning and deed restrictions as they pertain to the property. *Lewis* v. *Long & Foster Real Estate, Inc.*, 584 A.2d 1325 (M.D. App.—1991). Another case has held that the broker has the fiduciary duty to confirm the property meets with the client's standards or to disclose that no such investigation has been made. *Salhutdin* v. *Valley of California, Inc.*, 29 Cal. Rptr. 2d 463 (Cal. App.—1994). The easier answer to all of these questions is that the duties of care of buyer's brokerage have not really been clearly defined under either case law or under traditional theories of agency as applied in the practical marketplace. Buyer agency is still a new concept, and, as such, there are many unanswered questions.

The TAR® Buyer's Representation Agreement (Form 1501, see Fig. 8.2), enables a broker's compensation to be paid under three possible scenarios: (1) paid by the seller or seller's broker; (2) paid by the buyer; and (3) additional compensation. Under our traditional agency relationships, sellers have been liberal about allowing listing brokers to share commissions with the other broker (presumably including the buyer's brokers) so, from a practical standpoint, if the system doesn't change, we may come to expect normal seller compensation for both listing and buyer's brokers.

The key thing to remember, however, is that who pays the commission is not determinative. A broker can represent either party and get paid by either party, or both parties, provided that all commissions are disclosed. Some sellers may argue that they are paying the commission and expect the brokers to represent them. The buyers' counterargument is that the seller is including the broker's commission in the sales price; therefore, the buyer is paying it indirectly. If the seller has built a commission payment into his sales price, who gets that commission should logically not be of concern, since the property is marketed and the deal is made. The split of commissions between the brokers is merely that: an agreement between brokers. The seller and buyer are not normally a part of that agreement.

## Compensation

As stated previously, who pays the commission is not determinative of whom the agent represents so long as the compensation is disclosed. It would be anticipated that listing brokers would still be willing to split their commissions under the MLS system. If, however, a listing broker refuses to split the commission because of a buyer's representation of a purchaser, the buyer's broker would have to look to the purchaser or some other source (whatever that is!) for recovery. Remember that a cooperating broker does not have an agreement with a seller and therefore cannot sue him for a commission. *Boyert* v. *Tauber*, 834 S.W.2d 60 (Tex. 1992); *Trammell Crow No. 60, et al.*, v. *Harkinson*, 944 S.W.2d 631 (Tex. 1997), although the listing broker may be sued by the "other" broker. See Art. 6573a, §20(d).

**Fee for Services.** A hot new topic has arisen in compensation issues. Many brokers now choose to provide a "**fee for services.**" A fee for services is a new concept of charging compensation which is not based on the sales price of the property, but rather on services performed (i.e., instead of charging 3% of the sales price, they would charge an hourly rate). This has opened up a number of alternatives for buyers who prefer to do their own research, obtain their own financing, and may not need any actual help until execution of the contract for sale or going to closing. Sellers, too, may choose to pay a lower fee to the listing broker if the broker provides a more limited range of services (i.e., the broker doesn't show the house, or provide traditional advertising). This method of compensation has added a whole new level of competition in the marketplace as well as provided a number of cheaper alternatives. Some companies are publishing a list of fees for various services, others are merely offering a rebate of part of their commission back to the buyer or seller. Again, rebates of commission to principals do not violate the Texas Real Estate License Act, and if a broker chooses to share their commission with a principal in return for providing fewer services, this arrangement is perfectly legal.

**Minimal Level of Services.** What if a broker refuses to perform any services, but expects to split the commission? For instance, a broker can access the MLS system to split the commission (let's assume 3%), rebate part of that commission back to the buyer and perform no services, leaving the listing broker with all the responsibility (and liability) in handling the transaction. The Texas legislature has addressed this situation by requiring a minimum level of service under the Real Estate License Act. These new minimum requirements provide that a broker who represents a party or who lists real property under an exclusive agreement must: (1) inform the party of material information relating to the transaction, including the receipt of an offer by the broker; (2) answer the party's questions; and (3) present an offer to or from the party.

This presents another issue. The Texas Real Estate License Act specifically prohibits a broker from contacting another party who they know is represented by another broker. If, however, you have the consent of the other broker to contact the other party, a licensee may do so, but he may not negotiate with that party. He apparently can only deliver the documents to the other party (note §1101.557, Texas Occupations Code).

# Dual Agency

As previously mentioned, real estate brokers have traditionally represented sellers. The development of the concept of buyer brokerage has indicated a niche in the marketplace for buyers who feel they want representation, or for buyers who have particularly close relationships with real estate brokers (relative, business partner, close friend, previous working relationship) such that a buyer agency is almost presumed.

Real-life issues, however, complicate this situation. If a potential buyer walks into a broker's office looking for a property and wants buyer representation and employs the broker to be the buyer's agent, can the broker show his own listings to that buyer? Recall that this creates a fiduciary duty owed to both the buyer and seller, and the resulting potential conflict. Note that the seller's broker has the duty to get the highest price on the market for the seller; the buyer's broker focuses on buying product— obtaining the real estate that best fits the buyer's needs, and maybe for a lower price. As seller's agents, brokers may feel the temptation of a buyer "slipping away" because they cannot represent them with their own listings. What results is the pressure to represent both parties, and become a **dual agent**.

The License Act now provides "a broker must agree to act as an intermediary . . . if the broker agrees to represent in the transaction: (1) a buyer or tenant; and (2) a seller or a landlord." This puts a duty on the broker who represents both parties to get written consent from each party to act as an intermediary in the transaction, which also must contain a written consent of the parties concerning the source of any expected compensation to the broker. This could create a very dangerous situation. If a broker casually represents both parties because of prior personal relationships, and doesn't get the written consents from both parties to be an intermediary, it's a violation of the License Act.

# Single Agency

Single agency is another agency concept that has developed. In a single agency situation, a broker would be limited to representing only one party in any given transaction. In this situation, the buyer may employ the broker, but the broker could not show the buyer any of the broker's own listings. Similarly, a seller may request that the broker have 100% allegiance to her, and not show her home to any buyers that the broker represents. In either of these cases, there will be a segment of the market that will be omitted. For instance, the broker should explain to the seller that if he cannot show the property to any buyers the brokerage company represents, it may eliminate a potential buyer for that listing. In the opposite situation, the buyer would have to be informed that the broker will not show any of his own listings to the buyer, so the broker may want to show all the broker's listings before being employed by the buyer.

# Intermediaries

The 1995 Texas legislature introduced a new concept into Texas real estate brokerage law called an intermediary. An **intermediary** is defined under the License Act as "a broker who is employed to negotiate a transaction between the parties . . . and for that purpose may be an agent to the parties to the transaction."

A real estate broker who acts as an intermediary between the parties: (1) may not disclose to the buyer or tenant that the seller or landlord will accept a price less than the asking price unless otherwise instructed in a separate writing by the seller or landlord; (2) may not disclose to the seller or landlord that the buyer or tenant will pay a price greater than the price submitted in a written offer to the seller or landlord unless otherwise instructed in a separate writing by the buyer or tenant; (3) may not disclose any confidential information or any other information parties specifically instruct the real estate broker in writing not to disclose unless otherwise instructed in a separate writing by the prospective party or required to disclose such information by this act [the Real Estate License Act] or a court order, or if the information materially relates to the condition of the property; and (4) shall treat all parties to the transaction honestly, *§1101.651*. Note that another provision of the new statute also requires that the intermediary be required to "act fairly so as not to favor one party over the other." See *§1101.559(c)*.

The statute provides that a real estate broker may act as an intermediary between the parties if: (1) the real estate broker obtains written consent from each party to the transaction for the real estate broker to act as an intermediary in the transaction; and (2) the written consent of the parties states the source of any expected compensation to the real estate broker. A written employment agreement, which also authorizes the real estate broker to act as an intermediary, is sufficient to establish that written consent if the written agreement sets forth, in conspicuous bold or underlined print, the real estate broker's obligations.

If a real estate broker obtains the consent of the parties to act as an intermediary, the broker may appoint, by providing written notice to the parties, one or more licensees associated with the broker to communicate with and carry out instructions of one party, as well as one or more other licensees associated with the broker to communicate with and carry out instructions of the other party or parties, so long as the parties consent and authorize the broker to make the appointment, which is presumably done in the listing agreement.

One might explain it this way:

The intermediary concept involves two approaches. One is the statutes' definitions and duties of intermediary; the other involves the process of getting to be an intermediary (obtaining the consents and appointing the agents). The Real Estate License Act has created three "window periods" that a licensee will go through to create intermediary status:

The first window period is the exclusive agency wherein the licensee has an exclusive right to sell and an exclusive buyer's representation agreement. During this phase there is a 100% fiduciary duty and a 100% disclosure to the principal that the agent represents.

The second window period is that time when the buyer and the seller, both represented by the same broker, are going into the same transaction. When this potential conflict arises, the licensee is a dual agent (or an unappointed intermediary, whatever that is) until the intermediary process has been completed.

The third window period is when the buyer and seller have been notified and have accepted that notification that they now have an agent that represents them. At that point, the appointed agent can give advice and opinion. Presumably, during the second window period (as a dual agent) the agent cannot give advice and opinion. Is it a 100% fiduciary to both? Probably not. What percentage would you fill in? Is a whole fee being charged for less than 100% fiduciary duty? Hmm.

From a liability standpoint, the trick seems to be to keep the second window period as narrow as possible (i.e., as soon as the potential for conflict arises, the agent diligently pursues the intermediary appointments).

The following chart may help visualize this issue.

| 1st. Window Period | | 2nd Window Period | | 3rd Window Period |
|---|---|---|---|---|
| Exclusive Buyer/Tenant and Exclusive Seller/Tenant Representation | uh oh! → | Buyer/Tenant and Seller/Tenant both Represented by Same Broker | "may" appoint agent to represent both parties → | Seller and Buyer Notified of Intermediary Status |
| 100% Fiduciary Duty to Each | | Unappointed intermediary | no appointment ↓ | __?__ % fiduciary duty |
| Can give advice and opinion | | Dual agency! No advice or opinion Did you get consent? | what is an unappointed intermediary? | Can give advice and opinion |

It does leave the lingering question. If the broker is defined as an "intermediary," but doesn't go through the appointment process, what is that broker's status? An intermediary without appointment? A dual agent? Is there a difference?

The net effect of this statute is yet to be determined. We have not yet been able to even get the final results of the dual agency legislation before this legislation was passed in 1995. It does pose some interesting questions, however. The statute also provides that the duties of a licensee acting as an intermediary supersede or are in lieu of the licensee's duties under common law or any other law; however, no duties are defined under the statute other than the above-referenced five duties (which are really no different from those required of a dual agent, discussed previously). Presumably, a licensee could be both a dual agent and an intermediary the way the statute is currently written.

# Middlemen

One exception to the agency theory has been the "**middleman**" concept. In a pure middleman situation, the broker brings the buyer and seller together and may receive a commission for it, but the broker represents neither party. If such a transaction is contemplated, it is very important that the broker be a mere middleman. If the court, or the jury, construes that the agent is acting on behalf of either party, he owes fiduciary duties to that party even though he is a "middleman." *West* v. *Touchstone*, 620 S.W.2d 687 (Tex. Civ. App.—Dallas, 1981).

It may well be more difficult to be a middleman than to be a party's agent. A few other states have created a statutory provision for a "transactional" broker. It has not yet been determined, though, whether this limits the broker's liability, nor has there been any clear definition as to what the limited scope of the broker's duties is. For instance, if the broker provides fewer services (which seems to be necessary in this case as well as in dual agency), should the broker be compensated the same amount?

# Agency Disclosures

How do we reconcile all of these potential situations and conflicts? The Texas Real Estate License Act provides for two levels of agency disclosure.

## If the Licensee Does Not Represent a Party

The licensee is required to furnish a party in a real estate transaction *at the time of the first substantive dialogue* with the party, the following written statement:

> Before working with a real estate broker, you should know that the duties of a broker depend on whom the broker represents. If you are a prospective seller or landlord (owner) or a prospective buyer or tenant (buyer), you should know that the broker who lists the property for sale or lease is the owner's agent. A broker who acts as a subagent represents the owner in cooperation with the listing broker. A broker who acts as a buyer's agent represents the buyer. A broker may act as an intermediary between the parties if the parties consent in writing. A broker can assist you in locating a property, preparing a contract or lease, or obtaining financing without representing you. A broker is obligated by law to treat you honestly.

IF THE BROKER REPRESENTS THE OWNER: The broker becomes the owner's agent by entering into an agreement with the owner, usually through a written listing agreement, or by agreeing to act as a subagent by accepting an offer of subagency from the listing broker. A subagent may work in a different real estate office. A listing broker or subagent can assist the buyer but does not represent the buyer and must place the interests of the owner first. The buyer should not tell the owner's agent anything the buyer would not want the owner to know because an owner's agent must disclose to the owner any material information known to the agent.

IF THE BROKER REPRESENTS THE BUYER: The broker becomes the buyer's agent by entering into an agreement to represent the buyer, usually through a written buyer representation agreement. A buyer's agent can assist the owner but does not represent the owner and must place the interests of the buyer first. The owner should not tell a buyer's agent anything the owner would not want the buyer to know because a buyer's agent must disclose to the buyer any material information known to the agent.

IF THE BROKER ACTS AS AN INTERMEDIARY: A broker may act as an intermediary between the parties if the broker complies with the Texas Real Estate License Act. The broker must obtain the written consent of each party to the transaction to act as an intermediary. The written consent must state who will pay the broker and, in conspicuous bold or underlined print, set forth the broker's obligations as an intermediary. The broker is required to treat each party honestly and fairly and to comply with the Texas Real Estate License Act. A broker who acts as an intermediary in a transaction: (1) shall treat all parties honestly; (2) may not disclose that the owner will accept a price less than the asking price unless authorized in writing to do so by the owner; (3) may not disclose that the buyer will pay a price greater than the price submitted in a written offer unless authorized in writing to do so by the buyer; and (4) may not disclose any confidential information or any information that a party specifically instructs the broker in writing not to disclose unless authorized in writing to disclose the information or required to do so by the Texas Real Estate License Act or a court order or if the information materially relates to the condition of the property. With the parties' consent, a broker acting as an intermediary between the parties may appoint a person who is licensed under the Texas Real Estate License Act and associated with the broker to communicate with and carry out instructions of one party and another person who is licensed under that Act and associated with the broker to communicate with and carry out instructions of the other party.

If you choose to have a broker represent you, you should enter into a written agreement with the broker that clearly establishes the broker's obligations and your obligations. The agreement should state how and by whom the broker will be paid. You have the right to choose the type of representation, if any, you wish to receive. Your payment of a fee to a broker does not necessarily establish that the broker represents you. If you have any questions regarding the duties and responsibilities of the broker, you should resolve those questions before proceeding.

What is first substantive dialogue? Substantive dialogue is defined by the Real Estate License Act as a meeting or written communication that involves a substantive discussion relating to specific real property. It does not include a meeting that occurs at a property held open for prospective purchasers or tenants or a meeting that occurs after the parties of the transaction have signed the contract to sell, buy, rent, or lease the real property concerned. It clearly includes the first written correspondence involving a specific property.

**Exemptions.** A licensee is not required to provide this written information if: (1) the proposed transaction for a residential lease is not for more than one year and no sale is being considered; or (2) the licensee meets with the party who is represented by another licensee. See *Sec. 15C(e)*.

### If the Licensee Represents a Party

The 1995 legislature has also modified the disclosure process under a new *§15C* of the Texas Real Estate License Act. The statute now provides that a licensee *who represents a party in a proposed real estate transaction* must disclose that representation at the time of the licensee's first contact with: (1) another party to the transaction; or (2) another licensee who represents another party to the transaction. The disclosure may be orally or in writing. It would seem to be a prudent business practice, however, to do it in writing so the that agent could confirm that the disclosure was properly made.

# Management Responsibilities

Different problems arise if a broker is acting as a manager of real estate, rather than simply as a broker in a sales transaction. His duties to owners and third parties in this situation relate to service contracts for services to be performed on a particular project, as well as to properly maintaining the property such that no one suffers any injury caused by the broker's negligence in maintaining the property. The liability problems for real property managers to owners and third parties are clearly covered under the Deceptive Trade Practices Act. *Lerma* v. *Brecheisen*, supra. The problem of management liability may also occur when the property management company, or broker, does not want to become obligated for the payment of the expenses of a project. On the other hand, the vendors and suppliers who must perform the services must know whom they should pursue in the event they are not paid. The fundamentals of principal and agent again apply, and the liabilities can be summarized as follows:

1.  Where an agent (the broker) acts on behalf of a principal who is known to the service company performing the work, and the agent is acting within the scope of his authority, the principal is liable, and the agent will not ordinarily be personally liable to the third party. If the agent exercises **ostensible** (apparent) authority that he does not have, and the third party reasonably relied on such representation, an agency will be presumed, and the principal is still liable, rather than the agent. The principal may also **ratify** an agent's acts after they have been performed (even if they were wrongfully performed by the agent) and become liable for the agent's acts. The collector of legal terms may wish to add to his collection this doctrine of **respondeat superior**. However, if the agent was not acting within his scope of authority, the principal has a cause of action against the agent to recover whatever losses may have been incurred.

2.  If the broker discloses the fact that he is an agent but does not disclose the identity of the principal, the broker will generally be considered personally liable on the agreement. Thus it logically follows that the third party is advancing services only on the agent's good name and promise to pay, even though the third party knows that the broker is acting only as an agent. A third party performing services should not expect to be paid by a principal when he does

not know who that principal is or anything about that principal's ability to pay. If the third party subsequently discovers the identity of the principal, both the principal and the agent may be liable to that third party.

3. It follows, then, that if the principal is undisclosed, and the agency is also undisclosed, the agent is liable to third parties for all acts that he performs, as if they were the principal's.

And finally, the agent is always liable for his torts or contracts if he commits an act constituting deceit or misrepresentation. Even if the third party sues the principal and recovers, the agent would still be liable to the principal.

# Termination of Agency

Once it has been determined that an agency agreement exists, there are two basic ways it can be terminated:

1. By acts of the parties; and
2. By operation of law.

Termination of an agency agreement by acts of the parties can be accomplished by either party or by both parties. If both parties agree to terminate the agency agreement, it is simple to agree to the termination by **mutual consent**. The termination can also be accomplished by **completion of the agency objective** (i.e., the property being sold) or by expiration of the stipulated length of time as set out in the listing agreement or agency contract.

Termination of the contract by one of the parties tends to be more complicated. A principal may unilaterally **revoke** the agency or listing agreement at any time if she has cause to do so. If she does not have cause to do so and her reasons appear to be arbitrary, the agent has the right to recover the reasonable value of his services and reimbursement for his agency expenses. Conversely, the agent can **renounce** the contract if he feels that the principal is not helping him to complete his agency objective. The agent may then be liable for damages if the agent does not have just cause to terminate the contract. In both cases, what is "just cause" is a fact question that has to be determined by a jury. In either case this creates, at best, a difficult situation.

Termination of the agency relationship by operation of law occurs upon the **death** of either the principal or the agent, **insanity** of either party, or **change of law**. Since the agency contract is a contract for personal services and is often purely unilateral, the death of either party terminates the obligations of either party. This can always be modified, however, if the broker is a corporation, the seller is a corporation, or either are entities rather than natural persons (i.e., a trust or limited partnership). Similarly, insanity of either party limits the contractual capacity of either party to the point that the principal–agent relationship cannot be completed. Of course, determinations and definitions of sanity are difficult to determine. If a change of law (called **supervening illegality**) makes a contract become illegal, any contract that is illegal is void. An excellent example of this arose in the recent case of *Centex Corporation* v. *Dalton*, 840 S.W.2d 952 (Tex. 1994). In that case, the listing broker earned a substantial commission by negotiating the sale of several savings and loans. While the transaction was pending, however, Congress made the payment of commissions to brokers for this type of sale illegal. The broker was then denied his commission because of supervening illegality. It was legal initially but became illegal during the pendency of the transaction.

Once the confidential relationship is established, it cannot just be disregarded or ignored. If the agent takes advantage of the principal because of this "insider" information, or if he advises someone else to do so, he still may breach his fiduciary duty. Therefore, even if the agency terminates, the fiduciary duty may not end. *Swallows* v. *Laney*, 691 P.2d 874 (N. Mex. 1984). For instance, a broker cannot become a principal on the same transaction and shed his fiduciary obligations. The agency relationship is presumed to continue once it is established. *Southern Cross Industries, Inc.* v. *Martin*, supra. The agency liabilities may continue far beyond the termination of the agency relationship.

The law of principal and agent has always been difficult. There are a number of fact situations that are always involved, making trial proceedings difficult. It is important to note that the expanding duties to third parties are currently drawing the most attention and controversy pertaining to broker liability. Many attorneys consider this to be a trend and a substantial change to the existing theories of agency law.

# Power of Attorney

There is an often misunderstood type of agency relationship created when a principal employs an **attorney-in-fact**. This creates a general agency, and the attorney-in-fact is given the authority to act on behalf of his principal pursuant to an express document called a **power of attorney**. The power of attorney may be global (to do any and all acts as if the attorney-in-fact were the principal) or very specific (to sell one's house).

It is *very* important to understand that a power of attorney merely creates an agency by express agreement. It gives no special or extraordinary power to the attorney-in-fact. An attorney-in-fact does not have to be an attorney-at-law, either; it can be anyone (relative or friend) whom a principal wishes to employ to be her agent. Powers of attorney have always been very difficult for title companies to deal with. It is so easy to terminate them (death, insanity, or revocation) that they have difficulty knowing whether or not the power of attorney is enforceable at the time documents are signed. The Texas Probate Code has always allowed for powers of attorney to survive the incompetence of the principal, provided that the power of attorney specifically provided for this. It has always created significant uncertainty, however, when insuring land titles.

A durable power of attorney is defined by statute as a written instrument that: (1) designates another person as attorney-in-fact or agent; (2) is signed by an adult principal; (3) contains the words "This Power of Attorney is not effected by the subsequent disability or incapacity of the principal," or "This Power of Attorney becomes effective on the disability or incapacity of the principal," or similar words showing the principal's intent that the authority conferred on the attorney-in-fact or agent shall be exercised notwithstanding the principal's subsequent disability or incapacity; and (4) is acknowledged by a principal before an officer authorized to take acknowledgments to deeds of conveyances and to administer oaths under the law of this or any other state.

In addition, the durable power of attorney is timeless. It does not lapse because of the passage of time unless the instrument creating the power of attorney specifically states that there is a time limitation (see *V.T.C.A., Probate Code, §483*).

Except for express revocation or termination by its own terms, there are three ways a durable power of attorney can be terminated: (1) the death of the principal; (2) the appointment of a guardian for the principal; or (3) the divorce or annulment of the principal and agent if the agent has been appointed by the principal *and* the innocent third party had been put on notice of the change of status. An affidavit by the attorney-in-fact stating that he or she did not have actual knowledge of the revocation of the power of attorney at the time of the execution of documents is conclusive proof of such fact for such purposes. Even those terminations are limited. However, the statute clearly states that the revocation, death, or qualification of a guardian of the estate of the principal doesn't revoke or terminate the agency as to the attorney-in-fact who doesn't have actual knowledge of the termination. How does the attorney-in-fact prove he didn't have knowledge? The statute merely requires that he sign an affidavit saying that he did not have, at the time of the exercise of his power, actual knowledge of the termination of the power of attorney by revocation, death, or qualification of the guardian, and that the affidavit is "conclusive proof as between the attorney-in-fact or agent and a person other than the principal." The same is true of people's reliance on the durable power of attorney when the principal becomes disabled or incapacitated. The affidavit is, again, "conclusive proof" of a disability or incapacity of the principal at the time (see *V.T.C.A., Probate Code, §487*).

A revocation of the durable power of attorney is not effective as to a third party relying on the power of attorney unless the third party receives *actual notice* of the revocation.

If the durable power of attorney is for a real property transaction, the durable power of attorney is required to be recorded in the office of the county clerk of the county in which the real property is located. The statute even provides a power of attorney form to be used, shown here as Figure 8.2. The form is not exclusive, and other forms of power of attorney can be used. Third parties who rely in good faith on the acts of the agent within the scope of the power of attorney may do so *without fear of liability to the principal* (see *V.T.C.A., Probate Code, §490*). Section 492 of the Probate Code gives very broad definitions as to what a durable power of attorney can cover and authorize, which is virtually anything.

## ■ SUMMARY

The parties necessary to establish an agency relationship are the principal, the agent, and third parties. An agency relationship can be created by actual authority, by ostensible authority, or by ratification. The agent owes certain duties to his principal, including the duties of performance, reasonable care, loyalty, and accounting. The principal owes the agent the duties of care including performance, compensation, reimbursement, and indemnification. The agent also owes duties of care to third parties. The primary duty of care to third parties is honesty and integrity, although there are other requirements of disclosure pursuant to the Texas Real Estate License Act.

In a special agency, a principal is not responsible for the acts of his agent. In a general agency, the principal is responsible for the acts of his agent. The agency relationship may be terminated by acts of parties or operation of law.

**FIGURE 8.2  POWER OF ATTORNEY.**

## STATUTORY DURABLE POWER OF ATTORNEY

NOTICE:   THE POWERS GRANTED BY THIS DOCUMENT ARE BROAD AND SWEEPING. THEY ARE EXPLAINED IN THE DURABLE POWER OF ATTORNEY ACT, CHAPTER XII, TEXAS PROBATE CODE.  IF YOU HAVE ANY QUESTIONS ABOUT THESE POWERS, OBTAIN COMPETENT LEGAL ADVICE.  THIS DOCUMENT DOES NOT AUTHORIZE ANYONE TO MAKE MEDICAL AND OTHER HEALTH-CARE DECISIONS FOR YOU.  YOU MAY REVOKE THIS POWER OF ATTORNEY IF YOU LATER WISH TO DO SO.

I,_____, appoint _____ as my agent (attorney-in-fact) to act for me in any lawful way with respect to all of the following powers except for a power that I have crossed out below.

TO WITHHOLD A POWER, YOU MUST CROSS OUT EACH POWER WITHHELD.
Real property transactions;
Tangible personal property transactions;
Stock and bond transactions;
Commodity and option transactions;
Banking and other financial institution transactions;
Business operating transactions;
Insurance and annuity transactions;
Estate, trust, and other beneficiary transactions;
Claims and litigations;
Personal and family maintenance;
Benefits from Social Security, Medicare, Medicaid, or other governmental programs or civil or military service;
Retirement plan transactions;
Tax matters.

IF NO POWER LISTED ABOVE IS CROSSED OUT, THIS DOCUMENT SHALL BE CONSTRUED AND INTERPRETED AS A GENERAL POWER OF ATTORNEY, AND MY AGENT (ATTORNEY-IN-FACT) SHALL HAVE THE POWER AND AUTHORITY TO PERFORM OR UNDERTAKE ANY ACTION I COULD PERFORM OR UNDERTAKE IF I WERE PERSONALLY PRESENT.

SPECIAL INSTRUCTIONS:

Special instructions applicable to gifts (initial in front of the following sentence to have it apply):

I grant my agent (attorney-in-fact) the power to apply my property to make gifts, except that the amount of a gift to an individual may not exceed the amount of annual exclusions allowed from the federal gift tax for the calendar year of the gift.

ON THE FOLLOWING LINES YOU MAY GIVE SPECIAL INSTRUCTIONS LIMITING OR EXTENDING THE POWERS GRANTED TO YOUR AGENT.

_____
_____
_____
_____

UNLESS YOU DIRECT OTHERWISE ABOVE, THIS POWER OF ATTORNEY IS EFFECTIVE IMMEDIATELY AND WILL CONTINUE UNTIL IT IS REVOKED.

FIGURE 8.2 **CONTINUED.**

CHOOSE ONE OF THE FOLLOWING ALTERNATIVES BY CROSSING OUT THE ALTERNATIVE NOT CHOSEN:
- (A)   This power of attorney is not affected by my subsequent disability or incapacity.
- (B)   This power of attorney becomes effective upon my disability or incapacity.

YOU SHOULD CHOOSE ALTERNATIVE (A) IF THIS POWER OF ATTORNEY IS TO BECOME EFFECTIVE ON THE DATE IT IS EXECUTED.

IF NEITHER (A) NOR (B) IS CROSSED OUT, IT WILL BE ASSUMED THAT YOU CHOSE ALTERNATIVE (A).

If Alternative (B) is chosen and a definition of my disability or incapacity is not contained in this power of attorney, I shall be considered disabled or incapacitated for purposes of this power of attorney if a physician certifies in writing at a date later than the date this power of attorney is executed that, based on the physician's medical examination of me, I am mentally incapable of managing my financial affairs. I authorize the physician who examines me for this purpose to disclose my physical or mental condition to another person for purposes of this power of attorney. A third party who accepts this power of attorney is fully protected from any action taken under this power of attorney that is based on the determination made by a physician of my disability or incapacity.

I agree that any third party who receives a copy of this document may act under it. Revocation of the durable power of attorney is not effective as to a third party until the third party receives actual notice of the revocation. I agree to indemnify the third party for any claims that arise against the third party because of reliance on this power of attorney.

If any agent named by me dies, becomes legally disabled, resigns, or refuses to act, I name the following (each to act alone and successively, in the order named) as successor(s) to that agent: _____

Signed this _____ day of _____, 1998.

_____
Principal's Signature

STATE OF TEXAS               §
                             §
COUNTY OF _____         §

This document was acknowledged before me on _____, 1998, by _____.

_____
NOTARY PUBLIC

THE ATTORNEY-IN-FACT OR AGENT, BY ACCEPTING OR ACTING UNDER THE APPOINTMENT, ASSUMES THE FIDUCIARY AND OTHER LEGAL RESPONSIBILITIES OF AN AGENT.

## CASE STUDIES FOR DISCUSSION

1. A listing agent for a broker prepared a brochure regarding a house for sale. The brochure contained numerous misrepresentations about various features of the house. The purchaser was given a free opportunity to inspect the house during his various visits, and no efforts were made to hide anything from him. The purchaser, the morning of the closing, visited the house for the purposes of checking all mechanical operations. After closing, the purchaser then sued the broker to recover the difference between the actual value of the house and the value of the house as represented in the brochure prepared by the broker. The purchaser alleged misrepresentation and deceptive trade practices. The broker argued that the purchaser had sufficient time to inspect and the broker should not be liable. What legal ramifications do you foresee?

2. A broker negotiated a sale for some property that was consummated at the title company. The title company issued a title insurance policy for the site. Upon closing, the seller refused to pay the commission to the broker since he did not advise the purchaser in writing that he had to obtain an abstract of title insurance or procure a policy of title insurance. The broker contends that since the insurance was obtained, there was no need to give the purchaser the advice in writing. The seller argues that the Texas Real Estate License Act is very clear and that he must advise the purchaser according to the statute in order to maintain an action for his commission. What arguments do you see for both sides?

3. Mr. Houston obtained an exclusive right to sell a listing from Mr. Water. Mr. Houston diligently endeavored to find purchasers for the property, but the sale of the property was negotiated without the aid of Mr. Houston and directly to a purchaser during the time the listing agreement was in effect. The seller contends that the broker did not endeavor to find a purchaser, that he found the purchaser himself, and that the broker, although available, was never asked to perform any services in the sale and therefore did not earn any commissions. The broker contends that under his exclusive right to sell listing agreements, he deserves the full 6% commission contracted for plus attorney's fees. What legal ramifications do you foresee?

4. In July, Gilmore received an earnest money deposit from the Browns in connection with the contract for their purchase of property from the Hearns. The deal fell through, and there was a dispute between the parties as to who was entitled to the earnest money. In August, the Real Estate Commission informed Gilmore that he should remit the money to one of the parties. Gilmore's attorney notified the Hearns and the Browns in September that the money was in Gilmore's escrow account and Gilmore ultimately interpleaded the money into a registry of the court while the parties were contesting who was to receive the money. In November, the Real Estate Commission instituted proceedings to remove Gilmore's license because of his violation of Section 15(6)(Z) of the Texas Real Estate License Act. There was evidence that Gilmore knew about the dispute between the parties in April and waited until September to do anything about the earnest money. Gilmore alleges that he was trying to hold the earnest money until the parties settled their differences. The Real Estate Commission alleges that Gilmore waited too long to allow for the escrow money to be properly distributed. What is the result?

## CHAPTER 9

# Contracts for the Sale of Real Estate

The law of contracts is one of the most complex areas of the law to study. A complete discussion of the law of contracts requires volumes of thorough study, explanation, and history. Contracts normally used in real estate include listing agreements, earnest money contracts, installment land contracts, leases, easement agreements, deeds, mortgages, security agreements, liens, construction contracts, and partnership agreements. For the purposes of this chapter, the discussions of contract law will be centered around the creation and construction of contracts, generally, earnest money contracts, option contracts, rights of first refusal, and installment land contracts.

## Contracts, Generally

It is important that some of the fundamental elements of contracts be understood before discussing the specific requirements and peculiarities of real estate contracts. A **contract** can most simply be defined as a deliberate or voluntary agreement between competent parties, made on a sufficient legal consideration, to do or not to do a particular act or thing. Contracts may be oral or express, although in matters involving real estate, Texas law requires that some contracts be in writing in order to be enforceable. The Texas statute applied to this principle is in Sections 26.01 and 26.02 of the Texas Business and Commerce Code, more commonly called the **Statute of Frauds**, discussed later in this chapter.

### Creation

Four essential elements must exist for a contract to be present. They include *competent parties, legal subject matter, consideration* for the promises contained in the contract, and *mutual assent*.

**Competent Parties.** Competence and authority of business entities were discussed in Chapter 5, How Ownership Is Held. The same rules apply in contract law, covering their ability to sign as competent parties. There are additional concerns involving individual competence, which deserve further discussion at this point.

The general rule of law is that all parties to a contract have read it and understood it. *First City Mortgage Co.* v. *Gillis*, 694 S.W.2d 144 (Tex. Civ. App.—Houston, 1985). This is true even if they are "slow" or are illiterate. Certain persons do not have full contractual capacity, however. The most obvious of these are minors, mental defectives, and persons under the influence of drugs or alcohol.

**Minors** are defined by the Texas Family Code as people who have not yet attained the age of 18 years. Contracts executed by a minor are generally considered to be voidable at the option of the minor. This power of avoiding the contract lies only with the minor; the option is not available to the other contracting party of legal age. Therefore, anyone who contracts with a minor always contracts at their peril with the possibility that the minor may choose to avoid his contract, which the minor has a legal right to do. However, when the minor achieves the legal age, and continues to perform on the contract, it becomes valid and binding.

Contracts with the **mentally infirmed** can be either void or voidable. If the person has been adjudicated to be insane, the contract is void because the person never had capacity to enter into the contract. When such an adjudication has not been made, however, and the contracting party is attempting to prove insanity, mental infirmity, senility, or mental retardation, the contract becomes voidable at the option of the infirm party, their agent, or guardian. Proof of insanity may be difficult since it may have been temporary or not "apparent" to the third party dealing with the insane claimant.

Parties under the **influence of drugs** are generally treated the same as people who are mentally infirmed. Cases permitting avoidance when the party voluntarily becomes under the influence, however, are rare. It is only when the party is induced at the instigation of the other contracting party prior to entering into the contract that the courts may allow avoidance.

**Legal Subject Matter.** A contract for an **illegal purpose** is void, and the law treats the contract as if it were never created. A change of law terminates the offer prior to its being accepted. Similarly, if the contract is for an illegal purpose as to commit a tort, the courts treat it as if it never existed.

**Consideration.** People often think of **consideration** as the money or good exchanged by the parties. Legally, however, consideration is defined as the obligation that each party makes to the other in order to make the contract enforceable. It is sometimes defined as something of value given in exchange for a promise. Alternatively, it is sometimes said that a benefit and a detriment must exist for each promise contained in the contract. The consideration does not have to be stated, either, in order to be enforceable. *Horner* v. *Bourland*, 724 F.2d 1142 (5th Cir.—1984). To determine whether the essential element of consideration is present, it is helpful to first determine whether a contract is unilateral or bilateral in nature.

In a **unilateral contract**, only one party makes a promise, and the other party completes their half of the contract by performance. The simplest example of a unilateral contract is the promise of a cash payment for crossing a bridge. One party promises to pay the cash when the bridge is crossed. The other party does not promise to cross the bridge, he crosses it. Upon the second party's performance, he has completed his obligation under the contract and has earned his cash payment, which is now due from the other party. In some respects an open listing agreement might be thought of as an example (when it is initially executed) because only one party (the seller) makes a promise. The seller conditionally promises to pay a commission if the broker produces a ready, willing, and able buyer, but the other party (the broker) does not promise to sell the property. The broker accepts the offer (promise to pay a commission) when he secures a ready, willing, and able buyer because this is the performance that meets the offer. Thus, the legal requirement of consideration (the broker's performance) is present.

A common example of a **bilateral contract** is an earnest money contract in which the seller promises to sell and the buyer promises to buy the described real property. The seller suffers a detriment on her promise, in that she must give up the land. The buyer realizes a benefit on this same promise because he will receive the land. The buyer experiences a detriment on his promise to buy because he must give up his money. At the same time the seller benefits because she receives the money. The law generally does not concern itself with the "sufficiency" of the consideration. It is sometimes said that "mere peppercorn" can be enough to constitute legal consideration. Similarly, if a broker promises to perform certain functions under their listing agreement, or has partially performed as promised, some compensation may be due, either pursuant to the contract terms or the law of agency (duty to reimburse and/or compensate).

On the other hand, if there is great disparity between the values of the bargain received by each party, a court of equity may grant relief to avoid treating one party unfairly. When this occurs, it is because fairness and good conscience dictate that one party should be relieved of his legal obligation. The important point to remember is that the sufficiency of the consideration generally does not prevent a contract from being created, although it may give grounds for equitable relief.

**Mutual Assent.** **Mutual assent** is an essential prerequisite to the formation of a contract and is often the most difficult factor to determine. There must have been a "meeting of the minds" between parties, meaning that they must objectively have appeared to have reached an agreement on all material items in the contract. Since this involves acts of the parties, the determination of mutual assent is usually a question of fact and is completed by the process of **offer and acceptance**. As discussed later, these facts also give rise to many defenses to mutual assent, making this prerequisite an often litigated area of contracts.

*Offer* The person making the offer is called the **offeror**. The person to whom the offer is made is called the **offeree**. One might say that if all of the other elements of the contract are present, the offeror completes the first half of the contractual obligation. To be effective, however, the offer must meet certain legal requirements. It must be: (1) communicated to a specific offeree, (2) intended to be a serious offer, and (3) definite and certain enough to be accepted by the offeree. That is, its communication must be such that it creates a **power of acceptance** in the offeree. It cannot be merely an invitation for offers (as in a newspaper advertisement). It cannot be made in jest, while drunk, or as a "dare," as this destroys the requisite intent. It must also be specific so that the offeree, in exercising his power of acceptance, knows exactly what he is accepting. In most real estate situations, the offer is usually completed upon the purchaser's signing and submitting the earnest money contract to the seller. *Freeman* v. *Greenbriar Homes, Inc.*, 715 S.W.2d 394 (Tex. App.—Dallas, 1986).

*Termination of offers* If an offer has been made, it can be terminated prior to acceptance by the offeree, due to: (1) the **acts of the parties** or (2) **operation of law**. It is important to remember that, at this point, no contract is in existence, only the unilateral offer extended by the offeror. While one of the following criteria can terminate an *offer*, it does not necessarily terminate a contract.

Acts of the parties depend on the conduct of the offeror and offeree. As discussed earlier, when the offer is made it is deemed to create a *power of acceptance* in the offeree. The offer, if no time is specified, remains open for a reasonable period of time, and the offeree may accept this offer within that reasonable time period. If there is a specified time period, the offer terminates when the time period is expired. Similarly, an offer may be terminated by the offeror **revoking** his offer prior to it being accepted, *Dempsey* v. *King*, 662 S.W.2d 725 (Tex. Civ. App.—Austin, 1983), by **rejection** of the offeree, or by the offeree partially rejecting a contract (perhaps changing some of the terms), which creates a **counteroffer**. A counteroffer is a rejection, unless the offeree expressly states that the original offer is still being considered. *Thurmond* v. *Wieser*, 699 S.W.2d 680 (Tex. Civ. App.—Waco, 1985).

An offer may also be terminated by operation of law prior to acceptance by the offeree. The law terminates the offer upon the *death* of the offeror or offeree prior to the acceptance, *insanity* of either of the parties prior to acceptance, or a *change in the law* that renders the contract illegal. *Centex Corp.* v. *Dalton*, 840 S.W.2d 952 (Tex. 1992).

*Acceptance* In determining whether or not there was an effective **acceptance** of the contract, the points generally considered are those of **intent**, whether or not that acceptance was **unconditional**, and the **communication** of that acceptance to the offeror.

**Intent**, also one of the main criteria for an effective offer, speaks to the intent of the parties' bargain. Did the person accepting the contract intend, by his words and conduct, to create a contractual relationship by accepting the offer?

To effect a proper acceptance, there also must be an **unqualified, unconditional acceptance** of the offer. Any acceptance that is not an acceptance of the whole offer becomes conditional acceptance, and a conditional acceptance becomes a *counteroffer*. Therefore, the contract is not completed until the offeror (counter-offeree) has accepted the counteroffer to complete the agreement.

Finally, to achieve acceptance there must also be a **communication** of that acceptance to the offeror. Until the acceptance has been communicated to the offeror, the parties' minds have not met and there can be no contract. Therefore, the offeree must communicate that acceptance to the offeror at any time before the offer is terminated. *Jatoi* v. *Park Center, Inc.*, 616 S.W.2d 399 (Tex. Civ. App.—Ft. Worth, 1981).

*Defenses to mutual assent* Very often one finds that there has been a written contract, signed by all parties, which leads to the assumption that the requirement of mutual assent has been satisfied and that a contract is valid. However, this is not necessarily the case. Either party may wish to assert, at a later date, that they entered into the contract as a result of *fraud, mutual mistake of material fact, duress, menace, undue influence*, or because of some act of the other party that constitutes *misrepresentation* or deceit. If proven, this could be a valid defense to the formation of the contract, and the contract would be voidable because the essential element of mutual assent did not, in fact, exist. These defenses need to be explained in a little more detail to help describe how they can arise.

**Fraud** in real estate consists of:

1. False representation of a past or existing material fact, when the false representation is:
    a. Made to a person for the purpose of inducing that person to enter into a contract.
    b. Relied on by that person in entering into that contract.
2. False promise to do an act, when the false promise is:
    a. Material.
    b. Made with the intention of not fulfilling it.

c. Made to a person for the purpose of inducing that person to enter into a contract.

d. Relied on by that person in entering into that contract.

The measure of actual damages suffered by the aggrieved party is the difference between the value of the real estate as represented or promised and its actual value in the condition in which it is delivered at the time of the contract. Any person who commits the fraud is additionally liable to the person defrauded for exemplary damages not to exceed twice the amount of the actual damages. In order for this type of fraud to exist, there must be an intent to induce the defrauded party. *Dobbs* v. *Camco, Inc.*, 445 S.W.2d 565 (Tex. Civ. App.—Houston, 1969).

**Mutual mistake of material fact** is the assertion that the parties were both in error as to some integral fact in the contract. A discrepancy in price alone does not constitute material mistake; however, it must be a factor that materially affects the performance of the parties, such as the amount of property to be purchased. *Stewart* v. *Jones*, 633 S.W.2d 544 (Tex. Civ. App.—Texarkana, 1982); *Horner* v. *Bourland*, supra. It is not grounds for relief if only one of the parties made a mistake, *Turberville* v. *Upper Valley Farms, Inc.*, 616 S.W.2d 676 (Tex. Civ. App.—Corpus Christi, 1981), unless the mistake is of such great consequence that to enforce the contract would be unconscionable. *Harry Brown, Inc.* v. *McBryde*, 622 S.W.2d 596 (Tex. Civ. App.—Tyler, 1981).

**Duress** is the use of physical force to induce a party to sign a contract, whereas **menace** is the mere threat (mere threat?) of physical violence, although Texas courts do not always distinguish them so clearly. *Tower Contracting Co., Inc.* v. *Burden Brothers, Inc.*, 482 S.W.2d 330 (Tex. Civ. App.—Dallas, 1972). One would think that when the samurai sword is pointed at one's kidney, it is menace; when the sword touches, it is duress. In either event, it must be an action that the threatening or performing party had no right to do, and that causes the other party to do an act he otherwise would not have done. *Bailey* v. *Arlington Bank & Trust Co.*, 693 S.W.2d 787 (Tex. Civ. App.—Ft. Worth, 1985).

**Undue influence** results from a breach of trust or fiduciary capacity. There must be dominion and control exercised over the mind of the person executing the instrument. This may occur, for instance, when a broker fails to inform her principal of an increase in value of the property and takes advantage of the bargain herself. *Ramsey* v. *Gordon*, supra.

**Misrepresentation** or deceit has a whole new meaning since the passage of the infamous Texas Deceptive Trade Practices Act. It is sufficient to say only that the aggrieved party could probably avoid his contractual obligation if the other party violated this sacrosanct pillar of legislation.

It is important to remember that even if the foregoing defenses are not true allegations, the lawsuit that can result can be a lengthy, expensive, and difficult proceeding. In the meantime, the property may be "tied up" so that no sale can occur.

**Delivery.** There is often a question arising as to whether **delivery** is required in contracts. Delivery is usually required, but it is usually not material if the instrument is silent and the parties demonstrate a contrary intent by their acts. *Awad Tex. Enterprises, Inc.* v. *Homart Development Co.*, 589 S.W.2d 817 (Tex. Civ. App.—Dallas, 1979). The key terms to remember are the "offer" and "acceptance," which constitute the mutual assent. Remember that the contract is generally considered to be enforceable when the acceptance of the offer has been communicated to the offeror. This must occur prior to the offer being revoked. Because the intent of the parties can usually be determined during this period of mutual assent, the requirement of delivery isn't material.

# Rules for the Construction of Contracts

Once it has been determined that a legal contract has been formed, the court will make every effort not to strike down the contract unless it was illegal or was made under fraud, duress, or by mistake. *ABS Sherman Properties, Ltd.* v. *Sarris*, 626 S.W.2d 538 (Tex. Civ. App.—Texarkana, 1981). The underlying theory is that if two parties care enough to make a binding contract, and each performs to some extent on that contract, there must have been sufficient intent to warrant enforcement of that contract. As an introduction to contracts, it is helpful to understand some basic "rules of thumb" that courts generally use in interpreting and construing the intent of contracts.

## Reasonable Time

There is a general rule in the law that if the time is not specified, the contract must be performed within a "reasonable" period of time. What is "reasonable" is usually a fact question for the jury to decide and is said to be such time as is necessary and convenient to do what the contract requires to be done, and as soon as circumstances will permit. *Carter* v. *Gerald*, 577 S.W.2d 797 (Tex. Civ. App.—Austin, 1979). It never means an unnecessary delay and needs to be determined by the jury as it applies to the facts of the particular case. *Price* v. *Horace Mann Life Insurance Co.*, 590 S.W.2d 644 (Tex. Civ. App.—Amarillo, 1979).

## Validity

Contracts are always construed in favor of upholding the contract. Forfeitures of contracts are not favored in the law, and if given an equal choice, the court will always choose to uphold the contract rather than strike it down. If there are two contracts that seem to conflict, or two provisions of one contract that seem to conflict, the court will attempt to construe them so that each will be permitted to stand. *Ogden* v. *Dickinson State Bank*, 622 S.W.2d 380 (Tex. 1983).

## Four Corners Doctrine

Another standard construction of contracts is called the **Four Corners Doctrine**. This doctrine states that the instrument must be read in its entirety. No particular provision may be lifted out of context and be construed on its own merits. When you are reading each provision in the contract, every other provision of that contract must be kept in mind also, so that no inequitable constructions will be made on a clause or paragraph contrary to the intent of the rest of that contract. This also applies to separate instruments executed at the same time for the same purpose (deed, deed of trust, and note, for instance), and in the same transaction. They are to be read and construed together. *ABS Sherman Properties, Ltd.* v. *Sarris*, supra.

## Interlineations, "Fill-in-the-Blanks"

All **interlineations** (writing between the lines) of contracts are deemed part of that contract and stand on an equal footing with the remainder of the contract. The same is true of addenda or other instruments that are incorporated by reference in the contract, or attached to the back thereof. There is a difficult problem of proof when there are interlineations and addenda. Good practice suggests that when an interlineation, addendum, or incorporation by reference is made, said interlineation should be initialed by all parties to the contract. In addition, all addenda, or documents incorporated by reference, should be indicated on the face of the contract. Addenda to the document should also be initialed, indicating that all parties to the contract knew which documents were being incorporated.

## Against Maker

When a contract is unclear or ambiguous, and both possible interpretations stand on an equal footing, the court will construe the instrument most strictly against the party who drafted it and is responsible for the language used. This does not mean the court chooses to penalize the person who drew the contract, but merely that in a case of reasonable doubt as to interpretation, the equities will be construed against the drafter of the ambiguous contract. *ABS Sherman Properties, Ltd.* v. *Sarris*, supra.

## Parol Evidence Rule

In construing a contract, as well as in courtroom proceedings, one of the critically important factors in determining interpretations of contractual instruments is what is termed the **parol evidence rule**. Very simply explained, the parol evidence rule stands for the theory that when an agreement has been reduced to writing, parol evidence (oral or additional writings) is not admissible to add to or vary the promises contained in the original instrument. However, the contract must be clear and certain as to its terms, and not ambiguous in order for the parol evidence rule to apply.

This rule is critically important when drafting earnest money contracts. There is very often underlying intent in areas of financing, fixtures, and repairs, which can be agreed to orally and with the best of intentions. However, when one party fails to perform on an implied or oral agreement (even though the agreement may have been considered an important part of the earnest money contract), the court will not allow this evidence to be introduced so that it can construe the terms of the earnest money contract if it is otherwise unambiguous. To be found to be unambiguous, only one meaning must clearly emerge in interpretation of the provision. *Laguarta, Gavrel & Kirk, Inc.* v. *R & P Enterprises*, 596 S.W.2d 517 (Tex. Civ. App.—Houston, 1979). In other words, a person can say whatever he wishes, but if it is not in the contract, he will have a very difficult time of proof and enforcement.

An often overlooked area of the parol evidence rule is that of modifying existing contracts. If the subsequent modification or amendment of an existing unambiguous contract does not properly incorporate or amend the previous contract, it is considered a new and separate agreement and cannot be used as evidence to construe the terms of that contract. To amend a previous contract properly, one must achieve the same formalities as making the original contract; that is, there must be a meeting of the minds, both parties must execute it, and they must have all of the other attributes as if the agreement were a new contract. *Mandril* v. *Kasishke*, 620 S.W.2d 238 (Tex. Civ. App.—Amarillo, 1981). The Statute of Frauds also requires that the modification be in writing, unless it only involves minor, inconsequential changes. *Garcia* v. *Karam*, 276 S.W.2d 255 (Tex. 1955); *Givens* v. *Dougherty*, supra.

## Printed Versus Typed

When a contract uses a printed form contract and typed provisions are put into the contract that conflict with a statement in the form of the contract, the typed provisions will control over the printed provisions since it was the language the parties used and should carry more weight than that of the printed form. *Friedrich* v. *Amoco Production Co.*, 698 S.W.2d 748 (Tex. Civ. App.—Corpus Christi, 1985). The same is true of a handwritten provision versus a typed or printed provision in a contract. The changes usually imply the intent of the parties, possibly done as a last-minute change, to give more effect to prior provisions in the contract, or to clarify same.

## Effective Date

The standard rule for the effective date of the contract is not when the contract is delivered (this is true of deeds and leases, but not of contracts generally). The contract takes effect when it is dated or when both parties have signed it. Note that the TREC-promulgated contract forms are effective when the broker fills in the date!

The foregoing general rules are by no means conclusive, as each fact situation can, of course, impose its own equities and variations. Inevitably, conflicts will arise, and even the foregoing general rules can conflict in many situations. In one case, the court had to construe a conflict between the foregoing general rules when a real estate broker used a form contract on which he typed special provisions. The court had to decide which rule should be applied—the rule that says that typed matter controls over printed matter, or the rule that says the contract should be construed against the maker (the broker). In this particular case, the court held that the rule should be applied that typed matter controls over printed matter instead of the rule of construction against the author. *Innes* v. *Webb*, 538 S.W.2d 237 (Tex. Civ. App.—Corpus Christi, 1976). Unfortunately, this type of problem with earnest money contracts comes up far too often, and great care should be taken to help avoid such situations.

## Legal Effect

There is a lot of confusion as to the validity of a contract once it has been agreed to. In determining the validity and enforceability of a contract, it is generally construed to have one of four legal effects: It may be *valid, void, voidable,* or *unenforceable*.

A **void** contract is a contract that never was and has no legal effect. These contracts lack one of the essential contract elements (legal subject matter, competent parties, consideration, or mutual assent) to the extent that the parties knew it was void on its face. Therefore, a contract for an illegal act is void, as is a contract with a person judicially declared to be insane. Similarly, a forged contract is void, as the party signing the contract was not the legitimate party to enter into the contractual obligation.

The vast majority of contracts held to be invalid are held to be **voidable**. These contracts do not have a patent defect that renders the contract void but have latent defects that can be discovered upon further inquiry and disclosure of additional facts. Contracts by minors are considered to be voidable in Texas at the option of the minor, as are those where a party is determined to be insane at the time of their execution. In the latter case, the insane is not an adjudicated insane (making the contract void) but one who is later determined to have been insane or temporarily insane at the time he signed the contract. When the jury determines that there has been a valid defense to mutual assent (fraud, duress, menace, undue influence, misrepresentation), the contractual obligations are voidable and can be avoided at the option of the aggrieved party. Similarly, Texas law looks at contracts in violation of the Statute of Frauds as voidable when the statute of limitations for the contracts' enforcement has expired.

Texas law recognizes that if contracts are not performed on within the statutory period (generally two years for oral agreements and four years for written agreements), the contracts are no longer enforceable by either party. There is a similar equitable doctrine called **laches**, which is a period of unreasonable delay in enforcing a contract, causing detriment to the other party. *Murray* v. *Murray*, 611 S.W.2d 172 (Tex. Civ. App.—El Paso, 1981); *Mandril* v. *Kasishke*, supra. Instead of a statutory period, however, the period of time is what is "reasonable." That is, if the contract is not performed within a reasonable amount of time, the doctrine of laches may be imposed by a court to render the contract **unenforceable**. Laches cannot be asserted against a governmental entity, however. *Waller* v. *Sanchez*, 618 S.W.2d 407 (Tex. Civ. App.—Corpus Christi, 1981).

The major difference between a contract that is voidable and one that is unenforceable lies in the fact that if an unenforceable obligation has been performed, it may not be avoided. A voidable contract can be avoided after performance if the proper facts can be proven. The remedy for an unenforceable contract is cancellation, while the remedy for a void or voidable contract is reversion, which restores the parties to their former position. *Manges* v. *Guerra*, 621 S.W.2d 652 (Tex. Civ. App.—Waco, 1981).

## Statute of Frauds

The Texas Statute of Frauds specifically provides that any agreement as described in that statute is not enforceable unless the promise or agreement, or a memorandum of it, is: (1) in writing and (2) signed by the person to be charged with the promise or agreement or by someone lawfully authorized to sign for him. The contracts and agreements in the Texas Statute of Frauds that are specifically pertinent for real estate transactions are: (1) a contract for the sale of real estate; (2) a lease of real estate for a term longer than one year; (3) an agreement that is not to be performed within one year from the date of making the agreement; (4) a promise or agreement to pay a commission for the sale or purchase of (a) an oil or a gas mining lease to an oil or gas royalty; (b) minerals; or (c) a mineral interest; and (5) a loan agreement in which the amount involved in the loan exceeds $50,000 in value. The statute applies to modification of contracts, as well as to the contracts themselves. *Vendig* v. *Traylor*, 604 S.W.2d 424 (Tex. Civ. App.—Dallas, 1980); *Givens* v. *Dougherty*, supra.

**Federal Pre-emption—Electronic Transactions.** The federal government has preempted the Texas Statute of Frauds somewhat by authorizing electronic signatures and documents. The **Electronic Records in Global and National Commerce Act** ("UETA") was signed on October 1, 2000 and became effective on March 1, 2001.

This act, popularly referred to as "Esign," has as one of its primary purposes to repeal state law requirements for written instruments as they apply to electronic agreements. The operative language is clear:

"Notwithstanding any statute, regulation, or other rule of law with respect to any transactions in or affecting interstate or foreign commerce

(1) a signature, contract, or other record relating to such transaction may not be denied legal effect, validity or enforceability solely because it is in electronic form; and

(2) a contract relating to such transaction may not be denied legal effect, validity or enforceability solely because an electronic signature or electronic record was used in its formation."

The key term is "transaction." Esign provides a very broad definition:
"The term 'transaction' means an action or set of actions relating to the conduct of a business, consumer or commercial affairs between two or more persons, including any of the following types of conduct.

(A) the sale, lease, exchange, or other disposition of property and intangibles

(B) the sale, lease, exchange or other disposition of any interest in real property, or any combination thereof."

Congress has provided that almost anything can be an electronic signature, binding a party to an agreement. The statutory language states:

> The term 'electronic signature' means an electronic sound, symbol, or process, attached to or logically associated with a contract or other record and executed or adopted by a person with the intent to sign the record.

For instance, if you were sent an email that said: "I'll buy your property at 450 W. Meyer in Dallas for $50,000, and you typed at the top of this message "OK" and hit "return," you might have a binding real estate contract. All you'd have to show is that the typing of the words "OK" indicated my intent to express agreement. The fact that you didn't even type out your name would not matter, since you attached an electronic symbol to a contract. The contract would still have to meet standards of clarity and certainty. Perhaps an informal exchange would not meet those standards in some states. The point, however, is that a relatively simple and perhaps thoughtless act arguably could result in the formation of a relatively serious contract.

Note that the Act only applies to transactions in "interstate commerce." An email message, when it left your computer, could conceivably bounce to Hoboken, then to Geneva, then to Mexico City all on its way to your computer, even if your computer was located in the building next door. Further, it was carried on a variety of communications media commonly associate with interstate transactions. The likelihood is quite strong that the Supreme Court will have difficulty interpreting around the conclusion that email transactions are in interstate commerce.

But many real estate owners are not "well advised" at the time that they are in the throes of negotiating real estate deals. Agents know that all too often there is something on the table before the client shows up for legal advice. Frequently, the presence of the Statute of Frauds has protected such clients basically against themselves. If It's not in writing, it can always be changed to make a more comfortable agreement. Frequently, these situations arise when there has been no part performances or estoppel, and the parties can work out an agreement in a more formal negotiating environment.

**Texas esign.** Texas responded by enacting its own Uniform Electronic Transaction Act. Briefly stated, the federal law preempted state law concerning paper and ink writing and signature requirements to allow both electronic authentication and electronic records. The Federal esign law provides that the federal law preemption of state law may in turn be superseded by state law if the state passes the Uniform Electronic Transactions Act with no substantial modifications. Texas passed the UETA largely intact, so the controlling law for electronic transactions in Texas should no longer be the federal esign law, but the Texas Uniform Electronic Transaction Act. It preempts the state of frauds requirement that real estate documents must be in writing and signed, but only to the extent of allowing the writing and signing to be done electronically.

Texas' modification to the federal esign law provides that (1) notices of default, acceleration, repossession, foreclosure, eviction, or the right to cure, under a credit agreement secured by, or a rental agreement for, a primary residence of the individual and (2) notices of utility cut-off must continue and be in writing under the old statute of frauds. The bill also does not apply to transactions governed by other laws concerning the creation or execution of wills, codicils, or testamentary trusts.

One certainly needs to look to the future in this matter. Electronic closings, recordings and commercial contracts and leases have become common.

# Texas Contracts for the Sale of Real Estate

Now that there has been a preliminary introduction to contracts, it may be a little easier to comprehend the requirements of a contract for the sale of real estate, more commonly called the **earnest money contract**.

The earnest money contract is by far the most important instrument that a real estate agent comes into contact with in the general day-to-day business of real estate practice. Earnest money contracts are, of course, binding obligations; they normally involve substantial amounts of money and very often control the biggest investment a family makes in its lifetime. The importance of this document simply cannot be overemphasized.

## Use of Forms

Even though the earnest money contract has such important legal significance, the drafting of these instruments is usually done by real estate agents and is seldom left to the expertise of attorneys. Attorneys are specifically trained in the field of drafting contracts, and there has been some objection to this practice as performed by real estate agents. An attorney general's opinion, drafted November 1, 1972, stated that:

> The drawing up or supplying of any preliminary or earnest money contract form and the filling in of the blanks for the parties by a real estate dealer may reasonably be deemed suspect and possibly in violation of Section 17 [now Section 1101.654] of the Occupations Code under the existing state court decisions in this field.

However, the attorney general's opinion went on to say that the use of the Texas Real Estate Commission's promulgated form would not constitute a violation of the Texas Real Estate License Act or constitute the illegal practice of law. Standard contract forms were promulgated and are now required by statute to be used when applicable by all licensees,[1] *V.T.C.A., Occupation Code, §1101.654.* In light of the foregoing, it can be ascertained that using the commission-promulgated form is clearly sanctioned, and such use is not a violation of the law. The commission may, however, revoke a license when a licensee fails to use a required contract form, or a form provided by the principal's attorney.

A copy of the commission-promulgated form (No. 20-7) is included in Figure 9.1. Real estate licensees are statutorily required to use, when appropriate, one or more of

---

[1] These forms are not required to be used in the following: (1) transactions involving a principal who provides a different contract form regularly used in the course of a principal's business; (2) transactions in which the licensee is functioning as a principal, not as an agent; and (3) transactions in which an agency of the U.S. government requires a different form to be used.

**FIGURE 9.1 ONE TO FOUR FAMILY RESIDENTIAL CONTRACT.**

02-13-06

PROMULGATED BY THE TEXAS REAL ESTATE COMMISSION (TREC)
**ONE TO FOUR FAMILY RESIDENTIAL CONTRACT (RESALE)**
NOTICE: Not For Use For Condominium Transactions

**1. PARTIES:** _____ (Seller) agrees to sell and convey to _____ (Buyer) and Buyer agrees to buy from Seller the Property described below.

**2. PROPERTY:**
A. LAND: Lot _____ Block _____, _____ Addition, City of _____ , County of _____ , Texas, known as _____ (address/zip code), or as described on attached exhibit.
B. IMPROVEMENTS: The house, garage and all other fixtures and improvements attached to the above-described real property, including without limitation, the following **permanently installed and built-in items,** if any: all equipment and appliances, valances, screens, shutters, awnings, wall-to-wall carpeting, mirrors, ceiling fans, attic fans, mail boxes, television antennas and satellite dish system and equipment, heating and air-conditioning units, security and fire detection equipment, wiring, plumbing and lighting fixtures, chandeliers, water softener system, kitchen equipment, garage door openers, cleaning equipment, shrubbery, landscaping, outdoor cooking equipment, and all other property owned by Seller and attached to the above described real property.
C. ACCESSORIES: The following described related accessories, if any: window air conditioning units, stove, fireplace screens, curtains and rods, blinds, window shades, draperies and rods, controls for satellite dish system, controls for garage door openers, entry gate controls, door keys, mailbox keys, above ground pool, swimming pool equipment and maintenance accessories, and artificial fireplace logs.
D. EXCLUSIONS: The following improvements and accessories will be retained by Seller and removed prior to delivery of possession: _____.

The land, improvements and accessories are collectively referred to as the "Property".

**3. SALES PRICE:**
A. Cash portion of Sales Price payable by Buyer at closing ............... $_____
B. Sum of all financing described below (excluding any loan funding fee or mortgage insurance premium) ........................... $_____
C. Sales Price (Sum of A and B) ........................... $_____

**4. FINANCING:** The portion of Sales Price not payable in cash will be paid as follows: (Check applicable boxes below)
❑ A. THIRD PARTY FINANCING: One or more third party mortgage loans in the total amount of $_____ (excluding any loan funding fee or mortgage insurance premium).
(1) Property Approval: If the Property does not satisfy the lenders' underwriting requirements for the loan(s), this contract will terminate and the earnest money will be refunded to Buyer.
(2) Financing Approval: (Check one box only)
❑ (a) This contract is subject to Buyer being approved for the financing described in the attached Third Party Financing Condition Addendum.
❑ (b) This contract is not subject to Buyer being approved for financing and does not involve FHA or VA financing.
❑ B. ASSUMPTION: The assumption of the unpaid principal balance of one or more promissory notes described in the attached TREC Loan Assumption Addendum.
❑ C. SELLER FINANCING: A promissory note from Buyer to Seller of $_____, secured by vendor's and deed of trust liens, and containing the terms and conditions described in the attached TREC Seller Financing Addendum. If an owner policy of title insurance is furnished, Buyer shall furnish Seller with a mortgagee policy of title insurance.

**5. EARNEST MONEY:** Upon execution of this contract by both parties, Buyer shall deposit $_____ as earnest money with _____, as escrow agent, at _____ (address). Buyer shall deposit additional earnest money of $_____ with escrow agent within _____ days after the effective date of this contract. If Buyer fails to deposit the earnest money as required by this contract, Buyer will be in default.

**6. TITLE POLICY AND SURVEY:**
A. TITLE POLICY: Seller shall furnish to Buyer at ❑ Seller's ❑ Buyer's expense an owner policy of title insurance (Title Policy) issued by _____ (Title Company) in the amount of the Sales Price, dated at or after closing, insuring Buyer

Initialed for identification by Buyer_____ _____ and Seller _____ _____    TREC NO. 20-7

Contract Concerning _____Page 2 of 8    02-13-06
(Address of Property)

against loss under the provisions of the Title Policy, subject to the promulgated exclusions (including existing building and zoning ordinances) and the following exceptions:

(1) Restrictive covenants common to the platted subdivision in which the Property is located.

(2) The standard printed exception for standby fees, taxes and assessments.

(3) Liens created as part of the financing described in Paragraph 4.

(4) Utility easements created by the dedication deed or plat of the subdivision in which the Property is located.

(5) Reservations or exceptions otherwise permitted by this contract or as may be approved by Buyer in writing.

(6) The standard printed exception as to marital rights.

(7) The standard printed exception as to waters, tidelands, beaches, streams, and related matters.

(8) The standard printed exception as to discrepancies, conflicts, shortages in area or boundary lines, encroachments or protrusions, or overlapping improvements. Buyer, at Buyer's expense, may have the exception amended to read, "shortages in area".

B. COMMITMENT:  Within 20 days after the Title Company receives a copy of this contract, Seller shall furnish to Buyer a commitment for title insurance (Commitment) and, at Buyer's expense, legible copies  of restrictive covenants and documents evidencing exceptions in the Commitment (Exception Documents) other than the standard printed exceptions.  Seller authorizes the Title Company to deliver the Commitment and Exception Documents to Buyer at Buyer's address shown in Paragraph 21.  If the Commitment and Exception Documents are not delivered to Buyer within the specified time, the time for delivery will be automatically extended up to 15 days or the Closing Date, whichever is earlier.

C. SURVEY:  The survey must be made by a registered professional land surveyor acceptable to the Title Company and any lender. (Check one box only)

❑ (1) Within _____days after the effective date of this contract, Seller shall furnish to Buyer and Title Company Seller's existing survey of the Property and a Residential Real Property Affidavit promulgated by the Texas Department of Insurance (Affidavit). If the existing survey or Affidavit is not acceptable to Title Company or Buyer's lender, Buyer shall obtain a new survey at ❑ Seller's ❑ Buyer's expense no later than 3 days prior to Closing Date. If Seller fails to furnish the existing survey or Affidavit within the time prescribed, Buyer shall obtain a new survey at Seller's expense no later than 3 days prior to Closing Date.

❑ (2) Within _____ days after the effective date of this contract, Buyer shall obtain a new survey at Buyer's expense. Buyer is deemed to receive the survey on the date of actual receipt or the date specified in this paragraph, whichever is earlier.

❑ (3) Within _____days after the effective date of this contract, Seller, at Seller's expense shall furnish a new survey to Buyer.

D. OBJECTIONS: Buyer may object in writing to defects, exceptions, or encumbrances to title: disclosed on the survey other than items 6A(1) through (7) above; disclosed in the Commitment other than items 6A(1) through (8) above; or which prohibit the following use or activity: _____
_____.
Buyer must object not later than (i) the Closing Date or (ii) _____ days after Buyer receives the Commitment, Exception Documents, and the survey, whichever is earlier. Buyer's failure to object within the time allowed will constitute a waiver of Buyer's right to object; except that the requirements in Schedule C of the Commitment are not waived. Provided Seller is not obligated to incur any expense, Seller shall cure the timely objections of Buyer or any third party lender within 15 days after Seller receives the objections and the Closing Date will be extended as necessary.  If objections are not cured within such 15 day period, this contract will terminate and the earnest money will be refunded to Buyer unless Buyer waives the objections.

E. TITLE NOTICES:

(1) ABSTRACT OR TITLE POLICY: Broker advises Buyer to have an abstract of title covering the Property examined by an attorney of Buyer's selection, or Buyer should be furnished with or obtain a Title Policy.  If a Title Policy is furnished, the Commitment should be promptly reviewed by an attorney of Buyer's choice due to the time limitations on Buyer's right to object.

(2) MANDATORY OWNERS' ASSOCIATION MEMBERSHIP: The Property ❑ is ❑ is not subject to mandatory membership in an owners' association. If the Property is subject to mandatory membership in an owners' association, Seller notifies Buyer under §5.012, Texas Property Code, that, as a purchaser of property in the residential community in which the Property is located, you are obligated to be a member of the owners' association. Restrictive covenants governing the use and occupancy of the Property and a dedicatory instrument governing the establishment, maintenance, and operation of this residential community have been or will be recorded in the Real Property Records of the county in which the Property is located. Copies of the restrictive covenants and dedicatory instrument may be obtained from the county clerk. You are obligated to pay

**FIGURE 9.1 CONTINUED.**

assessments to the owners' association. The amount of the assessments is subject to change. Your failure to pay the assessments could result in a lien on and the foreclosure of the Property. If Buyer is concerned about these matters, the TREC promulgated Addendum for Property Subject to Mandatory Membership in an Owner's Association should be used.

(3) STATUTORY TAX DISTRICTS: If the Property is situated in a utility or other statutorily created district providing water, sewer, drainage, or flood control facilities and services, Chapter 49, Texas Water Code, requires Seller to deliver and Buyer to sign the statutory notice relating to the tax rate, bonded indebtedness, or standby fee of the district prior to final execution of this contract.

(4) TIDE WATERS:  If the Property abuts the tidally influenced waters of the state, §33.135, Texas Natural Resources Code, requires a notice regarding coastal area property to be included in the contract.  An addendum containing the notice promulgated by TREC or required by the parties must be used.

(5) ANNEXATION: If the Property is located outside the limits of a municipality, Seller notifies Buyer under §5.011, Texas Property Code, that the Property may now or later be included in the extraterritorial jurisdiction of a municipality and may now or later be subject to annexation by the municipality. Each municipality maintains a map that depicts its boundaries and extraterritorial jurisdiction. To determine if the Property is located within a municipality's extraterritorial jurisdiction or is likely to be located within a municipality's extraterritorial jurisdiction, contact all municipalities located in the general proximity of the Property for further information.

(6) PROPERTY LOCATED IN A CERTIFICATED SERVICE AREA OF A UTILITY SERVICE PROVIDER:  Notice required by §13.257, Water Code:  The real property, described in Paragraph 2, that you are about to purchase may be located in a certificated water or sewer service area, which is authorized by law to provide water or sewer service to the properties in the certificated area. If your property is located in a certificated area there may be special costs or charges that you will be required to pay before you can receive water or sewer service.  There may be a period required to construct lines or other facilities necessary to provide water or sewer service to your property. You are advised to determine if the property is in a certificated area and contact the utility service provider to determine the cost that you will be required to pay and the period, if any, that is required to provide water or sewer service to your property. The undersigned Buyer hereby acknowledges receipt of the foregoing notice at or before the execution of a binding contract for the purchase of the real property described in Paragraph 2 or at closing of purchase of the real property.

(7) PUBLIC IMPROVEMENT DISTRICTS: If the Property is in a public improvement district, §5.014, Property Code, requires Seller to notify Buyer as follows: As a purchaser of this parcel of real property you are obligated to pay an assessment to a municipality or county for an improvement project undertaken by a public improvement district under Chapter 372, Local  Government Code. The assessment may be due annually or in periodic installments. More information concerning the amount of the assessment and the due dates of that assessment may be obtained from the municipality or county levying the assessment.  The amount of the assessments is subject to change.  Your failure to pay the assessments could result in a lien on and the foreclosure of your property.

**7. PROPERTY CONDITION:**
   A. ACCESS, INSPECTIONS AND UTILITIES:  Seller shall permit Buyer and Buyer's agents access to the Property at reasonable times. Buyer may have the Property inspected by inspectors selected by Buyer and licensed by TREC or otherwise permitted by law to make inspections. Seller at Seller's expense shall turn on existing utilities for inspections.
   B. SELLER'S DISCLOSURE NOTICE PURSUANT TO §5.008, TEXAS PROPERTY CODE (Notice): (Check one box only)
   ☐ (1) Buyer has received the Notice.
   ☐ (2) Buyer has not received the Notice.  Within _____ days after the effective date of this contract, Seller shall deliver the Notice to Buyer. If Buyer does not receive the Notice, Buyer may terminate this contract at any time prior to the closing and the earnest money will be refunded to Buyer. If Seller delivers the Notice, Buyer may terminate this contract for any reason within 7 days after Buyer receives the Notice or prior to the closing, whichever first occurs, and the earnest money will be refunded to Buyer.
   ☐ (3) The Seller is not required to furnish the notice under the Texas Property Code.
   C. SELLER'S DISCLOSURE OF LEAD-BASED PAINT AND LEAD-BASED PAINT HAZARDS is required by Federal law for a residential dwelling constructed prior to  1978.
   D. ACCEPTANCE OF PROPERTY CONDITION: Buyer accepts the Property in its present condition; provided Seller, at Seller's expense, shall complete the following specific repairs and treatments: _____
   _____
   E. LENDER REQUIRED REPAIRS AND TREATMENTS: Unless otherwise agreed in writing,  neither party is obligated to pay for  lender required repairs, which includes treatment for wood

**FIGURE 9.1 CONTINUED.**

destroying insects. If the parties do not agree to pay for the lender required repairs or treatments, this contract will terminate and the earnest money will be refunded to Buyer. If the cost of lender required repairs and treatments exceeds 5% of the Sales Price, Buyer may terminate this contract and the earnest money will be refunded to Buyer.

F. COMPLETION OF REPAIRS AND TREATMENTS:  Unless otherwise agreed in writing, Seller shall complete all agreed repairs and treatments prior to the Closing Date. All required permits must be obtained, and repairs and treatments must be performed by persons who are licensed or otherwise authorized by law to provide such repairs or treatments. At Buyer's election, any transferable warranties received by Seller with respect to the repairs and treatments will be transferred to Buyer at Buyer's expense. If Seller fails to complete any agreed repairs and treatments prior to the Closing Date, Buyer may do so and receive reimbursement from Seller at closing. The Closing Date will be extended up to 15 days, if necessary, to complete repairs and treatments.

G. ENVIRONMENTAL MATTERS: Buyer is advised that the presence of wetlands, toxic substances, including asbestos and wastes or other environmental hazards, or the presence of a threatened or endangered species or its habitat may affect Buyer's intended use of the Property. If Buyer is concerned about these matters, an addendum promulgated by TREC or required by the parties should be used.

H. RESIDENTIAL SERVICE CONTRACTS: Buyer may purchase a residential service contract from a residential service company licensed by TREC. If Buyer purchases a residential service contract, Seller shall reimburse Buyer at closing for the cost of the residential service contract in an amount not exceeding $_____.  Buyer should review any residential service contract for the scope of coverage, exclusions and limitations. **The purchase of a residential service contract is optional. Similar coverage may be purchased from various companies authorized to do business in Texas.**

8. **BROKERS' FEES:** All obligations of the parties for payment of brokers' fees are contained in separate written agreements.

9. **CLOSING:**
   A. The closing of the sale will be on or before _____, 20_____, or within 7 days after objections made under Paragraph 6D have been cured or waived, whichever date is later (Closing Date).  If either party fails to close the sale by the Closing Date, the non-defaulting party may exercise the remedies contained in Paragraph 15.
   B. At closing:
      (1) Seller shall execute and deliver a general warranty deed conveying title to the Property to Buyer and showing no additional exceptions to those permitted in Paragraph 6 and furnish tax statements or certificates showing no delinquent taxes on the Property.
      (2) Buyer shall pay the Sales Price in good funds acceptable to the escrow agent.
      (3) Seller and Buyer shall execute and deliver any notices, statements, certificates, affidavits, releases, loan documents and other documents required of them by this contract, the Commitment or law necessary for the closing of the sale and the issuance of the Title Policy.
   C. Unless expressly prohibited by written agreement, Seller may continue to show the Property and receive, negotiate and accept back up offers.
   D. All covenants, representations and warranties in this contract survive closing.

10. **POSSESSION:** Seller shall deliver to Buyer possession of the Property in its present or required condition, ordinary wear and tear excepted: ❑ upon closing and funding ❑ according to a temporary residential lease form promulgated by TREC or other written lease required by the parties. Any possession by Buyer prior to closing or by Seller after closing which is not authorized by a written lease will establish a tenancy at sufferance relationship between the parties. **Consult your insurance agent prior to change of ownership and possession because insurance coverage may be limited or terminated. The absence of a written lease or appropriate insurance coverage may expose the parties to economic loss.**

11. **SPECIAL PROVISIONS:** (Insert only factual statements and business details applicable to the sale. TREC rules prohibit licensees from adding factual statements or business details for which a contract addendum, lease or other form has been promulgated by TREC for mandatory use.)

**FIGURE 9.1  CONTINUED.**

Contract Concerning _____ Page 5 of 8    02-13-06
(Address of Property)

**12. SETTLEMENT AND OTHER EXPENSES:**
   A. The following expenses must be paid at or prior to closing:
   (1) Expenses payable by Seller (Seller's Expenses):
      (a) Releases of existing liens, including prepayment penalties and recording fees; release of Seller's loan liability; tax statements or certificates; preparation of deed; one-half of escrow fee; and other expenses payable by Seller under this contract.
      (b) Seller shall also pay an amount not to exceed $ _____ to be applied in the following order: Buyer's Expenses which Buyer is prohibited from paying by FHA, VA, Texas Veterans Housing Assistance Program or other governmental loan programs, and then to other Buyer's Expenses as allowed by the lender.
   (2) Expenses payable by Buyer (Buyer's Expenses):
      (a) Loan origination, discount, buy-down, and commitment fees (Loan Fees).
      (b) Appraisal fees; loan application fees; credit reports; preparation of loan documents; interest on the notes from date of disbursement to one month prior to dates of first monthly payments; recording fees; copies of easements and restrictions; mortgagee title policy with endorsements required by lender; loan-related inspection fees; photos; amortization schedules; one-half of escrow fee; all prepaid items, including required premiums for flood and hazard insurance, reserve deposits for insurance, ad valorem taxes and special governmental assessments; final compliance inspection; courier fee; repair inspection; underwriting fee; wire transfer fee; expenses incident to any loan; and other expenses payable by Buyer under this contract.
   B. Buyer shall pay Private Mortgage Insurance Premium (PMI), VA Loan Funding Fee, or FHA Mortgage Insurance Premium (MIP) as required by the lender.
   C. If any expense exceeds an amount expressly stated in this contract for such expense to be paid by a party, that party may terminate this contract unless the other party agrees to pay such excess. Buyer may not pay charges and fees expressly prohibited by FHA, VA, Texas Veterans Housing Assistance Program or other governmental loan program regulations.

**13. PRORATIONS:** Taxes for the current year, interest, maintenance fees, assessments, dues and rents will be prorated through the Closing Date. The tax proration may be calculated taking into consideration any change in exemptions that will affect the current year's taxes. If taxes for the current year vary from the amount prorated at closing, the parties shall adjust the prorations when tax statements for the current year are available. If taxes are not paid at or prior to closing, Buyer shall pay taxes for the current year.

**14. CASUALTY LOSS:** If any part of the Property is damaged or destroyed by fire or other casualty after the effective date of this contract, Seller shall restore the Property to its previous condition as soon as reasonably possible, but in any event by the Closing Date. If Seller fails to do so due to factors beyond Seller's control, Buyer may (a) terminate this contract and the earnest money will be refunded to Buyer (b) extend the time for performance up to 15 days and the Closing Date will be extended as necessary or (c) accept the Property in its damaged condition with an assignment of insurance proceeds and receive credit from Seller at closing in the amount of the deductible under the insurance policy. Seller's obligations under this paragraph are independent of any other obligations of Seller under this contract.

**15. DEFAULT:** If Buyer fails to comply with this contract, Buyer will be in default, and Seller may (a) enforce specific performance, seek such other relief as may be provided by law, or both, or (b) terminate this contract and receive the earnest money as liquidated damages, thereby releasing both parties from this contract. If, due to factors beyond Seller's control, Seller fails within the time allowed to make any non-casualty repairs or deliver the Commitment, or survey, if required of Seller, Buyer may (a) extend the time for performance up to 15 days and the Closing Date will be extended as necessary or (b) terminate this contract as the sole remedy and receive the earnest money. If Seller fails to comply with this contract for any other reason, Seller will be in default and Buyer may (a) enforce specific performance, seek such other relief as may be provided by law, or both, or (b) terminate this contract and receive the earnest money, thereby releasing both parties from this contract.

**16. MEDIATION:** It is the policy of the State of Texas to encourage resolution of disputes through alternative dispute resolution procedures such as mediation. Any dispute between Seller and Buyer related to this contract which is not resolved through informal discussion ☐will ☐will not be submitted to a mutually acceptable mediation service or provider. The parties to the mediation shall bear the mediation costs equally. This paragraph does not preclude a party from seeking equitable relief from a court of competent jurisdiction.

**17. ATTORNEY'S FEES:** The prevailing party in any legal proceeding related to this contract is entitled to recover reasonable attorney's fees and all costs of such proceeding incurred by the prevailing party.

Initialed for identification by Buyer_____  _____ and Seller _____  _____          TREC NO. 20-7

**FIGURE 9.1 CONTINUED.**

Contract Concerning _____ Page 6 of 8   02-13-06
(Address of Property)

**18. ESCROW:**

A. ESCROW: The escrow agent is not (i) a party to this contract and does not have liability for the performance or nonperformance of any party to this contract, (ii) liable for interest on the earnest money and (iii) liable for the loss of any earnest money caused by the failure of any financial institution in which the earnest money has been deposited unless the financial institution is acting as escrow agent.

B. EXPENSES: At closing, the earnest money must be applied first to any cash down payment, then to Buyer's Expenses and any excess refunded to Buyer. If no closing occurs, escrow agent may require payment of unpaid expenses incurred on behalf of the parties and a written release of liability of escrow agent from all parties.

C. DEMAND: Upon termination of this contract, either party or the escrow agent may send a release of earnest money to each party and the parties shall execute counterparts of the release and deliver same to the escrow agent. If either party fails to execute the release, either party may make a written demand to the escrow agent for the earnest money. If only one party makes written demand for the earnest money, escrow agent shall promptly provide a copy of the demand to the other party. If escrow agent does not receive written objection to the demand from the other party within 15 days, escrow agent may disburse the earnest money to the party making demand reduced by the amount of unpaid expenses incurred on behalf of the party receiving the earnest money and escrow agent may pay the same to the creditors. If escrow agent complies with the provisions of this paragraph, each party hereby releases escrow agent from all adverse claims related to the disbursal of the earnest money.

D. DAMAGES: Any party who wrongfully fails or refuses to sign a release acceptable to the escrow agent within 7 days of receipt of the request will be liable to the other party for liquidated damages of three times the amount of the earnest money.

E. NOTICES: Escrow agent's notices will be effective when sent in compliance with Paragraph 21. Notice of objection to the demand will be deemed effective upon receipt by escrow agent.

**19. REPRESENTATIONS:** Seller represents that as of the Closing Date (a) there will be no liens, assessments, or security interests against the Property which will not be satisfied out of the sales proceeds unless securing payment of any loans assumed by Buyer and (b) assumed loans will not be in default. If any representation of Seller in this contract is untrue on the Closing Date, Seller will be in default.

**20. FEDERAL TAX REQUIREMENTS:** If Seller is a "foreign person," as defined by applicable law, or if Seller fails to deliver an affidavit to Buyer that Seller is not a "foreign person," then Buyer shall withhold from the sales proceeds an amount sufficient to comply with applicable tax law and deliver the same to the Internal Revenue Service together with appropriate tax forms. Internal Revenue Service regulations require filing written reports if currency in excess of specified amounts is received in the transaction.

**21. NOTICES:** All notices from one party to the other must be in writing and are effective when mailed to, hand-delivered at, or transmitted by facsimile or electronic transmission as follows:

| **To Buyer** at: _____ | **To Seller** at: _____ |
|---|---|
| _____ | _____ |
| _____ | _____ |
| _____ | _____ |
| Telephone: ( ) _____ | Telephone: ( ) _____ |
| Facsimile: ( ) _____ | Facsimile: ( ) _____ |
| E-mail: _____ | E-mail: _____ |

**FIGURE 9.1 CONTINUED.**

Contract Concerning _____ Page 7 of 8    02-13-06
(Address of Property)

**22. AGREEMENT OF PARTIES:** This contract contains the entire agreement of the parties and cannot be changed except by their written agreement.  Addenda which are a part of this contract are (Check all applicable boxes):

❑ Third Party Financing Condition Addendum

❑ Seller Financing Addendum

❑ Loan Assumption Addendum
❑ Buyer's Temporary Residential Lease
❑ Seller's Temporary Residential Lease

❑ Addendum for Sale of Other Property by Buyer

❑ Addendum for Seller's Disclosure of Information on Lead-based Paint and Lead-based Paint Hazards as Required by Federal Law

❑ Addendum for Property Subject to Mandatory Membership in an Owners' Association

❑ Environmental Assessment, Threatened or Endangered Species and Wetlands Addendum

❑ Addendum for "Back-Up" Contract
❑ Addendum for Coastal Area Property
❑ Addendum for Property Located Seaward of the Gulf Intracoastal Waterway
❑ Addendum for Release of Liability on Assumption of FHA, VA, or Conventional Loan Restoration of Seller's Entitlement for VA Guaranteed Loan
❑ Other (list): _____
_____

**23. TERMINATION OPTION:** For nominal consideration, the receipt of which is hereby acknowledged by Seller, and Buyer's agreement to pay Seller $_____ (Option Fee) within 2 days after the effective date of this contract, Seller grants Buyer the unrestricted right to terminate this contract by giving notice of termination to Seller within _____ days after the effective date of this contract.  If no dollar amount is stated as the Option Fee or if Buyer fails to pay the Option Fee within the time prescribed, this paragraph will not be a part of this contract and Buyer shall not have the unrestricted right to terminate this contract. If Buyer gives notice of termination within the time prescribed, the Option Fee will not be refunded; however, any earnest money will be refunded to Buyer. The Option Fee ❑will ❑will not be credited to the Sales Price at closing. **Time is of the essence for this paragraph and strict compliance with the time for performance is required.**

**24. CONSULT AN ATTORNEY:** Real estate licensees cannot give legal advice. READ THIS CONTRACT CAREFULLY. If you do not understand the effect of this contract, consult an attorney BEFORE signing.

Buyer's
Attorney is: _____

_____

Telephone: (___) _____

Facsimile: (___) _____

E-mail: _____

Seller's
Attorney is: _____

_____

Telephone: (___) _____

Facsimile: (___) _____

E-mail: _____

EXECUTED the _____day of _____, 20____ (EFFECTIVE DATE).
(BROKER: FILL IN THE DATE OF FINAL ACCEPTANCE.)

_____    _____
Buyer                        Seller

_____    _____
Buyer                        Seller

The form of this contract has been approved by the Texas Real Estate Commission.  TREC forms are intended for use only by trained real estate licensees. No representation is made as to the legal validity or adequacy of any provision in any specific transactions. It is not intended for complex transactions. Texas Real Estate Commission, P.O. Box 12188, Austin, TX 78711-2188, 1-800-250-8732 or (512) 459-6544 (http://www.trec.state.tx.us) TREC NO. 20-7. This form replaces TREC NO. 20-6.

TREC NO. 20-7

**FIGURE 9.1 CONTINUED.**

Contract Concerning _____ Page 8 of 8   02-13-06
                              (Address of Property)

## BROKER INFORMATION AND RATIFICATION OF FEE

Listing Broker has agreed to pay Other Broker _____ of the total sales price when Listing Broker's fee is received. Escrow Agent is authorized and directed to pay Other Broker from Listing Broker's fee at closing.

| Other Broker _____ License No. | Listing Broker _____ License No. |
|---|---|
| represents ☐ Buyer only as Buyer's agent | represents ☐ Seller and Buyer as an intermediary |
| ☐ Seller as Listing Broker's subagent | ☐ Seller only as Seller's agent |

Associate _____ Telephone          Listing Broker _____ Telephone

Broker's Address _____             Listing Associate's Office Address _____ Facsimile

City _____ State _____ Zip              City _____ State _____ Zip

Facsimile _____                   Email Address _____

Email Address _____               Selling Associate _____ Telephone

                                            Selling Associate's Office Address _____ Facsimile

                                            City _____ State _____ Zip

                                            Email Address _____

### OPTION FEE RECEIPT

Receipt of $_____ (Option Fee) in the form of _____ is acknowledged.

_____        _____
Seller or Listing Broker                Date

### CONTRACT AND EARNEST MONEY RECEIPT

Receipt of ☐ Contract and ☐ $_____ Earnest Money in the form of _____ is acknowledged.

Escrow Agent: _____        Date: _____

By: _____        _____
                                                     Email Address

_____            Telephone (_____) _____
Address

_____            Facsimile: (_____) _____
City                    State          Zip

TREC NO. 20-7

the standard contract forms in real estate transactions. For a more in-depth discussion of filling in the blanks of these forms, there are other books that cover the topic in greater detail.[2]

**Computer Programs** A Real Estate Commission regulation provides that computer-driven printers can produce the TREC-promulgated forms under the following guidelines:

1. A computer filer program containing the form text must not allow the end-user direct access to the text of the form and may only permit the user to insert language in blanks in the forms.

2. Typefaces or fonts must appear to be identical to those used by the commission in printed proofs of the particular form.

3. The text and number of pages must be identical to those used by the commission in printed proofs of the particular form.

4. The spacing, length of blanks, borders, and placement of text on the page must appear to be identical to those used by the commission in printed proofs of the form.

5. The name and address of the person or firm responsible for the developing of the software program must be legibly printed below the border at the bottom of each page in no smaller than 6point type and in no larger than 10-point type.

6. The text of the form must be obtained from a proof of the form bearing a control number assigned by the commission.

7. The control number of each proof must appear on all forms reproduced from the proof, including forms reproduced by computer-driven printers.

8. Forms approved or promulgated by the commission would be reproduced with the following changes or additions only:

   a. The business name or logo of a broker, organization, or printer may appear at the top of the form outside the border; and

   b. The broker's name may be inserted in any blank provided for that purpose.[3]

# Requirements of Texas Contracts

**Oral Contracts** If you recall the discussion in a previous section of this chapter, you will remember that there was a general requirement that all contracts affecting the transfer of real estate must be in writing, in order to comply with the Statute of Frauds. We will depart from this basic underlying theory just long enough to prove that there are exceptions to every rule. There is such a thing as an **oral earnest money contract** (horror of horrors!). There are basically three requirements to enforce an oral earnest money contract, and these all must exist simultaneously. *Hooks* v. *Bridgewater*, 229 S.W. 1114 (Tex. 1921):

1. There must be payment of the consideration, whether it be in money or services; and

2. The possession of the subject property must be taken by the purchaser; and

---

[2] Charles J. Jacobus, Joseph E. Goeters, and John P. Wiedemer, Keeping Current with Texas Real Estate, updated annually, South-Western Publishing.

[3] TREC Rules §537.11(h).

3. The purchaser must have made payment and valuable improvements on the property with the seller's consent.

Payment of the consideration in full (item 1 above) is not required if the other requirements are met. *Cheatwood* v. *De Los Santos*, 561 S.W.2d 273 (Tex. Civ. App.—Eastland, 1978). While the reader is scratching his or her head in bewilderment, we will attempt to explain a fact situation under which an oral earnest money contract could be enforced:

> Vendee agrees to pay vendor $10,000 as full purchase price for vendor's house. Vendee moves in, takes possession of that house, and then constructs some valuable improvement to that property with the vendor's consent. Vendor subsequently tries to renounce the sale and get his property back. Since there was nothing in writing to enforce the conveyance by deed or other acceptable means of property transfer, the court will seek to uphold an oral earnest money contract that vendee can specifically enforce.

Although the above situation may seem rather bizarre, it must be remembered that there are a lot of people who buy real estate not knowing that they are supposed to have a deed or earnest money contract, or any other evidence of title. Most experienced real estate practitioners would probably not be involved in a situation of this type. It is important only to realize that oral earnest money contracts can exist, but under very strict guidelines. No reasonable real estate agent, attorney, or well-informed client should ever rely on an oral earnest money contract, except as a last resort.

**Express Contracts.** **Express contracts** are, of course, written contracts. As our discussion comes back into more identifiable current business practices, it should be pointed out that in earnest money contracts, as in all other real estate instruments, Texas courts have established specific and basic requirements that must be satisfied before such contracts will be considered to be enforceable in the State of Texas. These requirements are as follows:

1. *There must be a written instrument* (the only exceptions are esign, and is the one noted above); and

2. *The instrument must be signed by the party to be charged.* This means that the person against whom the instrument is being enforced must have signed the contract; for instance, if A and B contract to sell real estate, and only A has signed the contract, it can reasonably be assumed that B could enforce the contract against A, but A could not enforce the contract against B until B signs the contract. With one signature on the contract, it is now a standing offer, which B can accept at any time by simply signing his name (provided that this was within the guidelines of acceptances described above); and

3. *There must be evidence of an intent to convey an interest in the real estate at some time in the future.* This requirement generally meets the consideration guidelines in that one party offers to give up his money while the other party offers to convey her interest in some real estate at a future date; and

4. *There must be an identifiable grantor and grantee.* The grantor and grantee must, of course, be identifiable and be competent as described earlier; and

5. *The subject matter to be conveyed must be identifiable.* This, of course, is the requirement of a proper legal description so that there can be no mistake as to which property is the subject matter of the contract.

Once these formalities have been met, the contract is considered specific enough to be enforceable in a court of law.

# Provisions of Contracts for Sale

As real estate agents know, most earnest money contracts go into much greater depth than the foregoing requirements, and a much more in-depth discussion of each of these requirements, particularly as they pertain to the TREC-promulgated forms, is necessary to clarify and understand the need for each of these provisions.

**Legal Description.** Legal descriptions were discussed in detail in Chapter 4. Legal sufficiency of the description of the property is essential to any contract that relates to real estate. The legal description must be contained in the instrument itself, or it may refer to another instrument from which the data to describe the property may be obtained with reasonable certainty. It is not necessary that the property be described beyond all reasonable doubt, but it must be described with reasonable certainty so that a person familiar with the locality can identify the property. *Foster* v. *Bullard*, 496 S.W.2d 724 (Tex. Civ. App.—Austin, 1973); *Major Investments, Inc.* v. *De Castillo*, 673 S.W.2d 276 (Tex. Civ. App.—Corpus Christi, 1984). A recital of ownership may be sufficient, or a map attached to the contract may be used as long as the map contains the necessary descriptive information.

Generally, if a metes-and-bounds description is required, the foregoing rules will be sufficient. In most residential situations, a lot and block number in a specific, recorded, and identifiable subdivision within a county will be sufficient. *Riebe* v. *Foale*, 508 S.W.2d 175 (Tex. Civ. App.—Corpus Christi, 1974). Of course, as a general rule, a street address, by itself, is not sufficiently specific to be enforceable. The TREC-promulgated forms provide for a lot and block description as well as a street address. When filling in the blanks of the form, an agent should be careful the two references do not conflict.

One of the exceptions to the parol evidence rule, however, can help to clarify problems in legal descriptions. As long as the instrument does contain the legal description, the court will allow parol evidence to explain the words and to identify the land. *Littlejohn* v. *Kariel*, 568 S.W.2d 452 (Tex. Civ. App.—Waco, 1978).

The real estate agent must also remember to have adequate descriptions of any items of personalty that are to be included in the sale of the property, and he should also note a requirement for a bill of sale to be executed by the seller.

**Financial Considerations.** The TREC-promulgated form provides three choices: (1) Third Party Financing, (2) Assumption, or (3) Seller Financing. Rather than including all of the financing provisions in the body of the contract, it now refers to the applicable addenda, which can be attached to the contract.

This Third Party Financing provision breaks the financing contingency two different contingencies; one is whether or not the property (the condition of the house, or appraised value) satisfies the lender's underwriting requirements, notwithstanding the buyer's ability to qualify for the loan. There is no time limit on this contingency. If a lender determines on the day of closing that the property doesn't satisfy the lender's underwriting requirements, this contingency has not been satisfied (the buyer has an "out" until the day of closing, depending on the lender's underwriting requirements). The second contingency is for the buyer to qualify for the loan (credit history, credit score, etc.).

If there is a financing contingency, the contract requires the use of the new Third Party Financing Condition Addendum. Note that this Addendum creates contingencies for conventional financing, Texas Veterans Housing assistance Program Loans, FHA financing, and VA guaranteed financing.

There is also a provision (Paragraph 4.A.[2]) that eliminates the buyer's contingency for financing. Presumably, if Box 4.A.(2) is checked, the buyer either has the cash to close or has financing already in place. It might be construed as a representation to the seller of the buyer's financial ability to close. If you cannot qualify for a loan after making this representation, does it become a deceptive trade practice? This may create an unexpected liability for a buyer.

If the buyer is going to assume the loan, the contract now requires the utilization of the Loan Assumption Addendum. Note that it gives the seller (rather than the lender) the right to approve buyer's credit. If the assumed loan varies in an amount greater than $350 at closing, either party may terminate the contract and the earnest money will be refunded to the buyer unless the other party elects to eliminate the excess by an appropriate adjustment at the closing. There are also contingencies involved in any assumption fee that may be required by the lender. If there is an existing escrow account, the escrow account is required to be transferred to the buyer without any deficiency and the buyer is to reimburse the seller for the amount of the transferred account at closing.

In the Seller Financing Addendum, there are requirements for credit documentation and credit approval, and it gives the buyer the right to prepay the promissory note holder in part at any time without penalty. It also has automatic provisions for late payment fees along with the payment provisions that are required in the promissory note.

The addendum also has specific choices for the terms of the Deed of Trust regarding property transfers (due-on-transfer clauses) and tax and insurance escrows, so that the seller can be assured that the taxes and insurance are current and paid timely each year.

When the earnest money contract is contingent upon the buyer securing a third-party loan, the buyer implicitly promises to make application for the loan and to diligently pursue obtaining the loan. If the buyer fails to exercise this diligence, or causes a cancellation of his loan, he may not recover his earnest money because of his failure to obtain that loan. *Williford* v. *Walker*, 499 S.W.2d 190 (Tex. Civ. App.—Corpus Christi, 1973). If the purchaser has applied for the loan and is rejected, though, the deal is over. There is no duty to apply again. *Watkins* v. *Williamson*, 869 S.W.2d 383 (Tex. App.—Dallas, 1993).

However, if the sale is other than one for cash, and no third-party loan is involved, it probably involves an assumption of or "subject to" existing seller financing. When such is the case, it is very important that all the terms of the purchase price are clearly set out. These requirements include the down payment, the terms of the note (to be assumed or to be newly incurred), the balance remaining on the note, and the identification of the type of mortgage to be utilized.

On the other hand, if the purchaser is having difficulty securing financing approval, he has a right to terminate the contract at his option. There have been several Texas cases where the seller has attempted to take advantage of the buyer's inability to obtain financing to cancel the contract. Financing contingencies tend to run in favor of the purchaser. It only makes the contract avoidable at the purchaser's option in the event financing is not obtained. The seller cannot take advantage of this contingency. *Renouf* v. *Martini*, 577 S.W.2d 803 (Tex. Civ. App.—Houston, 1979); *Smith* v. *Nash*, 571 S.W.2d 372 (Tex. Civ. App.—Texarkana, 1978). It should also be pointed out that the Third Party Financing Addendum form provides that the purchaser's financing contingencies are not satisfied (financing is not approved by the lender) until *all* loan requirements are satisfied. There is no partial approval provided for, so the loan is not approved until it is approved!

**Title Matters.** Section 1101.555 of the Real Estate License Act requires certain title matters to be disclosed before the real estate agent can maintain an action for a commission. Therefore, from an agent's point of view, this is a critical inclusion in the earnest money contract. *Jones* v. *Del Anderson and Associates*, supra. The TREC-promulgated forms include this advice in paragraph 6.E.(1).

Beyond this, "title" means much more than a title policy or mere ownership of the property. It encompasses all matters that affect the title and use of the subject property. There are frequent considerations of reservations of mineral rights, restrictions on land use, homestead rights, leasehold interests, liens, and boundary disputes. The TREC-promulgated contract requires a title policy insuring the buyer against loss, and making all encumbrances (beyond the standard exceptions, specified in paragraph 6 of the TREC form) subject to the purchaser's approval, or the examination of the abstract by the purchaser's attorney. If no exceptions are specified in the contract, it may be interpreted to mean a title policy with no exceptions. *Suiter* v. *Gregory*, 279 S.W.2d 902 (Tex. Civ. App.—Galveston, 1955). The TREC earnest money contracts require the seller to cure all title defects to the buyer's satisfaction prior to closing the sale. If they cannot be cured, the buyer has the option to terminate the contract.

If a title company is to be used, the normal procedure is for the seller to purchase the title policy (it is his certification that the title is good), but it is usually the purchaser's prerogative as to which title company to use. Purchasers are the ones who are having the title insured. Therefore, they should be careful to select a title company that they know is solvent, reputable, and accommodating to their needs.

Paragraph 6.A.(8), provides that the buyer, at buyer's expense, to have the title insurance exception as to "discrepancies, conflicts, shortages in area for boundary lines, encroachments or protrusions, or overlapping of improvements" can be amended to read only "shortages in area." The issue presented is a rather complex one, and now real estate licensees are going to have to become very familiar with this issue because many buyers, particularly those from other states, might ask about this provision. The title commitment form contains an explanation of the coverage.

The initial issue involves title insurance coverage. The standard owner's policy of title insurance has an exception for "discrepancies, conflicts, shortages in areas for boundary lines, encroachments or protrusions, or overlapping of improvements," which means that the buyer does not have title insurance coverage for most minor encroachment issues (e.g., fences, garage eaves, deck encroachments onto power line easements, roof encroachments over building lines, and misaligned driveways). Many buyers are surprised that this coverage is not provided, but the coverage traditionally has not been available in Texas unless the buyer pays an additional premium and provides the title insurer with a staked, on-the-ground survey. This could mean a considerable additional expense for the Buyer. If this additional coverage is requested, the title insurance company will review the survey to determine whether there are any conflicts or encroachments. If a conflict exists, the title insurance company may except to a specific encroachment or choose to insure against enforcement of any third party's rights regarding that encroachment. If there is a subsequent attempt at enforcement, the title insurance company will defend them against that enforcement by another party.

If a licensee represents a buyer, they may want to pay particular attention to this new provision. Many buyers tend to be extremely picky, and they are firmly convinced that they do not have good title if there is a 3-inch encroachment of a pool deck into a power line right-of-way. The fact is, they don't have good title if this exists, but, as we just previously discussed, the title insurance company can insure against any damages as a result of the encroachment. Some buyers, however, will worry about their ability to sell the property in the future with the encumbrances and will choose not to purchase.

**Property Condition.** Paragraph 7.A. provides for an absolute right for the buyer to have inspections and access to utility by an inspector "licensed by TREC or otherwise permitted by law to make such inspections." This may prevent the "setup" of an uncle or cousin from doing a bad inspection to create a better negotiating position for the buyer. It does, however, allow for a qualified engineer who is permitted by law to make such inspections but is not licensed as an inspector to perform these inspections. Please note that this paragraph also provides for reinspection after the repairs have been made. *Paragraph 7.A. does not make inspections or re-inspections a contingency.* However, if the property does have significant defects, the buyer may have a cause of action against the seller for misrepresentation or failure to disclose those defects.

Paragraph 7.B. provides for the statutorily required seller's disclosure, including paragraph (3), to provide for those instances where a seller is not required to furnish the seller's disclosure form.

Paragraph 7.C. is also revised and confirms the seller's obligation to comply with the lead-based paint disclosure. There is a box to check as to whether or not the disclosure is attached.

Federal law does not require the addendum for property constructed after January 1, 1978; property sold at foreclosure; the sale of a zero bedroom dwelling with a sleeping unit that is not separated from the living area; and housing for the elderly or disabled where children under the age of six are not expected to reside.

Paragraph 7.D. provides that the buyer accepts the property "in its present condition." Subject to specified repairs the buyer may request, this paragraph has been interpreted as creating an "as is" provision. The burden of inspection and repairs falls on the buyer and the buyer's inspectors and/or agents. As a buyer's agent, this may be critically important that Paragraph 23 (discussed later) is utilized to provide an option for termination by the buyer.

Paragraph 7.E. provides for lender required repairs and provides that the buyer can terminate the contract if the lender required repairs exceed five percent of the sales price. If lender required repairs are not made, the loan won't be approved, and the buyer may avoid performance by exercising the financing contingency set out in Paragraph 4.A.(1). If the repair does not exceed 5 percent, what happens? As a practical matter, the buyer can't get the loan, so the deal is over (i.e., you probably can't successfully sue the buyer who can't get financing) because of the condition of the house, and the seller may have liability for failure to disclose the defect.

Paragraph 7.F. provides for completion of repairs and treatments, and additionally provides that the repairs and treatments must be performed by persons who regularly provide such services, hopefully eliminating "Uncle Elmo the Handyman" from making these repairs. There is also a provision for all transferable warranties to be transferred to the buyer, at the buyer's expense. Note that if the seller fails to complete any agreed repairs prior to the Closing Date, the buyer has the right to do so and receive reimbursement from the seller at closing. This apparently is without regard to the expense, and it seems to give the buyer the unilateral right to do any repairs that are "agreed to." It also allows the Closing date to be extended up to 15 days to complete those repairs and treatments. There is a practical problem to this. What if the seller won't let the buyer in to make the repairs? What if the buyer pays an unusually high price for repair. It may be wise to provide an "agreed to" value for those repairs in a contract amendment in order to eliminate conflicts at the closing.

**Earnest Money.** There is no legal requirement for **earnest money** in a contract. It has also been held that even the deposit of the earnest money is not a condition precedent to performance, *Hudson* v. *Wakefield*, 645 S.W.2d 427 (Tex. 1983), although the TREC-promulgated forms make the failure to deposit the earnest money a default on the part of the buyer. It is customary to put in a certain amount of earnest money to assure the seller that the purchaser is, in fact, serious about buying the property. Provisions in most earnest money contracts provide that in the event a purchaser does not perform, the earnest money should go to the seller as liquidated damages. The amount of escrow deposited, or even the requirement of escrow deposited, is always subject to negotiation between the parties.

When the earnest money is deposited, the title company normally serves as the escrow agent. However, other parties may perform this function if it is acceptable to the parties. One party's attorney, a broker, or a financial institution can serve this same function, particularly when the closing is not to take place at a title company. The escrow agent usually represents neither party and is trusted by both sides of the transaction.

Another consideration concerning the earnest money provision of the contract may involve the type of earnest money to be used. Earnest money deposits other than cash often include a letter of credit, a certificate of deposit, a check or bank draft, and sometimes a promissory note, made due and payable upon the date of closing.

Normally, if the seller defaults, the earnest money is returned to the purchaser. However, a significant factor concerning the deposit of earnest money involves the escrow agent's obligation to protect the earnest money and the interests of the parties involved. Regardless of the facts surrounding a default in an earnest money contract, most escrow agents are very reluctant to release the earnest money to either party without the other party's written consent. No matter how blatant or obvious the breach of the contract may be, one will seldom find that an escrow agent will readily forward the earnest money to either party unless he (the escrow agent) is adequately protected by some other agreement, affidavit, bond, or other assurance. It happens all too often that a purchaser simply backs out of a sale but will not sign a written consent to allow the earnest money to be forwarded to the seller. When this happens, there is very little available to the seller as a remedy except at the courthouse. Note that paragraph 18 of the TREC form deals with this issue in some detail.

**Representations.** There are often representations in earnest money contracts that the property is in good condition. Note paragraph 19 of the TREC form. These representations are sometimes supported by a further representation that the seller will complete the repair of certain items in the house, building, or whatever might be the subject of the sale. It should be noted that there are distinct differences between a representation and a warranty. A representation may hinder the closing or create certain verbal adversities, whereas a warranty generally gives the purchaser a certain damage claim. *Fant* v. *Howell*, 547 S.W.2d 261 (Tex. 1977).

Although the number of representations or warranties that could be contained in earnest money contracts are as vast as the imagination could conceive, great care should be taken by the agent to see that both parties have their representations very clearly stated. There should be specific provisions made for remedies in the event one of the representations is not true or is not performed as required by the contract.

Representations and covenants are often omitted altogether by granting the purchaser a right of inspection prior to the closing, and agreeing to buy the property "as is."

**Closing. Closing** is the term normally given to the process of consummating the sale of real estate. The provision in the TREC form pertaining to a closing specifies the date, an automatic extension if needed for completing the loan requirements, and a provision that the contract becomes voidable at the option of either party if the other party fails to close. Other specific provisions relating to the closing include right to possession of the real estate and requirements for the documentation needed at the closing (usually including the deed, mortgage procedures, assignments, bills of sale, and application of escrow funds). There may be additional provisions for surveys, delivery of title policy, and allocation of expenses to be borne by each party. The expenses include the attorney's fees, brokerage fees, survey fees, inspection fees, proration of taxes, utilities and insurance, and recording and escrow fees. These provisions are found in paragraph 12 of the TREC form.

**Option to Terminate.** This paragraph is somewhat unique. It gives the Buyer (in consideration for the payment of an option fee to the seller) the right to terminate the contract within the specified number of days. Note that if the blanks of this contract are not filled in, the buyer does not have the termination option; or if, for whatever reason, the buyer has not paid the option fee, there is no right to terminate. Therefore, if the seller does not receive the option money (or the check bounces) or the contract blanks are not filled in, *this is a binding earnest money contract on both parties, subject to the conditions of the agreement.*

The burden is on the buyer to give notice of the termination within the time specified, and there is a choice as to whether or not the option fee will be credited to the sales price at closing. The appropriate form has been promulgated by TREC as Form No. 38-1. If the buyer fails to give the notice, the right to terminate is waived. Buyer's agents, mark your calendars!

The size of the option fee is always negotiable, and it is always prudent to negotiate an option period long enough to allow for inspections and to obtain costs for repairs. BUT . . . if the buyer finds that the need for extensive repairs exist, the buyer should timely give notice of termination, or amend the Earnest Money Contract.

**Time Is of the Essence.** Unless a contract clearly indicates that time is of the essence, it will not be construed to be so. *Helsley* v. *Anderson*, 519 S.W.2d 130 (Tex. Civ. App.—Dallas, 1975). However, in an option contract, time is always of the essence, *Tabor* v. *Ragle*, 526 S.W.2d 670 (Tex. Civ. App.—Ft. Worth, 1975), although the stipulated time limit may be extended by agreement of the parties. The TREC-promulgated form does not provide that time is of the essence (except for Paragraph 23), and, except in very rare circumstances, it should never be added.

**Assignment.** Unless otherwise provided for, contracts for the sale of real property are assignable. However, when the sale is to be made on credit or other condition of performance by one of the parties, the contract is normally not considered to be assignable unless made specifically assignable by its terms. *Farrell* v. *Evans*, 517 S.W.2d 585 (Tex. Civ. App.—Houston, 1974).

**Contingencies.** Purchasers often desire to tie up the seller's property for a "free look" by putting unreasonable or frivolous contingencies in the contract for sale. These contingencies may be solely at the purchaser's option, such that the purchaser has no obligation at all. For instance, the purchaser may make his contract:

> . . . contingent upon the approval of purchaser's attorney. In the event said
> approval is not obtained, this contract shall become null and void, at the purchaser's
> option.

This type of contingency contains no time for performance, does not name the attorney, and gives no rights at all to the seller.

Such contingencies are not only vague and ambiguous, but they may also be complicated by unexpected legal problems. If there is a contingency, the law generally imposes a standard of reasonable diligence on the purchaser, regardless of the terms of the contract. *Black Lake Pipe Line Co.* v. *Union Construction Co., Inc.*, 538 S.W.2d 80 (Tex. 1976). If the terms are too one-sided, the court may even refuse to enforce them because of a lack of mutuality and construe them to be an option to purchase, not a contract for sale. *Donahoe* v. *Allen*, 608 S.W.2d 745 (Tex. Civ. App.—Beaumont, 1980). Similarly, if one of the parties causes the default (intentionally causing the refusal of financing, for instance), the court will enforce the performance and not allow that party to benefit from his own default. *Renouf* v. *Martini*, supra. So trying for the "free look" is not always as simple as it may seem.

**Default and Remedies.** In the event of material default of the terms of an earnest money contract, there are usually remedies provided for in the contract for the purchaser and the seller, respectively. In the event of the purchaser's default, the remedies are normally that the seller retain the earnest money as **liquidated damages** (a stated predetermined sum of money awarded to the seller for holding his property off the market for the requisite period of time) and a liability for damages. In the event the seller defaults because he cannot deliver title to the property as agreed to, the purchaser is normally limited to an action for damages and a return of her earnest money. Note paragraph 15 of the TREC form.

A remedy that both parties may seek to enforce is one called **specific performance**, although this provision is sometimes specifically deleted in a contract—which probably limits a party's action to one for money damages. *Brewer* v. *Meyers*, 545 S.W.2d 235 (Tex. Civ. App.—Tyler, 1976). It must be remembered that specific performance is an equitable remedy, and the party seeking specific performance must have acted in good faith and not himself have committed a material breach of the contract. Specific performance is not an easy remedy to pursue because there are a number of requirements that must be met before specific performance can be decreed. The essential terms of the contract must be expressed with reasonable certainty, and the court order must conform to the terms of the contract. *Smith* v. *Hughes*, 540 S.W.2d 485 (Tex. Civ. App.—Houston, 1976); *Glass* v. *Anderson*, 596 S.W.2d 507 (Tex. 1980). Adequate damages must be virtually impossible to ascertain, and the default must result in irreparable harm and hardship to the party seeking specific performance. *Cowan* v. *Allen Monuments, Inc.*, 500 S.W.2d 223 (Tex. Civ. App.—Texarkana, 1973); *American Housing Resources* v. *Slaughter*, 597 S.W.2d 13 (Tex. Civ. App.—Dallas, 1980). However, some courts have seen fit to pursue this remedy because of the traditionally "unique" nature of real estate.

Although the foregoing is not intended to be an exhaustive review of all the provisions that may be contained in contracts, it must be remembered that each contract stands on its own and must be read very carefully to determine the rights of the parties involved. Whenever a party signs a contract, he is deemed by law to have read and understood all the provisions, even if that party is illiterate. It is always wise to have a party's attorney review his contract. This puts the burden of interpretation and reliance on the attorney, and not on the broker, who may be liable for misrepresentations, as well as being prohibited (by statute) from the practice of law. If a broker's client relied on certain representations or promises made by the real estate broker or sales agent (conditions that were not met by the broker), said agent may further be liable for deceptive trade practices.

## Statutory Disclosures

**Water District Disclosure.** In recent years, Texas has had a requirement to disclose to purchasers that the property being conveyed from the seller to the purchaser was in a water district. This kept the purchaser from being surprised when water district taxes were levied. The law also required that the water district notice disclose the bond amount so that the purchaser would be aware that there were obligations of the water district, and aware of the size of those obligations. This statute was frequently criticized because purchasers were not aware of the additional taxing authority, or the amount of those taxes, until closing. This was often too late because the purchaser was already obligated to purchase the property. The new statute, however, says that the notice to purchasers must be attached to any contract in which a party proposes to sell or convey the property. This means that the new water district notice will have to be attached to the earnest money contract forms. The statute even provides the format the notice is to take. The information must be current as of January 1 of the year of disclosure.

**Residential Lead-Based Paint Hazard Reduction Act of 1992.** The final rule has been issued from the Environmental Protection Agency concerning lead-based paint disclosures. To facilitate compliance with the federal rules, the Texas Real Estate Broker-Lawyer Committee has developed a contract addendum for use with TREC-promulgated contract forms. A copy is shown in Figure 9.2 at the end of this chapter.

*What is required?* Before the buyer or tenant becomes obligated under the contract for sale or lease:

1. Sellers and landlords must disclose known lead-based paint and lead-based paint hazards and provide available reports to buyers or tenants.
2. Sellers and landlords must give buyers and renters the pamphlet titled *Protect Your Family from Lead in Your Home*.
3. Home buyers will get a 10-day period to conduct a lead-based paint inspection or risk assessment at their own expense, if desired. The number of days can be changed by mutual consent. **This inspection period is not required for prospective tenants**.
4. Sales contracts and leasing arrangements must include certain language to ensure that disclosure and notification actually take place.
5. Sellers, lessors, and real estate agents share responsibility for ensuring compliance.
6. Proof of compliance must be retained for THREE YEARS.

*Note that the rule does not require testing, removal, or abatement of lead-based paint, nor does it invalidate leasing and sales contracts.*

The statute targets housing built prior to 1978, and specifically does *not* cover the following:

1. Housing built after 1977.
2. Zero-bedroom units, such as efficiencies, lofts, and dormitories.
3. Leases for less than 100 days, such as vacation houses or short-term rentals.
4. Houses exclusively for the elderly (unless there are children living there).
5. Housing for the handicapped (unless there are children living there).

6. Rental houses that have been inspected by a certified inspector and found to be free of lead-based paint.

7. Houses being sold because of foreclosure.

8. Renewals of existing leases in which the landlord has previously disclosed all required lead-based paint information.

*Agent responsibilities* There are specific requirements for real estate agents under the final rule. The agents must ensure that:

1. Sellers and landlords are aware of their obligations.

2. Sellers and landlords disclose the proper information to buyers and tenants.

3. Sellers give buyers the 10-day opportunity to conduct an inspection (or other mutually agreed-upon period).

4. Agents should see that leases and sales contracts include proper disclosure language and proper signatures.

5. The agent must comply with the law if sellers or landlords fail to do so.

*New penalties* The penalties can be severe. The EPA issued a guidance document clarifying its enforcement policy for violations or federal disclosure requirements in January of 1998. Under this policy, the EPA establishes a procedure to issue a first-time violator a Notice of Noncompliance ("NON"), in lieu of a civil penalty, unless the violation is considered egregious (a child or pregnant woman "put at risk").

The penalties are set up in two stages: the Gravity-Based Penalty stage and the Adjustment stage. The Gravity-Based Penalty stage can reach an upper limit of $11,000 per violation. The Adjustment stage adjusts the Gravity-Based Penalty stage up or down, based on various factors (the violator's ability to pay, history of prior violations, degree of culpability, and whether or not the violator qualifies as a "small business").

Each requirement of the disclosure is separate from the others and penalties will be assessed on each violation; therefore, a landlord with 10 apartments who fails to distribute a pamphlet and fails to disclose lead-based paint could be liable for 20 violations, each carrying a potential $11,000 penalty!

**Tax Rollback.** Currently codified under Section 5.010 of the Texas Property Code, this section requires that contracts for the sale of vacant land include a statutory notice about the potential liability for rollback taxes if the property has a special tax classification, such as agricultural or open space use. If the seller fails to include the required notice, the seller is liable to the purchaser for any rollback tax liability. This requirement does not apply if the sales contract separately allocates responsibility between seller and purchaser for any future rollback tax liability. The TREC Farm and Ranch Contract (25-5), New Home Contract (23-7), and Unimproved Property contracts provide for this new disclosure.

**Pipelines.** Section 5.013 of the Property Code requires that a seller of unimproved land to be used for residential property must disclose in writing to the purchaser the location of any transportation pipeline on the property, including a pipeline for the transport of natural gas, natural gas liquids, synthetic gas, liquefied petroleum gas, petroleum, petroleum products, or hazardous substances. The notice must state the information to the best of the seller's belief and knowledge as of the date the notice is signed and given to the purchaser. If the seller does not know whether pipelines exist under the property, that fact must be stated. The notice must be delivered to the purchaser on or before the effective date of the contract. If a contract is entered into without the notice, the purchaser may terminate it for any reason not later than the seventh day after the effective date of the contract. This notice doesn't need to be given if the seller is obligated, under the terms of the earnest money contract, to delivery of title commitment to the purchaser, and if the purchaser has a right to terminate the contract if objections to title are not cured. TREC forms already provide for this approval, but the exception does not apply if the seller is going to supply an abstract of title.

**Seller's Disclosure—Potential Annexation.** A person who sells an interest in real property located in an extra-territorial jurisdiction of the city is required to give the purchaser of the property a written notice that the property is located outside the limits of the municipality, but may now, or later, be included in the extra-territorial jurisdiction of the municipality and is therefore subject to the annexation by the city at some future date. The seller must deliver the notice to the purchaser before the date of the execution of the contract for sale. This notice is already contained in the TREC contract form. *V.T.C.A., Property Code §5.011.*

**Seller's Notice of Obligations to Membership in Property Owners' Association.** If a seller of residential property is subject to membership in a property owners' association and the property is comprised of not more than one dwelling unit, the seller is required to give the purchaser of the property a written statement indicating that the purchaser is obligated to be a member of the property owners' association. The TREC forms have also been revised to include this new provision. The seller must deliver the notice to the purchaser before the date of this contract is executed. *V.T.C.A., Property Code §5.012.*

**Property Owners' Association Disclosures.** Later than the 10th day after the written request for subdivision information is received from an owner, owner's agent, or title insurance company or its agent acting on behalf of the owner, a property owners' association must deliver to the owner, owner's agent, or title insurance company or its agent, current copies of the restrictions, a copy of the bylaws and rules of the property owners' association and a resale certificate.

The property owners' association may charge a reasonable fee for this service. If the property owner's association fails to deliver the resale certificate after two (2) requests, the owner can seek a court order and judgment against the property owners' association for up to $500.00, plus attorney's fees and costs.

## The Merger Doctrine

It is a well-understood point of law that the earnest money contract is a contract for sale and performs precisely that function. Most contracts for sale contain a provision that the written contract must embody the entire agreement of the parties and that there is no other oral or written agreement between the parties. This provision is commonly called a **merger** provision; it is enforced by excluding parol evidence, unless the intention of the parties indicates otherwise. *Humber* v. *Morton*, supra. Once the sale has been closed and the deed has been transferred, the earnest money contract has no force or effect whatsoever on either party because the purpose of the contract (the sale) has been fulfilled.

One may often find that an earnest money contract has certain representations and warranties that are intentionally specified to extend beyond the closing (properly termed **survive the closing**). However, unless these provisions are carefully drawn and unless the parties understand the intention to survive the closing, such provisions will not survive. Upon closing, it is normally determined that the terms of the earnest money contract are merged into the deed, or other instrument executed at the closing, and any cause of action for representation or warranties must be on the basis of the deed, rather than on the basis of the earnest money contract. *Scull* v. *Davis*, 434 S.W.2d 391 (Tex. Civ. App.—El Paso, 1968). The doctrine of merger, however, cannot be used to defeat a cause of action under the Deceptive Trade Practices Act. *Alvarado* v. *Bolton*, 749 S.W.2d 47 (Tex. 1988).

There has been erosion of this **doctrine of merger** because of builders' warranties and agreements to perform services. Cases are indicating that merger depends upon the intent of the parties, which is a fact issue. *Rowe* v. *Harris*, 576 S.W.2d 172 (Tex. Civ. App.—Waco, 1979). So, in the case of builders' or contractors' warranties, the doctrine of merger may not apply in Texas. In addition, the TREC-promulgated forms provide that representations will "survive the closing." This further maximizes merger problems.

# Option Contracts

An **option contract** is an agreement by which the owner of property gives another the right to purchase his property at a fixed price, on specified terms, within the time specified within the option contract, or within a reasonable period of time. *Maxwell* v. *Lake*, 674 S.W.2d 795 (Tex. Civ. App.—Dallas, 1984). This agreement creates an irrevocable offer to sell the property at a fixed price. It requires consideration before the contract can be binding. *Culbertson* v. *Brodsky*, 778 S.W.2d 156 (Tex. App.—Ft. Worth, 1990), even if the contract states "Ten Dollars," the ten dollars needs to be delivered. *Joppich* v. *1464-Eight, Ltd.* 965.10.3d 614 (Tex. App.—Houston [14th Dist.] 2002). However, the parties may agree that the payment for the option can be applied to the purchase price in the event the option is exercised. *Echols* v. *Bloom*, 485 S.W.2d 798 (Tex. Civ. App.—Houston [14th Dist.], 1972). The option contract is a **unilateral** contract, normally only signed by the seller (optionor) because he is the only party to be charged in performance. It should be noted, however, that since the purchaser has no obligation to perform, she gets no title of any kind to the property (neither equitable nor legal), and time is always of the essence in an option contract. *Lafevere* v. *Sears*, 629 S.W.2d 768 (Tex. Civ. App.—El Paso, 1981).

There has been some litigation in recent years concerning the difference between (1) an option contract and (2) an **earnest money contract** in which the seller's sole remedy is to accept the earnest money as liquidated damages. The legal difference between the two instruments is insignificant. *Texlouana Producing and Refining Co.* v. *Wall*, 257 S.W.2d 875 (Comm. App.—1924). In fact, several Texas courts have held that if the seller's only contractual remedy in the event of the purchaser's default in an earnest money contract is retention of the earnest money, the agreement constitutes a unilateral option rather than a **bilateral** contract for sale. *Broady* v. *Mitchell*, 572 S.W.2d 36 (Tex. Civ. App.—Houston, 1978). The same is true of one-sided or vague contingencies (see the "contingencies" portion of this chapter). So in an option contract, the only effective remedy is the buyer's right to force the seller specifically to perform. The seller has no right to force the buyer specifically to perform.

## Right of First Refusal

A **right of first refusal** is a preemptive right to purchase in event the landowners should decide to sell. It requires the owner, when and if the owner decides to sell, to offer the property first to the person entitled to the preemptive right at the stipulated price.

A right of first refusal ripens into an option when the owner decides to sell the real estate. In that case, the holder of the right of first refusal is to be notified that the sale is taking place and that the holder has the right to exercise this right. The owner is required to make a reasonable disclosure of the terms of the proposed sale then the holder of the right of first refusal has the duty to undertake a reasonable investigation of any terms that are unclear to him. If he refuses to exercise his right, he cannot revive the right he declined. *Comeaux* v. *Suderman*, 93 S.E.3d 215 (Tex. App.—Houston [14th Dist.] 2003).

From time to time a seller may find some benefit in granting a right of first refusal to another. This can be a significant interest in that the holder of the right of first refusal has the right to match any subsequent offers, therefore, a seller should be careful to keep the right of first refusal a very short period of time to respond. Otherwise, the holder of the right of first refusal can basically "trump" any offer and bind the seller's hands for an extended period of time. In most circumstances, a seller would want to grant a right of first refusal for no longer than fifteen days.

In a nutshell, this creates three potential contract right:

1. the seller can grant a right of first refusal;
2. when the seller receives the offer, he needs to notify the holder of that right, which creates an option in the holder to buy the property;
3. if the holder chooses to exercise that right, his option converts into an enforceable earnest money contract.

# Installment Land Contracts

An **installment land contract** is a contract for the sale of real estate that extends over a long period of time. It is called an **executory contract** because the terms of the contract are not to be completed in the near future—this contrasts with an **executed contract** in which the terms of the contract are satisfied as of signing (e.g., a deed). The installment land contract is also called a **contract for deed**, and it is precisely that. It is a contract entered into between the buyer and seller to deliver a deed at some future date. *Texas American Bank/Levelland* v. *Resendez*, 706 S.W.2d 343 (Tex. Civ. App.—Amarillo, 1986). This contract may last as long as 10 years, or longer, depending on the terms. An installment land contract has been likened to a marital agreement in that the parties have just entered into an agreement for a long period of time that may produce adverse results they had not anticipated at the time they made the deal. There is very little difference between a vendor–buyer relationship under an installment land contract situation and a landlord–tenant relationship, except that the purchaser (unlike the lessee) expects to gain title to the property at some future date. The seller retains **legal title**, and the purchaser gets an **equitable title** to the property. *Lafevere* v. *Sears*, supra. All of the purchaser's rights to the property are defined by that contract, just as a lessee's rights are defined by a lease.

Installment land contracts are a two-edged sword. They are an excellent **mortgaging technique** as well as a **marketing tool**. Historically, we have used installment land contracts as a type of mortgage. In its simplest format, there is the seller of a farm who had probably been in possession of the premises and had been farming the property for many years. When he decided to sell the property, there was no lending source available to loan the money to the purchaser, so the farmer simply financed it himself by using the installment land contract.

To do this, the farmer signed a long-term contract in which he agreed to convey title to the purchaser at some time in the future, after the full purchase price had been paid. The purchaser got possession of the property, farmed it, and used the income from the farm to make his payments. To protect himself, the seller retained title to the real estate until the purchase price was paid in full. The buyer, being in possession, could use the property as he wished so long as he continued to pay the agreed purchase price. This could also provide a passive income for the seller in his later years.

In more current usage, however, the installment land contract has been more of a marketing technique for developers rather than a mortgaging technique. In these situations, a developer might buy 1,000 acres from a farmer, receiving title to the real estate by deed and executing a mortgage in favor of the farmer to secure the future payments. The developer then subdivides the property (borrowing money to finance this construction also) and builds roads, clubhouses, and other recreational amenities to make his real estate development more desirable. Since the developer now has two mortgages on the property, he may not be able to transfer clear title to the purchaser until those mortgages are satisfied. Therefore, in his marketing effort, he simply transfers an equitable interest (also referred to as **equitable title**) to a prospective purchaser using the installment land contract. As in the previous example, the developer retains legal title; the purchaser gets equitable title and the right to possess the property. Eventually, the purchaser will make all his payments to the developer, and the developer will then transfer title to the purchaser at that later date, hopefully when the mortgages have been released and title is clear of any encumbrances.

Considering these two examples, one can see how the installment land contract can be used as the same legal document to transfer equitable title, but for two very different purposes. One (the developer's parcel) is somewhat riskier than the other (the farmer's parcel).

**New Statutory Changes.** There have been massive changes in the last several legislatures concerning installment land contracts. These changes apply only to transactions involving an "executory contract for conveyance" (another term for installment land contracts) by a seller of real property to be used or to be used as the purchaser's residence or as a residence of a person related to a purchaser within the second degree of consanguinity or affinity. If the negotiations that proceed the execution of an executory contract are conducted primarily in a language other than English, the Seller must provide a copy in that language of all written documents relating to the transaction, including the contract, disclosure notices, annual accounting statements, and a notice of default required under this new law.

Before an executory contract is signed by the purchaser, the seller must provide the purchaser with: (1) A tax certificate from the collector for each taxing unit that collects taxes on the property; and (2) a legible copy of the insurance policy, binder, or other evidence relating to the property that indicates: (a) the name of the insurer and the insured, (b) a description of the property insured and (c) the amount for which the property is insured. If the seller fails to provide this information, it constitutes a deceptive trade practice and entitles the purchaser to cancel and rescind the executory contract and receive a full refund of all payments made to the seller.

Similar disclosures are required for disclosure of property condition. A specific seller's disclosure notice for financing is also required. If the seller fails to utilize this disclosure, it is also a violation of the Deceptive Trade Practices Act.

In addition, the seller must also provide prospective purchasers with a bold faced notice in 14 point type, in the contract, or in a separate document, that oral agreements for the conveyance of real estate are invalid and that the contract may not be varied by any oral agreement or discussions that occur before or contemporaneously with the execution of the contract. Again, if seller fails to provide this notification, it constitutes a deceptive trade practice.

Section 5.077 provides for an annual accounting statement by the owner of the property to the purchaser. The statement must be post-marked not later than January 31st of each year. The accounting statement must provide for:

(1) The amount paid under the contract.

(2) The remaining amount owed under the contract.

(3) The number of payments remaining under the contract.

(4) The amounts paid to taxing authorities on the purchaser's behalf, if collected by the seller.

(5) The amounts paid to insure the property on the purchaser's behalf, if collected by the seller.

(6) If the property has been damaged and the seller has received insurance proceeds, an accounting of the proceeds applied to the property.

(7) If the seller has changed insurance coverage, a legible copy of the insurance, binder, or other evidence as satisfies the requirements of the statute.

If the seller has sold more than one property in the last 12 month period, and fails to comply with this provision, he is liable for liquidated damages in the amount of $250.00 for each day after January 31st that the seller fails to provide the purchaser with a statement, and also for reasonable attorney's fees. There are some exceptions to these penalties if the seller has died and the heirs have to go to court to probate the estate. See Section 5.079. In effect, the legislature is telling us not to use executory contracts. If the statue is not strictly adhered, to, the penalties are severe. Most of the new provisions apply to executory contract signed after September 1, 2001. See generally, Section 5.069-5.079.

## Default and Remedies

The default and remedy provisions were also changed dramatically. Under the new legislation "default" means the failure to (1) make a timely payment; (2) comply with terms of an executory contract.

The statute requires a notice in the event of default which must be in writing and must be delivered by registered or certified mail, return receipt requested. The notice must be conspicuous and printed on a 14-point bold-faced type or 14-point upper case typewritten letters and must include, on a separate page, the statement:

**NOTICE**
**YOU ARE NOT COMPLYING WITH THE TERMS OF THE CONTRACT TO BUY YOUR PROPERTY. UNLESS YOU TAKE THE ACTIONS SPECIFIED IN THIS NOTICE BY (DATE) THE SELLER HAS THE RIGHT TO TAKE POSSESSION OF YOUR PROPERTY.**

The foregoing notice must also identify and explain the remedy the Seller intends to enforce and if the purchaser has failed to make a timely payment. Also specify the delinquent amount, (1) itemized into principal and interest; (2) any additional charges, claims, such as late charges or attorney's fees; and (3) the period to which the delinquency and additional charges relate.

If the purchaser has failed to comply with the terms of the contract, the notice must also identify the terms violated and the action required to cure the violation. The notice by mail is given when it is mailed to the purchaser's address or place of business.

**Remedies.** The seller has the right to enforce the remedy of rescission or of forfeiture in acceleration against purchaser only if the seller notifies the purchaser of the seller's intent to enforce the remedy under this section and the purchaser's right to cure the default within the 30 days described under the statute and if the purchaser fails to cure the default within the 30 days, and the seller has paid less than 40% or more of the amount due or less than the equivalent of 48 monthly installments under the executory contract.

If the purchaser defaults and has paid 40% or more of the amount, or the equivalent of 48 monthly installments under the executory contract, the seller is granted the power to sell, through a trustee designated by the seller, the purchaser's interest in the property, and may not enforce the traditional remedy of rescission or of forfeiture and acceleration.

In this event, the seller must notify the purchaser of a default under the contract and allow the purchaser at least 60 days to cure the default. Notice of default is different from any other notice in that it allows a trustee designated by the seller to sell the property at a public auction. The property is then sold pursuant to an auction under Section 51.002 of the Property Code, the traditional foreclosure procedure pursuant to a public sale at the county courthouse under a deed of trust.

The Texas courts have been very liberal in construing this act, both on the part of the vendor and on the part of the purchaser; *Wentworth* v. *Medellin*, 529 S.W.2d 125 (Tex. Civ. App.—San Antonio, 1975) indicated that as far as the vendor's rights were concerned, substantial compliance with the statute was enough to warrant enforcement. However, in the interest of the purchaser, there have been several cases that provide for the protection of the purchaser. *DeLeon* v. *Aldrete*, 398 S.W.2d 160 (Tex. Civ. App.—San Antonio, 1965) forced a vendor who exercised her right of forfeiture to make restitution under the principles of equity and to reimburse some funds that the purchaser had expended on the residence. In a more significant decision, Texas courts have held that the statutory forfeiture provisions apply to all contracts entered into before 1969, as long as they are still in effect after passage of the statute. *Pratt* v. *Story*, 530 S.W.2d 325 (Tex. Civ. App.—Tyler, 1975). It has also been held that the statutory forfeiture provisions also apply to raw land as well as improved real property. *Sanchez* v. *Brandt*, 567 S.W.2d 254 (Tex. Civ. App.—Corpus Christi, 1978). There may also be prohibitions against forfeiture and acceleration of an installment land contract if the vendor has made a practice of accepting late payments in the past, and if no installments were delinquent at the time the vendor attempted to effect forfeiture. *Jordan* v. *Crockett*, 511 S.W.2d 618 (Tex. Civ. App.—Austin, 1974).

## Seller's Considerations

**Advantages.** The benefit to the seller of the installment land contracts is that he does not give legal title. The seller may prohibit the purchaser from recording the contract, so that it will not cloud the title in the event the purchaser defaults in his payments. The parcel may also be somewhat easier to sell (this is the marketing advantage) since no traditional lending sources are required and, therefore, no loan application, credit approval, or appraisal. The new Seller disclosures required by the new legislation, however, may eliminate this advantage.

**Disadvantages.** The seller's primary disadvantage with the installment land contract is that a sophisticated purchaser may attempt to cloud title by assigning the contract or recording a memorandum of it in the county clerk's office. The purchaser may also be evasive when the seller attempts new enforcement procedures for default under the contract. The purchaser may also consistently make late payments, knowing that the rights to cure the default under the Texas statute work in the purchaser's favor.

## Buyer's Considerations

**Advantages.** The primary advantage for a buyer using an installment land contract is the ease of acquisition. She simply signs her contract and, if desired, moves onto the premises with very few additional obligations. She can pay for the property over a period of years, ultimately acquiring title without being forced to use traditional lending sources. In real estate transactions, this is the original easy credit purchase plan!

**Disadvantages.** The disadvantages of this type of financing technique for the buyer are extensive. First, the buyer seldom checks title to see if the seller has good title and is really buying an unknown quantity and quality of interest in real estate. Second, the seller may not be able to deliver clear title in the future after the purchaser has made all of her payments. The third problem concerns multiple sales. Since the purchaser does not check title and the contract is frequently not recorded, there is no way for a purchaser to determine if the seller has sold the property to somebody else. There may be two contract purchasers for the same parcel of real estate and no sure way to discover this at the time of the purchase. Fourth, the seller may die, go bankrupt, move to New Jersey, or sell the project to a six-year-old boy in El Reno, Oklahoma. The purchaser has virtually no control over how the development will be handled in the future. If the seller is unscrupulous, the purchaser has big problems.

## Good Points

This is not to say that installment land contracts are inherently bad. If the seller provides title insurance to the buyer, the buyer can take comfort that title is good and that the seller has the ability to perform in the future. A buyer can also require that the seller deliver a general warranty deed into escrow with the title company. The seller may also allow the buyer to record her contract so that all subsequent purchasers and creditors will be on notice of her intent to acquire title to the real estate and eliminate the potential problem of multiple purchasers with unrecorded interests. The equitable title received by the buyer may also even be superior to the seller's subsequent lien creditors. *Texas American Bank/Levelland* v. *Resendez*, supra.

In its purest sense, the installment land contract is an excellent mortgaging technique. It is particularly useful when a purchaser cannot otherwise qualify for a mortgage or has no down payment, and an honest seller is willing to extend credit by retaining title to the property as security for the loan. Under the new statutory changes, the bigger risk seems to fall on the seller.

## ■ SUMMARY

The law of contracts is one of the most complex areas of the law to study. The fundamental elements of the contract consist of the offer, acceptance, and consideration. There are standard rules of construction for contracts that, while not controlling, usually give guidance as to how the contract will be interpreted by the courts.

Earnest money contracts have particular application to real estate transactions. They may be oral or expressed and, in each case, have very specific requirements in order to be valid and enforceable. At closing, it is said that the earnest money contract "merges" into the deed and other instruments because the purpose of that contract "sale" has been accomplished.

Installment land contracts are also known as contracts for deed or executory contracts. They are contracts for the sale of real estate that normally extend over a period of years. There are many disadvantages to an installment land contract, and they have often been abused by unscrupulous land developers. There have been new statutory provisions enacted in Texas that provide additional rights for purchasers under installment land contracts in the event of default. Installment land contracts are not all bad, however, and have been used to effect a convenient method of financing for low-income housing.

## CASE STUDIES FOR DISCUSSION

1. Edwards obtained from Kelly an option to purchase a tract of land in consideration of $7,500 paid to Kelly by Edwards. Two months later Edwards notified Kelly of his election to exercise the option. In the next month Edwards attempted to terminate his exercise of the option and demand return of his $7,500. Kelly sued for damages in the amount of $110,000, which represented the price to be paid for the property. Edwards maintains that he merely had an option and Kelly's total liquidated damages were only $7,500. Kelly alleges that at the time Edwards exercised his option to purchase, his option became a bilateral contract to purchase the real estate, and therefore he is entitled to damages for the full amount of the breach. What legal ramifications do you foresee?

2. Elwood Longfellow entered into a contract for the sale of land from Stevens. When the closing date arrived, Elwood Longfellow had decided not to close and Stevens brought suit for specific performance. Prior to the final trial date, Stevens lost title to the property through foreclosure. Longfellow alleges that now he does not have to perform since Stevens no longer holds title. Stevens contends that he should still be required to perform since title may still be obtainable at the original sales price. What legal ramifications do you foresee?

**FIGURE 9.2 ADDENDUM FOR SELLER'S DISCLOSURE OF INFORMATION ON LEAD-BASED PAINT AND LEAD-BASED PAINT HAZARDS AS REQUIRED BY FEDERAL LAW.**

APPROVED BY THE TEXAS REAL ESTATE COMMISSION                    02-09-2004

## ADDENDUM FOR SELLER'S DISCLOSURE OF INFORMATION ON LEAD-BASED PAINT AND LEAD-BASED PAINT HAZARDS AS REQUIRED BY FEDERAL LAW

CONCERNING THE PROPERTY AT _____
(Street Address and City)

A. **LEAD WARNING STATEMENT:** "Every purchaser of any interest in residential real property on which a residential dwelling was built prior to 1978 is notified that such property may present exposure to lead from lead-based paint that may place young children at risk of developing lead poisoning. Lead poisoning in young children may produce permanent neurological damage, including learning disabilities, reduced intelligence quotient, behavioral problems, and impaired memory. Lead poisoning also poses a particular risk to pregnant women. The seller of any interest in residential real property is required to provide the buyer with any information on lead-based paint hazards from risk assessments or inspections in the seller's possession and notify the buyer of any known lead-based paint hazards. A risk assessment or inspection for possible lead-paint hazards is recommended prior to purchase."
   **NOTICE: Inspector must be properly certified as required by federal law.**

B. **SELLER'S DISCLOSURE:**
   1. PRESENCE OF LEAD-BASED PAINT AND/OR LEAD-BASED PAINT HAZARDS (check on box only):
      ☐ (a) Known lead-based paint and/or lead-based paint hazards are present in the Property (explain): _____
      _____ .
      ☐ (b) Seller has no actual knowledge of lead-based paint and/or lead-based paint hazards in the Property.
   2. RECORDS AND REPORTS AVAILABLE TO SELLER (check one box only):
      ☐ (a) Seller has provided the purchaser with all available records and reports pertaining to lead-based paint and/or lead-based paint hazards in the Property (list documents):_____
      _____ .
      ☐ (b) Seller has no reports or records pertaining to lead-based paint and/or lead-based paint hazards in the Property.

C. **BUYER'S RIGHTS** (check one box only):
   ☐ 1. Buyer waives the opportunity to conduct a risk assessment or inspection of the Property for the presence of lead-based paint or lead-based paint hazards.
   ☐ 2. Within ten days after the effective date of this contract, Buyer may have the Property inspected by inspectors selected by Buyer. If lead-based paint or lead-based paint hazards are present, Buyer may terminate this contract by giving Seller written notice within 14 days after the effective date of this contract, and the earnest money will be refunded to Buyer.

D. **BUYER'S ACKNOWLEDGMENT** (check applicable boxes):
   ☐ 1. Buyer has received copies of all information listed above.
   ☐ 2. Buyer has received the pamphlet *Protect Your Family from Lead in Your Home*.

E. **BROKERS' ACKNOWLEDGMENT:** Brokers have informed Seller of Seller's obligations under 42 U.S.C. 4852d to: (a) provide Buyer with the federally approved pamphlet on lead poisoning prevention; (b) complete this addendum; (c) disclose any known lead-based paint and/or lead-based paint hazards in the Property; (d) deliver all records and reports to Buyer pertaining to lead-based paint and/or lead-based paint hazards in the Property; (e) provide Buyer a period of up to 10 days to have the Property inspected; and (f) retain a completed copy of this addendum for at least 3 years following the sale. Brokers are aware of their responsibility to ensure compliance.

F. **CERTIFICATION OF ACCURACY:** The following persons have reviewed the information above and certify, to the best of their knowledge, that the information they have provided is true and accurate.

_____    _____    _____    _____
Buyer                        Date      Seller                      Date

_____    _____    _____    _____
Buyer                        Date      Seller                      Date

_____    _____    _____    _____
Other Broker                 Date      Listing Broker              Date

The form of this addendum has been approved by the Texas Real Estate Commission for use only with similarly approved or promulgated forms of contracts. Such approval relates to this contract form only. TREC forms are intended for use only by trained real estate licensees. No representation is made as to the legal validity or adequacy of any provision in any specific transactions. It is not suitable for complex transactions. Texas Real Estate Commission, P.O. Box 12188, Austin, TX 78711-2188, 1-800-250-8732 or (512) 459-6544 (http://www.trec.state.tx.us)

**Form OP-L    01A**

## CHAPTER 10

# Voluntary Conveyances

For centuries there has been a legal and practical method by which an owner can convey, alienate, transfer, or dispose of his interest in real estate; he can have it conveyed in his absence, or even without his consent. It was obviously apparent from the initial concepts of individual real estate ownership that something had to evidence title, and something had to transfer that title, short of armed combat. The scope of Chapters 10 and 11 is to study these means of conveyance. The types of conveyances discussed in this chapter will be **voluntary conveyances**, which encompass deeds and wills (wills are a voluntary means of conveyance, although the means to effect that conveyance may not be so voluntary). **Involuntary conveyances**, which include condemnation, adverse possession, intestacy (death of the owner leaving no will), foreclosure, tax sales, escheat, dedication, and transfer by natural causes, will be discussed in Chapter 11.

## Deeds

A **deed** is a written instrument by which a landowner transfers the ownership of his land. The quality of title that the landowner (grantor) conveys to the purchaser (grantee) is controlled by the type of deed utilized, by the warranties included, and by the restrictions and exceptions to the title contained in that deed.

### Types of Deeds

Before getting into the legal requirements, details, and interpretations of deeds, one should be familiar with the different types of deeds in order to establish the proper basis for a more in-depth discussion. The types of deeds to be discussed, in their descending order of warranty, are: general warranty deeds, special warranty deeds, trustee's deeds, court-ordered deeds, bargain and sale deeds (also called deeds without warranties), and quitclaim deeds. Copies of these various deed forms and notation as to their various clauses are included in Figures 10.1 through 10.5 for your reference.

**FIGURE 10.1  SAMPLE GENERAL WARRANTY DEED.**

**NOTICE OF CONFIDENTIALITY RIGHTS:  IF YOU ARE A NATURAL PERSON, YOU MAY REMOVE OR STRIKE AN OF THE FOLLOWING INFORMATION FROM THIS INSTRUMENT BEFORE IT IS FILED FOR RECORD IN THE PUBLIC RECORDS: YOUR SOCIAL SECURITY NUMBER OR YOUR DRIVER'S LICENSE NUMBER.**

**GENERAL WARRANTY DEED**
**(Cash)**

| | | |
|---|---|---|
| THE STATE OF TEXAS | § | |
| | § | KNOW ALL MEN BY THESE PRESENTS: |
| COUNTY  OF  HARRIS | § | |

THAT THE UNDERSIGNED, Ben Dover, hereinafter referred to as "Grantor," whether one or more, for and in consideration of the sum of TEN DOLLARS ($10.00) cash, and other good and valuable consideration in hand paid by the Grantee, herein named, the receipt and sufficiency of which is hereby fully acknowledged and confessed, has GRANTED, SOLD and CONVEYED, and by these presents does hereby GRANT, SELL and CONVEY unto Neil Down, herein referred to as "Grantee," whether one or more, the real property described on attached Exhibit "A."

This conveyance, however, is made and accepted subject to any and all validly existing encumbrances, conditions and restrictions, relating to the hereinabove described property as now reflected by the records of the County Clerk of Harris County, Texas.

TO HAVE AND TO HOLD the above described premises, together with all and singular the rights and appurtenances thereto in anywise belonging unto the said Grantee, Grantee's heirs, executors, administrators, successors and/or assigns forever; and Grantor does hereby bind Grantor, Grantor's heirs, executors, administrators, successors and/or assigns to WARRANT AND FOREVER DEFEND all and singular the said premises unto the said Grantee, Grantee's heirs, executors, administrators, successors and/or assigns, against every person whomsoever claiming or to claim the same or any part thereof.

Current ad valorem taxes on said property having been prorated, the payment thereof is assumed by Grantee.

EXECUTED this _____ day of _____, 2003.

_____
Ben Dover

Grantee's Address:

_____

_____

**FIGURE 10.2  SAMPLE SPECIAL WARRANTY DEED.**

**NOTICE OF CONFIDENTIALITY RIGHTS: IF YOU ARE A NATURAL PERSON, YOU MAY REMOVE OR STRIKE AN OF THE FOLLOWING INFORMATION FROM THIS INSTRUMENT BEFORE IT IS FILED FOR RECORD IN THE PUBLIC RECORDS: YOUR SOCIAL SECURITY NUMBER OR YOUR DRIVER'S LICENSE NUMBER.**

**SPECIAL WARRANTY DEED**

THE STATE OF TEXAS          §

                            §          KNOW ALL MEN BY THESE PRESENTS:

COUNTY  OF  HARRIS          §

   THAT THE UNDERSIGNED, Ben Dover, hereinafter referred to as "Grantor," whether one or more, for and in consideration of the sum of TEN DOLLARS ($10.00) cash, and other good and valuable consideration in hand paid by the Grantee, herein named, the receipt and sufficiency of which is hereby fully acknowledged and confessed, has GRANTED, SOLD and CONVEYED, and by these presents does hereby GRANT, SELL and CONVEY unto Neil Down, herein referred to as "Grantee," whether one or more, the real property described on attached Exhibit "A."

   This conveyance, however, is made and accepted subject to any and all validly existing encumbrances, conditions and restrictions, relating to the hereinabove described property as now reflected by the records of the County Clerk of Harris County, Texas.

   TO HAVE AND TO HOLD the above described premises, together with all and singular the rights and appurtenances thereto in anywise belonging unto the said Grantee, Grantee's heirs, executors, administrators, successors and/or assigns forever; and Grantor does hereby bind Grantor, Grantor's heirs, executors, administrators, successors and/or assigns to WARRANT AND FOREVER DEFEND all and singular the said premises unto the said Grantee, Grantee's heirs, executors, administrators, successors and/or assigns, against every person whomsoever claiming or to claim the same or any part thereof, by, through, or under Grantor, but not otherwise.

   Current ad valorem taxes on said property having been prorated, the payment thereof is assumed by Grantee.

   EXECUTED this _____ day of _____, 2003.


                                        _____
                                        Ben Dover

Grantee's Address:

_____

_____

**FIGURE 10.3 SAMPLE BARGAIN AND SALE DEED.**

---

**NOTICE OF CONFIDENTIALITY RIGHTS:  IF YOU ARE A NATURAL PERSON, YOU MAY REMOVE OR STRIKE AN OF THE FOLLOWING INFORMATION FROM THIS INSTRUMENT BEFORE IT IS FILED FOR RECORD IN THE PUBLIC RECORDS: YOUR SOCIAL SECURITY NUMBER OR YOUR DRIVER'S LICENSE NUMBER.**

**DEED**
**(Without Warranties)**

THE STATE OF TEXAS           §
                             §        KNOW ALL MEN BY THESE PRESENTS:
COUNTY  OF  HARRIS           §

THAT the undersigned, Ben Dover and wife, Eilene Dover, hereinafter referred to as "Grantor," whether one or more, of the County of Harris and State of Texas, for and in consideration of the sum of TEN AND NO/100 DOLLARS ($10.00) and other good and valuable consideration in hand paid by Neil Down, hereinafter referenced "Grantee," whether one or more, the receipt and sufficiency of which is hereby acknowledged, have granted, sold and quitclaimed, and by these presents do grant, sell and convey unto Grantee, of the County of Harris and State of Texas, the real property described on attached Exhibit "A."

TO HAVE AND HOLD the above described property and premises unto the said Grantee, Grantee's heirs, administrators, executors, successors and/or assigns forever. This conveyance is made without warranty, express or implied.

EXECUTED this _____ day of _____, 2003.


_____
Ben Dover


_____
Eilene Dover

Grantee's Address:
_____
_____

---

**General Warranty Deeds.** The **general warranty deed** is the most widely used deed in this state and, by both statute and case law, ensures the highest warranty the law recognizes. A general warranty deed is shown in Figure 10.1. Statutorily, since the general warranty deed uses the words "**grant**" or "**convey**," the law implies that the grantor gives two covenants. One of these is called the **covenant of seizin**. This means that the grantor has not conveyed the same estate previously, has good title to the property, and will indemnify the grantee against any claims due to failure of title. *Childress* v. *Stiles*, 272 S.W.2d 417 (Tex. Civ. App.—Waco, 1954). The second covenant is the **covenant against encumbrances**. This covenant warrants that there are no other encumbrances affecting the property other

FIGURE 10.4  SAMPLE QUITCLAIM DEED.

**NOTICE OF CONFIDENTIALITY RIGHTS: IF YOU ARE A NATURAL PERSON, YOU MAY REMOVE OR STRIKE AN OF THE FOLLOWING INFORMATION FROM THIS INSTRUMENT BEFORE IT IS FILED FOR RECORD IN THE PUBLIC RECORDS: YOUR SOCIAL SECURITY NUMBER OR YOUR DRIVER'S LICENSE NUMBER.**

**QUITCLAIM DEED**

THE STATE OF TEXAS　　　　§
　　　　　　　　　　　　　§　　KNOW ALL MEN BY THESE PRESENTS:
COUNTY OF HARRIS　　　　 §

That the undersigned, Ben Dover, hereinafter referred to as "Grantor," whether one or more, for and in consideration of the sum of TEN AND NO/100 DOLLARS ($10.00) in hand paid by Grantee herein named, and other good and valuable consideration, the receipt and sufficiency of which is hereby acknowledged, has QUITCLAIMED, and by these presents does QUITCLAIM unto Neil Down, of the County of Harris State of Texas, herein referred to as "Grantee," whether one or more, the real property described on attached Exhibit "A."

TO HAVE AND TO HOLD all of Grantor's right, title and interest in and to the above described property and premises unto the Grantee, and Grantee's heirs, administrators, executors, successors and/or assigns forever; so that neither Grantor nor Grantor's heirs, administrators, executors, successors and/or assigns shall have, claim or demand any right or title to the aforesaid property, premises or appurtenances or any

EXECUTED this ____ day of _____, 2003.

_____
Ben Dover

Grantee's Address:

_____

_____

than those shown in the deed, if any. This covenant implies that the grantor will indemnify the grantee from claims arising from any third party seeking to establish an interest in the real estate. It also imposes a duty on the grantor to discharge all liens and encumbrances incurred prior to the conveyance. *Triplett* v. *Shield*, 406 S.W.2d 941 (Tex. Civ. App.—Eastland, 1966). One court has also held that a breach of an implied warranty of title can create a violation of the Deceptive Trade Practices Act. *Medallion Homes, Inc.* v. *Thermar Investments, Inc.*, 698 S.W.2d 400 (Tex. Civ. App.—Houston [14th Dist.], 1985).

In addition, when using the general warranty deed, the grantor warrants not only that the title is free of these encumbrances, but also that he is well seized of the premises and that this covenant is through his entire chain of title. To help soften the impact of this warranty, there are certain adverse possession statutes (to

**FIGURE 10.5  SAMPLE TRUSTEE'S DEED.**

**NOTICE OF CONFIDENTIALITY RIGHTS:  IF YOU ARE A NATURAL PERSON, YOU MAY REMOVE OR STRIKE AN OF THE FOLLOWING INFORMATION FROM THIS INSTRUMENT BEFORE IT IS FILED FOR RECORD IN THE PUBLIC RECORDS: YOUR SOCIAL SECURITY NUMBER OR YOUR DRIVER'S LICENSE NUMBER.**

**TRUSTEE'S DEED**

THE STATE OF TEXAS            §

                             §       KNOW ALL MEN BY THESE PRESENTS:

COUNTY  OF  HARRIS            §

WHEREAS, M.T. Pockets ("Maker," whether one or more), whose address is 123 Looscan Lane, executed a Deed of Trust dated February 30, 1999, to Charles J. Jacobus, Trustee, to secure the payment of that one certain promissory note of even date therewith in the original principal sum of $150,000.00 (the "Note"), payable to the order of Friendly Mortgage Company, which Deed of Trust was filed for record in the Official Public Records of Real Property of Harris County, Texas, under County Clerk's File No. Q107636, and which Deed of Trust covers the property described on attached Exhibit "A"; and

WHEREAS, default has been made in the payment of the above-referenced Note and Friendly Lender Mortgage Company, the present owner and holder of the Note, has declared the Note to be fully due and payable; and

WHEREAS, said Deed of Trust provides that the Beneficiary thereunder is authorized to appoint a Trustee by designating such Trustee in writing; and

WHEREAS, Beneficiary has, pursuant to the Appointment of Trustee attached hereto as Exhibit "B," named, appointed and designated Charles J. Jacobus, the Trustee, and requested him to foreclose said Deed of Trust and to advertise and sell the property in accordance with all terms and provisions thereof and the laws of the State of Texas;

NOW, THEREFORE, KNOW ALL MEN BY THESE PRESENTS:

THAT I, Charles J. Jacobus, Trustee, in performance of my duty under the Deed of Trust, after advertising the time and place and terms of sale of all the above-described real property and in accordance with the terms of the Deed of Trust and as required by law, by posting a written notice of such sale at the courthouse door of Harris County, Texas, said notice having been posted for at least twenty-one days successively next before the date of sale as reflected by the affidavit attached hereto as Exhibit "C," and having confirmed that written notice of said sale has been mailed to the Maker of the Note and all other obligors thereon according to the records of Beneficiary, said notice having been mailed at least twenty-one days successively next before the date of the sale, with said notices specifying the time, place and terms of sale of the above-described property, and with full description of the property to be sold; and

*(continued)*

**FIGURE 10.5 CONTINUED.**

THAT after full compliance by Beneficiary, and the undersigned as Trustee, with all prerequisites required by law and by the Deed of Trust, on October 6, 1999, at the hour of 10:00 or within three hours thereof, I did offer for sale and did sell at public venue, the property above-described at the courthouse door of Harris County, Texas, in the area designated by the County Commissioner's of said County, to Friendly Lender Mortgage Company, the highest and best bidder therefore, as purchaser of said property, and sold to it by me for the sum of Twenty-five Thousand and no/100 Dollars ($25,000.00) applied under the terms of the Deed of Trust; and

I, Charles J. Jacobus, Trustee, in consideration of the premises and of the application of the above-mentioned sum pursuant to the Deed of Trust have GRANTED, SOLD and CONVEYED, and by these presents do GRANT, SELL and CONVEY, unto Friendly Lender Mortgage Company, hereinafter Grantee, whether one or more, all of the hereinabove described real property and appurtenances thereto, being the same property described in and covered by the Deed of Trust.

TO HAVE AND TO HOLD the above-described property and premises, together with the rights, privileges and appurtenances thereto belonging unto the said Grantee, his heirs, executors, administrators, successors and assigns forever; and I, by virtue of the authority vested in me by the Deed of Trust, do hereby bind the Maker, Maker's heirs, executors and administrators, to warrant and forever defend the title to said property to the Grantee, Grantee's executors, administrators, successors and assigns, against every person whomsoever, lawfully claiming or to claim the same or any part thereof as fully as I, Charles J. Jacobus, Trustee, can lawfully do; however, without covenants or warranties, expressed or implied, or any liabilities whatsoever on me personally.

EXECUTED this _____ day of October, 1999.

_____
Charles J. Jacobus, Trustee

Grantee's Address:

_____

_____

be discussed later in this chapter) that maintain that the title cannot be litigated after somebody has been in possession of the property for a certain period of years. Since title can be perfected by adverse possession, title is not necessarily guaranteed back to the original land grant. This is discussed in more depth in the discussion of "Chain of Title" in Chapter 12.

**Special Warranty Deeds.** A **special warranty deed** has basically the same language as the general warranty deed, as shown in Figure 10.2. The only difference is that in the **habendum and warranty clause** of the special warranty deed, the warranty extends only to the ownership of the grantor; that is, the grantor does not warrant any chain of title beyond himself. The grantor's warranty is to warrant the title against all claimants to the title that was acquired "by or through me" but not further back in the chain. *Owen* v. *Yocum*, 341 S.W.2d 709 (Tex. Civ. App.—Ft. Worth, 1960). Note the difference in the habendum and warranty paragraph in the special warranty deed in Figure 10.2, as compared to that of the general warranty deed in Figure 10.1.

Special warranty deeds have a particularly useful application for trustees in bank trust departments, in major corporations, and in governmental entities. These entities are generally owners who acquired title without title insurance (through trust documentation or mergers) or who have held the property for a particular use, which has expired, and they now wish to sell it to a new owner. In the event title fails, and the title company (if one is used) balks at paying the claim, these entities do not want to be bound by whatever discrepancies in the title may have plagued the property prior to their purchase of it. However, they are willing to say that the warranties of title passed by and through them are good and that they have not clouded or encumbered title to that property. It does not necessarily mean a lesser quality of deed, but the warranties are not as good as a general warranty since the grantee effectively waives his rights against the grantor as to any encumbrances existing prior to the grantor's ownership. There is always a risk that discrepancies may materialize at some future date because of a deficiency in title caused by an owner prior to the immediate grantor.

**Bargain and Sale Deeds.** The deed of **bargain and sale** (sometimes called a **deed without warranties**) contains no warranties at all; however, it has a particular value in that it does purport to convey property. Therefore, the After Acquired Title Doctrine (discussed later in this chapter) does apply to bargain and sale deeds, even though there are no warranties on the part of the grantor. *Blanton* v. *Bruce*, 688 S.W.2d 908 (Tex. Civ. App.—Eastland, 1985). The grantor in a bargain and sale deed conveys whatever interest that grantor has in the land but is not giving any warranty of title. A bargain and sale deed is shown in Figure 10.3. Note the disclaimer of any warranty in the habendum clause in the bargain and sale deed. The use of words "grant" or "convey," you will recall, reflects two general warranties. The exception to this is if the warranty is expressly modified, as it is here. *City of Beaumont* v. *Moore*, 202 S.W.2d 448 (Tex. 1947).

**Quitclaim Deeds.** The **quitclaim deed** is a deed by which the grantor quitclaims unto the grantee all of his rights, title, and interests in the property. A quitclaim deed is shown in Figure 10.4. Note that the grantor does not claim to have any interest in that particular piece of property (the words "grant" or "convey" are not used) but is saying that if he does have any interest in that property, he conveys it to the grantee by virtue of the quitclaim deed.

Quitclaim deeds have a valuable use in clearing up clouds on title. A title company or abstractor, in searching the chain of title to a property, may determine that some heir or some grantee in the chain of title may have some interest in that property as the result of a previous transaction. Often however, this heir, or possible title holder, does not know that he has any interest (and maybe he does not actually have any). Therefore, to clear up this cloud on the title, the title company will request that this "possible heir" execute a quitclaim deed, which contains no warranties whatsoever and is not binding as to any warranties on the grantor. The individual with the outstanding interest, then, can convey the interest, if there is any, but without worry that anybody will hold him to any type of warranty as to the title that is being conveyed. The purchaser, however, cannot be a bona fide purchaser for value (discussed in Chapter 12) and takes title with notice of all defects.

An interesting thing about quitclaim deeds is that since there is no warranty or representation of ownership, one can literally give a quitclaim deed to anything. For instance, one can quitclaim the Brooklyn Bridge to convey whatever right, title, and interest one had, if any, in the Brooklyn Bridge to the grantee. It is a perfectly valid deed, and if the grantee is willing to pay consideration for it, the grantee obtains whatever right, title, and interest that the grantor happens to have in the Brooklyn Bridge (which, of course, is nothing beyond what the normal taxpayer has).

It is important to understand, however, that if a person conveys his house to somebody by virtue of a quitclaim deed (or by any of the other kinds of deeds described herein), whatever right, title, and interest he has in his house are certainly conveyed along with that deed. *Thomas v. Rhodes*, 701 S.W.2d 943 (Tex. Civ. App.—Ft. Worth, 1986). The only difference is the warranty of the grantor. Therefore, a quitclaim deed can pass good title if the grantor has good title at the time of the conveyance. *Lott v. Lott*, 370 S.W.2d 463 (Tex. 1963).

**Trustee's Deeds.** A **trustee's deed** is generally thought of, in this state, as a foreclosure deed. A trustee's deed is shown in Figure 10.5. The trustee's warranty binds the owner because the trustee is generally liable only in his representative capacity, and recovery is only against the trust assets, whatever they may be. The trustee normally operates as a pure nominee (legal title holder) for another person or persons, whom we term **beneficial owners**, and acts only on their behalf. The title is, of course, perfectly valid, and it contains all the covenants of general warranty, which bind the previous owner, not the trustee. Title is also passed subject to any encumbrances superior to those of the beneficial owner. The risk to the grantee, generally, is whether or not the trustee is acting in the proper capacity, or that the foreclosure sale was improperly held.

**Court-Ordered Deeds.** A **court-ordered deed** or **sheriff's deed** is a deed given pursuant to a court order or a forced sale by execution (that is, a creditor is probably selling a property because of a debt owed to him by the property owner), and the title, of course, in this case has a good warranty. However, the court does not want to take the obligation of generally warranting title to the property. Therefore, conveyance exists of only the right, title, interest, and claim that the defendant in execution had in the property sold. A sheriff's deed is substantially the same as the trustee's deed.

## Requirements of a Deed

Although it is not particularly beneficial for the average nonlaw student to go into the details of requirements and legal technicalities of a deed, it is important that the average real estate professional be familiar with enough of the details of these instruments to be able to discuss them with his attorneys or the clients' attorneys in a professional manner.

The statutory requirements for a deed are very simple. The deed must be in writing, be subscribed to, and be properly delivered, *V.A.T.S., Property Code, §5.021.* **Delivered** is a key word. If the deed is not properly delivered, it is not a valid conveyance.

In general, case law has held that a deed by its nature is a contract, and it must have all the essential elements of a contract before it can be supported either in law or in equity. If you refer to Chapter 9, you will recall that there are certain provisional requirements for the enforcement of an earnest money contract since it deals with real estate and also has to satisfy the Statute of Frauds in order to be upheld. It follows that since a deed is also a contract, and one that purports to transfer an interest in real estate, then, like an earnest money contract, it also should have specific requirements above and beyond the normal contract requirements required in most non–real estate situations.

In a well-known Texas case, the court, in determining the existence of a valid deed, stated that:

> if from the whole instrument, the *grantor* and *grantee* can be ascertained and there are *operative words of grant showing intent to grant title and sufficiently describing the land* and it is *signed and acknowledged* by the grantor, it is a deed [emphasis supplied], *Brown v. Byrd,* 512 S.W.2d 753 (Tex. Civ. App.—Tyler, 1974).

Now let's compare this statement with the same requirements for earnest money contracts. The requirements for an earnest money contract are as follows:

1. It must be a written instrument.
2. It must be signed by the party to be charged.
3. There must be operative words of grant showing intent to convey an interest at some time in the future.
4. The grantor and grantee must be identifiable.
5. The subject matter to be conveyed must be identifiable.

You will note the only difference between the two instruments, as far as the legal requirements are concerned, is that the deed must show a **present intent to convey**, whereas the earnest money contract has a **future intent to convey**. Aside from this, the legal requirements of the two instruments are basically the same. This similarity also serves to reinforce the Merger Doctrine discussed in the previous chapter. The change in time of the intent to convey, along with the statutorily required delivery, logically merges the terms of the earnest money contract into the deed.

Therefore, the legal requirements of a deed can be summarized as:

1. It must be a written instrument.
2. It must be signed by the party to be charged (the grantor).
3. There must be operative words of grant showing a present intent to convey.
4. The grantor and grantee must be identifiable (legal entities).
5. The subject matter to be conveyed must be identifiable (sufficient legal description).
6. It must be delivered, *V.A.T.S., Property Code, §5.021.*

Of course, the terminology, format, and net effect of the two instruments are entirely different. There has been a considerable amount of discussion as to why a real estate licensee, for instance, can fill in the blanks of an earnest money contract but cannot fill in the blanks of a deed. One must remember that there is a certain finality in a properly executed and delivered deed. If there is a mistake in the deed, the mistake can only be corrected by subsequent correction deed or by subsequent trips to the courthouse to try to get the deed reformed. If there is a mistake in an earnest money contract, on the other hand, it can often be renegotiated, changed, or rescinded with considerably less effort and legal formality.

To keep these statutory and case law requirements from appearing too simple, one must realize that each of these requirements, of course, has further requirements. It is not so simple to determine who an identifiable grantor or grantee may be, what constitutes delivery, and so forth. So to make these matters clearer, we will attempt to discuss each of these requirements to help determine how any given fact situation may affect each of these requirements.

**Requirements of Grantor and Grantee.** The **grantor** is the owner and seller of the property. The grantor must have sufficient mental capacity to reasonably understand the transaction, or else the deed is voidable. The name of the grantor must appear on the document, but it is not necessary that it appear on the body of the deed. The name of the grantor could be just a signature, but it must be somewhere on the instrument, and the grantor must be identifiable. Texas community property laws present an additional concern. It is a generally accepted practice to put the marital status of the grantor into the deed so that the grantee will be on notice of any conflicts of community property laws that may arise as a result of a husband conveying his property without the joinder of his wife, or vice versa. A more complete discussion of how the community property laws affect this is found in previous chapters.

A deed must also have an identifiable **grantee**; if it does not, it is void—not voidable, but void. If the instrument does not purport to convey property to any particular grantee, it simply is not a conveyance. The grantee, of course, must be a legal entity. This does not preclude, of course, the deed being put into the hands of an agent for delivery at a later date. For instance, it can be left with any third-party escrow agent with the provision that it is to be delivered to "the first person who donates $5,000 to my church," or with some other similar contingency. Providing it was properly delivered to the agent, such a conveyance would be considered valid because of the Relation Back Doctrine, discussed later. An interesting note is that the grantee must be alive; a dead man cannot be a grantee. If the grantee dies before the deed is delivered, the conveyance is void.

Texas law requires that, in a deed or other conveyance, the document must contain the mailing address of each grantee appearing on a document, or it must appear in a separate instrument signed by the grantor and grantee and attached to the document. This has no bearing on the legality of the document but provides for a penalty filing fee when the document is filed for record with the county clerk's office, *V.A.T.S., Property Code, §11.003(2)*.

**Intent to Grant Title.** Intent to grant title can generally be construed from the consideration recited and the words of conveyance. The words "grant" and "convey" (operative words of grant) are sufficient to convey, as are other words of positive command or direction. Reciting a mere wish that someone have the property is not sufficient. *Harlan* v. *Vetter*, 732 S.W.2d 390 (Tex. Civ. App.—Eastland, 1987).

Consideration occupies a peculiar position in regard to the deed as a contract in that it is *not* necessary to effect the conveyance of real estate. *Medley* v. *Medley*, 683 S.W.2d 877 (Tex. Civ. App.—Corpus Christi, 1984). Therefore, intent to convey title does not necessarily mean consideration but would include consideration if any is given. For instance, "$1 or $10," "love and affection," or "support and maintenance" are consideration and can effect the conveyance of property. This type of conveyance, supported without valuable consideration, is generally used to transfer property to a loved one, heir, or other situation where a gift or donation suffices for intent and consideration.

However, none of the foregoing is considered "valuable consideration" in a legal sense. "Ten dollars and other good and valuable consideration" may not even be enough in a true legal sense, *Crane* v. *Glenney*, 352 S.W.2d 773 (Tex. Civ. App.—Houston, 1961), because to effect a valid contract in the true legal sense (and not as a gift), there must be true mutuality. If a conveyance is contested by a third party, it has been held that the consideration, at law, must be substantially equal to value; however, the inadequacy of price must be extreme to obtain relief in equity unless coupled with concealment or misrepresentation. A deed, then, is both a contract and a conveyance. In effect, a deed without valuable consideration may be valid as a conveyance (as in a gift to a child), but as a contractual obligation, it may be subject to contest.

**Legal Description.** The deed must have an adequate legal description. There are a lot of "gray areas" surrounding what is considered an adequate legal description. The general maxim is that the property must be sufficiently described so that it is distinct from any other property, and so that it can be reasonably ascertained exactly which property is being conveyed. *Hancock* v. *Booker*, 608 S.W.2d 811 (Tex. Civ. App.—Waco, 1980). If the description of the real property is so indefinite that it cannot be identified with some certainty, the deed is void. *Young* v. *Gharis*, 170 S.W.2d 796 (Tex. Civ. App.—Dallas, 1914). This is discussed in greater detail in Chapter 4.

**Signature of Grantor.** The deed, of course, as discussed before, must be signed by the party to be charged (the grantor), and by the party's spouse if it is community property or homestead property. A forged deed does not pass title. *First Coppell Bank* v. *Smith*, 742 S.W.2d 454 (Tex. App.—Dallas, 1987). The grantee is not generally a signatory party to the deed. The grantee's possession of the deed, constituting acceptance of delivery, is enough to hold the grantee to any responsibilities or liabilities expressed in that deed.

**Delivery.** To be effective as a valid conveyance, a deed must be properly **delivered** and be **accepted** by the grantee. In the actual delivery of a deed, intention of the parties is the primary factor, and this is a fact question for the jury to decide. *DeGrassi* v. *DeGrassi*, 533 S.W.2d 81 (Tex. Civ. App.—Amarillo, 1976). If a deed has been recorded, it is prima facie evidence that proper delivery has been effected. *Austin* v. *Bice*, 586 S.W.2d 931 (Tex. Civ. App.—Waco, 1979). The more serious delivery problems arise when there is a grantee who refuses delivery or there is a partial delivery of the deed to several grantees. In addition, there may be a fact question as to whether or not delivery to a third person as agent for the grantee is a proper delivery, or whether the agent can operate in that fiduciary capacity. The particular facts involved play a key role in determining the question of delivery, and the questions of law generally hinge on these facts. If the deed is placed in an escrow, delivery takes place at that time if (1) the grantee can then exercise final control over delivery and (2) the grantor intended for that delivery to be effective as a conveyance. *Stout* v. *Clayton*, 674 S.W.2d 821 (Tex. Civ. App.—San Antonio, 1984). See Chapter 16, Closings, concerning the Relation Back Doctrine.

**Acknowledgment.** An **acknowledgment** is not necessary for the valid conveyance of real estate and is necessary only for recording. Therefore, even if a valid deed is not acknowledged or recorded, it is still good and binding between the parties, *Haile* v. *Holtzclaw*, 414 S.W.2d 916 (Tex. 1967); *Drake* v. *McGalin*, 626 S.W.2d

786 (Tex. Civ. App.—San Antonio, 1982), although it does not constitute public notice and may not be good in enforcing rights against third parties who may acquire rights in the same property.

Similarly, a date is not required on a deed, since the only important dates are delivery and recordation. The date actually written on the deed is therefore not significant. *Rosestone Properties* v. *Schliemann*, 662 S.W.2d 49 (Tex. Civ. App.—San Antonio, 1983).

## After Acquired Title Doctrine

To give proper effect to certain conveyances, the courts have developed an equitable doctrine that is termed the **After Acquired Title Doctrine**. This doctrine basically sets out that if the grantor conveys the property to the grantee when, in fact, the grantor did not have title to same, title would be conveyed whenever the grantor subsequently obtained titled. The theory is that the grantor is estopped from claiming a title that he has assumed to convey. *Scarmardo* v. *Potter*, 613 S.W.2d 756 (Tex. Civ. App.—Houston, 1981).

For instance, grantor A conveys a property to grantee B by general warranty deed. Grantor A, at the time of conveyance and delivery of the deed, does not have title to the mineral rights of the property; however, he has every expectation of obtaining same. Although there are a number of fact questions involved in a problem like this, the After Acquired Title Doctrine stands for the principle that when grantor A does acquire the mineral rights, the conveyance of those mineral rights will be valid to the first grantee B because of the grantor's initial conveyance. The subsequently required property rights will pass immediately to the grantee, and be binding on the original grantor. *Houston First American Savings Assoc.* v. *Musick*, 650 S.W.2d 764 (Tex. 1983). Note that the After Acquired Title Doctrine does not apply to quitclaim deeds because quitclaim deeds do not purport to convey title to real estate; however, the doctrine does presumably apply to bargain and sale deeds. It is for purposes of this After Acquired Title Doctrine that a bargain and sale deed is often used instead of a quitclaim deed. If there is a question of grantor's title in a bargain and sale deed, it may be later clarified by the After Acquired Title Doctrine concept. The same is not true of a quitclaim deed.

The After Acquired Title Doctrine also is very effective in eliminating problems of fraudulent conveyance. If a grantor induced the grantee to enter into a transaction and conveyed the property to the grantee while the property was still under contract to the grantor, the law would not allow the grantor to obtain title to the property adverse to the present grantee's interest.

## Exceptions, Reservations, and Covenants in Deeds

You may recall that if an estate is not expressly limited, Texas law presumes fee simple title. Exceptions, reservations, and covenants are limitations on the title being passed from the grantor to the grantee. These limitations are significantly different. **Exceptions** are deficiencies in the existing title as part of the grant, which are excepted at the time of the conveyance; that is, they are deficiencies in the title that the grantor has at the time of conveyance. Exceptions would include easements, mineral rights held by third parties, rights-of-way, deed restrictions, or other encumbrances on the grantor's property. They would be excepted from the legal title conveyed because they are not part of the fee title that the grantor holds.

A **reservation**, on the other hand, is a paragraph in a deed creating or reserving an interest to the grantor out of the title being conveyed. Reservations might be mineral rights reserved to the seller. For instance, the grantor would convey the surface of some property but reserve the mineral rights to himself. Often an easement may be reserved to the grantor, by selling the frontage but reserving an easement for the grantor's benefit across the property being conveyed in the grantor's deed. All exceptions and reservations are part of the deed and are enforced under purely contractual principles.

**Covenants** are clauses in deeds that are usually given or received as consideration for the transfer of title. For instance, a deed may contain a covenant that, as part of the conveyance, the grantee agrees not to construct any noxious or odorous industrial plants on the property. Other covenants have often included prohibitions for construction of slaughtering houses, chemical plants, wastewater facilities, cesspools, and the like. Since they are a part of the consideration of the conveyance, these covenants are enforced by theories of contract law. As such, they are enforced by injunctive relief or suit for damages. A breach of a covenant, however, does not result in a loss of title. *Humphrey* v. *C. G. Jung Educational Center of Houston*, supra. For a loss of title to occur, you may recall, one must give a deed with a condition in it, as discussed in Chapter 2.

# Wills

The conveyance of property by virtue of a **will** is a voluntary conveyance in that the person conveying the property by will (the "**testator**") does purport to convey his property to a definite grantee. In the strict application to real estate law, I do not think conveyance by wills needs to be discussed in any great depth, especially as the vast majority of the law involved in this area is best considered in other works on probate law and estate planning. However, it is important to understand the basis of wills as these pertain to certain real estate interests.

## Types of Wills

Texas law basically recognizes two types of wills:

1.  A **witnessed will**, by statute, must:
    a.  Be in writing.
    b.  Be signed by the testator or by another person for him by his direction and in his presence.
    c.  Be attested by two or more creditable witnesses above the age of 14 years.

    This is generally what we consider as a **formal will**, drawn by a lawyer, with the formality, self-proving affidavit, and other more particular requirements and details that competent estate-planning attorneys utilize in performing their services for their clients.

2.  A **holographic will** is a will written wholly in the handwriting of the testator. It does not require any subscribing witnesses, may also have a self-proving affidavit, and is by all means a valid, binding will.

## Conveyance by Will

Once it has been conclusively established that a will exists, the most pertinent point that needs to be made is that encompassed by Section 37 of the Probate Code of the Texas Revised Civil Statutes, which states quite succinctly:

> When a person dies, leaving a lawful will, *all of his estate* devised or bequeathed by such will, and all powers of appointment granted in such will, *shall vest immediately* in the devisees or legatees of such estate and the donees of such power; and all the estate of such person, not devised or bequeathed, shall vest immediately in his heirs at law; *subject, however, to the payments of the debts of the testator or intestate, except such as exempted by law* [emphasis supplied].

Therefore, unless there is a contest of the will or other probate complications, the estate of the deceased passes immediately, subject to the settling of the affairs of that estate. It is particularly important for a licensee to acknowledge the fact that complications may exist in the estate of the deceased and to be sure that listing agreements, contracts, and all other legal instruments pertinent to any real estate involved in this estate are signed by all heirs at law or beneficiaries of the will, to protect both the real estate agent and the purchaser in any subsequent transaction. When an estate is involved, it is very important that the real estate agent rely heavily on the activities of the decedent's lawyers to assure himself of proper compliance with any legal technicalities that may be pertinent.

## ■ SUMMARY

Conveyancing can generally be divided into two categories: voluntary conveyances and involuntary conveyances. Voluntary conveyances are conveyanced by deed and will. Involuntary conveyances include adverse possession, condemnation, foreclosure, intestacy, tax sales, and escheat.

The deed is by far the most voluntary form of conveyance. The types of deeds normally used in Texas include the general warranty deed, special warranty deed, bargain and sale deed, quitclaim deed, trustee's deed, and court-ordered deed. Deeds, like all other real estate contracts, have specific requirements in order to be enforceable and to be upheld. The requirements are construed by case law and by statute.

Wills are basically of three types: a witnessed will, a holographic will, and a nuncupative will. Each type has its own requirements in order to be enforceable and upheld.

## CHAPTER 11

# Involuntary Conveyances

**Involuntary conveyances** are generally categorized as those conveyances over which the grantor has little or no control. The conveyance is generally controlled by statute (as in eminent domain, escheat, and intestacy), but the discretion of third parties is sometimes an important factor in matters concerning tax sales and foreclosures.

## Eminent Domain

**Eminent domain** is a complicated and multifaceted issue. It is an area involved with litigation procedures and damage issues as well as the substantive real estate law. By enactment of eminent domain statutes, legislators have established an expeditious procedure whereby possession of property may quickly be taken for **public purpose**. Eminent domain is exercised through a legal process called **condemnation**. The condemnation procedures are in the interest of the general public and do not require the balancing of the relative interests of the parties involved. The test is merely to see if some definite right results for the public benefit. *Tenngasco Gas Gathering Co.* v. *Fischer*, 624 S.W.2d 301 (Tex. Civ. App.—Corpus Christi, 1983). There must, of course, be **just compensation**, and there are eminent domain statutes that provide for the proper procedure for awarding these damages in the event that just compensation cannot be reached by agreement between the parties.

### Public Purpose

The power of eminent domain vests in the state, county, or political subdivision of a county; in a city or town; in the U.S. government; in irrigation districts, water improvement districts, or water power control districts created by authority of law; or in any other corporation or entity that has been granted the right of eminent domain by the state. *Benat* v. *Dallas County*, 266 S.W.2d 539 (Tex. Civ. App.—Dallas, 1924). It can readily be ascertained that there are a number of different organizations that can exercise their power of eminent domain; these basically include any sort of entity that has been granted that authority by state law, including privately owned authorities such as gas companies, electric companies, and utility districts that are not owned by, or under direct control of, state or governmental agencies.

Once it has been determined that the condemning authority has the authority to condemn, the more complicated question involves what constitutes **public purpose** to justify the taking of the property. Court cases have determined that condemning authorities can take property for public use even if the ultimate purpose of the property is to convey it to a private developer. *Hawaii Housing Authority* v. *Midkiff*, 104 Sup. Ct. 2321 (1984). This has been given specific application in Texas for tax increment financing districts, whose primary legislative authority is to preserve the tax base of certain blighted communities. State law allows the condemning authority to take the property from nonproductive owners and convey it to developers. The net effect is an overall increase in the city's ad valorem tax base, as well as generation of additional sales tax revenues in the new, redeveloped areas. *City of El Paso, Texas* v. *El Paso Community College Dist.*, 729 S.W.2d 296 (Tex. 1987). There has even been a case that implies a professional football team can be a public use because of city subsidization and support for the sport, and because of the revenues generated for the city. *City of Oakland* v. *Oakland Raiders*, 646 P.2d 835, 843 (Cal. 1982).

## Just Compensation

The compensation rights of the grantor under eminent domain proceedings are basically founded in the Fifth and Fourteenth Amendments to the Constitution of the United States, and Article I, Section 17, of the Texas Constitution. The Fifth Amendment states that no one can be denied the right to his property without due process of law. Therefore, if required by the property owner, the condemning authority must go to the court to secure the condemnation if an agreed compensation cannot be reached between the parties. The Fifth Amendment is applied to the individual states by virtue of the Fourteenth Amendment. The Texas Constitution specifies that adequate compensation must be made. *Durden* v. *City of Grand Prairie*, 616 S.W.2d 345 (Tex. Civ. App.—Ft. Worth, 1982). The value that is determined is the value as of the time of the taking and cannot reflect potential value, or increase in value, as a result of the condemnation. *United States* v. *Miller*, 317 U.S. 369 (1943). Therefore, the basis for the just compensation requirement is not something that can be changed by legislative enactment, judicial order, or executive decision. Although the constitutional interpretations may vary from time to time, changes in these rights can only be properly made by an amendment to the respective constitutions.

# Adverse Possession

**Adverse possession** is statutorily defined as:

> An actual and visible appropriation of real property, commenced and continued under a claim of right inconsistent with and hostile to the claim to another person. *Civil Practices, and Remedies Code, §16.021(1).*

This means basically that somebody can enter upon the property of another, peaceably establish his claim of right to that property, and if the true owner is not diligent enough in trying to effect removal of the adverse claim to his property, the adverse claimant's right to the property can ripen into full legal title against the interest of the true owner. The adverse possession statutes are intended to settle and support land titles and are not designed to create a method by which someone may deviously appropriate property for his own use. *Alvarado* v. *Gonzales*, 552 S.W.2d 539 (Tex. Civ. App.—Corpus Christi, 1977). The possession, therefore, must be such open and unambiguous acts that knowledge on the part of the owners is presumed. *Stafford* v. *Jackson*, 687 S.W.2d 784 (Tex. Civ. App.—Houston, 1985). Mere grazing of cattle, for instance, is not open and notorious enough if the land has not been fenced, *Welch* v. *Matthews*, 642 S.W.2d 829 (Tex. Civ. App.—Tyler, 1982), unless the property was "designedly" enclosed for such purpose. *Shouse* v. *Roberts*, 737 S.W.2d 354 (Tex. App.—Houston [14th Dist.], 1987 writ ref'd n.r.e.). Planting a hedge would be enough to claim adverse possession, though mere maintenance is not enough. *Bywaters* v. *Gannon*, 686 S.W.2d 593 (Tex. 1985); *Julien* v. *Baker*, 758 S.W.2d 873 (Tex. App.—Houston [14th Dist.], 1988). The same is true of fence encroachments. Minor fence encroachments in subdivisions are not adverse possession; they are merely encroachments. *McAllister* v. *Samuels*, 857 S.W.2d 768 (Tex. App.—Houston [14th Dist.], 1993, writ den.). If a person is in possession under a claim of right recognized by the owner (such as a co-tenant, leasehold estate, or conditional title), adverse possession cannot exist unless the claim to possession is blatant and obvious. *Hernandez* v. *Hernandez*, 611 S.W.2d 732 (Tex. Civ. App.—San Antonio, 1981); *Humphrey* v. *C. G. Jung Educational Center of Houston*, supra, *King Ranch, Inc.* v. *Chapman*, 118 S.W.3d 742 (Tex. 2003). The use must also be continuous. If the land is allowed to lie fallow and not be used periodically, it does not toll the statute of limitations because the land must be in constant use. *Parker* v. *McGinnis*, 842 S.W.2d 357 (Tex. App.—Houston [1st Dist.], 1992, writ den.).

Texas has provisions for 3-, 5-, 10-, and 25-year statutes of limitations under which an adverse claimant can gain title of the property adversely to the true owner.

## Three-Year Statute

The three-year statute of limitations is as follows.

> **§16.024. Adverse Possession: Three-Year Limitations Period**
> A person must bring suit to recover real property held by another in peaceable and adverse possession under title or color of title not later than three years after the day the cause of action accrues.

**Title** refers to a regular chain of transfers from or under the sovereignty of the soil, and **color of title** is meant as a consecutive chain of such transfers down to the person in possession that: (1) is not regular because of a muniment that is not properly recorded or is only in writing or because of a similar defect that does not want of intrinsic fairness or honesty; or (2) is based on a certificate of head-right, land warrant, or land scrip. This chain of transfers might even be "irregular" (that is, one or more of the documents of title may not be duly registered), but "irregular" does not include any documents obtained that may have been obtained through fraudulent or dishonest means. Therefore, under the three-year adverse possession statute, if the party has taken possession of the property under some color of title or some chain of title, the owner of the real estate cannot institute suit to dispossess him of that property after three years after the cause of action accrued. The cause of action is presumed to have accrued upon entry of the adverse claimant to the property. *Hickman* v. *Ferguson*, 164 S.W.2d 1085 (Tex. Civ. App.—Austin, 1914).

## Five-Year Statute

The five-year adverse possession statute is set out as follows.

### §16.025. Adverse Possession: Five-Year Limitations Period

(a) A person must bring suit not later than five years after the day the cause of action accrues to recover real property held in peaceable and adverse possession by another who:

(1) cultivates, uses, or enjoys the property.

(2) pays applicable taxes on the property.

(3) claims the property under a duly registered deed.

(b) This section does not apply to a claim based on a forged deed or a deed executed under a forged power of attorney.

Note that the five-year possession statute does not require a title or color of title requirement, as the three-year possession statute does. It requires only the cultivating, using, or enjoying of the property; paying taxes on it (which must be paid before they become delinquent); and claiming under a deed. However, as in all other cases, a void deed or one obtained through fraudulent or dishonest practices is not allowed the benefits of the five-year adverse possession statute. Although a quitclaim deed is not sufficient to perfect adverse possession under the five-year statute, *Bell* v. *Ott*, 606 S.W.2d 942 (Tex. Civ. App.—Waco, 1980), the requirements of a deed are minimal. The whole object of the statute is to define the boundaries of the claim and give notice to the owner of such adverse claim. An instrument in the form of a deed not void on its face, even though the grantor is wholly without title, satisfies the requirement of the statute. *Hunter* v. *Dodds*, 624 S.W.2d 365 (Tex. Civ. App.—Waco, 1981).

## 10-Year Statute

The 10-year adverse possession statute is set out as follows.

### §16.026. Adverse Possession: 10-Year Limitations Period

(a) A person must bring suit not later than 10 years after the day the cause of action accrues to recover real property held in peaceable and adverse possession by another who cultivates, uses, or enjoys the property.

(b) Without a title instrument, peaceable and adverse possession is limited in this section to 160 acres, including improvements, unless the number of acres actually enclosed exceeds 160. If the number of enclosed acres exceeds 160 acres, peaceable and adverse possession extends to the real property actually enclosed.

(c) Peaceable possession of real property held under a duly registered memorandum of title other than a deed that fixes the boundaries of the possessor's claim extends to the boundaries specified in the instrument.

The burden of proof in the 10-year adverse possession statute is considerably less than even that of the five-year statute. Again, the adverse possessor must only be cultivating, using, or enjoying the real estate. However, the real estate cannot exceed 160 acres unless it has been actually enclosed by a fence or some other barricade that would manifest the adverse possessor's claim to that property that is in excess of 160 acres.

The same claim to an amount of property in excess of 160 acres can also be held to ripen into full title when a written **memorandum of title** (which includes an instrument other than a deed) is recorded. The adverse possessor's claim of the property shall be presumed to be coextensive with the boundary.

Therefore, the requirements under the 10-year adverse possession statute really require very little effort other than occupying, cultivating, and enjoying the premises. If the adverse possessor wants more than 160 acres, his right to the excess acreage is presumed if it is actually enclosed by a fence, or a written memorandum of title duly recorded reflects such excess acreage.

## 25-Year Statutes

The 25-year adverse possession statutes are set out as follows.

### §16.027. Adverse Possession: 25-Year Limitations Period Notwithstanding Disability

A person, regardless of whether the person is or has been under a legal disability, must bring suit not later than 25 years after the day the cause of action accrues to recover real property held in peaceable and adverse possession by another who cultivates, uses, or enjoys the property.

### §16.028. Adverse Possession With Recorded Instrument: 25-Year Limitations Period

(a) A person, regardless of whether the person is or has been under a legal disability, may not maintain an action for the recovery of real property held for 25 years before the commencement of the action in peaceable and adverse possession by another who holds the property in good faith and under a deed or other instrument purporting to convey the property that is recorded in the deed records of the county where any part of the real property is located.

(b) Adverse possession of any part of the real property held under a recorded deed or other recorded instrument that purports to convey the property extends to and includes all of the property described in the instrument, even though the instrument is void on its face or in fact.

(c) A person who holds real property and claims title under this section has a good and marketable title to the property regardless of a disability arising at any time in the adverse claimant or a person claiming under the adverse claimant.

### §16.029. Evidence of Title to Land by Limitations

(a) In a suit involving title to real property that is not claimed by this state, it is prima facie evidence that the title to the property has passed from the person holding apparent record title to an opposing party if it is shown that:

(1) for one or more years during the 25 years preceding the filing of the suit the person holding apparent record title to the property did not exercise dominion over or pay taxes on the property.

(2) during that period the opposing parties and those whose estate they own have openly exercised dominion over and have asserted a claim to the land and have paid taxes on it annually before becoming delinquent for as long as 25 years.

(b) This section does not affect a statute of limitations, a right to prove title by circumstantial evidence under the case law of this state, or a suit between a trustee and a beneficiary of the trust.

The 25-year statute of limitations is logically the one that requires the least burden of proof on the part of the adverse possessor. Note that the only thing required to ripen adverse possession after 25 years is any instrument (or instruments) purporting to convey the property to the adverse possessor that has been recorded in the deed records of the county in which the real estate is situated. Such title can even vest unto the adverse possessor's successors as long as there is a privity of estate between them, that is, some sort of conveyance reflected to the successor.

It is also important to note that the 25-year statute is the only statute that runs against title holders who may be minors, insane, or suffering from other disability.

As a general rule, adverse possession cannot run against property dedicated to public use, or to people who are minors, imprisoned, of unsound mind, or serving in the armed forces of the United States during time of war, *V.T.C.A., Civil Practice and Remedies Code, §§16.030, 16.022.*

## Other Issues

Other issues relevant to adverse possession are discussed in the following paragraphs.

**Recording.** One issue is the question as to the time of recordation of the deed and conflicting interests between various deed holders. The law in Texas is that title given by adverse possession of the property is equivalent to that of constructive notice, *Bell* v. *Smith*, 532 S.W.2d 680 (Tex. Civ. App.—Ft. Worth, 1976), so that actual possession of the property is enough to put any purchaser or true owner on constructive notice that said adverse possessor may have a claim, and therefore it is equivalent to recording. There is no requirement that the adverse possessor be openly defiant.

**Nature of Claim.** The adverse claim must be peaceable, which means possession of real property that is continuous and is not interrupted by an adverse suit to recover the property. Although the adverse possession statutes specify hostile claim, the adverse possessor cannot sit with a rifle, gun, or other military paraphernalia to try to establish the adverse claim. The mere fact that the claim is against the wishes of the landowners is enough to determine that the possession is hostile. All Texas real estate agents who have grown up in the shadow of the great Texas land barons should now understand why it was so necessary to ride the range on a regular basis. If the owners of land did not keep their property fenced and remove the poachers on a regular basis, they would be forever fighting claims of adverse possession. An owner may acknowledge the existence of a tenancy, however. Absent other facts, a **tenant** is occupying the premises with the landlord's consent and therefore cannot be an adverse possessor. If a tenant wants to assert an adverse possession claim, he must put the owner on notice of the hostile nature of the claim. *Wright* v. *Wallace*, 700 S.W.2d 269 (Tex. Civ. App.—Corpus Christi, 1985).

**Tacking.** There is a basic concept in adverse possession called "**tacking.**" The theory of tacking provides that anyone in adverse possession of the property may tack on his years of adverse possession with those of his predecessor in interest so that the adverse possessions can cumulatively total the requisite number of years to acquire title by limitation. The tacking only requires a privity of estate and not a privity of title; so as long as the adverse possessors maintain this privity of estate or possession, two or more adverse possessors may tack enough consecutive years to acquire good title, *V.T.C.A., Civil Practice and Remedies Code, §16.023.*

In more modern times, it can be understood that the title companies, on examining title to a piece of property back to the sovereign, can generally rely on a three-year adverse possession statute in the event there is a claim at a later date concerning title discrepancies to any given parcel of real estate on which they have insured title.

## Encroachments

One of the more novel problems of adverse possession is what constitutes adverse possession in a subdivision. There has been a common misconception that when a fence is a few feet (or inches) on somebody else's property, there is an ultimate claim to title to the adjacent property by adverse possession. It should be noted that most small misalignments of fence are cosmetic or "casual" fencing. Such casual fencing is not adverse possession. *Rhodes* v. *Cahill*, 802 S.W.2d 643, 646 (Tex. 1990). In rural environments such casual fencing is not adverse possession. In an urban environment (subdivisions) this is often a mere encroachment and not a true claim of adverse possession as would ripen under the 3-, 5-, 10-, or 25-year statutes. *McAllister* v. *Samuels*, supra.

# Intestate Succession

When a person dies leaving no will, it is said that she has died **intestate**. Therefore, all of her property passes purely by operation of statutory law, often called the statutes of **descent and distribution**. The specific statutes that control how the property is distributed are as follows:

### §38. Persons Who Take Upon Intestacy

(a) Intestate Leaving No Husband or Wife. Where any person, having title to any estate, real, personal or mixed, shall die intestate, leaving no husband or wife, it shall descend and pass in parcenary to his kindred, male and female, in the following course:

1. To his children and their descendants.

2. If there be no children nor their descendants, then to his father and mother, in equal portions. But if only the father or mother survive the intestate, then his estate shall be divided into two equal portions, one of which shall pass to such survivor, and the other half shall pass to the brothers and sisters of the deceased, and to their descendants; but if there be none such, then the whole estate shall be inherited by the surviving father or mother.

3. If there be neither father nor mother, then the whole of such estate shall pass to the brothers and sisters of the intestate, and to their descendants.

4. If there be none of the kindred aforesaid, then the inheritance shall be divided into two moieties, one of which shall go to the paternal and the other to the maternal kindred, in the following course: To the grandfather and grandmother in equal portions, but if only one of these be living, then the estate shall be divided into two equal parts, one of which shall go to such survivor, and the other shall go to the descendant or descendants of such deceased grandfather or grandmother. If there be no such descendants, then the whole estate shall be inherited by the surviving grandfather or grandmother. If there be no surviving grandfather or grandmother, then the whole of such estate shall go to their descendants, and so on without end, passing in like manner to the nearest lineal ancestors and their descendants.

(b) Intestate Leaving Husband or Wife. Where any person having title to any estate, real, personal or mixed, other than a community estate, shall die intestate as to such estate, and shall leave a surviving husband or wife, such estate of such intestate shall descend and pass as follows:

1. If the deceased have a child or children, or their descendants, the surviving husband or wife shall take one-third of the personal estate, and the balance of such personal estate shall go to the child or children of the deceased and their descendants. The surviving husband or wife shall also be entitled to an estate for life, in one-third of the land of the intestate, with remainder to the child or children of the intestate and their descendants.

2. If the deceased have no child or children, or their descendants, then the surviving husband or wife shall be entitled to all the personal estate, and to one-half of the lands of the intestate, without remainder to any person, and the other half shall pass and be inherited according to the rules of descent and distribution; provided, however, that if the deceased has neither surviving father nor mother nor surviving brothers or sisters, or their descendants, then the surviving husband or wife shall be entitled to the whole of the estate of such intestate.

Constitutional provisions. Const. art. 3, §56, provides, in part, that the Legislature shall not, except as otherwise provided in this Constitution, pass any local or special law changing the law of descent or succession.

There was a major change on intestate death of a spouse in the 1993 legislature:

### §45. Community Estate

(a) On the intestate death of one of the spouses to a marriage, the community property estate of the deceased spouse passes to the surviving spouse if:

(1) no child or other descendant of the deceased spouse survives the deceased spouse.

(2) all surviving children and descendants of the deceased spouse are also children or descendants of the surviving spouse.

(b) On the intestate death of one of the spouses to a marriage, if a child or other descendant of the deceased spouse survives the deceased spouse and the child or descendant is not a child or descendant of the surviving spouse, one-half of the community estate is of the deceased spouse. The descendant shall inherit only such portion of said property to which they would be entitled under Section 43 of this code. In every case, the community estate passes charged with the debts against it.

When someone dies intestate, the heirs of the decedent must take the affirmative approach to have the estate of the decedent probated and to have a final determination as to how the estate is to be divided. The court normally appoints an **administrator** or **administratrix** (in testate succession, the decedent's will appoints an **executor** or **executrix**) to oversee the proper distribution of the decedent's estate. Without going into a great amount of detail, it is only important to realize that the estate of the decedent is generally split amongst her heirs, depending on whether or not she had a spouse, or children, or both, and whether or not that property was separate or community property. Even an illegitimate child can inherit property under certain circumstances. *Reed* v. *Campbell*, 682 S.W.2d 697 (Tex. Civ. App.—El Paso, 1984). There is very little chance that all of the property will go to one individual if the decedent dies intestate, unless it is community property and the decedent has no children. The distribution of intestate succession is graphically shown in Figure 11.1.

There is a perennial question as to who are heirs of the decedent's community property. The new statute provides that on the death of one spouse, the community property of the deceased passes to the surviving spouse if all of the children are the children of that marriage. If the child is not a child of the surviving spouse, one-half of the community estate is retained by the surviving spouse and the other one-half passes to the children or decedents of the deceased spouse. Therefore, if upon one spouse's death, there are children by another spouse, the surviving spouse owns, outright, one-half of the community property, not as an heir but as a survivor in the

**FIGURE 11.1  DISTRIBUTION OF INTESTATE SUCCESSION.**

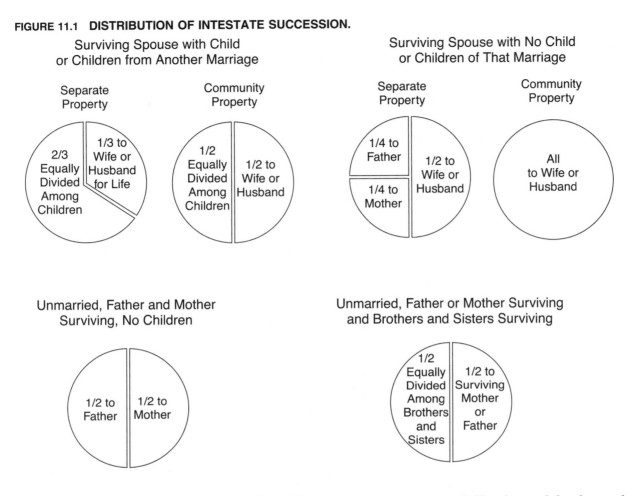

community, and the children own the remaining one-half as heirs of the deceased mother or father. *Forrest* v. *Moreno*, 161 S.W.2d 364 (Tex. Civ. App.—San Antonio, 1942).

This is in contrast to separate property, where the spouse does inherit a life estate in one-third of the deceased spouse's property. *Walker* v. *Young*, 37 T. 519 (Tex. 1873). For instance, if a husband and wife own 100 shares of stock and the husband dies, 33⅓ shares of the stock would go to the spouse and the other 66⅔ shares would be divided equally among the children as his heirs. To add further complications, the statute also provides that an illegitimate child may petition the court to determine his rights of inheritance. This statute may create a few worries!

Beyond these few initial facts, it is obviously wise for anybody interested in acquiring real estate through the estate of an intestate decedent to be absolutely sure that all the legal aspects are properly taken care of through the courts before taking any action.

# Foreclosure

The Texas standard deed of trust form (to be discussed in greater detail in Chapter 13), used in the great majority of mortgage transactions, contains a "**power of sale**" clause. Although this mortgage instrument has consistently been held to be a contractual obligation between the parties, and not under authority of the state, the procedure for the **foreclosure** proceedings is codified under *V.T.C.A., Property Code, §51.002*. Generally, all sales by execution conferred by any deed of trust or other lien shall be made:

1. At the door of the county courthouse.

2. In the county in which the land is located.

3. At public vendue between 10:00 a.m. and 4:00 p.m. of the first Tuesday of any month.

4. After proper notice has been posted at said courthouse door, and notice of sale has been mailed by certified mail to each debtor at least 21 days preceding the date of sale.

In practice, the holder of the note (mortgage lender or, in some cases, the mortgage servicer) acts through a **trustee**, who literally holds a public auction between 10:00 a.m. and 4:00 p.m. on the first Tuesday of the month, after proper notice has been posted. Anyone can bid for and buy the real estate providing the purchaser has enough cash to buy the property at the auction. The purchaser, by means of a trustee's deed, buys whatever interest the lien holder has in the real estate. The lien holder, through his trustee, can sell the property for whatever price he deems sufficient.

Once the sale has been made and the trustee's deed has been delivered, the new purchaser succeeds to the lien holder's rights. Conceivably, the lien holder can then sell the property for $10 and take a judgment against the debtor for the deficiency (the difference between the amount owed and the foreclosure sale price received for the property). This procedure can, of course, lead to abuses when a valuable parcel of real estate can be sold for a grossly inadequate price to a nominee of the lien holder, leaving the debtor liable for a personal judgment for the difference. However, providing there is no irregularity in the sale, the deed of trust foreclosure sale will not be avoided merely because of inadequacy of price. The mortgagee can purchase the property at the sale so long as the sale is conducted fairly and in accordance with the terms of the deed of trust. If there are any excess funds, they are forwarded to the borrower after the expenses of the sale have been paid.

There are always additional questions of presentment, payment acceleration of all the payments, and other technical legal aspects of the sale, abuse of which can set aside the foreclosure sale. It is well advised, however, to take foreclosure proceedings seriously. They are seldom set aside. The law clearly seems to favor the mortgagee in a foreclosure. It must be remembered that if the rights of the debtor or the mortgagee have to be balanced, the mortgagee often has more interest in the land than the debtor, and in order to encourage real estate loans, the lender needs to be protected. Without this type of protection, mortgagees might prefer to place their lendable sources of cash into other types of investments.

# Tax Sales

The only sale of real property for property taxes in Texas is for ad valorem taxes pursuant to state law. There are no federal ad valorem taxes, and tax sales of real property for other than state ad valorem taxes are not going to be considered here.

It is sufficient to say that the federal government can sell virtually anything to recover its tax debt.

It is generally understood that all property in this state is liable for taxes. That is, if **ad valorem taxes** have not been paid, the owner's property, whether real or personal, may be levied against to satisfy all delinquent taxes. Sales of real property for delinquent taxes of any type are specifically provided for in this state by statute. There are exceptions to this rule—one is the sacred cow of Texas, the homestead. Statutorily, the homestead cannot be sold for taxes other than the taxes due on such homestead. The other exception is the elderly. If the homeowner is older than 65 years of age, no sale can take place while the person still owns the house, *V.T.C.A., Tax Code, §33.06.*

As in most other involuntary sales of real estate, the property must be properly advertised. In the case of **tax sales**, the advertisements for the sale must occur for three consecutive weeks in some newspaper published in the county where the land is to be sold. The advertisement must state the time, place, and terms of sale; and like the foreclosure sale, it must be held at public outcry at the courthouse door, between legal hours on the first Tuesday of the month.

To effect the sale, then, a **tax deed** is used. The tax deed provides for conveyance of all the rights and interest the former owner had at the time when the assessment was made. The deed also specifically provides for the redemption period and penalties specified in *V.T.C.A., Tax Code, §32.06.* A copy of a tax deed is shown in Figure 11.2.

The biggest difference between the tax sale and any other type of execution or foreclosure is that the tax sale provides for a specific right of the debtor, termed the **right of redemption**; that is, the debtor has the right to buy back his property if he pays the statutory penalties for doing so.

The debtor may assert the limitation statutes as his defense to stop the tax sale. These limitations are very liberal, however. The taxing authority must file suit for taxes due on personal property within four years. The suit must be filed within 20 years for taxes due on real property. The owner of the property may request that certain, specific property be sold first, *V.T.C.A., Tax Code, §34.01(b).* The subject of tax sales is discussed in greater detail in Chapter 21.

## Escheat

**Escheat** is the statutory provision of the State of Texas that provides for the transfer of real estate belonging to any person who dies without a will and has no heirs, or where the owner of any real property shall be absent for a term of seven years and is not known to exist, leaving no heirs or will. Such real estate shall escheat to and vest in the State of Texas. This simply provides for the State of Texas to get title to real estate so that no parcels of property will be unaccounted for. It is a tool to effect valid conveyance of real estate when there are no other possible means of conveyance. The methods for this conveyance are controlled very strictly by statute. It is generally safe to assume that the state does not want to become the proprietor of various odd tracts of land throughout the state, and so escheat is used only as a last resort. The process of escheating land is done through a court proceeding in a district court in the county in which the land is located. Upon such final judgment being rendered, title to the land is forwarded to the commissioner of the General Land Office in Austin, Texas, and is **dedicated** to the **Permanent Free School Fund** for the State of Texas. The commissioner may lease or sell this property as he sees fit if it is determined (by the commissioner) to be in the state's best interest.

**FIGURE 11.2 TAX DEED.**

**TAX DEED**

THE STATE OF TEXAS                    §

                                     § KNOW ALL MEN BY THESE PRESENTS

COUNTY OF _____           §


        THAT WHEREAS, by virtue of an Order of Sale issued by the
Clerk of the District Court in and for _____ County,
dated _____, on a certain judgment rendered in said Court
on _____, in a certain suit No. _____ styled

_____
_____ I, _____ Sheriff
of said County, did upon _____, levy upon and advertise
the said premises as described in said Order of Sale, by giving public notice
of the time and place of said sale by an advertisement in the English Language, published once a week for three consecutive weeks preceding such
sale, the first publication appearing not less than twenty days immediately
preceding the day of sale, beginning on the _____ day of _____ A.D.
20_____, in the _____ a newspaper published in the
County of _____, stating in said advertisement the
authority by virtue of which said sale was to be made, the time of levy, the
time and place of sale, a brief description of the property to be sold, the
number of acres, the original survey, its locality in the County, and the name
by which the land is generally known, and by delivering a similar notice
to each of the above named defendants, and on the first Tuesday in
_____, 20_____, within the hours prescribed by law, sold said
hereinafter described land or lots at public vendue, at the Courthouse door
of said County, at which sale the premises hereinafter described were struck
off to:


for the sum of

(he, she, they) being the highest bidder(s) therefore, and that being the
highest bid for the same,

        NOW, THEREFORE, in consideration of the premises aforesaid,
and of the payment of the said sum of

the receipt of which is hereby acknowledged, I, _____,
Sheriff as aforesaid, have Granted, Sold and Conveyed, and by these

*(continued)*

**FIGURE 11.2  CONTINUED.**

presents do Grant, Sell and Convey unto the said all of the estate, right, title and interest which the defendants in such suit had on the date said judgment was rendered or at any time afterwards, in and to the following described land and premises, as described in the Order of Sale, viz:

TO HAVE AND TO HOLD the above described premises, subject, however, to the defendant's right to redeem the same in the manner prescribed by law within two years from the date of recordation of this deed, unto the said _____, heirs and assigns, forever, as fully and as absolute as I, as Sheriff aforesaid, can convey by virtue of said Order of Sale. It is understood and agreed that by virtue of said Judgment and Order of Sale, writ of possession will issue within twenty days after the period of redemption shall have expired, but not until then.

IN TESTIMONY WHEREOF, I have hereunto set my hand this _____ day of _____ , A.D. 20_____ .

_____

Sheriff _____ County
Texas

– – – – – – – – – – – – – –

THE STATE OF TEXAS

COUNTY OF _____

Before me, the undersigned authority, on this day personally appeared _____ , Sheriff, known to me to be the person whose name is subscribed to the foregoing instrument and acknowledged to me that he executed the same as Sheriff aforesaid, for the purposes, consideration and in the capacity therein expressed.

Given under my hand and seal of office, this _____ day of _____ , AD. 20 _____ .

_____

_____

_____ County, Texas

# Gain or Loss of Title by Natural Causes

In Texas, gain or loss of title by natural causes has been an object of some controversy over the years. Some people have termed the gain of property accession. **Accession**, however, applies only to personal property and refers to the acquisition of title to personal property by its incorporation into the real property. The natural causes that may affect title are evidenced by accretion, alluvion, reliction, erosion, avulsion, and subsidence. When these natural forces occur, sometimes one loses title and sometimes one does not, depending on the form in which the natural force occurs.

## Accretion and Alluvion

**Accretion** is the increase in land area by the gradual and imperceptible deposition of solid material from the operation of natural causes. **Alluvion** normally applies to the solid material that is deposited, although the terms are often used interchangeably. Title may be acquired by accretion or alluvion. *Giles* v. *Basore*, 278 S.W.2d 830 (Tex. 1955).

## Reliction

**Reliction** applies to an increase in land area caused by the withdrawal of waters contiguous to it. This is contrasted with alluvion or accretion where the silt, mud, or other material is deposited. In reliction, the waters gradually withdraw from the subject property, perhaps through the change of a bed of a river, creek, or stream. Title may be acquired by reliction.

## Erosion

**Erosion** is defined as the gradual washing away (decrease in area) of land bordering on a stream or body of water by the action of the water. Title to the eroded land is lost as long as the erosion is imperceptible.

## Avulsion

**Avulsion** is the sudden and perceptible loss of or addition to land by the action of water due to the sudden change in the bed or course of a stream. In the case of avulsion, the dividing line between the property owners remains in accordance with the former boundaries and not in accordance with the boundaries created by the avulsion. Title is neither lost nor acquired.

The general rule appears to be that if the loss of the land is gradual or imperceptible, title is lost. "Gradual" or "imperceptible" has been characterized as a change that a person could not notice while it was happening but could, from time to time, notice the result of the process. *Denny* v. *Cotton*, 22 S.W. 122 (Tex. Civ. App.—1893).

The more difficult question is defining "gradual." Does a hurricane gradually erode a coastline and result in loss of title? Additional questions of gaining title are posed when the property of a riverbed is owned by the State of Texas. If reliction occurs and the streambed is owned by the state, Texas law generally favors retention of title of the streambed by the State of Texas. *Dolan* v. *Walker*, 49 S.W.2d 695 (Tex. 1932). It has already been well settled that title of property owned by the state may not be acquired by adverse possession, *Tex. Rev. Civ. Stat. Ann., Art. 5517.*

## Subsidence

**Subsidence** or **submergence** occurs when the water advances to Subsidence cover the previously dry land. This is accomplished by the rising level of water or by lowering the elevation of the land. Title is not lost through submergence. *Coastal Industrial Water Authority* v. *York*, 532 S.W.2d 949 (Tex. 1976).

## ■ SUMMARY

Eminent domain is a right by which some public entity with the power of condemnation can take an individual's property for public use provided that there is just compensation. Adverse possession, on the other hand, is the right of a private individual to obtain full title to someone else's property by virtue of his possession of that property. Intestate succession is a statutory procedure that determines who has the right to the decedent's estate if a person dies leaving no will. Foreclosure is a statutory method of selling property because of a default on a mortgage. Tax sales are sales by some governmental entity for past due and delinquent taxes. Escheat is the statutory provision of the State of Texas that provides for the transfer of real estate to the capital estate of Texas when a person dies leaving no will and no heirs.

## CHAPTER 12

# Recording, Constructive Notice, and Acknowledgments

## Recording and Constructive Notice

The State of Texas, through a series of laws in the Property Code, provides for a means of recordation that is available to all individuals who have an interest in real estate. Through these laws, anyone who has an interest in real estate may put the world on notice of their interest in the real estate by recording the instrument reflecting that interest in the real property records of the county in which the land is located.

Virtually all instruments may be recorded, *V.T.C.A., Property Code, §12.001(a)*. If the document to be recorded is a deed or another conveyance conveying an interest in real property, it should contain the mailing address of each grantee appearing on the document, or in a separate instrument signed by a grantor or grantee and attached to the document. Failure to include such an address does not render the instrument void or voidable, but it substantially raises the recording fee for that instrument, *V.T.C.A., Property Code, §11.003(2)(b)*.

The effect of recording one's interest in real estate is to put all subsequent purchasers for valuable consideration and all creditors on notice of the claimant's interest in that particular piece of property, and that the instrument is subject to inspection by the public. *V.T.C.A., Property Code, §13.002*. Subsequent purchasers and creditors, then, are under a duty of care to search the records of real property in the county in which the land is located to assure themselves of proper title or of priority lien interests in the real estate that may adversely affect them. Texas law further provides that unless these instruments are recorded, they are void as to all such subsequent purchasers and creditors, *V.T.C.A., Property Code, §13.001(a)*.

Therefore, the basic premises behind the **Recording Act** are:

1. To protect the individual who owns an interest in real estate (because by recording he establishes the priority of his interest).

2. To assure subsequent purchasers and creditors as to the status of the title of that real estate (third parties can search the title to be sure there are no interests recorded that are superior to theirs).

**It is important to note, however, that any instrument that is not recorded is still binding between the parties; but it is not notice to third**

**parties or subsequent creditors or purchasers of the property and therefore would not be binding against them**, *V.T.C.A., Property Code, §13.001(b)*. The process of recording the interest in the real estate is performed in the county clerk's office in the county courthouse in the county in which the land is situated. Once the instrument has been properly recorded in the county clerk's office and made public record, the entire world is legally on notice of that interest in the real estate. This type of notice is termed **constructive notice** and is considered to be as good as actual notice because the law requires subsequent purchasers and creditors to search the records. *Clear Lake Apartments, Inc.* v. *Clear Lake Utilities Co.*, 537 S.W.2d 48 (Tex. Civ. App.—Houston, 1976).

Constructive notice differs from actual notice. **Actual notice** exists when the subsequent purchaser or creditor has express information about something—something that reasonable, diligent inquiry and exercise of the means of information would disclose. *O'Farrel* v. *Coolidge*, 225 S.W.2d 582 (Tex. Civ. App.—Texarkana, 1949). Constructive notice is information or knowledge of a fact imputed by law to a person. Knowledge of the county real property records, as well as knowledge of anyone in actual possession of the property, constitutes constructive notice. *Park* v. *Sweeten*, 270 S.W.2d 687 (Tex. Civ. App.—San Antonio, 1954).

If a person acquires real property without either type of notice (actual or constructive), he is considered to be a **bona fide purchaser for value without notice** and acquires title to that real property free and clear of any other claims. Therefore, in order to obtain the status of bona fide purchaser for value without notice, the prospective purchaser has the obligation to: (1) search the record and (2) look at the property to see who is in possession, in order to satisfy the requirements of constructive notice. The purchaser also needs to inquire diligently into the resolution of any apparent defects or conflicting interests of which he may have to satisfy the requirement of actual notice. *Raposa* v. *Johnson*, 693 S.W.2d 43 (Tex. Civ. App.—Ft. Worth, 1985).

## The Recording Process

Therefore, recording a document is the simplest method of creating notice. There are four basic requirements that an instrument must have to be properly recorded:

1. The instrument must be the original instrument, not a copy (which means that the signature must be original).
2. The instrument must be in English and not a foreign language.
3. The instrument must be properly acknowledged, properly witnessed (acknowledgment and witnessing will be discussed in more depth later in this chapter), or sworn to with a proper jurat.
4. It must be recorded in the county where the property is located.
5. If it is an "instrument" (deed or deed of trust) it must contain a notice on the first page of the instrument in 12 point bold-faced type or 12 point upper case letters and read substantially as follows:

**NOTICE OF CONFIDENTIALITY RIGHTS: IF YOU ARE A NATURAL PERSON, YOU MAY REMOVE OR STRIKE ANY OF THE FOLLOWING INFORMATION FROM ANY INSTRUMENT THAT TRANSFERS AN INTEREST IN REAL PROPERTY BEFORE IT IS FILED FOR RECORD IN THE PUBLIC RECORDS: YOUR SOCIAL SECURITY NUMBER OR YOUR DRIVER'S LICENSE NUMBER.**

If federal law requires a document contain a social security number or driver's license number, it overrules this requirement.

When the foregoing requirements are complied with and the instrument is recorded, the recording process is determined to have been "perfected" such that subsequent purchasers and creditors are on notice, *V.T.C.A., Property Code, §11.07.*

**Electronic Filing** New changes were recently enacted by the Texas Legislature that allow authorized persons to file documents electronically with a county clerk that accepts electronic filing. Those who may file electronically include: (1) an attorney licensed in Texas; (2) a bank, savings and loan association savings bank, or a credit union doing business under the laws of the United States or the State of Texas; (3) a federally chartered lending institution, a federal government-sponsored entity, an instrumentality of the federal government, or a person approved as a mortgagee by the United States to make federally insured loans; (4) a person licensed to make regulated loans in Texas; (5) a title insurance company or title insurance agent licensed to do business in Texas; or (6) an agency of the State of Texas.

A county clerk that accepts electronic filing must confirm or reject the electronic filing not later than the first business day after the date the instrument is filed. This notice of confirmation or rejection must be made by electronic means, if possible, or if not possible, by telephone or electronic facsimile machine. If the county clerk fails to provide a notice of rejection within the time provided, the instrument is considered accepted for filing and may not subsequently be rejected. The county recorder is required to charge the same fee for filing electronically as recording a document under traditional recording procedures.

Is there a potential for confusion? Obviously; so the State Legislature has provided for an electronic recording advisory committee to recommend to the Texas State Library and Archives Commission rules to provide guidance as to how this new system is to work effectively. Many have predicted that we will soon have "paperless" closings. If, after the closing, the party wants a copy of a document, he can simply access it through the county records on his computer. The times, they are a changing.

## Chain of Title

In the less populated Texas counties, the instruments are recorded in the county clerk's records in books provided specifically for that purpose. When recordation is referred to in describing an instrument in those counties, one refers to a deed recorded by the volume and page number of the deed records of the county in which the land is located. The entries are often made by hand in separate volumes, one volume kept for deed records, one for mortgage records, and so forth. Recordation of such instruments is reflected in the following manner:

. . . recorded in Volume, _____

Page _____ of the _____

Records of _____ County, Texas.

In more populated counties, the Texas legislature has provided for a method of recording by microfilming the documents, rather than keeping the entries recorded in large volumes. In these counties, the interest in the real estate is recorded in one main microfilm library, known as the **Official Public Records of Real Property**. When referring to the recording information on deeds recorded in this manner, one refers to a deed recorded under the clerk's file number and film code number of the Official Public Records of Real Property of the county in which the real estate is located. Recordation of these instruments is reflected in the following manner:

Filed for record in the Official Public Records of Real Property of

_____ County, Texas, under Clerk's File

No._____ and recorded under Film Code

No_____.

When the proper recording has been made by the county clerk, it becomes apparent that the real property records of that county would have a list of the grantors and grantees, as well as of all of the instruments that have been recorded against the subject property as far back as records have been kept. This, of course, goes back to the original grant (called a **patent**) from the Sovereign of Texas in 1836. This **list** of grantor–grantee records is established in chronological order. It creates a **chain of title**, which establishes a complete line of fee title from the original grant from the Sovereign of Texas down to the most current property owner. When all of the recorded **instruments** (as contrasted to **list** of same) relating to a parcel of real estate are assembled in chronological order, these are collectively referred to in Texas as an **abstract of title**.

Individuals who wish to search the title records of the county are allowed to do so since all of these records are public. All courthouses keep what is called an **index of grantors and grantees**, and an individual may trace the chain of title through the **grantee–grantor index** in order to perform his own title search. Once the grantee-to-grantor search has been made back to the original land patent, the title examiner then performs a grantor-to-grantee index search (coming forward from the patent) to be sure the chain coincides with the grantee-to-grantor search, and that there are no "breaks" or strangers in the chain. The examiner is not only held to a duty of care of examining the chain, but also of having read and understood the terms of every document in the chain. *Cooksey* v. *Sinder*, 682 S.W.2d 252 (Tex. 1984). After the chain has been established, the examiner is not required to search for inferior claims or documents filed outside the chain (such as court records, divorce proceedings, or unrecorded contracts). *Swanson* v. *Grassedonio*, 647 S.W.2d 716 (Tex. Civ. App.—Corpus Christi, 1983). These documents do not constitute notice, so a subsequent purchaser would be a bona fide purchaser for value of the real estate as long as he did not have actual notice of any defects to title or other outstanding interests.

Private abstract companies, in addition to the grantor–grantee index, also keep records of the titles of real property for each particular tract of land. This type of indexing system is called a **tract indexing system** and is most convenient when one is trying to determine who has interests in a particular parcel of real estate. The Texas Department of Insurance requires all title companies to maintain this type of title plant.

## Lis Pendens

In addition to the recording information in the Official Public Records of Real Property, or the volume and page reference, there are additional records that allow for the recordation of other instruments, such as the **plat record** (recording of subdivision plats); **condominium records** (recording of condominium regimes); and another, rather unique, recording of instruments called **lis pendens notices**. Literally translated, "lis pendens" means that the "law is pending." This establishes constructive notice to subsequent creditors, purchasers, and other third parties that there is a lawsuit pending that directly involves an interest to that property. *Helmsley-Spear of Texas, Inc.* v. *Blanton*, 699 S.W.2d 643 (Tex. Civ. App.—Houston, 1985). Anyone who buys that property with notice of the lis pendens buys it subject to the outcome of the lawsuit affecting the property.

Although lis pendens serves as a very effective method of protecting parties in litigation, it can be abused when used to cloud the title to somebody's property because the claim has virtually no adverse effect on the claimant. This is because a lis pendens is considered "privileged" since it is part of a lawsuit that has been filed and is currently pending. *Kropp* v. *Prather*, 526 S.W.2d 283 (Tex. Civ. App.—Tyler, 1975). To clarify the theory underlying this concept, it should be explained that **privilege** is an exemption from libel and slander given to a party during judicial proceedings. It is well understood that during litigation any allegations can be made in pleadings, or in the courtroom, and no individual can be liable for libel or slander if those allegations are made in good faith. This encourages the free exchange of ideas and attitudes in the courtroom and helps solicit certain facts that otherwise might not be brought into the legal proceeding. A lis pendens notice, being a part of a lawsuit, is given the same status, unless filed maliciously, or in bad faith. Believe it or not! Even if a lis pendens is filed in bad faith, the plaintiff must show a specific loss of sale in order to recover damages. *Belo* v. *Sanders*, 632 S.W.2d 145 (Tex. 1982).

This whole issue is complicated by the 1997 legislature, which passed a new provision creating liability for a person using a fraudulent court document as a claim against real estate if it constitutes an intent to cause another person to suffer financial injury or mental anguish. This may create some liability for spurious lis pendens claims. *Tex. Civ. Prac. and Rem. Code, §11.002.*

# Acknowledgments

As previously discussed, an **acknowledgment** is one of the requirements for making instruments recordable. This, and only this, is the primary purpose of an acknowledgment. It does not make the instrument "official" or "legal"; it simply makes the instrument recordable. Acknowledgments are not the only method of making an instrument recordable, however; instruments can also be made recordable by signatures of two subscribing witnesses or by the testimony of a person to the handwriting of the signatory party and witnesses.

The requirements to make an effective acknowledgment consist of the following:

1. The person who executed the instrument must appear before the person authorized to take the acknowledgment.

2. The officer taking the acknowledgment must know or have satisfactory evidence that the person making such acknowledgment is the individual who executed the instrument.

3. The signer must acknowledge to the officer taking the acknowledgment that he executed the instrument for the purposes and consideration therein expressed, and in the capacity therein stated.

4. The acknowledgment must be signed by the authorized officer, and be sealed with his seal of office.

The foregoing requirements of an acknowledgment are self-explanatory if one takes the time to read an acknowledgment carefully. The statutory form for an ordinary certificate of acknowledgment, V.A.T.S., *Civil Practices and Remedies Code, §121.007*, is shown in Figure 12.1. Note that it provides for the means of identifying the signatory party. If the acknowledgment is taken outside of Texas, a seal is not required unless that local jurisdiction requires it.

The 2001 Legislature also passed an amendment to the Civil Practice and Remedies Code which eliminates the requirement for an embossed seal on an electronically transmitted certificate of acknowledgement (see Section 121.004). Another change in the Government Code though does require an electronically transmitted authenticated document to legibly reproduce the required elements of the seal (see Section 406.103).

A short-form acknowledgment can also be used as an alternative to the other authorized form (see Figure 12.2). It is a much shorter form of acknowledgment and only indicates that the instrument "was acknowledged" by the signatory party. The term "was acknowledged" is now defined under the statute.

## Persons Authorized to Take Acknowledgments

The acknowledgment or proof of an instrument of writing may be made in this state before:

1. A clerk of the district court.

2. A judge or a clerk of the county court.

3. A notary public.

**FIGURE 12.1  A SAMPLE CERTIFICATE OF ACKNOWLEDGMENT.**

A sample certificate of acknowledgment.

THE STATE OF                              §

                                          §

COUNTY OF                                 §

BEFORE ME, _____, on this day personally appeared _____, known to me [or proved to me on the oath of _____, or through _____ (description of identity card or other document)] to be the person whose name is subscribed to the foregoing instrument and acknowledged to me that _____ executed the same for the purposes and consideration therein expressed.

Given under my hand and seal of office this _____ day of _____, _____.

_____

NOTARY PUBLIC

### FIGURE 12.2  A SAMPLE SHORT-FORM ACKNOWLEDGMENT.

A sample short-form acknowledgment.

State of Texas

County of _____

    This instrument was acknowledged before me on (date) by (name or names of person or persons acknowledging).

        (Signature of officer)

        (Title of officer)

        My commission expires: _____

An acknowledgment may be made outside of the State of Texas, but within the physical limits of the United States, before:

1. A clerk of some court of record having a seal.
2. A commissioner of deeds duly appointed into the laws of this state.
3. A **notary public** or any other official authorized to administer oaths in the jurisdiction where the acknowledgment or proof is taken.

An acknowledgment or proof of an instrument may be made outside the physical limits of the United States and its territories before:

1. A minister, commissioner, or chargéd'affaires of the United States, resident and accredited in the country where the proof of the acknowledgment is made.
2. A consul general, consul, vice consul, commercial agent, vice commercial agent, deputy consul, or consular agent of the United States, resident in the country where the proof of acknowledgment is made.
3. A notary public.

In addition to the above methods, the acknowledgment may be made by a member of the armed forces of the United States before any commissioned officer of the armed forces of the United States or the auxiliaries thereof. Acknowledgments of this type do not necessarily require a seal as do other types of acknowledgments.

The certificate of acknowledgment must be substantially the same as provided for by the statute. An officer authorized to take acknowledgments must be a disinterested party. If he has an interest in the transaction, the acknowledgment is void; but this does not qualify or make the instrument itself void.

The law even allows the notary public to sign the name of an individual who is physically unable to do so or to make a mark on behalf of the individual, if authorized to do so by the disabled person in the presence of a disinterested witness. The notary must write the following under the signature: "Signature affixed by notary in the presence of the [name of witness], a disinterested witness, under Section 406.0165 Government Code." When signed in this manner, the signature is effective as the signature on whose behalf the signature is made for any purpose.

**Notario Publico**  Apparently there have been abuses in the notary public system as a result of the influx of Mexican nationals into Texas. In Mexico, the term "notario" or "notario publico" is a very high-ranking public official. The requirements for becoming a notary public in the State of Texas are not nearly so stringent.

The 2001 Legislature passed new legislation that creates criminal liability if a notary public (1) states or implies that the person is an attorney licensed to practice law in this state; (2) solicits or accepts compensation to prepare documents for or otherwise represent the interest of another in a judicial or an administrative proceeding, including a proceeding relating to immigration to the United States, United States Citizenship or related matters; (3) solicits or accepts compensation to obtain relief of any kind on behalf of another, from any officer, agency or employee of this state or the United States; (4) uses the phrase "notario" or "notario publico" to advertise the services of a notary public or by using signs, pamphlets, stationery or other written communication or by radio or television; or advertises the services of a notary public in a language other than English, whether by signs, pamphlets, stationery, or other written communication or by radio or telephone.

If the person posts or otherwise includes with the advertisement a notice that does not include a statement that the person is not an attorney licensed to practice law in Texas and can not give legal advice, it is a criminal offense.

The first offense is a Class A misdemeanor and the second offence is a third-degree felony (see Government Code Section 406.017 et seq.).

## Venue

In an average transaction, most acknowledgments are taken by a notary public. The **venue** (jurisdiction) of a notary public is coextensive with the boundaries of the state, irrespective of the county in which he (the notary public) is appointed. Note, however, that the notary's jurisdiction is confined to the State of Texas. For instance, consider a deed signed in Massachusetts to convey title to real property in Harris County, Texas. If that deed is acknowledged in Massachusetts, a Massachusetts notary public would take the acknowledgment, and the jurisdiction of that notary would be the State of Massachusetts. There is no requirement that an instrument conveying property in a particular country be notarized in that country. It can be acknowledged anywhere before any authorized officer in any country, so long as his jurisdiction is properly noted on the acknowledgment, and the acknowledgment is in English or is officially translated.

## Construction of an Acknowledgment

Since the acknowledgment performs a particularly important function (to accomplish the requirements of proper recordation), the courts have rather liberally construed the requirements of an effective acknowledgment. For instance, the failure of a notary to show the date of his commission expiration does not invalidate the certificate, but the certificate is invalid without the official seal. There has even been a Texas case where the name of the person making the acknowledgment (signer of the instrument) was omitted, but it did not render it fatally defective. *Sheldon* v. *Farinacci*, 535 S.W.2d 938 (Tex. Civ. App.—San Antonio, 1976). It appears that as long as the acknowledgment is signed by the person *taking* the acknowledgment (i.e., the notary public), sealed, and in substantially the same form as prescribed by statute, it will be considered an effective and valid acknowledgment, and the acknowledgment will not be literally construed so as to render it ineffective.

# Proofs Other than by Acknowledgment

The proof of an instrument for the purpose of being recorded may be given by one or more subscribing witnesses personally appearing before some officer authorized to take said proof, and stating under oath that he or they saw the person who executed the instrument subscribe to same and that this person had executed the same for the purposes and consideration therein stated. The witnesses appearing to testify to said proof must be personally known to the officer taking the proof, or must prove by their oath that they are the witnesses testifying to said proof. A form of a certificate where the execution of the instrument is proved by a witness is substantially as shown in Figure 12.3.

An execution of an instrument may also be established for record by proof of the handwriting of the grantor and of at least one subscribing witness under certain circumstances, as when the signatory party of the instrument and the witnesses are dead, or nonresidents, or their residences are unknown, or for some reason the signatory parties and witnesses are incompetent to testify. The same general rules apply if there is a signatory party who has made his mark rather than signed his name.

# Record of Acknowledgment

Section 121.012 of the *Civil Practices and Remedies Code* requires that all officers authorized or permitted by law to take acknowledgments shall keep a well-bound book. The book should contain the true date on which the acknowledgment was taken, the name of the grantor of the instrument, and, if proved by the subscribing witness, the name of the witness, the residence of the witness, and whether such witness is personally known or unknown to the officer. Recent changes in this statute also require that the notary keep a record of the acknowledging party's signature, and the notary's method of identifying that person.

Any person injured by the failure, refusal, or neglect of any officer to comply with the requirements of the law shall have a cause of action against the officer so failing, before any court of competent jurisdiction for recovery of all damages resulting from such neglect, failure, or refusal.

**FIGURE 12.3**

The State of _____

County of _____

    Before me, _____ (here insert the name and character of the officer), on this day personally appeared _____, known to me (or proved to me on the oath of _____), to be the person whose name is subscribed as a witness to the foregoing instrument of writing, and after being duly sworn by me stated on oath that he saw _____, the grantor or person who executed the foregoing instrument, subscribe the same (or that the grantor or person who executed such instrument of writing acknowledged in his presence that he had executed the same for the purposes and consideration therein expressed), and that he had signed the same as a witness at the request of the grantor (or person who executed the same).

    (Seal) Given under my hand and seal of office this _____ day of _____, A.D., _____.

# Jurat

A **jurat** is a certificate of an officer or person before whom a writing was sworn to. This certificate is made before the same people who have the authority to take acknowledgments. However, a jurat is not, and should not be confused with, an acknowledgment. A jurat normally simply states:

Subscribed and sworn to before me on this _____ day of _____,

_____.

Notary Public in and for _____ County, Texas

In a jurat, the signatory party is swearing that the facts contained in the instrument are true, and not simply that he signed same for the purposes and consideration therein expressed. The acknowledgment and the jurat are entirely different certificates for entirely different purposes. The acknowledgment makes the instrument recordable. The jurat verifies the facts contained in the instrument and is usually used in affidavits when testimony is taken for court proceedings or other evidentiary use.

## ■ SUMMARY

The State of Texas has the Recording Act, a means of registration that is available to all individuals who have an interest in real estate. The effect of recording one's interest in real estate is to put all subsequent purchasers for valuable consideration and all creditors on notice of the claimant's interest in that particular piece of real estate. The public is then on constructive notice of the claimant's interest in that property. Through recording each claimant's interest in real estate, we establish what is referred to as a chain of title. When all of the instruments have been assembled in chronological order, it is called an abstract of title.

A lis pendens notice is a notice that a lawsuit is pending that involves title to the real estate. It may only be filed after a lawsuit has been commenced.

An acknowledgment is one of the requirements for making instruments recordable. An acknowledgment may be taken before a notary public, a judge, or a clerk of the district court. A notary's jurisdiction encompasses the entire State of Texas. Acknowledgments are liberally construed, and there are other methods of proving the veracity of an instrument besides an acknowledgment.

A jurat, often confused with an acknowledgment, is a statement by the notary that the document has been sworn to as true. A jurat will make an instrument recordable, as an acknowledgment will.

## CASE STUDIES FOR DISCUSSION

1. On August 9, 2003, Arnold D. Smith executed a quitclaim deed to Cristine Smith. On October 17, 2003, Arnold D. Smith executed a general warranty deed to Lucille Bell on the same property. Both deeds were acknowledged at the same time. Mrs. Bell claims that she had good title by virtue of her general warranty deed. Mrs. Smith claims that she has good title by her prior quitclaim deed and that Mrs. Bell could not be a bona fide purchaser since Mrs. Smith was in possession at the time the deed was executed and delivered. What legal ramifications do you foresee?

2. Plaintiffs filed suit against Mr. Kropp alleging embezzlement of funds. Kropp claimed that Plaintiffs owed him money, asserted an equitable title in some property held by Plaintiffs, and filed a lis pendens against same. Plaintiffs lost their cause of action but asserted a slander of title action against Kropp since their property was encumbered and any subsequent conveyances were forbidden because of the lis pendens notice. Defendant alleges that he has privilege because the lis pendens was part of a lawsuit. Assuming that neither cause of action reached final adjudication, what legal ramifications do you foresee?

3. On July 11, 2001, a deed was recorded from Sunshine Corporation to Empire Construction Company. On January 29, 2002, Snidely Whiplash recovered a judgment against Sunshine Corporation. On April 29, 2002, Snidely Whiplash recorded an abstract of judgment against Sunshine Corporation. On November 27, 2002, Sunshine Corporation recorded a correction deed to Empire Construction Company because of an allegedly defective acknowledgment. The acknowledgment did not contain the name of the grantor of the deed on July 11, 2001. Snidely Whiplash alleges that the correction deed passed with notice of the judgment lien and he therefore has the right to recover from the transfer of the property. Empire Construction Company alleges that the correction deed was valid and that the incorrect acknowledgment was not a fatal defect on the original transfer. What legal ramifications do you foresee?

## CHAPTER 13

# Mortgages

The financing of real estate is one of the key factors in the ability to consummate a sale. The real estate agent who understands the key details and legal ramifications of various methods of financing real estate has a clear advantage over his competitors because he can advise his clients on much more than just the fair market value and sales price. Since many deals may be contingent upon the purchaser obtaining financing, agents should understand the value of the various financing techniques. To understand these various financing techniques, one must also understand the basics of the various types of **mortgages** in Texas, since these are the primary legal documents that secure the purchaser's indebtedness.

## Instruments

Most mortgage procedures in Texas require the execution of two instruments: the **promissory note** and the **deed of trust**. In financing real estate transactions, the promissory note used is generally referred to as a real estate lien note. This note is the actual promise to pay. The only difference between a **real estate lien note** and other forms of promissory notes is that the real estate lien note references the real estate used as security for the payment of the note.

### Real Estate Lien Note

Figure 13.1 shows a simple form **real estate lien note**. Notice that it contains the actual promise to pay to the order of the **mortgagee** [1], the amount [2], the interest rate [3], and the additional interest provisions for past due unpaid principal and interest [4]. (The term **matured** as used in the note in Figure 13.1 indicates that the entire amount of the note is due and payable.)

In this particular real estate lien note, the payment clause is a simple one for monthly payments for the term of the note [5], and, for illustration purposes, there is a clause for prepayment (prepayment clause) [6], which specifies a penalty for the prepayment and a provision for the application of said prepayments for the remainder of the note.

**FIGURE 13.1 REAL ESTATE LIEN NOTE.**

## REAL ESTATE LIEN NOTE

$150,000.00

(2)

Houston, Texas
February 30, 2008

(1)

FOR VALUE RECEIVED, the undersigned Maker, whether one or more, promises to pay to the order of FRIENDLY LENDER SAVINGS BANK, at 99 Hirate Boulevard, Houston, Harris County, Texas 77009, or such other address as Payee may from time to time designate, the sum of One Hundred Fifty Thousand and no/100 Dollars ($150,000.00) in legal and lawful money of the United States of America, together with interest thereon from date hereof until maturity at the rate of seven and one-half percent (7½%) per annum; matured, unpaid principal and interest shall bear interest at the rate of eighteen percent (18%) per annum until paid.

(3)

(4) This Note is due and payable as follows, to-wit:

(5) In monthly installments of One Thousand Forty-Eight Dollars And 82/100 ($1,048.82) each, including interest on the 1st day of each calendar month hereafter, beginning on the 1ˢᵗ day of April, 1999, and continuing until the principal and interest are fully paid.

Payment hereof is secured by, among other security, a Deed of Trust of even date herewith executed by Maker to CHARLES J. JACOBUS, (10) TRUSTEE, against the following described real property:

Lot 1, Block 1, Shakey Acres Subdivision, Harris County, Texas, as shown of record at Volume 7, Page 3 of the Map Records of (11) Harris County, Texas.

(6) Privileged is reserved to prepay on any monthly installment paying dates but before maturity of this note, all or any part of the unpaid principal hereof, by paying a penalty of one percent (1%) of the amount so prepaid.

(7) It is expressly provided that upon default in the punctual payment of this Note or any part thereof, principal or interest, as the same shall become due and payable, or default in the performance of any of Maker's obligations under the referenced Deed of Trust, then at the option of the holder, the entire indebtedness secured by the herein before mentioned lien shall be matured, and in the event default is made in the prompt payment of this Note when due or declared due, and the same is placed in the hands of an attorney for collection, or suit is brought on same, or the same is collected through probate, bankruptcy or other judicial proceedings, then the Makers agree and promise to pay five percent (5%) additional on the amount of principal and interest
(8) then owing, as attorney's fees.

If default occurs in the payment of any principal or interest when due hereunder, or upon the occurrence of any default or failure to perform any covenant, agreement or obligation to be performed under any document or instrument executed in connection with or as security for this Note, or upon Maker's insolvency or business failure, the appointment of a receiver of all or any part of Maker's property, an assignment for the benefit of creditors of Maker, a calling of a meeting of creditors of Maker, the commencement of any proceeding under any bankruptcy, insolvency or debtor relief laws by or against Maker or any guarantor or surety for Maker, the holder hereof may, at its option, declare the entirety of this Note, principal and interest, immediately due and payable, and pursue any and all other remedies available to it at law or in equity, but failure to do so at any time shall not constitute a waiver of such holder's right to do so at any other time. Failure to exercise this option upon any default shall not constitute a waiver of the right to exercise it in the event of any subsequent defaults.

(9) Each Maker, surety and endorser of this Note expressly waives all notices of any kind or character, demands for payment, presentations for payment, notices of intention to accelerate, notice of acceleration, the maturity, protest and notice of protest, as to this Note and as to each, every and all installments hereof.

The parties intend to conform strictly to the applicable usury laws. All agreements between Lender and Borrower (or any other party liable with respect to any indebtedness under the Loan Documents) are hereby limited by the provisions of this paragraph which shall override and control all such agreements, whether now existing or hereafter arising and whether written or oral. In no way, nor in any event or contingency (including but not limited to prepayment, default, demand for payment, or acceleration of the maturity of any Obligations or any part thereof), shall the interest contracted for, charged or received under the Note or otherwise exceed the maximum amount permissible under applicable law. If, from any possible construction of any document, interest would otherwise be payable to Lender in excess of the maximum lawful amount, any such construction shall be subject to the provisions of this paragraph and such document shall be automatically reformed and the interest payable to Lender shall be automatically reduced to the maximum amount permitted under applicable law, without the necessity of execution of any amendment or new document. If Lender shall ever receive anything of value which is characterized as interest under applicable law and which would apart from this provision be in excess of the maximum lawful amount, an amount equal to the amount which would have been excessive interest shall, without penalty, be applied to the reduction of the principal amount owing in the inverse order of its maturity and not to the payment of interest, or refunded to Borrower to the extent that the amount which would have been excessive interest exceeds unpaid principal. The right to accelerate maturity of the Note or any other indebtedness does not include the right to accelerate any interest which has not otherwise accrued on the date of such acceleration, and Lender does not intend to charge or receive any unearned interest in the event of acceleration. All interest paid or agreed to be paid to Lender shall, to the extent permitted by applicable law, be amortized, prorated, allocated and spread throughout the full stated term (including any renewal or extension) of such indebtedness so that the amount of interest on account of such indebtedness does not exceed the maximum permitted by applicable law.

Maker may prepay all or any part hereof at anytime without penalty, and interest shall immediately cease on all amounts so prepaid. All prepayments shall be applied first to accrued but unpaid interest, the balance to installments due hereon in inverse order of maturity.

This Note shall be governed by and construed in accordance with the laws of the State of Texas.

MAKER

(12) _____
MAY B. DEBTED

_____
N. DEBTED

The default clause [7] is standard in most promissory notes and provides for the entire indebtedness to be matured in the event of default at the option of the holder. The note also provides for payment of attorney's fees in the event legal proceedings are required in order to enforce payment [8].

Another clause, normally referred to as the **waiver** [9], is also considered to be standard. It provides for two waivers: (1) the waiver of notice for payment (the payment obligations are absolute), and (2) the waiver of notice to accelerate the maturity of the note in the event there is a default. This second waiver has been the subject of a number of lawsuits. The way this note is written, a borrower can default on a single payment of his note, and the lender can post the property for foreclosure without notifying the borrower that the note has been matured and is now payable in full. The lender's right to accelerate without notice is even more serious because the Texas foreclosure procedure (discussed later) is a harsh one. The Texas rule, however, is to enforce these waiver provisions as written. *Cruce* v. *Eureka Life Ins. Co.*, 696 S.W.2d 656 (Tex. Civ. App.—Dallas, 1985).

If there is no waiver in the note, the noteholder (lender) must give the borrower the opportunity to cure the default. *Diversified, Inc.* v. *Walker*, 702 S.W.2d 717 (Tex. Civ. App.—Houston, 1985). In addition, if a noteholder has accepted late payments consistently, he cannot accelerate the indebtedness for a single late payment. *Highpoint of Montgomery Corp.* v. *Vail*, 638 S.W.2d 624 (Tex. Civ. App.—Houston, 1982). The logical result, then, is that the lender must rigorously enforce his payments, or he may lose his right to accelerate at a later date.

The security clause [10], in this case, specifies the lien created by the deed of trust, and the legal description of the real estate [11] to be used as security for the payment of the note.

The last item in this real estate lien note is the space provided for the signatures [12] of the makers of the note.

The real estate lien note is normally not a recorded instrument since it does not create the lien interest in the real estate. It therefore does not usually contain an acknowledgment. The lien interest in the real estate is created by the mortgage instrument. The legal effect of a note will be discussed later in this chapter.

## Deed of Trust

The mortgage is the document that offers the property as security for the debt. The most commonly used mortgage in Texas is referred to as the **deed of trust**. A deed of trust is often described as a three-party mortgage with a **power of sale**. A typical deed of trust form is shown in Figure 13.2. You will note that it has many of the characteristics of the deed. However, as you recall in the discussion in Chapter 2, legal title does not pass in a deed of trust. The lender gets only a lien, as Texas is a **lien theory** state.

The deed of trust is most easily defined as a conveyance by the borrower (called the **grantor** in the deed of trust) to a third-party **trustee** (usually a nominee of the lender) as security for a debt for money loaned by the lender (called the **beneficiary** in the deed of trust), subject to a condition of defeasance; that is, the conveyance of the trustee does not become effective until there has been a default in the payments of the promissory note, and the trustee must exercise the powers conferred upon him in the deed of trust. When the note has been paid in full, the deed of trust, by its own terms, renders the conveyance to the trustee null and void and of no further force and effect. Note the underlined area in Figure 13.2. This is called the **defeasance clause**. The more common practice, however, is to

**FIGURE 13.2 DEED OF TRUST.**

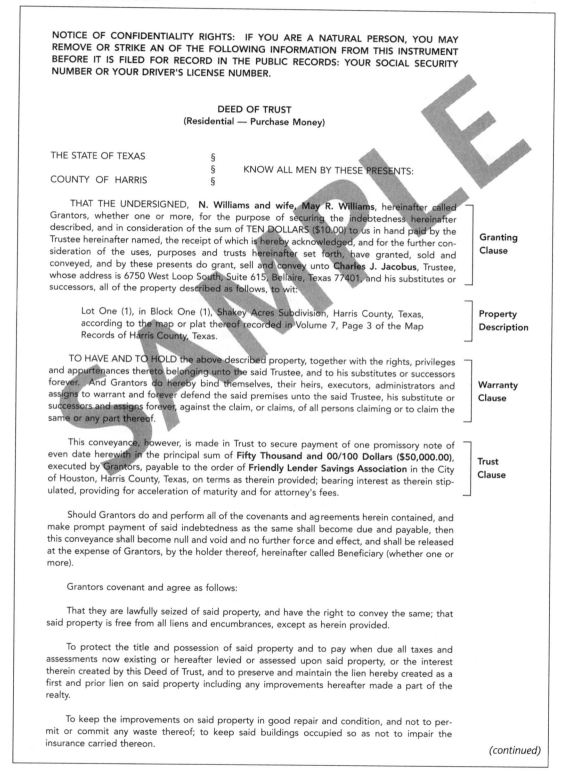

NOTICE OF CONFIDENTIALITY RIGHTS:  IF YOU ARE A NATURAL PERSON, YOU MAY REMOVE OR STRIKE AN OF THE FOLLOWING INFORMATION FROM THIS INSTRUMENT BEFORE IT IS FILED FOR RECORD IN THE PUBLIC RECORDS: YOUR SOCIAL SECURITY NUMBER OR YOUR DRIVER'S LICENSE NUMBER.

### DEED OF TRUST
(Residential — Purchase Money)

| | | |
|---|---|---|
| THE STATE OF TEXAS | § | |
| | § | KNOW ALL MEN BY THESE PRESENTS: |
| COUNTY OF  HARRIS | § | |

THAT THE UNDERSIGNED,  **N. Williams and wife, May R. Williams**, hereinafter called Grantors, whether one or more, for the purpose of securing the indebtedness hereinafter described, and in consideration of the sum of TEN DOLLARS ($10.00) to us in hand paid by the Trustee hereinafter named, the receipt of which is hereby acknowledged, and for the further consideration of the uses, purposes and trusts hereinafter set forth, have granted, sold and conveyed, and by these presents do grant, sell and convey unto **Charles J. Jacobus**, Trustee, whose address is 6750 West Loop South, Suite 615, Bellaire, Texas 77401, and his substitutes or successors, all of the property described as follows, to wit:

— **Granting Clause**

Lot One (1), in Block One (1), Shakey Acres Subdivision, Harris County, Texas, according to the map or plat thereof recorded in Volume 7, Page 3 of the Map Records of Harris County, Texas.

— **Property Description**

TO HAVE AND TO HOLD the above described property, together with the rights, privileges and appurtenances thereto belonging unto the said Trustee, and to his substitutes or successors forever.  And Grantors do hereby bind themselves, their heirs, executors, administrators and assigns to warrant and forever defend the said premises unto the said Trustee, his substitute or successors and assigns forever, against the claim, or claims, of all persons claiming or to claim the same or any part thereof.

— **Warranty Clause**

This conveyance, however, is made in Trust to secure payment of one promissory note of even date herewith in the principal sum of **Fifty Thousand and 00/100 Dollars ($50,000.00)**, executed by Grantors, payable to the order of **Friendly Lender Savings Association** in the City of Houston, Harris County, Texas, on terms as therein provided; bearing interest as therein stipulated, providing for acceleration of maturity and for attorney's fees.

— **Trust Clause**

Should Grantors do and perform all of the covenants and agreements herein contained, and make prompt payment of said indebtedness as the same shall become due and payable, then this conveyance shall become null and void and no further force and effect, and shall be released at the expense of Grantors, by the holder thereof, hereinafter called Beneficiary (whether one or more).

Grantors covenant and agree as follows:

That they are lawfully seized of said property, and have the right to convey the same; that said property is free from all liens and encumbrances, except as herein provided.

To protect the title and possession of said property and to pay when due all taxes and assessments now existing or hereafter levied or assessed upon said property, or the interest therein created by this Deed of Trust, and to preserve and maintain the lien hereby created as a first and prior lien on said property including any improvements hereafter made a part of the realty.

To keep the improvements on said property in good repair and condition, and not to permit or commit any waste thereof; to keep said buildings occupied so as not to impair the insurance carried thereon.

*(continued)*

**FIGURE 13.2** **CONTINUED.**

To insure and keep insured all improvements now or hereafter created upon said property against loss or damage by fire and windstorm, and any other hazard or hazards as may be reasonably required from time to time by Beneficiary during the term of the indebtedness hereby secured, to the extent of the original amount of the indebtedness hereby secured, or to the extent of the full insurable value of said improvements, whichever is the lesser, in such form and with such Insurance Company or Companies as may be approved by Beneficiary and to deliver to Beneficiary the policies of such insurance having attached to said policies such mortgage indemnity clause as Beneficiary shall direct; to deliver renewals of such policies to Beneficiary at least ten days before any such insurance policies shall expire; and any proceeds which Beneficiary may receive under any such policy or policies, may be applied by Beneficiary, at his option, to reduce the indebtedness hereby secured, whether then matured or to mature in the future, and in such manner as Beneficiary may elect, or Beneficiary may permit Grantors to use said proceeds to repair or replace all improvements damaged or destroyed and covered by said policy.

That in the event Grantors shall fail to keep the improvements on the property hereby conveyed in good repair and condition, or to pay promptly when due all taxes and assessments, as aforesaid, or to preserve the prior lien of this Deed of Trust on said property, or to keep the buildings and improvements insured, as aforesaid, or to deliver the policy, or policies, of insurance or the renewal thereof to Beneficiary, as aforesaid, then Beneficiary may, at his option, but without being required to do so, make such repairs, pay such taxes and assessments, purchase any tax title thereon, remove any prior liens, and prosecute or defend any suits in relation to the preservation of the prior lien of this Deed of Trust on said property, or insure and keep insured the improvements thereon in an amount not to exceed that above stipulated; that any sums which may be so paid out by Beneficiary and all sums paid for insurance premiums, as aforesaid, including the costs, expenses and attorney's fees paid in any suit affecting said property when necessary to protect the lien hereof shall bear interest from the dates of such payments at the rate stated in said note and shall be paid by Grantors to Beneficiary upon demand, at the same place at which said note is payable, and shall be deemed a part of the debt hereby secured and recoverable as such in all respects.

Grantor represents and warrants and covenants and agrees that (i) Grantor has not used and will not use and, to the best of Grantor's knowledge, no prior owner or current or prior tenant, subtenant, or other occupant of all or any part of the Property has used or is using hazardous material (as that term is hereinafter defined) on, from or affecting the Property in any manner that violates any laws pertaining to hazardous materials applicable to Grantor or to the Property; (ii) to the best of Grantor's knowledge, no hazardous materials have been disposed of on the Property nor have any hazardous materials migrated onto the Property, in either event in violation of any laws pertaining to hazardous materials applicable to Grantor or to the Property; and (iii) Grantor will not permit or suffer any such violation of any laws pertaining to hazardous materials applicable to Grantor or to the Property.

In the event that any investigation, site monitoring, containment, clean-up, removal, restoration or other remedial work of any kind or nature (hereinafter referred to as the "remedial work") is required under any laws pertaining to hazardous materials applicable to Grantor or to the Property, because of, or in connection with, the current or future presence, suspected presence, release or suspected release of a hazardous material in or about the air, soil, ground water, surface water or soil vapor at, on, about, under or within the Property (or any portion thereof), Grantor shall within the time periods required by the applicable laws pertaining to hazardous materials, commence and thereafter diligently prosecute to completion, all such remedial work. All remedial work shall be performed by contractors reasonably approved in advance by Lender and under the supervision of a consulting engineer reasonably approved by Lender. All costs and expenses of such remedial work shall be paid by Grantor including, without limitation, Lender's reasonable attorneys' fees and costs incurred in connection with monitoring or review of such remedial work. In the event Grantor shall fail to timely prosecute to completion such remedial work, Lender may, but shall not be required to, cause such remedial work to be performed and all costs and expenses thereof or incurred in connection therewith, shall be immediately due and payable by Grantor to Lender and shall become part of the indebtedness.

*(continued)*

**FIGURE 13.2  CONTINUED.**

Grantor shall provide Lender with prompt written notice: (a) upon Grantor's becoming aware of any release or threat of release of any hazardous materials upon, under or from the Property in violation of any laws pertaining to hazardous materials applicable to Grantor or to the Property; (b) upon Grantor's receipt of any notice from any federal, state, municipal or other governmental agency or authority in connection with any hazardous materials located upon or under or emanating from the Property; and (c) upon Grantor's obtaining knowledge of any incurrence of expense, for which Grantor or the Property could be liable, by any governmental agency or authority in connection with the assessment, containment or removal of any hazardous materials located upon or under or emanating from the Property.

That in the event of default in the payment of any installment, principal or interest, of the note hereby secured, in accordance with the terms thereof, or of a breach of any of the covenants herein contained to be performed by Grantors, then and in any of such events Beneficiary may elect, Grantors hereby expressly waiving presentment and demand for payment, to declare the entire principal indebtedness hereby secured with all interest accrued thereon and all other sums hereby secured immediately due and payable, and in the event of default on the payment of said indebtedness when due or declared due, it shall  thereupon, or at any time thereafter, be the duty of the Trustee, or his successor or substitute as hereinafter provided, at the request of Beneficiary (which request is hereby conclusively presumed), to enforce this trust; and after advertising the time, place and terms of the sale of the above described and conveyed property, then subject to the lien hereof, and mailing and filing notices, as required by section 51.002, Texas Property Code, as then amended (successor to article 3810, Texas Revised Civil Statutes), and otherwise complying with that statute, the Trustee shall sell the above described property, then subject to the lien hereof, at public auction in accordance with such notices on the first Tuesday in any month between the hours of 10:00 a.m. and 4:00 p.m., to the highest bidder for cash, selling all of the property as an entirety or in such parcels as the Trustee acting may elect, and make due conveyance to the Purchaser or Purchasers, with general warranty binding Grantors, their heirs and assigns; and out of the money arising from such sale, the Trustee acting shall pay first, all the expenses of advertising the sale and making the conveyance, including a commission of five percent to himself, which commission shall be due and owing in addition to the attorney's fees provided for in said note, and then to Beneficiary the full amount of principal, interest, attorney's fees and other charges due and unpaid on said note and all other indebtedness secured hereby, rendering the balance of the sales price, if any, to Grantors, their heirs or assigns; and the recitals in the conveyance to Purchaser or Purchasers shall be full and conclusive evidence of the truth of the matter therein stated, and all prerequisites to said sale shall be presumed to have been performed, and such sale and conveyance shall be conclusive against Grantors, their heirs and assigns.

Power of Sale Clause

It is agreed that in the event a foreclosure hereunder should be commenced by the Trustee, or his substitute or successor, Beneficiary may at any time before the sale of said property direct the said Trustee to abandon the sale, and may then institute suit for the collection of said note, and for the foreclosure of this Deed of Trust lien; it is further agreed that if Beneficiary should institute a suit for the collection thereof, and for a foreclosure of this Deed of Trust lien, that he may at any time before the entry of a final judgment in said suit dismiss the same, and require the Trustee, his substitute or successor to sell the property in accordance with the provisions of this Deed of Trust.

Beneficiary, if he is the highest bidder, shall have the right to purchase at any sale of the property, and to have the amount for which such property is sold credited on the debt then owing.

Beneficiary in any event is hereby authorized to appoint a substitute trustee, to act instead of the Trustee named herein without other formality than the designation in writing of a substitute or successor trustee; and the authority hereby conferred shall extend to the appointment of other successor and substitute trustees successively until the indebtedness hereby secured has been paid in full, or until said property is sold hereunder, and each substitute trustee shall succeed to all of the rights and powers of the original trustee named herein.

In the event any sale is made of the above described property, or any portion thereof, under the terms of this Deed of Trust, Grantors, their heirs and assigns, shall forthwith upon the

*(continued)*

**FIGURE 13.2  CONTINUED.**

making of such sale surrender and deliver possession of the property so sold to the Purchasers at such sale, and in the event of their failure to do so they shall thereupon from and after the making such sale be and continue as tenants at will of such Purchaser, and in the event of their failure to surrender possession of said property upon demand, the Purchaser, his heirs or assigns, shall be entitled to institute and maintain an action for forcible detainer of said property in the Justice of the Peace Court in the Justice Precinct in which such property, or any part thereof, is situated.

It is agreed that the lien hereby created shall take precedence over and be a prior lien to any other lien of any character whether vendor's, materialman's or mechanic's lien hereinafter created on the above described property, and in the event the proceeds of the indebtedness secured hereby as set forth herein are used to pay off and satisfy any liens heretofore existing on said property, then Beneficiary is, and shall be, subrogated to all of the rights, liens and remedies of the holder of the indebtedness so paid.

It is further agreed that if Grantors, their heirs or assigns, while the owner of the herein-above described property, should commit an act of bankruptcy, or authorize the filing of a voluntary petition in bankruptcy, or should an act of bankruptcy be committed and involuntary proceedings instituted or threatened, or should the property hereinabove described be taken over by a Receiver for Grantors, their heirs or assigns, the note hereinabove described shall, at the option of Beneficiary, immediately become due and payable, and the acting Trustee may then proceed to sell the same under the provisions of this Deed of Trust.

As further security for the payment of the hereinabove described indebtedness, Grantors hereby transfer, assign, and convey unto Beneficiary all rents issuing or to hereafter issue from said real property, and in the event of any default in the payment of said note or hereunder, Beneficiary, his agent or representative, is hereby authorized, at his option, to collect said rents, or if such property is vacant to rent the same, and collect the rents, and apply the same, less the reasonable costs and expenses of collection thereof, to the payment of said lien without altering or affecting the priority of the lien created by this Deed of Trust in favor of any junior indebtedness, whether then matured or to mature in the future, and in such manner as Beneficiary may elect.  The collection of said rents by Beneficiary shall not constitute a waiver of his rights to accelerate the maturity of said indebtedness nor of his right to proceed with the enforcement of this Deed of Trust.

It is agreed that an extension, or extensions, may be made of the time of payment of all, or any part, of the indebtedness secured hereby, and that any part of the above described property may be released from this lien without altering or affecting the priority of the lien created by this Deed of Trust in favor of any junior encumbrancer, mortgagee or purchaser, or any persons acquiring an interest in the property hereby conveyed, or any part thereof; it being the intention of the parties hereto to preserve this lien on the property herein described and all improvements thereon, and that may be hereafter constructed thereon, first and superior to any liens that may be placed thereon, or that may be fixed, given or imposed by law thereon after the execution of this instrument notwithstanding any such extension of the time of payment, or the release of a portion of said property from this lien.

In the event any portion of the indebtedness hereinabove described cannot be lawfully secured by this Deed of Trust lien on said real property, it is agreed that the first payments made on said indebtedness shall be applied to the discharge of that portion of said indebtedness.

Beneficiary shall be entitled to receive any and all sums which may become payable to Grantors for the condemnation of the hereinabove described real property, or any part thereof, for public or quasi-public use, or by virtue of private sale in lieu thereof, and any sums which may be awarded or become payable to Grantors for damages caused by public works or construction on or near the said property. All such sums are hereby assigned to Beneficiary, who may, after deducting therefrom all expenses actually incurred, including attorney's fees, release same to Grantors or apply the same to the reduction of the indebtedness hereby secured, whether then matured or to mature in the future, or on any money obligation hereunder, as and in such

*(continued)*

**FIGURE 13.2 CONTINUED.**

manner as Beneficiary may elect. Beneficiary shall not be, in any event or circumstances, liable or responsible for failure to collect, or exercise diligence in the collection of, any such sums.

The parties intend to conform strictly to the applicable usury laws. All agreements between lender and Borrower (or any other party liable with respect to any indebtedness under the Loan Documents) are hereby limited by the provisions of this paragraph which shall override and control all such agreements, whether now existing or hereafter arising and whether written or oral. In no way, nor in any event or contingency (including but not limited to prepayment, default, demand for payment, or acceleration of the maturity of any Obligations or any part thereof), shall the interest contracted for, charged or received under the Note or otherwise exceed the maximum amount permissible under applicable law. If, from any possible construction of any document, interest would otherwise be payable to lender in excess of the maximum lawful amount, any such construction shall be subject to the provisions of this paragraph and such document shall be automatically reformed and the interest payable to lender shall be automatically reduced to the maximum amount permitted under applicable law, without the necessity of execution of any amendment or new document. If lender shall ever receive anything of value which is characterized as interest under applicable law and which would apart from this provision be in excess of the maximum lawful amount, an amount equal to the amount which would have been excessive interest shall, without penalty, be applied to the reduction of the principal amount owing in the inverse order of its maturity and not to the payment of interest, or refunded to Borrower to the extent that the amount which would have been excessive interest exceeds unpaid principal. The right to accelerate maturity of the Note or any other indebtedness does not include the right to accelerate any interest which has not otherwise accrued on the date of such acceleration, and lender does not intend to charge or receive any unearned interest in the event of acceleration. All interest paid or agreed to be paid to lender shall, to the extent permitted by applicable law, be amortized, prorated, allocated and spread throughout the full stated term (including any renewal or extension) of such indebtedness so that the amount of interest on account of such indebtedness does not exceed the maximum permitted by applicable law.

If this Deed of Trust is executed by only one person or by a corporation the plural reference to Grantors shall be held to include the singular, and all of the covenants and agreements herein undertaken to be performed by and the rights conferred upon the respective Grantors named herein, shall be binding upon and inure to the benefit of not only said parties respectively, but also their respective heirs, executors, administrators, grantees, successors and assigns.

If Grantor transfers any part of the property, or any interest therein, without Beneficiary's prior written consent, Beneficiary may declare the debt secured by this deed of trust immediately payable. In that event Beneficiary will notify Grantor that the debt is payable and may, without further notice or demand to Grantor, invoke any remedies provided in this instrument for default. Exceptions to this provision for declaring the note due on sale or transfer are limited to the following: (a) creation of a lien or encumbrance subordinate to this deed of trust; (b) creation of a purchase-money security interest for household appliances; (c) transfer by devise, descent, or operation of law on the death of a joint tenant; and (d) grant of a leasehold interest of three years or less without an option to purchase.

If Grantor transfers any part of the property, or any interest therein, without Beneficiary's prior written consent, Beneficiary may declare the debt secured by this deed of trust immediately payable. In that event Beneficiary will notify Grantor that the debt is payable and may, without further notice or demand to Grantor, invoke any remedies provided in this instrument for default. Exceptions to this provision for declaring the note due on sale or transfer are limited to the following: (a) creation of a lien or encumbrance subordinate to this deed of trust; (b) creation of a purchase-money security interest for household appliances; (c) transfer by devise, descent, or operation of law on the death of a joint tenant; and (d) grant of a leasehold interest of three years or less without an option to purchase.

The indebtedness, the payment of which is hereby secured, is in part payment of the purchase price of the real property herein described and is also secured by a vendor's lien retained in deed of even date herewith to the undersigned, and this Deed of Trust is given as additional security for the payment of said indebtedness.

*(continued)*

**FIGURE 13.2  CONTINUED.**

EXECUTED this ____ day of February, 2003.

GRANTOR:

_____

N. Williams

_____

May R. Williams

THE STATE OF TEXAS      §
                                    §

COUNTY OF HARRIS      §

This instrument was acknowledged before me on this the _____ day of February, 2003, by **N. Williams**.

_____

NOTARY PUBLIC, STATE OF TEXAS

THE STATE OF TEXAS      §
                                    §

COUNTY OF HARRIS      §

This instrument was acknowledged before me on this the _____ day of February, 2003, by May R. Williams.

_____

NOTARY PUBLIC, STATE OF TEXAS

file a **release of lien**, a copy of which is shown in Figure 13.3. Figure 13.4 may help orient your thoughts about the deed of trust, the release of lien, and the parties' interrelationships in the standard deed of trust situation.

**Requirements.** There are basically five requirements that make a deed of trust legally enforceable in Texas. If you refer to the deed of trust form in Figure 13.2, it may be helpful in showing how these five requirements coordinate with each other to create the enforceable obligation. The individual clauses are discussed below.

*Granting clause and property description* The **granting clause** and **property description** define the grantor (this is the grantee of the deed—and purchaser of the property). The clause effects a conveyance, in trust, of the described real estate. As stated previously, true legal title does not pass to the trustee, only title sufficient to create an interest in the property, in the event of a default. Note that in Figure 13.2 there is a legal description of the real estate. It may also include a description of some personal property that is to pass with that real estate. With both legal descriptions, the deed of trust form can be used not only as a mortgage that secures the

**FIGURE 13.3 RELEASE OF LIEN.**

NOTICE Prepared by the State Bar of Texas for use by Lawyers only. 9-73-10M
*To select the proper form, fill in blank spaces, strike out form provisions or insert special terms constitutes the practice of law. No "standard form" can meet all requirements.*

### RELEASE OF LIEN

THE STATE OF TEXAS

COUNTY OF HARRIS } KNOW ALL MEN BY THESE PRESENTS:

THAT the undersigned, of the County of _____ Harris _____, and State of Texas, the legal and equitable owner and holder of that one certain promissory note in the original principal sum of __ FIFTY THOUSAND AND NO/100--------- Dollars ( $50,000.00 ) dated __ February 24, 2003 __, executed by N. Debted and wife, May B. Debted ,
payable to the order of Friendly Lender Savings and Loan Association, more fully described in a deed of trust, duly recorded under Clerk's File No. O123456 and Film Code No. 45880618 of the Official Public Records of Real Property of Harris County, Texas; said note being secured by said deed of trust lien against the following described property, to wit:

Lot 1, Block 1, Shakey Acres Subdivision, Harris County, Texas, as shown of Record at Volume 7, Page 3 of the Map Records of Harris County, Texas.

for and in consideration of the full and final payment of all indebtedness secured by the aforesaid lien or liens, the receipt of which is hereby acknowledged, has released and discharged, and by these presents hereby releases and discharges, the above described property from all liens held by the undersigned securing said indebtedness.

EXECUTED this __4th__ day of __April__, A.D. _2003_.

Friendly Lender Savings and Loan Association

By: Adam Baum, President

**FIGURE 13.4   TYPICAL TEXAS DEED OF TRUST TRANSACTION.**

LENDER

Loan

Note and
Deed of Trust

BORROWER ⟶ TRUSTEE

(Technical Conveyance Only)

When Loan is Made

LENDER

Money

Release
of Lien

BORROWER --------- TRUSTEE

(Conveyance Becomes Void
by Terms of Deed of Trust)

When Loan is Repaid

debt with the real property, but also as a security agreement and financing statement for personal items to perfect the mortgagee's interest in the personalty. These types of provisions are normally used in loans when the personalty is to be secured by the deed of trust as part of the entire financing agreement. This is often done when purchasing income-producing property or when constructing new improvements. Please recall that some of these conflicts were discussed in Chapter 6, Fixtures and Easements.

*Habendum and warranty clause*  The **habendum and warranty clause** is very similar to that of a deed, as discussed in Chapter 10, and basically binds the grantor to the warranty, so that his legal title in the real estate is good and sufficient.

*Trust clause*  The **trust clause** specifically sets out that this conveyance is made **in trust** to secure the payment of the promissory note. This limits the title that is being passed and clearly sets out the trust relationship and reinforces the limited nature of the conveyance. This language does *not* create a true trust, such as the ones discussed in Chapter 5; it only creates an enforceable right in the trustee in the event of a default in the note and debt secured.

*Note and debt secured*  The **note and debt provision** indicates the amount of the note that is being secured and defines the beneficiary (this is the lender or mortgagee). The terms of the note may be specified in this provision. However, since the terms of an individual's payments may be quite lengthy and confidential, the words "as therein provided" are often used as sufficient reference to the terms of the note.

*Power of sale*  The **power of sale clause** is the specific provision that makes the deed of trust mortgage unique when compared with other types of mortgages. The clause provides for an out-of-court **foreclosure** in the event of a default in the payments of the real estate lien note. Recall Chapter 3 on home equity loans, though, where some judicial process is required before those foreclosure proceedings. The power of sale provision, of course, must comply with the Texas law of executions, pursuant to sales under a deed of trust.

*Notice of sale—generally* The power of sale clause provides that in the event of default in the payment of the real estate lien note, the trustee, upon request, will post a notice at the courthouse door (there are generally bulletin boards located near the courthouse door for such purposes), informing the public of the sale of the property referenced in the deed of trust, and a copy of the notice must also be filed in the county clerk's office. The notice must state the earliest time the sale will begin. A copy of this notice must be sent by certified mail to the last known address of the grantor in the deed of trust so that he will have notice that such sale is to take place. If the property is the grantor's residence, this notice must also be *preceded* by a 20-day notice to cure his default. It has been construed that notice to the husband and wife can be sent to only one of them to satisfy the statute. *Forestier* v. *San Antonio Savings Assoc.*, 564 S.W.2d 160 (Tex. Civ. App.—El Paso, 1978). The notice must be posted at least 21 days preceding the date of the sale, although these deadlines can be delayed up to 48 hours because of inclement weather, natural disaster, or other act of God. In computing the 21-day time period, the day the notice is posted is the first day of the required time period. *Concrete, Inc.* v. *Sprayberry*, 691 S.W.2d 771 (Tex. Civ. App.—El Paso, 1985). The date of the sale, pursuant to the power of sale clause, is always on the first Tuesday of the month following the required notice posted at the courthouse door. Then, believe it or not, on the first Tuesday of the following month after the notice has been posted (including holidays!), the trustee holds a public sale of the real estate on the courthouse steps or at such other location as the County Commissioner's Court may designate. Anyone is allowed to purchase at the sale, including the grantor (defaulting borrower) or the lender, but the purchase price must be paid in cash, unless otherwise agreed to. If the purchaser doesn't have cash at the sale, the trustee must give the highest bidder a "reasonable" time to provide the cash. *First Texas Service Corporation* v. *McDonald*, 762 S.W.2d 935 (Tex. App.—Ft. Worth, 1988). The sale is held between 10:00 a.m. and 4:00 p.m., and the trustee must designate where the sale will be held. The sale must be held within the area designated by the county commissioners court. *AG Op. No. JM-1044* (1989).

If there is an intention to buy property at a foreclosure sale, it is suggested that one find the trustee (he can hold the sale at any time between the hours of 10:00 a.m. and 4:00 p.m., but not later than three hours after the earliest time indicated in the posted notice of sale, discussed above) to determine how much he will accept for the property, and at which courthouse door (if more than one) he will be holding the sale. However, once these facts have been determined, and the buyer produces cash to the trustee, the conveyance is made to the subsequent purchaser by use of a trustee's deed, which passes full legal title to the purchaser, subject only to superior interests, if any.

*Notice of sale—debtor* There have been several court decisions in foreclosures concerning notice of the sale to the debtor, centering around whom notice must be given to and the last known address of the grantor (borrower). The general rule is that notice must not be given to anybody who is not a debtor and that notice need not be given to a debtor against whom no deficiency is sought. The purpose behind the notice requirement is to give each debtor an opportunity to protect his own interest. Since no notice need be given to somebody who is no longer considered a debtor or who has no further liability in a foreclosure, it only stands to reason that anybody who purchases the property subject to the mortgage (which would include wraparound mortgages) would not be entitled to the notice in the event of a foreclosure. *Hausmann* v. *Texas Savings & Loan Association*, 585 S.W.2d 796 (Tex. Civ. App.—El Paso, 1979). It is clear that the statute is being interpreted only to provide a minimum level of protection for the debtor. If the lender has no knowledge of the debtor's whereabouts, he is under no obligation to search for the address of the debtor if none is shown in his records. *Krueger* v. *Swann*, 604 S.W.2d 454 (Tex. Civ. App.—Tyler, 1980). One of the more interesting cases was a case in which the debtor wrote the lender a certified letter indicating that there was going to be a change of address and to please forward all correspondence to the new address. Upon foreclosing, the lender did not send notice to the new address but only to the old address. The Texas Court of Civil Appeals held that the notice, even to the wrong address, was sufficient. The Texas Supreme Court reversed this holding, indicating that it would defeat the legislative purpose of the statute if the debtor could not change his address after executing the deed of trust. *Lido International, Inc.* v. *Lambeth*, 611 S.W.2d 622 (Tex. 1981). Therefore, it is very, very important that anyone obligated on a deed of trust be sure to keep his lender informed of his current address. Otherwise, a foreclosure could take place, the notice requirements could have been satisfied, and the debtor could still have no knowledge of the default.

*Inadequate price* As stated in Chapters 10 and 11 on conveyancing, there are always technical legal questions involving foreclosure sales concerning the conduct of the sale, the notice of acceleration of indebtedness, and other irregularities or wrongful foreclosures. A lender, for instance, used to have the power to sell the property at a grossly inadequate price and then seek a deficiency judgment against the debtor. This effectively gave the lender the double recovery of getting the property back and requiring payment by the debtor. You can't get blood out of a turnip, but you might be able to get blood out of a dead beet [sic]. If the grossly inadequate price was coupled with an irregularity, however, the sale could be set aside. In at least one Texas case, the trial court cancelled a trustee's deed because the public sale was not loud enough. It appeared the debtor was standing three feet away from the trustee at the time of the sale but could not hear him "cry out" the sale of the property. This was enough of an irregularity to set aside the sale. *Dodson* v. *McCoy*, 601 S.W.2d 128 (Tex. Civ. App.—Houston [1st Dist.], 1980). An inadequacy to bid price, by itself, is not enough to set aside the sale. *BFP* v. *Resolution Trust Corporation*, 114 S.Ct. 1757 (1994). Courts may also set aside the sale if the debtor has been misled by the creditor into believing that the foreclosure will not take place, *Jinkins* v. *Chambers*, 622 S.W.2d 614 (Tex. Civ. App.—Tyler, 1981), or if less than all of the property could be sold to satisfy the creditor. *Stanglin* v. *Keda* 713 S.W.2d 94 (Tex. 1986).

As courts become more consumer-oriented, the issue of inadequacy of price, coupled with potential bankruptcy problems, creates a more delicate issue. One recent case has even held that the mortgagor (borrower) could sue for damages if the lender "chilled" the bidding at the foreclosure sale to result in an inadequate sales price, even though the sales price was not "grossly" inadequate. *Charter Bank–Houston* v. *Stevens*, 781 S.W.2d 368 (Tex. App.—Houston [14th Dist.], 1989).

*The "Antideficiency" Statute* Sections 51.003, 51.004, and 51.005 of the Texas Property Code do not change the **foreclosure** process as established in the statute (set out in Section 51.002 of the Property Code) but do address the case of a deficiency judgment that a mortgagee may pursue after a nonjudicial foreclosure sale. If the mortgagee chooses to pursue a deficiency against the borrower, the deficiency lawsuit must be filed within two years after the date of the foreclosure sale (the prior rule was a four-year statute of limitations). The most significant aspect of the statute, however, is that the borrower is given the opportunity of challenging the price paid by the purchaser at the foreclosure sale. The debtor can have the trier of the fact (judge or jury) determine whether or not less than fair market value was paid at the foreclosure sale. If the evidence presented by the borrower establishes that the fair market value was greater than the price paid at the foreclosure sale, the court will offset the debt by the fair market value instead of the foreclosure price in order to determine the amount of the deficiency, if there is any. For instance, if a house is sold at a foreclosure sale for $60,000 and the debt owed is $80,000, the mortgagee may pursue a $20,000 deficiency. If, however, the borrower produces evidence that the fair market value of the house is $80,000, he is entitled to a full offset against the deficiency balance.

Another provision of the statute provides that the monies received by the mortgagee from private mortgage insurance must be credited before the mortgagee begins a deficiency lawsuit, an additional hedge against a deficiency for the benefit of the borrower. An important exception, however, is that the credit required against a deficiency does *not* apply to the exercise of a private mortgage insurer of its subrogation rights against a borrower or any other person liable for a deficiency. That is, if the private mortgage insurance company pays a portion of the deficiency, it may then pursue that deficiency against the borrower. This may result in many lenders crediting up to the amount of private mortgage insurance and then allowing the private mortgage insurer to pursue the deficiencies instead of the mortgagee.

The new statutes apply to all foreclosures, both judicial and nonjudicial, and to all guarantors of the obligation.

**The Deed-in-Lieu Statute.** The Property Code (§51.006) provides for a lender's ability to accept a deed-in-lieu of foreclosure. Frequently, a borrower will be in default of her loan and want to avoid the embarrassment of public notice of the foreclosure sale. As an accommodation to the lender, she will simply deed the property back to the lender to avoid the foreclosure sale at the courthouse steps. One may logically assume that by accepting the deed, the lender acquired the same rights she would have acquired had she foreclosed at the courthouse steps, including the elimination of subordinate interests. The Texas Supreme Court held, however, that this was not so in *Flag-Redfern Oil Co.* v. *Humble Exploration Company, Inc.*, 744 S.W.2d 6 (Tex. 1988), and since that time lenders have been reluctant to accept deeds-in-lieu of foreclosure, preferring instead to foreclose on the debtor.

This statute provides that the lender may void a deed conveying real property and satisfaction of debt before the fourth anniversary of the date that the deed is executed and foreclosed under the original deed of trust if: (1) the debtor fails to disclose to the holder of the debt a lien or other encumbrance of the property before executing the deed conveying the property to the holder of the debt in satisfaction of the debt; and (2) the holder of the debt has no personal knowledge of the undisclosed lien or encumbrance on the property. If the lender looks to void the deed-in-lieu of foreclosure, the priority of its deed of trust will not be affected or impaired by the deed-in-lieu of foreclosure. As an alternative, the lender can accept the deed-in-lieu of foreclosure but still foreclose on its deed of trust without electing to void the deed, and the priority of the deed of trust will not be affected.

This statute may give lenders comfort in allowing them to preserve a little dignity for a borrower and not pursue a public foreclosure.

**Redemption.** In many other states, there are statutes (or case law) that provide for a **right of redemption**. This right basically means that the borrower has the right to bring the payments up-to-date even after the foreclosure sale, and reacquire title to the property. These periods of redemption may range from 30 days to several months. In Texas there is no right of redemption unless this right was specifically granted to the borrower when he executed his note. *Joy Corp.* v. *Nob Hill North Properties, Ltd.*, 543 S.W.2d 691 (Tex. Civ. App.—Tyler, 1976). The only right the borrower has in the event of default is to pay the note in full or to buy the property at the foreclosure sale. *Lusher* v. *First National Bank of Fort Worth*, 260 S.W.2d 621 (Tex. 1953).

An old common law doctrine has always existed in Texas that created an **equity of redemption**. This doctrine is to provide relief against penalties and forfeitures; it gives the mortgagor a reasonable time to cure a default and requires a reconveyance of the mortgaged property. To enforce an equity of redemption, one must sue and plead the equities that would authorize the recovery: (1) the party must prove that he has a legal or equitable interest in the property subject to the mortgage; (2) the party asserting an equity of redemption must prove that he is "ready, able, or willing to redeem the property in controversy by paying off the amount of valid and subsisting liens to which the parties are subject"; and (3) one must assert his equity of redemption before the foreclosure sale because the equity of redemption terminates once the foreclosure sale occurs. It is seldom that one finds a mortgagor able to pay off the full amount of the loans *and* pay all expenses incurred with the default, but this equitable right continues to exist in Texas. *Scott* v. *Dorothy B. Schneider Estate Trust*, 783 S.W.2d 26 (Tex. App.—Austin, 1990).

The out-of-court foreclosure is a very harsh remedy. There is some comfort, however, in that courts may hesitate to foreclose for nonmonetary defaults. *SARA-NEC* v. *Slape*, 546 S.W.2d 703 (Tex. Civ. App.—El Paso, 1977). There is also some comfort in the fact that before the lender can accelerate the note, he may have to give proper notice to the borrower of his intent to accelerate, and afford the borrower an opportunity to cure the default, although this requirement of notice can be waived in the promissory note. *Ogden* v. *Gibraltar Savings Assoc.*, 640 S.W.2d 232 (Tex. 1982); *Crow* v. *Heath*, 516 S.W.2d 225 (Tex. Civ. App.—Corpus Christi, 1974).

One last thought on foreclosures. In the case of a declining Texas economy (which many have never seen before), people have tended not to take their foreclosures seriously, thinking they can "walk away" from their mortgage and give the property back to the lender. It should be pointed out that lenders do not hesitate to pursue deficiencies, nor do the private mortgage insurers, FHA, VA, or other guarantors. A choice to breach one's contract to pay his mortgage payments can result in some serious repercussions on a borrower's credit and subsequent home purchases. Recording self-serving deeds back to the lender is not a simple, easy answer as these deeds do not convey title if they are not accepted by the mortgagee. *Martin* v. *Uvalde Savings and Loan Assoc.*, 773 S.W.2d 808 (Tex. App.—San Antonio, 1989).

## Lien Priority

When a valid foreclosure sale of property secured by a deed of trust takes place, all other lien interests that are inferior to the deed of trust are "wiped out," and the inferior lien holders, as well as the grantor, lose all of their interest in the property. If the foreclosure sale is invalid, the person who bids for the property on the foreclosure sale does so at his own peril. The buyer at a foreclosure sale cannot be a bona fide purchaser for value and take superior title. If there is a defective or irregular sale that can be set aside, the purchaser at sale cannot acquire title to the property at that sale, *Henke* v. *First Southern Properties, Inc.*, 586 S.W.2d 617, 620 (Tex. Civ. App.—Waco, 1979), although it may create a cause of action under the Deceptive Trade Practices Act against the lender. *Diversified, Inc.* v. *Gibraltar*

*Savings Association*, 762 S.W.2d 620 (Tex. App.—Houston [14th Dist.], 1988). If the grantor declares bankruptcy (even after the sale!!), the sale may be set aside by the bankruptcy court. So there is always a high degree of risk in purchasing at a foreclosure sale.

Lien priorities, in any situation, follow what has been called the "barber shop rule"; that is, the first in time gets priority. The first lien in time is generally the lien created by the purchase money mortgage, usually created by the first lien deed of trust. The **second lien** in time (which may be a second lien note to acquire funds to aid in purchasing the property, or perhaps to construct additional improvements on the property) then takes a second position in priority, and so forth.

If the deed of trust foreclosure is a second lien deed of trust, and a first lien deed of trust is outstanding, the purchaser at the second lien foreclosure sale also purchases the **equity of redemption**, which gives the purchaser the right to redeem (make payments on, or pay off) the grantor's equity interest in the first lien note. *North Texas Building & Loan Association* v. *Overton*, 86 S.W.2d 738 (Tex. 1935); *Churchill* v. *Bussey*, 692 S.W.2d 596 (Tex. Civ. App.—Ft. Worth, 1985). He is considered to be **subrogated** (put in the place of) the original grantor on said second lien deed of trust. The purchaser, therefore, acquires good title and the right to pay off the previously existing note. In the foreclosure process, the purchaser is said to **redeem up** and the trustee **forecloses down**, indicating that all the inferior interests are dissolved, and the purchaser acquires the right to pay off the superior interests.

Since the penalties in foreclosure are so harsh, and establishing lien priorities may be difficult, the most obvious question is how to stop the foreclosure of a superior interest. The only two remedies available to an inferior lien holder would be: (1) to file an injunction to prevent the foreclosure of the superior lien holder until a settlement or other alternative can be agreed to, or (2) after the foreclosure has been completed, file a lawsuit to set aside the foreclosure sale. Both remedies are difficult to pursue, are time-consuming, and ultimately depend on the equities and facts in any given case.

**Additional Deed of Trust Provisions.** It is often said that lenders operate under what is called the "golden rule"; that is, they have the gold, so they make the rules! Remember that the mortgage is a contract between the lender and the borrower and is inclined to be strictly construed in accordance with the terms of the instrument. This is not necessarily as one-sided as it seems, as lenders may also be subject to deceptive trade practice violations, but they are also entitled to be sure that their debt is adequately secured. *Levitt Mortgage and Investment Co., Inc.* v. *Thomas*, 626 S.W.2d 611 (Tex. Civ. App.—El Paso, 1981). Therefore, one often finds that there are additional provisions in a deed of trust that are added to protect the lender's interest. The lender needs to be sure that no additional conflicting claims may arise in his security and that the real estate is kept in good enough condition so that the value of his security in the real estate is not impaired. Provisions included in the deed of trust instrument in Figure 13.2 include the requirements for payment of all taxes and assessments, requirements to keep the property adequately insured, provisions for a substitute trustee, and provisions for bankruptcy. Other common provisions that one may encounter while reading various deed of trust instruments include the following.

*Assignment of rentals* Assignment of rentals normally assures the lender that in the event that the subject property is leased or rented, he is entitled to the rentals obtained from that property if he so requests.

*Condemnation* Condemnation generally provides that upon condemnation, all the proceeds of said condemnation are to go to the lender and are to be applied to the unpaid balance of the note, since the lender has provided the money to purchase the property. If any part of the property is lost by means of condemnation or other damage claim, the lender deserves to get the proceeds instead of the owner of the property.

*Partial releases* **Partial releases** provide that certain elements of the property may be released without releasing the entire property. These releases are very common when one has a deed of trust against a very large piece of property and wishes to construct improvements on only a portion of the property at a time.

*Due-on-transfer clause* The **due-on-transfer clause** normally provides that the grantor of the deed of trust may not convey the property to another party without paying off the note or obtaining the mortgagee's approval. This could effectively preclude any chance of the grantor selling the real estate if the mortgagee refused to give its prior written consent. *Sonny Arnold, Inc.* v. *Sentry Savings Assoc.*, 633 S.W.2d 811 (Tex. 1982, note concurring opinion). Provisions like this protect the mortgagees from having a noncreditworthy purchaser assume the responsibilities of the individual to whom the loan was made. Although there has been some question as to the legality of this particular clause, it has been consistently upheld as being a valid method of protecting a mortgagee's interest. *Ashley* v. *Leitch*, 533 S.W.2d 831 (Tex. Civ. App.—Eastland, 1975); *A. R. Clark Investment Co.* v. *Green*, 375 S.W.2d 425 (Tex. 1964); *Sonny Arnold, Inc.* v. *Sentry Savings Assoc.*, supra.

There have been some convincing arguments and Supreme Court decisions in other states that indicate that a due-on-transfer clause may be illegal. You may recall that fee simple ownership gives the owner of the property the uncontrolled right of disposition. Some states have taken the position that this due-on-transfer clause is an unreasonable restriction on fee simple ownership. Various other states have taken the position that the lender must prove that his security is in jeopardy or that the new purchaser is uncreditworthy before he can enforce the clause. *Wellenkamp* v. *Bank of America*, 582 P.2d 970 (Cal. 1978); *Patton* v. *First Fed. Sav. and Loan Assoc.*, 578 P.2d 152 (Ariz. 1979). The federal government has passed a statute that presumes these clauses to be enforceable in accordance with the terms of the contract, 12 C.F.R. 545.8–3(f); *Fidelity Federal Savings & Loan Assoc.* v. *de la Cuesta*, 102 S. Ct. 3014 (1982). Texas has held that it is not a restraint on sale, so long as the contractual provision in the mortgage is clear and unequivocal. *Sonny Arnold, Inc.* v. *Sentry Savings Assoc.*, supra. If the mortgage contains a penalty for prepayment, however, it may be such an unreasonable restraint. *Metropolitan Savings & Loan Assoc.* v. *Nabours*, 652 S.W.2d 820 (Tex. Civ. App.—Tyler, 1983).

There has also been some question as to whether or not something less than a full conveyance of the property will give the lender the right to accelerate on a due-on-transfer clause. For instance, is the transfer of property by contract for deed or possession of the property by a lease with an option to purchase a conveyance of title to the property such that it gives the lender the right to accelerate the note? These and many other questions have not yet been addressed by the courts in Texas because the actual language in these clauses frequently varies from contract to contract. So the enforceability of many of these clauses has yet to be ultimately determined by the Texas courts.

*No personal liability* On occasion, a purchaser is fortunate enough to have a lender who is so confident as to the value of the real estate that he will provide that, in the event of default, he will not seek a money judgment against the purchaser but will limit his remedies to foreclosing and retaking possession of the real estate. This is also referred to as a **nonrecourse** provision. It is generally considered to extend to other obligations in the mortgage as well as to the payments themselves (such as obligations to pay taxes). *Smart* v. *Tower Land & Investment Co.*, 597 S.W.2d 333 (Tex. 1980); *Wood* v. *Henry S. Miller Co.*, 597 S.W.2d 332 (Tex. 1980). The non-recourse provision also destroys the negotiability of the note. *Hinckley* v. *Eggers*, 587 S.W.2d 448 (Tex. Civ. App.—Dallas, 1979). Since a nonrecourse note is not negotiable, it must be assigned rather than negotiated. This prevents the assignee of the note from being a holder in due course, discussed later in this chapter.

*Insurance clause* An insurance clause generally provides that the mortgagor will keep the property insured so that in the event the property is ever destroyed, there will be proceeds available to rebuild the structure and maintain the value of the secur-ity. These clauses vary widely from mortgage to mortgage, however, and should be carefully read. The clause usually assigns the insurance proceeds to the lender and may give the lender the option of either rebuilding the structure or accepting the pro-ceeds of the insurance policy to pay off the loan (the homeowner gets to keep any excess proceeds and title to the lot). A rather harsh result was reached in a Texas case where the clause in the mortgage indicated that all of the insurance proceeds were to be paid to the lender. The court strictly construed this paragraph by saying the parties agreed that all insurance proceeds would go to the lender and all the pro-ceeds (which consisted of an excess over the debt) had to be paid over to the lender. That particular case involved a loan balance of only $62,500 and insurance proceeds of $110,000, resulting in an excess of $48,000 going to the lender. *English* v. *Fischer*, 660 S.W.2d 521 (Tex. 1983).

It should also be noted that if there is a clause in the mortgage that runs to the benefit of the mortgagee, which is breached by the mortgagor, the mortgagee has the right to foreclose. This right to foreclose may be due to the mortgagor's failure to pay ad valorem taxes, provide insurance coverage, or maintain the property in good con-dition and repair. *Chapa* v. *Herbster*, 653 S.W.2d 594 (Tex. Civ. App.—Tyler, 1983).

Although there are many variations of each of the foregoing clauses, the ones shown in Figure 13.2 are illustrative of clauses of this type generally found in deeds of trust.

## Why Have Two Instruments?

There is one question that is anticipated when discussing mortgages: Why are there two separate instruments—the promissory note and the deed of trust? The reason for this is fairly simple but is often overlooked.

**Negotiability.** The promissory note, being the actual promise to pay, is considered a **negotiable instrument** (the mortgage is not). This means that the promissory note, similar to a bank draft, can be endorsed on the back and sold to an investor, who then becomes the new noteholder. This is a very common practice in the mortgage busi-ness where mortgage companies will often sell millions of dollars in loans using the endorsed promissory note as the primary instrument of transfer. The new noteholder then becomes subrogated to the rights of the previous noteholder, giving it the right to enforce payment. The purchaser of the promissory note also becomes a **holder in due course**, which means he takes the note free and clear of all defenses that the maker may have, except for fraud in the inducement. This gives the purchaser of the note a privileged status since all the endorsers of this note, including the pri-mary lender, have guaranteed that the payments will be made on the note. A mort-gagee is not required to give the mortgagor notice of the assignment of the mortgage.

*Wagner* v. *GMAC Mortgage Corp.*, 775 S.W.2d 71 (Tex. App.—Houston [1st Dist.], 1989), unless it is covered by RESPA (discussed later in Chapter 16).

**Foreclosure.** Legally, since a promissory note is a negotiable instrument, it is an unconditional promise to pay by the maker of the note. There should be no conditions to payment, and the obligation of the maker to pay the note is absolute. There can be exceptions when a noteholder consistently accepts late payments, but the general rule is that a noteholder has the absolute right to accelerate all the payments (call the total amount of the note due) when one payment is a day late. This, in turn, gives him the right to foreclose under the deed of trust, which secures the payment of that note. *Highpoint of Montgomery Corp.* v. *Vail*, supra; *Dhanani Investments, Inc.* v. *Second Masterbilt Homes, Inc.*, 650 S.W.2d 220 (Tex. Civ. App.—Ft. Worth, 1983). This is true even if the mortgage has not been assigned to the new noteholder. The right to foreclose under the mortgage passes to the new noteholder by endorsement of the note. *West* v. *First Baptist Church of Taft*, 42 S.W.2d 1078 (Tex. Civ. App.—1931).

**Refinancing.** The separate promissory note document also creates other misconceptions. For instance, a person frequently talks about refinancing his house. As you may recall from the discussion of homesteads in Texas, one cannot refinance a house above the then-existing principal balance of the debt. In Texas, therefore, when a person refinances his house, he does not get a new mortgage up to the 95% value (which is frequently done in other states); he merely renegotiates his note to reflect different payments, different interest rate, different term, or other method of payment. The note is still secured by the same deed of trust that was originally in existence, which is usually extended (or renewed) to include the payments on the new note in place of the previous note.

**Deed of Trust.** The deed of trust, on the other hand, is a mortgage that evidences a lien interest against the real estate. This is normally recorded to reflect the lender's interest in the real estate and becomes part of the official public records of the county in which the property is located. In effect, the lender forecloses on the lien created by the deed of trust and sues on the note for the debt.

Both instruments serve entirely different functions but are dependent on each other to effect a sufficient promise to pay and perfect a lien interest in real estate.

Although the deed of trust per se may be a rather difficult concept to grasp, there is one misunderstanding that always seems to creep into the student's mind. This is the concept that the deed of trust is a deed. The deed of trust *is not a deed—it is a mortgage.*

# Other Types of Mortgages

Although the deed of trust is by far the most commonly used mortgage instrument in Texas, there are a number of other types of mortgages and mortgaging techniques. Some of these mortgages are different types of mortgage instruments altogether (regular mortgages, sale lease-back, contract for deed, etc.), whereas others are considered financing techniques, which may be deeds of trust or other mortgages with special provisions to achieve a particular purpose.

## Regular Mortgage

Since the deed of trust is so widely used in Texas as a mortgage (Texas law is unique in this area) and the foreclosure remedies are so simple and expedient, the so-called **"regular" mortgage** is seldom used in Texas. The regular mortgage is a two-party mortgage where the mortgagor offers his property as security for the loan and the mortgagee is the lender and holder of the note. These mortgages are similar to a deed of trust except there is no third-party trustee and there is no power of sale clause. Some states have held that a power of sale clause is unconstitutional because it denies the borrower his right to his property without due process of law. Therefore, in most of these other states we find the regular mortgage in common use. In most circumstances the regular mortgage must be foreclosed through judicial proceedings. That is, there must be a lawsuit filed, a service of process, and an ultimate judgment in favor of the lender before the property can be sold pursuant to a **writ of execution** (a writ of **execution** is an order by a judge to force the sale of the property to satisfy the obligation of the debtor). The courts have consistently upheld the power of sale clause under Texas law, so this type of mortgage is seldom used in Texas.

## Absolute Deed as a Mortgage

There are times when a lender will request that the mortgagor (borrower–purchaser) give the lender a deed to the property as a method of mortgaging. Although a transfer of legal title does take effect, the parties intend the transfer to be security for a loan rather than to effect a complete sale of the property. *Crow* v. *Williams*, 596 S.W.2d 310 (Tex. Civ. App.—Waco, 1980). When such a situation exists, one normally finds that the grantor of the real estate retains possession of the premises, and that the market value of the property is in excess of the consideration given for the transfer. This is similar to mortgages in title theory states (where the lender is determined to have legal title and the mortgagor merely a lien on the real estate). In such a case, when the property is fully paid for, the mortgagee executes another deed, sometimes called a **release deed**, to reconvey the property back to the original owner.

When an **absolute deed** is used as a mortgage, it is a necessity that parol evidence be allowed to show the clear import of the deed, even though the deed may be clear and unambiguous on its face. *Johnson* v. *Cherry*, 726 S.W.2d 4 (Tex. 1987). This is one of the few exceptions to the parol evidence rule discussed in Chapter 9.

Remember that Texas is a lien theory state, where the lender gets a lien on the property and the grantee named in the deed retains true legal title. There is an old common-law theory that says "once a mortgage—always a mortgage," which means that a mortgage is always a mortgage, regardless of the documentation used to create that mortgage. This confirms the theory that absolute deeds are merely mortgages and not a true transfer of title. There is no present intent to convey title to the real estate, other than for the sole purpose of obtaining a cash advance, by using the real property as security for the loan.

During difficult times in Texas, this created such serious problems that the 1987 legislature passed a statute concerning sales of homesteads, *V.T.C.A., Property Code, §41.006,* to protect the homeowners against loan sharks and scurrilous scuzz-buckets. The new statute provides that: (1) when there is a sale or purported sale of a homestead at a fixed purchase price that is less than the fair market value; and (2) the seller of the property executes a lease to continue his occupancy of the property, at lease payments that would exceed the fair rental value of the property, the transaction is considered to be a loan. The statute further provides that such a transaction is defined as a deceptive trade practice (see Chapter 7 for a discussion of deceptive trade practices), and the deed is void. The statute has done nothing more than merely put into statutory form what the law of Texas has always been in relation to deeds absolute as mortgages.

## Sale Lease-Back

The instruments used for a mortgage in the **sale lease-back** method normally include a deed and a lease; if the sale is not for cash, there may also be the execution of a deed of trust. In a typical sale lease-back situation, the owner of a property will sell the property for cash to a purchaser and then simultaneously execute a lease with the purchaser for the use and occupancy of the premises. This guarantees a definite rate of return on an investment for the purchaser. For instance, Manufacturing Company, Inc., may sell its plant, improvements, and other facilities to B. T. Operator for a cash payment of $100,000. At the same time the deed is signed, Manufacturing Company, Inc., executes a lease, as tenant, with B. T. Operator, as landlord, at a rate of $11,000 per year (which guarantees an 11% return cash-on-cash investment for B. T. Operator). Figure 13.5 graphically illustrates this transaction.

**Advantages.** In the above transaction, Manufacturing Company, Inc., obtains a free and clear $100,000 in working capital, which it can use to expand, make capital improvements, and streamline its manufacturing efficiency, rather than invest in real estate. Most companies would like to utilize their money in income-producing manufacturing methods rather than as a capital investment in non–income-producing real estate. To make the investment more attractive, there may be a provision in the lease for an option to buy the property back for $1 at the end of 30 years (the regular amortization period of a loan).

The sale lease-back transaction benefits the purchaser because he is allowed to have a definite return on his investment. He can also deduct the depreciation for the improvements on the property. If he has borrowed the money to finance the transaction, he can further deduct the interest paid on his loan. This offers a very good tax advantage for the purchaser.

The advantages for the seller, Manufacturing Company, Inc., are that it can pay a tax-deductible lease payment every month, and it receives a large influx of working capital (which is normally utilized to improve its monthly cash flow). It may also get a capital gains tax treatment upon the sale of the property and have an excellent chance to repurchase the property if repurchase options are included in the lease.

**Disadvantages.** Although the above sale lease-back example may indicate to the reader that there is a perfect relationship where everyone appears to come out ahead, it must be remembered that there are also disadvantages to this type of arrangement. The primary disadvantage is the possible adverse position of the Internal Revenue Service. If the transaction is not carefully done, or if there is too close a relationship between the buyer and the seller, the IRS may choose to treat the transaction as a loan rather than as a true sale. If such is the case, the tax breaks are dramatically different. In determining how to treat the sale lease-back transaction, the IRS normally looks to the intention of the parties surrounding the circumstances of the lease agreement itself, whether or not the option to repurchase is legitimate or appears to be a sham, whether or not the price of the sale is related to fair market value, and the appropriateness and size of the rental payments.

**FIGURE 13.5  A SALE LEASE-BACK TRANSACTION.**

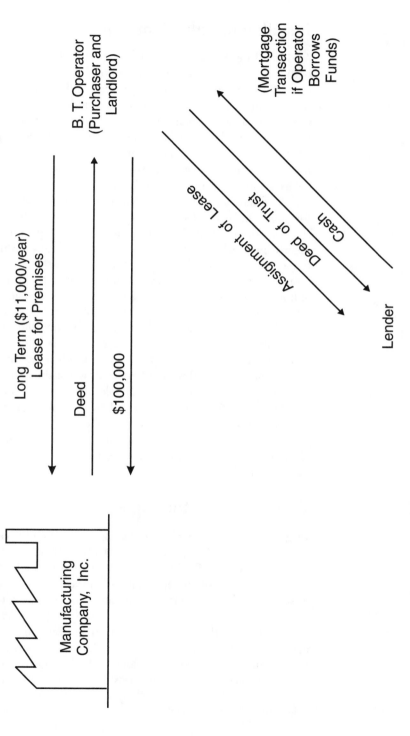

If done properly, the sale lease-back can be a very good benefit as a mortgaging technique, both for the purchaser and the seller, if they can avoid the pitfalls of the IRS code, and if the transaction is done in good faith and is not a sham transaction.

## Installment Sale Contracts

An **installment sale contract** is a very effective means of providing a mortgage, particularly for low-income transactions. An installment sale contract provides for seller financing pursuant to the terms of the installment land contract. Since the seller is financing the sale himself, he can establish his own criteria as to the credit-worthiness of and risks involved in evaluating the purchaser. The purchaser buys the house in accordance with the installment land contract, usually for a small down payment, and when he has completed the full number of monthly payments, normally for a term of years, the seller will convey the property to the purchaser by his execution of a deed.

As discussed in Chapter 9, in the event of foreclosure, the contract is simply forfeited and rescinded in the event of default. Although there are risks involved for the purchaser, if the seller operates in good faith, it provides a very efficient means by which lower-income families can buy housing without having to qualify for a loan or go through the red tape of mortgage insurance and financial statements, or having to sit across from the glare of a suspicious lender's investigation, although the contract document itself is the mortgage instrument and may contain many onerous provisions. Again, the "golden rule" applies.

There are also additional tax breaks for the seller in that he can use the installment sale method of reporting his income over a period of years, rather than taking all of his profit on the sale of the house in his first year. However, there are pitfalls, in that the Internal Revenue Service may consider the installment land contract to be a lease rather than an actual sale. The seller would then have to declare the income as normal income rather than as capital gains. Or, if there is an existing mortgage on the property, the installment sale tax benefits may be minimized under the provisions of the Internal Revenue Code of 1986. As in the sale lease-back situation, great care should be taken to be sure that the transaction is truly bona fide and not a sham.

## Construction Mortgages

In general, a **construction mortgage** normally utilizes the standard deed of trust form, but it contains special provisions because of: (1) the short-term nature of this type of mortgage; (2) the requirements of partial advances while construction is in progress; and (3) the incorporation of certain items of personalty into the real estate in which the lender wants to maintain prior security interest.

Mortgages of this type are often set up as "**tri-party agreements**"—where the **permanent lender**, the **construction lender**, and the **mortgagor** enter into an agreement by which the permanent lender promises to pay off the construction lender's mortgage upon completion of the construction to the permanent mortgagee's satisfaction. When the construction lender is paid by the permanent lender, the mortgagor then begins making his monthly payments to the permanent lender. The interest rate on construction loans is generally somewhat higher than that of the permanent loan, and the construction lender is normally a local financing institution that can personally inspect the construction on a daily basis, whereas the permanent lender is often located in another state and is not staffed to maintain this type of inspection policy on a day-to-day basis.

Special provisions that one may find in a construction loan deed of trust normally include what we call a **dragnet clause** or **future advance clause**, which secures all sums loaned or advanced by the beneficiary (construction lender) to the account of the mortgagor (regardless of the use of those funds). The deed of trust may also include an **additional property clause** (often referred to as a **"Mother Hubbard" clause**), which provides for any property attached to the premises at a later date also to be secured by the deed of trust. However, it should be pointed out that even if there are additional property clauses contained in the construction deed of trust, a mechanic's and materialman's lien is superior to that deed of trust if the additional property placed there by the mechanic or materialman can be removed without material injury to the property. *First National Bank of Dallas* v. *Whirlpool Corp.*, supra. There was a major change in residential construction loans in 1997. This will be discussed in a later chapter on liens.

## Home Equity Mortgages

You'll recall in Chapter 3 on Statutory Estates, we discussed the limited number of enforceable liens on Texas homesteads. In 1997, the citizens of Texas amended their homestead law to provide for enforceable home equity liens. While these loans utilize a Texas deed of trust form, the statute requires certain other procedural requirements in order for these loans to be valid.

The loans can only be made by designated lending institutions. These include banks, savings & loans, federally chartered institutions, persons licensed to make loans, licensed mortgage brokers, and a person who is related to the homestead property owner within the second degree of affinity or consanguinity (i.e., a close relative). See generally, §50(a)(6)(P).

A loan also has specific conditions. The owner can not be required to apply the proceeds of the extension of credit to repay another debt, except the debt to another lender (not the lender making the home equity loan). The owner of the homestead may not assign wages for the extension of the credit; may not sign any instrument which blanks are left to be filled in; may not sign a confession of judgment or power of attorney to the lender; and in addition, lenders are required to give copies of all documents signed by the owner related to the extension of the home equity loan and all the documents must contain a disclosure that it's a home equity loan. The homeowner and their spouse is also given a three day right of rescission after the extension of credit is made, and must also sign a written acknowledgment as to the fair market value of the homestead on the date the extension of credit is made.

The penalties for non-compliance with the home equity legislation are severe. The lender, or any holder of the note or extension of credit will forfeit all principal and interest to the extension of credit if the lender fails to comply with the constitutional provisions and fails to correct or comply within sixty days after the date they are notified of the non compliance. These are not your standard home equity loans that one finds in other states!

Prior to closing the home equity loan, all owners and their spouses must be given a final statement of settlement costs not later than one business day prior to closing the home equity loan. Once the owners and their spouses have received their advance copy, any change and any fee or other charge by the broker, lender, title company, or other settlement service provider, would delay the closing by at least one additional business day because the closing would have to be rescheduled.

**Line of Credit Loans.** Texas has also expanded home equity loans by voting in another constitutional amendment that allowed for **home equity line of credit**

loans. This allows a home owner to have a pre-approved loan (i.e. $50,000.00) that he can draw down in increments, repay in increments, and generally keep an open loan up to the $50,000.00 limit. Predictably, we have a number of requirements for the line of credit loan, which further complicates the home equity mortgage procedure. Each advance under the line of credit must be in an amount of at least $4,000.00 and the lender may not charge any fees with each advance. The only fees that may be charged are those collected at the time the line of credit is established. The maximum of principal amount that may be extended when added to all other debts secured by the homestead claimant may not exceed 80% of the fair market value of the property on the date the line of credit is established. The principal balance under the line of credit, however, may not exceed 50% of the fair market value of the home as determined on the date the line of credit is established. Payments can be made no less often than monthly, nor more often than every fourteen (14) days.

As a final thought on this matter, a home equity loan is a home equity loan and every time a loan is made the compliance procedures are the same (one cannot refinance a home equity loan with a purchase money loan). Another new constitutional amendment passed in 2003 does, however, allow the refinance of a home equity lien with a reverse mortgage. This will allow a homeowner to use the equity in their home for cash advances and then convert this loan to scheduled advances from the lender for the term of the reverse mortgage loan. Both loans have to be based on the equity in the homestead claimant's house (Tex. Const., §50(f)).

# Assumptions and Subject To

If there is no enforceable due-on clause in a mortgage, or if the lender chooses not to exercise his rights under the due-on clause in that mortgage, there are two methods by which property can be conveyed without having to change the terms of, or pay off, the mortgage. Both of these methods anticipate a full conveyance of the property by deed and not just transfer of an interest in the property, such as a contract for deed or lease with an option to purchase. This is accomplished through the means of an **assumption** of the existing indebtedness, or buying the property **subject to** the existing indebtedness.

## Assumption

In the **assumption** loan situation, the grantee of the property becomes primarily liable on the note and deed of trust, whereas the grantor in the situation operates as a surety in the event the note is not paid in full. In this situation, if there is a default on the note, the lender must pursue his remedy against the grantee; but if the grantee cannot satisfy the indebtedness, the lender has the remedy of also pursuing a cause of action against the original grantor, who is also the original signatory party on the note and deed of trust. It is sometimes a surprise to the grantor (when he sells his house on an assumption) that if there is a subsequent default, he may still be liable on that note at some later date. This surprised a lot of people in Texas's recessionary economic cycle. Figure 13.6 graphically shows how the assumption procedure takes effect.

The concern over the rights of the seller (shown as purchaser 1 in Figure 13.6) has prompted many questions as to his rights in the event of a foreclosure by the

**FIGURE 13.6  HOW THE ASSUMPTION PROCEDURE TAKES EFFECT.**

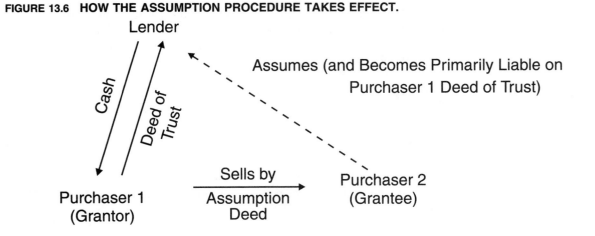

lender on purchaser 2. It is generally an accepted principle that purchaser 2 has the right to pay off the loan prior to the foreclosure sale. *Lusher* v. *First National Bank of Fort Worth*, supra. The question has arisen, however, as to whether or not purchaser 1 has the right to pay off the note to protect his interest.

Upon conveyance, Texas law has generally considered the grantor to become a guarantor of the obligation assumed by the grantee. Therefore, under most theories, purchaser 1 has the right to pay off the lender and subrogate to (put himself in place of) the rights of the lender. Therefore, purchaser 2 would have to make his payments to purchaser 1. Some lenders have taken the position that if they release purchaser 1 from liability (this is properly termed a **novation**), purchaser 1 has no right to pay off the note and subrogate himself to the lender's rights.

Another difficulty is in determining whether or not purchaser 1 even has notice of the foreclosure on purchaser 2. By law (note §51.002, discussed previously in this chapter), the lender is supposed to give notice of the foreclosure to each debtor at the debtor's last known address. This has been interpreted to provide only a minimum level of requirements for private foreclosure sales. *Forestier* v. *San Antonio Savings Assoc.*, supra. Since purchaser 1 is a guarantor, there is a question as to whether or not he is a "debtor" as specified by §51.002. In addition, if purchaser 1 has sold his home by assumption and has moved once or twice since this sale, there is a very good chance that he will never get notice and be aware of the foreclosure sale such that he could protect his rights. If purchaser 2 "walks" his mortgage, purchaser 1 may find himself liable many years after the sale. In a declining economy, this has surprised a lot of homeowners who have "moved up" to a new home, only to find that their purchaser has defaulted on the old one. Aaugh! (And the seller is still liable!!)

There has been some attempt to remedy the situation by the use of a legal instrument called a deed of trust to secure assumption. This is basically nothing more than an agreement between purchaser 1 and purchaser 2 that in the event purchaser 2 defaults, purchaser 1 has the right to subrogate himself to the lender and make the payments on behalf of purchaser 2. It may also give purchaser 1 the right to foreclose on purchaser 2 and retake possession of the premises and reassume the payments to the lender. It must be remembered, however, that this instrument is not signed by the lender and was not agreed to by the lender. It is not prudent to rely on this instrument as giving purchaser 1 any rights against the lender. A deed of trust to secure assumption, creating a cloud on title when recorded, often creates more problems than it solves.

All of the disadvantages of the assumption of the mortgage are further magnified if purchaser 1 takes a second mortgage back for the remainder of the purchase price. If the lender forecloses on purchaser 2, purchaser 1 may lose his second lien interest at the foreclosure sale.

## Subject To

When property is sold **subject to** an existing mortgage, the grantee does not become obligated to pay the mortgage but merely has the option of paying that mortgage if he chooses to do so.

In the "subject to" situation, the grantor still remains primarily liable on the note, and the grantee has no obligation at all to the original lender. *Lyons* v. *Montgomery*, 701 S.W.2d 641 (Tex. 1985). Figure 13.7 graphically illustrates how the "subject to" mortgage situation takes effect. Purchaser 2 typically makes the mortgage payments to purchaser 1, and purchaser 1 forwards these payments to the lender. If there is an excess amount due to purchaser 1, purchaser 2 may execute an additional note and deed of trust "subject to" the first lien deed of trust and make these payments to purchaser 1 in addition to those of the original mortgage payment.

If there is a due-on clause in the original deed of trust, the assumption situation normally cannot take effect until the subsequent grantee has been approved by the lender. This is also true in the "subject to" situation.

## Wraparound Mortgage

Commercial transactions and land syndication schemes have made widespread use of a more complicated type of "subject to" mortgage, more commonly called a **wraparound mortgage**. The property is conveyed by a deed "subject to" the existing

**FIGURE 13.7 HOW THE SUBJECT-TO MORTGAGE TAKES EFFECT.**

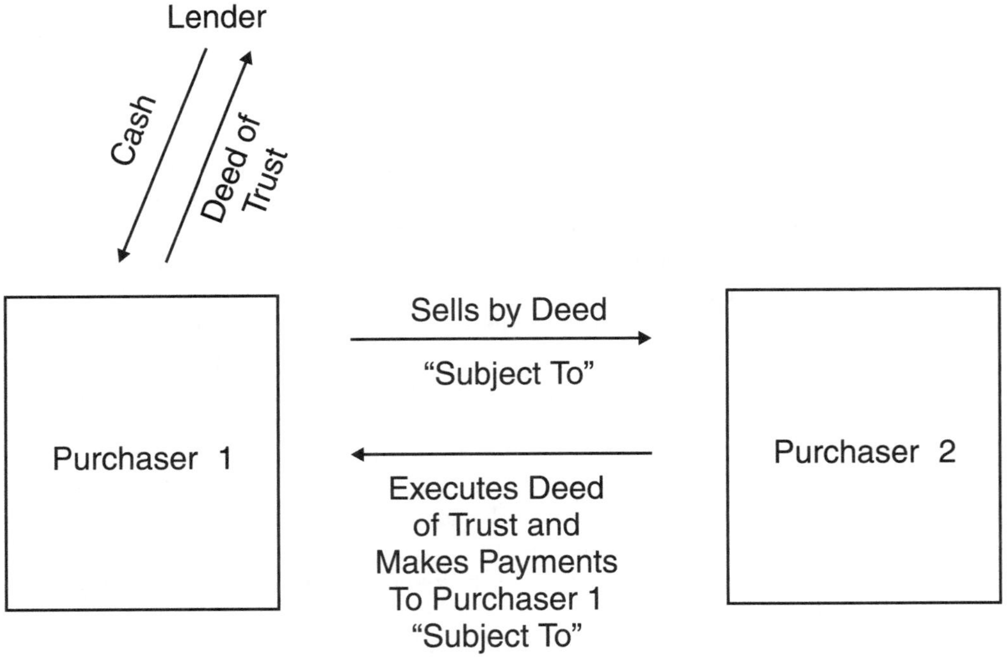

mortgage, and, of course, the second mortgage between the grantor and grantee is signed by the grantee "subject to," but not promising to pay, the prior existing mortgage. The wraparound mortgage has basically the same effect as creating a second lien deed of trust, except that the obligation of the grantee is to pay the entire mortgage amount to the grantor, and the grantor, in turn, pays the lender (first lien holder).

When purchaser 2 executes the second lien wraparound deed of trust (sometimes also called an "all-inclusive" deed of trust), it is normally a deed of trust in a larger amount, which encompasses both the first lien note and the additional obligation to pay purchaser 1 any excess. For instance, if purchaser 1's remaining balance on his note was in the amount of $40,000 and the purchase price was $60,000, purchaser 2 could pay $10,000 down and execute the second lien deed of trust to purchaser 1 in the amount of $50,000. In this manner it encompasses the $40,000 indebtedness as well as the $10,000 difference, which he owes to purchaser 1 as part of the purchase price of the property.

This type of financing became so common during the rampant real estate syndication craze in the early 1970s that it was not uncommon to see extended chains of wraparound mortgages, similar to the illustration in Figure 13.8.

**Advantages.** The wraparound mortgage provides advantages similar to those of installment land contracts to both the buyer and the seller. Since the grantor is selling to the grantee subject to the existing mortgage, there is normally no outside financing that has to be obtained by the grantee, and this results in basic seller financing. Since the grantee pays the grantor, this method also avoids the risks of the more typical second lien situation in assumptions, since the grantee must pay the grantor directly. The grantor, then, is always sure that the first lien mortgage payments are being made. If there is a default in the initial payment, the grantor is immediately on notice and can exercise his right of foreclosure to reinstate his interest in the property before there is a default to the primary lender. The terms on a sale of this kind are usually more attractive than sales utilizing more conventional financing techniques: The sale price is normally higher; there is a higher interest yield; and the seller can take an installment sale advantage as a tax benefit.

The buyer's advantage generally centers around the fact that he deals with the seller directly, so he can get more attractive terms (interest only, or perhaps longer terms), and there are no credit requirements or loans to apply for.

**Disadvantages.** The disadvantages to a wraparound note and mortgage are basically that the buyer runs the risk that the seller may not pay off the prior lien note(s) and may default. Thus, even though the purchaser has paid his note, he may lose his interest when the prior lender forecloses. This problem can sometimes be overcome by the use of a third-party escrow agent. In that event, the grantee pays the escrow agent, and the escrow agent pays part of the payment to the lender and the remainder to the grantor. This assures the subsequent grantee that all obligations pursuant to the prior existing mortgages have been met.

There has been little case law to date and little information as to the effect that the court will give these mortgages. Each grantee may also find additional liability as he changes his status from grantee to grantor because he may undertake the additional obligation to assure his grantee that the prior mortgage payments are made. *Newsom* v. *Starkey*, supra.

Another Texas case to construe wraparound mortgages is *Tanner Development Co.* v. *Ferguson*, 561 S.W.2d 777 (Tex. 1977). This case was the first such case to construe wraparound mortgages in a usury context. This will be described in greater detail in Chapter 14, Interest and Finance Charge.

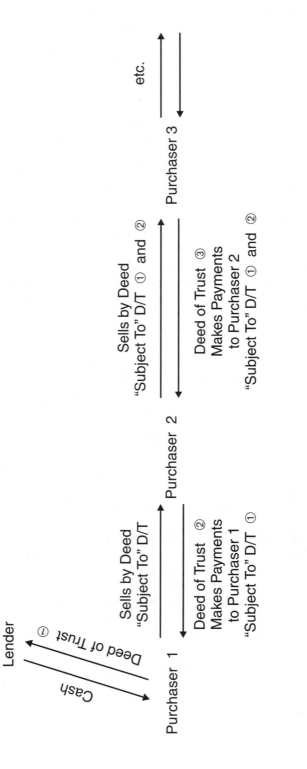

**FIGURE 13.8**

Foreclosures of wraparound mortgages have always been a complicated issue. If A sells to B, seller financing a mortgage for $4,000,000, then B sells to C, and B seller finances a mortgage for $6,000,000, there is always a chance of default. If C defaults and B forecloses on C, how much does he sell it for at the foreclosure sale? He could bid $6,000,000 (the amount of the note), but he actually only loaned $2,000,000 (because it was subject to the prior $4,000,000). If he sells it for $6,000,000 at the foreclosure sale, must he apply the $4,000,000 to the outstanding first lien balance or can B keep it? Some clarification was given by the Texas Supreme Court in 1989, wherein the Supreme Court stated that in such cases the law should imply a covenant into the parties' agreement requiring the trustee at the foreclosure sale to apply the proceeds first to the satisfaction of the preexisting debt before making any distribution to the mortgagor. *Summers* v. *Consolidated Capital Special Trust*, 783 S.W.2d 580 (Tex. 1989).

The wraparound mortgage has proved to be a very effective tool for creating installment sales and for obtaining easy financing. For investment groups, it has not been at all uncommon for the property to be conveyed using the wraparound mortgage several times without the primary lien holder ever being paid in full. The more this type of mortgage is used in a sequencing chain of sales and purchases, however, the bigger the risks the subsequent grantees are forced to take.

## ■ SUMMARY

The most common mortgage procedure in Texas requires the execution of two instruments: the promissory note and the deed of trust. The promissory note is the purchaser's promise to pay, and the deed of trust is the mortgage instrument most commonly used in Texas. The deed of trust is basically a mortgage with a power of sale provision. The power of sale provision allows the lending institution, by request to the trustee, to sell the property at public auction in the event of a default by the mortgagor (borrower). Other types of mortgages in Texas include the absolute deed as a mortgage, the sale lease-back, installment land contracts, and construction mortgages.

There are two methods by which property can be conveyed without paying off the original mortgage. One is selling the property on an "assumption," where the subsequent purchaser assumes the existing mortgage. The second method is "subject to," which allows the subsequent purchaser to purchase the property without assuming the mortgage but simply acknowledging the mortgage's existence and excepting it from title. A common utilization of the "subject to" mortgage is the wraparound mortgage.

## CASE STUDIES FOR DISCUSSION

1. The First National Bank of Dimebachs sought to foreclose on Green Acres Apartment Complex. Upon foreclosure, the contractor arrived to remove all the fixtures he had installed in the premises. The First National Bank of Dimebachs alleged that its deed of trust was prior in time and, therefore, had a prior interest in the fixtures. The contractor claimed he had a right to remove them or recover all severable fixtures because of his claim as a mechanic and materialman, even though his claim was second in time. What legal ramifications do you foresee?

2. Mr. and Mrs. Niland owned a large single-family residence on an acre and a half lot in Dallas, Texas. They also owned a condominium in the same general area of town. They went to Lender No. 1 and claimed that their single-family residence was their homestead and used the condominium as security for a loan. They signed a non-homestead affidavit and a designation of homestead for their single-family residence. They then went to Lender No. 2 and claimed the condominium was their homestead and borrowed money using the single-family residence as security for the loan. They used part of the proceeds to pay off Lender No. 1 and then defaulted to Lender No. 2. Upon Lender No. 2's foreclosure, the Nilands alleged that the house was their homestead, the loan was invalid, and the lender could not foreclose. Lender No. 2 foreclosed and Mr. Deeson bought the property at the foreclosure sale. Mr. Deeson alleges the house is his because he was the purchaser at the foreclosure sale. Mr. Niland alleges the house is his because it was his homestead, and the lender is worried. What legal ramifications do you foresee?

## CHAPTER 14

# Interest and Finance Charge

The mortgagor–mortgagee relationship is one of those last vestiges of true free enterprise. The lender (mortgagee) makes an effort to maximize the return on investment, and the borrower (mortgagor) "shops around" at various banks, mortgage companies, and other primary lending sources in an effort to find the best rates for the loan. There has been serious effort, however, on the part of the State of Texas and the U.S. government to protect borrowers and consumers from loan sharks, "sharpies," and con artists who abuse their expertise in the mortgage and lending business. The tongue-in-cheek "golden rule" that has been referred to in the previous chapter cannot extend itself to violate public policy, to discriminate, or to promote unconstitutional objectives. In addition, the legislatures (both state and federal) have made a concerted effort to effect disclosure of loan costs (finance charges) and to limit the amount of interest that can be charged. There are few areas of lending that have been more often litigated, or that more directly affect the consumer, than the areas of interest and finance charge.

## Finance Charge

To begin with, there are two distinctly separate areas of the law that deal with the cost of obtaining money. One is a state law; the other is a federal law.

### Regulation Z

Originally passed in 1968, the **Federal Consumer Credit Protection Act**, under Title I of the **Truth-in-Lending Act** (T-i-L Act), required extensive disclosure by creditors when making loans to consumers. The T-i-L Act placed the job of implementing the act on the Board of Governors of the Federal Reserve System. This was accomplished by the **Federal Reserve Board's** promulgation of **Regulation Z** (Reg. Z), an exhaustive publication dealing with almost every imaginable area of extension of credit. There are entire sets of books written on these regulations alone (not to mention the interpretative rulings, public information letters, staff opinions, and published forms), and there will be little attempt made here to explain anything but the most general applications of the T-i-L Act.

The purpose of the T-i-L Act is to ensure that everyone being extended commercial credit by a creditor covered by the act is given meaningful disclosures with respect to the cost of the credit being extended. The disclosures must be clear and according to the statutory forms published pursuant to the T-i-L Act and Reg. Z.

Creditors covered by the T-i-L Act must comply fully with all Reg. Z requirements if four conditions are met:

1. The credit is offered or extended to consumers (must be natural persons).

2. The credit is offered and extended regularly (more than five times for transactions secured by dwellings in a preceding year).

3. The credit is subject to "finance charge" or payable by written agreement in more than four installments.

4. The credit is extended primarily for personal, family, or household purposes.

The disclosures must be made in terms of deferred **finance charge** and **annual percentage rate** (APR), so that the consumer will clearly understand what is being disclosed to him.

**Finance charge** is defined as:

> . . . the sum of all charges, payable directly or indirectly by the creditor as an incident to or as a condition of the extension of credit, whether paid or payable by the customer, the seller, or any other person on behalf of the customer to the creditor or a third party . . . [Reg. Z, Section 226.4(a)].

The APR is the rate charged (expressed as a percentage) as determined by applying the federal government's definition of **finance charge** to the federal government's definition of **consumer credit**. The finance charge is not necessarily **interest** as defined by Texas statute. *Rotello* v. *Twin City International, Inc.*, 616 S.W.2d 318 (Tex. Civ. App.—Houston, 1981). A form Reg. Z disclosure is shown in Figure 14.1. It is important to note that there are exemptions and exclusions from the determination of finance charges as they apply to certain real estate transactions (primarily in buying homes). However, good practice favors disclosure of the items, to ensure compliance. One should also note that there is no ceiling (limitations) to finance charges; the requirements only specify that the charges be disclosed.

The federal Truth-in-Lending Act and Regulation Z were both changed in 1980 by the Truth-in-Lending Simplification and Reform Act. This statute became effective on April 1, 1982. It was changed again in 1983 to comply with the Depository Institutions Act of 1982. The most significant changes affecting real estate, however, are the definitions of creditor and arrangers of credit. A **creditor** is basically a person who extends credit more than five times for a transaction secured by a dwelling in a preceding calendar year or in a current calendar year, *Reg. Z, §226.2(a)(17)*. An **arranger** of credit could include real estate brokers who arrange for sellers to take second lien loans.

The important point to remember is that a violation of the T-i-L Act creates an unavoidable liability by the party violating the act. It must be strictly complied with, and verbal disclosures are not effective. *Smith* v. *Chapman*, 614 F.2d 968 (5th Cir.—1980).

## Right of Rescission

One of the most effective parts of the T-i-L Act is the **right of rescission**. The right of rescission applies to all consumer loans, although mortgages for acquisition of residential real estate (or initial construction) are exempt. When a consumer

**FIGURE 14.1   REGULATION OF DISCLOSURE FORM.**

### CREDITOR'S TRUTH-IN-LENDING DISCLOSURES TO CONSUMERS (FEDERAL DISCLOSURE BOX)

| *ANNUAL PERCENTAGE RATE<br>The cost of my credit as a yearly rate. | FINANCE CHARGE<br>The dollar amount the credit will cost me. | Amount Financed<br>The amount of credit provided to me or on my behalf. | Total of Payments<br>The amount I will have paid after I have made all payments as scheduled. |
|---|---|---|---|
| _____ % | E $ _____ | $ _____ | E $ _____ |

\* The **ANNUAL PERCENTAGE RATE** disclosed above:

☐ is a fixed rate for the life of my loan.

☐ is the initial interest rate in my variable rate loan that may change (increase or decrease) from time to time based upon movements up or down of the "Prime Rate" (the highest of multiple "Prime Rates") published in the MONEY RATES column of **The Wall Street Journal** (the "Journal Prime Rate") which is in effect on the 15th day of each calendar month (or on the next publication date if **The Wall Street Journal** is not published on the 15th day of any month). For example, a change in the Journal Prime Rate of one percentage point on the 15th day of any calendar month (or the next publication date) will result in a one percentage point change in the same direction in my **Annual Percentage Rate** on the first day of the following calendar month. My interest rate on this loan is and will remain _____ percentage points above the Journal Prime Rate, which presently is _____ %.

An example of the effect on my interest rate of an increase in the Journal Prime Rate is as follows: If my loan were for $5,000, with an initial interest rate of 11.00% per year, payable in 36 consecutive monthly installments of $163.69, and the Journal Prime Rate increased to 13.00% at the end of one year, the amount of my final monthly payment would increase by $89.50 to $253.19.

**My payment schedule will be:**

| Number of Payments | Amount of Payments | When Payments Are Due |
|---|---|---|
| 1 | | _____ days after date, on _____ 19 _____ |
| | | Monthly, or ☐ Quarterly   ☐ Semi-Annually   ☐ Annually Beginning _____<br>(Date) |

☐ If checked here, my loan is payable on demand and all disclosures are based on an assumed maturity of one year.
**Security:** Collateral securing other loans with you may also secure this loan.
**Late Charge:** If a payment is more than 15 days late, I will be charged 4% of the payment amount.
**Prepayment:** If I pay off early, I will not have to pay a penalty.
I can see my contract documents for any additional information about nonpayment, default, any required repayment in full before the scheduled date, and prepayment refunds and penalties.

E means an estimate

### ACKNOWLEDGMENT OF RECEIPT OF DISCLOSURES

We affirm that the above Contract was complete, with all blanks filled in, before we signed below and that one of us that was a primary Debtor received a copy of it Witness our Hands(s) and Seal(s), this sealed instrument being signed and delivered on the date first above written. Each us us adopts as his/her/its seal the word "(SEAL)" appearing beside or near his/her/its signature below.

WITNESS _____   Debtor _____ (SEAL)

WITNESS _____   Debtor _____ (SEAL)

WITNESS _____   Debtor _____ (SEAL)

WITNESS _____   Debtor _____ (SEAL)

BOM-CONS-1 (6-89)

enters into a credit transaction, she is given the right to rescind (back out of) the transaction by midnight of the third business day after: (1) she has signed the documents to secure the credit; or (2) delivery of the notice of right to rescind; or (3) delivery of all material disclosures. If the consumer exercises this right, the documents are void, and any money advanced by the consumer (other than for the lender's actual expenses) must be returned to the consumer. The consumer can waive this right to rescind for a bona fide financial emergency.

**High Cost Mortgages.** In an attempt to regulate predatory lending, Congress enacted the Home Owners Equity Protection Act of 1994 (**HOEPA**). Among other things, this statute regulates **High Cost Mortgages** which are defined as "a consumer credit transaction," secured by consumer's principal dwelling, and in which either: (1) the annual percentage rate at consummation will exceed by more than eight (8) percentage points, the yield on Treasury Securities having comparable periods of maturity to the loan maturity as of the 15th day of the month immediately preceding the month in which the application for the extension of credit is received by the creditors (it is a 10% point margin for subordinate lien mortgages); or (2) the total points and fees payable by the consumer at or before loan closing will exceed the greater of eight percent (8%) of the total loan amount, or $480.00 (this figure is subject to adjustment by Congress). HOEPA requires a special disclosure, similar to a Regulation Z Disclosure. Similar to Regulation Z, the high cost mortgage regulations do not apply to "**Residential Mortgage Transactions**," which are defined as "loans used to finance the purchase or initial construction of the borrower's principal dwelling."

Creditors who extend high cost mortgages cannot include certain items in their loan documents such as balloon payments of less than 5 years, negative amortization, increased interest after default and certain calculations of payment rebates and penalties. In addition, creditors cannot extend credit for high costs mortgages if, considering the consumer's current and expected income, current obligations, and employment status, the consumer will be unable to make the scheduled payments to repay the obligation. High cost home improvement loans cannot be funded directly to the Contractor, but must, instead, be paid jointly to the Contractor and owner or to a third party escrow agent through an escrow agreement.

# Interest

In contrast to the federal government's determination of finance charge is the Texas definition of interest. The 1997 legislature enacted massive changes in the usury laws. References to those statutes are now contained in the newly adopted Finance Code and a renumbered series of civil statutes. **Interest** is defined as "the compensation allowed by law for the use or forbearance or detention of money," *Finance Code, §301.002.*

## Usury

**Usury** is defined as the charging of an interest rate that is in excess of that allowed by law. It has three essential elements: (1) a loan of money; (2) an absolute obligation that the principal be repaid; and (3) the exaction of a greater compensation than allowed for by law. *Bray* v. *Neeley*, 682 S.W.2d 615 (Tex. Civ. App.—Houston, 1984). The "charging" of interest is liberally construed. The charge is usurious when the rate of interest is in excess of the legal rate as invoiced, demanded, or received. *Fisher* v. *Westinghouse Credit Corporation*, 760 S.W.2d 802 (Tex. App.—Dallas, 1988). It can include any charge unilaterally placed on an account as interest and can even include a payoff quote. *Danziger* v. *San Jacinto Savings Association*, 732 S.W.2d 300 (Tex. 1987). The Texas statute may not apply, however. Texas courts have upheld the theory that parties can agree in their contract to enforce the usury law in *any* state applicable to their transaction so long as there is significant contact with that state. For instance, a Texas resident buying property in Utah could agree to apply the Utah usury statute. If, however, a Texas resident contracts to buy property in Minnesota, it would be a subterfuge to avoid the Texas usury laws to apply the usury laws of the state of Kentucky. *Cook* v. *Frazier*, 765 S.W.2d 546 (Tex. App.—Ft. Worth, 1989).

Except as otherwise fixed by law, the maximum rate of interest in Texas is 10% per year. Of course, there are many other interest rates "otherwise fixed by law." There are extensions of credit where the original principal (or a series of advances, which total the principal amount) is $250,000 or more. That maximum interest rate is 18% per year, *Finance Code, §302.102*. There are also optional interest ceilings. They do not apply to a loan secured by a lien on the borrower's homestead, *Finance Code §303.101*. The ceilings can be calculated weekly, monthly, or quarterly, or they can be annualized.

The weekly ceiling is computed by: (1) multiplying the auction rate by 2; and (2) rounding a result obtained to the nearest 1/4 of 1%. The "auction rate" means the auction average rate quoted on a bank discount basis for 26-week treasury bills issued by the U.S. government, as published by the Board of Governors of the Federal Reserve System, for the week preceding the week in which the weekly ceiling is to take effect.

The quarterly and annualized ceilings are computed by the Consumer Credit Commissioner on December 1, March 1, June 1, and September 1 of each year for the calendar quarter beginning the following January 1, April 1, and October 1. The quarterly ceiling or annualized ceiling is computed by averaging all of the weekly ceilings using average rates for auctions held during the three calendar months preceding the computation date of the ceiling. Isn't this fun and interesting?

The Consumer Credit Commissioner must compute the monthly ceiling on the first business day of the calendar month in which the rate applies. The monthly ceiling is computed by averaging all of the weekly ceilings, computed using rates from auctions held during the calendar month preceding the computation date of the monthly ceiling! The minimum ceiling is 18% per year, *Finance Code, §303.304*. The maximum ceiling is a little more complicated (?!?). In general terms, the maximum ceiling rate is 24% per year. If, however, the contract for credit is extended for a business, commercial, investment, or similar purpose, but excluding a contract that is not any of those purposes; it is primarily for personal, family, household, or agricultural use; and the amount of credit extension is more than $250,000, then the ceiling is 28% per year, *Finance Code, §303.305*.

There are other statutory provisions that allow for other rates of interest in special situations (i.e., consumer credit transactions, FHA insured and VA guaranteed loans, *Finance Code, §302.202*). However, for most loans secured by real estate that are not consumer credit transactions, or controlled by federal statute, the above interest statutes are controlling.

## Federal Intervention of State Usury Laws

On March 31, 1980, and October 8, 1980, federal laws were passed that declared that the constitutional laws of any state expressly limiting the rate or amount of interest shall not apply to any loan that is:

1. Secured by a first lien on residential property, by a first lien on stock in residential cooperative housing corporations, or by a first lien on a residential manufactured home.

2. Made after March 31, 1980.

3. Described in Section 527(b) of the National Housing Act, 12 U.S.C. 1735f-5(b).

Another provision of the federal statute that is applicable to business or agricultural loans provides a new ceiling for loans made for business or agricultural purposes in the amount of $1,000 or more. These loans may charge a rate of interest of not more than 5% per annum in excess of the discount rate, including any surcharge thereon, on 90-day commercial paper in effect at the Federal Reserve Bank in the federal reserve district where the person is located. There are also provisions for the state to preempt this provision under conditions similar to that of a prior statute.

## Determination of Interest

The most difficult question to date has been: What constitutes interest as a charge for the "forbearance or detention" of money? There are an almost indeterminable number of fees that have been tacked on, added to, credited to, paid collaterally with, and given in exchange for all kinds of loan transactions. Most of these charges incurred when obtaining a loan are clearly established and understood. The lender must be very careful in requiring these charges, so that the interest charged will not be considered to be usurious. Therefore, the determination of these charges as "interest" is very important to the lender's business practice. Some of the more common charges for obtaining a loan may constitute interest and deserve more detailed discussion.

**Late Charges.** The most controversial determination of interest in recent years involves the use of late charges. Earlier cases in Texas tended to indicate that late charges could be usurious in certain circumstances. A controlling issue seems to be whether or not the late fee is charged for a service performed or is a charge for a detention of money past the due date. Secondly, if it is a charge for the detention of money past the due date, the controlling concern is how to calculate the interest rate. Recent Texas legislation has eliminated this conflict. The federal law (late charges are interest but covered by the federal preemption) controls, *V.A.T.S., Art. 5069-1C.103.*

**Points, Commitment Fees, and Loan Brokerage Fees.** Points, commitment fees, and loan brokerage fees are fees paid to a lender or loan broker when obtaining a loan. The value of these fees is normally measured in points, each point being 1% of the loan value. For instance, a $100,000 loan requiring three points would require a fee of $3,000. Although often used interchangeably, points, commitment fees, and loan brokerage fees are for separate and distinct purposes.

The definition of **points**, for the purposes of this discussion, will be deemed to be a fee charged for entering into a loan contract charged by, and paid to, the lending institution that is making the loan. Generally, whether or not points are construed to be interest is determined by what the points are to be used for. If the points are not directly attributable to expenses incurred by the lender in making such loan, the points will constitute interest. *Terry* v. *Teachworth*, 431 S.W.2d 917 (Tex. Civ. App.—Houston, 1968); *Gonzales County Savings and Loan Association* v. *Freeman*, 534 S.W.2d 903 (Tex. 1976). However, if the points are charged for a definite expense, rationally related to making the loan, they will *not* constitute interest.

A **commitment fee**, on the other hand, is normally a fee charged for the promise of securing funds at some future date. This does not fall within the definition of interest. A commitment fee can be characterized as an option to enter into a future loan, and as long as the fee was reasonably related to the risks taken by the lender, it will not be construed to be interest. *Gonzales County Savings and Loan Association* v. *Freeman*, supra.

**Loan brokerage fees** (fees charged by mortgage brokers for placing the loan with a lender) will not normally be considered interest if the fee does not go to the lender itself, and if there is no joint control or agreement between the lender and the broker (as in the case of points as defined above). It is common for a mortgage company or savings and loan association to operate as a mortgage broker and to charge one to five points as a fee for finding another lender to make the loan. In this capacity, the institution is serving only as a mortgage broker. In such case, the fee is not used as a cost for obtaining the loan but instead is a fee for paying the broker for finding a lender. *Crow* v. *Home Savings Association*, 522 S.W.2d 457 (Tex. 1975); *Greever* v. *Persky*, 165 S.W.2d 709 (Tex. 1942).

**Prepayment Penalties and Partial Release Fees. Prepayment penalties** (also measured in points) are the fees that a lender charges the borrower for paying off a loan prematurely. It may seem unreasonable for a lender to charge a fee to pay off a loan. However, as a practical matter, when a borrower has entered into a contract to pay 9% interest over a period of 30 years, he has normally contracted to pay a certain determinable amount of interest over that 30-year period. Thus, if the contract is terminated prematurely (by prepayment), there is a certain amount of interest that will not be paid. Therefore, the lender charges a certain number of points as a prepayment penalty. This charge would appear to be within the legitimate expectation of damages on the lender's part.

There has been some indication that Texas courts would not construe prepayment penalties as interest but rather as consideration for the termination of the loan contract. *Boyd* v. *Life Ins. Co.*, 546 S.W.2d 132 (Tex. Civ. App.—Houston, 1977); *Gulf Coast Investment Corp.* v. *Prichard*, 438 S.W.2d 658 (Tex. Civ. App.—Dallas, 1969). New Texas legislation now makes it clear that prepayment charges are *not* interest, *V.A.T.S., Art. 5069-1H.005.*

There is a similar theory regarding the payment of **partial release fees**. Normally, when a borrower requests that the lender release a portion of the secured real estate, the lender would charge not only a premium for the portion to be released, but also a partial release fee. This fee is normally attributable to the preparation of instruments, bookkeeping, and clerical costs for releasing the security and for the resulting adjustment of the principal balance due under the terms of the loan. Partial release fees of this type are not considered to be interest.

**Compensating Balances.** It is also a common practice for a lending institution to require the borrower to make certain deposits or to purchase certificates of deposit to be pledged to the lender. These arrangements are often verbal transactions and are not made part of the loan documents themselves. The **compensating balances** generally create a separate and independent obligation (on which interest is paid by the lender) and are not deemed interest. *Commerce Savings Association* v. *GGE Management Company*, 543 S.W.2d 862 (Tex. 1976); *Moss* v. *Metropolitan National Bank*, 533 S.W.2d 397 (Tex. Civ. App.—Houston, 1976); *Texas International Mortgage Company* v. *Crum*, 564 S.W.2d 421 (Tex. Civ. App.—Dallas, 1978). However, if the lender freezes the loan proceeds or requires the compensating balance in the loan document, it may be considered interest; but the authorities on this theory of interest revolve closely around the fact situations of each case. *Miller* v. *First State Bank*, 551 S.W.2d 89 (Tex. Civ. App.—Ft. Worth, 1977); *Community Finance and Thrift Corp.* v. *State of Texas*, 343 S.W.2d 232 (Tex. 1961).

**Matured Interest.** Most promissory notes have penalty provisions in the event there is a default on the payments. Figure 13.1 in the previous chapter shows a typical provision of this type. The provision usually states that the entire principal amount is matured; and matured unpaid principal and interest will bear interest at the rate of 10% per annum until paid. This is sometimes referred to as **interest on interest**. However, this penalty provision does not constitute interest as far as the loan transaction itself is concerned. In a very old Texas case, *Crider* v. *San Antonio Real Estate Building and Loan Association*, 34 S.W.2d 1047 (Tex. 1896), the Texas Supreme Court held that such a provision represents a new obligation once the default has taken place, and the interest on the note and the interest on the past due principal payments do not, together, constitute a new, higher rate of interest.

**Compulsory Loan Retirement.** It is also a common practice for a lender to require **compulsory loan retirement**, which means the borrower pays off all of his preexisting indebtedness before obtaining a new loan. This normally is not considered interest. However, such a requirement *may* be considered interest if there is a required prepayment penalty on the loan to be paid off.

**Turnaround Sales.** In the interesting case of *Commerce Savings Association* v. *GGE Management Company*, supra, there was a requirement that the borrower sell a project to the lender for $349,000. The lender resold the property to the borrower for $400,000. Not surprisingly, the extra costs charged in this **turnaround sales** transaction were determined by the jury to be interest and the transaction disguised to evade the usury statute.

**Equity Participation.** Lenders have become increasingly aware of their ability to participate in the equity and development of the project without any additional cost to themselves as lenders. The key determination when a lender is involved in **equity participation** is whether or not the lender is taking a risk similar to that of the borrower. If the lender gets a preferred return on his investment, this may be determined to be interest, and possibly usurious, *Johns* v. *Jabe*, 518 S.W.2d 857 (Tex. Civ. App.—Dallas, 1974), but such is not always the case. If the lender shares in the risks, and the return on his investment is not readily ascertainable, he is considered to be a true equity participant. See *V.A.T.S., Art. 5069-1H.101*.

**Required Incorporation.** Since the law allows businesses to pay interest at higher rates than those of noncorporate borrowers, lenders sometimes simply require that the noncorporate borrower either incorporate or guarantee a corporation's indebtedness. In one of the more profound cases, *Skeen* v. *Glenn Justice Mortgage Co.*, 526 S.W.2d 252 (Tex. Civ. App.—Dallas, 1975), the court held that the requirement by a lender for the borrower to form a corporation as a condition of the loan does not, by itself, indicate that the corporation was created to cover up for a fraudulent transaction or to evade usury statutes. The mere fact that a corporation was formed to obtain the loan did not, in itself, render the transaction void or illegal, unless the corporation was an obvious sham that had no corporate function or purpose. This theory has been consistently upheld, although the Texas Supreme Court has not yet spoken to this issue. *Hutchison* v. *Commercial Trading Co., Inc.*, 427 F. Supp. 662 (N.D. Tex. 1977); *Peters* v. *Lomas & Nettleton Financial Corporation*, 572 S.W.2d 809 (Tex. Civ. App.—Houston, 1978); *Shook* v. *Republic National Bank of Dallas*, 627 S.W.2d 741 (Tex. Civ. App.—Tyler, 1981).

Another practice permitted that the lender require that an individual guarantee a corporation's indebtedness. There was some speculation that perhaps this might constitute usury. However, there have been two very recent cases that indicate that since the loan was made to the corporation and not to the individual, the transaction did not constitute usury. *Loomis Land and Cattle Co.* v. *Diversified Mortgage*, 533 S.W.2d 420 (Tex. Civ. App.—Tyler, 1976); *Micrea, Inc.* v. *Eureka Life Ins. Co. of America*, 534 S.W.2d 348 (Tex. Civ. App.—Ft. Worth, 1976).

**Seller's Points.** A Texas case (which was settled prior to the actual trial) considered an interesting point as to whether or not seller's points constituted interest under Texas law. In the judge's opinion (which denied a motion for summary judgment), seller's points should be construed to be interest under Texas law since the seller raised the sales price of his property to cover the cost of the points charged by the lender. *American Savings and Loan Assoc. v. U.S.A. and King Parkway, Ltd.*, C. A. H-77-833 (U.S.D.C.—S.D. Tex. H. D., Nov. 13, 1978). This is not a precedent-setting decision but is considered by most to be well reasoned under Texas law. This is a primary reason many lenders require sellers to sign affidavits at closing indicating that the seller did not raise his purchase price to cover the cost of the points.

# Spreading

Once it has been determined that these extra charges, such as points, turnaround sales, and other additional payments to secure loans, are, in fact, "interest," there is a question as to how that interest is to be calculated to determine whether or not it is usurious. Texas has adopted the concept of "**spreading**," *V.A.T.S., Art. 5069-1C.101.* The spreading doctrine refers to the fact that the points for fees and commitments and other charges attributable to the loan transaction itself (although they are one-time charges) can be "spread" over the life of the loan to determine whether or not it would constitute usury over the entire period. For instance, if one made a loan at 9% per annum but had to pay three points to the lender as consideration for making the loan, the charge for making the loan would be determined by taking the 9% interest and adding to it 1/30 of the three points for each year. The 9% is then added to the 1/30 times three points to determine whether or not the annual interest charge would exceed 10% per annum. Since the loan is made for a period of 30 years, it is assumed that the three points paid prior to obtaining the loan can be spread over this 30-year period to determine the true effective interest rate. Calculating the interest in this manner, it can be seen that a large number of points can be calculated and be added to an interest rate before it can achieve the actual 10% ceiling.

**Penalties for Usury.** The statutory penalties for usury were significantly decreased by the Texas legislature in 1997. The penalty that the lender shall forfeit to the maker of the note is three times the interest, time price differential, or other charges that exceed the amount of interest allowed by law, and reasonable attorney's fees. In no event, however, shall the amount forfeited be less than $2,000 or 20% of the principal, whichever is smaller. There shall be no penalty for any usurious interest that results from accidental or bona fide error by the lender, *V.A.T.S., Art. 5069-1F.101.*

Any person who contracts for or receives interest in excess of double the amount of interest allowed by the law shall forfeit all principal as well as interest and all other charges, *V.A.T.S., Art. 50691F.002.*

A creditor is not liable to usury if, no later than the 60th day after the date the creditor actually discovered the violation, the creditor corrects the violation by taking any necessary action and making a necessary adjustment (including the payment of interest on a refund), and the creditor gives written notice to the borrower of the violation before the borrower gives notice of the violation or files alleging the violation, *V.A.T.S., Art. 5069-1F.103; Sotelo v. Interstate Financial Corporation*, 224 S.W.3d 517 (Tex. App.—El Paso, 2007).

The impact of the statute has been further softened because of court decisions that indicate that if there is a "savings clause" (a clause that states the lender does not intend to charge usurious interest or provides for a rebate of any excess interest to the borrower, or both), the lender may not be liable for the statutory penalties for usury. *5636 Alpha Rd.* v. *NCNB Texas Nat'l Bank*, 879 F. Supp. 655 (N.D. Dallas, 1995).

## ■ SUMMARY

There are few areas of lending that have been litigated more often than the areas of interest and finance charge. Finance charge is a term used under the Federal Consumer Credit Protection Act (commonly called the Truth-in-Lending Act). The law requires extensive disclosures by creditors when making loans to consumers.

Interest, on the other hand, is covered by state law. Charging a fee for money in excess of the maximum allowable interest rate in Texas is called usury. There are criminal and civil penalties for charging usurious interest. Many lenders have tried to get around charging "interest" by charging additional fees to produce or maintain a loan. There have been various constructions by courts in Texas as to what does or does not constitute "interest" as a fee charge for procuring a loan.

## CASE STUDIES FOR DISCUSSION

1. McGee borrowed money from Friendly Lender Savings and Loan Association to build two homes. She borrowed $38,400 at 9% per annum. Upon closing, she noticed there was a charge on the closing statement for a "commitment fee" of $768, or 2% of the principal. McGee alleges that it was interest under Texas law. The savings and loan contends that it is, in fact, a "commitment fee" and is not interest. What legal ramifications do you foresee?

# CHAPTER 15

# Methods of Title Assurance

## Evidence of Title

Once a purchaser has made up his mind that he wants to purchase an interest in real estate, he wants to be absolutely sure that he is fully advised of the status of the title to that real estate, and to assure himself that there is no "**cloud on title**," which would adversely affect his interest. The real estate agent's function is important in this area because although the licensee cannot give advice as to the quality of the title, it is part of the real estate agent's obligation to inform the purchaser, in writing, that he (the purchaser) should have the abstract to real estate examined prior to closing or that he should obtain title insurance to assure himself of the status of the title to that real estate. There are generally two things the purchaser should be concerned about: (1) the solvency of the defendant should title fail; and (2) the expertise of those investigating the status of title.

There are a number of ways that a purchaser can assure himself that title is satisfactory. Title is typically considered to be satisfactory when it is a marketable title. **Marketable title** has not been statutorily defined in Texas, but case law defines it as "one that is free from reasonable doubt as to matters of law and fact, such title is such that a prudent man, advised of the facts and the legal significance, would willingly accept, although a title need not be absolutely free from every technical and possible suspicion in order to be marketable." *Medallion Homes, Inc.* v. *Thermar Investments, Inc.*, supra. In Texas, it is basically synonymous with the term **merchantable title**. Utilizing our concept of constructive and actual notice, one usually thinks of marketable title as a title that is free of defects of record. Those methods of title assurance to be discussed in this chapter will include the Torrens system of title registration, personal warranty of the grantor, a lawyer's title opinion, an abstractor's certificate, and title insurance policies.

### The Torrens System of Title Registration

The **Torrens system** of title registration is not utilized in Texas, but it is a rather interesting method of title assurance that has been used in a few other states. In this method of title assurance, the title to the real estate is reflected by a registration certificate, similar to that used in Texas for an automobile title. The registration certificate would have a proper legal description of the real estate. All adverse claims against the real estate would also be reflected. When a lien is placed on the property, one turns in his title registration certification and receives a new one reflecting the new lien. The old registration certificate is then destroyed. Therefore, for each parcel of real estate, there is only one registration certificate outstanding, and there can never be any doubts as to the status of the title since it is reflected on the face of that certificate, unless due to fraud or forgery. An official copy of the certificate is held by the County Registrar's office.

Although this system seems to greatly facilitate the passage of title and the assurance of proper title, there are certain drawbacks as to its effectiveness, particularly in a State like Texas. The primary difficulty in the Torrens registration system involves the final determination of title. If one is going to convert to the Torrens registration system, the final status of title must be judicially determined in order to ensure proper title in every single case as it pertains to every ascertainable parcel of real estate. Unless a special judicial system could be set up to ascertain property title, the burden on the existing court system, and accompanying costs, would probably be insurmountable in order to achieve a proper shift from our existing methods of title assurance to the Torrens system. In addition, there would have to be certain changes in our recording act, in the insurance code as it relates to title insurance, and in methods of recordation in the county courthouses. Such changes, of course, would require legislative action, which would mean another very difficult procedure of shifting to the Torrens system.

The most significant drawbacks to the Torrens system involve the practical application and day-to-day operation of a Torrens registration system. Basically, the system is very slow. The County Registrar must accept the current certificate, reflect the change in the status of that certificate if there is an additional encumbrance affecting the property (such as involuntary liens that may not be posted to the owner's certificate), compare it with the old certificate, change both certificates, and then mail the new certificate out to the current property owner. The physical time involved in this may take two to three hours. The actual act of recording under the Texas Recording Act takes only a few minutes. In a county where a large number of transactions are recorded on a daily basis, the backlog is enormous. Where a document may be recorded and returned within a few days when recorded, the registration may take several months in a Torrens system. Therefore, if a property changes hands several times in a year, the Torrens backlog on that particular piece of property can create significant problems.

The other difficulty is the recovery you may obtain under the Torrens system. If there is a failure of title, one must sue the county, which is, at best, a long and tedious process. The county is supposed to keep a capital reserve fund for paying claims. If this fund is insufficient, however, there is normally no other provision for recovery.

## Personal Warranty of the Grantor

A second method of title assurance is the personal warranty of the grantor. As discussed in Chapter 10, Voluntary Conveyances, and depending on the type of deed utilized in the conveyance, the grantor usually gives warranties of the title of the real estate upon execution of the deed. If there is a defect in the title, the purchaser has the right to pursue a cause of action against the grantor on his warranty. The difficulty here, of course, involves the quality of the warranty of the grantor, who may not be alive, in existence (if a corporation or other business entity), or financially solvent enough to stand behind the warranty or to pay damages to an aggrieved purchaser. However, the personal warranty of the grantor, coupled with the effect of the adverse possession statutes, does provide some method of title assurance after the purchaser has maintained possession of the real estate beyond the 3-, 5-, 10-, and 25-year statutes of limitations.

There are situations, of course, when the personal warranty of the grantor is a very good method of title assurance, especially when the grantor is large, solvent, and reputable. A solvent grantor (Exxon Mobile) probably provides better assurance than some title companies (but remember Enron!).

## Lawyer's Title Opinion

The **lawyer's title opinion** at one time was one of the most common methods of title assurance. It is still quite frequently used in some of the rural areas of Texas. It is also used in cases where the chain of title and abstracts to a parcel of property may be so involved and complicated that the purchaser would prefer his own attorney's opinion as to the effect of each document, rather than a policy of title insurance or personal warranty of the grantor. It is commonly thought that the attorney's title opinion ensures "marketable title," reasonably free of defects of record.

The lawyer's title opinion is a functional and effective method of title assurance, but it has several disadvantages:

1. Most lawyers, in an effort to do a good job, often find that reading the abstracts and writing opinions is a very time-consuming process; and many purchasers find that it is too slow when trying to complete or consummate the closing of a fairly complicated real estate transaction.

2. The lawyer, in reading an abstract, always runs the risk that the abstract compiled for his review may have been improperly prepared or may be missing some instruments in the chain of title.

3. There is no guarantee in the event that title fails that the purchaser can have any recovery. Although most lawyers carry malpractice insurance in the event of errors and omissions, the purchaser may still find that his recovery may not be enough to cover the damages he may have incurred.

4. As in every other profession, there are always the problems of incompetence, errors in judgment, and mistakes.

There has been an effort on the part of the legal community to reinstate lawyers in the business of insuring title to real property. It is felt by some members of the legal community that the role of the lawyer has become too diminished in the function of assuring title because of the widespread use of title insurance companies. In 1975, the Texas legislature passed an act creating the Attorney's Title Insurance Company, regulated by Article 9.56 of the Texas Insurance Code. The Attorney's Title Insurance Company has regulations similar to those of title insurance companies generally. However, there has not been a significant shift toward utilizing this method to date.

## Abstractor's Certificate

An **abstractor** is a person who is employed to compile abstracts that affect certain parcels of real estate. The **abstract** reflects a complete chain of title to a particular piece of real estate from the current date back to the origin of title to the property, but it gives the purchaser no protection in and of itself.

An abstract is usually furnished to an attorney as a basis for the lawyer's title opinion, as discussed above. An experienced abstractor has a high level of expertise, particularly in small, rural counties where this system is in wide use (there may be no title companies). An abstractor is normally bonded, and in the event there is an error or omission in the abstract, one may proceed against his (the abstractor's) bond in order to effect a recovery. If the abstractor's bond is sufficient, it will cover the damages suffered by the purchaser. However, there is no requirement that an abstractor carry bonds in any great amount. Therefore, there is probably a good chance that the bond would not be sufficient to reimburse the purchaser's damages. In addition, the purchaser might have to prove negligence on the part of the abstractor. There is no malpractice insurance available for abstractors. Furthermore, an abstractor's opinion normally only lists the instruments affecting the property, rather than the specific encumbrances that are reflected by those instruments. In addition, as you may recall, interpreting an instrument and its effect on the property is a legal function, and unless the abstractor is a lawyer, an interpretation of the instruments is practicing law without a license, so the abstractor will probably not offer a legal opinion.

## Title Insurance

**Title insurance** is by far the most common method of title assurance used in Texas. Title companies originally grew as the result of the need for an insurance policy for a lawyer's title opinion. Today, title insurance is the insurance business, period. Insurance companies (termed **underwriters**) write insurance policies through their own companies or through **title insurance agents** who issue policies on behalf of those underwriters. Title insurance allows for spreading of the risk and offers a greater possibility of solvency in the event that damages are incurred by the purchaser. Solvency of title insurance companies is monitored by annual filings of their financial condition to the Texas Department of Insurance. Title insurance companies have their own abstract plans and their own abstractors. They also have their own lawyers for title opinions. In addition, each title is insured by a solvent insurance company that has been authorized to do business in Texas.

The title insurance industry is very tightly regulated by the Texas Department of Insurance. All forms are the same, and all procedures and rates are the same. Since titles are necessarily long-term problems, such tight regulation ensures solvency in the industry and is considered by most to be a benefit to the consumer public, as it minimizes the chances of "fly-by-night" title operations. So, for practical purposes, this is probably the most efficient method of title assurance, with the greatest probability of solvency for the buyer's benefit.

A title insurance policy is a contract of indemnity. *Chicago Title Insurance Co.* v. *McDaniel*, 875 S.W.2d 310 (Tex. 1994). For a one-time premium charge, it guarantees that the insured will be indemnified (protected) from any cause of action or loss in the event his title fails for any defect that accrued prior to the effective date of the policy. In addition, the Insurance Code creates an affirmative duty on the title company to investigate claims, *V.A.T.S., Insurance Code, §9.57*. The rates for title policies are set by the Texas Department of Insurance, so there is no advantage to "shopping around" for a better price on a title insurance policy. It should be remembered also that title insurance and title insurance commitments are not transactions in real estate, but merely transactions incidental to a transaction in real estate. The provisions of the title insurance policy are governed by the Insurance Code and not Texas real estate law. *American Title Ins. Co., et al.* v. *Byrd, et al.*, 348 S.W.2d 683 (Tex. 1964).

**The Solvency Issue.** In bad economic times title insurance claims always increase, and there have been concerns about the solvency of title insurers. To ensure solvency, the Texas Department of Insurance sets the premiums for title insurance based on risk, losses, profits, and overall operating expenses of title insurance companies in Texas. If title fails, the underwriter (through retained capital reserves) will stand good for the loss. If the title insurance company becomes insolvent, the Texas Department of Insurance then places the title insurance company into receivership and provides a fund for claimants to pursue their damages.

In addition, the Texas Department of Insurance further limits how much insurance any title insurance company can write. In any given transaction, no title company may insure more than its stated limit as established by the Department. If it is a very large transaction, one may have to utilize the services of two or more title insurance companies to either **co-insure** (each company takes a percentage of the liability) or **reinsure** (the primary insuring company takes the risk up to its allowable limit, then the reinsuring company insures only the risk in excess of that primary policy limit). It should be emphasized that the Texas Department of Insurance has done an exceptional job in maintaining standards and ensuring solvency in the title insurance industry.

*Preliminary Title Information* The procedures for obtaining preliminary title information from a title insurance company usually include obtaining a **title commitment**. It is *not* an opinion or report of the status of title. It is a form, promulgated by the Texas Department of Insurance, which obligates the title insurer to issue title policies in favor of the proposed insured subject to its terms and requirements. The commitments terminate 90 days after the effective date of the commitment, or when the policy committed for finally issues, whichever occurs first.

There are other preliminary methods of obtaining title information. One, obtained through the title insurance company for the benefit of the mortgagee, is getting a **mortgagee title policy binder**, which applies to interim construction loans. Since the cost of title insurance may be substantial for large projects, a lender may require only a binder from the title insurance company (rather than the more expensive mortgagee's title policy) to assure itself that the borrower has good title. The binder indicates that good and indefeasible title to the property is vested in the owner at a given time. This form basically provides no coverage and no liability for the insurance company. It is therefore not often used, except for very large construction loans. Since the Texas Department of Insurance amended its regulations to allow for installment payments for premiums on mortgagee policies, we may find the title insurance binder being used even less.

A **title report** is typically nothing more than a representation by the title company as to who has good title (in effect, an abstractor's certificate). Similarly, one may require a **nothing-further certificate**. Frequently, an owner may simply want his title updated for pending construction loans, peace of mind, or to assure himself that disputed liens have been removed from the record. The nothing-further certificate is typically issued for a nominal charge by the same company that issued the original title policy.

**Types of Title Insurance Policies.** There are normally two policies issued: one issued for the benefit of the lender, and one issued for the benefit of the mortgagor (new owner). The **loan title policy** (for the purpose of this discussion, this policy will not be discussed in great detail) is generally issued at a nominal cost (if issued simultaneously with the owner's policy), and it insures that the mortgagee's (the lender's) lien priority is good. This policy has different title coverage than the **owner's title policy**, which is issued to insure the mortgagor's title.

Both policies also continue coverage for a period of time, even after the subsequent resale. Upon the sale of the real estate, the owner's policy of title insurance converts to a warrantor's policy. If the mortgage is foreclosed by the mortgagee, the mortgagee's title insurance policy continues in force effective to provide title insurance to the lender as of the original date of issuance. The mortgagee can also assign the mortgage to another lender, and the policy stays effective for that new lender.

In contrast to the concept of marketable title, the owner's policy of title insurance guarantees to the owner **good and indefeasible** title. This term has never been legally defined. By some interpretations, this is a higher duty of care to the owner than marketable title. Marketable title usually means that the title is reasonably free of defects of record. Indefeasible title has been defined as a title that cannot be defeated, set aside, or made void. Therefore, the title insurance policy guarantees much more than just marketable title. It guarantees against forgeries in the chain of title, incapacity of parties in the chain of title, unrecorded interests that may affect the property, and virtually any other defect of which the owner had no actual knowledge or constructive notice.

**Scope of Coverage.** The basic duty of a title company is not to disclose the defects of the title, but only to indemnify the insured against any loss from defects in the title. *Prendergast* v. *Southern Title Guaranty Co.*, 454 S.W.2d 802 (Tex. Civ. App.—Houston, 1970). It insures the real estate at the purchase price. It does not increase in coverage as the value of the real estate increases, unless an additional premium is paid. The duty to defend any causes of action against that title is generally set out in the terms of the title policy. The title insurance coverage does ensure access to the parcel of real estate, although it does not guarantee the quality of that access.

*Obligation to defend* A copy of the Texas residential owner's title insurance form is shown in Figure 15.1 for your reference, with some of the pertinent parts underlined for emphasis. Note that in this standard form, the title insurance company insures, as of the date of the policy, against loss or damage incurred as a result of the five items specified on the face of the policy. The company is not required to defend any claims excluded from coverage or excepted in the policy under Schedule B of the standard form (the standard exceptions).

*Notice to company* It should also be noted that the parties entitled to defense (the insured party) must, within a reasonable time after any action against the title of that property has commenced, give the company written notice of the pendency and authority to defend. The company is not liable for any damages until it has reached the court of last resort and such adverse interest or claim has been established. This provision has been construed strictly in favor of the title company. If it appears that a defect in the title is cured, the damages would be no more than nominal, regardless of the complications this defect might have caused between the time it was apparent and the time the company cured same. *Southern Title Guaranty Co.* v. *Prendergast*, 494 S.W.2d 154, 158 (Tex. 1973).

*Continuing coverage* An often overlooked area of coverage is the continuing warranty, underlined in Figure 15.1. If any title problems arise in the future, after the insured has sold the property, he still has title insurance coverage. **The coverage extends into perpetuity**.

The company insures against the specific loss or damage stated in the policy, not exceeding the amount of insurance stated on the face of the policy, apparently making the title company liable for damages as of the date of the title loss (not the date of the policy). Note also that instead of the broad, general coverage of "good and indefeasible" title, the policy form lists those items insured against.

**FIGURE 15.1   TEXAS OWNER'S TITLE INSURANCE FORM.**

## OWNER'S COVERAGE STATEMENT

This Policy insures your title to the land described in Schedule A—if that land is a one-to-four family residential property or condominium unit.

Your insurance, as described in this Coverage Statement, is effective on the Policy Date shown in Schedule A.

This document is title insurance. It is not an opinion or report of your title. it is a contract of indemnity, meaning a promise to pay you or take other action if you have loss resulting from a covered title risk.

Your insurance under this contract is limited by the following:

- Exclusions on page _____.
- Exceptions on Schedule B, page _____.
- Conditions on pages _____.

We insure you against actual loss resulting from:

- Any title risks covered by this Policy—up to the Policy Amount, and
- Any costs, attorneys' fees and expenses we have to pay under this Policy. We must approve the attorney before the attorney begins to work. You have the right to disapprove our choice of attorney for reasonable cause.

## COVERED TITLE RISKS

This Policy covers the following title risks subject to the Exceptions (p. _____) and Exclusions (p. _____), if they affect your title to the land on the Policy Date. We do not promise that there are no covered risks. We do insure you if there are covered title risks.

1. Someone else owns an interest in your title.
2. A document is invalid because of improper signature, acknowledgment, delivery, or recording.
3. A document is invalid because of forgery, fraud, duress, incompetency, incapacity or impersonation.
4. Restrictive covenants apply to your title.
5. There is a lien on your title because of:
    - a mortgage or deed of trust,
    - a judgment, tax, or special assessment, or
    - a charge by a homeowner's or condominium association.
6. There are liens on your title for labor and material which have their inception before the policy date. However, we will not cover liens for labor and material that you agreed to pay for.
7. Others have rights in your title arising our of leases, contracts or options.
8. Someone else has an easement on your land.
9. You do not have good and indefeasible title.
10. There are other defects in your title.
11. There are other liens or encumbrances on your title.

**This Policy also covers the following title risk:**

You do not have any legal right of access to and from the land.

**FIGURE 15.1  CONTINUED.**

## OUR DUTY TO DEFEND AGAINST COURT CASES

We will defend your title in the part or parts of a court case involving a Title Risk covered by this Policy. We will pay the costs, attorneys' fees, and expenses that we incur in that defense. We will not pay for the parts of a case not involving a covered title risk. You may disapprove our choice of attorney for reasonable cause.

We can end this duty to defend your title by exercising any of our options listed in Item 4 of the Conditions, see page _____ .

This Policy is not complete without Schedules A and B.

BLANK TITLE INSURANCE COMPANY

BY:_____

President

An authorized party also must countersign this Policy.

[Witness clause optional]

_____

(Authorized Signature)

BY:_____

Secretary

_____

(Authorized Signature)

## SCHEDULE A

Policy Number:                                      File Number:

Policy Date:

Policy Amount:

Premium:

1.  Name of Insured:

2.  We insure your interest in the land covered by this Policy is:

3.  Legal Description of land:

## SCHEDULE B

## EXCEPTIONS

We do not cover loss, costs, attorneys' fees and expenses resulting from:

1.  The following restrictive covenants of record itemized below (We must either insert specific recording data or delete this exception.):

2.  Any discrepancies, conflicts, or shortages in area or boundary lines, or any encroachments or protrusions, or any overlapping of improvements.

3.  Homestead or community property or survivorship rights, if any of any spouse of any insured. (Applies to the Owner Policy only.)

4.  Any titles or rights asserted by anyone, including, but not limited to, persons, the public, corporations, governments or other entities,

    a.  to tidelands, or lands comprising the shores or beds of navigable or perennial rivers and streams, lakes, bays, gulfs or oceans, or

    b.  to lands beyond the line of the harbor or bulkhead lines as established or changed by any government, or

    c.  to filled-in lands, or artificial islands, or

    d.  to statutory water rights, including riparian rights, or

    e.  to the area extending from the line of mean low tide to the line of vegetation, or the rights of access to that area or easement along and across that area.

5.  Standby fees, taxes and assessments by any taxing authority for the year 19 ____ , and subsequent year, and subsequent taxes and assessments by any taxing authority for prior years due to change in land usage or ownership.

6.  The following matters and all terms of the documents creating or offering evidence of the matters (We must insert matters or delete this exception.):

**FIGURE 15.1 CONTINUED.**

## EXCLUSIONS

In addition to the Exception in Schedule B, we do not insure you against loss, costs, attorneys' fees, and expenses resulting from these Exclusions:

1. We do not cover loss caused by the exercise of governmental police power or the enforcement or violation of any law or government regulation. This includes building and zoning ordinances and laws and regulations concerning:

   a. land use

   b. Improvements on the land

   c. Land division

   d. Environmental protection

This exclusion does not apply to notices of violations or notices of enforcement that appear in the public records at Policy Date. However, there may be an Exception in Schedule B.

2. We do no cover the right to take the land by condemning it, unless:

   a. a notice of exercise of the right appears in the public records on the Policy Date, or

   b. the taking happened before the Policy Date and is binding on you if you bought the land without knowing of the taking.

3. We do not cover title risks:

   a. that are created, allowed, or agreed to by you,

   b. that are known to you, but not to us on the Policy Date unless they appeared in the public records,

   c. that result in no loss to you, or

   d. that first affect your title after the Policy Date—this does not limit the labor and material lien coverage in Item 6 of the Covered Title Risks.

4. We do not cover the effect of failure to pay value for your title.

5. We do not cover lack of a right:

   a. to any land outside the area specifically described and referred to in item 3 of Schedule A.

   b. in streets, alleys, or waterways that touch your land.

This exclusion does not limit the access coverage in the Covered Title Risks.

6. We do not cover any claim based upon allegations that your purchase of title (or acquisition of title by gift or otherwise):

   a. was a fraudulent conveyance, fraudulent transfer, voidable distribution, or voidable dividend;

   b. should be subordinated or recharacterized as a result of equitable subordination;

   c. was a preferential transfer unless

   (1) the Company or its issuing agent failed to timely file for record the deed to you after delivery or

   (2) the recordation of the deed to you is not legal record notice.

   (We do cover the two types of claims described in c.(1) and c.(2) above.)

7. We do not cover the refusal of any person to buy, lease or lend money on your land because of unmarketability of the title.

8. We do not cover claims concerning the physical condition of your land or of the access to your land.

**FIGURE 15.1 CONTINUED.**

## CONDITIONS

1. DEFINITIONS

   a. **Actual Loss.** This is the difference between the value of your land without the covered title risk and the value of your land with the covered title risk. These values are the respective values at the time you must furnish proof of your loss.

   b. **Document.** A deed or other conveyance of title to you or a prior owner.

   c. **Easement.** A portion of your land someone else has the right to use for a special purpose.

   d. **Government Regulation.** Any federal, state, or local law, constitutional provision, regulation, ordinance, or guideline.

   e. **Land.** The land or condominium unit described in Schedule A and any improvements on the land that are real property.

   f. **Knowledge or known.** Actual knowledge, not constructive knowledge or notice that may be imputed to an insured by the public records.

   g. **Mortgage.** A type of lien on the land such as a deed of trust or other security instrument.

   h. **Public Records.** Those records required by Texas law and maintained by public officials in the county where the property is located that give legal notice of matters affecting your title.

   i. **Title.** The ownership interest in the land, as shown in Schedule A.

   j. **We, us or our.** The title insurance company. This is _____
      (Insert name of company.)

   k. **You, your.** The insured.

2. CONTINUATION OF COVERAGE

   We insure you as long as you:

   a. own your Title,

   b. own a mortgage from anyone who buys your Title, or

   c. are liable for and Title warranties you make.

   We insure anyone who receives your title because of your death.

   We do not insure your transferee or assignee.

3. YOUR DUTIES IF YOU MAKE A CLAIM.

   You must follow this process to make a claim:

   a. You Must give Us Notice Of Your Claim

      If anyone claims a right against your insured title, you must notify us promptly.

      Send the notice to _____ or call 1-800- _____ and ask for a claims attorney. If you initially notify us by phone, we recommend that you also notify us in writing. Please include the Policy number shown in Schedule A, and the county where the land is.

      Our obligation to you is reduced or ended if:

      (1) you fail to give prompt notice, and

      (2) your failure affects our ability to dispose of or to defend you against the claim.

      Our obligation is reduced only the extent that your failure affects our ability to dispose of or to defend you against the claim.

   b. You Must Give Us Proof of Your Loss if We Request It

      You must send to us, if we request, your signed proof of loss within 91 days of our request on a standard form supplied by us. Within 15 days after we receive your notice of claim, we must request a signed proof of loss. If not, we waive our right to require a proof of loss. This waiver will not waive our other rights under the policy. The statement must have the following information to the best of your knowledge:

      (1) the Covered Title Risks which resulted in your loss,

      (2) the dollar amount of your loss, and

      (3) the method you used to compute the amount of your loss.

**FIGURE 15.1 CONTINUED.**

    c.  You Must Provide Papers We Request

        We may require you to show us your records, checks, letters, contracts, and other papers that relate to your claim of loss. We may make copies of these papers.

        If you tell us this information is confidential, we will not disclose it to anyone else unless we reasonably believe the disclosure is necessary to administer the claim.

    d.  You Must Answer Questions Under Oath

        We may require you to answer questions under oath.

    e.  Effect of Failure to Cooperate.

        Our obligation to you reduces or ends if you fail or refuse to:

        (1)  (a)  provide a statement of loss,

               (b)  answer our questions under oath, or

               (c)  show us the papers we request, and

        (2)  your failure or refusal effects our ability to dispose of or to defend you against the claim.

4.  OUR CHOICES WHEN YOU NOTIFY US OF A CLAIM

    a.  After we receive your claim notice or in any other way learn of a matter for which we are liable, we can do one or more of the following:

        (1)  Pay the claim against your title.

        (2)  Negotiate a settlement.

        (3)  Prosecute or defend a court case related to the claim.

        (4)  Pay you the amount required by this Policy.

        (5)  Take other action under Section 4b.

        (6)  Cancel this policy by paying the Policy Amount, then in force, and only those costs, attorneys' fees and expenses incurred up to that time that we are obligated to pay.

    We can choose which of these to do.

    b.  If you report to us that a covered title risk exists, we will promptly investigate to determine if that covered title risk is valid and not barred by law or statute. A covered title risk is a title risk that this Policy does not exclude or except.

    If we conclude that your claim, or any part of your claim, is covered by the policy, we will take one or more of the following actions to the extent that it is covered:

        (1)  Institute all necessary legal proceedings to clear the title to the property.

        (2)  Indemnify you pursuant to the terms of the policy;

        (3)  Issue a new title policy without making exception to the covered title risk. If another insurer issues the new title policy to your purchaser, lender or other transferee without making exception to the covered title risk, we will indemnify the other insurer.

        (4)  Secure a release of the covered title risk.

    c.  If we deny your claim, or any part of your claim, not more than 15 days after we deny the claim, we will:

        (1)  notify you in writing, and

        (2)  give you the reasons for denial of your claim in writing.

5.  HANDLING A CLAIM OR COURT CASE

You must cooperate with us in handling any claim or court case and give us all relevant information.

We must repay you only for those settlement costs, attorneys' fees and expenses that we approve in advance.

When we defend or sue to clear your title, we have a right to choose the attorney. You have the right to disapprove our choice of attorney for reasonable cause. We can appeal any decision to the highest court. We do not have to pay your claim until your case is finally decided. We do not agree that the matter is a covered title risk by defending.

6.  LIMITATIONS OF OUR LIABILITY

Our liability is limited by the following:

    a.  We will pay up to your actual loss of the Policy Amount in force when the claim is made—whichever is less.

    b.  If we remove the claim against your title with reasonable diligence or take other action under this policy after receiving notice of it, we will have no further liability for it.

    c.  All payments we make under this policy—except for costs, attorneys' fees and expenses—will be subtracted from your Policy Amount.

---

**FIGURE 15.1 CONTINUED.**

    d.   If the Covered Title Risk is an easement, we may pay an insured mortgage holder instead of paying you when a written agreement between you and the mortgage holder allows. If the claim involves another Covered title Risk, we may pay the mortgage holder instead of paying you. The amount paid to the mortgage holder is considered a payment to you under your policy and will be subtracted from your policy amount.

    e.   If you do anything to affect any right of recovery or defense you may have, we can subtract from our liability the amount by which you reduced the value of that right or defense. But we must add back to our liability any amount by which our expenses are reduced as a result of your action.

7.   TRANSFER OF YOUR RIGHTS

When we settle a claim, we have all the rights you had against any person or property related to the claim. You must transfer these rights to us when we ask, and you must not do anything to affect these rights. You must let us use your name in enforcing these rights.

We will not be liable to you if we do not pursue these rights or if we do not recover any amount that might be recoverable.

With the money we recover from enforcing these rights, we will pay whatever part of your loss we have not paid. We have a right to keep what is left.

8.   ARBITRATION

If it is permitted under Texas or federal law, you and we may agree to arbitration when you file a claim.

The arbitration may decide any matter in dispute between you and us.

Arbitration is one means of alternative dispute resolution. it may lessen the time and cost of claims settlement. You may wish to consider another form of mediation or use the court system. If you choose arbitration, you may give up some discovery rights and your right to sue.

The arbitration award may:

    a.   include attorneys' fees if allowed by state law, and/or

    b.   be entered as a judgment in the proper court.

The arbitration shall be under the Title Insurance Arbitration Rules of the American Arbitration Association. You may choose current Rules or Rules in existence on Policy Date.

The law used in the arbitration is the law of the place where the property is located.

You can get a copy of the Rules from us.

9.   ENTIRE CONTRACT PROVISION

This policy and any endorsements we attach are the entire contract between you and us.

Any claim you make against us must be under this Policy and is subject to its terms.

10.  COMPLAINT NOTICE

Should any dispute arise about your premium or about a claim that you have filed, contact the agent or write to us. OUR TOLL-FREE NUMBER IS _____. If we do not resolve the problem, you also may write the Texas Department of Insurance, P.O. Box 149091, Austin, TX 78714-9091, FAX No. (512) 475-1771. THE TOLL-FREE NUMBER FOR THE TEXAS DEPARTMENT OF INSURANCE IS 1-800-252-3439.

This notice of complaint procedure is for information only. It does not become a part of condition of this policy.

**Standard Exceptions.** There are certain standard title exceptions included in the title policy against which the title policy will not insure the purchaser, unless an additional premium is paid or unless special riders are attached to the policy. These exceptions are listed under Schedule B of the standard owner's policy of title insurance shown in Figure 15.1. They are as follows (italics indicate actual wording as shown in Schedule B):

1. *The following restrictive covenants of record itemized below (the Company must either insert specific recording data or delete this exception).*

2. *Any discrepancies, conflicts, or shortages in area or boundary lines, or any encroachments or protrusions, or any overlapping of improvements.* This exception clearly states in both the owner and mortgagee title policies that any shortages in area, encroachments, or overlapping improvements simply are not insured against. This exception might come as quite a shock to people who buy homes and find that the neighbors have an encroachment on their property, or perhaps that they, as the new home purchasers, have an encroachment on their neighbor's property. This exception (except for the "shortages-in-area" exception) can be deleted in residential policies for an additional premium in an amount equivalent to 5% of the basic rate or a minimum fee of $20. This would normally require the title company to use an approved surveyor, and to make the determination of whether or not it feels that the title to the property is an insurable risk. Of course, the title company always has the option of not insuring the title to the property in the event it finds the encroachment or overlapping improvements. Courts have been rather hard on title companies in the past and generally construe the title insurance policy against the insurer in the event there is a title defect due to a shortage or boundary conflict. *Clements* v. *Stewart Title Co.*, 537 S.W.2d 126 (Tex. Civ. App.—Austin, 1976); *Dallas Title and Guaranty Co.* v. *Valdes*, 445 S.W.2d 26 (Tex. Civ. App.—Austin, 1969); *Chanoux* v. *Title Insurance Company*, 258 S.W.2d 866 (Tex. Civ. App.—El Paso, 1953). Although if the discrepancy is due to the surveyor's error, the title company has no liability. *Larson* v. *Cook Consultants, Inc.*, 690 S.W.2d 567 (Tex. 1985).

3. *Homestead or community property or survivorship rights, if any, of any spouse of any insured.*

4. Any titles or rights asserted by anyone including, but not limited to, persons, corporations, governments, or other entities, to tidelands, or lands comprising the shores or beds of navigable or perennial rivers and streams, lakes, bays, gulfs, or oceans, or to any land extending from the line of mean low tide to the line of vegetation, or to lands beyond the line of the harbor or bulkhead lines as established or changed by any government, or to filled-in lands, or artificial islands, or to riparian rights or other statutory water rights, or the rights or interests of the State of Texas, or the public generally in the area extending from the line of mean low tide to the line of vegetation or the right of access thereto, or right of easement along and across the same.

5. *Standby fees and taxes for the year 20__ and subsequent years, and subsequent assessments for prior years due to change in land usage or ownership.*

   Everyone is considered by law to be on notice of taxes and tax liens. Taxes arise at the first of every year and will stay with the property until paid. The title insurance policy, though, does insure that all taxes prior to the current year have been paid and that the only taxes that the purchaser will be liable for are those for the current year and subsequent years.

6. The sixth exception notes all liens and instruments creating any evidence of said liens in the property, and normally it lists whatever might still be of record at the time the title search is performed.

There is an additional exception that most title companies include in the title insurance form even though it is not part of the standard form, and that is the exception to the **rights of parties in possession**. The title company may add this exception to either the owner's or mortgagee's title policy where the purchaser contractually waives the inspection of the land by the title company. If the purchaser is not willing to waive the inspection by the title company, the title company may charge an additional fee for personal on-site inspection of the property. It should also be pointed out that the first paragraph of Schedule B indicates that the policy is subject to the conditions and stipulations of any leases or easements shown in Schedule A, which works hand in hand with the "rights of parties in possession" exception to the title policy. The courts have consistently held that a purchaser has a duty of inspection to the property because the right of parties in possession is equivalent to that of constructive notice as required by the recording act. *Bell* v. *Smith*, supra. This exception also applies to easements or any other obvious encumbrance on the property that would have been obvious to the purchaser had he personally inspected the property. *Jupe* v. *City of Schertz*, 604 S.W.2d 405 (Tex. Civ. App.—San Antonio, 1980). Upon a personal inspection of the property, the purchaser would have known of such rights of parties in possession, even though the title insurance company does not. *Halvorson* v. *National Title and Abstract Co.*, 391 S.W.2d 112 (Tex. Civ. App.—Tyler, 1965).

Although it may appear that the title insurance business seems to be "ducking" most obvious liabilities and limiting its exposure to liability to such a great extent, it should also be pointed out that compared to other methods of title assurance, title insurance is the quickest, cheapest, and most available type for most real estate transactions.

**Disadvantages.** Title insurance does have certain limitations, but these are usually conditions that are out of the ordinary for most standard real estate transactions. The most obvious limitation in a title insurance policy would be the insuring of a very valuable piece of property, the value of which may exceed the value of the title insurance company's assets. This is often the case in purchasing an office building that is worth hundreds of millions of dollars. A similar exception would be the purchase of a block of a downtown major metropolitan center like Houston. If the block cost $800 per square foot and the title policy is limited to the cost of the property, it would not cover the cost of the subsequent improvements erected on that property, unless the title policy has specific provisions for renewal in the event of construction of the specified improvements. Since the title policy is for a fixed amount, the same disadvantage applies to normal inflationary increases in real estate values (these are not covered by a title policy), unless the additional premium is paid to increase the owner's coverage.

Another major exception is one in which the grantor of a piece of property is probably more solvent than the title company (but don't forget Enron—it may not last as long as the title company). In such event, one may well find that the grantor would be a better insurer of the title of that property through his personal warranty than the title insurance company would be using the proportionate reduction clause formula. However, in this circumstance, the purchaser would have the affirmative duty and expense of filing the lawsuit, whereas the title insurance company is required to provide the indemnification at no expense to the purchaser.

## ■ SUMMARY

It is part of the real estate agent's obligation in Texas to inform the purchaser in writing that the purchaser should have the abstract to real estate examined prior to closing or that title insurance should be obtained to assure himself of the status of the title to that real estate.

The Torrens system is a system of title registration that is not utilized in Texas. The personal warranty of the grantor gives a full warranty as to the title of the property, but it is only as good as the solvency of the grantor. A lawyer's title opinion is a commonly used method of title assurance. However, in the event of default or title failure, there is little ability for recovery short of a suit for malpractice, unless the lawyer has insurance on his opinions. An abstractor's certificate, or a certificate of title, does not give a legal opinion, nor is there a solvent fund for recovery in the event of mistakes, omissions, or errors. Title insurance is a method by which a state-regulated insurance company, with a proven source of solvent funds, provides an insurance policy to assure the purchaser that his title is good and indefeasible. Title insurance is issued on standard forms, which are promulgated by the Insurance Board of the State of Texas.

## CHAPTER 16

# Closings

## The Closing Process

The final consummation of a real estate transaction is commonly termed the **closing**. It is at the closing that the documents are signed and transmitted to the parties, the funds are distributed, and, hopefully, all obligations of all parties have been fulfilled. A closing is not a purely legal function; it is considered by most to be a business function. In a well-planned closing, the papers are normally prepared by the attorneys and are reviewed by the clients prior to the closing to eliminate potential misunderstandings.

The vast majority of closings in Texas are held at title companies, or a third-party escrow agent serves as a depository for instruments and funds. The escrow agent is normally a disinterested third party who accumulates the various and sundry instruments and funds into "escrow" for final distribution upon consummation of the sale, pursuant to the terms of the earnest money contract or formal escrow instrument. The widespread use of escrows and escrow agents during closings creates very little need for all the parties to attend the closing together. In fact, it is suggested by some that all parties should not attend the closing at the same time. Depending on the circumstances surrounding the sale (especially residential sales), there is often an air of tension or emotionalism that may serve to hinder the actual closing process rather than help it.

In the typical residential transaction, there are actually two closings involved rather than just one. First, there is the closing of the sale from the seller to the purchaser; and second, there is the closing of the loan, involving the mortgagee and the purchaser. In the actual sale closing between the seller and the purchaser, the mortgagee is not interested in any part of the transaction except the fact that the purchaser is getting a clear, unencumbered title, subject only to the mortgagee's new lien to be created at the closing. For the loan-closing transaction, the seller has no concern as to the papers and documents to be signed between the purchaser and the lender, only with the papers he (the seller) is supposed to secure to complete the actual sale of the property.

It should be noted at this point that there are closings in which *no* sale transaction takes place. This type of closing, referred to as a **loan closing**, only involves the refinancing of real estate by the owner, or the borrowing of money that is to be secured by the owner's real estate. The loan closing (very common among real estate developers, contractors, and investors) does not involve a sale of property at all, just the borrowing of money to be secured by the real estate.

# Escrows

The **escrow** function, whether it is served by a title company or by a disinterested attorney, is one of the keys to a successful closing. The escrow officer is normally one who is trusted by both parties; he helps ease the air of suspicion or distrust that may exist in a transaction when the parties think of themselves as adversaries. The agent represents neither party and has a duty to both parties. He cannot give legal advice nor explain the legal effect of the documents at the closing. *Bell* v. *Safeco Title Insurance Co.*, 830 S.W.2d 157 (Tex. App.—Dallas, 1992, writ den.). The escrow should be created pursuant to an escrow agreement with specific instructions for the escrow officer. If not written as specific escrow instructions, the intent and specifications for the escrow may be contained in the earnest money contract. *Covert* v. *Calvert*, 287 S.W.2d 117 (Tex. Civ. App.—Amarillo, 1926); *Campbell* v. *Barber*, 272 S.W.2d 750 (Tex. Civ. App.—Ft. Worth, 1954). Such escrows are generally considered irrevocable. Although this general rule may seem to be harsh, it must be remembered that the escrow officer, in placing himself in a position of trust, is a fiduciary to both parties and cannot act detrimentally to the interest of either party. *Watkins* v. *Williamson*, supra. Since the escrow is irrevocable, it may somewhat ease the burden of the escrow officer having to respond to the whims and capricious desires of either party. The escrow officer holds the instruments and funds in trust from the time they are deposited with him until the conditions and specific obligations required in the earnest money contract or escrow instructions are performed. At the time that all conditions have been performed, he distributes the funds and signed instruments, and the transaction is considered to be completed.

There may be new liabilities on the horizon. The prevalence of mortgage fraud and predatory lending has created situations where title companies handle the escrow for these closings. Does the title company have the duty to be a policeman and discover fraud in these fraudulent transactions? At least one case indicated that they do, because their fiduciary duty of one hundred percent disclosure extends to all parties to the transaction, *Home Loan Corp.* v. *Texas American Title Co.* 191 S.W.3d 728 (Tex. App.—Houston [14th Dist.], 2006, pet. den.). This creates a very difficult situation. How can a title company disclose one hundred percent of everything they know to all parties, particularly when the title company is "trusted" by a party and has to maintain confidentiality? This case did note, however, that the lender's funding of money into the closing was irrevocable. If fraud occurs, it is usually between the lender and borrower. The question remains, then, as to whether or not a title company is a part of the fraud if they have not made representations concerning the fraud to any parties of the closing. This is a hot area of the law, with more to come.

## Relation Back Doctrine

Since escrow agreements are normally considered to be irrevocable, and since the escrow function is dictated by certain obligations and performances that must be completed prior to distribution, a legal doctrine has been applied to the escrow function relating to the time of performance. This doctrine is called the **Relation Back**

**Doctrine**. This can be briefly summarized by stating that when a document is given to an escrow officer (when authorized by the escrow agreement) for delivery to the grantee upon compliance with specified conditions, the date of delivery relates back to the time of deposit into escrow so as to constitute delivery to the grantee upon delivery into escrow. *Roach* v. *Roach*, 672 S.W.2d 524 (Tex. Civ. App.—Amarillo, 1984). However, title does not pass to the grantee until all the conditions have been performed and the document has been delivered by the escrow agent. Basically, after the document is placed in escrow, the grantee has control over its ultimate delivery (that is, if he satisfies the escrow conditions). This document has particularly pertinent application when instruments are disposed into escrow and the grantor subsequently dies or becomes insane. The Relation Back Doctrine supports the theory of irrevocability by vesting delivery from the grantor at the time of deposit into escrow.

## Closing into Escrow

The escrow function also performs a very valuable accommodation to the parties by allowing different closing times for each of the parties. One party who may be forced to leave town at an early date can sign all the instruments as required by the contract and leave them with the escrow agent. This is called *closing into escrow*. The other party, then, upon performance of his obligations as required by the contract, may go in at some later date and close at his convenience. As long as all contracting parties performed their obligations within the time specified, there normally should not be any conflicts in utilizing the escrow function in this manner. As stated previously, it is sometimes recommended that the parties not close at the same time because of the amount of emotion and tension that sometimes exists at a closing. One only needs to leave a closing once with all the parties crying (including the real estate agents and escrow officer) to realize how valuable this escrow function can be.

## Liability of Escrow Agent

The **escrow agent** is held to a duty of due care, honesty, and integrity when operating as an escrow agent. Normally, the full liability of the escrow officer in the event of a mistake or negligent error is to pay the expense of restoring the status quo. *Texas Reserve Life Ins. Co.* v. *Security Title Co.*, 352 S.W.2d 347 (Tex. Civ. App.—San Antonio, 1961). The Texas Insurance Code requires that escrow agents for title companies be licensed and bonded. As a result, most people in Texas use title companies as escrow agents. Unfortunately, there were some serious title insurance scams, primarily in Houston and Dallas. In those cases, it was a matter of misplaced trust with the title insurance agent, and the losses were "escrow" losses, rather than title insurance losses. For this type of loss, the escrow agent is liable, rather than the title insurer, in most circumstances. *3Z Corporation* v. *Stewart Title Guaranty Co.*, 851 S.W.2d 933 (Tex. App.—Beaumont, 1993). The Texas Department of Insurance now provides an available fund for consumers to pursue when they have suffered losses as a result of misapplication of trust funds or shortages in escrow accounts, *V.T.C.A., Insurance Code, §2602.002*.

One of the more perilous undertakings by the escrow officer in a closing is when one of the parties indicates that the other party has breached the contract. When certain obligations and functions have not been performed, the escrow agent normally waits for a judicial determination before returning any of the documents or escrowed funds to either party. For example, consider the case where one party claims that there has been a breach of the transaction, but the other party denies that such breach has taken place. The escrow agent, as a third party, normally will choose not to take sides and will only perform his function as ordered by a court of competent jurisdiction. This is a very important thing to remember. Even though the earnest money contract may be very clear as to the parties' obligations, if one of the parties claims a breach, the escrow agent is not going to undertake the responsibility of disbursing funds or instruments. This would be running the risk of breaching one's duty of care in the escrow function.

## Funding

Even experienced real estate brokers can feel confused as to how funding occurs during a real estate closing. In an effort to provide good service, many title companies have routinely offered "table funding" so that real estate brokers and sellers could get their cash at closing. It tends to keep good customers happy and, in some cases, makes sellers feel more comfortable if they can receive their proceeds at closing.

There is a problem with this procedure, however. A title company has no better access to funds than anyone else. If the buyer brings a personal check to closing and the check bounces, the title company does not have the funds to pay out of escrow to the seller or to the real estate brokers. The title companies have no magic source of funds, cannot get immediate credit for checks, or fund any differently than household bank accounts. This was often overlooked, however, as title companies, in an effort to keep customers satisfied, routinely ran the risks of insufficient checks to "table fund."

The problem became so severe that the Texas Department of Insurance finally adopted rules and regulations as to how title companies can fund at closing. This has come to be known as the "good funds" rule, which establishes guidelines by which title companies can issue checks out of their escrowed funds at closing. "Good funds" means:

1. Cash or wire transfer.
2. Certified checks, cashier's checks, and teller's checks.
3. Uncertified funds in amounts of less than $1,500, including checks, traveller's checks, money orders, and negotiate orders of withdrawal, provided multiple items shall not be used to avoid the $1,500 limitation.
4. Uncertified funds in amounts of $1,500 or more, drafts, and any other items when collected by the financial institution.
5. State of Texas warrants.
6. United States treasury checks.
7. Checks drawn on a bank, savings bank, or savings and loan association insured by the FDIC and for which a transaction code has been issued pursuant to, and in compliance with, a fully executed immediately available funds procedure agreement (Form T-37) and such bank or savings and loan association.
8. Checks by city and county governments located in the State of Texas.

These requirements now bring *all* title companies into the same funding procedures for closings.

However, even though there are some areas of good funds that are approved by the Texas Department of Insurance, it needs to be emphasized that the banks do not have to honor each of these items unless they choose to do so. Therefore, the ultimate decision on whether or not funds are "good" is made by the bank receipting these evidences of funds. The old rules are still the most reliable: "Good funds" is cash in the bank; nothing else can actually be verified. Table funding at closings will be difficult without making prior arrangements.

# Documents for the Closing

Virtually all documents needed for a closing are deposited into escrow. Sometimes there are difficulties in determining exactly what instruments are supposed to be at the closing. Therefore, it is good advice for realtors and lawyers to make a closing checklist before attending the closing. This is a very simple thing to do and can save tremendous embarrassment. There are few situations more humiliating than to leave the closing (after representing a client) and discover that certain documents have not been properly signed or the proper amount of funds has not been distributed.

The closing checklist is very simply created by sitting down and carefully reading the earnest money contract and making a list of which documents and which funds your client should have in his possession upon leaving the closing. In creating this list you should also keep in mind that there are going to be certain documents that will not leave the closing but will be transferred to the courthouse for recordation before being distributed to the proper parties. A typical closing checklist may include the following items if representing the seller:

1. Cash in an amount that should be predetermined (this may be delayed upon funding of the purchaser's loan).
2. The deed of trust (if the seller is going to finance the transaction, but will usually be sent to the courthouse to record).
3. A promissory note (if the seller is going to finance the transaction).
4. A closing statement.
5. Hopefully, a smile.

If representing the purchaser, the checklist would include:

1. The deed (which is normally forwarded to the courthouse for recording before being delivered to the purchaser).
2. Warranties as requested or required [(1) mechanical equipment inspection, (2) termite inspection, (3) slab inspection, (4) roof inspection].
3. The owner's title policy.
4. A bill of sale (if any personalty is to be transferred).
5. Estoppel certificates to evidence the payoff figure for the underlying indebtedness, if any.
6. A receipt for the purchase price paid.
7. A closing statement.
8. Seller Disclosure Form.
9. Disclosures required in the contract for sale or required by state law.

If the purchase concerns income-producing property, the buyer may walk away with the following additional items:

1. Estoppel letter by tenants.
2. Landlord's estoppel certificates signed by the prior landlord.
3. Assignments, which may include the following:
   a. Service contracts.
   b. Warranties on mechanical equipment.
   c. Rents and deposits.

      d. Escrow funds that may be contained in the seller's mortgage account.

      e. Insurance policies.

4. A letter from the seller to the tenants indicating the new ownership.

5. A letter to the building manager indicating the change in ownership.

6. The rental rolls (normally certified).

7. Original leases.

8. Employment contracts.

9. Assignment of trade name.

If the property purchased is a condominium, the following additional items may be obtained:

1. The master deed or condominium declaration.

2. The bylaws of the condominium homeowners' association.

3. Builders' warranties.

4. Condominium Resale Certificate.

# Parties to a Closing

Two of the more important aspects of a smooth closing transaction that all parties should understand are: (1) what the closing is supposed to accomplish, and (2) what role or function each of the parties should assume to ensure a proper closing and adequate representation of the client.

The various roles of the parties at a closing normally include these four categories:

1. The escrow officer.

2. The seller and purchaser.

3. The real estate agent(s).

4. The attorneys.

(This is assuming the worst of all possible situations when all the parties show up at the same time!)

The escrow agent, especially if a title company, performs only two functions: that of being an escrow agent and that of being the agent of the title guarantor, as previously discussed. The escrow agent's duties are not to be a "gofer," negotiator, soothsayer, or salver of all wounds. The escrow agent's job is a professional one, and he should not be involved with the problems of either party, or of the respective real estate agents or attorneys, unless such involvement relates to his particular function as an escrow agent or title insurer. It is not his job to make phone calls, check on loan proceeds, or talk to anyone's relatives or friends with respect to said closing. The escrow officer normally has enough responsibility without having to be concerned with all the other parties' problems.

The seller or purchaser is normally a client whose property and funds are involved in consummating the sale. He is represented by a real estate agent and preferably also by an attorney. It is anticipated that this client is a true "consumer," one who is not a professional real estate licensee, attorney, or individual involved in the business of transacting real estate. It is the interest of the consumer that must be protected.

The real estate agent's role is primarily one of being the chief negotiator and arbiter between the parties. He can be of tremendous help in making sure that all parties stay convinced that they have each made a good deal, and that there is a complete understanding of all the facts involved. The transfer of real estate is normally considered a very personal transaction; that is, it is people-oriented. Therefore, the assistance of a qualified real estate agent should help to solve many problems, since he understands the relationship between the parties and what each party is expecting to obtain from the consummation of the sale.

Although the closing is not particularly a legal function, it is the author's personal opinion that all clients should be represented by an attorney (just as they should also be represented by their real estate agent). It is the attorney who understands the technical legal ramifications of the escrow agent's function, the representations made by both parties, and the interpretations of the instruments used at the closing. He is uniquely valuable in being the only individual at the closing who is capable of explaining an individual's legal rights as these pertain to the transaction. Anyone else who attempts to interpret the documents or to explain an individual's legal rights is practicing law without a license. This applies to the escrow agent as well as to the real estate agent (provided that neither is licensed to practice law).

All four of the above separate roles and functions overlap to a certain degree. However, each one can be maintained separately, individually, and in coordination with each of the other parties' rights, providing all parties can maintain their professional attitudes.

# The Real Estate Settlement Procedures Act

Most closings are relatively simple and do not last very long, depending on the complications involved and the number of parties required to consummate the transaction. However, there have been a number of severe criticisms of closings generally because of the amount of fees and costs that are taken out of the purchaser's and seller's funds—expenses that were not disclosed prior to the closing. It was as a result of some of these imprudent practices across the country that Congress felt compelled to pass a new law called the **Real Estate Settlement Procedures Act**, which required certain disclosures to all parties prior to a closing and the use of certain forms during the closing. These requirements are of particular importance in residential transactions and therefore will be discussed here in some detail.

The Real Estate Settlement Procedures Act (RESPA) was originally passed in 1974. Amendments to the act, as well as to the applicable regulations, were passed in 1975 and 1976. Most of the provisions of RESPA were passed to control practices of certain states that had a large number of fees going to the escrow officer, attorneys, and other various and sundry parties—fees that came as a surprise to the consumer when he attended the closing. As in most other cases, the statutes were passed at the national level for the benefit of all people who needed this protection. On a national scope, Texas is not considered one of the states with a reputation for charging a large amount of closing costs. In fact, Texas passed regulations affecting title companies that are very similar to those of RESPA; these regulations are contained in Articles 9.53 and 9.54 of the Insurance Code. However, all the provisions of the federal act, of course, apply to Texas, as they do to all the other states.

## Transactions Covered

Just as the federal Truth-in-Lending Act passed Regulation Z to establish guidelines for the enforcement of the Truth-in-Lending Act, so the Department of Housing and Urban Development passed what we call **Regulation X**, which establishes the guidelines for enforcement of the Real Estate Settlement Procedures Act (RESPA). There were significant changes to RESPA in 1992. Under Regulation X, RESPA is construed to apply to all "federally related loans," which are loans that meet the following requirements:

1. Any loan (other than temporary financing, such as a construction loan) that is secured by a first or subordinate lien on residential real property, including a refinancing of any secured loan on residential real property.

2. The loan must be secured by a lien on property upon which there is located a one-to four-family residential structure, either presently existing or to be constructed from the loan proceeds, or a condominium or co-op unit.

3. The mortgaged property must be located in a state.

4. The loan must be made by a lender whose accounts are insured by, or the lender regulated by, an agency of the federal government. RESPA also requires that the lender, other than a state agency, invest in more than $1 million per year in residential real estate loans; or the loan must be insured, guaranteed, or assisted by the federal government; or the loan must be made in connection with the Housing and Urban Development program administered by the government; or the loan must be intended to be sold to FNMA, GNMA, FHLMC, or to a lender who intends to sell the mortgage to FHLMC.

Any installment sales contract, land contract, or other contract for otherwise qualifying residential property is a federally regulated mortgage loan if the contract is being funded in whole or in part by proceeds of the loan made by any maker of mortgage loans specified under the act.

It is not difficult to see that RESPA applies to all institutional lenders and to virtually all residential transactions.

## Exemptions from RESPA

Originally, there were eight exemptions to the application of RESPA. The Housing and Community Development Act of 1992, however, limited those exceptions to: (1) farms of 25 acres or more; (2) home equity line of credit transactions; (3) transactions involving only modification of existing obligations (excluding new obligations created to satisfy an existing obligation or loans for increased amounts); (4) "bridge" loans; (5) assumptions, if no lender approval is required; (6) temporary financing such as a construction loan; and (7) secondary market transactions.

The general requirements of RESPA, similar to those of the Truth-in-Lending Act, simply involve disclosure of all costs and items applicable to a particular closing transaction. We will now discuss some of these disclosures that are important to the purchaser—disclosures that involve the lender, the escrow agent, and the title companies.

## Lender Requirements

The requirements of RESPA imposed on the lender consist primarily of the lender giving a "special information booklet in any RESPA-covered transaction to every person who submits a loan application in writing," *Rev. Reg. X, §3500.6(a)*. The purpose of the booklet is to provide as much information as possible about the borrower's rights and obligations in connection with the closing of the loan transaction. The booklet must be provided to the borrower not later than the third business day after the lender receives the loan application, *Rev. Reg. X, §3500.6(a)*. The book is basically in the format provided by HUD, although certain variations are allowed to be made by the lender as long as they are HUD-approved.

In addition to the special information booklet, the lender must also furnish the borrower with a good faith estimate of the settlement charges that the borrower is likely to incur in connection with the loan transaction, *Rev. Reg. X, §3500.7(a)*. Although there is some discretion allowed for the "good faith estimate," it is required that the form used must include the lender's name, must be clear and concise, and must inform the borrower that other charges may be incurred at the time of closing, *Rev. Reg. X, §3500.7(d)*.

Regulations effective April 1, 1991, require lenders and servicers of loans to provide borrowers disclosure statements concerning the establishment and maintenance of escrow accounts. The lender must provide an "initial escrow account statement" within 45 days of closing, or show it on the HUD-1 statement at closing. The form to be used is promulgated by the federal government and is required to be used, *12 U.S.C. 2609, §10(c)(1)(C)*.

## Settlement Agent's Requirements

Whereas Texas requires the settlement agent (escrow agent) to use the Texas Department of Insurance–promulgated closing forms in all non-RESPA transactions, RESPA requires that the escrow agent must use the standard settlement or closing statement, often referred to as **HUD-1** (or HUD-1A for refinancings), *Rev. Reg. X, §3500.8(a)*. There are exceptions provided where the borrower is not required to pay any closing costs; but, at least to date, this option has not been widely utilized in the State of Texas. There have been some complaints about the use of the HUD forms because they are confusing in parts and sometimes difficult to explain to prospective purchasers during the closing transaction.

There is a basic requirement to itemize all charges paid by the borrower and seller, except for those that are not imposed by the lender and are paid for outside of the closing. If there are any costs required by the lender, even if paid outside the closing, they must still be noted on the settlement form; these would be marked "P.O.C." to indicate their payment outside of the closing. It is interesting to note that both the buyer's and seller's expenses are noted on the same form. There have been some complaints that the buyer and the seller preferred to keep their parts of the transaction confidential. Therefore, RESPA regulations provide that the seller's columns may be deleted from the buyer's copy and the buyer's columns may be deleted from the seller's copy, *Rev. Reg. X, §3500.8(b)*. There is additionally a general requirement that the settlement agent must provide the lender with a copy of each settlement statement.

One of the more fundamental disclosures that is required is that upon the buyer's request, the settlement agent must permit the borrower to inspect the HUD forms at any time during the business day before the scheduled closing. There is some limitation on this, however, in that the escrow officer need only complete the items known at the time and has no obligation to furnish information not available prior to the closing date. With a few exceptions, the final settlement statement is to be delivered to the borrower and seller, or to their agents, at or before the time of the settlement.

## Controlled Business and Referral Fees

There have evidently been some problems in closings as to the seller requiring the buyer to purchase title insurance from a particular title company. Since the seller in Texas normally purchases the title insurance (and the rates are set by the Texas

Department of Insurance), it is rather questionable whether or not this requirement has any technical application under normal Texas real estate practice. Similar prohibitions apply to other "controlled businesses" wherein a lender or other person is in the position to refer business as a part of a real estate settlement service. This simply prevents "kickbacks" and unearned fees from going to a party in a position of control who might take advantage of the other person's lack of bargaining power.

These prohibitions are a particular concern for real estate agents because they may often find themselves in situations where somebody providing a settlement service (appraisal, inspection, title examination, preparation of documents, origination fees for loans) may be willing to pay the broker a referral fee for "networking" that business. These kinds of referral fees are strictly prohibited. The purpose of RESPA is to eliminate those kickbacks or referral fees that tend to unnecessarily increase the cost of settlement services to the consumer. The interpretations under the statute are very broad. A "referral" includes any oral or written action that has the effect of affirmatively influencing the selection by any person of a provider of a settlement service when such person will pay for such settlement service or business. It also refers to a person being required to pay for a settlement service to a particular provider of that settlement service, or business incident thereto.

There are specific exceptions to Section 8 that also affect a real estate licensee. Controlled business arrangements are an exception, provided that:

1. At or prior to the time of the referral, a disclosure is made of the existence of such an arrangement to the person being referred, and, in connection with such referral, such person is provided a written estimate of the charge or range of charges generally made by the provider to which the person is referred, except that when a lender makes a referral, this requirement may be satisfied at the time that the estimates of settlement charges are required.

2. Such person is not required to use any particular provider of settlement services.

3. The only thing of value that is received from the arrangement, other than the permitted payments, is a return on the ownership interest or franchise relationship.

A controlled business arrangement is defined by the statute as an arrangement in which a person who is in a position to refer business incident to or a part of a real estate settlement service involving a federally related mortgage loan, or an associate of such person, has either an affiliate relationship with or a direct or beneficial ownership interest of more than 1 percent in the provider of settlement services; and such person directly or indirectly refers such person to that provider or affirmatively influences the selection of that provider.

Any person who violates RESPA "shall be fined not more than $10,000.00 or imprisoned for not more than one year, or both." Those who violate the prohibitions are also jointly and severally liable to the person or persons charged with the settlement service involved in the violation in an amount equal to three times the amount of any charge paid for such settlement service. (See *RESPA §8(b)*.) There are separate provisions for referrals to title insurance companies.

Anyone who violates this provision is liable to the buyer in an amount equal to three times the charge for such title insurance, or other damages received, *RESPA, §9(b)*.

## Escrow Accounts

There has been a common practice among lenders to require the borrower to maintain an escrow account for the payment of taxes and insurance during the term of the mortgage. There have been some complaints made by the borrowers that they are required to pay certain advanced amounts into the escrow account that exceed the amount that would be required to pay for the tax and insurance requirements. The RESPA rules provide that any amounts collected for escrow accounts for payments of taxes and insurance can only be so much as would equal the amount to be sufficient to pay such taxes, insurance premiums, and other charges attributable to the period between the closing and the time the amount is to be paid, plus one-sixth (two months) of the estimated annual amount to be paid. All future collections for payment into the escrow account are limited to one-twelfth of the charges to become due within the next year.

The foregoing is, of course, not even a slight attempt at explaining all the RESPA rules. As in the case of the Truth-in-Lending Act, there are many publications available that explain most of the provisions of the RESPA Act and Regulation X in much greater detail than can be given here.

## Payment Shock

On January 21, 1998, a new RESPA rule was passed addressing "payment shock." It involves the proper accounting method to calculate escrow payments where the servicer anticipates the disbursements (such as property taxes) will increase substantially in the second year of the escrow account. This situation frequently occurs in new home construction, wherein the taxes calculated for the initial year were on a substantially lower value than the newly constructed home, which may be reevaluated for tax purposes in the following year. Many homeowners (who are stretching the limit for monthly payments with escrow account estimates created in the first year) suffer "payment shock" in the second year when their escrow account contributions are substantially increased. The increase is not only because of the increased value but also to make up escrow shortages if the increased tax was not collected in prior months.

The new rule allows the servicer, with the consent of the borrower, the option of calculating the escrow payments over a 24-month basis, allowing the servicer to look ahead to the second year and estimate the payment that would be due, thereby mitigating the deficiency or shortage after the first year and leaving a smaller deficiency or shortage after the second year. It is not required, but it is encouraged as a best practice. The servicers may disclose the problems to the borrowers, and the borrowers then may make "voluntary" overpayments to their escrow account.

## ■ SUMMARY

The closing is the final consummation of a real estate transaction. The vast majority of closings in Texas are held at title companies, where a third-party escrow agent serves as a depositary for instruments and funds. In the typical residential transaction, there are actually two closings involved rather than one. There is closing of the sale (from the seller to the purchaser), and there is closing of the loan (involving the contractual relationship between the mortgagee and the mortgagor–purchaser).

The escrow function involves the use of a disinterested third party, which helps ease the air of suspicion and distrust that may exist in a transaction. By utilizing escrow, the parties may also "close into escrow," which greatly facilitates most closing transactions.

Since there is a diversity of documents utilized in a closing, it is often helpful for the real estate agent to prepare a closing checklist to help him monitor the instruments that are to be signed. It is also important that all parties to a transaction recognize what functions each party to the closing is to perform.

In an attempt to clarify and disclose some of the pertinent closing functions, the federal government passed the Real Estate Settlement Procedures Act (RESPA), which covers virtually all residential transactions and all institutional lenders, although there are specific exemptions.

## CHAPTER 17

# Liens

A **lien**, generally defined, is a charge on the property of a person for the payment or discharge of a debt or duty owed by that person. It is also defined as a claim against a person's real estate that exists as a security interest for some obligation to be discharged. It has long been understood that when one party is indebted to a creditor, the creditor has the right to an interest in the first party's real estate under certain specified circumstances. In some circumstances, the creditor may even force the sale of that real estate to satisfy the debt. The only liens to be discussed in this chapter will consist of liens that attach directly to real estate, since UCC and chattel mortgage liens have been discussed in Chapter 6. Liens are often referred to as **general liens** (those attached to all of the property a debtor owns) or **specific liens** (those attached only to specific parcels of real estate).

Real estate liens are generally categorized according to the source from which they are derived. For the purposes of this discussion, equitable liens (implemented upon principles of equity), statutory liens (implemented by statute), constitutional liens (implemented by the state constitution), and contractual liens (liens created by contracts) will be discussed.

## Equitable Liens

An **equitable lien**, as its name implies, is recognized and enforced by courts under equitable principles. As in other equitable principles, this lien is founded on an express or implied contract pertaining to some specific real property and will not be applied when there is an adequate remedy at law. The only significant requirement of an equitable lien is that the lien holder must show an intention on his part to charge the property with a debt. An equitable lien, since it is not usually recorded, is not good against a subsequent purchaser or creditor without notice of the lien.

Equitable liens normally fall into two categories. One is a **vendor's lien**, and the other is normally referred to as a **tenant's lien**. In Texas, a vendor's lien is well established as being implied every time there is a transfer of real property by a deed. The deed with a vendor's lien is interpreted as a mortgage, coupled with a power of rescission (right to rescind the contract) in the event of default. The vendor's lien must be judicially foreclosed and can only operate as security for payment of the purchase price or other obligations resulting from the purchase of the real estate. *McInroe* v. *Lloyd*, 847 S.W.2d 362 (Tex. App.—Ft. Worth, 1993). In most transactions, there are deed of trust liens, mechanics' and materialmen's liens, and other express liens that can be recorded and are good against innocent purchasers and subsequent creditors. A vendor's lien is totally separate and distinct from these types of liens, however, even in the same transaction. *Goidl* v. *North American Mortgage Investors*, 564 S.W.2d 493 (Tex. Civ. App.—Dallas, 1978). These other methods of creating liens are so widely accepted that the vendor's lien enforcement only occurs in the most severe fact situations. The vendor's lien is normally felt to be the "last resort" to create a lien interest in real estate if there is a default by the purchaser. When such situations occur, the courts generally hold that the purchaser holds title to the property in trust for the seller until the purchase price is paid. However, the vendor's lien is often expressly reserved and is assigned to financing institutions to create a record on the face of the deed.

Another equitable lien, a tenant's lien, is easy to envision and sometimes creates unanticipated headaches for negligent landlords. In the typical tenant lien situation, the tenant constructs some improvement on the real property (with the landlord's knowledge, and with the expectation of being paid) that increases the value of that property such that the landlord would be unjustly enriched if the tenant were not adequately reimbursed. One can easily envision a tenant constructing an improvement with the landlord's full knowledge, and the landlord refusing to reimburse the tenant for the cost of the improvement. In this type of situation, the tenant's only recourse may be to petition a court of equity to ensure his reimbursement at some future date.

# Statutory Liens

There are basically four types of statutory liens that affect real property in Texas: (1) ad valorem tax liens, (2) federal tax liens, (3) judgment liens, and (4) mechanics' and materialmen's liens. There are also statutory liens for landlords and tenants, but those will be discussed in Chapter 18.

## Ad Valorem Tax Liens

**Ad valorem tax liens** in Texas are both constitutional and statutory. They are given an automatic priority and become liens on the real estate on January 1 of each and every year. In short, ad valorem taxes must be paid. They not only have a statutory priority, but they also have a practical priority. In the event any property is going to be sold, the title company always obtains tax certificates in order to be sure that the taxes are paid and to provide information to prorate taxes for the current year. If any taxes are delinquent, the taxing authority informs the title company at that time, and all delinquent taxes must be paid in order for the seller to convey free and clear title. If a foreclosure or other forced sale occurs, the taxes are still due and payable at the end of each calendar year, regardless of who then holds title to the property. All suits to collect ad valorem taxes must be filed within 20 years after the taxes become delinquent, *V.T.C.A., Tax Code, §33.05.*

## Federal Tax Liens

A lien for any income taxes due to the United States arises from the date the assessment is made and continues upon all property of the taxpayer until the amount so assessed is satisfied or becomes unenforceable by lapse of time, *26 U.S.C.A., §6321.* However, this **general lien** is not effective against any subsequent purchasers and creditors unless the notice of the tax lien is filed with the real property records in the county where the real property is located. If the taxes remain unpaid, the **Internal Revenue Service** can collect them by levy upon the property belonging to the taxpayer. The owner of the property that is sold, or any of his heirs, executors, administrators, or anyone who has lien interests, can redeem the property sold within 180 days after the sale, *26 U.S.C.A., §6337.* If the property is not redeemed, the District Director of the Internal Revenue Service then executes a deed to the person who purchased at the sale. This deed conveys all rights, title, and interest of the delinquent taxpayer to the real estate, operating similarly to the tax deed discussed in Chapter 11.

More difficult problems occur if property is foreclosed on by a superior lien (for instance, a first lien purchase money mortgage, which was on record prior to the **federal tax lien**). If the purchase money lien is foreclosed and the notice of tax lien is filed less than 30 days before the sale, the foreclosure sale has priority over the federal tax lien. If, however, the federal tax lien is filed more than 30 days before the foreclosure sale, the foreclosing lender must give the IRS in Austin, Texas, at least a 25-day advance notice of the sale, and a **right of redemption** exists in the United States for 120 days after the foreclosure sale. If proper notice is not given to the United States, the lien remains on the property even after the foreclosure sale has taken place, *26 U.S.C.A., §7425.* All suits to foreclose on property that is subject to the federal tax lien must be filed within 10 years after the lien has been filed of record. Tax liens filed prior to December 1, 1990 have a limitation of six years.

## Federal Judgment Liens

The Federal Debt Collection Procedure Act of 1990 (FDCPA) applies to judgment liens obtained by the United States or an agency, department, commission, board, or other entity of the United States. The federal judgment lien becomes a lien upon the property of the judgment debtor upon the filing of a certified copy of the judgment or an abstract thereof in the real property records of the county in which the real property is located. The lien is effective for 20 years, *28 U.S.C.A., §3201(c)(2),* and applies to all judgments entered on or after May 21, 1981, *28 U.S.C.A., §3005.*

The United States, as a judgment lienholder, has a right of redemption for a period of one year from the date of foreclosure of any superior lien, *28 U.S.C.A., §2410.*

## State Judgment Liens

In order to obtain a **judgment lien** under Texas law, the creditor must obtain a judgment of a state or federal court of competent jurisdiction against the debtor. After the judgment has been obtained, it takes 30 days for it to become final. When the judgment is final, the creditor must then cause the judgment to be "abstracted" and indexed in the judgment records maintained by the county clerk in the county in which the land is located. This recording process is called filing an abstract of judgment. Obtaining the judgment, by itself, does not create a lien until the **abstract of judgment** has been filed. *Citicorp Real Estate, Inc.* v. *Banque Arab Internationale D'Investissement*, 747 S.W.2d 926 (Tex. App.—Dallas, 1988). Once the abstract of judgment has been filed, however, the lien becomes a **general lien** that attaches to all nonexempt real estate owned by the judgment debtor within the county, as well as to any other real estate acquired by that debtor in the county during the life of the judgment lien. The abstract of judgment may be filed in as many counties as the judgment creditor desires, and it creates an independent lien in each county where it is recorded. Judgment liens generally follow the "barber shop rule" and have priority against all subsequent liens and interests in the real property, with the exception of federal tax liens and state and county tax liens provided for by Texas law, *Tex. Rev. Civ. Stat. Ann., Art. 7172*. A judgment lien is valid for 10 years following the date of recording and indexing the abstract of judgment, *V.T.C.A., Property Code, §52.006*. To maintain its validity, it must be renewed before the expiration of each 10-year period.

It is important to note that judgment liens do not attach to exempt homestead property. Likewise, you may recall that as a general rule, the proceeds of the sale of the homestead remain exempt from garnishment for six months after the homestead is sold. If the proceeds are reinvested in another homestead, the new home is also exempt from forced sale. Texas has such liberal exemptions from judgment liens that it has often been called a **debtor's state**. When a judgment lien has been attached to the real estate, however, most title companies will not guarantee title until the lien has been satisfied. Therefore, as a practical matter, the judgment lien is often given more credence than the law may technically provide for, which is something of a problem.

There are special provisions for the judgment liens against debtors that are recorded on or after September 1, 1993. The lien is discharged and released without further action if the debtor obligation evidenced by the judgment is discharged in bankruptcy, *V.T.C.A., Property Code, §52.042*. This automatically clears the record title of a lot of judgment liens. If the judgment was recorded before September 1, 1993, however, the liens will still cloud title until they are either released or removed by court order.

**Attachments.** A **writ of attachment** is not actually a lien, but a legal seizure of property issued by judges and clerks of the district and county courts, and justices of the peace, which operates as a lien on a person's property. This is sometimes done if a person has filed suit for damages and he feels the defendant will hide or sell his property in an effort to liquidate his property before final judgment is rendered. To properly effect an **attachment**, the plaintiff must first file suit and post a bond in an amount fixed by a judge, *Tex. Rev. Civ. Stat., Art 279*. When the suit has been fully prosecuted and a final judgment has been rendered, the writ of attachment is no longer effected, and it is replaced by a judgment lien when the abstract of judgment is filed.

## Mechanics' and Materialmen's Liens

**Mechanics' and materialmen's liens** (more commonly called **M and M liens**) were created by the legislature to protect the **mechanic** or **materialman** in the event of nonpayment of funds due him for material or labors he supplied to improve or demolish real property. Except for homestead property (which requires a written contract), virtually anyone who furnishes labor or materials pursuant to an agreement for construction of improvements on real property can claim the benefit of this statutory lien, *V.T.C.A., Property Code, §53.021*. The benefits of the statute do not extend to the claimant unless there has been some visible, on the ground, labor performed or materials delivered. To eliminate confusion, Texas law now provides that an original contractor and owner can file an affidavit of commencement with the county clerk not later than the 30th day after the date of actual commencement of structural improvements or delivery of materials to the land. This creates a presumption for the date the lien arises, *V.T.C.A., Property Code, §53.124*.

In addition to contractors, the statute also applies to engineers, architects, and surveyors, so long as their work product is incorporated into the improvements placed on the property. The liens must be perfected in the manner prescribed by law and are strictly construed, although "substantial compliance" may be enough to allow enforcement. *T.D. Industries, Inc.* v. *NCNB National Bank*, 837 S.W.2d 270 (Tex. App.—Eastland, 1992, writ den.).

The procedure for recording the liens is specifically described by statute, *V.T.C.A., Property Code, §53.051*. The **original contractor** (one who has a direct contractual relationship with the owner) or a **subcontractor** (one who has a direct contractual relationship with the original contractor) files a lien affidavit. The lien claimant must send one copy of the affidavit by registered or certified mail to the owner (or to the original contractor, if a subcontractor is filing) not later than the 10th business day after the date of filing the affidavit in the public records or after the date the affidavit is required to be filed, whichever is earlier, *V.T.C.A., Property Code, §53.055*. The M and M lien (including those liens of engineers, architects, and surveyors) takes inception from the time that labor or materials are furnished to the job, so the lien arises and is valid *before* the lien is filed for record. The prudent lien claimant, however, should "perfect" that lien interest by recording it in the county courthouse in the manner prescribed by law. The lien attaches to *all* of the property of the owner on which the work was performed, not just the portion on which the work was performed. *Valdez* v. *Diamond Shamrock*, 842 S.W.2d 273 (Tex. 1992).

**Special Homestead Requirements.** A lien affidavit relating to a homestead must contain the notice at the top of each page in 10-point boldface type as follows:

### NOTICE: THIS IS NOT A LIEN.
### THIS IS ONLY AN AFFIDAVIT CLAIMING A LIEN.

This notice must be at the top of each page of the lien.

The notice required to be given to the owner by the subcontractor must contain a statement that the owner's property may be subject to a lien if he fails to withhold sufficient money from the payment to the contractor, or fails to retain 10% of the contract price or 10% of the value of the work performed by the contractor.

**Original Contractors' Liens.** If there is an original contractor who wishes to perfect a lien, he must do so by filing an affidavit with the county clerk not later than the 15th day of the fourth calendar month after the date on which the indebtedness accrues. Indebtedness accrues to the original contractor on the last day of the month in which the written declaration by the original contractor or the owner is received by the other party to the original contract, stating that the original contract has been terminated, completed, finally settled, or abandoned. The indebtedness to a derivative claimant accrues on the last day of the last month in which labor was performed or the material furnished. Please note that this is different from the definition given to the original contractor. He must additionally send two copies of the affidavit to the owner by certified mail. The affidavit must be substantially in the same form as provided by statute, *V.T.C.A., Property Code, §53.054*, and must contain the following:

1. A sworn statement of the contractor's claim, including the amount; a copy of the written agreement or contract, if any, may be attached.

2. The name of the owner or reputed owner, if known.

3. A general statement of the kind of work done or materials furnished.

4. The name of the person by whom the contractor was employed or to whom he furnished the materials or labor.

5. The name of the original contractor.

6. A description of the property to be charged with the liens legally sufficient for identification (an adequate legal description).

It should be noted that there are two important facts concerning the original contractor's perfecting his lien: (1) there is no advance notice required to be given to the owner of the property before the affidavit is filed; and (2) the lien, as far as money accrued is concerned, is considered to relate back to the date of inception, which is the day that materials were delivered or labor was first performed on the project. This protects the contractor and ensures that he gets paid the full amount for labor and materials used in constructing improvements on the property. This doctrine of the lien arising as of the time of inception is referred to as the **Relation Back Doctrine**. However, it should not be confused with the Relation Back Doctrine referred to when speaking of escrow accounts.

**Subcontractors' Liens.** A **subcontractor** is defined by statute as a person, firm, or corporation who has furnished labor or materials to fulfill an obligation to an original contractor, or another subcontractor, to perform all or part of work required by an original contractor. These include suppliers, artisans, and materialmen.

Before discussing the legal requirements for perfecting a lien by a derivative claimant, it is important to understand that such liens are rather technical, but for a special reason; that is, there is no original contract between the subcontractor and the owner of the property. In a normal situation, the owner of the property contracts with an original contractor, who in turn employs the subcontractors. Therefore, there is no **privity of contract** (direct contractual relationship) between the owner and subcontractor. Since the subcontractor has the ability to cloud the title to the owner's property, he is held to a high degree of care in perfecting his claim to a lien on that property.

For a subcontractor to perfect his lien he must, in addition to the notice of lien required as to lien claimants generally (§53.055), also give the required notice to the owner in order to secure his lien as provided by statute under Section 53.056 of the Property Code. (Remember that the original contractor is not required by statute to give notice prior to filing his lien.) The statute provides for three different types of notices from the subcontractor.

*Notice—retainage* According to the conditions under which the work was performed, notice under §53.057 of the Property Code provides that if an agreement for a **retainage** (escrowed funds) exists between the claimant and the original contractor, or between the claimant and any other subcontractor, the derivative claimant may give written notice to the owner of his right to perfect a lien. The notice must be given not later than the 15th day of the second month following delivery of materials or the performance of labor by the claimant. A copy of the notice must also be given to the original contractor. The notices must be sent by certified or registered mail, properly addressed to the owner and to the original contractor. The notice must state the amount to be retained and indicate the nature of the retainage agreement. This type of notice does not impound any funds and only serves as a proceeding to collect against a bond or retainage agreement, if such agreement is in full force and effect and funds have not been disbursed out of the retainage or bond funds to another claimant. This is not considered one of the more protective provisions of notices required by the statute.

*Notice—withholding funds* A notice under §53.056 of the Property Code, on the other hand, is generally considered to be one of the most protective for the subcontractor because it has the effect of impounding funds that are in the hands of owners and are owing to the original contractor. Normally, when this happens, the owner will withhold any funds from the original contractor until he is sure that the subcontractor has been paid. It is not uncommon for an owner to make the check payable to both the original contractor and the subcontractor to be sure that both parties are aware that payment has been made by the owner and that the funds have been properly distributed. When making a check out jointly, the owner is at least assured that the proper funds have been paid, and if the subcontractor does not get his share of those funds, it was not due to the owner's negligence or lack of diligence.

To authorize the owner to withhold funds, the notice to the owner must state that if the bill remains unpaid, the owner may be personally liable and his property may be subjected to a lien unless he withholds payment from the contractor for the payment of such statement or unless the bill is otherwise paid or settled. *Brown* v. *Dorsett Bros. Concrete Supply, Inc.*, 705 S.W.2d 765 (Tex. Civ. App.—Houston, 1986). If there is a debt incurred by a subcontractor, the claimant must give the original contractor written notice of the unpaid balance not later than the 15th day of the second month following each month in which all or a part of the claimant's labor was performed or material delivered. Thereafter the claimant must give the same notice to the owner and the original contractor (again) not later than the 15th day of the third month following each month in which all or a part of the claimant's labor was performed or materials delivered. This notice is an absolute requirement to authorize the owner to retain funds. *Trinity Universal Ins. Co.* v. *Palmer*, 412 S.W.2d 691 (Tex. Civ. App.—San Antonio, 1967). The notice must also be given to the original contractor not later than the 15th day of the third month following each month in which the claimant's labor was performed or materials delivered. These notices to the contractor must be given each and every month that work is performed or materials are delivered and the derivative claimant is not paid.

There is an additional problem for the subcontractor, in that if he waits too long after the work was performed before he sends his notice, all funds could have already been distributed to the original contractor upon completion of the work. In this case, it may be too late to trap any substantial amount of funds to assure the derivative claimant of payment. Therefore, it is sometimes common practice for a subcontractor to file his notice automatically at the end of the month, to be sure to protect his interest and to impound any funds that may be available before distribution to the original contractor. This sometimes serves to put the owner on notice that the lien may exist in the event of nonpayment. Of course, the owner does not know the terms of the contract between the original contractor and subcontractor, and the subcontractor may be sending the notice without any right to do so. However, its use normally only serves to effect proper notice to the owner, as required by statute, and does not serve to cloud the title to the property.

*Notice—fabricated items* A notice under §53.058 of the Property Code is used when the derivative claimant's claim is for a specially fabricated item. The notice must also be given to the owner not later than the 15th day of the second month after the month in which the claimant receives and accepts the order for such specially fabricated material. This notice must be sent by certified or registered mail addressed to the owner, and to the original contractor where required. It does not provide for impoundment of funds and must be followed by a notice under §53.056 of the Property Code to perfect the lien after the material has been delivered to the job.

In addition to the foregoing notices, the subcontractor must also file an affidavit pursuant to the same requirements that the original contractor must file (not later than the 15th day of the fourth calendar month after the day on which the indebtedness accrues). If there is a debt incurred by a subcontractor, the claimant must give the original contractor written notice of the unpaid balance not later than the 15th day of the second month following each month in which all or a part of the claimant's labor was performed or materials delivered. Thereafter the claimant must give the same notice to the owner and the original contractor (again) not later than the 15th day of the third month following each month in which all or a part of the claimant's labor was performed or materials delivered. Two copies of the affidavit are sent to the owner, and the lien must be filed in the lien records of the county courthouse.

It is fairly well settled in Texas that if the owner disburses all of his funds to the contractor before receiving the required notice of any materialmen's claim, his liability is limited such that the maximum amount of lien that can be claimed by the subcontractor or materialman is: (1) the amount required to be retained under the retainage statute (discussed next); plus (2) any additional amount the materialman might be entitled to that was paid to the contractor after the owner received statutory notice and warning to retain funds owing to the contractor. *McKalip* v. *Smith Building and Masonry Supply, Inc.*, 599 S.W.2d 884 (Tex. Civ. App.—Waco, 1980).

**Statutory Retainage.** An often overlooked area of mechanics' and materialmen's liens is the statute that provides for the claimant's fund with preference to mechanics and artisans, *V.A.T.S., Property Code, §53.102*. The purpose of this statute is to create a special fund for the benefit of mechanics and artisans, and to grant them a preference over materialmen and subcontractors. The statute basically provides that it is the duty of the owner, or his agent, to retain in his hands, during the progress of work and for 30 days after the work is completed, 10% of the contract price of such work (or 10% of the value of same) for each original contract. It applies only to the original contract, not a new, subsequent contract when the first one has been terminated. *Page* v. *Structural Wood Components, Inc.*, 102 S.W.3d 720 (Tex. 2003). This secures the payment of artisans and mechanics who perform labor and services and also secures the payment of any other claimant furnishing material, material and labor, or specially fabricated material for any contractor, subcontractor, agent, or receiver.

All persons who send notice as required by the mechanics' and materialmen's lien statute shall have a lien upon that retained fund with preference given to artisans and mechanics. Remember, though, that the statute now requires claims be filed by the 15th day of the second month following the delivery of materials. This may be later than the 30th day after completion. The claimants share ratably to the extent of their claims, so there is a good chance that a claimant may only get a small proportional part of the money due him. However, he will have a preference claim to the funds remaining if he files his claim within 30 days. After the artisans and mechanics are paid, the remainder of the fund, if any, goes to the other participating claimants, also ratably shared.

The statute further states that if the owner fails to comply with this statutory provision, he shall be liable for the liens, at least to the extent of the 10%, implying that there might be unlimited liability on the part of the owner for failing to keep this statutory 10% **retainage**. There have been quite a number of cases that support the artisan's claim to the statutory retainage, implying that the owner may have an unlimited liability, *Hayek* v. *Western Steel Co.*, 478 S.W.2d 786 (Tex. 1972), and, further, that if the statutory retainage is not properly kept, the 30-day period for claiming liens is not applicable as a limitation time for lien claimants. *General Air Conditioning Co.* v. *Third Ward Church of Christ*, 426 S.W.2d 541 (Tex. 1968).

**Affidavit of Completion.** The owner may, if he so chooses, file an **affidavit** of completion with the county clerk of the county in which the property is located. The notice must contain the address of the owner, the name of the original contractor, a description of the property, a description of the improvements, and the date of completion in a conspicuous statement that the claimant may not have a lien on the retained funds unless the claimant files the lien affidavit not later than the 30th day after completion. A copy of the affidavit must be sent by certified mail to the original contractor not later than the 10th day after the date the affidavit is filed and to each claimant who has sent a notice of lien to the owner not later than the 10th day after the owner receives the notice of the lien, *V.T.C.A., Property Code, §53.106.*

**Prompt Payment to Contractors or Subcontractors.** The 1993 legislature gave additional protection to the contractor by requiring prompt payment for properly performed work or soon-to-be-stored materials. Under this new statutory provision, the owners are required to pay the amount stated in the written payment request to the contractor, less any statutory offsets (retainage) not later than the 45th day after the owner receives the request for payment. The contractor or subcontractor, then, is required to make payment to other subcontractors not later than the seventh day after the date the contractor or subcontractor receives payment.

The statute has two exceptions. If a good faith dispute exists concerning the amount owed for the payment, the owner may withhold from the payment not more than 110% of the difference between the amount the contractor claims is due and the amount the owner claims is due. The other exception relates to bank funds. Once the owner has properly requested bank funds, but the bank fails to disburse, the owner is in compliance with the statute so long as he disburses the funds not later than the fifth day after the owner receives the loan proceeds. This gets complicated, doesn't it?

**Bonds to Pay Liens or Claims.** The foregoing requirements for statutory retainage may be waived if a proper **bond** is filed by any person to ensure payment to the subcontractors, materialmen, and other claimants. There are a number of requirements to perfect the bond, but they can basically be broken down as follows:

1. A written contract exists between the owner and the original contractor.
2. The contractor must have furnished a bond in favor of the owner in a penal sum of not less than the total of the original contract amount executed by the original contractor and a corporate surety.
3. The bond must have the written approval of the owner.
4. The bond must be filed with a written contract between the owner and the original contractor with the county clerk of the county wherein the owner's property on which the construction or repairs are being performed is situated.

Any bond issued must be executed by a corporate surety authorized and admitted to do business under the laws of Texas *and* must be licensed to execute such bonds under Texas law. After the bond has been filed, a claim by a subcontractor or materialman against the owner can be perfected by the provisions of the M and M lien statutes, or by giving notice to the corporate surety in lieu of the owner of the property. If a claim still remains unpaid for 60 days after the notice is given to the surety, a claimant may file suit against the surety in the county where the bond and contract were filed for the amount of his claim and court costs.

If the foregoing bond requirements have been met, the statute specifically provides that no causes of action can be filed against the owner or the property. Any subsequent purchaser can rely upon the record of such bond or contract on file in the county courthouse as proof that all claims and liens have been paid, *V.T.C.A., Property Code, §53.204.*

**Construction Trust Funds.** In a further effort to protect the contractor and other lien claimants, additional statutory provisions provide that all monies or funds paid to a contractor or subcontractor under a construction contract are considered to be **construction trust funds** for the benefit of the contractors or derivative claimants who may labor or furnish labor for construction or repair of any improvement of any real property. This statute effectively makes any officer of a contractor or subcontractor a trustee for all funds to be paid to the subcontractors and imposes upon them the responsibility to see that the claimants are paid. *Nuclear Corp. of America* v. *Hale*, 355 F. Supp. 193 (N.D. Tex. 1973). If a contractor or subcontractor misapplies any of these trust funds, he may be fined and sentenced to prison in the Department of Corrections for a period not exceeding 10 years.

The statute provides additional protection in that federal tax liens and other claims are not subject to levy by execution or attachment by third-party creditors. *Owens* v. *Drywall & Acoustical Supply Corp.*, 325 F. Supp. 397 (S.D. Tex. 1971).

**Mechanics' and Materialmen's Lien Priorities—Severable Improvements.** With the foregoing statutory mechanics' and materialmen's lien provisions, both for notice and affidavits, along with the statutory retainage provision, one would normally think that the mechanic and materialman, particularly the artisan and laborer, would be well protected under Texas law. However, this is not necessarily the case. Owners who have to keep the statutory retainage are often corporations with little or no assets. These owners may be construction companies, or developers' subsidiaries, and claims for damages against them may be difficult to recover. This problem is compounded by the fact that the subcontractors or contractors do not have to file their claims for 90 days or 120 days, respectively, so these claims for liens may be too late to be constructive notice to a subsequent purchaser for value. Therefore, the law puts a high duty of care on the contractor, subcontractor, and mechanic and materialman in perfecting their interest.

In an effort to protect the mechanic's and materialman's interest, the courts have liberally construed the statutes so as to protect them when possible. Starting with one of the oldest landmark cases in Texas, *Oriental Hotel Co.* v. *Griffiths*, 33 S.W.2d 652 (Tex. 1896), the courts have consistently held that the lien, regardless of when filed, relates back to the date of inception, that is, the date that any work was done or materials were brought to the premises, so that the mechanic's and materialman's claim would be prior in time to anything brought subsequently. Derivative claimants take the same inception date as that of the general contractor.

The mechanics' and materialmen's lien is also superior to a prior recorded deed of trust lien, where the improvements can be removed without material injury to the land and preexisting improvements. *First National Bank of Dallas v. Whirlpool Corp.*, supra; *Exchange Savings & Loan Association* v. *Monocrete Pty., Ltd.*, 629 S.W.2d 34 (Tex. 1982). It is interesting to note that there have been a number of cases that distinguish what can be removed without material injury to the building (these improvements are termed **severable improvements**). Severable improvements have been held to include a ticket booth, a speaker stand and a screen at a drive-in theatre, a partially completed structure attached to a concrete foundation and frame building, garbage disposals, built-in dishwashers, heating and air-conditioning systems, carpets, burglar alarms, smoke detectors, light fixtures, door locks, and compressors and air-handling units inside of air-conditioning units. In one Texas case, a court also held that windows and doors can be removed and foreclosed upon separately if they can be removed with no ultimate damage to the land or preexisting improvements. *First Cont. Real Estate Inv. Trust* v. *Continental Steel Co.*, 569 S.W.2d 42 (Tex. Civ. App.—Ft. Worth, 1978). Nonseverable improvements have included a house, roofing, fireplace, brick veneer, chimney, painting and plastering, roof repairs, and cabinets. There will probably be much litigation in the future to determine what other improvements could be construed as being severable.

One may recall that there is also a specified priority interest for fixture filings under UCC security interests (see Chapter 6, Fixtures and Easements). There have been a number of concerns over the priority of the mechanics and materialmen versus that of the supplier of the fixture. There is some authority that the mechanics' and materialmen's lien does have priority over a conflicting UCC security interest. *Justice Mortgage Investors* v. *C. B. Thompson Constr. Co.*, 533 S.W.2d 939 (Tex. Civ. App.—Amarillo, 1976). There is some conflicting authority, however, over whether or not a contractor can remove an item he did not supply. In one case, it was determined that the contractor must identify the materials as having been furnished by him in order to remove them from the premises. *Kasper* v. *Cockrell-Riggens Lighting Co.*, 511 S.W.2d 109 (Tex. Civ. App.—Eastland, 1974).

This doctrine of mechanics' and materialmen's lien priority, plus the concept of severable improvements, is virtually absolute except in a circumstance where the interim lender (the bank) may have a deed of trust that specifies a prior lien for money advanced to the general contractor (future advance clause). If such a mortgage is filed before the materialman begins delivery of his materials, that deed of trust lien is prior to the materialman's lien with respect to the advances made, with notice, actual or constructive, of the materialman's lien. *Coke Lumber & Mfg. Co.* v. *First National Bank in Dallas*, 529 S.W.2d 612 (Tex. Civ. App.—Dallas, 1975). The doctrine favoring the interim lender is fairly limited and is construed according to the covenants contained in the deed of trust instrument with respect to future advances.

In addition to the foregoing, it should be pointed out that mechanics and materialmen are also protected by the attorney's fees statute, *Tex. Rev. Civ. Stat. Ann., Art. 2226*. This statute entitles the lien holder to attorney's fees in the event he is forced to hire legal counsel to represent him in pursuing a cause of action for payment of his services.

**Statute of Limitations.** Except as provided under residential construction liens (discussed next), a contractor or subcontractor must bring a suit to foreclose his lien within **two years** after the date of the filed lien affidavit or within one year after completion of the work under the original contract on which the lien is claimed, whichever is later, *V.A.T.S., Property Code, §53.052*. Under the residential construction contracts, the statute of limitations has been shortened to **one year**.

**Residential Construction Liens.** The mechanics' and materialmen's lien laws have always been confusing, and the loser was often the homeowner who couldn't understand the details and complexities of these statutes. A major lobbying effort in the 1997 legislature resulted in a number of pro-consumer statutes that will, hopefully, benefit homeowners:

1.  Before a residential construction contract (defined as a contract for construction or repair of a new or existing residence) is executed by the owner, the original contractor must deliver to the owner a disclosure statement (roughly three pages long) that informs the consumer of his rights under the mechanics' and materialmen's lien statutes. See Sec. 53.255.

2.  For the construction of improvements under a residential construction contract, the original contractor must attach to the disclosure statement set out above, or furnish to the owner before the commencement of construction a written list that identifies by name, address, and telephone number each subcontractor and supplier that the contractor intends to use in the work to be performed. The contractor must provide the owner with an updated list of subcontractors and suppliers not later than the 15th day after the day the subcontractor or supplier is added or deleted from the list. The owner can waive their right to receive the list of subcontractors and suppliers. The waiver must be in writing and must be conspicuously printed in at least 10 point bold-faced type. See Sec. 53.256.

3.  If the owner is obtaining third-party financing for the construction of improvements under a residential construction contract, the lender is required to deliver to the owners all documentation relating to the closing of the loan not later than one business day before the date of the closing. There are exceptions for this requirement for (1) a "bona fide" emergency, or (2) "another good cause," provided that the lender obtains the written consent of the owner. At the closing the lender also has to provide the same disclosure statement discussed in 1 above. See Sec. 53.257.

4.  The original contractor must then provide to the owner a signed periodic statement that lists the bills or expenses that the original contractor represents will be paid, or that have been paid, and for which the original contractor is requesting payment. If the owner finances the construction of improvements through a third party that advances proceeds directly to the original contractor, the lender must obtain the signed periodic statements from the original contractor and provide to the owner a statement of funds disbursed by the lender since the last statement was provided to the owner. The lender is not responsible for the accuracy of the information contained in the disbursement statement obtained from the original contractor. See Sec. 53.258.

5.  As a condition of final payment under a residential construction contract, the original contractor shall, at the time the final payment is tendered, execute and deliver to the owner an affidavit stating that the original contractor has paid each person in full for all labor and materials used in the construction of improvements on the real property. A lender or contractor who doesn't comply with the lien affidavit requirements, bills paid affidavit requirements, disclosure statements, or final bills paid affidavits requirements is subject to a fine of up to $4,000 or confinement in jail for a term not to exceed one year, or both, and the contractor is personally liable, and cannot hide behind a corporation or partnership status.

In addition, a contractor may not require an owner of real property to convey the real property to the contractor, or an entity controlled by the original contract, as the condition for the performance of residential construction contracts for improvements for the real property. See Sec. 53.260.

Lien rights also changed. The original contractor must file the lien affidavit by the 15th day of the **third** calendar month, and a copy of the affidavit must be sent to the owner **one business day** after the affidavit is filed with the county clerk. Similarly, subcontractor's notice provisions have been shortened. The notice under residential construction contracts must be given by the 15th day of the **second** month following each month in which labor was performed or material delivered.

Other new amendments to the Texas Property Code to help consumers were made in 1997. The law now provides that, in a "cost plus a fee" construction contract entered into before the commencement of construction, the fee paid to the contractor is not considered trust funds. See Sec. 162.001(c).

New laws also require that a contractor on a residential homestead construction project of more than $5,000 deposit trust funds received from the owner into an escrow account at a financial institution (that must be referred to on the statement as a "construction account"). The contractor is required to maintain certain information regarding the construction escrow account, including source and amount of funds and deposits; date and amount of disbursements, and to whom; current balance; a breakdown of "direct costs" (costs that are specific to the construction of the improvements) and "indirect costs" (costs included under a construction contract that are not specific to the construction of the improvements); and to retain invoices and other supporting documentation relating to disbursements. See Sec. 162.006–.007. Failure to establish or maintain a construction account, including the record-keeping requirements, constitutes at least a Class A misdemeanor and perhaps a third-degree felony (e.g., the contractor also retains, uses, disburses, or diverts trust funds of $500 or more). See Sec. 162.032.

The notice provisions have also been shortened; if a subcontractor is not paid, he must give notice by the 15th day of the second month following each month in which all or part of the claims labor was performed or materials or especially fabricated materials were delivered. This alerts the homeowner at least two months sooner than the notice provisions for other liens, discussed earlier in this chapter.

## The Texas Residential Construction Commission Act

The 2003 Legislature enacted a sweeping statutory changes regarding residential construction. This legislation creates the Texas Residential Construction Commission composed of 9 members appointed by the Governor (consisting of 4 homebuilders, 3 public members, one engineer, one architect and one architect or residential inspector). The commission has six primary responsibilities: (1) register home-builders, in order to keep track of undisciplined homebuilding; (2) oversee a state sponsored home defect inspection process; (3) prepare and adopt building performance standards; (4) oversee three task force groups (mold, arbitration, and rain harvesting); (5) provide a voluntary certification program for arbitrators; and (6) provide for a filing of arbitration awards.

The new commission and the new building performance standards also mandates a method of resolving construction disputes. The homeowner or building can file a claim with the commission and any pending lawsuit is abated. The commission then assigns a state-approved inspector to inspect the alleged defect and determine whether the construction complies with the conditions building performance standards. The builder can offer to repair the defect as provided under the Residential Construction Liability Act. If the homeowner refuses the offer and elects to proceed with the suit, the homeowner has the burden of overcoming the inspector's determination.

All builders will be registered with this new commission, and be subject to its disciplinary authority. The statute also provides a mechanism for an agreement between the builder and homeowner for the terms by which a builder may voluntarily decide to buy back a home.

This legislation, by its terms, replaces any implied warranty of good workmanlike construction with a limited statutory warranty and statutory warranty of habitability. It seems the litigation in this area of the law has just begun.

## Fraudulent Lien Claims

Recently, some wayward members of society have fraudulently filed liens, delivered legal-looking court papers alleging service in a nonexistent court proceeding, and passed bad (although official-looking) warrants and checks in real estate transactions. To put it bluntly, some sought to create confusion and chaos in the existing systems of recording, closing, and purchasing real estate.

Section 12.003 of the Civil Practices and Remedies Code, referred to informally as the "Republic of Texas" bill, provides civil remedies against those who have made fraudulent filings, including the filing of fraudulent judgment liens issued by so-called "common-law courts," and fraudulent documents purporting to create liens or claims on the personal and real property with the Secretary of State and many county and district clerks throughout the state. In addition, amendments to other statutes (not the Property Code) provide for criminal sanctions to be levied against those who seek to file such fraudulent claims. The Penal Code was also amended, making it an offense to file a fraudulent court document or record, to exercise a function of a public office that has no lawful existence, to cause or induce a public servant to record a fraudulent court document, to deliver or cause to be delivered a document that simulates legal process, and to refuse to execute a release of a fraudulent instrument purporting to create a lien or claim.

The offenses range from a Class C misdemeanor to a first-degree felony depending on the value of the property, service, or pecuniary interest. The statutes also make it a violation of the organized crime provisions of the Penal Code to exercise as a function of a public office that has no lawful existence and create an expedited judicial process that permits someone aggrieved by a fraudulent filing to obtain a court order declaring the filing to be fraudulent. The law also creates a private cause of action against a person who files fraudulent judgment liens or fraudulent documents purporting to create a lien or claim against real or personal property in favor of a person aggrieved by the filing or an attorney representing the state, county, or municipality.

## The Broker's and Appraiser's Lien on Commercial Real Estate Act

The 1999 Legislature enabled real estate brokers and appraisers to put liens on real estate for commissions due. It applies to most commercial real estate transactions, but it specifically does not apply to:

1. A transaction involving a claim for a commission of less than $2,500.00 or
2. A transaction involving a claim for a commission of $5,000.00 or less if the commercial real estate:

   (a) Is the principal place of business of the record title owner.
   (b) Is occupied by more than one and few than five tenants.

(c)  Is improved with 7500 square feet or less of total gross building area.

The statute defines "commercial real estate" as:

(a)  All real estate except real estate improved with one to four residential units.

(b)  A single family residential unit including a condominium or townhouse.

(c)  Real estate that includes the person's homestead.

(d)  Real estate that is not improved with a structure and is (i) zoned for single family residential use, or (ii) restricted for single family use under restrictive covenants that will remain in effect for at least the next two years.

(e)  Real estate that (i) is primarily used for farming and ranching purposes, (ii) will continue to be used primarily for farming and ranching purposes, and (iii) is located more than three miles from the corporate boundaries of any municipality.

In general terms, the lien statute applies to only commercial real estate, not residential or agricultural real estate. See Property Code §62.002.

A critical issue, and one of extensive litigation, is when the commission is earned. The statute provides that a commission is earned on the *earlier* of the date that: (i) the date defined under the Commission Agreement; or (ii) the person obligated to pay the commission enters into a purchase contract or lease during the period prescribed by the commission agreement. In commercial lease transactions, the statute provides that when a broker has earned a commission under a commission agreement relating to a lease transaction, and the commission agreement provides that the broker may receive an additional commission when the lease is modified to expand the lease space or renewed, the additional commission is earned: (i) when the broker performs all the defined services related in the commission agreement, or (ii) when the broker first earned a commission under the commission agreement if the commission agreement does not specifically require the broker to perform additional services (it relates back to the original commission payment date). The commission is apparently earned when the initial services are performed, but not payable until the later date when the lease is renewed or extended. See Property Code §62.004.

**Filing the Lien.** The broker has a lien on the commercial real estate interest of a seller, or lessor, if the broker has earned the commission and the notice of lien is filed and recorded in the county clerk's office in the county in which the commercial real estate is located. The lien is available only to the broker named in the commission agreement (not to an employee or independent contractor of the broker) and must be disclosed in the commission agreement. **So a commercial broker, wanting to pursue the lien claim, must make sure the lien right is clearly stated in the commission agreement**.

The broker's lien cannot be waived in a sales transaction. It will be automatically waived if the commission is earned in a lease transaction and the commission agreement is included as a provision in the lease agreement.

QUERY: If the lien right is not contained in the employment agreement, isn't it effectively waived?

**The Lien Document.** The Notice of Lien must be signed by the broker by a person authorized to sign on behalf of the broker and must contain the following:

1.  A sworn statement of the nature and amount of the claim, including:

   (a)  The commission amount or the formula used to determine the commission.

   (b)  The type of commission at issue, including a deferred commission.

(c) The month and year in which the commission was earned.

2. The name of the broker and real estate license number of the broker.

3. The names reflected on the broker's records of any person who the broker believes is obligated to pay the commission under the Commission Agreement.

4. The name reflected in the broker's records of any person the broker believes to be the owner of the commercial real estate interest on which the lien is claimed.

5. A description legally sufficient for identification of the commercial real estate interest sought to be charged with the lien.

6. The name of any cooperating broker or principal in the transaction with whom the broker intends to share the commission and the dollar or percentage amount to be shared.

7. A copy of the commission agreement in which the lien is based.

After the broker files the lien, the broker must mail a copy of the notice of lien by certified mail, return receipt requested, or registered mail, to the owner of record of the commercial real estate on which the lien is claimed, or the owner's authorized agent, and the perspective buyer or tenant, and any escrow agent named in the contract for the sale or lease of the commercial real estate interest in which the lien is claimed. The notice is deemed sent when deposited into the United States Mail, postage prepaid, and addressed to the persons entitled to receive the notice.

**Lien Priority.** A recorded lien, mortgage, or other encumbrance on commercial real estate including a recorded lien securing a revolving credit and future advances for a loan recorded before the date the broker's lien is recorded has priority over the broker's lien. Basically, the "barber shop rule" (first in time, first in right) still applies. There are two exceptions: (1) A purchase money mortgage lien executed by the buyer of the commercial real estate has priority over the broker's lien, as does (2) a mechanic's lien that is recorded after a broker's lien but relates back to the date before the broker's lien is recorded (similar to other mechanic's liens priorities). If requested, the broker must execute and acknowledge a subordination agreement of the above-referenced liens before a notary public not later than the 7th day after the date the broker receives the subordination agreement.

The broker's lien is extinguished if the property is zoned single-family use or restricted for single-family use within 360 days after the broker's commission is payable, and those zoning ordinances or restrictive covenants are in effect until at least the second anniversary of the date the commission is payable.

**Time for Filing the Lien.** If representing the seller, the lien must be filed after the commission is earned and before the conveyance of the commercial real estate interest. If representing the buyer, the lien must be filed after the buyer acquires legal title to the commercial real estate interest and before the buyer conveys that commercial real estate interest. If it is a lease transaction, the broker must record the notice of lien after the commission is earned and the *earlier* of: (i) the 91st day after the date the event in which the commission becomes payable, or (ii) the date the person obligated to pay the commission records a subsequent conveyance of that person's commercial real estate after executing the lease agreement.

If the notice of lien is not filed within the time required, the lien is **void**.

**Suit to Foreclose the Lien.** The broker can bring a suit to foreclose lien in any district court in the county in which the commercial real estate is located, which suit must be filed on or before the second anniversary of the date the notice of lien is recorded. If it is a deferred commission, the suit must be filed before the second anniversary date on which the commission is payable or the 10th anniversary of the date the lien is recorded, or the 10th anniversary date the broker records a subsequent notice of the lien as a renewal of the broker's right to the lien, whichever date is later.

As an alternative, the broker claiming the lien must bring suit to foreclose the lien not later than the 30th day after the date the broker receives a written demand to bring a suit to foreclose the lien. If the suit to foreclose the lien is not brought within the above-referenced time periods, the lien is **void**.

QUERY: Can the landowner demand that the broker sue within 30 days, or the lien the void?

**Release of Lien.** A broker's lien is discharged only by:

1. a court order discharging the lien.
2. paying the broker the commission named in the Commission Agreement.
3. establishing an escrow account in which an escrow agent can deposit amounts sufficient to satisfy the lien, plus 15% of that amount.

The escrow account will be maintained by the escrow agent until the matter is resolved, the lien is no longer enforceable, or the funds are interplead into the district court in the county in which the commercial real estate is located.

**Broker Liability.** The new statute also gives the court the right to discharge the broker's lien if the broker fails to timely comply with any of the provisions of the statute. It additionally awards the owner or tenant damages (actual damage, including attorney's fees and court costs) and can additionally award a civil penalty in an amount not to exceed three times the amount of the commission claimed. Not much help against an insolvent broker, however.

Nothing in the statute prevents a person from filing a complaint with the Texas Real Estate Commission, nor prevents the Texas Real Estate Commission's investigation or disciplinary proceedings.

This is a complicated statute. While potentially protecting the broker's interest, it does create liability if the terms of the statute are not strictly adhered to.

## Other Statutory Liens

The foregoing statutory liens are the most common liens one will encounter. There are other liens, however, which are statutory and may have a very high priority but are seldom encountered. One of these is a lien created by the relocation or replacement of sewer lines. It has the same priority as an assessment for paving or ad valorem taxes, *Tex. Rev. Civ. Stat. Ann., Art. 1110g*. Street improvements also have a very high priority, and their lien relates back to the original notice of impending sewer or paving work and shall be a "first and prior lien thereon from the date the improvements are ordered," *Tex. Rev. Civ. Stat. Ann., Art. 1105b*.

Another lien, commonly referred to in Texas as the "weed-cutting" lien, is considered by statute to be "privileged" and subject only to the tax liens and liens for street improvements, *Tex. Rev. Civ. Stat. Ann., Art. 4436*. As a practical matter, all three of these liens are established by the city, and although they are not construed to be "taxes" that enable them to be foreclosed against a homestead, they eventually must be paid. In any event, since the ad valorem taxes are the prior lien, the city is always in a good position to enforce these liens. Priority of these liens is always a problem. In one case a city passed a hotel occupancy tax, which was passed after the filing of the first lien deed of trust. When the first lien holder foreclosed, he alleged that there was no obligation to pay the tax because it was not imposed until after the mortgaged lien had been perfected. The law, however, can be harsh. A city's constitutionally granted power to levy, assess, and collect taxes, as well as the specific legislative authorization granted the city to levy and collect taxes, preempts any other document lien priority. *City of Amarillo* v. *Ray Berney Enterprises, Inc.*, 764 S.W.2d 861 (Tex. App.—Amarillo, 1979).

Even the State of Texas establishes superpriorities. The Texas Workforce Commission can file a Wage Lien on property which is a special labor law administrative lien, *V.T.C.A., Texas Labor Code,* § 61.0825.

One federal lien, filed in the local county records, has recently become an issue. The **Superfund Amendment and Reauthorization Act of 1986** is a federal law that creates a lien in favor of the United States upon property subject to or affected by hazardous substance removal or remedial action by the superfund statute. The superfund amendments and hazardous waste disposal are discussed in greater detail in Chapter 20, Regulation of Real Estate.

# Constitutional Liens

The Texas Constitution provides for an automatic **constitutional lien** under Article 16, Section 37, as another means of protecting the mechanic, materialman, and artisan. This type of lien is available only to an **original contractor** (one who is in direct contractual relationship with the owner), but it does apply to all mechanics, artisans, and materialmen, and those who furnish labor and materials for the erection and repair of a building.

The lien becomes effective automatically, although it is subordinate to the homestead exemption provided by Article 16, Section 50, of the Texas Constitution. *Moray Corp.* v. *Griggs*, supra. This lien becomes effective as of the time the owner entered into the contract or at the time of first delivery of material or labor, whichever is first. However, like a vendor's lien, if it is not recorded, it would not be good against an innocent purchaser unless the contractor filed his affidavit in accordance with the mechanics' and materialmen's lien statutes. *Dee's Cabinet Shop* v. *Weber*, 562 S.W.2d 945 (Tex. Civ. App.—Ft. Worth, 1978). In this manner, a filed constitutional lien becomes a statutory lien.

The importance of a constitutional lien, of course, is that one does not have to rely on the whims and caprices of the legislature, and the lien exists regardless of whether or not one meets the filing deadlines as provided under the mechanics' and materialmen's lien statutes. Even if the lien is filed late, and not within the statutory guidelines, one still has a constitutional basis for establishing that lien as a mechanic or materialman.

# Contractual Liens

The liens discussed thus far have been those provided for by statute or by law of equity. The **contractual lien**, on the other hand, can exist simply when two parties wish to establish the lien as security for some type of obligation. Examples of contractual liens would be mortgages, in that they offer proper security for money to be loaned. Leases are also a very common source of contractual liens. Or one often finds that the tenant offers his furniture and personalty in the leased premises as security for his payment of his rental obligations under his lease. There are also provisions for statutory landlords' liens and owners' of buildings liens, which will be discussed in greater detail in the next chapter.

# Redemption

In the event of default on any secured obligation in Texas, including liens, the only right one has is to pay the obligation (full amount of the note), or buy the property at the foreclosure sale, which is generally for cash. Except for tax liens (Chapter 21) or installment land contracts (Chapter 9), *Texas law provides for no right of redemption unless specifically provided for by agreement.* As you recall from Chapter 13, debtors do have the right to "redeem up" if they are not in default and have an equity of **redemption** in the property. However, if such equity of redemption is in default, and the property is subject to foreclosure, there is no right to pay the entire indebtedness except by buying at the foreclosure sale. Recall also that the holders of federal liens also retain a right of redemption.

From a practical standpoint, the lender or lien holder normally allows the debtor to pay the obligations rather than having to go through the foreclosure procedure. However, this is not always the case. One must remember that mere lack of adequate consideration, by itself, is not enough to set aside a foreclosure sale, and that the law is that the foreclosure is proper unless there are some material irregularities in that foreclosure.

## ■ SUMMARY

A lien is a charge on the property of a person for the payment or discharge of a debt or duty owed by that person. An equitable lien is imposed by a court of jurisdiction to help prevent an unfair result; since it is not recorded, it is not valid against a subsequent purchaser or creditor without notice of the lien. Statutory liens have a significant impact in Texas. They consist of judgment liens and mechanics' and materialmen's liens. A judgment lien is a lien that is perfected by the proper party filing an abstract of judgment. This abstract of judgment can only be filed after a court of competent jurisdiction rules in favor of the creditor. Mechanics' and materialmen's liens were created by the legislature to protect mechanics or materialmen in the event of nonpayment of funds owed to them. The methods of perfecting liens are very specifically set out by statute. There are different requirements for perfecting the lien, depending on whether the contractor is a general contractor or a subcontractor. There are complicated questions of priorities when dealing with mechanics' and materialmen's liens. The ability to sever the improvements and remove them without material injury to the building is another effective method of protecting the contractor.

Constitutional liens protect the contractor and artisan. These liens have no recording requirements and become effective automatically after the work is performed on all property except homestead property. Texas has no right of redemption for defaults unless specifically provided for by an agreement.

# Landlord and Tenant Relationships

The existence of a **landlord (lessor)** and **tenant (lessee)** relationship creates a nonfreehold estate, called a **leasehold estate**. A leasehold estate is also referred to as a **tenancy**. Tenancy implies more than just a mere use of the premises because it includes occupancy and possession of the premises superior to the rights of anyone else. Even the landlord's rights are limited, both by statute and by case law. At common law, the landlord was given very high priority in determining rights between the landlord and tenant. Statutes, however, have given much greater effect to the rights of the tenant in possession of the property. In most cases, the landlord finds that his hands are tied when making an effort to remove the tenant from the premises very quickly. The tenant, if he is represented by good lawyers, often finds he can maintain his occupancy for several months before he would ever have to leave the premises. This chapter will discuss the statutory law and case law relating to landlord and tenant relationships, the law applicable to forcible entry and detainer proceedings, and some procedural court problems that arise in a normal eviction proceeding.

## Tenancies

There are four types of tenancies, leasehold estates, and **nonfreehold** estates:

1. An estate for years.
2. An estate from period to period.
3. An estate at will.
4. An estate at sufferance.

### Estate for Years

An **estate for years** has a definite termination date (it may be less than a year in length) and almost necessarily implies the existence of a lease. The Statute of Frauds (§26.01) specifically provides that a lease for real estate for a term longer than one year is not enforceable unless it is in writing and is signed by the person to be charged. One normally envisions estates for years as being long-term office leases, ground leases, or those rare instances when one may find a residential lease for longer than one year. One of the more interesting examples of an estate for years was created as a lifetime tenancy for a lessee under an oral lease. The tenant, in this case, contended that the entire estate for years was dependent on whether or not she lived for longer than one year and, therefore, was not within the Statute of Frauds. Believe it or not, this contention was upheld. *McCloud* v. *Knapp*, 507 S.W.2d 644 (Tex. Civ. App.—Dallas, 1974). The basic fundamentals of leases will be discussed later in this chapter as a separate topic.

## Estate from Period to Period

An **estate from period to period** normally includes an estate from month to month (common in apartment rentals), or an estate from year to year (common in rural leases—because of harvest year), renewable at the option of the parties. It has an indefinite duration. The estate from month to month is not normally in writing and is probably the most common form found in Texas. Unless there is a written agreement to the contrary, tenancies from month to month must have a 30-day notice before they are terminated.

## Estate at Will

An **estate at will** is an estate that is terminable at the will of either the lessor or the lessee. It has an indefinite duration. The most typical estate at will would be a share-cropper or migrant farm worker. The worker's right to occupy the premises is his "will" to work.

## Estate at Sufferance

An **estate at sufferance** is an estate that exists when a person wrongfully continues possession of the land after the termination of his right to possession. Normally, in an estate at sufferance, the tenant's right to possession is the result of the landlord's neglect or lack of diligence. The tenant, as a tenant at sufferance, has no obligation to pay rent, or any other rights under his estate at sufferance until he has utilized the services of the landlord. It is equal to having no estate at all. In Texas, a tenant in this holdover capacity is normally liable for rents during his occupancy under the same terms and conditions that he enjoyed prior to the end of his lease term and before the holdover period, and exemplary damages may also be obtained. *Williams* v. *Garnett*, 608 S.W.2d 794 (Tex. Civ. App.—Waco, 1980). An interesting question was addressed by the Texas Supreme Court in *Bockelman* v. *Maryneck*, 788 S.W.2d 569 (Tex. 1990). There were two tenants (possessing the premises as co-tenants) during the term of the lease. At the termination of the lease, only one tenant held over. The landlord sued both tenants for damages. The Texas Supreme Court held that holding over did not create a new co-tenancy and only the one holdover tenant was liable for damages. A typical tenant at sufferance would be a seller of a home that remained in possession after closing, or a tenant who lawfully entered the premises but refused to leave at lease termination.

# Statutes

As a general rule, the rights of landlord and tenant are set out either by statute or by the requirements of the lease. Since these statutes are so specific, and so important in interpreting day-to-day landlord and tenant problems, some of the more pertinent ones are reproduced here in their entirety for the student's benefit, with some additional comment as to the application of the statutes.

## General Statutes

**Chapter 91**

### Provisions Generally Applicable to Landlords and Tenants

#### §91.001. Notice for Terminating Certain Tenancies

(a) A monthly tenancy or a tenancy from month to month may be terminated by the tenant or the landlord giving notice of termination to the other.

(b) If a notice of termination is given under Subsection (a) and if the rent-paying period is at least one month, the tenancy terminates on whichever of the following days is the later:

(1) the day given in the notice for termination; or

(2) one month after the day on which the notice is given.

(c) If a notice of termination is given under Subsection (a) and if the rent-paying period is less than a month, the tenancy terminates on whichever of the following days is the later:

(1) the day given in the notice for termination; or

(2) the day following the expiration of the period beginning on the day on which notice is given and extending for a number of days equal to the number of days in the rent-paying period.

(d) If a tenancy terminates on a day that does not correspond to the beginning or end of a rent-paying period, the tenant is liable for rent only up to the date of termination.

(e) Subsections (a), (b), (c), and (d) do not apply if:

(1) a landlord and a tenant have agreed in an instrument signed by both parties on a different period of notice to terminate the tenancy or that no notice is required; or

(2) there is a breach of contract recognized by law.

Please note that the foregoing statute provides for a specified notice for terminating the tenancy, primarily in the event that there is no written agreement or lease between the landlord and tenant that provides for other terms of termination.

#### §91.004. Landlord's Breach of Lease; Lien

(a) If the landlord of a tenant who is not in default under a lease fails to comply in any respect with the lease agreement, the landlord is liable to the tenant for damages resulting from the failure.

(b) To secure payment of the damages, the tenant has a lien on the landlord's nonexempt property in the tenant's possession and on the rent due to the landlord under the lease.

This is a statutory tenant's lien!

### §91.005. Subletting Prohibited

During the term of a lease, the tenant may not rent the leasehold to any other person without the prior consent of the landlord.

The foregoing statute makes it quite clear that no tenant may sublet his premises without the prior approval of the landlord, and tenants should always be encouraged to get this approval in writing. This has been held to include assignments also (even assignments between partners). *Heflin* v. *Stiles*, 663 S.W.2d 131 (Tex. Civ. App.—Ft. Worth, 1983). It has also been held that if a landlord gives consent, he does not become a party to the sublease. The landlord's consent, even though it may be attached to the lease, is only a method to comply with this statute, not a blanket approval of any of the terms contained in the sublease. If a landlord does not consent to an assignment or sublease of a lease agreement, he may also be entitled to recover from the assignee or sublessee the fair rental value of the leased premises. *Reynolds* v. *McCullough*, 739 S.W.2d 424 (Tex. App.—San Antonio, 1987, writ den.).

## Residential Statutes

**Chapter 92**

### Residential Tenancies
### Subchapter A. General Provisions

#### §92.001. Definitions

Except as otherwise provided in this chapter, in this chapter:

(1) "Dwelling" means one or more rooms rented for use as a permanent residence under a single lease to one or more tenants.

(2) "Landlord" means the owner, lessor, or sublessor of a dwelling, but does not include a manager or agent of the landlord unless the manager or agent purports to be the owner, lessor, or sublessor in an oral or written lease.

(3) "Lease" means any written or oral agreement between a landlord and tenant that establishes or modifies the terms, conditions, rules, or other provisions regarding the use and occupancy of a dwelling.

(4) "Normal wear and tear" means deterioration that results from the intended use of a dwelling, including, for the purposes of Subchapters B and D, breakage or malfunction due to age or deteriorated condition, but the term does not include deterioration that results from negligence, carelessness, accident, or abuse of the premises, equipment, or chattels by the tenant, by a member of the tenant's household, or by a guest or invitee of the tenant.

(5) "Premises" means a tenant's rental unit, any area or facility the lease authorizes the tenant to use, and the appurtenances, grounds, and facilities held out for the use of tenants generally.

(6) "Tenant" means a person who is authorized by a lease to occupy a dwelling to the exclusion of others and, for the purposes of Subchapters D, E, and F, who is obligated under the lease to pay rent.

#### §92.003. Landlord's Agent for Service of Process

(a) In a lawsuit by a tenant under either a written or oral lease for a dwelling or in a suit to enforce a legal obligation of the owner as landlord of the dwelling, the owner's agent for service of process is determined according to this section.

(b) If written notice of the name and business street address of the company that manages the dwelling has been given to the tenant, the management company is the owner's sole agent for service of process.

(c) If Subsection (b) does not apply, the owner's management company, on-premise manager, or rent collector serving the dwelling is the owner's authorized agent for service of process unless the owner's name and business street address have been furnished in writing to the tenants.

This provision provides generally for the same type of protection and privilege for service of process that the law of principle and agency provides. In this instance, the landlord is considered the agent for the owner.

### §92.005. Attorney's Fees

(a) A party who prevails in a suit brought under Subchapter B, E, or F may recover the party's costs of court and reasonable attorney's fees in relation to work reasonably expended.

(b) This section does not authorize a recovery of attorney's fees in an action brought under Subchapter D, E, or F for damages that relate to or arise from property damage, personal injury, or a criminal act.

### §92.006. Waiver or Expansion of Duties and Remedies

(a) A landlord's duty or a tenant's remedy concerning security deposits, security devices, the landlord's disclosure of ownership and management, or utility cutoffs, as provided by Subchapter C, D, E, or G, respectively, may not be waived. A landlord's duty to install a smoke detector under Subchapter F may not be waived, nor may a tenant waive a remedy for the landlord's noninstallation or waive the tenant's limited right of installation and removal. The landlord's duty of inspection and repair of smoke detectors under Subchapter F may be waived only by written agreement.

(b) A landlord's duties and the tenant's remedies concerning security devices, the landlord's disclosure of ownership and management, or smoke detectors, as provided by Subchapter D, E, or F, respectively, may be enlarged only by specific written agreement.

(c) A landlord's duties and the tenant's remedies under Subchapter B, which covers conditions materially affecting the physical health or safety of the ordinary tenant, may not be waived except as provided in Subsections (d), (e), and (f) of this section.

(d) A landlord and a tenant may agree for the tenant to repair or remedy, at the landlord's expense, any condition covered by Subchapter B.

(e) A landlord and a tenant may agree for the tenant to repair or remedy, at the tenant's expense, any condition covered by Subchapter B if all of the following conditions are met:

(1) at the beginning of the lease term the landlord owns only one rental dwelling;

(2) at the beginning of the lease term the dwelling is free from any condition which would materially affect the physical health or safety of an ordinary tenant;

(3) at the beginning of the lease term the landlord has no reason to believe that any condition described in Subdivision (2) of this subsection is likely to occur or recur during the tenant's lease term or during a renewal or extension; and

(4) (A) the lease is in writing;

(B) the agreement for repairs by the tenant is either underlined or printed in boldface in the lease or in a separate written addendum;

(C) the agreement is specific and clear; and

(D) the agreement is made knowingly, voluntarily, and for consideration.

(f) A landlord and tenant may agree that, except for those conditions caused by the negligence of the landlord, the tenant has the duty to pay for repair of the following conditions that may occur during the lease term or a renewal or extension:

(1) damage from wastewater stoppages caused by foreign or improper objects in lines that exclusively serve the tenant's dwelling;

(2) damage to doors, windows, or screens; and

(3) damage from windows or doors left open.

This subsection shall not affect the landlord's duty under Subchapter B to repair or remedy, at the landlord's expense, wastewater stoppages or backups caused by deterioration, breakage, roots, ground conditions, faulty construction, or malfunctioning equipment. A landlord and tenant may agree to the provisions of this subsection only if the agreement meets the requirements of Subdivision (4) of Subsection (e) of this section.

### §92.008. Interruption of Utilities

(a) A landlord or a landlord's agent may not interrupt or cause the interruption of utility service paid for directly to the utility company by a tenant unless the interruption results from bona fide repairs, construction, or an emergency.

(b) Except as provided by Subsections (c) and (d), a landlord may not interrupt or cause the interruption of water, wastewater, gas, or electric service furnished to a tenant by the landlord as an incident of the tenancy or by other agreement unless the interruption results from bona fide repairs, construction, or an emergency.

(c) A landlord may interrupt or cause the interruption of electrical service furnished to a tenant by the landlord as an incident of the tenancy or by other agreement if:

(1) the electrical service furnished to the tenant is individually metered or sub-metered for the dwelling unit;

(2) the electrical service connection with the utility company is in the name of the landlord or the landlord's agent; and

(3) the landlord complies with the rules adopted by the Public Utility Commission of Texas for discontinuance of sub-metered electrical service.

(d) A landlord may interrupt or cause the interruption of electrical service furnished to a tenant by the landlord as an incident of the tenancy or by other agreement if:

(1) the electrical service furnished to the tenant is not individually metered or submetered for the dwelling unit;

(2) the electrical service connection with the utility company is in the name of the landlord or the landlord's agent;

(3) the tenant is at least seven days late in paying the rent;

(4) the landlord has mailed or hand-delivered to the tenant at least five days before the date the electrical service is interrupted a written notice that states:

(A) the earliest date of the proposed interruption of electrical service;

(B) the amount of rent the tenant must pay to avert the interruption; and

(C) the name and location of the individual to whom or the location of the on-site management office where the delinquent rent may be paid during the landlord's normal business hours;

(5) the interruption does not begin before or after the landlord's normal business hours; and

(6) the interruption does not begin on a day, or on a day immediately preceding a day, when the landlord or other designated individual is not available or the on-site management office is not open to accept rent and restore electrical service.

(e) A landlord who interrupts electrical service under Subsection (c) or (d) shall restore the service not later than two hours after the time the tenant tenders, during the landlord's normal business hours, payment of the delinquent electric bill or rent owed to the landlord.

(f) If a landlord or a landlord's agent violates this section, the tenant may:

(1) either recover possession of the premises or terminate the lease; and

(2) recover from the landlord an amount equal to the sum of the tenant's actual damages, one month's rent or $500, whichever is greater, reasonable attorney's fees, and court costs, less any delinquent rents or other sums for which the tenant is liable to the landlord.

(g) A provision of a lease that purports to waive a right or to exempt a party from a liability or duty under this section is void.

### §92.0081. Removal of Property and Exclusion of Residential Tenant

(a) A landlord may not remove a door, window, or attic hatchway cover or a lock, latch, hinge, hinge pin, doorknob, or other mechanism connected to a door, window, or attic hatchway cover from premises leased to a tenant or remove furniture, fixtures, or appliances furnished by the landlord from premises leased to a tenant unless the landlord removes the item for a bona fide repair or replacement. If a landlord removes any of the items listed in this subsection for a bona fide repair or replacement, the repair or replacement must be promptly performed.

(b) A landlord may not intentionally prevent a tenant from entering the leased premises except by judicial process unless the exclusion results from:

(1) bona fide repairs, construction, or an emergency;

(2) removing the contents of premises abandoned by a tenant; or

(3) changing the door locks of a tenant who is delinquent in paying at least part of the rent.

(c) If a landlord or a landlord's agent changes the door lock of a tenant who is delinquent in paying rent, the landlord or the landlord's agent must place a written notice on the tenant's front door stating:

(1) an on-site location where the tenant may go 24 hours a day to obtain the new key or a telephone number that is answered 24 hours a day that the tenant may call to have a key delivered within two hours after calling the number;

(2) the fact that the landlord must provide the new key to the tenant at any hour, regardless of whether or not the tenant pays any of the delinquent rent; and

(3) the amount of rent and other charges for which the tenant is delinquent.

(d) A landlord may not intentionally prevent a tenant from entering the leased premises under Subsection (b)(3) unless:

(1) the landlord's right to change the locks because of a tenant's failure to timely pay rent is placed in the lease;

(2) the tenant is delinquent in paying all or part of the rent; and

(3) the landlord has locally mailed not later than the fifth calendar day before the date on which the door locks are changed or hand-delivered to the tenant or posted on the inside of the main entry door of the tenant's dwelling not later than the third calendar day before the date on which the door locks are changed a written notice stating:

(A) the earliest date that the landlord proposes to change the door locks;

(B) the amount of rent the tenant must pay to prevent changing of the door locks; and

(C) the name and street address of the individual to whom, or the location of the on-site management office at which, the delinquent rent may be paid during the landlord's normal business hours.

(D) in underlined or bold print, the tenant's right to receive a key to the new lock at any hour, regardless of whether the tenant pays the delinquent rent.

(e) A landlord may not change the locks on the door of a tenant's dwelling under Subsection (b)(3) on a day, or on a day immediately before a day, on which the landlord or other designated individual is not available, or on which any on-site management office is not open, for the tenant to tender the delinquent rent.

(e-1) A landlord who changes the locks or otherwise prevents a tenant from tenant's individual rental unit may not change the locks or otherwise prevent a tenant from entering a common area of residential property.

(f) A landlord who intentionally prevents a tenant from entering the tenant's dwelling under Subsection (b)(3) must provide the tenant with a key to the changed lock on the dwelling without regard to whether the tenant pays the delinquent rent.

(g) If a landlord arrives at the dwelling in a timely manner in response to a tenant's telephone call to the number contained in the notice as described by Subsection (c)(1) and the tenant is not present to receive the key to the changed lock, the landlord shall leave a notice on the front door of the dwelling stating the time the landlord arrived with the key and the street address to which the tenant may go to obtain the key during the landlord's normal office hours.

(h) If a landlord violates this section, the tenant may:

(1) either recover possession of the premises or terminate the lease; and

(2) recover from the landlord a civil penalty of one month's rent plus $1000, actual damages, court costs, and reasonable attorney's fees in an action to recover property damages, actual expenses, or civil penalties, less any delinquent rent or other sums for which the tenant is liable to the landlord.

(i) If a landlord violates Subsection (f), the tenant may recover, in addition to the remedies provided by Subsection (h), an additional civil penalty of one month's rent.

(j) A provision of a lease that purports to waive a right or to exempt a party from a liability or duty under this section is void.

(k) A landlord may not change the locks on the door of a tenant's dwelling place under Subsection (b)(3):

(1) when the tenant or any other legal occupant is in the dwelling; or

(2) more than once during a rental payment period.

(l) This section does not affect the ability of a landlord to pursue other available remedies, including the remedies provided by Chapter 24.

This imposes very strong restrictions on the landlord in that he cannot willfully interrupt any utilities if paid for by the tenant directly to the utility company and may not exclude a tenant from the premises without due process of law. **Due process of law** means court action. This means the landlord must take a tenant to court and have a formal eviction proceeding before he can exclude that tenant from his premises. This applies even if the lease provides for an automatic eviction, since Section (j) of the statute prohibits any waiver or oral or written agreement for the rights contained in this particular statute.

Section (c) specifies that the landlord can change the locks on a tenant's doors but must provide a key for the tenant so that he (the tenant) can gain entrance into his apartment at any time of the day or night. There is no requirement that the notice stay posted for a specified period. *Causey* v. *Catlett*, 605 S.W.2d 719 (Tex. Civ. App.—Dallas, 1980). The net effect of this particular provision is that the tenant must approach the landlord and at least talk to him on a face-to-face basis before he can get the key to his apartment. Although this statute might seem to be totally unfair to the landlord, there are methods of making this provision a little more effective for the landlord's benefit. Section (d) requires that the tenant's right to receive the key must be in the lease, in bold or underlined print.

A particularly important provision of this statute is Section (h), which provides for the damages that the tenant may recover in the event of a violation of that statute by the landlord. Note that the tenant may recover actual damages, plus one month's rent, plus reasonable attorney's fees, less any delinquent rentals or other sums for which the tenant is liable. Those are pretty stiff penalties for noncompliance on the part of the landlord.

### §92.009. Residential Tenant's Right of Reentry After Unlawful Lockout

(a) If a landlord has locked a tenant out of leased premises in violation of Section 92.008, the tenant may recover possession of the premises as provided by this section.

(b) The tenant must file with the justice court in the precinct in which the rental premises are located a sworn complaint for reentry, specifying the facts of the alleged unlawful lockout by the landlord or the landlord's agent. The tenant must also state orally under oath to the justice the facts of the alleged unlawful lockout.

(c) If the tenant has complied with Subsection (b) and if the justice reasonably believes an unlawful lockout has likely occurred, the justice may issue, ex parte, a writ of reentry that entitles the tenant to immediate and temporary possession of the premises, pending a final hearing on the tenant's sworn complaint for reentry.

(d) The writ of reentry must be served on either the landlord or the landlord's management company, on-premises manager, or rent collector in the same manner as a writ of possession in a forcible detainer action. A sheriff or constable may use reasonable force in executing a writ of reentry under this section.

(e) The landlord is entitled to a hearing on the tenant's sworn complaint for reentry. The writ of reentry must notify the landlord of the right to a hearing. The hearing shall be held not earlier than the first day and not later than the seventh day after the date the landlord requests a hearing.

(f) If the landlord fails to request a hearing on the tenant's sworn complaint for reentry before the eighth day after the date of service of the writ of reentry on the landlord under Subsection (d), a judgment for court costs may be rendered against the landlord.

(g) A party may appeal from the court's judgment at the hearing on the sworn complaint for reentry in the same manner as a party may appeal a judgment in a forcible detainer suit.

(h) If a writ of possession is issued, it supersedes a writ of reentry.

(i) If the landlord or the person on whom a writ of reentry is served fails to immediately comply with the writ or later disobeys the writ, the failure is grounds for contempt of court against the landlord or the person on whom the writ was served, under Section 21.002, Government Code. If the writ is disobeyed, the tenant or the tenant's attorney may file in the court in which the reentry action is pending an affidavit stating the name of the person who has disobeyed the writ and describing the acts or omissions constituting the disobedience. On receipt of an affidavit, the justice shall issue a show cause order, directing the person to appear on a designated date and show cause why he should not be adjudged in contempt of court. If the justice finds, after considering the evidence at the hearing, that the person has directly or indirectly disobeyed the writ, the justice may commit the person to jail without bail until the person purges himself of the contempt in a manner and form as the justice may direct. If the person disobeyed the writ before receiving the show cause order but has complied with the writ after receiving the order, the justice may find the person in contempt and assess punishment under Section 21.002(c), Government Code.

(j) This section does not affect a tenant's right to pursue a separate cause of action under Section 92.008.

(k) If a tenant in bad faith files a sworn complaint for reentry resulting in a writ of reentry being served on the landlord or landlord's agent, the landlord may in a separate cause of action recover from the tenant an amount equal to actual damages, one month's rent or $500, whichever is greater, reasonable attorney's fees, and costs of court, less any sums for which the landlord is liable to the tenant.

(l) The fee for filing a sworn complaint for reentry is the same as that for filing a civil action in justice court. The fee for service of a writ of reentry is the same as that for service of a writ of possession. The fee for service of a show cause order is the same as that for service of a civil citation. The justice may defer payment of the tenant's filing fees and service costs for the sworn complaint for reentry and writ of reentry. Court costs may be waived only if the tenant executes a pauper's affidavit.

(m) This section does not affect the rights of a landlord or tenant in a forcible detainer or forcible entry and detainer action.

### §92.010. Occupancy Limits

(a) Except as provided by Subsection (b), the maximum number of adults that a landlord may allow to occupy a dwelling is three times the number of bedrooms in the dwelling.

(b) A landlord may allow an occupancy rate of more than three adult tenants per bedroom:

(1) to the extent that the landlord is required by a state or federal fair housing law to allow a higher occupancy rate; or

(2) if an adult whose occupancy causes a violation of Subsection (a) is seeking temporary sanctuary from family violence, as defined by Section 71.01, Family Code, for a period that does not exceed one month.

(c) An individual who owns or leases a dwelling within 3,000 feet of a dwelling as to which a landlord has violated this section, or a governmental entity or civic association acting on behalf of the individual, may file suit against a landlord to enjoin the violation. A party who prevails in a suit under this subsection may recover court costs and reasonable attorney's fees from the other party. In addition to court costs and reasonable attorney's fees, a plaintiff who prevails under this subsection may recover from the landlord $500 for each violation of this section.

(d) In this section:

(1) "Adult" means an individual 18 years of age or older.

(2) "Bedroom" means an area of a dwelling intended as sleeping quarters. The term does not include a kitchen, dining room, bathroom, living room, utility room, or closet or storage area of a dwelling.

### §92.011. Cash Rental Payments

(a) A landlord shall accept a tenant's timely cash rental payment unless a written lease between the landlord and tenant requires the tenant to make rental payments by check, money order, or other traceable or negotiable instrument.

(b) A landlord who receives a cash rental payment shall:

(1) provide the tenant with a written receipt; and

(2) enter the payment date and amount in a record book maintained by the landlord.

(c) A tenant or a governmental entity or civic association acting on the tenant's behalf may file suit against a landlord to enjoin a violation of this section. A party who prevails in a suit brought under this subsection may recover court costs and reasonable attorney's fees from the other party. In addition to court costs and reasonable attorney's fees, a tenant who prevails under this subsection may recover from the landlord the greater of one month's rent or $500 for each violation of this section.

### §92.016. Right to Vacate and Avoid Liability Following Family Violence

(a) For purposes of this section:

(1) "Family violence" has the meaning assigned by Section 71.004, Family Code.

(2) "Occupant" means a person who has the landlord's consent to occupy a dwelling but has no obligation to pay the rent for the dwelling.

(b) A tenant may terminate the tenant's rights and obligations under a lease and may vacate the dwelling and avoid liability for future rent and any other sums due under the lease for terminating the lease and vacating the dwelling before the end of the lease term if the tenant complies with Subsection (c) and obtains and provides the landlord or the landlord's agent a copy of one or more of the following orders protecting the tenant or an occupant from family violence committed by a cotenant or occupant of the dwelling:

(1) a temporary injunction issued under Subchapter F, Chapter 6, Family Code; or

(2) a protective order issued under Chapter 85, Family Code.

(c) A tenant may exercise the rights to terminate the lease under Subsection (b), vacate the dwelling before the end of the lease term, and avoid liability beginning on the date after all of the following events have occurred:

(1) a judge signs an order described by Subsection (b);

(2) the tenant has delivered a copy of the order to the landlord; and

(3) the tenant has vacated the dwelling.

(d) Except as provided by Subsection (f), this section does not affect a tenant's liability for delinquent, unpaid rent or other sums owed to the landlord before the lease was terminated by the tenant under this section.

(e) A landlord who violates this section is liable to the tenant for actual damages, a civil penalty equal in amount to the amount of one month's rent plus $500, and attorney's fees.

(f) A tenant who terminates a lease under Subsection (b) is released from all liability for any delinquent, unpaid rent owed to the landlord by the tenant on the effective date of the lease termination if the lease does not contain language substantially equivalent to the following:

"Tenants may have special statutory rights to terminate the lease early in certain situations involving family violence or a military deployment or transfer."

(g) A tenant's right to terminate a lease before the end of the lease term, vacate the dwelling, and avoid liability under this section may not be waived by a tenant.

### §92.017 Right to Vacate and Avoid Liability Following Certain Decisions Related to Military Service

(a) For purposes of this section, "dependent," "military service," and "servicemember" have the meanings assigned by 50 App. U.S.C. Section 511.

(b) A tenant who is a servicemember or a dependent of a servicemember may vacate the dwelling leased by the tenant and avoid liability for future rent and all other sums due under the lease for terminating the lease and vacating the dwelling before the end of the lease term if:

(1) the lease was executed by or on behalf of a person who, after executing the lease or during the term of the lease, enters military service; or

(2) a servicemember, while in military service, executes the lease and after executing the lease receives military orders:

(A) for a permanent change of station; or

(B) to deploy with a military unit for a period of 90 days or more.

(c) A tenant who terminates a lease under Subsection (b) shall deliver to the landlord or landlord's agent:

(1) a written notice of termination of the lease; and

(2) a copy of an appropriate government document providing evidence of the tenant's entrance into military service if Subsection (b)(1) applies or a copy of the servicemember's military orders if Subsection (b)(2) applies.

(d) Termination of a lease under this section is effective:

(1) in the case of a lease that provides for monthly payment of rent, on the 30th day after the first date on which the next rental payment is due after the date on which the notice under Subsection (c)(1) is delivered; or

(2) in the case of a lease other than a lease described by Subsection (1), on the last day of the month following the month in which the notice under Subsection (c)(1) is delivered.

(e) A landlord, not later than the 30th day after the effective date of the termination of a lease under this section, shall refund to the residential tenant terminating the lease under Subsection (b) all rent or other amounts paid in advance under the lease for any period after the effective date of the termination of the lease.

(f) Except as provided by Subsection (g), this section does not affect a tenant's liability for delinquent, unpaid rent or other sums owed to the landlord before the lease was terminated by the tenant under this section.

(g) A tenant who terminates a lease under Subsection (b) is released from all liability for any delinquent, unpaid rent owed to the landlord by the tenant on the effective date of the lease termination if the lease does not contain language substantially equivalent to the following:

"Tenants may have special statutory rights to terminate the lease early in certain situations involving family violence or a military deployment or transfer."

(h) A landlord who violates this section is liable to the tenant for actual damages, a civil penalty in an amount equal to the amounts of one month's rent plus $500, and attorney's fees.

(i) Except as provided by Subsection (j), a tenant's right to terminate a lease before the end of the lease term, vacate the dwelling, and avoid liability under this section may not be waived by a tenant.

(j) A tenant and a landlord may agree that the tenant waives a tenant's rights under this section if the tenant or any dependent living with the tenant moves into base housing or other housing within 30 miles of the dwelling. A waiver under this section must be signed and in writing in a document separate from the lease and must comply with federal law. A waiver under this section does not apply if:

(1) the tenant or the tenant's dependent moves into housing owned or occupied by family or relatives of the tenant or the tenant's dependent; or

(2) the tenant and the tenant's dependent move, wholly or partly, because of a significant financial loss of income caused by the tenant's military service.

(k) For purposes of Subsection (j), "significant financial loss of income" means a reduction of 10 percent or more of the tenant's household income caused by the tenant's military service. A landlord is entitled to verify the significant financial loss of income in order to determine whether a tenant is entitled to terminate a lease if the tenant has signed a waiver under this section and moves within 30 miles of the dwelling into housing that is not owned or occupied by family or relatives of the tenant or the tenant's dependent. For purposes of this subsection, a pay stub or other statement of earnings issued by the tenant's employer is sufficient verification.

## Subchapter B. Repair or Closing of Leasehold

### §92.052. Landlord's Duty to Repair or Remedy

(a) A landlord shall make a diligent effort to repair or remedy a condition if:

(1) the tenant specifies the condition in a notice to the person to whom or to the place where rent is normally paid;

(2) the tenant is not delinquent in the payment of rent at the time notice is given; and

(3) the condition:

(A) materially affects the physical health or safety of an ordinary tenant; or

(B) arises from the landlord's failure to provide and maintain in good operating condition a device to supply hot water of a minimum temperature of 120 degrees Fahrenheit.

(b) Unless the condition was caused by normal wear and tear, the landlord does not have a duty during the lease term or a renewal or extension to repair or remedy a condition caused by:

(1) the tenant;

(2) a lawful occupant in the tenant's dwelling;

(3) a member of the tenant's family; or

(4) a guest or invitee of the tenant.

(c) This subchapter does not require the landlord:

(1) to furnish utilities from a utility company if as a practical matter the utility lines of the company are not reasonably available; or

(2) to furnish security guards.

(d) The tenant's notice under Subsection (a) must be in writing only if the tenant's lease is in writing and requires written notice.

### §92.053. Burden of Proof

(a) Except as provided by this section, the tenant has the burden of proof in a judicial action to enforce a right resulting from the landlord's failure to repair or remedy a condition under Section 92.052.

(b) If the landlord does not provide a written explanation for delay in performing a duty to repair or remedy on or before the fifth day after receiving from the tenant a written demand for an explanation, the landlord has the burden of proving that he made a diligent effort to repair and that a reasonable time for repair did not elapse.

### §92.054. Casualty Loss

(a) If a condition results from an insured casualty loss, such as fire, smoke, hail, explosion, or a similar cause, the period for repair does not begin until the landlord receives the insurance proceeds.

(b) If after a casualty loss the rental premises are as a practical matter totally unusable for residential purposes and if the casualty loss is not caused by the negligence or fault of the tenant, a member of the tenant's family, or a guest or invitee of the tenant, either the landlord or the tenant may terminate the lease by giving written notice to the other any time before repairs are completed. If the lease is terminated, the tenant is entitled only to a pro rata refund of rent from the date the tenant moves out and to a refund of any security deposit otherwise required by law.

(c) If after a casualty loss the rental premises are partially unusable for residential purposes and if the casualty loss is not caused by the negligence or fault of the tenant, a member of the tenant's family, or a guest or invitee of the tenant, the tenant is entitled to reduction in the rent in an amount proportionate to the extent the premises are unusable because of the casualty, but only on judgment of a county or district court. A landlord and tenant may agree otherwise in a written lease.

### §92.055. Closing the Rental Premises

(a) A landlord may close a rental unit at any time by giving written notice by certified mail, return receipt requested, to the tenant and to the local health officer and local building inspector, if any, stating that:

(1) the landlord is terminating the tenancy as soon as legally possible; and

(2) after the tenant moves out the landlord will either immediately demolish the rental unit or no longer use the unit for residential purposes.

(b) After a tenant receives the notice and moves out:

(1) the local health officer or building inspector may not allow occupancy of or utility service by separate meter to the rental unit until the officer certifies that he knows of no condition that materially affects the physical health or safety of an ordinary tenant; and

(2) the landlord may not allow reoccupancy or reconnection of utilities by separate meter within six months after the date the tenant moves out.

(c) If the landlord gives the tenant the notice closing the rental unit:

(1) before the tenant gives a repair notice to the landlord, the remedies of this subchapter do not apply;

(2) after the tenant gives a repair notice to the landlord but before the landlord has had a reasonable time to make repairs, the tenant is entitled only to the remedies under this section; or

(3) after the tenant gives a repair notice to the landlord and after the landlord has had a reasonable time to make repairs, the tenant is entitled only to the remedies under Subdivisions (3), (4), and (5) of Subsection (b) of Section 92.056 and under this section.

(d) If the landlord closes the rental unit after the tenant gives the landlord a notice to repair and the tenant moves out on or before the end of the rental term, the landlord must pay the tenant's actual and reasonable moving expenses, refund a pro rata portion of the tenant's rent from the date the tenant moves out, and, if otherwise required by law, return the tenant's security deposit.

(e) A landlord who violates Subsection (b) or (d) is liable to the tenant for an amount equal to the total of one month's rent plus $100 and attorney's fees.

(f) The closing of a rental unit does not prohibit the occupancy of other apartments, nor does this subchapter prohibit occupancy of or utility service by master or individual meter to other rental units in an apartment complex that have not been closed under this section. If another provision of this subchapter conflicts with this section, this section controls.

### §92.056. Landlord Liability and Tenant Remedies; Notice and Time for Repair

(a) A landlord's liability under this section is subject to Section 92.052(b) regarding conditions that are caused by a tenant and Section 92.054 regarding conditions that are insured casualties.

(b) A landlord is liable to a tenant as provided by this subchapter if:

(1) the tenant has given the landlord notice to repair or remedy a condition by giving that notice to the person to whom or to the place where the tenant's rent is normally paid;

(2) the condition materially affects the physical health or safety of an ordinary tenant;

(3) the tenant has given the landlord a subsequent written notice to repair or remedy the condition after a reasonable time to repair or remedy the condition following the notice given under Subdivision (1) or the tenant has given the notice under Subdivision (1) by sending that notice by certified mail, return receipt requested, or by registered mail;

(4) the landlord has had a reasonable time to repair or remedy the condition after the landlord received the tenant's notice under Subdivision (1) and, if applicable, the tenant's subsequent notice under Subdivision (3);

(5) the landlord has not made a diligent effort to repair or remedy the condition after the landlord received the tenant's notice under Subdivision (1) and, if applicable, the tenant's notice under Subdivision (3); and

(6) the tenant was not delinquent in the payment of rent at the time any notice required by this subsection was given.

(c) For purposes of Subsection (b)(4) or (5), a landlord is considered to have received the tenant's notice when the landlord or the landlord's agent or employee has actually received the notice or when the United States Postal Service has attempted to deliver the notice to the landlord.

(d) For purposes of Subsection (b)(3) or (4), in determining whether a period of time is a reasonable time to repair or remedy a condition, there is a rebuttable presumption that seven days is a reasonable time. To rebut that presumption, the date on which the landlord received the tenant's notice, the severity and nature of the condition, and the reasonable availability of materials and labor and of utilities from a utility company must be considered.

(e) Except as provided in Subsection (f), a tenant to whom a landlord is liable under Subsection (b) of this section may:

(1) terminate the lease;

(2) have the condition repaired or remedied according to Section 92.0561;

(3) deduct from the tenant's rent, without necessity of judicial action, the cost of the repair or remedy according to Section 92.0561; and

(4) obtain judicial remedies according to Section 92.0563.

(f) A tenant who elects to terminate the lease under Subsection (e) is:

(1) entitled to a pro rata refund of rent from the date of termination or the date the tenant moves out, whichever is later;

(2) entitled to deduct the tenant's security deposit from the tenant's rent without necessity of lawsuit or obtain a refund of the tenant's security deposit according to law; and

(3) not entitled to the other repair and deduct remedies under Section 92.0561 or the judicial remedies under Subdivisions (1) and (2) of Subsection (a) of Section 92.0563.

(g) A lease must contain language in underlined or bold print that informs the tenant of the remedies available under this section and Section 92.0561.

### §92.0561. Tenant's Repair and Deduct Remedies

(a) If the landlord is liable to the tenant under Section 92.056(b), the tenant may have the condition repaired or remedied and may deduct the cost from a subsequent rent payment as provided in this section.

(b) The Tenant's deduction for the cost of the repair or remedy may not exceed the amount of one month's rent under the lease or $500, whichever is greater. However, if the tenant's rent is subsidized in whole or in part by a governmental agency, the deduction limitation of one month's rent shall mean the fair market rent for the dwelling and not the rent that the tenant pays. The fair market rent shall be determined by the government agency subsidizing the rent, or in the absence of such a determination, it shall be a reasonable amount of rent under the circumstances.

(c) Repairs and deductions under this section may be made as often as necessary so long as the total repairs and deductions in any one month do not exceed one month's rent or $500, whichever is greater.

(d) Repairs under this section may be made only if all of the following requirements are met:

(1) The landlord has a duty to repair or remedy the condition under Section 92,052, and the duty has not been waived in a written lease by the tenant under Subsection (e) or (f) of Section 92.006.

(2) The tenant has given notice to the landlord as required by Section 92.056(b)(1), and, if required, a subsequent notice under Section 92.056(b)(3), and at least one of those notices states that the tenant intends to repair or remedy the condition. The notice shall also contain a reasonable description of the intended repair or remedy.

(3) Any one of the following events has occurred:

(A) The landlord has failed to remedy the backup or overflow of raw sewage inside the tenant's dwelling or the flooding from broken pipes or natural drainage inside the dwelling.

(B) The landlord ha expressly or impliedly agreed in the lease to furnish potable water to the tenant's dwelling and the water service to the dwelling has totally ceased.

(C) The landlord has expressly or impliedly agreed in the lease to furnish heating or cooling equipment; the equipment is producing inadequate heat or cooled air; and the landlord has been notified in writing by the appropriate local housing, building, or health official or other official having jurisdiction that the lack of heat or cooling materially affects the health or safety of an ordinary tenant.

(D) The landlord has been notified in writing by the appropriate local housing, building, or health official or other official having jurisdiction that the condition materially affects the health or safety of an ordinary tenant.

(e) If the requirements of Subsection (d) of this section are met, a tenant may:

(1) have the condition repaired or remedied immediately following the tenant's notice of intent to repair if the condition involves sewage or flooding as referred to in Paragraph (A) of Subdivision (3) of Subsection (d) of this section;

(2) have the condition repaired or remedied if the condition involves a cessation of potable water as referred to in Paragraph (A) of Subdivision (3) of Subsection (d) of this section and if the landlord has failed to repair or remedy the condition within three days following the tenant's delivery of notice of intent to repair;

(3) have the condition repaired or remedied if the condition involves inadequate heat or cooled air as referred to in Paragraph (C) of Subdivision (3) of Subsection (d) of this section and if the landlord has failed to repair the condition within three days after delivery of the tenant's notice of intent to repair; or

(4) have the condition repaired or remedied if the condition is not covered by Paragraph (A), (B), or (C) of Subdivision (3) of Subsection (d) of this section and involves a condition affecting the physical health or safety of the ordinary tenant

as referred to in Paragraph (D) of Subdivision (3) of Subsection (d) of this section and if the landlord has failed to repair or remedy the condition within seven days after delivery of the tenant's notice of intent to repair.

(f) Repairs made pursuant to the tenant's notice must be made by a company, contractor, or repairman listed in the yellow or business pages of the telephone directory or in the classified advertising section of a newspaper of the local city, county, or adjacent county at the time of the tenant's notice of intent to repair. Unless the landlord and tenant agree otherwise under Subsection (g) of this section, repairs may not be made by the tenant, the tenant's immediate family, the tenant's employer or employees, or a company in which the tenant has an ownership interest. Repairs may not be made to the foundation or load-bearing structural elements of the building if it contains two or more dwelling units.

(g) A landlord and a tenant may mutually agree for the tenant to repair or remedy, at the landlord's expense, any condition of the dwelling regardless of whether it materially affects the health or safety of an ordinary tenant. However, the landlord's duty to repair or remedy conditions covered by this subchapter may not be waived except as provided by Subsection (e) or (f) of Section 92.006.

(h) Repairs made pursuant to the tenant's notice must be made in compliance with applicable building codes, including a building permit when required.

(i) The tenant shall not have authority to contract for labor or materials in excess of what the tenant may deduct under this section. The landlord is not liable to repairmen, contractors, or material suppliers who furnish labor or material to repair or remedy the condition . A repairman or supplier shall not have a lien for materials or services arising out of repairs contracted for by the tenant under this section.

(j) When deducting the cost of repairs from the rent payment, the tenant shall furnish the landlord, along with payment of the balance of the rent, a copy of the repair bill and the receipt for its payment. A repair bill and receipt may be the same document.

(k) If the landlord repairs or remedies the condition or delivers an affidavit for delay under Section 92.0562 to the tenant after the tenant has contacted a repairman but before the repairman commences work, the landlord shall be liable for the cost incurred by the tenant for the repairman's trip charge, and the tenant may deduct the charge from the tenant's rent as if it were a repair cost.

### §92.0562. Landlord Affidavit for Delay

(a) The tenant must delay contracting for repairs under Section 92.0562 if, before the tenant contracts for the repairs, the landlord delivers to the tenant an affidavit, signed and sworn to under oath by the landlord or his authorized agent and complying with this section.

(b) The affidavit must summarize the reasons for the delay and the diligent efforts made by the landlord up to the date of the affidavit to get the repairs done. The affidavit must state facts showing that the landlord has made and is making diligent efforts to repair the condition, and it must contain dates, names, addresses, and telephone numbers of contractors, suppliers, and repairmen contacted by the owner.

(c) Affidavits under this section may delay repair by the tenant for:

(1) 15 days if the landlord's failure to repair is caused by a delay in obtaining necessary parts for which the landlord is not at fault; or

(2) 30 days if the landlord's failure to repair is caused by a general shortage of labor or materials for repair following a natural disaster such as a hurricane, tornado, flood, extended freeze, or widespread windstorm.

(d) Affidavits for delay based on grounds other than those listed in Subsection (c) of this section are unlawful, and if used, they are of no effect. The landlord may file subsequent affidavits, provided that the total delay of the repair or remedy extends no longer than six months from the date the landlord delivers the first affidavit to the tenant.

(e) The affidavit must be delivered to the tenant by any of the following methods:

(1) personal delivery to the tenant;

(2) certified mail, return receipt requested, to the tenant; or

(3) leaving the notice inside the dwelling in a conspicuous place if notice in that manner is authorized in a written lease.

(f) Affidavits for delay by a landlord under this section must be submitted in good faith. Following delivery of the affidavit, the landlord must continue diligent efforts to repair or remedy the condition. There shall be a rebuttable presumption that the landlord acted in good faith and with continued diligence for the first affidavit for delay the landlord delivers to the tenant. The landlord shall have the burden of pleading and proving good faith and continued diligence for subsequent affidavits for delay. A landlord who violates this section shall be liable to the tenant for all judicial remedies under Section 92.0563 except that the civil penalty under Subdivision (3) of Subsection (a) of Section 92.0563 shall be one month's rent plus $1,000.

(g) If the landlord is liable to the tenant under Section 92.056 and if a new landlord, in good faith and without knowledge of the tenant's notice of intent to repair, has acquired title to the tenant's dwelling by foreclosure, deed in lieu of foreclosure, or general warranty deed in a bona fide purchase, then the following shall apply:

(1) The tenant's right to terminate the lease under this subchapter shall not be affected, and the tenant shall have no duty to give additional notice the new landlord.

(2) The tenant's right to repair and deduct for conditions involving sewage backup or overflow, flooding inside the dwelling, or a cutoff of potable water under Subsection (e) of Section 92.0561 shall not be affected, and the tenant shall have no duty to give additional notice to the new landlord.

(3) For conditions other than those specified in Subdivision (2) of this subsection, if the new landlord acquires title as described in this subsection and has notified the tenant of the name and address of the new landlord or the new landlord's authorized agent and if the tenant has not already contracted for the repair or remedy at the time the tenant is so notified, the tenant must deliver to the new landlord a written notice of intent to repair or remedy the condition, and the new landlord shall have a reasonable time to complete the repair before the tenant may repair or remedy the condition. No further notice from the tenant is necessary in order for the tenant to repair or remedy the condition after a reasonable time has elapsed.

(4) The tenant's judicial remedies under Section 92.0563 shall be limited to recovery against the landlord to whom the tenant gave the required notices until the tenant has given the new landlord the notices required by this section and otherwise complied with Section 92.056 as to the new landlord.

(5) If the new landlord violates this subsection, the new landlord is liable to the tenant for a civil penalty of one month's rent plus $2,000, actual damages, and attorney's fees.

(6) No provision of this section shall affect any right of a foreclosing superior lienholder to terminate, according to law, any interest in the premises held by the holders of subordinate liens, encumbrances, leases, or other interests and shall not affect any right of the tenant to terminate the lease according to law.

### §92.0563. Tenant's Judicial Remedies

(a) A tenant's judicial remedies under Section 92.056 shall include:

(1) an order directing the landlord to take reasonable action to repair or remedy the condition;

(2) an order reducing the tenant's rent, from the date of the first repair notice, in proportion to the reduced rental value resulting from the condition until the condition is repaired or remedied;

(3) a judgment against the landlord for a civil penalty of one month's rent plus $500;

(4) a judgment against the landlord for the amount of the tenant's actual damages; and

(5) court costs and attorney's fees, excluding any attorney's fees for a cause of action for damages relating to a personal injury.

(b) A landlord who knowingly violates Section 92.006 by contracting orally or in writing with a tenant to waive the landlord's duty to repair under this subchapter shall be liable to the tenant for actual damages, a civil penalty of one month's rent plus $2,000, and reasonable attorney's fees. For purposes of this subsection, there shall be a rebuttable presumption that the landlord acted without knowledge of the violation. The tenant shall have the burden of pleading and proving a knowing violation. If the lease is in writing and is not in violation of Section 92.006, the tenant's proof of a knowing violation must be clear and convincing. A mutual agreement for tenant repair under Subsection (g) of Section 92.0561 is not a violation of Section 92.006.

(c) The justice, county, and district courts have concurrent jurisdiction of an action under Subsection (a) of this section except that the justice court may not order repairs under Subdivision (1) of Subsection (a) of this section.

### §92.058. Landlord Remedy for Tenant Violation

(a) If the tenant withholds rents, causes repairs to be performed, or makes rent deductions for repairs in violation of this subchapter, the landlord may recover actual damages from the tenant. If, after a landlord has notified a tenant in writing of (1) the illegality of the tenant's rent withholding or the tenant's proposed repair and (2) the penalties of this subchapter, the tenant withholds rent, causes repairs to be performed, or makes rent deductions for repairs in bad faith violation of this subchapter, the landlord may recover from the tenant a civil penalty of one month's rent plus $500.

(b) Notice under this section must be in writing and may be given in person, by mail, or by delivery to the premises.

(c) The landlord has the burden of pleading and proving, by clear and convincing evidence, that the landlord gave the tenant the required notice of the illegality and the penalties and that the tenant's violation was done in bad faith. In any litigation under this subsection, the prevailing party shall recover reasonable attorney's fees from the nonprevailing party.

### §92.060. Agents for Delivery of Notice

A managing agent, leasing agent, or resident manager is the agent of the landlord for purposes of notice and other communications required or permitted by this subchapter.

### §92.061. Effect on Other Rights

The duties of a landlord and the remedies of a tenant under this subchapter are in lieu of existing common law and other statutory law warranties and duties of landlords for maintenance, repair, security, habitability, and nonretaliation, and remedies of tenants for a violation of those warranties and duties. Otherwise, this subchapter does not affect any other right of a landlord or tenant under contract, statutory law, or common law that is consistent with the purposes of this subchapter or any right a landlord or tenant may have to bring an action for personal injury or property damage under the laws of this state. This subchapter does not impose obligations on a landlord or tenant other than those expressly stated in this subchapter.

Subchapter B was passed as the Texas legislature's answers to *Kamarath* v. *Bennett*, 568 S.W.2d 658 (Tex. 1978) and *Sims* v. *Century Kiest Apts.*, 567 S.W.2d 526 (Tex. Civ. App.—Dallas, 1978), discussed later. The landlord's duty to repair or remedy any condition is only for those defects that materially affect the physical health or safety of an ordinary tenant. Since the statute does not define the terms "materially affect" or "ordinary tenant," it is assumed that one would have to look to the *Kamarath* case for guidance as to what "habitable" would mean when referring to these two terms. The tenant has affirmative burdens that he must perform in Section 92.053 of this statute, although this burden of proof may shift as provided in the statute. The statute further specifies both nonjudicial and judicial remedies for the tenant. At least one case has held that when a landlord refuses to repair an apartment and where the court finds there is certain reduced value in the premises because of that refusal to repair, the tenant is entitled to actual damages for the past reduction in value. *Waldon* v. *Williams*, 760 S.W.2d 833 (Tex. App.—Austin, 1988, no writ). While this provision is specifically applicable to residential tenancies, it has also been held to apply to commercial tenancies. *Davidow* v. *Inwood North Professional Group—Phase I*, 747 S.W.2d 373 (Tex. 1988). In commercial tenancies, however, the warranty is to "suitability," not habitability of the premises. The warranty of suitability, at least at this time, covers only latent defects in the nature of the physical or structural defect within the leased premises that the landlord has the duty to repair. It does not extend to negotiated terms of the lease agreement in which the tenant may have made a bad bargain. *Coleman* v. *Rotana, Inc.*, 778 S.W.2d 867 (Tex. App.—Dallas, 1989, writ den.). A landlord can pass the duty to repair and maintain the premises to the tenant in the lease, however. *Barnes* v. *Wendy's International, Inc.*, 857 S.W.2d 728 (Tex. App.—Houston [14th Dist.], 1993).

### §92.331. Retaliation by Landlord

(a) A landlord may not retaliate against a tenant by taking an action described by Subsection (b) because the tenant:

(1) in good faith exercises or attempts to exercise against a landlord a right or remedy granted to the tenant by lease, municipal ordinance, or federal or state statute;

(2) gives a landlord a notice to repair or exercises a remedy under this chapter; or

(3) complains to a governmental entity responsible for enforcing building or housing codes, a public utility, or a civic or nonprofit agency, and the tenant:

(A) claims a building or housing code violation or utility problem; and

(B) believes in good faith that the complaint is valid and that the violation or problem occurred.

(b) A landlord may not, within six months after the date of the tenant's action under Subsection (a), retaliate against the tenant by:

(1) filing an eviction proceeding, except for the grounds stated by Section 92.332;

(2) depriving the tenant of the use of the premises, except for reasons authorized by law;

(3) decreasing services to the tenant;

(4) increasing the tenant's rent or terminating the tenant's lease; or

(5) engaging, in bad faith, in a course of conduct that materially interferes with the tenant's rights under the tenant's lease.

### §92.332. Nonretaliation

(a) The landlord is not liable for retaliation under this subchapter if the landlord proves that the action was not made for the purposes of retaliation, nor is the landlord liable, unless the action violates a prior court order under Section 92.0563, for:

(1) increasing rent under an escalation clause in a written lease for utilities, taxes, or insurance; or

(2) increasing rent or reducing services as part of a pattern of rent increases or service reductions for an entire multidwelling project.

(b) An eviction or lease termination based on the following circumstances, which are valid grounds for eviction or lease termination in any event, does not constitute retaliation:

(1) the tenant is delinquent in rent when the landlord gives notice to vacate or files an eviction action;

(2) the tenant, a member of the tenant's family, or a guest or invitee of the tenant intentionally damages property on the premises or by word or conduct threatens the personal safety of the landlord, the landlord's employees, or another tenant;

(3) the tenant has materially breached the lease, other than by holding over, by an action such as violating written lease provisions prohibiting serious misconduct or criminal acts, except as provided by this section;

(4) the tenant holds over after giving notice of termination or intent to vacate;

(5) the tenant holds over after the landlord gives notice of termination at the end of the rental term and the tenant does not take action under Section 92.331 until after the landlord gives notice of termination; or

(6) the tenant holds over and the landlord's notice of termination is motivated by a good faith belief that the tenant, a member of the tenant's family, or a guest or invitee of the tenant might:

(A) adversely affect the quiet enjoyment by other tenants or neighbors; or

(B) materially affect the health or safety of the landlord, other tenants, or neighbors; or

(C) damage the property of the landlord, other tenants, or neighbors.

### §92.333. Tenant Remedies

(a) In addition to other remedies provided by law, if a landlord retaliates against a tenant under this subchapter, the tenant may recover from the landlord a civil penalty of one month's rent plus $500, actual damages, court costs, and reasonable attorney's fees in an action for recovery of property damages, moving costs, actual expenses, civil penalties, or declaratory or injunctive relief, less any delinquent rents or other sums for which the tenant is liable to the landlord. If the tenant's rent payment to the landlord is subsidized in whole or in part by a governmental entity, the civil penalty granted under this section shall reflect the fair market rent of the dwelling plus $500.

### §92.334. Invalid Complaints

(a) If a tenant files or prosecutes a suit for retaliatory action based on a complaint asserted under Section 92.331 (a) (3), and the government building or housing inspector or utility company representative visits the premises and determines in writing that a violation of a building or housing code does not exist or that a utility problem does not exist, there is a rebuttable presumption that the tenant acted in bad faith.

(b) If a tenant files or prosecutes a suit under this subchapter in bad faith, the landlord may recover possession of the dwelling unit and may recover from the tenant a civil penalty of one month's rent plus $500, court costs, and reasonable

attorney's fees. If the tenant's rent paymen
or in part by a governmental entity, the civi
reflect the fair market rent of the dwelling

### §92.335. Eviction Suits

In a eviction suit, retaliation by the landlord
a rent deduction lawfully made by the tenant
nonpayment of the rent to the extent allowed
under the chapter may not be joined with an
or crossclaim in an eviction suit.

The concept of retaliatory eviction is relativ
*Century Kiest Apts.*, supra, opened a whole ne ........................ to sue
their landlords for damages in the event they w ............ evicted from their premises for
no purpose other than retaliation by the landlord. The new statute specifies that the
landlord shall not, within six months from the date of the tenant's repair notice, do
any acts to evict the tenant that may constitute retaliation. There are certain acts
that the tenants can commit, which would allow the landlord to evict them and
which would not constitute retaliation, which are specified in Section 92.057(b). If
the landlord does retaliate against the tenant in violation of Section 92.057(b), the
statute imposes fairly severe penalties.

An important portion of the act is Section 92.056, which provides that any party
who prevails in the lawsuit shall be entitled to recover from the other party reasonable attorney's fees.

One should note that Subchapter B is specifically applicable to residential
tenancies. In a landmark Texas case, however, the Texas Supreme Court held that
this warranty of habitability also applies to commercial leases. This is a new, emerging area of the law, which deserves to be closely monitored. It is a significant addition to the causes of action available to a commercial tenant.

## Subchapter C. Security Deposits

### §92.102. Security Deposit

A security deposit is any advance of money, other than a rental application deposit
or an advance payment of rent, that is intended primarily to secure performances
under a lease of a dwelling that has been entered into by a landlord and a tenant.

### §92.103. Obligation to Refund

(a) Except as provided by Section 92.107, the landlord shall refund a security deposit to
the tenant on or before the 30th day after the date the tenant surrenders the premises.

(b) A requirement that a tenant give advance notice of surrender as a condition for
refunding the security deposit is effective only if the requirement is underlined or
is printed in conspicuous bold print in the lease.

(c) The tenant's claim to the security deposit takes priority over the claim of any
creditor of the landlord except a trustee in bankruptcy.

### §92.1031. Conditions for Retention of Security Deposit or Rent Prepayment

(a) Except as provided in Subsection (b), a landlord who receives a security deposit
or rent prepayment for a dwelling from a tenant who fails to occupy the dwelling
according to a lease between the landlord and the tenant may not retain the security deposit or rent prepayment if:

(1) the tenant secures a replacement tenant satisfactory to the landlord and the
replacement tenant occupies the dwelling on or before the commencement date
of the lease; or

(2) the landlord secures a replacement tenant satisfactory to the landlord and the replacement tenant occupies the dwelling on or before the commencement date of the lease.

(b) If the landlord secures the replacement tenant, the landlord may retain and deduct from the security deposit or rent prepayment either;

(1) a sum agreed to in the lease as a lease cancellation fee; or

(2) actual expenses incurred by the landlord in securing the replacement, including a reasonable amount for the time of the landlord in securing the replacement tenant.

## §92.104. Retention of Security Deposit; Accounting

(a) Before returning a security deposit, the landlord may deduct from the deposit damages and charges for which the tenant is legally liable under the lease or as a result of breaching the lease.

(b) The landlord may not retain any portion of a security deposit to cover normal wear and tear.

(c) If the landlord retains all or part of a security deposit under this section, the landlord shall give to the tenant the balance of the security deposit, if any, together with a written description and itemized list of all deductions. The landlord is not required to give the tenant a description and itemized list of deductions if:

(1) the tenant owes rent when he surrenders possession of the premises; and

(2) there is no controversy concerning the amount of rent owed.

## §92.1041. Presumption of Refund or Accounting

A landlord is presumed to have refunded a security deposit or made an accounting of security deposit deductions if, on or before the date required under this subchapter, the refund or accounting is placed in the United States mail and postmarked on or before the required date.

## §92.105. Cessation of Owner's Interest

(a) If the owner's interest in the premises is terminated by sale, assignment, death, appointment of a receiver, bankruptcy or otherwise, the new owner is liable for the return of security deposits according to this subchapter from the date title to the premises is acquired, regardless of whether notice is given to the tenant under subsection (b) of this section.

(b) The person who no longer owns an interest in the rental premises remains liable for a security deposit received while the person was the owner until the new owner delivers to the tenant a signed statement acknowledging that the new owner has received and is responsible for the tenant's security deposit and specifying the exact dollar amount of the deposit.

(c) Subsection (a) does not apply to a real estate mortgage lienholder who acquires title for foreclosure.

## §92.106. Records

The landlord shall keep accurate records of all security deposits.

## §92.107. Tenant's Forwarding Address

(a) The landlord is not obligated to return a tenant's security deposit or give the tenant a written description of damages and charges until the tenant gives the landlord a written statement of the tenant's forwarding address for the purpose of refunding the security deposit.

(b) The tenant does not forfeit the right to a refund of the security deposit or the right to receive a description of damages and charges merely for failing to give a forwarding address to the landlord.

### §92.108. Liability for Withholding Last Month's Rent

(a) The tenant may not withhold payment of any portion of the last month's rent on grounds that the security deposit is security for unpaid rent.

(b) A tenant who violates this section is presumed to have acted in bad faith. A tenant who in bad faith violates this section is liable to the landlord for an amount equal to three times the rent wrongfully withheld and the landlord's reasonable attorney's fees in a suit to recover the rent.

### §92.109. Liability of Landlord

(a) A landlord who in bad faith retains a security deposit in violation of this subchapter is liable for an amount equal to the sum of $100, three times the portion of the deposit wrongfully withheld, and the tenant's reasonable attorney's fees in a suit to recover the deposit.

(b) A landlord who in bad faith does not provide a written description and itemized list of damages and charges in violation of this subchapter:

(1) forfeits the right to withhold any portion of the security deposit or to bring suit against the tenant for damages to the premises; and

(2) is liable for the tenant's reasonable attorney's fees in a suit to recover the deposit.

(c) In an action brought by a tenant under this subchapter, the landlord has the burden of proving that the retention of any portion of the security deposit was reasonable.

(d) A landlord who fails either to return a security deposit or to provide a written description and itemization of deductions on or before the 30th day after the date the tenant surrenders possession is presumed to have acted in bad faith.

This statute is very specific with respect to security deposits and provides very stiff penalties under Section 92.109 in the event that the landlord fails to comply with the statute. The subject of security deposits was an area of heavy conflict prior to the passage of this statute. The statute, coupled with the new Deceptive Trade Practices Act, makes the landlord's liability far greater than any enrichment he might receive from the amount of the deposit. The tenant's obligations under Sections 92.107 and 92.103 must be complied with in order to maintain an action under the statute. *Minor* v. *Adams*, 694 S.W.2d 148 (Tex. Civ. App.—Houston, 1985). The tenant need not give his own forwarding address, however, and can give the address of his agent or attorney to receive the security deposits. *Johnson* v. *Huie Prop.*, 599 S.W.2d 488 (Tex. Civ. App.—Dallas, 1980); *Tammen* v. *Page*, 584 S.W.2d 914 (Tex. Civ. App.—Eastland, 1979).

There have been a number of recent cases that have dealt with the obligations of both the landlord and the tenant with respect to their security deposits. The failure to return a security deposit, by itself, is not a conclusive presumption of bad faith on the part of the landlord. This is particularly important under Section 92.109, which requires bad faith as a requirement for damages. *Wilson* v. *O'Connor*, 555 S.W.2d 776 (Tex. Civ. App.—Dallas, 1977). The burden is on the landlord to show that his retention of the security deposit was reasonable. *Byler* v. *Garcia*, 685 S.W.2d 116 (Tex. Civ. App.—Austin, 1985). The landlord does not have to return the security deposit if there is any back rent owing, but if he induces the tenant to return and clean the apartment and then refuses the refund, he may be acting in bad faith, and the tenant may sue. *Koelzer* v. *Pizzirani*, 718 S.W.2d 420 (Tex. Civ. App.—Ft. Worth, 1986); *Alltex Construction Inc.* v. *Alereksoussi*, 685 S.W.2d 93 (Tex. Civ. App.—Dallas, 1984).

## Subchapter D. Security Devices

### §92.151. Definitions

In this subchapter:

(1) "Doorknob lock" means a lock in a doorknob, with the lock operated from the exterior by a key, card, or combination and from the interior without a key, card, or combination.

(2) "Door viewer" means a permanently installed device in an exterior door that allows a person inside the dwelling to view a person outside the door. The device must be:

(A) a clear glass pane or one-way mirror; or

(B) a peephole having a barrel with a one-way lens of glass or other substance providing an angle view of not less than 160 degrees.

(3) "Exterior door" means a door providing access from a dwelling interior to the exterior. The term includes a door between a living area and a garage but does not include a sliding glass door or a screen door.

(4) "French doors" means a set of two exterior doors in which each door is hinged and abuts the other door when closed. The term includes double-hinged patio doors.

(5) "Keyed dead bolt" means:

(A) a door lock not in the doorknob that:

(i) locks with a bolt into the doorjamb; and

(ii) is operated from the exterior by a key, card, or combination and from the interior by a knob or lever without a key, card, or combination; or

(B) a doorknob lock that contains a bolt with at least a one-inch throw.

(6) "Keyless bolting device" means a door lock not in the doorknob that locks:

(A) with a bolt into a strike plate screwed into the portion of the doorjamb surface that faces the edge of the door when the door is closed or into a metal doorjamb that serves as the strike plate, operable only by knob or lever from the door's interior and not in any manner from the door's exterior, and that is commonly known as a keyless dead bolt;

(B) by a drop bolt system operated by placing a central metal plate over a metal doorjamb restraint that protrudes from the doorjamb and that is affixed to the doorjamb frame by means of three case-hardened screws at least three inches in length. One-half of the central plate must overlap the interior surface of the door and the other half of the central plate must overlap the doorjamb when the plate is placed over the doorjamb restraint. The drop bolt system must prevent the door from being opened unless the central plate is lifted off of the doorjamb restraint by a person who is on the interior side of the door.

The term "keyless bolting device" does not include a chain latch, flip latch, surface-mounted slide bolt, mortise door bolt, surface-mounted barrel bolt, surface-mounted swing bar door guard, spring-loaded night-latch, foot bolt, or other lock or latch; or

(C) by a metal bar or metal tube that is placed across the entire interior side of the door and secured in place at each end of the bar or tube by heavy-duty metal screw hooks. The screw hooks must be at least three inches in length and must be screwed into the door frame stud or wall stud on each side of the door. The bar or tube must be capable of being secured to both of the screw hooks and must be permanently attached in some way to the door frame stud or wall stud. When secured to the screw hooks, the bar or tube must prevent the door from being opened unless the bar or tube is removed by a person who is on the interior side of the door.

(7) "Landlord" means a dwelling owner, lessor, sublessor, management company, or managing agent, including an on-site manager.

(8) "Multiunit complex" means two or more dwellings in one or more buildings that are:

(A) under common ownership;

(B) managed by the same owner, agent, or management company; and

(C) located on the same lot or tract or adjacent lots or tracts of land.

(9) "Possession of a dwelling" means occupancy by a tenant under a lease, including occupancy until the time the tenant moves out or a writ of possession is issued by a court. The term does not include occupancy before the initial occupancy date authorized under a lease.

(10) "Rekey" means to change or alter a security device that is operated by a key, card, or combination so that a different key, card, or combination is necessary to operate the security device.

(11) "Security device" means a doorknob lock, door viewer, keyed dead bolt, keyless bolting device, sliding door handle latch, sliding door pin lock, sliding door security bar, or window latch in a dwelling.

(12) "Sliding door handle latch" means a latch or lock:

(A) located near the handle on a sliding glass door;

(B) operated with or without a key; and

(C) designed to prevent the door from being opened.

(13) "Sliding door pin lock" means a lock on a sliding glass door that consists of a pin or nail inserted from the interior side of the door at the side opposite the door's handle and that is designed to prevent the door from being opened or lifted.

(14) "Sliding door security bar" means a bar or rod that can be placed at the bottom of or across the interior side of the fixed panel of a sliding glass door and that is designed to prevent the door from being opened.

(15) "Tenant turnover date" means the date a new tenant moves into a dwelling under a lease after all previous tenants have moved out. The term does not include dates of entry or occupation not authorized by the landlord.

(16) "Window latch" means a device on a window that prevents the window from being opened and that is operated without a key and only from the interior.

## §92.152. Application of Subchapter

(a) This subchapter does not apply to: (1) a room in a hotel, motel, or inn or to similar transient housing; (2) residential housing owned or operated by a public or private college or university accredited by a recognized accrediting agency as defined under Section 61.003, Education Code; (3) residential housing operated by preparatory schools accredited by the Texas Education Agency, a regional accrediting agency, or any accrediting agency recognized by the commissioner of education; or (4) a temporary residential tenancy created by a contract for sale in which the buyer occupies the property before closing or the seller occupies the property after closing for a specific term not to exceed 90 days.

(b) Except as provided by Subsection (a), a dwelling to which this subchapter applies includes:

(1) a room in a dormitory or rooming house;

(2) a mobile home;

(3) a single family house, duplex, or triplex; and

(4) a living unit in an apartment, condominium, cooperative, or townhome project.

**§92.153. Security Devices Required Without Necessity of Tenant Request**
(a) Except as provided by Subsections (b), (e), (f), (g), and (h) and without necessity of request by the tenant, a dwelling must be equipped with:

(1) a window latch on each exterior window of the dwelling;

(2) a doorknob lock or keyed dead bolt on each exterior door;

(3) a sliding door pin lock on each exterior sliding glass door of the dwelling;

(4) a sliding door handle latch or a sliding door security bar on each exterior sliding glass door of the dwelling; and

(5) a keyless bolting device and a door viewer on each exterior door of the dwelling.

(b) If the dwelling has French doors, one door of each pair of French doors must meet the requirements of Subsection (a) and the other door must have:

(1) a keyed dead bolt or keyless bolting device capable of insertion into the doorjamb above the door and a keyless bolting device capable of insertion into the floor or threshold, each with a bolt having a throw of one inch or more; or

(2) a bolt installed inside the door and operated from the edge of the door, capable of insertion into the doorjamb above the door, and another bolt installed inside the door and operated from the edge of the door capable of insertion into the floor or threshold, each bolt having a throw of three-fourths inch or more.

(c) A security device required by Subsection (a) or (b) must be installed at the landlord's expense.

(d) Subsections (a) and (b) apply only when a tenant is in possession of a dwelling.

(e) A keyless bolting device is not required to be installed at the landlord's expense on an exterior door if:

(1) the dwelling is part of a multiunit complex in which the majority of dwelling units are leased to tenants who are over 55 years of age or who have a physical or mental disability;

(2) a tenant or occupant in the dwelling is over 55 years of age or has a physical or mental disability; and

(3) the landlord is expressly required or permitted to periodically check on the well-being or health of the tenant as a part of a written lease or other written agreement.

(f) A keyless bolting device is not required to be installed at the landlord's expense if a tenant or occupant in the dwelling is over 55 years of age or has a physical or mental disability, the tenant requests, in writing, that the landlord deactivate or not install the keyless bolting device, and the tenant certifies in the request that the tenant or occupant is over 55 years of age or has a physical or mental disability. The request must be a separate document and may not be included as part of a lease agreement. A landlord is not exempt as provided by this subsection if the landlord knows or has reason to know that the requirements of this subsection are not fulfilled.

(g) A keyed dead bolt or a doorknob lock is not required to be installed at the landlord's expense on an exterior door if at the time the tenant agrees to lease the dwelling:

(1) at least one exterior door usable for normal entry into the dwelling has both a keyed dead bolt and a keyless bolting device, installed in accordance with the height, strike plate, and throw requirements of Section 92.154; and

(2) all other exterior doors have a keyless bolting device installed in accordance with the height, strike plate, and throw requirements of Section 92.154.

(h) A security device required by this section must be operable throughout the time a tenant is in possession of a dwelling. However, a landlord may deactivate or remove the locking mechanism of a doorknob lock or remove any device not qualifying as a keyless bolting device if a keyed dead bolt has been installed on the same door.

(i) A landlord is subject to the tenant remedies provided by Section 92.164(a) (4) if the landlord:

(1) deactivates or does not install a keyless bolting device, claiming an exemption under Subsection (e), (f), or (g); and

(2) knows or has reason to know that the requirements of the subsection granting the exemption are not fulfilled.

### §92.154. Height, Strike Plate, and Throw Requirements—Keyed Dead Bolt or Keyless Bolting Device

(a) A keyed dead bolt or a keyless bolting device required by this subchapter must be installed at a height:

(1) not lower than 36 inches from the floor; and

(2) not higher than:

(A) 54 inches from the floor, if installed before September 1, 1993; or

(B) 48 inches from the floor, if installed on or after September 1, 1993.

(b) A keyed dead bolt or a keyless bolting device described in Section 92.151(6)(A) or (B) in a dwelling must:

(1) have a strike plate screwed into the portion of the doorjamb surface that faces the edge of the door when the door is closed; or

(2) be installed in a door with a metal doorjamb that serves as the strike plate.

(c) A keyed dead bolt or keyless dead bolt, as described by Section 92.151(6)(A), installed in a dwelling on or after September 1, 1993, must have a bolt with a throw of not less than one inch.

(d) The requirements of this section do not apply to a keyed dead bolt or a keyless bolting device in one door of a pair of French doors that is installed in accordance with the requirements of Section 92.153(b)(1) or (2).

### §92.155. Height Requirements—Sliding Door Security Devices

A sliding door pin lock or sliding door security bar required by this subchapter must be installed at a height not higher than:

(1) 54 inches from the floor, if installed before September 1, 1993; or

(2) 48 inches from the floor, if installed on or after September 1, 1993.

### §92.156. Rekeying or Change of Security Devices

(a) A security device operated by a key, card, or combination shall be rekeyed by the landlord at the landlord's expense not later than the seventh day after each tenant turnover date.

(b) A landlord shall perform additional rekeying or change a security device at the tenant's expense if requested by the tenant. A tenant may make an unlimited number of requests under this subsection.

(c) The expense of rekeying security devices for purposes of the use or change of the landlord's master key must be paid by the landlord.

(d) This section does not apply to locks on closet doors or other interior doors.

**§92.157. Security Devices Requested by Tenant**
(a) At a tenant's request made at any time, a landlord, at the tenant's expense, shall install:

(1) a keyed dead bolt on an exterior door if the door has:

(A) a doorknob lock but not a keyed dead bolt; or

(B) a keyless bolting device but not a keyed dead bolt or doorknob lock; and

(2) a sliding door pin lock or sliding door security bar if the door is an exterior sliding glass door without a sliding door pin lock or sliding door security bar.

(b) At a tenant's request made before January 1, 1995, a landlord, at the tenant's expense, shall install on an exterior door of a dwelling constructed before September 1, 1993:

(1) a keyless bolting device if the door does not have a keyless bolting device; and

(2) a door viewer if the door does not have a door viewer.

(c) If a security device required by Section 92.153 to be installed on or after January 1, 1995, without necessity of a tenant's request has not been installed by the landlord, the tenant may request the landlord to immediately install it, and the landlord shall immediately install it at the landlord's expense.

**§92.158. Landlord's Duty to Repair or Replace Security Device**
During the lease term and any renewal period, a landlord shall repair or replace a security device on request or notification by the tenant that the security device is inoperable or in need of repair or replacement.

**§92.159. When Tenant's Request or Notice Must Be in Writing**
A tenant's request or notice under this subchapter may be given orally unless the tenant has a written lease that requires the request or notice to be in writing and that requirement is underlined or in boldfaced print in the lease.

**§92.160. Type, Brand, and Manner of Installation**
Except as otherwise required by this subchapter, a landlord may select the type, brand, and manner of installation, including placement, of a security device installed under this subchapter. This section does not apply to a security device installed, repaired, changed, replaced, or rekeyed by a tenant under Section 92.164(a)(1) or 92.165(1).

**§92.161. Compliance with Tenant Request Required Within Reasonable Time**
(a) Except as provided by Subsections (b) and (c), a landlord must comply with a tenant's request for rekeying, changing, installing, repairing, or replacing a security device under Section 92.156, 92.157, or 92.158 within a reasonable time. A reasonable time for purposes of this subsection is presumed to be not later than the seventh day after the date the request is received by the landlord.

(b) If within the time allowed under Section 92.162(c) a landlord requests advance payment of charges that the landlord is entitled to collect under that section, the landlord shall comply with a tenant's request under Section 92.156(b), 92.157(a), or 92.157(b) within a reasonable time. A reasonable time for purposes of this subsection is presumed to be not later than the seventh day after the date a tenant's advance payment is received by the landlord, except as provided by Subsection (c).

(c) A reasonable time for purposes of Subsections (a) and (b) is presumed to be not later than 72 hours after the time of receipt of the tenant's request and any required advance payment if at the time of making the request the tenant informed the landlord that:

(1) an unauthorized entry occurred or was attempted in the tenant's dwelling;

(2) an unauthorized entry occurred or was attempted in another unit in the multiunit complex in which the tenant's dwelling is located during the two months preceding the date of the request; or

(3) a crime of personal violence occurred in the multiunit complex in which the tenant's dwelling is located during the two months preceding the date of the request.

(d) A landlord may rebut the presumption provided by Subsection (a) or (b) if despite the diligence of the landlord:

(1) the landlord did not know of the tenant's request, without the fault of the landlord;

(2) materials, labor, or utilities were unavailable; or

(3) a delay was caused by circumstances beyond the landlord's control, including the illness or death of the landlord or a member of the landlord's immediate family.

(e) This section does not apply to a landlord's duty to install or rekey, without necessity of a tenant's request, a security device under Section 92.153 or 92.156(a).

### §92.162. Payment of Charges; Limits on Amount Charged

(a) A landlord may not require a tenant to pay for repair or replacement of a security device due to normal wear and tear. A landlord may not require a tenant to pay for other repairs or replacements of a security device except as provided by Subsections (b), (c), and (d).

(b) A landlord may require a tenant to pay for repair or replacement of a security device if an underlined provision in a written lease authorizes the landlord to do so and the repair or replacement is necessitated by misuse or damage by the tenant, a member of the tenant's family, an occupant, or a guest, and not by normal wear and tear. Misuse of or damage to a security device that occurs during the tenant's occupancy is presumed to be caused by the tenant, a family member, an occupant, or a guest. The tenant has the burden of proving that the misuse or damage was caused by another party.

(c) A landlord may require a tenant to pay in advance charges for which the tenant is liable under this subchapter if a written lease authorizes the landlord to require advance payment, and the landlord notifies the tenant within a reasonable time after the tenant's request that advance payment is required, and:

(1) the tenant is more than 30 days delinquent in reimbursing the landlord for charges to which the landlord is entitled under Subsection (b); or

(2) the tenant requested that the landlord repair, install, change, or rekey the same security device during the 30 days preceding the tenant's request, and the landlord complied with the request.

(d) A landlord authorized by this subchapter to charge a tenant for repairing, installing, changing, or rekeying a security device under this subchapter may not require the tenant to pay more than the total cost charged by a third-party contractor for material, labor, taxes, and extra keys. If the landlord's employees perform the work, the charge may include a reasonable amount for overhead but may not include a profit to the landlord. If management company employees perform the work, the charge may include reasonable overhead and profit but may not exceed the cost charged to the owner by the management company for comparable security devices installed by management company employees at the owner's request and expense.

(e) The owner of a dwelling shall reimburse a management company, managing agent, or on-site manager for costs expended by that person in complying with this subchapter. A management company, managing agent, or on-site manager may reimburse itself for the costs from the owner's funds in its possession or control.

### §92.163. Removal or Alteration of Security Device by Tenant

A security device that is installed, changed, or rekeyed under this subchapter becomes a fixture of the dwelling. Except as provided by Section 92.164(a)(1) or 92.165(1) regarding the remedy of repair-and-deduct, a tenant may not remove, change, rekey, replace, or alter a security device or have it removed, changed, rekeyed, replaced, or altered without permission of the landlord.

### §92.164. Tenant Remedies for Landlord's Failure to Install or Rekey Certain Security Devices

(a) If a landlord does not comply with Section 92.153 or 92.156(a) regarding installation or rekeying of a security device, the tenant may:

(1) install or rekey the security device as required by this subchapter and deduct the reasonable cost of material, labor, taxes, and extra keys from the tenant's next rent payment, in accordance with Section 92.166;

(2) serve a written request for compliance on the landlord, and, except as provided by Subsections (b) and (c), if the landlord does not comply on or before the third day after the date the notice is received, unilaterally terminate the lease without court proceedings;

(3) file suit against the landlord without serving a request for compliance and obtain a judgment for:

(A) a court order directing the landlord to comply, if the tenant is in possession of the dwelling;

(B) the tenant's actual damages;

(C) court costs; and

(D) attorney's fees except in suits for recovery of property damages, personal injuries, or wrongful death; and

(4) serve a written request for compliance on the landlord, and, except as provided by Subsections (b) and (c), if the landlord does not comply on or before the third day after the date the notice is received, file suit against the landlord and obtain a judgment for:

(A) a court order directing the landlord to comply and bring all dwellings owned by the landlord into compliance, if the tenant serving the written request is in possession of the dwelling;

(B) the tenant's actual damages;

(C) punitive damages if the tenant suffers actual damages;

(D) a civil penalty of one month's rent plus $500;

(E) court costs; and

(F) attorney's fees except in suits for recovery of property damages, personal injuries, or wrongful death.

(b) A tenant may not unilaterally terminate the lease under Subsection (a)(2) or file suit against the landlord to obtain a judgment under Subsection (a)(4) unless the landlord does not comply on or before the seventh day after the date the written request for compliance is received if the lease includes language underlined or in boldface print that in substance provides the tenant with notice that:

(1) the landlord at the landlord's expense is required to equip the dwelling, when the tenant takes possession, with the security devices described by Sections 92.153(a)(1)–(4) and (6);

(2) the landlord is not required to install a doorknob lock or keyed dead bolt at the landlord's expense if the exterior doors meet the requirements of Section 92.153(f);

(3) the landlord is not required to install a keyless bolting device at the landlord's expense on an exterior door if the landlord is expressly required or permitted to periodically check on the well-being or health of the tenant as provided by Section 92.153(e)(3); and

(4) the tenant has the right to install or rekey a security device required by this subchapter and deduct the reasonable cost from the tenant's next rent payment, as provided by Subsection (a)(1).

(c) Regardless of whether the lease contains language complying with the requirements of Subsection (b), the additional time for landlord compliance provided by Subsection (b) does not apply if at the time the tenant served the written request for compliance on the landlord the tenant informed the landlord that an unauthorized entry occurred or was attempted in the tenant's dwelling, an unauthorized entry occurred or was attempted in another unit in the multiunit complex in which the tenant's dwelling is located during the two months preceding the date of the request, or a crime of personal violence occurred in the multiunit complex in which the tenant's dwelling is located during the two months preceding the date of the request, unless despite the diligence of the landlord:

(1) the landlord did not know of the tenant's request, without the fault of the landlord;

(2) materials, labor, or utilities were unavailable; or

(3) a delay was caused by circumstances beyond the landlord's control, including the illness or death of the landlord or a member of the landlord's immediate family.

### §92.1641. Landlord's Defenses

The landlord has a defense to liability under Section 92.164 if:

(1) the tenant has not fully paid all rent then due from the tenant on the date the tenant gives a request under Subsection (a) of Section 92.157 or the notice required by Section 92.164; or

(2) on the date the tenant terminates the lease or files suit the tenant has not fully paid costs requested by the landlord and authorized by Section 92.162.

### §92.165. Tenant Remedies for Other Landlord Violations

If a landlord does not comply with a tenant's request regarding rekeying, changing, adding, repairing, or replacing a security device under Section 92.156(b), 92.157, or 92.158 in accordance with the time limits and other requirements of this subchapter, the tenant may:

(1) install, repair, change, replace, or rekey the security devices as required by this subchapter and deduct the reasonable cost of material, labor, taxes, and extra keys from the tenant's next rent payment in accordance with Section 92.166;

(2) unilaterally terminate the lease without court proceedings; and

(3) file suit against the landlord and obtain a judgment for:

(A) a court order directing the landlord to comply, if the tenant is in possession of the dwelling;

(B) the tenant's actual damages;

(C) punitive damages if the tenant suffers actual damages and the landlord's failure to comply is intentional, malicious, or grossly negligent;

(D) a civil penalty of one month's rent plus $500;

(E) court costs; and

(F) attorney's fees except in suits for recovery of property damages, personal injuries, or wrongful death.

### §92.166. Notice of Tenant's Deduction of Repair Costs from Rent

(a) A tenant shall notify the landlord of a rent deduction attributable to the tenant's installing, repairing, changing, replacing, or rekeying of a security device under Section 92.164(a)(1) or 92.165(1) after the landlord's failure to comply with this subchapter. The notice must be given at the time of the reduced rent payment.

(b) Unless otherwise provided in a written lease, a tenant shall provide one duplicate of the key to any key-operated security device installed or rekeyed by the tenant under Section 92.164(a)(1) or 92.165(1) within a reasonable time after the landlord's written request for the key.

### §92.167. Landlord's Defenses

(a) A landlord has a defense to liability under Section 92.165 if on the date the tenant terminates the lease or files suit the tenant has not fully paid costs requested by the landlord and authorized by this subchapter.

(b) A management company or managing agent who is not the owner of a dwelling and who has not purported to be the owner in the lease has a defense to liability under Sections 92.164 and 92.165 if before the date the tenant is in possession of the dwelling or the date of the tenant's request for installation, repair, replacement, change, or rekeying and before any property damage or personal injury to the tenant, the management company or managing agent:

(1) did not have funds of the dwelling owner in its possession or control with which to comply with this subchapter;

(2) made written request to the dwelling owner that the owner fund and allow installation, repair, change, replacement, or rekeying of security devices as required under this subchapter and mailed the request, certified mail return receipt requested, to the dwelling owner; and

(3) not later than the third day after the date of receipt of the tenant's request, provided the tenant with a written notice:

(A) stating that the management company or managing agent has taken the actions in Subdivisions (1) and (2);

(B) stating that the owner has not provided or will not provide the necessary funds; and

(C) explaining the remedies available to the tenant for the landlord's failure to comply.

### §92.168. Tenant's Remedy on Notice from Management Company

The tenant may unilaterally terminate the lease or exercise other remedies under Sections 92.164 and 92.165 after receiving written notice from a management company that the owner of the dwelling has not provided or will not provide funds to repair, install, change, replace, or rekey a security device as required by this subchapter.

### §92.169. Agent for Delivery of Notice

A managing agent or an agent to whom rent is regularly paid, whether residing or maintaining an office on-site or off-site, is the agent of the landlord for purposes of notice and other communications required or permitted by this subchapter.

### §92.170. Effect on Other Landlord Duties and Tenant Remedies

The duties of a landlord and the remedies of a tenant under this subchapter are in lieu of common law, other statutory law, and local ordinances relating to a residential landlord's duty to install, change, rekey, repair, or replace security devices and a tenant's remedies for the landlord's failure to install, change, rekey, repair, or replace security devices, except that a municipal ordinance adopted before January 1,

1993, may require installation of security devices at the landlord's expense by an earlier date than a date required by this subchapter. This subchapter does not affect a duty of a landlord or a remedy of a tenant under Subchapter B regarding habitability.

Security has always been a problem for residential tenancies. The general rule is that unless the landlord is on notice of a problem, he is not responsible for the criminal conduct of a third party on the premises. *Walker* v. *Harris*, 924 S.W.2d 375 (Tex. 1996). If, however, the landlord is aware of certain deficiencies in security or existing dangerous conditions, he does have a duty of care to exercise prudent judgment in providing security. *Blaustein* v. *Gilbert-Dallas Co., Inc.*, 749 S.W.2d 633 (Tex. App.—Eastland, 1988, no writ); *Nixon* v. *Mr. Property Management Co., Inc.*, 690 S.W.2d 546 (Tex. 1985).

## Subchapter E. Disclosure of Ownership and Management

### §92.201. Disclosure of Ownership and Management

(a) A landlord shall disclose to a tenant, or to any government official or employee acting in an official capacity, according to this subchapter:

(1) the name and either a street or post office box address of the holder of record title, according to the deed records in the county clerk's office, of the dwelling rented by the tenant or inquired about by the government official or employee acting in an official capacity; and

(2) if an entity located off-site from the tenant's dwelling is primarily responsible for managing the dwelling, the name and street address of the management company.

(b) Disclosure to a tenant under Subsection (a) must be made by:

(1) giving the information in writing to the tenant on or before the seventh day after the day the landlord receives the tenant's request for the information;

(2) continuously posting the information in a conspicuous place in the dwelling or the office of the on-site manager or on the outside of the entry door to the office of the on-site manager on or before the seventh day after the date the landlord receives the tenant's request for the information; or

(3) including the information in a copy of the tenant's lease or in written rules given to the tenant before the tenant requests the information.

(c) Disclosure of information to a tenant may be made under Subdivision (1) or (2) or Subsection (b) before the tenant requests the information.

(d) Disclosure of information to a government official or employee must be made by giving the information in writing to the official or employee on or before the seventh day after the date the landlord receives the request from the official or employee for the information.

(e) A correction to the information may be made by any of the methods authorized for providing the information.

(f) For the purposes of this section, an owner or property manager may disclose either an actual name or names or an assumed name if an assumed name certificate has been recorded with the county clerk.

### §92.202. Landlord's Failure to Disclose Information

(a) A landlord is liable to a tenant or a governmental body according to this subchapter if:

(1) after the tenant or government official or employee makes a request for information under Section 92.201, the landlord does not provide the information; and

(2) the landlord does not give the information to the tenant or government official or employee before the eighth day after the date the tenant, official, or employee

gives the landlord written notice that the tenant, official, or employee may exercise his remedies under this subchapter if the landlord does not comply with the request by the tenant, official, or employee for the information within seven days.

(b) If the tenant's lease is in writing, the lease may require the tenant's initial request for information to be written. A request by a government official or employee for information must be in writing.

### §92.203. Landlord's Failure to Correct Information

A landlord who has provided information under Subdivision (2) or (3) of Subsection (b) of Section 92.201 is liable to a tenant according to this subchapter if:

(1) the information becomes incorrect because a name or address changes; and

(2) the landlord fails to correct the information on or before the seventh day after the date the tenant gives the landlord written notice that the tenant may exercise the remedies under this subchapter if the corrected information is not provided within seven days.

### §92.204. Bad Faith Violation

A landlord acts in bad faith and is liable according to this subchapter if the landlord gives an incorrect name or address under Subsection (a) of Section 92.201 by willfully:

(1) disclosing incorrect information under Section 92.201(b)(1) or (2) or Section 92.201(d); or

(2) failing to correct information given under Section 92.201(b)(1) or (2) or Section 92.201(d) that the landlord knows is incorrect.

### §92.205. Remedies

(a) A tenant of a landlord who is liable under Sections 92.202, 92.203, or 92.204 may obtain or exercise one or more of the following remedies:

(1) a court order directing the landlord to make a disclosure required by this subchapter;

(2) a judgment against the landlord for an amount equal to the tenant's actual costs in discovering the information required to be disclosed by this subchapter;

(3) a judgment against the landlord for one month's rent plus $100;

(4) a judgment against the landlord for court costs and attorney's fees; and

(5) unilateral termination of the lease without a court proceeding.

(b) A governmental body whose official or employee has requested information from a landlord who is liable under Section 92.202 or 92.204 may obtain or exercise one or more of the following remedies:

(1) a court order directing the landlord to make a disclosure required by this subchapter;

(2) a judgment against the landlord for an amount equal to the governmental body's actual costs in discovering the information required to be disclosed by this subchapter;

(3) a judgment against the landlord for $500; and

(4) a judgment against the landlord for court costs and attorney's fees.

### §92.206. Landlord's Defense

A landlord has a defense to liability under Section 92.202 or 92.203 if the tenant owes rent on the date the tenant gives a notice required by either of those sections. Rent delinquency is not a defense for a violation of Section 92.204.

### §92.207. Agents for Delivery of Notice

(a) A managing or leasing agent, whether residing or maintaining an office on-site or off-site, is the agent of the landlord for purposes of:

(1) notice and other communications required or permitted by this subchapter;

(2) notice and other communications from a governmental body relating to a violation of health, sanitation, safety, or nuisance laws on the landlord's property where the dwelling is located, including notices of:

(A) demands for abatement of nuisances;

(B) repair of a substandard dwelling;

(C) remedy of dangerous conditions;

(D) reimbursement of costs incurred by the governmental body in curing the violation;

(E) fines; and

(F) service or process.

(b) If the landlord's name and business street address in this state have not been furnished in writing to the tenant or government official or employee, the person who collects the rent from a tenant is the landlord's authorized agent for purposes of Subsection (a).

### §92.208. Additional Enforcement by Local Ordinance

The duties of a landlord and the remedies of a tenant under this subchapter are in lieu of the common law, other statutory law, and local ordinances relating to the disclosure of ownership and management of a dwelling by a landlord to a tenant. However, this subchapter does not prohibit the adoption of a local ordinance that conforms to this subchapter but which contains additional enforcement provisions.

## Subchapter F. Smoke Detectors

### §92.251. Definition

In this subchapter, "dwelling unit" means a home, mobile home, duplex unit, apartment unit, condominium unit, or any dwelling unit in a multiunit residential structure. It also means a "dwelling" as defined by Section 92.001.

### §92.252. Application of Other Law; Municipal Regulation

(a) The duties of a landlord and the remedies of a tenant under this subchapter are in lieu of common law, other statutory law, and local ordinances regarding a residential landlord's duty to install, inspect, or repair a smoke detector in a dwelling unit. However, this subchapter does not:

(1) affect a local ordinance adopted before September 1, 1981, that requires landlords to install smoke detectors in new or remodeled dwelling units before September 1, 1981, if the ordinance conforms with or is amended to conform with this subchapter.

(2) limit or prevent adoption or enforcement of a local ordinance relating to fire safety as a part of a building, fire, or housing code, including any requirements relating to the installation of smoke detectors or the type of smoke detectors; or

(3) otherwise limit or prevent the adoption of a local ordinance that conforms to this subchapter but which contains additional enforcement provisions, except as provided by Subsection (b); or

(4) affect a local ordinance that requires regular inspections by local officials of smoke detectors in dwelling units and that requires smoke detectors to be operational at the time of inspection.

(b) If a smoke detector powered by battery has been installed in a dwelling unit built before September 1, 1987, in compliance with this subchapter and local ordinances, a local ordinance may not require that a smoke detector powered by alternating current be installed in the unit unless:

(1) the interior of the unit is repaired, remodeled, or rebuilt at a projected cost of more than $2,500 and the repair, remodeling, or rebuilding requires a municipal building permit;

(2) an addition occurs to the unit at a projected cost of more than $2,500;

(3) a smoke detector powered by alternating current was actually installed in the unit at any time prior to September 1, 1987; or

(4) a smoke detector powered by alternating current was required by lawful city ordinance at the time of initial construction of the unit.

### §92.253. Exemption

(a) This subchapter does not apply to:

(1) a dwelling unit that is occupied by its owner, no part of which is leased to a tenant;

(2) a dwelling unit in a building five or more stories in height in which smoke detectors are required or regulated by local ordinance; or

(3) a nursing or convalescent home licensed by the Texas Department of Health and certified to meet the Life Safety Code under federal law and regulations.

(b) Notwithstanding this subchapter, a person licensed by the State Board of Insurance to install fire alarms or fire detection devices under Article 5.43-2, Insurance Code, shall comply with that article when installing smoke detectors.

### §92.254. Smoke Detector

(a) A smoke detector must be:

(1) designed to detect both the visible and invisible products of combustion;

(2) designed with an alarm audible to the bedrooms it serves;

(3) powered by battery, alternating current, or other power sources as required by local ordinance;

(4) tested and listed for use as a smoke detector by Underwriters Laboratories, Inc., Factory Mutual Research Corporation, or United States Testing Company, Inc.; and

(5) in good working order.

(b) The power system and installation procedure of a security device that is electrically operated rather than battery operated must comply with applicable local ordinances.

### §92.255. Installation and Location in New Construction

(a) Before the first tenant takes possession of a dwelling unit, the landlord shall install at least one smoke detector outside, but in the vicinity of, each separate bedroom in the dwelling unit, except:

(1) if the dwelling unit is designed to use a single room for dining, living, and sleeping, the smoke detector must be located inside the room;

(2) if the bedrooms are served by the same corridor, at least one smoke detector must be installed in the corridor in the immediate vicinity of the bedrooms; and

(3) if at least one bedroom is located on a level above the living and cooking area, the smoke detector for the bedrooms must be placed in the center of the ceiling directly above the top of the stairway.

(b) In this section, "bedroom" means a room designed with the intent that it be used for sleeping purposes.

### §92.256. Installation in Units Constructed or Occupied on or Before September 1, 1981

(a) If the dwelling unit was occupied as a residence on or before September 1, 1981, or the building permit for the unit was issued on or before that date, the landlord shall install at least one smoke detector in accordance with Sections 92.255 and 92.257 on or before September 1, 1984.

(b) Before September 1, 1984, a tenant may install a battery-operated smoke detector in the tenant's dwelling unit without the landlord's prior consent if the installation is made according to Sections 92.255 and 92.257. When the tenant's lease terminates, including after a renewal or extension, the tenant may remove the smoke detector, but the tenant is liable to the landlord for any unnecessary damages to the dwelling unit caused by the removal.

### §92.257. Installation Procedure

(a) Subject to Subsections (b) and (c), a smoke detector must be installed according to the manufacturer's recommended procedures.

(b) A smoke detector must be installed on a ceiling or wall. If on a ceiling, it must be no closer than six inches to a wall. If on a wall, it must be no closer than six inches and no farther than 12 inches from the ceiling.

(c) A smoke detector may be located other than as required by Subsection (b) if a local ordinance or a local or state fire marshal approves.

### § 92.2571 Alternative Compliance

A landlord complies with the requirements of this subchapter relating to the provision of smoke detectors in the dwelling unit if the landlord:

(1) has a fire detection device, as defined by Article 5.43-2, Insurance Code, that includes a smoke detection device installed in a dwelling unit; or

(2) for a dwelling unit that is a one-family or two-family dwelling unit, installs smoke detectors in compliance with Chapter 766, Health and Safety Code (special smoke detectors for the deaf).

### §92.258. Inspection and Repair

(a) The landlord shall inspect and repair a smoke detector according to this section.

(b) The landlord shall determine that the smoke detector is in good working order at the beginning of the tenant's possession by testing the smoke detector with smoke, by operating the testing button on the smoke detector, or by following the recommended test procedures of the manufacturer for the particular model.

(c) During the term of a lease or during a renewal or extension, the landlord has a duty to inspect and repair a smoke detector, but only if the tenant gives the landlord notice of a malfunction or requests to the landlord that the smoke detector be inspected or repaired. This duty does not exist with respect to damage or a malfunction caused by the tenant, the tenant's family, or the tenant's guests or invitees during the term of the lease or a renewal or extension, except that the landlord has a duty to repair or replace the smoke detector if the tenant pays in advance the reasonable repair or replacement cost, including labor, materials, taxes, and overhead.

(d) The landlord must comply with the tenant's request for inspection or repair within a reasonable time, considering the availability of material, labor, and utilities.

(e) The landlord has met the duty to inspect and repair if the smoke detector is in good working order after the landlord tests the smoke detector with smoke, operates the testing button on the smoke detector, or follows other recommended test procedures of the manufacturer for the particular model.

(f) The landlord is not obligated to provide batteries for a battery-operated smoke detector after a tenant takes possession if the smoke detector was in good working order at the time the tenant took possession.

(g) A smoke detector that is in good working order at the beginning of a tenant's possession is presumed to be in good working order until the tenant requests repair of the smoke detector as provided by this subchapter.

### §92.259. Landlord's Failure to Install, Inspect, or Repair

(a) A landlord is liable according to this subchapter if:

(1) the landlord did not install a smoke detector at the time of initial occupancy by the tenant as required by this subchapter or a municipal ordinance permitted by this subchapter; or

(2) the landlord does not install, inspect, or repair the smoke detector on or before the seventh day after the date the tenant gives the landlord written notice that the tenant may exercise his remedies under this subchapter if the landlord does not comply with the request within seven days.

(b) If the tenant gives notice under Subsection (a)(2) and the tenant's lease is in writing, the lease may require the tenant to make the initial request for installation, inspection, or repair in writing.

### §92.260. Tenant Remedies

A tenant of a landlord who is liable under Section 92.259 may obtain or exercise one or more of the following remedies:

(1) a court order directing the landlord to comply with the tenant's request if the tenant is in possession of the dwelling unit;

(2) a judgment against the landlord for damages suffered by the tenant because of the landlord's violation;

(3) a judgment against the landlord for a civil penalty of one month's rent plus $100 if the landlord violates Section 92.259 (a)(2);

(4) a judgment against the landlord for court costs;

(5) a judgment against the landlord for attorney's fees in an action under Subdivision (1) or (3); and

(6) unilateral termination of the lease without a court proceeding if the landlord violates Section 92.259 (a)(2).

### §92.261. Landlord's Defenses

The landlord has a defense to liability under Section 92.259 if:

(1) on the date the tenant gives the notice required by Section 92.259 the tenant has not paid all rent due from the tenant; or

(2) on the date the tenant terminates the lease or files suit the tenant has not fully paid costs requested by the landlord and authorized by Section 92.258.

### §92.2611. Tenant's Disabling of a Smoke Detector

(a) A tenant is liable according to this subchapter if the tenant removes a battery from a smoke detector without immediately replacing it with a working battery or knowingly disconnects or intentionally damages a smoke detector, causing it to malfunction.

(b) Except as provided in Subsection (c), a landlord of a tenant who is liable under Subsection (a) may obtain a judgment against the tenant for damages suffered by the landlord because the tenant removed a battery from a smoke detector without immediately replacing it with a working battery or knowingly disconnected or intentionally damaged the smoke detector, causing it to malfunction.

(c) A tenant is not liable for damages suffered by the landlord if the damage is caused by the landlord's failure to repair the smoke detector within a reasonable time after the tenant requests it to be repaired, considering the availability of material, labor, and utilities.

(d)(1) A landlord of a tenant who is liable under Subsection (a) may obtain or exercise one or more of the remedies in Subsection (e) if:

(A) a lease between the landlord and tenant contains a notice, in underlined or boldface print, which states in substance that the tenant must not disconnect or intentionally damage a smoke detector or remove the battery without immediately replacing it with a working battery and that the tenant may be subject to damages, civil penalties, and attorney's fees under Section 92.2611 of the Property Code for not complying with the notice; and

(B) the landlord has given notice to the tenant that the landlord intends to exercise the landlord's remedies under this subchapter if the tenant does not reconnect, repair, or replace the smoke detector or replace the removed battery within seven days after being notified by the landlord to do so.

(2) The notice in Subdivision (1) (B) must be in a separate document furnished to the tenant after the landlord has discovered that the tenant has disconnected or damaged the smoke detector or removed a battery from it.

(e) If a tenant is liable under Subsection (a) and the tenant does not comply with the landlord's notice under Subsection (d), the landlord shall have the following remedies against the tenant:

(1) a court order directing the tenant to comply with the landlord's notice;

(2) a judgment against the tenant for a civil penalty of one month's rent plus $100;

(3) a judgment against the tenant for court costs; and

(4) a judgment against the tenant for reasonable attorney's fees.

(f) A tenant's guest or invitee who suffers damage because of a landlord's failure to install, inspect, or repair a smoke detector as required by this subchapter may recover a judgment against the landlord for the damage. A tenant's guest or invitee who suffers damage because the tenant removed a battery without immediately replacing it with a working battery or because the tenant knowingly disconnected or intentionally damaged the smoke detector, causing it to malfunction, may recover a judgment against the tenant for the damage.

### §92.262. Agents for Delivery of Notice

A managing or leasing agent, whether residing or maintaining an office on-site or off-site, is the agent of the landlord for purposes of notice and other communication required or permitted by this subchapter.

If the landlord did not have notice of a nonworking smoke detector or other unsafe condition, he may not be liable for damages. See *Garza-Vale* v. *Kwiezien*, 796 S.W.2d 500 (Tex. App.—San Antonio, 1990).

## Subchapter G. Utility Cutoff

### §92.301. Landlord Liability to Tenant for Utility Cutoff

(a) A landlord who has expressly or impliedly agreed in the lease to furnish and pay for water, gas, or electric service to the tenant's dwelling is liable to the tenant if the utility company has cut off utility service to the tenant's dwelling or has given written notice to the tenant that such utility service is about to be cut off because of the landlord's nonpayment of the utility bill.

(b) If a landlord is liable to the tenant under Subsection (a) of this section, the tenant may:

(1) pay the utility company money to reconnect or avert the cutoff of utilities according to this section;

(2) terminate the lease if the termination notice is in writing and move-out is to be within 30 days from the date the tenant has notice from the utility company of a future cutoff or notice of an actual cutoff, whichever is sooner;

(3) deduct from the tenant's rent, without necessity of judicial action, the amounts paid to the utility company to reconnect or avert a cutoff;

(4) if the lease is terminated by the tenant, deduct the tenant's security deposit from the tenant's rent without necessity of lawsuit or obtain a refund of the tenant's security deposit pursuant to law;

(5) if the lease is terminated by the tenant, recover a pro rata refund of any advance rentals paid from the date of termination or the date the tenant moves out, whichever is later;

(6) recover actual damages, including but not limited to moving costs, utility connection fees, storage fees, and lost wages from work; and

(7) recover court costs and attorney's fees, excluding any attorney's fees for a cause of action for damages relating to a personal injury.

(c) When deducting for the tenant's payment of the landlord's utility bill under this section, the tenant shall submit to the landlord a copy of a receipt from the utility company which evidences the amount of payment made by the tenant to reconnect or avert cutoff of utilities.

(d) The tenant remedies under this section are effective on the date the tenant has notice from the utility company of a future cutoff or notice of an actual cutoff, whichever is sooner. However, the tenant's remedies under this section shall cease if:

(1) the landlord provides the tenant with written evidence from the utility that all delinquent sums due the utility have been paid in full; and

(2) at the time the tenant receives such evidence, the tenant has not yet terminated the lease or filed suit under this section.

There are also new requirements for rental applications. At the time an applicant is provided with a rental application, the landlord shall make available to the applicant printed notice of the landlord's tenant selection criteria and the grounds for which the rental application may be denied.

If the landlord makes the notice available, the applicant shall sign an acknowledgement indicating the notice was made available. If the acknowledgement is not signed, there is a rebuttable presumption that the notice was not made available to the applicant.

The acknowledgement must include a statement substantively equivalent to the following: "Signing this acknowledgment indicates that you have had the opportunity to review the landlord's tenant selection criteria. The tenant section criteria may include facts such as criminal history, credit history, current income, and rental history. If you do not meet the selection criteria, or if you provide inaccurate or incomplete information, your application may be rejected and your application fee will not be refunded."

## CHAPTER 93                   COMMERCIAL TENANCIES

### §93.002. Interruption of Utilities, Removal of Property, and Exclusion of Commercial Tenant

(a) A landlord or a landlord's agent may not interrupt or cause the interruption of utility service paid for directly to the utility company by a tenant unless the interruption results from bona fide repairs, construction, or an emergency.

(b) A landlord may not remove a door, window, or attic hatchway cover or a lock, latch, hinge, hinge pin, doorknob, or other mechanism connected to a door, window, or attic hatchway cover from premises leased to a tenant or remove furniture, fixtures, or appliances furnished by the landlord from premises leased to a tenant unless the landlord removes the item for a bona fide repair or replacement. If a landlord removes any of the items listed in this subsection for a bona fide repair or replacement, the repair or replacement must be promptly performed.

(c) A landlord may not intentionally prevent a tenant from entering the leased premises except by judicial process unless the exclusion results from:

(1) bona fide repairs, construction, or an emergency;

(2) removing the contents of premises abandoned by a tenant; or

(3) changing the door locks of a tenant who is delinquent in paying at least part of the rent.

(d) A tenant is presumed to have abandoned the premises if goods, equipment, or other property, in an amount substantial enough to indicate a probable intent to abandon the premises, are being or have been removed from the premises and the removal is not within the normal course of the tenant's business.

(e) A landlord may remove and store any property of a tenant that remains on premises that are abandoned. In addition to the landlord's other rights, the landlord may dispose of the stored property if the tenant does not claim the property within 60 days after the date the property is stored. The landlord shall deliver by certified mail to the tenant at the tenant's last known address a notice stating that the landlord may dispose of the tenant's property if the tenant does not claim the property within 60 days after the date the property is stored.

(f) If a landlord or a landlord's agent changes the door lock of a tenant who is delinquent in paying rent, the landlord or agent must place a written notice on the tenant's front door stating the name and the address or telephone number of the individual or company from which the new key may be obtained. The new key is required to be provided only during the tenant's regular business hours and only if the tenant pays the delinquent rent.

(g) If a landlord or a landlord's agent violates this section, the tenant may:

(1) either recover possession of the premises or terminate the lease; and

(2) recover from the landlord an amount equal to the sum of the tenant's actual damages, one month's rent or $500, whichever is greater, reasonable attorney's fees, and court costs, less any delinquent rents or other sums for which the tenant is liable to the landlord.

(h) A lease supersedes this section to the extent of any conflict.

**§93.003. Commercial Tenant's Right of Reentry After Unlawful Lockout**
(a) If a landlord has locked a tenant out of leased premises in violation of Section 93.002, the tenant may recover possession of the premises as provided by this section.

(b) The tenant must file with the justice court in the precinct in which the rental premises are located a sworn complaint for reentry, specifying the facts of the alleged unlawful lockout by the landlord or the landlord's agent. The tenant must also state orally under oath to the justice the facts of the alleged unlawful lockout.

(c) If the tenant has complied with Subsection (b) and if the justice reasonably believes an unlawful lockout has likely occurred, the justice may issue, ex parte, a writ of reentry that entitles the tenant to immediate and temporary possession of the premises, pending a final hearing on the tenant's sworn complaint for reentry.

(d) The writ of reentry must be served on either the landlord or the landlord's management company, on-premises manager, or rent collector in the same manner as a writ of possession in a forcible detainer action.

(e) The landlord is entitled to a hearing on the tenant's sworn complaint for reentry. The writ of reentry must notify the landlord of the right to a hearing. The hearing shall be held not earlier than the first day and not later than the seventh day after the date the landlord requests a hearing.

(f) If the landlord fails to request a hearing on the tenant's sworn complaint for reentry before the eighth day after the date of service of the writ of reentry on the landlord under Subsection (d), a judgment for court costs may be rendered against the landlord.

(g) A party may appeal from the court's judgment at the hearing on the sworn complaint for reentry in the same manner as a party may appeal a judgment in a forcible detainer suit.

(h) If a writ of possession is issued, it supersedes a writ of reentry.

(i) If the landlord or the person on whom a writ of reentry is served fails to immediately comply with the writ or later disobeys the writ, the failure is grounds for contempt of court against the landlord or the person on whom the writ was served, under Section 21.002, Government Code. If the writ is disobeyed, the tenant or the tenant's attorney may file in the court in which the reentry action is pending an affidavit stating the name of the person who has disobeyed the writ and describing the acts or omissions constituting the disobedience. On receipt of an affidavit, the justice shall issue a show cause order, directing the person to appear on a designated date and show cause why he should not be adjudged in contempt of court. If the justice finds, after considering the evidence at the hearing, that the person has directly or indirectly disobeyed the writ, the justice may commit the person to jail without bail until the person purges himself of the contempt in a manner and form as the justice may direct. If the person disobeyed the writ before receiving the show cause order but has complied with the writ after receiving the order, the justice may find the person in contempt and assess punishment under Section 21.002(c), Government Code.

(j) This section does not affect a tenant's right to pursue a separate cause of action under Section 93.002.

(k) If a tenant in bad faith files a sworn complaint for reentry resulting in a writ of reentry being served on the landlord or landlord's agent, the landlord may in a separate cause of action recover from the tenant an amount equal to actual damages, one month's rent or $500, whichever is greater, reasonable attorney's fees, and costs of court, less any sums for which the landlord is liable to the tenant.

(l) The fee for filing a sworn complaint for reentry is the same as that for filing a civil action in justice court. The fee for service of a writ of reentry is the same as that for service of a writ of possession. The fee for service of a show cause order is the same as that for service of a civil citation. The justice may defer payment of the tenant's filing fees and service costs for the sworn complaint for reentry and writ of reentry. Court costs may be waived only if the tenant executes a pauper's affidavit.

(m) This section does not affect the rights of a landlord or tenant in a forcible detainer or forcible entry and detainer action.

### §93.004. Security Deposit.

A security deposit is any advance of money, other than a rental application deposit or an advance payment of rent, that is intended primarily to secure performance under a lease of commercial rental property.

### §93.005. Obligation To Refund Security Deposit.

(a) The landlord shall refund the security deposit to the tenant not later than the 60th day after the tenant surrenders the premises and provides notice of the tenant's forwarding address under Section 93.009.

(b) The tenant's claim to the security deposit takes priority over the claim of any creditor of the landlord, including a trustee in bankruptcy.

### §93.006. Retention Of Security Deposit; Accounting.

(a) Before returning a security deposit, the landlord may deduct from the deposit damages and charges for which the tenant is legally liable under the lease or damages and charges that result from a breach of the lease.

(b) The landlord may not retain any portion of a security deposit to cover normal wear and tear. In this subsection, "normal wear and tear" means deterioration that results from the intended use of the commercial premises, including breakage or malfunction due to age or deteriorated condition, but the term does not include deterioration that results from negligence, carelessness, accident, or abuse of the premises, equipment, or chattels by the tenant or by a guest or invitee of the tenant.

(c) If the landlord retains all or part of a security deposit under this section, the landlord shall give to the tenant the balance of the security deposit, if any, together with a written description and itemized list of all deductions. The landlord is not required to give the tenant a description and itemized list of deductions if:

(1) the tenant owes rent when the tenant surrenders possession of the premises; and

(2) no controversy exists concerning the amount of rent owed.

The landlord's rights are significantly greater in commercial tenancies. One should be careful though. A commercial tenancy can become a residential tenancy. In *Warehouse Partners* v. *Gardner*, 910 S.W.2d 19 (Tex. App.—Dallas, 1995), a landlord was required to comply with the residential statutes when this happened.

**CHAPTER 54**

## LANDLORD'S LIENS
### Subchapter A. Agricultural Landlord's Lien

#### §54.001. Lien
A person who leases land or tenements at will or for a term of years has a preference lien for rent that becomes due and for the money and the value of property that the landlord furnishes or causes to be furnished to the tenant to grow a crop on the leased premises and to gather, store, and prepare the crop for marketing.

#### §54.002. Property to Which Lien Attaches
(a) Except as provided by Subsections (b) and (c), the lien attaches to:

(1) the property on the leased premises that the landlord furnishes or causes to be furnished to the tenant to grow a crop on the leased premises; and

(2) the crop grown on the leased premises in the year that the rent accrues or the property is furnished.

(b) If the landlord provides everything except labor, the lien attaches only to the crop grown in the year that the property is furnished.

(c) The lien does not attach to the goods of a merchant, trader, or mechanic if the tenant sells and delivers the goods in good faith in the regular course of business.

(d) A law exempting property from forced sale does not apply to a lien under this subchapter on agricultural products, animals, or tools.

#### §54.003. Exceptions
The lien does not arise if:

(1) a tenant provides everything necessary to cultivate the leased premises and the landlord charges rent of more than one-third of the value of the grain and one-fourth of the value of the cotton grown on the premises; or

(2) a landlord provides everything except the labor and directly or indirectly charges rent of more than one-half of the value of the grain and cotton grown on the premises.

### §54.004. Duration of Lien

The lien exists while the property to which it is attached remains on the leased premises and until one month after the day that the property is removed from the premises. If agricultural products to which the lien is attached are placed in a public or bonded warehouse regulated by state law before the 31st day after the day that they are removed from the leased premises, the lien exists while they remain in the warehouse.

### §54.005. Removal of Property

(a) If an advance or rent is unpaid, a tenant may not without the landlord's consent remove or permit the removal of agricultural products or other property to which the lien is attached from the leased premises.

(b) If agricultural products subject to the lien are removed with the landlord's consent from the leased premises for preparation for market, the lien continues to exist as if the products had not been removed.

### §54.006. Distress Warrant

(a) The person to whom rent or an advance is payable under the lease may apply to an appropriate justice of the peace for a distress warrant if the tenant:

(1) owes any rent or an advance;

(2) is about to abandon the premises; or

(3) is about to remove the tenant's property from the premises.

(b) The application for a warrant must be filed with a justice of the peace:

(1) in the precinct in which the leasehold is located or in which the property subject to the landlord's lien is located; or

(2) who has jurisdiction of the cause of action.

The distress warrant is issued pursuant to Article 54.025 of the Texas Property Code to preserve the statutory landlord's lien for rent. In many cases, this is the only immediate remedy a landlord may have in the event a tenant is about to abandon the premises and take some of the tenant's (or maybe landlord's) property that is then on the premises. The distress warrant procedures are set forth in Rules 610 through 620 of the Texas Rules of Civil Procedure. Although this may be construed as taking the property without "due process," the procedures have been held to be constitutional provided they satisfy the minimum constitutional requirements stated in *Mitchell* v. *W. T. Grant Co.*, 416 U.S. 600 (1974). These basic requirements are that (1) the distress warrant be issued by a judicial officer; (2) the affidavits and documents in support of the distress warrant were more than mere conclusions; (3) the debtor had immediate right to a hearing; and (4) dissolution of the writ would be granted absent proof at the hearing. *Lincoln Ten, Ltd.* v. *White*, 706 S.W.2d 125 (Tex. Civ. App.—Houston, 1986).

#### §54.007. Judgment on Replevin Bond

If a final judgment is rendered against a defendant who has replevied property seized under a distress warrant, the sureties on the defendant's replevy bond are also liable under the judgment, according to the terms of the bond.

## Subchapter B. Building Landlord's Lien

#### §54.021. Lien

A person who leases or rents all or part of a building for nonresidential use has a preference lien on the property of the tenant or subtenant in the building for rent that is due and for rent that is to become due during the current 12-month period succeeding the date of the beginning of the rental agreement or an anniversary of that date.

### §54.022. Commercial Building

(a) The lien is unenforceable for rent on a commercial building that is more than six months past due unless the landlord files a lien statement with the county clerk of the county in which the building is located.

(b) The lien statement must be verified by the landlord or the landlord's agent or attorney and must contain:

(1) an account, itemized by month, of the rent for which the lien is claimed;

(2) the name and address of the tenant or subtenant, if any;

(3) a description of the leased premises; and

(4) the beginning and termination dates of the lease.

(c) Each county clerk shall index alphabetically and record the rental lien statements filed in the clerk's office.

### §54.023. Exemption

This subchapter does not affect a statute exempting property from forced sale.

### §54.024. Duration of Lien

The lien exists while the tenant occupies the building and until one month after the day that the tenant abandons the building.

### §54.025. Distress Warrant

The person to whom rent is payable under a building lease or the person's agent, attorney, assign, or other legal representative may apply to the justice of the peace in the precinct in which the building is located for a distress warrant if the tenant:

(1) owes rent;

(2) is about to abandon the building; or

(3) is about to remove the tenant's property from the building.

The building landlord's lien has been held to renew each 12 months, effectively a series of yearly contracts. *FDIC* v. *Sears Roebuck & Company, Inc.*, 743 S.W.2d 772 (Tex. App.—El Paso, 1988, no writ). If another security interest is filed during the intervening period, the security interest may become superior to the building landlord's lien for rent at the expiration of any given 12-month period succeeding the date of the beginning of the rental agreement.

## Subchapter C. Residential Landlord's Lien

### §54.041. Lien

A landlord of a single or multifamily residence has a lien for unpaid rent that is due. The lien attaches to nonexempt property that is in the residence or that the tenant has stored in a storage room.

### §54.042. Exemptions

A lien under this subchapter does not attach to:

(1) wearing apparel;

(2) tools, apparatus, and books of a trade or profession;

(3) schoolbooks;

(4) a family library;

(5) family portraits and pictures;

(6) one couch, two living room chairs, and a dining table and chairs;

(7) beds and bedding;

(8) kitchen furniture and utensils;

(9) food and foodstuffs;

(10) medicine and medical supplies;

(11) one automobile and one truck;

(12) agricultural implements;

(13) children's toys not commonly used by adults;

(14) goods that the landlord or the landlord's agent knows are owned by a person other than the tenant or an occupant of the residence; and

(15) goods that the landlord or the landlord's agent knows are subject to a recorded chattel mortgage or financing agreement.

### §54.043. Enforceability of Contractual Provisions

(a) A contractual landlord's lien is not enforceable unless it is underlined or printed in conspicuous bold print in the lease agreement.

(b) A provision of a lease that purports to waive or diminish a right, liability, or exemption of this subchapter is void to the extent limited by this subchapter.

### §54.044. Seizure of Property

(a) The landlord or the landlord's agent may not seize exempt property and may seize nonexempt property only if it is authorized by a written lease and can be accomplished without a breach of the peace.

(b) Immediately after seizing property under Subsection (a) of this section, the landlord or the landlord's agent shall leave written notice of entry and an itemized list of the items removed. The notice and list shall be left in a conspicuous place within the dwelling. The notice must state the amount of delinquent rent and the name, address, and telephone number of the person the tenant may contact regarding the amount owed. The notice must also state that the property will be promptly returned on full payment of the delinquent rent.

(c) Unless authorized in a written lease, the landlord is not entitled to collect a charge for packing, removing, or storing property seized under this section.

(d) If the tenant has abandoned the premises, the landlord or the landlord's agent may remove its contents.

### §54.045. Sale of Property

(a) Property seized under Section 54.044 may not be sold or otherwise disposed of unless the sale or disposition is authorized in a written lease.

(b) Before selling seized property, the landlord or the landlord's agent must give notice to the tenant not later than the 30th day before the date of the sale. The notice must be sent to the tenant by both first class mail and certified mail, return receipt requested, at the tenant's last known address. The notice must contain:

(1) the date, time, and place of the sale;

(2) an itemized account of the amount owed by the tenant to the landlord; and

(3) the name, address, and telephone number of the person the tenant may contact regarding the sale, the amount owed, and the right of the tenant to redeem the property under Subsection (e) of this section.

(c) A sale under this section is subject to a recorded chattel mortgage or financing statement. The property shall be sold to the highest cash bidder. Proceeds from the sale shall be applied first to delinquent rents and, if authorized by the written lease, reasonable packing, moving, storage, and sale costs.

(d) Any sale proceeds remaining after payment of the amounts authorized in Subsection (c) of this section shall be mailed to the tenant at the tenant's last known address not later than the 30th day after the date of the sale. The landlord shall provide the tenant with an accounting of all proceeds of the sale not later than the 30th day after the date on which the tenant makes a written request for the accounting.

(e) The tenant may redeem the property at any time before the property is sold by paying to the landlord or the landlord's agent all delinquent rents and, if authorized in the written lease, all reasonable packing, moving, storage, and sale costs.

### §54.046. Violation by Landlord

If a landlord or the landlord's agent willfully violates this subchapter, the tenant is entitled to:

(1) actual damages, return of any property seized that has not been sold, return of the proceeds of any sale of seized property, and one month's rent or $500, whichever is greater, less any amount for which the tenant is liable; and

(2) reasonable attorney's fees.

### §54.047. Other Rights Not Affected

This subchapter does not affect or diminish any other rights or obligations arising under common law or any statute.

### §54.048. Tenant May Replevy

At any time before judgment in a suit for unpaid rent, the tenant may replevy any of the property that has been seized, if the property has not been claimed or sold, by posting a bond in an amount approved by the court, payable to the landlord, and conditioned that if the landlord prevails in the suit, the amount of the judgment rendered and any costs assessed against the tenant shall be first satisfied, to the extent possible, out of the bond.

These statutes apply to both oral and written tenancies. There is some question as to whether or not the foregoing statutes are constitutional, in that they do allow the landlord the right to certain properties of the tenant without due process of law. However, to date, there has not been a precedent-setting decision that holds the statutes unconstitutional. It is important to note the exemptions under Section 54.042 are rather broad, and there would probably be very little that a tenant would have that would be subject to the lien anyway. In this statute, similar to the previous one, we have nonwaiver of rights for the tenant, as well as a stiff penalty for the landlord in the event he violates any provision of the act.

It is important to emphasize, however, that if the landlord does attempt to seize the tenant's property, the landlord does have a duty to care for the property safely and to return it to the tenant when the rent is paid. *Johnson* v. *Lane*, 524 S.W.2d 361 (Tex. Civ. App.—Dallas, 1975); *Stein and Lieck* v. *Mauricio*, 580 S.W.2d 82 (Tex. Civ. App.—San Antonio, 1979). If there is no specific provision in the lease for foreclosure in the landlord's lien, the lien must be judicially foreclosed.

Note that any seizure of personal property must be pursuant to the terms of a written rental agreement and it must be in conspicuous bold print. What constitutes **"abandonment"** is a jury question. *H & L Enterprises* v. *Smith*, 625 S.W.2d 777 (Tex. Civ. App.—Ft. Worth, 1981). If the landlord does incorrectly seize property that is in violation of the statute or is contrary to the lease agreement, he is liable for damages. There is some indication that the market value of the item seized is not important as damages but rather as the value of that item to the owner. When personal property is held for the comfort and enjoyment of the owner, the measure of the damages is the value of its use to that owner, not its market value. If the personal property is **possessed** for the purpose of sale, the damages are the market value of the property. Therefore, the landlord may be liable for much more than he had previously anticipated. *Jay Fikes and Assoc.* v. *Walton*, 578 S.W.2d 885 (Tex. Civ. App.—Amarillo, 1979).

# Lease Agreements

A **lease** is a grant of an estate in land for a limited term with conditions attached. *Pioneer Oil Co.* v. *Vallejo*, 736 S.W.2d 227 (Tex. Civ. App.—Corpus Christi, 1987). Obviously, leases are also contracts involving the transfer of interest of real property. As such, the provisions of the Statute of Frauds are applicable for any lease in excess of one year. It is well accepted that the contractual nature of real property leases is interpreted pursuant to the strict construction of contracts, rather than the law of real property. Most leases, especially the more sophisticated varieties for office space and retail (shopping center) space, have become so detailed that it is necessary to secure the services of a lawyer to make sure that a party is adequately protected. The rules governing the interpretation of contracts and construction of contracts are the same when applied to leases.

A harsh result was reached in the recent case of *Reynolds-Penland Company* v. *Hexter & Lobello, et al.*, 567 S.W.2d 237 (Tex. Civ. App.—Dallas, 1978), which construed the lease in strict accordance with its terms and disallowed the intervention of equity, even though it resulted in hardship for one of the parties. The court stated that in the absence of circumstances such as fraud, misleading statements, or acts by the lessor, or waiver, the rules of equity could not be interposed to rewrite a lease.

## Lease Requirements

No particular form is necessary to create a lease. *Pioneer Oil Co.* v. *Vallejo*, supra. In discussing the requirements of a lease, we will find that they are very similar to those of other contracts for real estate generally. These requirements are as follows:

1. The lease must be in writing and must be signed by the party to be charged if the term is longer than one year.

2. It must include a specific, identifiable landlord and tenant (the parties to the lease).

3. It must contain the intent of the landlord to grant to the tenant the right to enter and possess the designated premises for a fixed consideration.

4. It must include an adequate description of the leasehold premises.

5. It must give a specific period of time of occupancy.

6. It must have been delivered and accepted.

Except for item 6, most of these provisions are self-explanatory. Delivery and acceptance, being a fact question, is normally implied when the lessee takes possession of the premises, which will bind him as effectively as an express acceptance. It is important to note that even if the lessor sells the property, the lease gives the lessee an estate in land that is not terminated by the sale unless it is expressly provided for in the lease. *Zale Corp.* v. *Decorama*, 470 S.W.2d 406 (Tex. Civ. App.—Waco, 1971). The lessee may further wish to protect his interest by recording the lease. If this is the case, the lease will also need to be acknowledged.

## Types of Leases

There are four types of leases, depending on the manner in which the rent is paid:

1. A lease for a fixed term (gross lease).
2. A percentage lease.
3. A net lease.
4. A ground lease.

It is important to note that any one of the above types of leases is going to have its own character, depending on the type of premises it is intended to transfer. For instance, the terms of a gross lease vary widely, depending on whether the premises are a single-family residence, office space, or an apartment. No one standard lease form is applicable to all situations.

**Gross Lease.** A **gross lease** is most often used for a fixed term and for a fixed sum of money. Typically, the landlord pays all costs for utilities, insurance, and maintenance. However, in more current years, the fixed rental provisions are subject to some rental adjustment for operation, costs, and utility escalation. This type of lease is commonly used when leasing office space and apartments.

**Percentage Lease.** A **percentage lease** is most often used for lessees in retail premises. Retail premises would include shopping malls, strip centers, and any other type of use that may deal directly with a lessee whose income is contingent upon access to the shopping public.

The unique rental payment provisions make the percentage lease different from most other types of leases. The lease normally provides that the lessee will occupy the space at a relatively low base rent. This rent is usually just enough for the lessor to meet his mortgage payment with perhaps a small amount of profit. The remainder of the lessee's lease payments are contingent upon a percentage of the gross sales that the lessee experiences. This percentage interest may vary from 2 to 11%, depending on the size of the lessee. Large, major lessees normally pay a much lower percentage because their volume of business is much higher and they are often a "draw" for smaller lessees. The percentage rentals may be paid monthly (after preliminary accounting of gross income), quarterly, or annually. Because of the volatile nature of costs in recent years, most lessors prefer that this percentage rental be paid monthly to cover the increasing uncontrolled costs for utilities, taxes, and insurance.

The percentage lease provides many advantages to both the lessor and the lessee by creating some dependence on each party. The lessee gets a lower base rate for his rentals and only has to pay an increased rent if, in fact, his volume of business justifies it. The lessor, on the other hand, is not only assured of having his mortgage payments paid but stands to make higher profits if the lessee makes higher profits. Therefore, it is to the advantage of the lessor to maintain his shopping center in such a manner as to make it attractive and accessible to all potential shoppers. There is an incentive on the part of both the lessor and the lessee to make their respective businesses as successful as possible. As a general rule, the percentage lease never creates a partnership agreement between the lessor and the lessee.

**Net Lease.** A **net lease** is generally one in which, in addition to rent, the lessee pays all of the expenses of operation, and the lessor's only obligation is to pay the mortgage payment. Although this type of lease has no true legal significance, the term "net lease" is standard jargon in the real estate business to describe certain types of leases. Normally, a net lease is one in which the tenant pays real estate taxes and special assessments in addition to his rent. A **net-net** lease usually implies that in addition to the foregoing, the tenant pays his own insurance premiums, both for hazard and liability insurance. A **net-net-net** lease (often called a **triple net** lease) usually implies that the tenant also pays the cost of repairs and maintenance of the property.

As one might have suspected, the net lease is the perfect investment tool for the passive investor–lessor who has a solvent, creditworthy tenant for the premises. Most retail fast-food establishments prefer to use triple net leases to give themselves absolute control over the maintenance and attractiveness of the premises, as well as over certain operating costs, in order to keep their rental rates at a minimum. The investor–lessor is normally guaranteed a fixed rate of return after his mortgage payment has been made. This lease plan also guarantees a fixed rental rate for the lessee. In some situations, the lender will even request that the lessee pay his lease payments directly to him (the lender), and the lender merely sends a difference check to the landlord (investor–lessor) after the mortgage payments and other costs have been deducted. This assures the lender of timely payments and provides the owner–lessor–investor with very little room to complain. In most of these situations, the lender loans money based on the quality of the tenant rather than on the financial statement of the investor.

**Ground Lease.** A **ground lease** is normally a long-term leasehold estate that has lease payment provisions similar to those of a gross lease. This type of lease is basically simple, providing primarily for a fixed monthly or annual payment to the lessor. The peculiarities of this type of lease, however, involve a rather complicated method of mortgaging the leasehold estate, so that the lessee can borrow money for the construction of improvements, subject to the underlying leasehold estate. This type of lease usually has provisions that allow for **subordination** of the leasehold premises, making the underlying lease inferior to the construction mortgage to provide an incentive for a lender to make the loan by giving him a first lien position. A ground lease often has fairly liberal provisions for assignment and subletting, since the lease is for such a long term. It is also one of the basic tools for the sale lease-back mortgaging technique discussed in Chapter 13.

## Assignment and Subletting

Although Texas has a statutory provision prohibiting the right of a lessee to assign or sublet the premises without the lessor's prior written consent, it should be understood that assignment and subletting are very functional and operational parts of the leasing process, and most lessors do not unreasonably withhold their consent. The transfer of interest of the lessee, however, can become rather complicated when the mortgaged premises involve a long-term ground lease. In this case, the parties would include the original landlord and the new lessee under the long-term ground lease. In the event there is a subsequent transfer of interest to the property, the lessee becomes either a **sublessor** or **assignor**. The subsequent interests are then held by the **sublessee** or the **assignee**, depending on the type of transfer used.

In the **sublease** situation, there is still a direct contractual relationship (privity of contract) between the lessor and the lessee. There is also a privity of contract between the lessee (sublessor) and the sublessee. There is no privity of contract between the sublessee and the original lessor. This makes the lessee (sublessor) still primarily liable on all obligations to the original lessor.

In the **assignment** situation, all rights, title, and interest of the original lessee (assignor) are assigned to the assignee, who then has a direct privity of contract with the original lessor. The liabilities change, then, in that the assignee has a direct obligation to the lessor. The original lessee, however, is not released from liability unless the landlord so agrees. *Martinez* v. *Ball*, 721 S.W.2d 580 (Tex. Civ. App.—Corpus Christi, 1986); *Franchise Stores Realty Corp.* v. *Dakri*, 721 S.W.2d 397 (Tex. Civ. App.—Houston, 1986).

Texas law tends to favor the sublease, and it has been held that if the original lessee (sublessor) maintains any right of reversion at all, the instrument will be held to be a sublease rather than an assignment. The original lessee (sublessor) is still held to be primarily liable on any breach of covenants to the original lessor. The diagram as shown in Figure 18.1 graphically illustrates how the assignment/sublease relationship exists.

## Special Provisions

A lease can have as many special provisions as one can possibly imagine. The scope of these lease provisions has become so large in recent years that one finds typical office leases or retail leases bound in book form, rather than stapled together as a short-form document. Because of the variety of applicable special provisions in any given situation, we will not discuss any of these special provisions in detail. There are extensive treatises on lease law that would be of greater benefit to the more

**FIGURE 18.1  ASSIGNMENT/SUBLEASE RELATIONSHIP.**

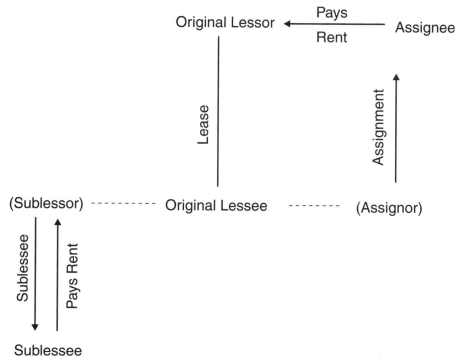

advanced student than any further discussion that could be given here. There are some recent case decisions, however, which have a bearing on certain lease provisions and deserve discussion.

**Options to Purchase.** If the lease contains an option to purchase, it has been held that when the **option to purchase** has been exercised in accordance with the terms of the lease, the relationship of landlord and tenant ceases and that of a vendor and purchaser begins. *Exxon Corp.* v. *Pollman*, 712 S.W.2d 230 (Tex. Civ. App.—Tyler, 1986). No rent is then payable, as the purchase and sale agreement becomes controlling. The tenant then has the right to enforce specific performance of his purchase contract. *Pitman* v. *Sanditen*, 626 S.W.2d 496 (Tex. 1981).

**Noncompetition.** There has also been considerable litigation recently over provisions for **noncompetition** clauses in leases. This type of clause typically prohibits a lessor from leasing to tenants in competition with each other. This allows a tenant to fully develop his own market share in the shopping center and provides for a more complementary tenant mix, which operates in the best interest of both the landlord and the tenant. There has been some concern that these violate federal and state antitrust laws as a restraint of trade. The general theory in Texas is that the noncompetition clause is legal if reasonably exercised. *City Products Corporation* v. *Berman*, 610 S.W.2d 446 (Tex. 1980); *Wettstein* v. *Love*, 583 S.W.2d 471 (Tex. Civ. App.—El Paso, 1979).

**Late Charges.** Another item of conflict that has frequently arisen is whether or not an agreed late charge in a lease agreement constitutes "interest" under Texas statutes. It is generally held that such a late charge is not a charge for the forbearance of money as defined by Texas statute and, therefore, is not a loan transaction that falls within the jurisdiction of Texas usury laws. *Maloney* v. *Andrews*, 483 S.W.2d 703 (Tex. Civ. App.—Eastland, 1972); *Apparel Manufacturing Company* v. *Vantage Properties, Inc.*, 597 S.W.2d 447 (Tex. Civ. App.—Dallas, 1980); *Potomac Leasing Company* v. *Housing Authority of the City of El Paso*, 743 S.W.2d 712 (Tex. App.—El Paso, 1988).

# Duties of Care

Since there has been a flurry of cases on duties of care as well as legislation imposing these duties of care on both the landlord and the tenant, it cannot be overemphasized how important these two areas have become. There will be extensive litigation in these areas in the next few years, which will undoubtedly be very complicated. A review of the fundamental concepts of these areas should help one understand the trend of the law.

## Duties of Landlord to Tenant

**Quiet Enjoyment.** Unless there is express language in the lease to the contrary, the tenant will have an implied covenant of **quiet enjoyment** in every lease of real estate. *L-M-S, Inc.* v. *Blackwell*, 233 S.W.2d 281 (Tex. 1950). What constitutes a breach of the covenant of quiet enjoyment is open to interpretation. These have included such things as the landlord threatening to kill a tenant and other personal violence, *Alford* v. *Thomas*, 238 S.W.2d (Tex. Civ. App.—Ft. Worth, 1922), as well as the landlord leasing the property to another party and allowing that third party to take possession in place of the current tenant. In one of the more interesting cases, it was considered a breach of this covenant when the landlord put the tenant's large dog into their apartment, which resulted in substantial damage. *Clark* v. *Sumner*, 559 S.W.2d 914 (Tex. Civ. App.—Waco, 1977). There is also significant authority that this obligation may include the obligation to provide security. *Nixon* v. *Mr. Property Management Co., Inc.*, supra.

**Repair.** There is no specific provision in Texas law to repair the premises, other than the statute already discussed. It should be noted, however, that the statute only applies to residential units and not to commercial units. The duty to repair, however, does extend to the landlord, presumably in all cases, under the landlord's duty to maintain the premises in a safe manner. Apparently, it extends to both residential and commercial leases, and is particularly applicable when the landlord has control over the premises (particularly common areas) and when he has knowledge of the defect. *Harvey* v. *Seale*, 362 S.W.2d 310 (Tex. 1962); *Rowlett* v. *McMillan*, 574 S.W.2d 625 (Tex. Civ. App.—Houston, 1978).

**Habitability and Suitability.** As a result of a Texas Supreme Court decision, *Kamarath* v. *Bennett*, supra, Texas now recognizes an implied **warranty of habitability**, which arises as a consequence of the landlord–tenant relationship. In this landmark case, the Texas Supreme Court held that the implied warranty of habitability exists and is imposed by law as a matter of public policy. It is very important to recognize, however, that the case specifically did not address the question of the landlord's breach of warranty constituting a deceptive trade practice in violation of the Deceptive Trade Practices Act.

The criteria constituting "habitability" are lengthy and indefinite. The court stated that in order to constitute a breach of the warranty, the defect must be:

> of a nature which will render the premise unsafe, or unsanitary, or otherwise unfit for living therein. The nature of the deficiency, its effect on habitability, the length of time which it persisted, the age of the structure, the amount of the rent, the area in which the premise is located, whether the tenant waived the defects, and whether the defects resulted from malicious, abnormal, or unusual use by the tenant are among the factors to be considered in deciding.

If there is a breach of the warranty, the court specifically stated that:

> the existence of a breach is usually a question of fact to be determined by the circumstance of each case.

Evidently, this makes any breach of implied warranty a fact to be decided at a trial and is not a question of law.

The Texas Supreme Court also has found that there was an implied warranty of *suitability* by the landlord in a commercial lease:

> We hold that there is an implied warranty of suitability by landlord in the commercial lease that the premises are suitable for their intended commercial purpose. *Davidow* v. *Inwood North Professional Group*, 747 S.W.2d 373 (Tex. 1988).

The parties can agree otherwise pursuant to the provisions of their lease, and the vast majority of commercial leases have a clause denying any express or implied warranties. Nonetheless, it continues to be a viable part of commercial lease litigation. The theory does not appear to apply to market conditions, but to the physical condition of the building. The defense of nonsuitability is a complete defense for liability for past due or future rents. *Neuro-Developmental Associates* v. *Corporate Hines Realty*, 908 S.W.2d (Tex. App.—Houston [1st Dist.], 1995).

**No Retaliatory Eviction.** Any tenant who exercises his rights under the law is protected from landlord retaliation by the new statute discussed previously, and if the tenant is the recipient of a subsidy under a federal housing program, the landlord must demonstrate good cause for termination. *Newhouse* v. *Settegast Heights Village Apts.*, 717 S.W.2d 131 (Tex. Civ. App.—Houston, 1986).

**Landlord's Duty to Mitigate.** In a landmark decision, the Texas Supreme Court held that the Texas landlord does have duty to mitigate damages and to use objectively reasonable efforts to fill the premises when a tenant breaches the lease. What does this mean? We really don't know a lot of the answers. *Austin Hill Country, Inc.* v. *Palisades Plaza, Inc.*, 948 S.W.2d 293 (Tex. 1997). In a prior case, the Texas Supreme Court indicated that there is a duty on the part of the landlord to mitigate damages by making reasonable efforts to relet after the tenant has vacated the premises. *Brown* v. *RepublicBank Midland, Tx.*, 766 S.W.2d 203 (Tex. 1988). The Texas legislature responded by passing a statute in 1997, which clearly states that the landlord has a duty to mitigate damages if the tenant abandons the leased premises in violation of the lease. The statute goes on to say that a provision of a lease that purports to waive a right, or to exempt the landlord from a liability or duty, is void, *V.T.C.A., Property Code, §91.006*. The statute seems to impose a much broader application of the landlord's duty to mitigate than the prior two Supreme Court cases. It is safe to say that the duty of the landlord to mitigate will be the subject of significant litigation over the next few years, to determine what mitigation efforts will be necessary. Does the landlord have a duty to lease at the same price, or can he choose to lease at a higher price? If he chooses to lease at the higher price, is the tenant responsible for the rent during the period while the space doesn't lease? There is a lot of law yet to be made here!

## Tenant's Duties to Landlord

**Payment of Rent.** Under the current Texas law, the tenant has an obligation to pay rent independent of the landlord's covenant to repair. Failure of the landlord to repair never justifies rent withholding. If the tenant holds over beyond the term of his lease, he is also liable for damages for his failure to vacate the premises. *Koelzer* v. *Pizzirani*, supra.

**Covenant Not to Damage.** While in possession, a tenant is under implied duty to prevent waste of the premises. Waste includes injury resulting from failure to exercise reasonable care by the tenant or any other party who is rightfully in possession. *R. C. Bowen Estate* v. *Continental Trailways*, 256 S.W.2d 71 (Tex. 1953).

# Remedies of Landlord and Tenant

In the event there is a breach of any implied duties of care or any express duties of care under one's lease agreement, the remedies seem to be slanted more in favor of the tenant than the landlord. It must be remembered that the landlord is usually a person of substance (he owns the real estate) and is not as transient and hard to locate as the tenant. Therefore, the remedies in favor of the tenant are a little easier to obtain and have much more practical application than those in favor of the landlord.

## Remedies of Landlord

**Suit for Damages.** In the event the tenant has committed waste of the premises or destroyed same, the landlord has a technical remedy of being able to sue the tenant for damages. However, as a practical matter, if the tenant has split for parts unknown or disappeared into the hinterland, there is very little chance of recovery. Second, if the tenant had any money, he probably would have paid his rent and stayed in possession. As a practical matter this is not considered to be a very effective remedy.

If a suit for damages is pursued, the measure of damages is typically the rental each month as it becomes due. If the landlord anticipates a breach of a contract for the remainder of the term, he can sue for the entire amount, although the value of the future rental installments would be discounted in determining the amount of damages the landlord is entitled to recover. *Look* v. *Werlin*, 590 S.W.2d 526 (Tex. Civ. App.—Houston, 1979); *Crabtree* v. *Southmark Commercial Management*, 704 S.W.2d 478 (Tex. App.—Houston [14th Dist.], 1986, writ ref'd, n.r.e.). If the landlord receives income from the premises because of a new lease, the landlord's damages must be offset by that income. *Miller* v. *Vineyard*, 765 S.W.2d 865 (Tex. App.—Austin, 1989).

**Specific Performance.** The landlord has the equitable remedy of specific performance. *Speedee Mart Incorporated* v. *Stovall*, 664 S.W.2d 174 (Tex. App.—Amarillo, 1983). However, the chances of recovering this would be relatively rare. The tenant would have to be solvent and the landlord would have to achieve some benefit from requiring the tenant to perform without running the risk of the tenant's negligent maintenance of the premises. It is typically not to the landlord's benefit to have a hostile tenant in possession of the premises.

**Landlord's Lien.** Statutorily, a landlord has a lien on all nonexempt property of the tenant, *V.T.C.A., Property Code, §54.021*. However, the landlord must comply with the statute in contractually establishing this lien in the tenant's lease. A statutory landlord's lien cannot be foreclosed by self-help. A distress warrant must be secured. In addition, the statutory landlord's lien is subject to the personal property exemptions under §42.001 of the Property Code (homestead exemptions). There is also the practical matter of attempting to find anything that the tenant owns that is nonexempt property. The few popular items that can have liens are stereos, television sets, and other "luxury" items, which would not be otherwise exempt. Wrongful exercise of this right can have serious consequences for the landlord. See the discussion under the landlord's liens and distress warrant provisions of this chapter.

Texas also recognizes a contractual landlord's lien, which arises upon agreement of the parties to the lease. This, in effect, becomes a perfection of the security interest of the Tex. Bus. & Comm. Code (see §9.102(c)). This can create a nonjudicial foreclosure pursuant of the contractual lien if the lessee refuses to peacefully surrender the personal property subject to that contractual landlord's lien. The landlord may turn to judicial proceedings as provided under §9.503 of the Tex. Bus. & Comm. Code.

**Eviction.** The landlord always has the duty to terminate the tenant's rights to occupy the premises. He must resort to due process to do this, however, and forcible entry and detainer proceedings are discussed in depth later in this chapter.

Damages can also be limited, depending on the conduct of the landlord. If the landlord reenters and relets the abandoned premises for his own benefit, the tenant's obligations cease. *Southmark Management Corp.* v. *Vick*, 692 S.W.2d 157 (Tex. Civ. App.—Houston, 1985). If, however, the landlord relets to mitigate his contractual damages while pursuing a cause of action against the tenant, the tenant's obligations to pay rent continue to accrue. *Harry Hines Medical Center, Ltd.* v. *Wilson*, 656 S.W.2d 598 (Tex. Civ. App.—Dallas, 1983).

## Remedies of Tenant

A tenant's damages are frequently raised as a defense to the suit by the landlord. There may be an event of default by the tenant and that tenant's defenses then become a condition precedent to the enforcement of the landlord's remedy.

**Damages.** The tenant has the right to sue for damages for **retaliatory eviction**. As discussed earlier, the tenant always has the right to sue the landlord for damages in the event he feels he has been retaliated against. Again, it should be remembered that the landlord is normally a solvent defendant and the chances of recovering money from the landlord are normally somewhat greater than recovering damages against the tenant. There is another cause of action for damages for what is termed **constructive eviction**. Constructive eviction occurs when the landlord intends that the tenant should no longer enjoy the premises so the landlord performs some act that substantially interferes with the use and enjoyment of the premises. *Fidelity Mutual Life Ins. Co.* v. *Kaminsky*, 768 S.W.2d 818 (Tex. App.—Houston [14th Dist.], 1989). That act must permanently deprive the tenant of the use and enjoyment of the premises, and the tenant must abandon the premises within a reasonable time after the commission of the act. *Stillman* v. *Youmans*, 266 S.W.2d 913 (Tex. Civ. App.—Galveston, 1954). The lessee may also be entitled to recover lost profits resulting from the lessor's constructive eviction to the extent the damage can be ascertained with reasonable certainty. *Downtown Realty, Inc.* v. *509 Tremont Building, Inc.*, 748 S.W.2d 309 (Tex. App.—Houston [14th Dist.], 1988).

There is support in more recent years that the tenant may recover from mental anguish even though there may not have been any actual physical injury. *Trevino* v. *Southwestern Bell Tel. Co.*, 582 S.W.2d 582 (Tex. Civ. App.—Corpus Christi, 1979); *Pargas of Longview, Inc.* v. *Jones*, 573 S.W.2d 571 (Tex. Civ. App.—Texarkana, 1978). In addition, a tenant may recover for a Deceptive Trade Practices Act violation caused by the lessor's misrepresentations, even for commercial premises, *Corum Management Co., Inc.* v. *Aguayo Enterprises, Inc.*, 755 S.W.2d 895 (Tex. App.—San Antonio, 1988, writ den.), although a breach of contract, by itself, will not support a DTPA claim. Another "gray" area of the law!

**Tenant's Lien.** The tenant has a judicial lien on all nonexempt property of the landlord as well as on all rent due the landlord for rental of the premises for any failure of the landlord to comply with the contract, *V.T.C.A., Property Code, §91.004*. There is virtually no case law on this subject. The statute was originally enacted in 1874 and was concerned with creating an agricultural landlord's lien on tenants' crops. The statute may now cover the residential and commercial situations.

**Move Out.** The tenant always has the remedy of moving out of the premises. Known as the "doctrine of surrender," this was statutorily enabled with the addition of Section 92.056(b) of the Property Code. The surrender may be accomplished by an abandonment of the premises if the landlord expressly or impliedly accepts this surrender, the lease is terminated, and the tenant has no further liability for rent. To constitute a surrender, however, there must be a mutual agreement between the landlord and the tenant where taking possession by the landlord on the abandonment by the tenant does not constitute an acceptance or surrender. One case has held that an attempt on the part of the landlord to re-lease the property at a higher rate of rental than in the lease of the defaulting tenant does not constitute an acceptance of the tenant's surrender. *Metroplex Glass Center, Inc.* v. *Vantage Properties, Inc.*, 646 S.W.2d 263 (Tex. App.—Dallas, 1983, writ ref'd n.r.e.). This doctrine may have been modified significantly, however, because of the landlord's duty to mitigate, discussed earlier.

If the tenant can "sneak out," the landlord typically has a very difficult time in finding him. While this should never be encouraged, as it breaches a contractual agreement, it is not difficult for one to understand the effectiveness of this self-help remedy.

# Forcible Entry and Detainer

Either an action for forcible entry and detainer or forcible detainer could be the proper cause of action for a lessor to pursue when he chooses to eject or remove a lessee from the premises. These are more commonly known as **eviction proceedings**. The 1985 and 1987 legislative sessions dramatically changed certain areas of these laws, giving landlords significantly more rights.

## Forcible Detainer Statutes

A person commits a **forcible entry and detainer** if the person enters the real property of another without legal authority or by force. A **forcible entry** is defined as either: (1) an entry without the consent of the person in actual possession of the property; or (2) as to the landlord, an entry onto the property in the possession of the landlord's tenant at will or by sufferance, whether with or without the tenant's consent, *V.A.T.S., Property Code, §24.001.*

A person who refuses to surrender possession of real property on demand commits a **forcible detainer** if the person, after demand for possession is made in writing by a person entitled to possession of the property: (1) is a tenant or a subtenant willfully and without force holding over after the expiration of the lease under which the person claimed; (2) is a tenant at will or by sufferance; (3) is a tenant of a person who acquired possession by forcible entry; (4) has made a forcible entry on the possession of the person who acquired possession by forcible entry; or (5) has made a forcible entry on the possession of a tenant whose term has expired, *V.A.T.S., Property Code, §24.002.*

Prior to bringing an action for forcible entry and detainer or forcible detainer, the lessor must give the lessee a minimum of three (3) days' written notice to vacate such premises, unless a landlord and a tenant contract otherwise in a written or an oral lease. The notice may be given by mail at the leased premises or in person. This three-day requirement should not be confused with the 30-day notice for terminating certain tenancies under the previously mentioned statutes. Rather, this is a notice requirement prior to filing a suit for forcible entry and detainer. You may recall that a lessee may not be dispossessed from the premises without due process of law. The forcible entry and detainer statutes provide the procedure to effect a valid due process of law by filing the suit for forcible entry and detainer, which initiates the court proceeding. These proceedings can be handled by the owner or the owner's authorized agent, *V.T.C.A., Property Code, §24.011.*

## Procedural Rules

Beyond the two basic statutory provisions, the law of forcible entry and detainer becomes one of procedural matters rather than one of substantive legal matters. Assuming the lessor has properly given notice and has filed his cause of action that the lessee has committed such acts as to constitute forcible entry and detainer, the procedure for evicting that lessee is then initiated. The rules for effecting the dispossession after filing the suit for forcible entry and detainer are contained in the Texas Rules of Civil Procedure (a part of the Texas Statutes).

Original jurisdiction for an action for forcible entry and detainer is vested in the justice of the peace in the precinct of the county in which the premises are located. When the suit has been filed, the justice is required to issue a citation to the defendants to appear not less than 6 days or more than 10 days after service of citation. Said service of citation can be left with anybody at the premises above the age of 16 years. Upon request, and supported by an affidavit, the trial may be postponed by either party showing good cause, for a period not to exceed six days. (One can see that there is at least a statutory attempt to make a quick proceeding out of the forcible entry and detainer process.)

The only issue that may be argued at the justice of the peace court is **possession** of the premises, which necessarily includes an interpretation of the lease, if there is one. Although the justice of the peace court may have a low maximum jurisdiction, the value of the lease rights is not involved when it comes to an issue of possession and of forcible entry and detainer. *Walther* v. *Anderson*, 114 S.W. 414 (Tex. Civ. App.—1908). However, the jurisdictional limit of the justice of the peace court does not prevent either party from suing for damages in excess of the justice court's jurisdictional limit in another court having the proper jurisdiction.

If judgment is awarded to the plaintiff (lessor), a **writ of possession** will be issued to give the plaintiff possession. The writ cannot be issued until the sixth day after the judgment is entered. If one of the parties appeals, however (which appeal must be perfected within five days after the judgment), and after a proper bond has been posted, the decision may be appealed to the county court where the issue of possession is tried once again. The second trial is not considered a true appeal process since the issue is tried once again as if the first trial had never happened. This process is called a trial *de novo*. After the appeal bond is filed, the judge in the justice of the peace court must file a transcript immediately, *Tex. Rul. Civ. Proc., Rule 751.* The trial in the county court is heard at any time after five full days from the date of filing the transcript in county court, *Tex. Rul. Civ. Proc., Rule 753.* If no answer is filed at the county court level, there is a judgment entered by default. When judgment is rendered at the county court level, the case is finally and completely disposed of as to the issue of possession, and no further appeals are allowed, except when the premises in question are being used for residential purposes only, *V.A.T.S., Property Code, §24.007; Woolley* v. *Burger*, 602 S.W.2d 116 (Tex. Civ. App.—Amarillo, 1980). The lessor may also maintain an action for attorney's fees if he gives a tenant 10 days' notice by registered or certified mail prior to filing the suit, or if the lease provides for recovery of attorney's fees.

## Post-Trial Procedures

Once the final issue of possession has been determined, the writ of possession (referred to above) orders the officer executing the writ to instruct the tenant to: (1) leave the premises; (2) remove, or allow the landlord or other person acting under the officer's supervision to remove, all personal property from the rental unit; and (3) place, or have an authorized person place, the removed personal property outside the rental unit at a nearby location, but not blocking a public sidewalk, passageway, or street and not while it is raining, sleeting, or snowing. At the officer's discretion, he may post a written warning on the exterior of the front door notifying the tenant that the writ has been issued and can engage the services of a bonded or insured warehouseman to remove and store all of the property at no cost to the landlord or the officer executing the writ. This statute does not impose a duty on the landlord or its agent to stand guard over the property until it is retrieved by the owner. The officer taking control over the property becomes state action, and he is not liable for damages as a result of the removal of those items. *Campos* v. *Investment Mgmt. Properties, Inc.*, 917 S.W.2d 315 (Tex. App.—San Antonio, 1996).

Understanding that the reader has just been exposed to a flurry of laws and procedural rules, the graphic illustration shown in Figure 18.2 may be helpful in illustrating the time concepts and some of the alternatives available in the forcible entry and detainer process. A good lessee, with a good lawyer, can sometimes postpone an actual dispossession of the premises for as long as 60 to 90 days, during which time

**FIGURE 18.2**

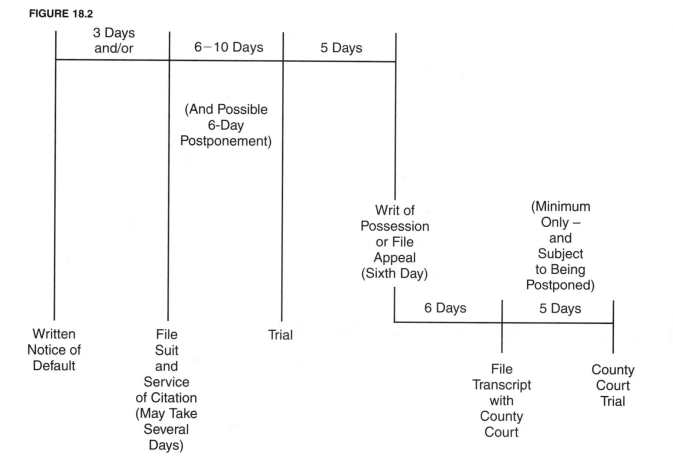

the lessee is usually not paying any rent. If there are substantial damages involved, as there often are, the lessor must bring a separate suit in either county or district court (depending on the amount of damages in controversy) in order to recover whatever damages he may have suffered.

## Warehouseman's Lien

A warehouseman's lien is provided when the tenant's property is stored in a bonded or insured public warehouse. The warehouseman is giving a lien on the property to the extent of any reasonable charge and moving charges incurred by the warehouseman. The lien does not attach to any property until the property has been stored by that warehouseman. If the property is to be removed and stored in a public warehouse under a writ of possession, the officer executing the writ shall, at the time of the execution, deliver in person to the tenant or by first-class mail to the tenant's last known address (not later than 72 hours after execution of the writ if the tenant is not present) a written notice stating the complete address and telephone number of the location at which the property may be redeemed. The notice must basically say that the tenant's property is to be removed, and that he can redeem the property without paying any moving or storage charges on demand during the time the warehouseman is removing the property. After the property has been stored, the tenant may redeem the property after paying moving and storing charges. The warehouseman has the right to sell the property to satisfy the reasonable charges after the 30-day requirement. The warehouseman, however, may not charge for moving or storing any tenant items that are exempt from a landlord's lien. He must also surrender the exempt items upon demand by the tenant.

## ■ SUMMARY

There are four types of nonfreehold estates: an estate for years, an estate from period to period, an estate at will, and an estate at sufferance. Many landlord and tenant relationships are construed by statute unless those rights are determined by an existing lease agreement. Lease agreements are construed similarly to other real estate contracts, and the same general rules of construction apply. There are four basic types of real estate leases: gross leases, percentage leases, net leases, and ground leases. Leases are not assignable by the lessee unless agreed to in writing by the landlord.

Forcible entry and detainer are commonly referred to as eviction proceedings. There must be a court proceeding in order to obtain a legal eviction proceeding. There are statutory requirements for notice and procedure, which can extend the time of eviction for several weeks if contested vigorously.

## CASE STUDIES FOR DISCUSSION

1. A landlord leased the premises in a shopping center to a tenant for its use as a veterinary clinic. Tenant subsequently abandoned the premises and landlord was unable to relet the premises because they would have to be completely renovated. Landlord says he is entitled to the full rental value of all future rental installments due under the lease, together with attorney's fees, as agreed to in the lease. Tenant alleges that full rental value for the remainder of the lease was unjust enrichment. What legal ramifications do you foresee?

2. Landlord leased a ranch to tenant for cattle grazing purposes only. After the tenant took possession, the landlord discovered that the tenant was cutting and removing timber from the property. The lease granted the landlord the right to retake possession of the premises along with a landlord's lien upon all personal property of tenant in the event of default. However, the lease was not very clear as to performance under the lease nor how the landlord's lien would be enforced. Upon the tenant's subsequent default, the landlord retook possession of the premises as well as all the personal property of the tenant. Landlord alleges that he had the right to do so under the terms of his lease. Tenant alleges that this violates his rights to due process and the landlord is not entitled to his lien on personal property. What legal ramifications do you foresee?

## CHAPTER 19

# Condominiums and Cooperatives

Condominiums have been one of the most interesting developments that the Texas housing industry has seen for a number of years. Particularly in more urban areas, the condominium has become one of the cheapest and more efficient methods of homeownership. Condominiums have also provided prestigious, high-security residences for the wealthy. Cooperatives, although not as common in Texas, have equally as good an attraction, but Texans have been a little more hesitant to accept cooperative ownership. Only a small amount of Texas has been urbanized to the point that condominiums and cooperatives could become a common means of homeownership.

There is no common-law derivation of the concept of condominium or cooperative in the United States. The creation of these two forms of housing has been one of statute and purely legal theory. As a result, this type of housing has been called **housing built on a statutory foundation**. Another term reflecting both of these forms of ownership has been **shared-facilities housing**.

## Condominiums

It is perhaps easier, for purposes of our explanation, to think of **condominiums** as ownership of single apartment units. If one can visualize the more typical garden-type apartment project, along with the individual ownership of each of those apartments, one begins to understand the true concept behind condominium ownership. Condominiums are generally cheaper to build than single-family houses or town-houses (for example, there are no major firewall requirements in most cities), and they (the condominiums) constitute a very high utilization of land. Also, more units can be built, and built faster, than comparable single-family residences. However, each unit has its own individual mortgage, as in other single-family residences. The condominium units may be either new construction or be converted to condominiums from existing apartment projects.

Texas has adopted the Texas Uniform Condominium Act (TUCA or the "Act"), which establishes the statutory guidelines for condominiums. The new condominium act applies to all commercial, industrial, residential, and other types of condominiums for which the declaration is recorded on or after January 1, 1994. If a condominium declaration was recorded before January 1, 1994, it may be required to conform with the new Uniform Condominium Act if the owners of the unit vote to amend the declaration. Since most condominium projects have elected to follow the new statute, only the new statute will be discussed.

## Statutory Definitions

Since condominiums are, by their nature, housing built on a statutory foundation, it stands to reason that the statute controlling the creation of a condominium and its function deals with a number of areas rather specifically. Before discussing any details of the three different types of ownership a condominium creates, it is imperative to understand how this act defines pertinent terms of condominiums and how these terms are used in relation to condominium ownership.

TUCA defines **condominium** as:

> a form of real property with portions of the real property designated for separate ownership or occupancy, and the remainder of the real property designed for common ownership or occupancy solely by the owners of those portions. Real property is a condominium only if one or more of the common elements are directly owned in undivided interests by the unit owners. Real property is not a condominium if all the common elements are owned by a legal entity separate from the unit owners, such as a corporation, even if the separate legal entity is owned by the unit owners. *V.T.C.A., Property Code, §82.003(a)(8).*

This implies that any condominium housing must consist of more than one unit. Note also that condominium projects can include much more than just residential units or apartments. They include office spaces or "other units," which indicates that even the parking sections in parking garages could be converted to condominiums (condominiumized). TUCA does not define "condominium project." The definition of condominium, however, seems to indicate that as long as there is more than one owner, a project can be a condominium.

TUCA defines **Unit** as:

> a physical portion of the condominium designated for separate ownership or occupancy, the boundaries of which are described by the declaration.

Any type of structure can become a condominium as long as it has individual apartments or units contained therein. Therefore, the physical structure itself has no bearing on whether or not a project is a condominium. A condominium can be a high-rise project, a townhouse project, a garden-type apartment project, or a fourplex unit, as long as the units meet the statutory criteria.

Now that the basics of apartment and its fee simple ownership, and condominium and its character, are understood, we can proceed to define **common elements**. Each owner holds his proportionate share of the common elements as a tenancy in common with the other apartment owners. There are two types of common elements, general common elements and limited common elements.

The Act defines **general common elements** as:

> common elements that are not limited common elements.

It is easy to see from the above that the bulk of the real estate in a condominium project is owned by the owners as shared facilities and as tenants in common.

**Limited common elements** is defined under the Act as:

a portion of the common elements allocated by the declaration or by operation of §82.052 [of the Uniform Condominium Act] for the exclusive use of one or more but less than all of the units.

A condominium association may not alter or destroy a limited common element without the consent of all owners affected and the first lien mortgagees of all affected owners.

## Types of Ownership and Ownership Rights

Once the concept of apartment (unit) ownership is understood, one needs to recall the more fundamental theory of "estates in land" to grasp the full meaning of this ownership. To begin with, the condominium owner gets three separate, indivisible, and distinct types of ownership:

1. Fee simple to a portion of the common elements, which must be shared in common with the others.

2. Fee simple title to the condominium unit (compartment).

3. An exclusive easement for air space, which that unit may occupy from time to time.

Each of these types of ownership will now be discussed separately.

**Tenancy in Common.** The fee simple ownership of a portion of the common elements is an undivided interest in the unit owner's proportionate share of the common elements. Common elements can generally be described as all of the real property existing outside of the individual's unit that technically belongs to all of the homeowners in undivided interests as tenants in common (it cannot be partitioned). The interests in the common elements must remain undivided and cannot be used such that they encroach upon the rights of the other owners. The concept of encroaching upon the rights of the others is probably one of the more important concepts for understanding what shared-facilities housing really means. The unit owner's portion of the common elements may be determined in two ways. First, it may be determined by the amount of square footage the owner occupies with respect to the entire condominium project, such as:

$$\text{Unit} = 1,500 \text{ square feet}$$
$$\text{Project} = 150,000 \text{ square feet}$$
$$\frac{1,500}{150,000} = 0.01 \times 100 = 1\%$$

(proportionate ownership of the common elements)

The owner of the 1,500-square-foot unit would thus own an undivided 1% of the common elements, shared in common with the other unit owners.

Second, the owner's proportionate share of the common elements may be determined by the unit versus the number of units in the project. For instance, if there are 300 units in the project and the unit owner owns 1 of the 300 units, his proportionate share of the common elements would be:

$$\frac{1}{300} = 0.00333 \times 100 = 0.333\%$$

(proportionate share of the common elements)

**Fee Simple to Unit.** The fee simple title to the unit refers only to the interior of the unit that the owner occupies. This is sometimes referred to as the **air space**

contained *inside* the apartment unit itself. Load-bearing walls are not included because a load-bearing wall is probably critical to the unit ownership of another apartment owner, and demolition or removal of a load-bearing wall may affect the other owner's rights significantly. More common theories of ownership indicate that the owner owns from **paint to paint** and from **ceiling to carpet**, not including the load-bearing walls. If a unit is purchased unfinished, however, the definition of unit could include all space to the unfinished building structure. Each definition is different and is defined in the condominium declaration and bylaws.

**Easement.** The third type of ownership is an easement to the air space that the unit may occupy from time to time. This concept of easement for air space is particularly functional in high-rise structures. It is understood that air space for the unit may shift due to a variety of factors, and this may affect the owner's use. Rather than worrying about older, more difficult concepts of metes-and-bounds descriptions and rights of parties in the property of others, it is simpler to consider the air space that the unit may occupy from time to time as an easement for reasonable enjoyment and use, so long as it does not affect the rights of other unit owners. This gives the unit owner particular rights to permit access through his unit to part of the common elements that may be contained therein, whether it be a roof, foundation, certain plumbing fixtures, or other common element items that the other owners may have a right to.

All three of these ownership rights must be conveyed together and cannot be conveyed separately under any circumstances, *V.T.C.A., Property Code, §82.057.* An example of a deed used to convey a condominium unit is shown in Figure 19.1.

## Creation

The creation of a condominium project is very similar to creating a subdivision. The statute provides that every county clerk shall provide a suitable well-bound book, to be called **condominium records**, in which shall be recorded all master deeds, master leases, or declarations. As a subdivision developer draws a survey and records the subdivision plat, the condominium developer files a **master deed**, **master lease**, or **declaration** to create the condominium regime, *V.T.C.A., Property Code, §81.101, §82.051.* The declaration must contain the legal description of the land with the location of each building or proposed building to be located thereon. Each building may be denoted by a letter (A, B, C, etc.). The declaration must also contain a general description of each unit, including its square footage, location, and other data necessary for its proper identification. The information is depicted by a plat of each floor of each building, showing the building and the number of the floor, along with the number of each unit. The declaration must also contain a general description of each garage, carport, or any other area subject to individual ownership and exclusive control; a description of the general common elements and limited common elements; and a statement of the fractional or percentage interest that the unit bears to the entire condominium regime expressed in fractions or percentages. The declaration may also provide for other provisions if desired by the developer. There are often a number of special provisions referring to peculiarities of each project that will change from project to project.

TUCA requirements for a declaration must include the following:

1. The name of the condominium, which must include the word "condominium," or be followed by the words "a condominium," or a phrase that includes the words "condominium," and the name of the association.

**FIGURE 19.1 WARRANTY DEED TO A CONDOMINIUM UNIT.**

---

### WARRANTY DEED TO A CONDOMINIUMUNIT

| | | |
|---|---|---|
| THE STATE OF TEXAS | § | |
| | § | KNOW ALL MEN BY THESE PRESENTS: |
| COUNTY OF HARRIS | § | |

THAT THE UNDERSIGNED, I.M. SELLER and wife, HAPPY SELLER, acting herein by and through its duly authorized agent, hereinafter called "Grantor," whether one or more, for and in consideration of the sum of TEN DOLLARS ($10.00) cash, and other good and valuable consideration in hand paid to Grantor by N. DEBTED and wife, MAY B. DEBTED, hereinafter called Grantee, whether one or more, whose mailing address is _____ and other good and valuable consideration, the receipt and sufficiency of which consideration are hereby acknowledged, has GRANTED, SOLD and CONVEYED, and by these presents does hereby GRANT, SELL and CONVEY unto Grantee of Harris County, subject to and upon the covenants, restrictions, limitations, conditions and other matters hereinbelow stated, the following described Apartment-type Unit, Parking Space and Undivided fractional interest in the Common Elements (together constituting and hereinafter collectively referred to as an "Apartment Unit") located in and being part of SHAKEY ACRES CONDOMINIUMS, a condominium project in the City of Houston, Harris County, Texas, according to the Enabling Declaration thereof (hereinafter called the "Declaration") and the survey plats and by-laws attached as Exhibits to such Declaration as part thereof, dated September 29, 1978, filed for record in the Office of the County Clerk of Harris County, Texas, on September 30th, 1978, under said Clerk's File No. Q106738, of the Condominium Records of Harris County, Texas, reference to all of which and said record thereto being hereby made for all purposes, which said condominium apartment project known as SHAKEY ACRES CONDOMINIUMS, is situated on the project tract of and described as 5.63 acres of land in the Charles Patrick Survey, Abstract No. 1076, City of Houston, Harris County, Texas, according to the plat thereof recorded in Volume 120, Page 97, of the Harris County Map Records, which constitutes the project tract of land for SHAKEY ACRES CONDOMINIUMS, and which said Apartment, Parking Space and Undivided fractional interest in the Common Elements constituting the Apartment Unit hereby conveyed are described:

(a) SHAKEY ACRES CONDOMINIUMS Apartment No. 301, and the space encompassed by the boundaries thereof, located in BUILDING H;

(b) PARKING SPACE NO. 301A, and the space encompassed by the boundaries thereof, located in BUILDING NO. H; and

(c) AN UNDIVIDED .956% ownership interest in and to the common elements of the Condominium Project known as SHAKEY ACRES CONDOMINIUMS;

*(continued)*

**FIGURE 19.1  CONTINUED.**

according to an as such Apartment Unit, Parking Space and Undivided fractional interest in the Common Elements are more particularly described in said Declaration and the survey plats attached as exhibits thereto.

This grant and conveyance is made and accepted subject to (a) the provisions of the Condominium Act of the State of Texas, hereby incorporated herein and made part hereof (b) the provisions, covenants, easements, restrictions, limitations, covenants and conditions contained and set out in said Declaration and/or shown on the survey plats attached as exhibits thereto, and all easements, covenants, restrictions and conditions otherwise appearing of record and affecting the project tract of land or part thereof, and (c) the said bylaws of SHAKEY ACRES CONDOMINIUMS and all amendments thereafter lawfully made thereto.

By acceptance of this deed and as part of the consideration therefore, the Grantees hereinabove named, their heirs, executors and administrators, personal representatives, successors, grantees, assigns and all future owners of said Apartment Unit or interest therein, covenant and agree and shall be bound and obligated (1) to abide by and comply with each of and all provisions of said Act, Declaration and bylaws and the government and administrations of said condominium apartment project in accordance therewith (2) to observe and comply with all lawful decisions and resolutions at any time made by the Board of Administration, the Council of Co-Owners and/or the unit owners of said condominium apartment project, and (3) to promptly pay, as the same becomes due and payable his prorata share and part of all common expenses and other valid charges and expenses assessed pursuant to the provisions of said Act, Declaration and/or bylaws, all of which common expenses and assessments shall be and constitute a lien upon and against the hereinabove described Apartment Unit at the time the same becomes due and payable, which lien shall be subject to, secondary and inferior to (a) all liens for taxes and special assessments levied by governmental and taxing authorities and (b) all liens securing sums due or to become due under any mortgage, Vendor's Lien or Deed of Trust filed for record prior to the time such prorata share of common expenses, charges and assessments become due, and (c) in general to fulfill and discharge all of his obligations, duties and responsibilities as an owner of an Apartment Unit in the condominium apartment project known as SHAKEY ACRES CONDOMINIUMS.

TO HAVE AND TO HOLD and said Apartment Unit, Parking Space and Undivided fractional ownership interest in Common Elements, hereinabove described and together constituting an Apartment Unit, together with all and singular the rights, hereditaments and appurtenances thereto in any wise belonging, unto the said Grantee hereinabove named, its successors and assigns forever. And, subject to each and all of the matters hereinabove stated, the Grantor herein does hereby bind himself, his heirs, executors and administrators, to WARRANT and DEFEND the title to said Apartment Unit herein and hereby conveyed unto the said Grantee, its successors and assigns, against every person whomsoever lawfully claiming or to claim the same of any part thereof.

*(continued)*

**FIGURE 19.1 CONTINUED.**

EXECUTED this the ___ day of _____, 1999.

_____
I.M. Seller

_____
Happy Seller

Grantee's Address;

_____

_____

THE STATE OF TEXAS          §
                             §
COUNTY OF                    §

The foregoing instrument was acknowledged before me on the _____ day of
_____, 20--, by _____.

_____
NOTARY PUBLIC, STATE OF TEXAS
PRINTED NAME OF NOTARY

MY COMMISSION EXPIRES:

_____

2. The name of each county in which any part of the condominium is located.

3. A legally sufficient description of the real property included in the condominium.

4. A description of the boundaries of each unit created by the declaration, including the unit's identifying number.

5. A statement of the maximum number of units that the declarant reserves the right to create.

6. A description of the limited common elements, other than those provided for by the statute.

7. A description of any real property, except real property subject to development rights, that may be allocated subsequently as limited common elements, together with a statement that the property may be so allocated.

8. An allocation of each unit of its allocated interests.

9. Any restriction on use, occupancy, or alienation of the unit.

10. A description of and the recording data for each recorded easement and licenses appurtenant to or included in the condominium or to which any portion of the condominium is or may be subject by reservation in the declaration.

11. The method of amending the declaration.

12. A plat or plan where the recording data of a plat or plan has been recorded under real property or condominium plat records.

13. A statement of the association's obligation under the statute to rebuild or repair any part of the condominium after a casualty or any other disposition of the proceeds of a casualty insurance policy.

14. A description of any developmental rights and other special declarant rights reserved by the declarant, together with a legally sufficient description of the real property to which each of those rights applies, and a time limit within which each of those rights must be exercised.

15. If any development right may be exercised with respect to different parcels of real property at different times, a statement to that effect, together (a) either a statement fixing the boundaries of those portions and regulating the order in which those portions may be subjected to the exercise of each development right, or a statement that no assurances are made in those regards; and (b) a statement as to whether, if any development right is exercised in any portion of the real property subject to that development right, that development right must be exercised in all or in any other portion of the remainder of that real property.

16. All matters required by the statute to be stated in the declaration.

17. Any other matter the declarant considers appropriate.

There are additional requirements for leasehold condominiums, which require that the declaration must state the recording date of the lease, the date on which the lease is scheduled to expire, the legal description of the property subject to the lease, and rights of the unit owners to remove improvements, renew the lease, or conditions of renewal, or a mere statement that the unit owners do not have the right to renew.

An important thing to remember is that the condominium declaration, which establishes the guidelines for the operation of the condominium project, creates significant contractual rights and obligations for the owners of the units in the project. Any purchaser of a unit in the project takes title to his unit subject to those restrictions. Virtually anything can be regulated, so long as it is not an unconstitutional provision. For instance, age restrictions can be imposed. *Preston Tower Condominium Association* v. *SB Realty, Inc.*, 685 S.W.2d 98 (Tex. Civ. App.—Dallas, 1985); *Covered Bridge Condominium Association* v. *Chambliss*, 705 S.W.2d 211 (Tex. Civ. App.—Houston, 1985). Late charges can even be imposed on maintenance fees without fear of usury. *Tygrett* v. *University Gardens Homeowners' Association*, 687 S.W.2d 481 (Tex. Civ. App.—Dallas, 1985). If the maintenance fees are not paid, there is some case precedent in Texas that the condominium unit can be foreclosed on even if it is a homestead. *Johnson* v. *First Southern Properties, Inc.*, 687 S.W.2d 399 (Tex. Civ. App.—Houston, 1985). The declaration may only be amended at a meeting of the apartment owners at which the amendment is approved by holders of at least 67% of the ownership interest in the condominium.

Most of the detailed information concerning maintenance and control of the condominium is contained in the condominium bylaws, which are administered through the "council of co-owners," or "unit owners' association," who may amend the bylaws if changes are needed.

## Control and Maintenance

The **council of co-owners** means all of the owners in a condominium project. As a practical matter, the council of co-owners forms a homeowners' association, which is usually a corporation with the specific function of maintaining the common elements and the day-to-day activity of the condominium project. Normally, if the project is a new one being built by the developer, the developer maintains control of the council of co-owners because of his ownership of the unsold number of apartments until the number of co-owners becomes sufficient to outvote the developer.

The maintenance of the common elements is one of the primary functions of the council of co-owners. Whether it chooses to appoint its own administrator (or board of administration) or to hire an outside management firm, the day-to-day maintenance of the common elements is determined by the council of co-owners. All **co-owners** are obligated to contribute pro rata toward the expense of the administration of the maintenance and repairs of the common elements. This is normally accomplished by the owners' monthly contributions to a **maintenance fund**, which is established by the condominium's bylaws. If a condominium dweller does not pay his share of the maintenance fee, it forces the other owners to pay his way. *San Antonio Villa Del Sol Homeowners' Association* v. *Miller*, 761 S.W.2d 460 (Tex. App.—San Antonio, 1988). The statute specifically provides that no owner shall be exempt from contributing toward such expenses by any waiver of his use of the enjoyment of the common elements or by abandonment of the apartment that he owns. Again, we see that the shared-facilities housing concept plays a very large part in creating an interdependence between the co-owners in the condominium project.

The council of owners decides how the premises are to be maintained (usually by majority vote). The premises maintained by the council of co-owners are the common elements, and, in applicable cases, the limited common elements. In addition to this, the bylaws normally specify that the individual unit owner may not maintain, change, or alter any of the general common elements or limited common elements without the approval of the council of owners.

The council of owners, then, takes the pro rata contributions made by all the owners into a general fund and uses this fund for maintenance and operation of the condominium project. It is up to the council to determine which area is going to be maintained and how well it is to be maintained. It is not uncommon for people to move into a condominium project and later find that their pro rata share of the contributions (generally referred to as the maintenance fund) increases drastically in an effort to maintain the condominium regime in a "first-class manner." If the exterior of the door to any condominium unit, or the windows, roof, foundation, or other common elements need any sort of alteration or repair, it is up to the council of co-owners to see that such repairs are taken care of properly. The obvious problem that arises from this maintenance by the council of co-owners is one in which an element of the common elements (for instance, the roof) is in need of repair, but it only affects one of the condominium owners (the man who lives on the top floor!). Sometimes it may be difficult for this one owner to convince the rest of the co-owners to spend the necessary capital funds to see that the roof is properly fixed. A condominium owner must simply relinquish some degree of freedom of choice and agree to subordinate some of his traditional ownership rights when he elects this type of ownership. *Raymond* v. *Aquarius Condominium Owners' Association*, 662 S.W.2d 82 (Tex. App.—Corpus Christi, 1983). One can expect similar problems from cracked slabs, cracked exterior walls, broken windows, and other similar common element repairs that may affect only a very small minority of the co-owners. An important, and perhaps harsh, rule is that only the council of co-owners can legally repair and maintain the unit. If a unit owner repairs the common elements, he is not entitled to an offset or credit for his maintenance fees. *Pooser v. Lovett Square Townhouse Owners' Assoc.*, 702 S.W.2d 226 (Tex. Civ. App.—Houston, 1985). An owner may force action or require an accounting. *Burton v. Cravey*, 759 S.W.2d 160 (Tex. App.—Houston [1st Dist.], 1988).

TUCA does not materially alter the duties of the council of co-owners. It renames the association as the "**Unit Owners' Association.**" It does, however, provide for a much more detailed coverage of their duties and obligations (see generally, *§82.102* and *§82.103*) and makes meetings of the association subject to open meetings requirements. See *§82.108.* The new statute also provides for termination of contracts and leases by the original condominium declarant; enforcement of bylaws; and a special provision for upkeep of the condominiums, meetings, quorums, votings, proxies, maintenance of insurance, assessments for condominium expenses, the association's lien for assessments, maintenance of association records, and a requirement that the association record a certificate in the real property records indicating who is responsible for the management of the association.

## Termination

TUCA has a very specific provision concerning the right to terminate. Unless the declaration provides otherwise, and except for a taking of all the units by condemnation, a condominium may be terminated only by the agreement of 100% of the votes in the association and each holder of a deed of trust or vendor's lien on a unit. The declaration may not allow a termination by fewer than 80% of the votes in the association if any unit is restricted exclusively to residential uses, *V.T.C.A., Property Code, §82.068.*

## Specific Problem Areas

Condominium ownership does, in fact, provide many of the benefits of homeownership along with the benefits of apartment ownership, which basically makes the project free from the worries that accompany the ownership of a single-family residence. However, there are specific issues relating to condominium ownership that need to be discussed in greater detail.

**Casualty Insurance.** A recurring problem of condominium ownership is casualty insurance. Normally, the council of co-owners maintains a casualty insurance policy in the event of fire, accident, or other hazard that may destroy the project or any individual unit. Therefore, there is a practical problem of whether or not the individual unit owner should also carry insurance in the event the policy owned by the council of co-owners lapses or is inadequate to protect the homeowner fully. This results in a duplication of insurance to ensure proper coverage for the same unit.

The Act specifically addresses these insurance issues. It requires the association to maintain property insurance on the insurable common elements and commercial general liability insurance, including medical payments insurance, covering all occurrences, insured against for death, bodily injury, and property damage arising out of or in connection with the use, ownership, or maintenance of the common elements. If insurance is not available, the association must give notice of that fact to all unit owners and lien holders, either by personal delivery or mail. In addition, the insurance policies must provide that each unit owner is an insured person under the policy, and that the insurer waives his right to subrogation under the policy against the unit owner. There are additional requirements that the proceeds be used to repair and restore the common elements, *V.T.C.A., Property Code, §82.111.*

**Consumer Protection.** The Uniform Condominium Act has enacted a special section for the protection of purchasers. The act requires that a declarant must prepare a condominium information statement before offering to the public any interest in the unit, *V.T.C.A., Property Code, §82.152.* While there are some limited exceptions to this rule, it appears to be absolute, although the declarant can transfer the responsibility for preparation of all or part of the condominium information statement to a successor declarant, or to a person in the business of selling real property who intends to offer units in the condominium for the person's own account. The **condominium information statement** must contain or accurately disclose at least 11 items required by the statute and also requires the disclosure of a projected or pro forma budget prepared in accordance with generally accepted accounting principles, including a projected monthly expense assessment for each type of unit, *V.T.C.A., Property Code, §82.153.* If a purchaser is buying a unit from an owner other than a declarant, the unit owner must provide to the buyer the declaration, bylaws, and association rules before the buyer executes a contract of sale, if the purchase contract does not contain in underlined or bold print a provision acknowledging the receipt of those documents or recommending that the purchaser read those documents before executing the contract. If not provided, the purchaser may cancel the contract before the sixth day after the date the purchaser received those documents. The unit owner (other than the declarant) must also furnish the purchaser a resale certificate that must have been prepared not earlier than three months before the date it is delivered to the purchaser. The **resale certificate** must be issued by the association and must contain the current operating budget of the association and statements of any right of first refusal that restrict transfer of the unit, the amount of any periodic common expense assessments, capital expenditures approved by the association for the next 12 months, and certain liabilities that may be pending against the association, *V.T.C.A., Property Code, §82.157.* It is anticipated that, similar to the owner disclosure statements discussed in Chapter 8 on Agency, the title company will not insure title until it has some confirmation that all these documents have been provided to the purchaser.

**Taxation.** Taxation provides another area of controversy in condominium ownership. The condominium owner will pay the ad valorem taxes for his individual unit along with the amount attributable to the owner's interest in the common elements. However, a critical problem arises about the monthly contributions from the homeowners to this maintenance fund. The homeowners' association must normally report this income for the maintenance fund (along with the other contributions for insurance, maintenance, etc.) each month as a taxable income, since this income is subject to taxation like any other income for an organization that falls under the jurisdiction of the Internal Revenue Service. Therefore, there is a double taxation achieved, once when income is taxed going to the individual co-owner, and again when it is contributed to the maintenance fund.

This problem has been solved to some extent, however, by the 1976 Tax Reform Act, which provides that a condominium management association may elect to be treated as a tax-exempt organization. If such an election is made, the association is not taxed on fees, membership dues, and assessments from the members of the association who own residential units in the particular condominium or subdivision, applicable to taxable years beginning after December 31, 1973, *I.R.C., §528(c)1(A).* The association's taxable income is only the excess of the gross income over actual operating costs, less any deductions and exempt income. To qualify for the tax-exempt qualification, substantially all of the units must be used as residences. There are additional requirements, too, in that the association must derive at least 60% of its gross income solely from dues, fees, and assessments; and at least 90% must be expended to acquire, construct, manage, maintain, care for, or improve association property, *I.R.C., §528(c)1(B)*. Although these provisions still leave many unanswered questions, at least some steps have been made toward eliminating a difficult problem.

**Tort Liability.** Tort liability is another area that has come under controversy in recent years. Take, for instance, the fact situation where a young 28-year-old neurosurgeon breaks his hands on a negligently maintained exercise machine owned by the homeowners' association. There is a good chance that the homeowners' association may have an insurance policy that would provide for certain coverage in that case. However, if the limit on that insurance policy is too low, one may wonder where the doctor will pursue additional causes of action once he has surpassed the limits of the insurance policy maintained by the homeowners' association. There is at least one authority who holds that a plaintiff may be able to take his cause of action against the homeowners individually, as the unit owners are proportionally liable for claims arising in the common areas. *Dutcher* v. *Owens*, supra; *White* v. *Cox*, 17 Cal. App. 3d 824 (1973).

**Security Regulations.** The most significant problem in purchasing a condominium unit is in the area of securities regulations. If the unit may be construed to be a security, rather than an interest in real estate, it will fall under the jurisdiction of the Securities and Exchange Commission and the acts of 1933 and 1934. In the often-cited case of *SEC* v. *Howey*, supra, it was determined that if one invests in a condominium unit that may be rented to others when it is not in use by the owner, and the owner expects profits from that investment through the efforts of a third-party manager, the unit will be construed to be a security. Therefore, condominium ownership is not simply an interest in real estate, and all offerings for sale may be subject to the regulation and disclosure requirements of the securities acts. This opinion has had particular application in regard to **timeshare condominiums** (contractual arrangements among co-tenants for an agreed-upon time of occupancy), **interval ownership condominiums** (fee title for a specified period—one to four weeks—that the owner is entitled to possession), resort condominiums, and other types of condominiums that lend themselves to investment opportunities. Even if a rental opportunity is available, the sale would be security. *Hocking* v. *Dubois, Vitousek, & Dick Realtors, Inc.*, 885 F.2d 1149 (9th Cir.—1989). Condominiums are considered good investments since they can be owned and operated with very low maintenance requirements for the owner. A private investor can buy a condominium and assure himself that at least the exterior and general common elements will be maintained in an acceptable manner. This is a luxury he does not have in a single-family residence because there is no homeowners' association to maintain the exterior and structural parts of the unit.

**Homestead Provisions.** The last problem to be discussed is one that is peculiar to Texas. Condominium ownership is protected by the constitutional homestead provisions available to all other residential units. The difficulty with the homestead statute exists when an owner owns his unit but refuses to pay his maintenance fund fees for maintenance and improvement of the common areas. It is logically assumed that due to the effect of the constitutional homestead laws, there is virtually no action one can take against such a unit owner. While this appears to be in contravention of the constitutional homestead exemptions, one can reason that the maintenance fees are required to maintain the common elements (which are intertwined with the unit ownership) and that a breach of the unit owner's payments to the homeowners' association is a violation of his purchase money mortgage.

## Timesharing

The objective of timesharing has been to provide the consumer with the exclusive right to use and occupy a structure during a particular time of year. Although timeshares are most often encountered in condominium projects, there is no requirement in Texas that they be condominiums. The arrangement can be of two types: (1) a fee ownership for the requisite ownership period, or (2) a "right-to-use" timeshare. The "right-to-use" type of timeshare is characterized as nothing more than a license allowing the owner to reserve his unit for a time period during his reservation season. No title is conveyed, and no definite time period is assigned to the purchaser. It is little more than an available hotel room. Regardless of the type of timeshare, however, all timeshare interests in Texas are considered to be "real estate" within the meaning of the Texas Real Estate License Act.

**Registration.** All timeshare properties must now be registered with the Texas Real Estate Commission, although a developer or person acting on his behalf may accept a reservation and a deposit from a prospective purchaser so long as the deposit is placed in an escrow account with an escrow agent and the deposit is fully refundable at any time at the request of the purchaser. All applications for registration must be accompanied by the timeshare disclosure statement, which is required by the statute, discussed next. The Real Estate Commission has the duty to investigate all matters relating to the application of the developer and may even require a personal inspection of the proposed timeshare. All expenses of registration must be borne by the timeshare developer.

**Disclosures—Promotions.** The Timeshare Act requires extensive disclosures to prospective purchasers, *§221.032*. Prior to the use of any promotion in connection with the offering of a timeshare, the person who intends to use the promotion must include the following information in advertisements to the prospective purchaser: (1) a statement to the effect that the promotion is intended to solicit purchasers of timeshare interests; (2) if applicable, a statement to the effect that any person whose name is obtained during the promotion may be solicited to purchase a timeshare interest; (3) the full name of the developer and seller of the timeshare property; (4) and, if applicable, the full name and address of any marketing company involved in the promotion of the timeshare property.

**Disclosures—Timeshare Fees.** The managing entity of any timeshare is required to make a written annual accounting of the operation of the timeshare properties managed by the managing entity to each purchaser who requests an accounting, not later than five months after the last day of each fiscal year. The statement must fairly and accurately represent the collection and expenditure of assessments and include a balance sheet, an income and expense statement, the current budget for the timeshare property, and the name, address, and telephone number of the designated representative of the managing entity. The managing entity shall also provide the owners with the name and address of each member of the board of directors of the owners' association, if one exists, if the owner requests it. In addition, they must provide an annual audit, which must be completed not later than five months after the last day of the fiscal year of the timeshare plan or timeshare property.

Knowingly furnishing false information in the annual timeshare fee and expense statement is a DTPA violation. The managing entity must post in the registration area of the accommodations a notice concerning the availability of the fee and expense statement. If they fail to provide the Timeshare Fee and Expense Statement, the managing entity may be liable for a penalty up to $1,500.00 per day, not to exceed $30,000.00 for any one statement period.

**Right to Cancel.** Any purchaser can cancel his contract to purchase a timeshare interest before the *sixth* day after the date his contract is signed *or* if the purchaser does not receive a copy of the contract at the time the contract is signed. The purchaser may not waive the right of cancellation. Any contract containing such a waiver is voidable at the option of the purchaser. The following statement must be contained in the contract or an exhibit to the contract or put in both:

**"PURCHASER'S RIGHT TO CANCEL."**
"(1) BY SIGNING THIS CONTRACT YOU ARE INCURRING AN OBLIGATION TO PURCHASE A TIMESHARE INTEREST. YOU MAY, HOWEVER, CANCEL THIS CONTRACT WITHOUT PENALTY OR OBLIGATION BEFORE THE SIXTH DAY AFTER THE DATE YOU SIGN THE CONTRACT. IF YOU DO NOT RECEIVE A COPY OF THE CONTRACT AT THE TIME THE CONTRACT IS SIGNED, YOU MAY CANCEL THIS CONTRACT WITHOUT PENALTY OR OBLIGATION BEFORE THE SIXTH DAY AFTER THE DATE YOU RECEIVE A COPY OF THE CONTRACT."

"(2) IF YOU DECIDE TO CANCEL THIS CONTRACT, YOU MAY DO SO BY EITHER HAND-DELIVERING NOTICE OF CANCELLATION TO THE SELLER OR BY MAILING NOTICE BY PREPAID UNITED STATES MAIL TO THE SELLER OR THE SELLER'S AGENT FOR SERVICE OF PROCESS. YOUR NOTICE OF CANCELLATION IS EFFECTIVE ON THE DATE SENT OR DELIVERED TO (INSERT NAME OF SELLER) AT (INSERT ADDRESS OF SELLER). FOR YOUR PROTECTION, SHOULD YOU DECIDE TO CANCEL YOU SHOULD EITHER SEND YOUR NOTICE OF CANCELLATION BY CERTIFIED MAIL WITH A RETURN RECEIPT REQUESTED OR OBTAIN A SIGNED AND DATED RECEIPT IF DELIVERING IT IN PERSON."

"(3) A PURCHASER SHOULD NOT RELY ON STATEMENTS OTHER THAN THOSE INCLUDED IN THIS CONTRACT AND THE DISCLOSURE STATEMENT."

The contract must also include the following: (1) the name and address of the developer and the address of the timeshare unit; (2) an agreement by the seller that if the purchaser timely exercises the right of cancellation under the contract, all payments made by the purchaser to the seller in connection with the contract shall be returned to such purchaser before the 21st day after the seller receives notice of cancellation; (3) the name of the person or persons actively involved in the sales presentation on behalf of the seller; (4) a statement disclosing the amount of the periodic assessments currently assessed against or collected from the purchasers of the timeshare interest, immediately followed by a statement providing that collected assessments will be used by the managing entity to pay for expenditures, charges, reserves, or liabilities relating to the operation of the timeshare plan or timeshare properties managed by the managing entities; (5) a statement disclosing that the timeshare common properties are not mortgaged, unless the mortgage contains a nondisturbance clause, which protects the timeshare owner in the event of foreclosure; (6) in the event such timeshare interests are sold under a lease, right to use or membership agreement where free and clear title to the timeshare unit is not passed to the buyer, then the contract must contain a warranty that the timeshare is free and clear, or if subject to a mortgage, the mortgage must contain a nondisturbance clause, which protects the timeshare owner in the event of foreclosure; (7) the date the purchaser signs the contract; and (8) a statement informing the timeshare purchaser that they have a right to an annual timeshare fee and expense statement.

A developer or seller who violates the Timeshare Act is guilty of a Class A misdemeanor.

Before the purchaser signs an agreement or contract to acquire a timeshare interest, the developer has to provide a timeshare disclosure statement to the prospective purchaser and must also obtain from that purchaser a written acknowledgment of the receipt of the timeshare disclosure statement. The disclosures under this portion of the statute include no fewer than 18 items, including a complete budget for the operation of the timeshare property, potential assessment liabilities, insurance coverage, tax liabilities, and administration expenses.

If the prospective purchaser is also offered participation in any exchange program, the developer must also give the prospective purchaser an exchange disclosure statement. This statement must explain the legal relationship between the exchange companies and the developers, conditions under which the exchange program might terminate or become unavailable, and other specific information affecting the consumer's interest in exchange programs.

There are exemptions where no disclosure statements are required, most of which involve dispositions pursuant to court orders, private individuals, foreclosures, or timeshare interests that are made to purchasers who are not within the State of Texas.

Unfortunately, the abusive timeshare sales have given timeshares a bad name. It should be remembered, however, that when there is an honest developer, timeshare interests can be a very attractive purchase. They are relatively inexpensive when compared to a year-round fee simple ownership. Many people get two weeks of vacation a year and can only utilize a vacation home for those two weeks. The owner can enjoy the tax benefits and ownership rights of the second home but not have the maintenance and management responsibilities of year-round fee simple ownership to a similarly located second home. The exchange programs can also be very successful in allowing greater flexibility to vacation areas other than the one in which the timeshare owner has purchased his unit.

Often, the risks of these investments are played down through marketing efforts or developers. This is a new, emerging area of real estate law and there are still many unanswered questions.

# Cooperative Housing

Cooperative ownership is another method of apartment ownership or shared-facilities housing. It is very similar to condominium ownership, but with a few major, distinct differences. The co-ownership and interdependence of the individual owners have much the same drawbacks of any multifamily housing project. However, there are distinct differences in methods of control and type of unit ownership as used by **cooperatives** in comparison to condominiums.

There have been some new cooperative housing developments in the Houston area, and, in 1987, the Texas legislature made some specific homestead provisions applicable to cooperative housing. It is anticipated that this will be an emerging area of real estate law in Texas.

# Creation

A cooperative can take one of three forms: (1) tenancy in common, (2) the trust form, or (3) the corporate form.

The **tenancy in common** form is fairly widespread in California and basically consists of the tenancy in common estates that were discussed in Chapter 5. In this form, the homeowner owns his share of the cooperative project in undivided proportionate shares, along with a lease, or certificate of occupancy, for a particular unit. Rights and liabilities of tenancy in common generally apply, and to some extent, this form does not create the problems of interdependence as much as do the other two forms of ownership.

The **trust** form of ownership is an ownership in severalty by a trust (a single entity), which executes a single blanket mortgage for the entire cooperative housing regime. The basis for the creation of this form of cooperative ownership is the trust instrument under which the trust derives its ownership and control. In the trust form of ownership, there is a single mortgage and management function, operated solely through the trust.

The **corporate** form of ownership, also an ownership in severalty, is similar to the corporate ownership of the homeowners' association in a condominium. The basis for this type of ownership arises out of the charter and bylaws of the corporation as created according to the laws of the State of Texas. Similar to the trust form of ownership, the corporation executes the mortgage on behalf of all the owners and maintains the actual control and ownership of the building throughout the life of the cooperative.

# Ownership and Control

The ownership and control under a tenancy in common cooperative is based on each individual owner's proportionate share of ownership in the cooperative regime. The owners normally elect a homeowners' association, which is primarily responsible for the maintenance and operation of the premises. The trust and corporate forms of ownership (both involving ownership in severalty) also have one blanket mortgage, which is secured by the entire cooperative as a unit. This type of cooperative ownership usually relies on the lender's being willing to take the proportionate liability of each of the owners as satisfactory security for the blanket mortgage that has been issued to cover the entire cooperative housing unit.

The trust (or board of trustees), or corporation, holds legal title to the property. The co-owners get a lease, or certificate of occupancy, under which they have the exclusive right to occupy their proportionate share of the property. To simplify this, you might want to think of a larger apartment project as an example. A corporation or trust would hold legal title to the project, and each of the occupants of the apartments, being a shareholder of the corporation (or beneficial owner of the trust), has the exclusive right of occupancy of his individual unit. This type of ownership normally involves obligations in the bylaws (or trust instruments) that require each individual unit owner to pay his fractional percentage of the mortgage each and every month, as well as his fractional percentage of the utilities, insurance, costs, and maintenance.

The certificate of occupancy (or lease) is regarded as personal property, not real estate. As in condominium ownership, there are fairly detailed and finite rules and regulations under the trust instrument or bylaws, which each and every unit owner must comply with, so that he will not have a detrimental effect on the other unit owners. Normally, upon termination of the certificate of occupancy, or the lease, the unit owner must surrender possession of the unit (by sale or otherwise) to the corporation or trust, who, in turn, may resell that interest to another subsequent occupant. The charter and bylaws (or trust instrument) usually contain provisions whereby the corporation or trust has the right of first refusal to buy the certificate of occupancy and proportionate interest when the unit owner decides to terminate his residency. Since there is a great amount of interdependence because of the proportionate payments of mortgages, maintenance fees, and expenses (much more so than in condominium ownership), it is critical that there be a strictly enforced agreement between the co-owners, carefully setting forth what all the rights and obligations are in order to ensure adequate functioning and maintenance of the cooperative housing development.

## Advantages

Cooperative housing developments have had particularly good application in retirement and resort areas. Because of the lower construction costs of cooperative housing, similar to those of condominiums, cooperatives are substantially cheaper to build than are other forms of single-or multifamily residential ownership; thus the cost of these units is likewise much cheaper. In the retirement situation, you can understand why a person, in his old age, may decide to retire to a senior citizens' cooperative housing development (normally restricted to people 65 years of age or over), buying a 1,200-to 1,500-square-foot unit for the price of $12,000 to $20,000 (perhaps his life savings). His future contributions, then, would be only to pay utilities and maintenance fund costs for the rest of his life. He would get all the benefits of living in an apartment, but with all the attributes of home ownership. He would have no mortgage payments to pay (assuming his unit was paid for), and any future conveyance of his cooperative unit would be subject only to the right of first refusal of the homeowners' association, corporation, or trust. Thus, he would be much more comfortable being able to live on a fixed retirement income. He also would probably have a higher quality of housing than he would have if he tried to buy a single-family residence or townhouse, or even a condominium unit, at the same price.

## Disadvantages

The disadvantages of cooperative housing stand out primarily because of the extreme interdependence in this type of housing. For instance, if each unit owner has the obligation to pay his proportionate share of the mortgage payment, what would happen if several unit owners could not make their payment for one month? The obvious answer is that the remaining unit owners must come up with the rest of the money in order to ensure that the mortgage payment is paid. The same is true of insurance, taxes, and other maintenance costs. In the condominium ownership situation, a mortgage company can foreclose on one unit. The cooperative form of ownership, however, does not allow for this type of independence, except possibly in the tenancy in common type of cooperative ownership.

Thus, **financing** is the first major disadvantage of cooperative ownership. For example, a loan can be made only to the corporation or trust, and not to any of the unit owners independently. This disadvantage also exists in all services, utilities, and other obligations that may be undertaken by the cooperative housing association. There is, of course, the usual problem of trying to ascertain the appraised value of the property for loan purposes because of the interdependence and multi-ownership facets of cooperative housing.

The second major difficulty and complication arising out of cooperative owner-ship is that of **securities**. Since this form of ownership is evidenced by a certificate of occupancy, or "shares" of ownership, one may think that it would automatically be affected by the securities laws. This was a very heavily litigated area for some time. In 1975, the Supreme Court of the United States, in a landmark decision involving coop-erative housing, *United Housing Foundation* v. *Foreman*, 421 U.S. 837 (1975), indi-cated that the housing aspect of a transaction that involved the purchase of stock in the cooperative corporation was not making an **investment**, as that term is used in securities law, even though it was possible for the cooperative owners to sell their "shares" at a later time and even for a profit. Since the housing units themselves were used as primary residences by the occupants, the purchaser is seeking a place to live, regardless of how the cooperative was financed or sold. The shares of stock in this case were completely tied to the proprietary leases, a fact that negates some of the attributes of ownership and investment that most stock shares exhibit. The Court also emphasized that the voting rights under the ownership in a cooperative unit were not one vote per share of stock, but rather, one vote per homeowner.

So at least in very closely identified situations, the shares of ownership in a cooperative will not automatically be considered to be securities. However, this does not indicate that all cooperatives are not securities. As in condominium owner-ship, there can always be a situation involving the marketing, selling, and retransfer of the interest in the cooperative housing that would make securities an extremely troublesome situation if handled improperly.

**Tort liability** for corporate or trust form cooperatives is not nearly the problem that it is under condominium ownership because the owners are, of course, insu-lated through the corporate veil or the trust form of ownership. Anyone who has a claim against the cooperative housing unit would have to sue the trust or corpora-tion, and the homeowners would understandably be sufficiently insulated from liabilities so that they would not be personally liable. The same is true of most con-tractual liabilities.

It is assumed that the tort or contractual liability of a tenancy in common coop-erative is the same as that of tenancy in common generally, rendering the owner liable only for his proportionate share, although the owners' personal liability may be unlimited.

In summary, it can be easily seen that both condominiums and cooperatives are heavily dependent on the shared-facilities housing concept and that the interdepen-dence of both types of ownership may create problems. However, we are going to have to learn to live with these problems because single-family housing is becoming more and more expensive in various parts of the country. In dealing with a pur-chaser or seller of a condominium or cooperative unit, the wise and astute attorney, and the real estate agent, must understand the various complications that are involved through securities, tort liability, organization of the ownership entity, and various aspects of interdependent living, all of which may make a substantial differ-ence (especially to the purchasing client). Recalling the terms of Section 15(4)(A) of the new Real Estate License Act, almost any of the facts and criteria listed above could be material consideration for a reasonable and prudent purchaser who is interested in purchasing a unit. It is therefore particularly important that the real estate agent be familiar with this type of housing if he chooses to concentrate his marketing efforts in this area.

■ **SUMMARY**

There is no common-law derivation of the concepts of condominium and cooperative ownership in the United States. The creation of these two forms of housing has been one of statute and legal theory. Condominium ownership involves the ownership of the fee to the apartment, ownership of the common elements as a tenant in common, and an easement to the space required for ingress and egress to that unit. The rights of the parties involved in condominiums are governed generally by the Texas Uniform Condominium Act. A condominium project in Texas must consist of more than one unit. The rights of condominium ownership necessarily involve the interdependence of the rights of the other unit owners in the condominium project. This creates specific problem areas, some of which have yet to be resolved.

Cooperative ownership is similar to condominium ownership with a few major, distinct differences in ownership and methods of control and operation of the project. The entire project is normally owned by one entity—a corporation or a trust. Each of the individual shareholders in that corporation or trust then has a right to occupancy of a specific unit. Cooperative ownership creates more interdependence in that, if one party defaults, the other parties are obligated to make up the difference to prevent a default in the obligations of the corporation or trust. Real estate agents should take particular care in representing the purchasing parties' rights when attempting to sell either condominium or cooperative housing because of the new provisions of the Real Estate License Act and provisions of the Deceptive Trade Practices Act.

## CHAPTER 20

# Regulation of Real Estate

In any form of government, there must be certain priorities that the government has with respect to the land contained within its jurisdiction that has a higher priority than any other individual or entity.

In the United States, the government has four chief methods for controlling land use or ownership. These are:

1. Eminent domain procedures.
2. Taxation.
3. Escheat.
4. Police power.

The fundamentals of eminent domain and escheat were discussed in Chapter 11. Taxation is discussed in Chapter 21. The scope of this chapter is to dwell on the fourth governmental power, which is government regulation pursuant to its police power.

It is by the use of **police power** that the government regulates and enforces laws and regulations that pertain to land-use control. This is a relatively inexpensive process because there is no "taking" of property (as in eminent domain), and therefore no requirement for just compensation.

There has been such a voluminous amount of land-use control legislation passed at the federal level that it cannot all be discussed within the scope of this chapter, or even within this text. Therefore, in discussing federal land-use control, we will attempt only to highlight some of the more important legislative efforts, just so the reader can keep his or her sanity. Beyond the federal land-use controls, we will discuss controls at the state and county level, as well as those at the municipal and local level.

## Federal Land-Use Control

In an attempt to categorize federal land-use control as succinctly as possible, we will discuss each federal agency under which land use is controlled. The agencies to be covered are the Securities and Exchange Commission, the Department of Housing and Urban Development, the Federal Trade Commission, and the Environmental Protection Agency. From a land-use control aspect, it should be remembered that every time a new restrictive regulatory law is passed, some developers and investors will stop investing in the type of project being regulated, forcing their funds into other areas, and ultimately changing certain land-use patterns.

## Securities and Exchange Commission

The **Securities and Exchange Commission** (SEC) regulates certain forms of land use, which, in its opinion, involve securities, investment contracts, or sale of equity interests. Thus, the SEC has been very effective in regulating real estate investment trusts, real estate syndications, and certain types of condominium offerings that involve investments, interstate sales promotions, and sales made with a promise of profit or a high rate of return.

In the eyes of the SEC, virtually any investment scheme or contract to purchase real estate with the expectation of profit makes that particular real estate transaction a security and requires certain disclosures pursuant to the **Securities and Exchange Acts of 1933 and 1934**. There are only two provisions of the 1934 act that exempt real estate investment transactions from being classified as securities. These are:

1. **Section 4(a)2** of the act, which exempts offerings that are made only to close friends, business associates, family relations, and other "close" offerings that are not made to the public in general.

2. **Section 3(a)11** of the act, which exempts offerings that do not go interstate, but are kept wholly as an intrastate offering. This means that the sales promotion cannot use any of the means of interstate commerce (the telephone, newspaper advertising, the U.S. mail, etc.).

The SEC has severely curtailed certain investment schemes and syndication offerings that became very common in Texas in the early 1970s. The expense of registering a security to comply with the Securities and Exchange Act is so great that most developers now prefer to restrict their offerings, or to go into a different type of real estate development altogether, instead of complying with the securities regulations. The exception is large real estate investment trusts and other large investment opportunities that can afford to be very attentive to compliance with these statutes. If any real estate offering has even the possibility of being considered a security, and the exemption may be in question, the real estate broker should work very closely with a lawyer well qualified in the area of real estate and securities laws.

## The Department of Housing and Urban Development

The **Department of Housing and Urban Development** (HUD) has made great strides in controlling and regulating real estate. The agencies under HUD control to be discussed include the Office of Interstate Land Sales Registration, the Federal Housing Administration, the Government National Mortgage Association, the Federal National Mortgage Association, and the Federal Insurance Administration.

The **Office of Interstate Land Sales Registration** was established to administer the rules, regulations, and statutes pertaining to the **Interstate Land Sales Full Disclosure Act**. This act makes it unlawful for any land developer (except for certain exempt developers) to sell or lease, by use of the mails or by use of any means of interstate commerce, any land offered as a part of a common promotional plan, unless such land has been registered with the Secretary of Housing and Urban

Development, *and* a printed property report (in a format established by HUD) is furnished to the purchaser or lessee in advance of the signing of any agreement for sale or lease. Although originally meant to affect sales of lots in resort-type subdivisions (an industry that badly needed regulating), the act has recently been changed to include a new definition of **lot**:

> … any portion, piece, division, unit, or undivided interest in land, if such interest includes the right to exclusive use of a specific portion of the land.

This means that literally any parcel of land, or "unit" of real estate, could ultimately be regulated by the Office of Interstate Land Sales Registration. Can you imagine having to register an office building for tenant leasehold space, or a parking garage for contract parking, or condominiums, or even apartments? This may sound ridiculous, but it is a real possibility since there are no clear guidelines limiting the government's authority.

The **Federal Housing Administration (FHA)** was originally established in 1933 to provide for and encourage improvement in housing standards and conditions and to provide for an adequate home-financing system. All homes qualifying for FHA loans must pass an FHA inspection to ensure adequate housing standards for the purchaser. This is also true of homes qualifying for loans guaranteed by the **Department of Veteran Affairs** (VA).

FHA also provides insurance for private lenders against loss on mortgage financing of homes, multifamily projects, and land-development projects. FHA covers virtually every area of the housing industry and has been one of the better incentives to induce lenders to make low equity loans. It has been a major contributor toward Americans being able to secure 90 to 95 percent loans when buying homes. When FHA changes its requirements of insurable loans, it affects the ability of certain segments of the American public to buy homes. When FHA is in an expansion posture, one will find that more loans are being made to stimulate the housing industry. When FHA chooses to take a less expansive posture, the housing industry will quickly feel the effect, as fewer people can qualify for loans.

The **Government National Mortgage Association** (GNMA), commonly called **Ginnie Mae**, and the **Federal National Mortgage Association** (FNMA), commonly called **Fannie Mae**, were originally created to purchase, service, and sell mortgages insured or guaranteed by FHA and VA in the **secondary market**. The secondary market is a market to purchase mortgages from the primary lending sources (banks, mortgage companies, and mortgage brokers). When the primary lending institutions sell their mortgages to Fannie Mae or Ginnie Mae, that gives the primary lending institutions more cash to make additional loans. Both Fannie Mae and Ginnie Mae put requirements on these primary lending institutions, such as requiring the lenders to buy back the mortgages if requested, and establish certain discount rates (sales price) for smaller mortgage lenders. This, in effect, allows Fannie Mae and Ginnie Mae to select the types of loans they will buy from the primary lender and automatically gives an incentive to the primary lender to make loans to the public in that area. For instance, if Fannie Mae and Ginnie Mae wish to increase the amount of money being made available for apartment construction, they have the ability to specify that they will purchase apartment loans rather than single-family loans. This, in turn, encourages the primary lender to lend on apartment projects rather than single-family residences.

In recent years, Ginnie Mae has taken a less active posture in purchasing in the secondary market and has turned more toward managing and liquidating the government's loan portfolios. The **Federal Home Loan Mortgage Corporation** (FHLMC), commonly called **Freddie Mac**, serves a function similar to that of

Fannie Mae. Freddie Mac was originally created as a secondary market for savings and loans associations. It is now allowed to buy any and all mortgages within its approved guidelines.

The Federal Insurance Administration was created to provide insurance for loss of properties as defined in standard insurance contracts. It has been particularly influential in providing for federal flood insurance under the **National Flood Insurance Act**. This act, along with the **Flood Disaster Control Act of 1973**, was designed to provide previously unavailable flood insurance to property owners in flood-prone areas. As almost all real estate agents know, the government's designation of flood-prone areas has taken a rather broad sweep along the Texas Gulf Coast and certain other areas near rivers, reservoirs, and even minor tributaries. The Flood Disaster Control Act basically makes it unlawful for any lending institution with funds underwritten or guaranteed by the federal government (which includes basically all lending institutions) to make loans on improvements in flood-prone areas unless the borrowers have flood insurance. There has been considerable controversy over how the "**flood-prone areas**" were designated by the U.S. Army Corps of Engineers, and a large amount of litigation has developed since the act was first passed.

One of the major concerns in the area of flood insurance has been the cost of obtaining the flood insurance. It was originally available at a relatively low cost. However, after major flooding in certain areas, the rates go up significantly; this is a cost that the homeowner must bear. If the rates do go up, the homeowner has no choice but to continue to purchase the flood insurance (regardless of the cost) to satisfy the requirements that have been imposed by the lender. It is arguable that this requirement for flood insurance makes a significant difference in the purchase price of a home built in a "flood-prone" area, since the purchaser may have undetermined future expenses. In addition, the flood prone area can change. If you're not in it now, you may be in the future. It can be unpredictable!

## The Federal Trade Commission

The **Federal Trade Commission** has recently come into the limelight because it has strongly expanded its scope from financial areas to those of consumer protection and consumer credit. The rules and regulations of the Federal Trade Commission are implemented and enforced by the Federal Reserve Board. Some of the primary functions of this board are to oversee the implementation and enforcement of such legislation as the Federal Truth-in-Lending Act, the Equal Credit Opportunity Act, the Fair Credit Reporting Act, and the Home Mortgage Disclosure Act.

The **Truth-in-Lending Act** was originally passed to require lenders to make certain meaningful disclosures as to interest rates and costs of obtaining loans. The **Equal Credit Opportunity Act** (ECOA) went into effect in 1975 to prohibit discrimination in any aspect of a credit transaction on the basis of sex or marital status. In 1976, amendments were added to the ECOA to prohibit discrimination on the basis of race, color, religion, national origin, age, and other arbitrary requirements. The **Fair Credit Reporting Act** has its most significant application to credit bureaus. Prior to the passage of this act, it was possible to have a "bad" credit rating, and the person who had the bad credit rating could not find out the source of that information, even if it was untrue. The Fair Credit Reporting Act has opened up the vaults of credit bureaus so that consumers can find out what their credit rating is, and hopefully correct any mistakes. The **Home Mortgage Disclosure Act** was passed in 1975 to force lenders to disclose in what areas of a town or metropolitan region they were making loans. This is to prevent "redlining" (making loans only to specified areas of town) and to encourage lenders to make loans in all areas of a town.

The most significant aspect of the FTC may be its attempt to *regulate* real estate brokerage through antitrust statutes, as discussed in Chapter 7, Real Estate Brokerage.

## The Environmental Protection Agency

In a continuing effort to make our environment more habitable, the **Environmental Protection Agency** (EPA) has passed voluminous laws and regulations to control the use of real property if such use is considered to be a direct source or an indirect source of environmental pollution. The EPA has made an effort to control virtually every area of air, water, and industrial pollution, and many of its regulations have resulted in extreme controversy. The EPA administers the **Clean Air Act**, which was designed to maintain a national air quality standard, whether the source of pollution was from a stationary, mobile, or indirect source of pollution. The EPA also passed land-use regulations under the **Federal Water Pollution Control Act**, which provides for area-wide planning. The EPA has not had very much success at the courthouse, however, and many of its attempts at regulating land-use control through these laws have been substantially altered or struck down altogether. The Clean Air Act and its indirect source rule have been somewhat more successful in controlling the construction of certain sources of pollution, such as shopping centers, office buildings, and so forth. These examples constitute indirect sources of pollution due to the number of cars that the structures attract, thereby creating a large amount of exhaust and carbon monoxide pollution.

New areas of land-use regulation are emerging in which the EPA is taking a very strong position. These include hazardous waste disposal, asbestos regulation, and regulation of ongoing waste facilities.

The **Comprehensive Environmental Response, Compensation, and Liability Act of 1980** (CERCLA), which was amended by the **Superfund Amendments and Reauthorization Act of 1986** (SARA), defines "hazardous substance," which is a very broad and potentially changing definition. This statute puts liability for cleanup of the site on: (1) the owner and operator of the facility, (2) the person who operates the facility, and (3) the person who arranges for disposal or the transportation of materials to that facility.

EPA enacted the "All Appropriate Inquiry" Rule, which became effective November 1, 2006. It requires more investigation than the prior rules and establishes new time limits for the regulations under CERCLA. The new rule specifically requires the hiring of an environmental professional who must develop opinions and conclusions about releases or threatened releases of hazardous substances concerning the subject property, sufficient to satisfy certain objectives and performance standards. The professional's research should seek to reveal present and historical uses of hazardous substances at the subject property as well as neighboring and adjoining properties. Searches for environmental clean up liens, government records, visual inspections, and interviews with past and present owners must be completed no more than 180 days prior to the date of the acquisition of the property.

Both EPA and OSHA now exercise certain regulations by promoting standards for asbestos insulation. This, in many instances, has resulted in significant changes in values of real estate when a potential purchaser realizes that the cost of complying with EPA and OSHA regulations can run into the millions of dollars for asbestos removal or encapsulation.

The **Resource Conservation and Recovery Act of 1976** (RCRA), which was amended by the **Hazardous Solid Waste Amendments of 1984** (HSWA), applies to the control of ongoing waste facilities. This statute creates significant liability for the property owner, without regard to fault, if an ongoing waste facility presents an imminent and substantial endangerment to health or environment. *United States* v. *Price*, 11 Envtl. L. Rep. 21047 (D.N.J.—1981).

The **Clean Water Act** authorizes the Corps of Engineers to issue permits for the discharge of dredged or filled material and also prohibits discharges of pollutants into navigable waters. The courts have further determined that the Clean Water Act was intended to apply to the full extent of Congress's power to "regulate among the several states." The Corps of Engineers and the Environmental Protection Agency have therefore defined "wetlands" by regulation, which is determined by the hydrology, soils, and vegetation in the field they are evaluating. **Wetlands**, then, come under specific federal jurisdiction of regulation of real estate development in that area. This has dramatic impact on properties along the Texas Gulf Coast. Almost any development now requires a Corps permit and the EPA can veto a Corps decision to grant a permit, if necessary. It goes without saying that obtaining permits in a wetlands area is a time-consuming process because it involves two federal agencies, *33 U.S.C.A., §1251.*

The Federal Endangered Species Act, *16 U.S.C.A., §1531*, creates a federal list of species that must be protected. The species include subspecies of fish or wildlife or plants as well as any distinct populations of a vertebrate species. The statute provides that the critical habitats may also be designated and prohibits a developer from "taking" property that would include harassing animals and disturbing their environment so they (the animals) won't want to live there. In many cases this requires a biological opinion.

One can also see how, by using the threat of public harm, the EPA can exercise broad jurisdiction over many other areas, establishing regulations for areas of environmental control for which, in many cases, acceptable standards have not yet been established.

The **Residential Lead-Based Paint Hazard Reduction Act of 1992** is a comprehensive statute applying to housing that is owned, subsidized, or the subject of mortgage guarantees by the federal government. It requires HUD to issue regulations for the disclosure of lead-based paint hazards in any target housing (housing constructed prior to 1978, except housing for the elderly or persons with disabilities, unless any child under six resides or is expected to reside in such housing, or any zero bedroom dwelling). The regulations must require that every contract for the purchase and sale of any interest in target housing shall contain a **Lead Warning Statement** and a statement signed by the purchaser that he has read the Lead Warning Statement and understands its contents, has received a lead hazard pamphlet, and has had a 10-day opportunity (unless the parties mutually agree upon a different period of time) before becoming obligated under the contract of purchase to conduct a risk assessment or inspection for the presence of lead-based paint hazards.

HUD has recently passed severe penalties for violation of this statute, with fines up to $11,000 per violation.

## Historic Preservation

The **National Historic Preservation Act**, *16 U.S.C.A., §470*, requires consultation between federal agencies and the Advisory Council on Historic Preservation before development can occur on certain sites. The consultation can be a lengthy process and must be completed prior to the approval of any action by a federal agency. In some cases it is necessary to have an archaeologist do a survey of the property, even if it is raw land. Once there has been a determination that the site is eligible for the National Register of Historic Places, the developer must determine whether development will affect the site, and define the area of potential effect. Texas also has similar protection under the **Texas Antiquities Code**, *V.T.C.A., Nat. Res. Code, §191.*

## Net Effect

One can easily see that in land-use control, the federal government has been fairly significantly involved in a number of different areas. Through the Securities and Exchange Commission, it controls the methods by which we can offer parcels of real estate for sale or present investment prospectuses and real estate promotional schemes. The federal government also regulates the sale of units of real estate through the Office of Interstate Land Sales Registration, the quality of housing and the availability of loans through the Federal Housing Administration, closing disclosure requirements through the Real Estate Settlement and Procedures Act, and availability of certain funds to primary lenders through Fannie Mae, Ginnie Mae, and Freddie Mac.

The federal government also protects the consumer from himself by requiring flood insurance for homes in government-designated flood-prone areas. Through the Federal Trade Commission, the federal government requires that certain disclosures be made to the consumer as provided by the federal Truth-in-Lending Act, it also requires disclosures under the Fair Credit Reporting Act, and it provides for additional disclosures to be made through the Home Mortgage Disclosure Act by the requirements imposed on lenders. The Environmental Protection Agency also helps in controlling land use by its regulations on construction through the Clean Air Act and the Federal Water Pollution Control Act. These acts significantly affect where factories and industry can be located, and major traffic patterns may be substantially altered if the federal government feels that these may hurt our pollution standards. Most of these regulations require extensive fees to be paid by the people regulated, and, ultimately, by you, the consumer, as these costs are passed on in the price of consumer products.

Some of the governmental functions have been outstanding in contributing to the overall welfare of the American public. However, this is not always the case. The most disturbing area of federal land-use control is the extended implementation of the acts as passed by Congress. Each of the foregoing federal agencies passes its own regulations in an attempt to clarify its positions, and sometimes an agency expands upon the authority given to it under the original statutes. It must be emphasized that although these regulations are not passed by Congress, they have the force of law until they are challenged in the federal courts. Challenging any federal regulation is an expensive, time-consuming, and high-risk process on the part of any private land developer. Not only does he run the risk of losing the case but risks incurring the wrath of that federal government agency he chooses to challenge. In addition, there is no control whatsoever on these federal government agencies as they pass these regulations. They are not subject to any system of checks and balances, and there is no authority to discipline them if there is any type of injustice or selective (unfair) enforcement involved, other than through the federal courts. If there is a basic injustice in any of the federal land-use controls, it is that there are no watchdogs over the federal government, whereas the federal agencies are acting as watchdogs over the private landowner and developer.

# State Land-Use Control

The Tenth Amendment to the U.S. Constitution reserves all powers not specifically delegated to the federal government to the states. So, subject to other constitutional provisions, the states do have the right to pass reasonable regulations and to exercise their police power to promote the health, safety, and welfare of the community. The states regulate land use through a number of different means, the most important of which are state agencies, land management, enabling acts, special-purpose districts, and regulation of natural resources.

The State of Texas has the **Texas Highway Commission**, the General Land Office, the **Texas Water Development Board**, the **Texas Natural Resources and Conservation Commission**, the **Texas Parks and Wildlife Department**, and other state agencies. Each agency has jurisdictional control over all lands that are maintained under the agency's specified scope of control. Most of these agencies are appointed by the governor and are relatively autonomous as to implementation and enforcement, and there is very little coordination between them.

Land management in Texas is accomplished through a number of different regional planning commissions, which have been inactive in recent years. Through independent authorities such as the **Houston-Galveston Area Council**, the **Coastal Zone Management Commission**, and other regional planning authorities, Texas is making its first attempt at regional land planning to achieve the best land use, both economically and environmentally, for areas of strategic environmental concern.

Special-purpose districts have been very important to the Texas development pattern. Through the authority of the legislature, special districts have been established whose boards ultimately regulate almost every type of land use imaginable. These districts have their own jurisdictional boundaries, which often overlap with other authorities' boundaries (cities, school districts, etc.). Special levee districts (to protect water hazards in flood-prone areas), water districts, water improvement districts, and utility districts have been instrumental in allowing vast expansion for most Texas cities when the municipal authorities did not have sufficient utility capacity to serve new subdivisions. Other special-purpose districts that have been particularly instrumental are the navigation districts, water conservation districts, soil conservation districts, and subsidence districts.

Regulation of natural resources has been the primary responsibility of the state **Railroad Commission**. The Railroad Commission has authority to regulate production capacities and to set restrictions on oil and gas production in Texas. The General Land Office has authority over certain uses of these resources offshore.

# County Regulations

Texas has traditionally not provided for county land-use control except for areas of road construction and maintenance. The county attorney or any other prosecuting attorney representing the county may file an action in the court of competent jurisdiction to enjoin a violation or threatened violation of any county requirement established or adopted under the new statute.

In counties with a population of more than 2.2 million, or in counties that are contiguous with a county with a population of more than 2.2 million, the county can require platting of certain subdivisions guaranteeing minimum street widths and plans for laying out the boundaries of certain lots. In establishing these plat guidelines, the statute expands the county's authority to be able to approve specifications for the construction of roads, and for adequate drainage to comply with standard engineering practices, and to require the owner or owners of any tract of land to supply a sufficient bond to ensure proper construction of the roadways.

In addition to allowing for the platting of the subdivision, there are also provisions for plat revision and cancellation of plats that had been approved by the county. Revision or cancellation requires the application of at least 75% of the ownership of the land area in the subdivision.

# Municipal Land-Use Control

Cities do not have any inherent lawmaking powers except those granted by the state. Therefore, the state has passed certain enabling acts that grant cities the authority to regulate land use. Typical examples of this type of delegation of power are reflected in the zoning statutes, indirect municipal land-use controls, municipal enforcement of deed restrictions, and certain powers of annexation. Enforcement often seems unfair, and landowners may want to sue the city. It should be noted that in exercising its governmental functions, the municipality has no liability for torts. *City of Round Rock* v. *Smith*, 687 S.W.2d 300 (Tex. 1985).

## Zoning

**Zoning** is the most extensive method of regulating land use in cities, and its use was upheld in Texas in 1934 in the case of *Lombardo* v. *City of Dallas*, 73 S.W.2d 475 (Tex. 1934). Zoning is a police power, and one of the strongest powers a city has to regulate land use. In fact, once a zoning ordinance has been passed, the law favors its validity. If a party contests the ordinance, the burden is on the complaining party to show that the city acted arbitrarily and capriciously in passing the ordinance. *Hunt* v. *City of San Antonio*, 462 S.W.2d 536 (Tex. 1971). This is a very difficult burden of proof. The zoning-enabling statutes are contained in the local government code. References later in this chapter are to sections contained in that code.

**Purpose** Sections 211.001 and 211.003 are the specific grants of authority to the cities by the state for the power of zoning. The statutes specifically set out that zoning is for the purpose of promoting health, safety, and morals; for the protection and preservation of places and areas of historical and cultural importance and significance; and for the general welfare of the community. The power of zoning specifically gives the municipality the authority to regulate and restrict the height, number of stories, and size of buildings and other structures; the percentage of a lot that may be occupied; the size of the yards, courts, and other open space; the density of population; and the location and use of buildings, structures, and land for trade, industry, residence, or other purposes. In the case of designated places and areas of historical and cultural importance, the city also has the power to regulate and restrict the construction, alteration, and reconstruction or razing of buildings and other structures. One case (non-Texas) has even given the zoning commission the right to legislate morality. It prevented a nonmarried couple from living together! *Zavala* v. *City of Denver*, 759 P.2d 664 (Col. 1988). One must always keep in mind the specific purpose of the zoning-enabling legislation because the purpose *per se* is one of the fundamental criteria the courts look to in determining whether or not a zoning ordinance will be upheld. The process relies on sound land-planning practices and is not subject to popular demand, or subject to a referendum. *San Pedro North, Ltd.* v. *City of San Antonio*, 562 S.W.2d 260 (Tex. Civ. App.—San Antonio, 1978).

The procedural aspects of zoning ordinances and zoning changes are critically important to the legality of any ordinance. If the proper procedures are not strictly adhered to, the ordinance is in imminent danger of being tested by opponents. One of the basic underlying principles of the zoning concept is that the zoning regulations (and changes thereto) must be made in accordance with a **comprehensive plan**, V.T.C.A., *Local Government Code, §211.004.* There is some question as to exactly what constitutes a comprehensive plan, and municipal planners often have their own ideas and criteria for what will constitute a valid comprehensive plan. There is no particular comprehensive plan format or criteria that must be followed, but the plan must be a uniform one that can act as a basis for justification to effect further zoning changes, or the refusal of same. The regulations, according to statute, must also be designed to accomplish the following:

1. To lessen congestion in the streets.
2. To secure safety from fire, panic, and other danger.
3. To promote health and the general welfare.
4. To provide adequate light and air.
5. To prevent the overcrowding of land.
6. To avoid undue concentration of population.
7. To facilitate adequate provision for transportation, water, sewage, schools, parks, and other public requirements.

A majority of the governing body may adopt or amend a comprehensive plan at any time. The policies of a comprehensive plan may only be implemented by ordinances duly adopted by the majority and shall not constitute land-use or zoning regulations, or establish zoning district boundaries.

Section 211.005 of the statute authorizes the city to divide the municipality into districts of such number, shape, and area as to carry out the purposes of the ordinance and to regulate and restrict construction and reconstruction, alteration, repair, and use of building structures or land inside of each district. All regulations are to be uniform for each class or kind of building throughout each district, but the regulations may differ from one district to the other.

**Zoning Procedure** The zoning regulations (as well as any amendments, supplements, or changes of same) cannot become effective until the legislative body holds a public hearing with respect to them, at which all parties and interested citizens can have an opportunity to be heard. At least 15 days' notice of the time and place of such hearing shall be published in an official paper in such municipality, V.T.C.A., *Local Government Code, §211.006.* In the event the proposed regulations are protested by the owners of 20% of the area of the lots covered by the proposed change, or the area of the lots or land within 200 feet of the property proposed to change, a three-fourths vote of the legislative body is necessary to enact the amendment or change, V.T.C.A., *Local Government Code, §211.006.*

The ultimate decision as to how an area is going to be zoned depends on the legislative body of the municipality, that is, the august body of elected officials who bear the burden of running the city. These individuals are aided by a group of appointed officials referred to as **zoning commissioners**, whose appointment and function are specifically authorized by statute.

In the normal zoning procedure, the applicant appears before the **zoning commission**, who, after a preliminary review, sets a public hearing for the applicant's proposed zoning changes. After proper statutory notice has been given, a public hearing is held to determine the public's views and attitudes on said proposed change. After the public hearing has taken place, the zoning commission then proceeds to make its recommendations and decisions on the proposed zoning change. It may propose the change exactly as it was proposed, or it can modify it and recommend a modified proposal, or it can reject the proposal entirely.

If the commission chooses to recommend the proposed change, the proposal then goes to the city council, who, after proper statutory notice, has its own public hearing and makes the final decision as to whether the zoning change will be accepted or rejected. The legislative body (city council, in this case) cannot make a decision until it has received a recommendation from the zoning commission. If the recommendation from the zoning commission were against the change, it would take a three-fourths majority of the council to overrule the recommendation of the zoning commission. The same is not true of a recommended change, however. If the zoning commission recommends the change, the city council can overrule it by mere majority vote.

If the applicant feels he has been unjustly treated, he may appeal his case to another appointed body, the **board of adjustment**. The board of adjustment is limited to hearing appeals from administrative decisions and to granting **special exceptions** and **variances**. The board is also empowered by statute to hear and decide appeals when there is an error in the decision by an administrative official in enforcing an ordinance. The board can also hear and decide special exceptions under the terms of the ordinance and can even authorize a variance from the terms of the ordinance when there are special circumstances, or if the ordinance creates an unnecessary hardship.

A **special exception** is a use that is permitted in a certain zone, but such use is subject to control or supervision by the municipal authorities. If there is an objection to the use in that zone, the special exception can be revoked, and the use is no longer permitted.

A **variance** is a use that literally violates the terms of the zoning ordinance, but the variance is permitted to stand because otherwise an unnecessary hardship would be created for the owner of the property. A variance can only be granted to solve location and construction violations.

Any appeal beyond the board of adjustment has to be taken to the nearest court of competent jurisdiction.

The ultimate benefactors of the zoning ordinance, the people of the community, do not have any direct say in the process. The enabling legislation does not provide for any initiative or referendum to repeal ordinances. Therefore, the power of the people to legislate directly does not extend to the subject of zoning. *City of Beaumont* v. *Salhab*, 596 S.W.2d 536 (Tex. Civ. App.—Beaumont, 1980).

**Zoning Issues.** There are a number of issues that continually recur in the zoning process that bear some additional discussion. Those to be considered will be "taking" issue, spot zoning, contract zoning, nonconforming use, and exclusionary land-use controls.

*"Taking" issue* There has long been an argument that zoning a property for a particular use is, in fact, "taking" that property from the owner, who can no longer determine its highest and best use and perhaps cannot even build for a profit. An example of this would be a piece of prime commercial frontage property, which, for various reasons, is rezoned for residential use. In this situation, the owner, expecting to sell the property for a commercial use, feels that his rights to build on the property profitably have been taken from him. The courts have, however, consistently held that this is a legal regulation of land use and *not* "taking." One Texas case has even held that the required dedication of park land by the developer is not "taking." *City of College*

*Station* v. *Turtle Rock Corp.*, 680 S.W.2d 802 (Tex. 1984). Therefore, there is no requirement for just compensation, and the city is not liable for any just compensation as it would be in an eminent domain proceeding, unless the city exercised its rights of police power arbitrarily. *City of Austin* v. *Teague*, 556 S.W.2d 400 (Tex. Civ. App.—Waco, 1977); *Agins et ux* v. *City of Tiburon*, 447 U.S. 255 (1980). In the event a city "takes" a property by eminent domain, it is not bound by its own zoning ordinance. *City of Lubbock* v. *Austin*, 628 S.W.2d 49 (Tex. 1982).

It should be pointed out that there have been recent trends in the **"taking" issue** that seem to be more supportive of landowners' rights. In two significant cases, the U.S. Supreme Court has held that a temporary regulation that prohibits the use of a landowner's property can constitute a "taking," and be compensable. *First English Evangelical Lutheran Church* v. *County of Los Angeles*, 107 S. Ct. 2378 (1987). The same "taking" issue was also upheld in a land-use regulation issue, when the Court held that refusing to issue a building permit was held to constitute a taking. *Nollan* v. *California Coastal Commission*, 107 S. Ct. 3141 (1987). Similarly, when a property has been zoned so that it no longer has an economic use, it is a taking. *Lucas* v. *South Carolina Coastal Council*, 112 S. Ct. 2886 (1992).

*Spot zoning* **Spot zoning** has been described as the process of singling out a small parcel of land for a use classification that is different and inconsistent with that of the surrounding zoned areas. Zoning of this type is normally to the benefit of the lot owner, but to the detriment of the surrounding area. An example of this would be to allow a townhouse zoning use in the middle of a single-family residential area (by permitting one of the owners to sell his lot off to a townhouse developer who may build four or five townhouses on that property). This use would not fit into the overall land use of the neighborhood or of that section of the city and creates a spot-zoning issue. Spot zoning is illegal and prohibited in Texas. *Burket* v. *City of Texarkana*, 500 S.W.2d 242 (Tex. Civ. App.—Texarkana, 1973).

*Contract zoning* **Contract zoning** is an agreement by a governing body to enact a change in land-use classification in exchange for certain concessions to be granted by the developer or applicant. It is "zoning by agreement," which does not fit into the criteria of providing for the health, safety, and welfare of the citizens. This has been held to be invalid as an improper "bargaining away" of the city's police power. *City of Farmers Branch* v. *Hawnco, Inc.*, 435 S.W.2d 298 (Tex. Civ. App.—Dallas, 1968). This should be distinguished, however, from **conditional zoning**, wherein the zoning authority unilaterally requires a property owner to subject his land to certain restrictions without a prior commitment to rezone. When the conditions of conditional zoning are not inconsistent with the underlying goals of zoning generally and are in conformance with the comprehensive plan of the city, conditional zoning provides for flexibility so that a city cannot be bound by traditionally more restrictive zoning regulations. This has recently been used in Texas to support the theory of planned unit development zoning. This is when a large tract may be zoned for flexible uses subject to proper plan submittals from the owner of the property. As long as the flexible conditions are imposed on the property itself and not the developer, the conditional zoning is legal in Texas. *Teer* v. *Duddlesten*, 664 S.W.2d 702 (Tex. 1984); *City of Pharr* v. *Tippitt*, 616 S.W.2d 173 (Tex. 1981).

*Nonconforming use* **Nonconforming use** relates to a zoning change or a new zoning designation. The nonconforming use is maintaining the previous use of an area, a use that does not properly fit into the new zoning classification. For instance, if a particular area of town were zoned R1-residential, and, at the time of the zoning change, there were two commercial uses in that zoning district, the two commercial uses would be allowed to remain, but they could not be materially changed or altered (or even improved) if they did not comply with the new existing zoning classification. The owner is allowed to repair the existing improvement but cannot materially alter it. *Nu-Way Emulsions, Inc.* v. *City of Dalworthington Gardens*, 610 S.W.2d 562 (Tex. Civ. App.—Ft. Worth, 1980). The theory behind this is that if the area has been properly planned, and a new zoning designation has been given, the nonconforming uses are supposed to cease to function eventually, and the new classification designated by the plan would be the only existing classification. There have been successful efforts at putting a limit to the use of the nonconforming structure by designating a certain number of years by which that nonconforming use must cease to exist. *City of Garland* v. *Valley Oil Co.*, 482 S.W.2d 342 (Tex. Civ. App.—Dallas, 1972).

*Exclusionary land-use control* There has been considerable litigation in recent years over what rights the city has to zone properties to exclude certain uses. This practice is referred to as **exclusionary zoning**. If zoning, for instance, is used to limit construction to homes on two-acre lots, and the city contains no apartments, no middle-income housing, or no low-income housing, that city may be determined to be using an exclusionary zoning technique, which would be illegal. Basically, the court would say that the city is excluding certain people from living in the town, which would be a violation of an individual's right to travel interstate, as provided for by the U.S. Constitution. *N.A.A.C.P.* v. *Button*, 371 U.S. 415; *Southern Burlington County N.A.A.C.P.* v. *Township of Mount Laurel*, 336 A.2d 713 (Sup. Ct.—N.J. 1975). Two cases, however, reaffirm the city's ability to use wide discretion in zoning its areas, as long as it has a permissible, constitutional objective for its land-use regulation. *Construction Industry Association of Sonoma County* v. *City of Petaluma*, 375 F. Supp. 574 (1975); *Village of Belle Terre* v. *Boraas*, 416 U.S. 1 (1974).

## Annexation—Extraterritorial Jurisdiction

The Texas legislature has passed an additional method of land-use control giving the city certain **annexation** powers and certain rights within its extraterritorial jurisdiction, *V.T.C.A., Local Government Code, §43.021.* **Extraterritorial jurisdiction** has been defined as the unincorporated area, not a part of any other city, that is contiguous with the corporate limits of any city. The size of the extraterritorial jurisdiction changes depending on the number of inhabitants in that city. The governing body of any city has the right, according to this statute, to extend by ordinance to all the area under its extraterritorial jurisdiction all the city's ordinances establishing rules and regulations governing the plats and subdivision of land. In addition to this, the city is given additional power to annex the area within its extraterritorial jurisdiction up to certain specified limits, after holding the required public hearings. Consent of the people whose property is being annexed is not required. *Woodruff* v. *City of Laredo*, 686 S.W.2d 692 (Tex. Civ. App.—San Antonio, 1985).

This statute has unusually broad application in a city like Houston, which has a five-mile extraterritorial jurisdiction (ETJ). When the city annexes additional property, it automatically increases its ETJ another five miles beyond the limits of the new annexed area. The Houston city limits are peculiar in that the city has adopted what is called **spoke annexation**. Houston has annexed a lot of property in satellite communities around it by doing this and has effectively increased its ETJ to include all of Harris County, plus a portion of each surrounding county. A city may not annex noncontiguous land, however. *City of Willow Park* v. *Bryant*, 763 S.W.2d 506 (Tex. App.—Ft. Worth, 1988).

There has been considerable litigation concerning Houston's power to annex and service these outlying areas. Similar statutes, however, have been held to be constitutional by the U.S. Supreme Court. The Court basically held that the city's right was not a voting rights question, but rather a legitimate interest in seeing that the segment of the population around the perimeters of cities does not go without such municipal services as police, fire, and health protection. *Holt Civic Club* v. *Tuscaloosa*, 439 U.S. 60 (U.S. Sup. Ct., 1978).

In Texas, the citizens of an annexed area have the right to petition for disannexation if the proper level of services is not provided by the city, *V.T.C.A., Local Government Code, §43.141.* The theory behind the annexation ordinance is a very solid one, however. One finds that in the Houston area, as the city continues to expand beyond its perimeters, it cannot be surrounded by other incorporated suburban communities. It has been the opinion of some land planners that this encirclement by suburban communities (of most cities) has been one of the major contributions to the decay of the inner city and "white flight" because the city's inhabitants can flee to the suburbs. In Houston, however, the inhabitants cannot escape to an outlying subdivision to escape the city's problems, tax base, or other municipal difficulties. Today, Houston is one of the few cities in the United States that has seen a revival of its downtown area, without special incentives from the city, so the ETJ and annexation ordinance may be significant factors in this development.

Any area owned by a municipality that is not contiguous to other territories owned by the municipality does not expand extraterritorial jurisdiction of the municipality (i.e., Waco can't buy a 40-acre tract of land two miles outside the city limits to expand the extraterritorial jurisdiction of Waco utilizing both tracts). Any land acquired with anticipated annexation must be contiguous to the existing city boundaries.

After annexation, a municipality may not prohibit a person from continuing to use the land in the manner in which the land was used prior to annexation, except for certain prohibited uses (sexually oriented businesses, public nuisances, flood control areas, storage and use of hazardous substances, fireworks, and firearms).

Probably the biggest restriction is that municipalities must give notice to all areas that they anticipate annexing a minimum of three years prior to the actual annexation. Before the 90th day after the date the municipality adopts or amends an annexation plan, the municipality must give notice to each property owner in the affected area and each public entity that provides services in areas proposed for annexation.

Under the old statute there was a theory of "spoke annexation" where the city could buy a one-foot strip of land 10 miles long, buy an adjacent land at the end of that strip, and dramatically increase its extraterritorial jurisdiction. The new statute eliminates that. A municipality may not annex an area that is located in the ETJ of the municipality that is less than one thousand feet in width at its narrowest point. This eliminates the "spoke annexation" concept.

In addition, there are requirements for municipal services that have to be provided to the area to be annexed. And the municipality must conduct two public hearings before it institutes the annexation proceedings.

## Indirect Municipal Land-Use Controls

Cities carry significant impact in being able to regulate land-use control through indirect sources, that is, sources that do not directly affect the use of property. One of these methods is the **building code**. This code regulates the minimum standards of construction for building within the city. The municipality has additional power through the control of **utility extensions** and capacities for those utilities as they are extended. For instance, if the city constructs a utility system in a particular subdivision that has just enough capacity for single-family homes, this literally denies the use for any multifamily homes or higher-density use for that property.

**Maintenance and construction of city streets** also have a particular impact on where and in what direction the city will expand and how fast. **Subdivisions' regulations** are controlled through the city planning department, through which all land plans and subdivision plats must be submitted for approval, so that the city can check the proposed development versus the capacity of existing utilities and traffic-control problems. New legislation for unzoned areas requires development plats to be filed before any new development can begin, *V.T.C.A., Local Government Code, §212.006, et seq.* Thus, major city concerns can be monitored to be sure that the new development would not be one that creates a difficulty for the city's existing facilities. The city is additionally given certain powers under the new federal statutes to enforce provisions of federal legislation such as the Clean Air Act and the Clean Water Act.

# Deed Restrictions

Most methods of land-use control are governmentally inspired and enforced. **Deed restrictions**, however, are the primary method of private land-use control and consist of an agreement between parties to limit the use and operation of one or more parcels of real estate. Originally, we had a situation in which one party was selling a portion of his real estate to another party. In an effort to protect himself from adverse use of this property, the grantor would restrict the grantee's use of the property in the deed that conveyed title to the grantee. These deed restrictions were then enforced as a private contractual agreement between the grantor and the grantee, and it ran to their heirs and assigns. In addition, anyone else who received a benefit from these restrictions could enforce them. *Giles* v. *Cardenas*, 697 S.W.2d 422 (Tex. Civ. App.—San Antonio, 1985).

## Creation

Over a period of time, the benefits of deed restrictions became obvious, and subdivision developers realized that they could control the quality of their developments to a great degree by establishing deed restrictions on entire subdivisions. In these cases, the developer (who was the original grantor of the lots) imposed deed restrictions on every single lot that, in most cases, were consistent throughout the subdivision. Therefore, either by incorporation by the grantor and his deed or by recording the restrictions applicable to an entire subdivision, a grantor can create deed restrictions on all of the property subsequently conveyed. Those restrictions are binding to all future purchasers and creditors as **covenants** running with the land. *Smith* v. *Bowers*, 463 S.W.2d 222 (Tex. Civ. App.—Waco, 1970); *Selected Lands Corp.* v. *Speich*, 702 S.W.2d 197 (Tex. Civ. App.—Houston, 1985); *Hicks* v. *Loveless*, 714 S.W.2d 30 (Tex. Civ. App.—Dallas, 1986).

## Control

Deed restrictions are particularly valuable in that they are construed as an agreement between parties rather than a governmental land-use control. There can be a lot more controls in deed restrictions since they can include more than just the health, safety, and welfare of the community. Common provisions in many deed restrictions include the quality requirements of roof shingles, minimum square footages, and building materials that must be used in the construction of a house. In contrasting these requirements with those of zoning or of building permits, it is apparent that deed restrictions go far beyond the health, safety, and welfare of the community. In fact, the only prohibitions of deed restrictions are those in violation of the rights under the U.S. Constitution (e.g., racial discrimination), *Shelley* v. *Kraemer*, 334 U.S. 1 (1948), and Texas statute. Those particular Texas statutes applicable are *V.T.C.A., Property Code, §5.026*, which invalidates deed restrictions based on race, color, religion, or national origin, and *V.T.C.A., Property Code, §5.025*, which makes deed restrictions requiring wood shingles invalid, although this is not interpreted to allow any kind of roof. *Hoye* v. *Shepherd's Glen Land Company*, 753 S.W.2d 226 (Tex. App.—Dallas, 1988). Similar restrictions on enforcement were passed in the 2003 legislature, prohibiting the enforcement of provisions prohibiting a property owner from composting vegetation, installing rain barrels or other similar types of conservation efforts. See §202.007. Since deed restrictions are private restrictions that are enforced by contract between the parties, it is important to note that only a party who gets a benefit from these deed restrictions (i.e., the other property owners in the subdivision) can maintain a cause of action to try to enjoin any violation of those restrictions, or attempt to enforce those restrictions, *Scott* v. *Rheudasil*, 614 S.W.2d 626 (Tex. Civ. App.—Ft. Worth, 1981); *Giles* v. *Cardenas*, supra, which includes the delegation of authority to an architectural control committee. *Whiteco Metrocom, Inc.* v. *Industrial Corp.*, 711 S.W.2d 81 (Tex. Civ. App.—Dallas, 1986).

## Enforcement, Generally

In **enforcing deed restrictions**, the rule of construction of contracts generally applies. When there is an ambiguity, the restrictive covenants will be construed in favor of the less restrictive use of the property and against the restriction. *Southhampton Civic Club* v. *Couch*, 322 S.W.2d 516 (Tex. 1958). However, this rule applies only if the intent of the parties cannot be ascertained from the terms of the restrictions and does not mean that the restrictions will not be strictly enforced. *Stephenson* v. *Perlitz*, 532 S.W.2d 954 (Tex. App.—Beaumont, 1976); *Davis* v. *Huey*, 620 S.W.2d 561 (Tex. 1981); *Shaver* v. *Hunter*, 626 S.W.2d 574 (Tex. Civ. App.—Amarillo, 1981). There is at least some authority that the covenants can run perpetually, *Moore* v. *Smith*, 443 S.W.2d 552 (Tex. 1969), but they are usually restricted by their own terms for a number of years. Changes to deed restrictions are also controlled by the restrictions' own terms; however, in the absence of specific procedure for change, it normally takes a vote of 100% of the people affected by those deed restrictions, *Norwood* v. *Davis*, 345 S.W.2d 944 (Tex. Civ. App.—Austin, 1961) to make a change.

Deed restrictions for subdivisions located in highly populated cities or counties can be changed, modified, or amended by a petition of the residents of that subdivision signed by 75% of the owners of the subdivision. See Property Code, §204.005; 201.006.

## Enforcement, Use

A number of issues have recently arisen concerning how to interpret deed restrictions properly as they pertain to specified uses. As one may imagine, deed restrictions that were written in the 1920s or 1930s did not anticipate the ultimate use of property in the 2000s. The traditional line of cases has always indicated that the property, where there were restrictive covenants, is to be construed in favor of the less restrictive use of the property. Recent statutory changes, however, indicate some conflict in that the law now provides that a restrictive covenant is to be liberally construed to give effect to its purposes and intent, *V.T.C.A., Property Code, §202.003(a)*. Specific issues concerning deed restrictions are litigated fairly frequently. Many cases are concerned with what constitutes a residential use and single family. One of the more complicating factors is whether or not "single family" indicates that all people must be of a single family or if it merely references the type of structure to be used on the property. In keeping with more liberal national trends, Texas courts have attempted to construe the definition of "family" liberally and "use" to a broader definition. For instance, the term "family home" is now defined by Texas statute as including a family home under the Community Home for Disabled Persons Location Act, *Vern. Tex. Civ. Stat., Art. 1011n*. Another recent case has also held that a "single-family-dwelling" restriction constitutes a type restriction, not a use restriction, and it did not prevent the use of a single-family dwelling as a family home for six mentally disabled persons. *Permian Basin Centers for Mental Health and Mental Retardation* v. *Alsobrook*, 723 S.W.2d 774 (Tex. Civ. App.—El Paso, 1986). Similar holdings have included a house used as a dwelling for four unrelated adult males and two house parents and housing used for temporary day-care centers. *Collins* v. *City of El Campo*, 684 S.W.2d 756 (Tex. Civ. App.—Corpus Christi, 1984) and *Mills* v. *Kubena*, 685 S.W.2d 395 (Tex. Civ. App.—Houston, 1985).

Business use has also seen common conflicts. The general rule seems to continue to restrict business activity unless that business activity is such that it is merely incidental to the residence, and there is no evidence of business activity outside the premises. *Whorton* v. *Point Lookout West, Inc.*, 736 S.W.2d 201 (Tex. Civ. App.—Beaumont, 1987). Similar restrictions have also been upheld excluding double-wide manufactured and mobile homes in a single-family subdivision. *Wilmoth* v. *Wilcox*, 734 S.W.2d 656 (Tex. 1987). Restrictions for single-family dwellings, however, do not prohibit the erection of a satellite dish, as this use is not contrary to single-family purposes, although the approval of the architectural control committee may be required before it can be constructed. *DeNina* v. *Bammel Forest Civic Club*, 712 S.W.2d 195 (Tex. Civ. App.—Houston, 1986).

## Enforcement, Remedies

You may recall that Chapter 2 discusses breach of conditions in deeds, which results in loss of title. Deed restrictions differ, however, in that they are purely contractual obligations and *not* conditions of transfer of title. Therefore, when a deed restriction is breached, the complaining parties are generally entitled to two remedies: (1) injunctive relief to stop the violator of the restrictive covenant from continuing the violation, or (2) damages to compensate those hurt as a result of the violation. These remedies typically develop out of a sense of fairness and justice to preserve the integrity and value of the property. Injunctive relief is simply to maintain the status quo until the applicability of the restrictive covenant is finally determined. *Guajardo* v. *Neece*, 758 S.W.2d 696 (Tex. App.—Ft. Worth, 1988). Bizarre and unrealistic remedies are generally not upheld, such as the removal of a home because of a small encroachment or other similar, minimal violations of those covenants. *Tanglewood Homeowners' Association, Inc.* v. *Hanke*, 728 S.W.2d 39 (Tex. Civ. App.—Houston, 1987). There has been a lot of case law discussing whether or not homeowners can waive enforcement of deed restrictions by not diligently enforcing them in a timely manner. It has been generally held that the enforcement of the deed restrictions may be refused on either of two theories. The first is a general change in the restricted area and surrounding area. The second is a waiver of the right to enforce by landowners who have violated or permitted violations of the restrictions. Both theories are jury issues and must be submitted to the jury as supported by the evidence in the case. *Traeger* v. *Lorenz*, 749

S.W.2d 249 (Tex. App.—San Antonio, 1988). The jury can then determine whether or not there has been a general change in the restricted area. The waiver issue, however, is a little more complicated. To establish a waiver of the deed restrictions, the non-conforming user must prove that the violations then existing are so great as to lead the mind of the "average man" to reasonably conclude that the restriction in question has been abandoned and this enforcement waived. There are a number of factors to be considered in determining the nature of that waiver, including the number of violations, the severity of the violation, prior acts of enforcement of the restriction, and whether it is still possible to realize a substantial benefit intended through the covenant that is attempting to be enforced. *Finklestein* v. *Southhampton Civic Club*, 675 S.W.2d 271 (Tex. App.—Houston [1st Dist.], 1984, writ ref'd n.r.e.).

There has been concern over enforcing these deed restrictions because of the expense of litigation involved in enforcement. Some relief to this has been given under *V.T.C.A., Property Code, §5.006*, which allows for attorney's fees to the prevailing party who asserted an action for a breach of restrictive covenant. *Inwood North Homeowners' Association, Inc.* v. *Meier*, 625 S.W.2d 742 (Tex. Civ. App.—Houston, 1981). The court may also assess a civil fine in an amount not to exceed $200 per day, *V.T.C.A., Property Code, §202.004(c)*.

## HOA Foreclosures

The Texas Legislature also enacted the Texas Residential Property Owners Protection Act in 2001 (the Blevins Bill), which applies to all residential subdivisions requiring membership in a property owners' association that may impose mandatory assessments. The Bill is lengthy and has built in a number of consumer protections for homeowners. The major provisions are as follows: (1) the property owners' association must record a management certificate providing subdivision recording data and the name and mailing address of the property owners' association. The property owners' officers, directors, employees, and agents are personally liable or willfully or grossly negligent in any delay of recording or failure to record a management certificate (see *Section 209.004*); (2) the property owners' association must make all of the books and records of the association available, including financial records, to an owner in accordance with the Texas Nonprofit Corporation Act (attorneys' files and records are excluded from that disclosure); (3) before a property owners' association can suspend an owner's right to use a common area, file a suit against the owner other than a suit to collect a regular or special assessment or foreclose under an association's lien, charge an owner for property damage, or levy a fine for violation of the restrictions or bylaws by rules of the association, the association or its agent must give written notice to the owner by certified mail, return receipt requested. The notice must describe the violation and then inform the owner that the owner is entitled to a reasonable period to cure the violation and that the owner may request a hearing within 30 days after the owner receives the notice. The statute even sets out procedures for hearings before the board, but also enables the association to collect reasonable attorneys' fees provided the proper notice has been given to the owner.

The property owners' association is authorized to conduct nonjudicial foreclosures, just as in the past. However, the attorney's fees are limited to the greater of one-third of actual costs and assessments or $2,500. The property owners' association may not foreclose on an assessment lien consisting solely of fines or attorney's fees associated with those fines. After the foreclosure sale, the property owners' association must send the owner a written notice stating the date and time the sale occurred and informing the property owner of the owner's right to redeem their property within 30 days. Those must be sent by certified mail, return receipt requested to the property owner's last known address. After the foreclosure, the property owner has the right to redeem the property after paying to the association: (a) all of the amounts due to the association at the time of the foreclosure sale; (b) interest from the date of the fore-closure sale to the date of redemption and all amounts owed to the association at an annual interest rate of 10 percent; (c) costs incurred by the association in foreclosing the lien, including reasonable attorney's fees for an assessment levied against the property by the association after the date of the foreclosure sale; (d) any reasonable costs incurred by the association, including mortgage payments and the cost of repair, maintenance, and leasing of the property; and (e) the purchase price paid by the asso-ciation's foreclosure sale less any amounts due the association that were satisfied out of the foreclosure sale proceeds. The right to redeem must be exercised within 180 days after the association mails the written notice of the sale to the owner.

## No Liability?

A new section (Article 2.22) was added to the Texas Nonprofit Corporation Act. (Nonprofit corporations may include homeowners' associations.) It provides that an officer, director, or any other person is not liable to the corporation for an action or omission made by the officer in the person's capacity as an officer, unless the offi-cer's conduct was not exercised: (1) in good faith, (2) in ordinary care, and (3) in a manner the officer reasonably believes to be in the best interest of the corporation.

## Governmental Enforcement of Deed Restrictions

Another method of municipal land-use control has surfaced in Texas, primarily due to Houston's lack of zoning and its abundance of subdivision deed restrictions, and that is municipal enforcement of deed restrictions. The Texas legislature has passed two enabling statutes to effect this method of land-use control, *V.T.C.A., Local Government Code, §230.001, et seq.* Under these statutes, the city is authorized to pass an ordinance that requires uniform application of the statutes to all property and citizens. These statutes also give the incorporated city the power to sue in any court of competent jurisdiction to enjoin or abate a violation of a deed restriction contained in a duly recorded plan, plat, replat, or other instrument affecting the subdivision inside its boundaries. Article 974a-2 specifically prohibits the issuance of commercial building permits if there is a violation of existing subdivision deed restrictions. This particular statute provides that the city may join with an interested property owner in a suit to enjoin further construction activity by someone who does not have a permit in compliance with the act. Thus, both of these statutes pro-vide a possible alternative to zoning in cities that rely primarily on deed restrictions as a means of land-use control. Although there has been a question as to the consti-tutionality of this statute, one court has held that it is constitutional. *Young v. City of Houston,* 756 S.W.2d 813 (Tex. App.—Houston [1st Dist.], 1988, writ den.).

In a recent case, *Truong v. City of Houston,* 99 S.W.3d 204 (Tex. App.—Houston [14th Dist.] 2002), the Court relied on a 2001 amendment to the Civil Practices and Remedies Code and the Local Government Code (§212.133) which added the enforcement of land-use restrictions under the list of activities defined as governmental functions. The Court went on to note that enforcement zoning ordinances is "akin" to enforcement of deed-restriction ordinances and that both accomplish the same objectives, noting further that zoning ordinances and land-use ordinances are valid exercises of the city's police power to safeguard the health, comfort, and general welfare of the citizens. When does a deed restriction become zoning? Deed-restrictions are usually created privately by land developers (in most cases to protect land values), not to guard the health, comfort and general welfare of the homeowners.

In the event there is a violation of deed restrictions in a county with a population of more than two million, the county attorney may sue in the court of competent jurisdiction to enjoin or abate the violations of the restriction. In the event a successful cause of action is maintained, the county can be awarded court costs and attorney's fees. This new statutory remedy is apparently in addition to the new $200 per day civil penalty, *V.T.C.A., §203.003, §202.004(c)*.

## ■ SUMMARY

It is by use of police power that the government regulates and enforces laws and regulations that pertain to land-use control. This involves no "taking" of the property, as in eminent domain, and therefore no requirement for just compensation to the landowner. Land-use controls are normally broken down into federal land-use controls, state land-use controls, county land-use controls, and municipal and local land-use controls.

Federal land-use regulations involve the Securities and Exchange Commission, Department of Housing and Urban Development, Federal Trade Commission, and Environmental Protection Agency. State land-use controls involve various state agencies in their control over parts of the real estate business. County regulations are minimal except for their road maintenance and construction authority. Municipal land-use control consists basically of zoning, building permit procedures, road construction, repair and maintenance, extraterritorial jurisdiction, and attempts at enforcing private deed restrictions. Deed restrictions are purely a private method of land-use control and are important in cities where there is no zoning.

## CHAPTER 21

# Real Estate Taxation

No one pretends that taxation of real estate is an easy subject. The tax laws affecting real estate are so complex that only a very basic approach to taxation will be made in this text. Hopefully, this chapter will provide the foundation for further research and inquiries for assistance from trained professionals, since tax advice often constitutes legal advice and is not within the scope of most licensees' employment. Advice from a competent tax lawyer and certified public accountant is indispensable to any licensee who plans a career in investment and income-producing property.

For the purposes of this chapter, the only areas of taxation considered are ad valorem taxation and certain provisions of federal income taxation that have unique application to real estate.

## Ad Valorem Taxes

In these times of general taxpayer dissatisfaction with the government, the most fundamental concepts of ad valorem taxation are often questioned. However, it is a system that will not easily be changed since there are numerous statutes and constitutional provisions dealing with ad valorem taxation, which have etched this concept in Texas law over many years.

### Constitutional Provisions

**Ad valorem** is a Latin phrase that translates literally to "according to value." Accordingly, ad valorem taxes are taxes that are assessed on real property, the tax being based on the property's fair market value. The Texas Constitution specifically provides for ad valorem taxation under Article VIII, Section 1, which states:

> all property in this state, . . . shall be taxed in proportion to its value, which shall be ascertained as may be provided by law.

It also provides that the taxes shall be "equal and uniform," *Art. VIII, §2.* The constitution further provides that each county is to elect an assessor and collector of taxes (or sheriff, depending on the size of the county) to perform all the duties necessary for the collection of taxes and equalization of taxes. The annual tax assessment is considered a prior lien, which arises automatically at the first of every year. The constitution also provides for seizure of the property for delinquent taxes, *Art. VIII, §13*, which will be discussed in greater detail later in this chapter.

On the lighter side, there is a constitutional limit to taxation in that the fair market value of the property may not be exceeded by the assessment. The constitution also provides for certain exemptions. These exemptions are primarily for land put to agricultural use, *Art. VIII, §1-d*, property owned by governmental entities for public purposes, and other property devoted exclusively to the use and benefit of the public, *Art. XI, §9*. The constitution also enables the legislature to exempt from taxation a large number of other properties, consisting primarily of those used for religious, charitable, and school purposes. Oddly enough, in light of all of the constitutional and statutory provisions, the state of Texas has abolished ad valorem taxes for state purposes, *Art. VIII, §1-e*.

## Statutory Provisions

The constitutional provisions have several enabling statutes authorizing the legislature to pass further tax laws. Specifically, procedures for assessment, foreclosure, determination of fair market value, tax equalization, and procedures for collecting delinquent accounts are left to the legislature's ability to balance government needs against the taxpayers' ability to pay. There were major changes in Texas's tax statutes made in 1979 when the legislature adopted the **Tax Code**. It effected some major changes in our taxing procedures and also helped clarify some of the conflicts we had in the law prior to the code being passed. For reference purposes, all citations used in this portion of the text will be referenced as sections to the Property Tax Code.

Before any of these statutory provisions are discussed in detail, we should understand the basic formula for calculating the tax an individual pays on the real estate. Simply stated, the formula is as follows:

Assessed Value × Tax Rate = Tax Payment

To understand the full meaning of the formula, one must first investigate the significance of each of its parts, as specifically determined by the statutes.

**Assessed Value.** As shown in the formula, one's taxes are a multiple of the **assessed value**. At one time most districts used assessing ratios and assessed the property at a percentage of fair market value. The use of assessing ratios has been specifically prohibited in the new Property Tax Code, *§26.02*, and all property must be assessed on the basis of 100% of its appraised value. There has always been a concern over the "equal" values as appraised in any tax district. Appraised values are now standardized under the Property Tax Code through the establishment of a State Property Tax Board and countywide appraisal districts.

*State Property Tax Board* The Property Tax Code provides that there will be a **State Property Tax Board** consisting of six members appointed by the governor, *§5.01*. This board shall adopt rules establishing minimum standards for the administration and operation of an appraisal district. The board shall also be responsible to conduct, sponsor, or approve courses of instruction for intern training programs on the aspects of property taxation, and to prepare and issue general appraisal manuals and pamphlets explaining the remedies available to dissatisfied taxpayers. The State Property Tax Board will also provide a minimum standard and guidelines for appraisals throughout the state as well as administration of the tax districts to ensure fair and equal tax procedures throughout the state.

*Appraisal districts* In a further attempt to provide for equalization, the Property Tax Code establishes **appraisal districts** in each county, *§6.02*. Each appraisal district's boundaries are the same as the county's boundaries, and each appraisal district is to be governed by a board containing a minimum of five directors serving two-year terms. The appraisal district is responsible for appraising property in the district for ad valorem tax purposes of the state and of each taxing unit that imposes ad valorem taxes on the property in the district. This requires all school districts, levee districts, water districts, and other taxing authorities to use the same appraised value on the property.

There are certain exceptions to the appraised values of property under the new statutes that specifically provide that land designated for agricultural use and timberland are to be appraised on a different basis other than fair market value. The appraised value of open-space agricultural land is determined on the basis of an accepted income capitalization method applied to the average net income of the land. The appraised value cannot exceed the market value as determined by other appraisal methods. The same basis theory is used for qualified timberland.

*Tax review* By April 15 or as soon thereafter as practicable, but in no event later than the 20th day before the date the **Appraisal Review Board** begins considering tax protests, the **chief appraiser** (the administrator of each district's appraisal office) shall deliver a written notice to the property owner indicating the appraised value of his property if the value is to be any greater than the previous year.

In the event a taxpayer chooses to protest or have his tax appraisal reviewed, he needs to appeal first to the Appraisal Review Board of the appraisal district as established by the Property Tax Code. Beyond this appeal, his case can be reviewed by the local district court. The taxpayer should realize, however, that any decisions made by any of the administrative or judicial bodies can also be appealed to the district court by the chief appraiser or the taxing authority. Believe it or not! There are two sides to this issue!

**Tax Rate.** The **tax rate** is set by the taxing authority in accordance with the following formula set out in Section 26.04 of the Texas Property Tax Code. It is a rather lengthy process and need not be discussed in detail here. Basically, the tax rate only operates as a function of what the taxing authority needs for operations in the current year.

For instance, the county has determined that, after all income is received, it will need $10 million more to provide an adequate budget to meet its needs. The Appraisal District has determined that the assessed valuation of the property in the county is worth $400 million. To determine the tax rate, the calculation would be as follows:

$$\$10,000,000 \div \frac{400,000,000}{100} = \text{Tax Rate}$$

$$\frac{10,000,000}{4,000,000} = \$\ 2.50$$

Therefore, the tax rate to be paid would be $2.50 per $100 of assessed valuation. All taxpayers would pay the same *rate* of taxation, but their total taxes would depend completely on the valuation of their properties.

The governing body may not adopt a tax rate that, if applied to the total taxable value, would impose an amount of taxes that exceeds last year's levy until it has had a public hearing on the proposed tax rate, *V.T.C.S., Tax Code, §26.05(d)*.

If any taxing unit adopts a tax rate that unlawfully exceeds the rollback tax rate (as defined under §26.04), the qualified voters of that taxing unit by petition may require that an election be held to determine whether or not to reduce the tax, *§26.07*.

**Tax Payment.** Once it has been finally determined that tax is due and payable by the taxing authority and all appeals have been exhausted, there is no provision for any reduction of taxes. However, the statutes provide that the taxing authority may allow a specified discount for early payment. State of Texas and county taxes are due upon receipt of the tax bill and are delinquent after the following January 31 of each year. A delinquent tax incurs a penalty of 6% of the amount of the tax for the first calendar month it is delinquent plus 1% for each additional month or portion of a month the tax remains unpaid prior to July 1 of the year in which it becomes delinquent. A tax delinquent on July 1 incurs a total penalty of 12% of the amount of the delinquent tax without regard for the number of months the tax has been delinquent. This results in a total penalty of 18%, plus interest, for only five months' delinquency!

State and county taxes may be paid in semiannual installments, §31.03. If a person pays one-half of the taxes imposed on or before December 1 for the year in which the assessment was made, he shall have until June 30 of the following year to pay the other one-half of the taxes without penalty or interest. Past-due taxes paid in this manner incur a penalty of 8% of the amount of the unpaid taxes. If the taxes are payable on the homestead of a taxpayer who is at least 65 years of age, the taxes can be paid in quarterly installments, §31.031. We now even allow taxes to be paid by credit card, although the taxing authority may require an additional processing fee if a credit card is used, §31.06.

*Delinquency* Interest penalties for delinquent taxes are now considered to be a serious penalty. While summary seizure and sale is provided for in both the constitution and the statutes, it has been effectively eliminated by the enactment of *Tex. Rev. Civ. Stat. Ann., Art. 732a*. This statute provides that all sales of real estate (personalty is not included) made for the collection of delinquent taxes can be made only after judicial foreclosure of the tax lien by a court of competent jurisdiction. The suit for the foreclosure of tax liens must also be in accordance with the existing statutes pertaining to tax suits, which are very specific as to notice, citation, and petition, to allow for adequate notice to and response from the property owner. Once judgment has been obtained, the court orders the sheriff to execute the sale. It is the sheriff who signs the deed effecting conveyance of the property.

**Transfer of the Tax Lien.** The statutes also provide for a transfer of the taxing authority's tax lien to any person or company that pays the taxing authority any taxes due upon real property at the request of the owner of said property. The holder of the transferred lien may foreclose by nonjudicial foreclosure. The owner then has the right to redeem within one year after said foreclosure after paying attorney's fees, amount of judgment at foreclosure, and costs and interest accrued in the judgment, plus interest not greater than 18% per annum, §32.06.

**Section 34.21.** The statute that covers **tax foreclosure** situations most comprehensively is Section 34.21. The procedure for sale is basically the same as provided for in Section 51.002 of the Property Code, which is used in foreclosure of deeds of trust, as discussed in Chapters 11 and 13. The property may not be sold to anyone other than the taxing unit for less than the adjudged value of the property or the aggregate amount of judgments against the property rendered in the tax foreclosure suit. If there is an excess at the sale, the proceeds are to go to the owner after all costs of sale have been paid. However, the burden is on the owner to file a petition and have a hearing to determine whether he is entitled to these funds. If there is no claim for the excess funds within four years, they are transferred to the state's general revenue.

The statute provides for a period of redemption in all suits brought under the authority of Section 34.21. Under the statute, the owner of a real property sold at a tax sale that was the residence homestead of the owner, or that was land designated for agricultural use when the suit to collect for tax was filed, may redeem the property within two years after the date on which the purchaser's deed is filed for record by paying to the purchaser the amount the purchaser bid for the property, the amount of the deed recording fee, and the amount paid by the purchaser as taxes, penalties, interest, and costs on the property, plus 25% of the aggregate total if the property is redeemed during the first year of the redemption period, or 50% of the aggregate total if the property is redeemed during the second year of the redemption period.

If the property is not the residence homestead, or designated for agricultural use, the owner may redeem the property within six months after the date on which the purchaser's deed is filed for record by paying the purchaser the amount the purchaser bid for the property, the amount of the deed recording fee, and the amount paid by the purchaser as taxes, penalties, interest, and costs on the property, plus 25% of the aggregate total.

The **tax deed** used to convey property at the sale vests good and perfect title in the purchaser to the interest owned by the defendant in the property, subject to the foreclosure, including the defendant's right to the use and possession of the property, subject only to the defendant's right of redemption. The deed may be impeached only for fraud, *§34.01(d)*.

## Tax Exemptions and Deferrals

The Property Tax Code specifies some **tax exemptions** and deferrals of ad valorem tax payments in certain areas in order to grant tax relief for those people specified by the statutes. Most of these exemptions are fairly complicated and some of them must be applied for. Any exemption should be investigated thoroughly before reliance on it.

**Homestead Old Age and Disability Tax Deferral** As a special note, it is comforting to know that Snidely Whiplash (that despicable character!) does not exist in Texas. The **homestead old age tax deferral** exempts from forced sale for taxes property that is: (1) a residence homestead and (2) occupied by a person 65 years or older claiming the homestead exemption. All that is required of the claimant is to file an affidavit containing the following information:

1. The birth date of the affiant.

2. Legal description of the homestead.

3. Signature of the affiant, along with an acknowledgment or proof of record, *§33.06*.

This exemption also extends to surviving spouses aged 55 or older that remain in their homestead, *§11.13*.

The effect of the statute is only to delay the proceeding. The taxes and interest (calculated at 8% per annum) continue to exist as a prior lien against the property, and the taxing unit can foreclose when the homestead is no longer held by the claimant. However, this exemption can provide a refuge from the increasing taxes that can be so burdensome on the elderly. Too often elderly people on fixed incomes cannot cope with the constantly increasing ad valorem taxes. This statute gives considerable relief from the problem, *§33.06*. In 2003, this same deferral was extended to disabled individuals, see *§11.26*.

**Appraisal Exemptions.** A single adult or family is entitled to an exemption from taxation for state purposes and for county purposes of $3,000 of the assessed value of the resident's homestead. An adult is also entitled to exemption from taxation by a school district of $15,000 of the appraised value of his residence homestead. If the adult is disabled or is 65 years or older, he is entitled to exemption from taxation of $10,000 of the appraised value of his residence homestead. *§11.13(a)(b)*. If you follow the calculation of tax payment as discussed previously in this chapter, you will note that a mere lowering of the appraised value is not necessarily a significant tax decrease, although it is some help.

Another rather unique exemption is one that prohibits the increase of ad valorem taxes imposed on a person's homestead for elementary and secondary public school purposes if the homestead is a residence of a person who is 65 years of age or older. This exemption also extends to the surviving spouse, providing that surviving spouse is 55 years of age at the time of the person's death. *§11.26(i)*.

Another exemption from appraised value is for disabled veterans. The technicalities of the exemption for disabled veterans are rather great and provide for varying types of disability, age, and additional provisions for the veteran's surviving spouse in the event of the veteran's death.

One of the more significant exemptions is the exemption for **religious use**, **agricultural use** and **timberland use**. To be available for the agricultural exemptions, the land must be devoted principally to agricultural or timber use to the degree of intensity generally accepted in the area for at least five of the seven preceding years. Its use cannot be merely recreational. *Tarrant Appraisal District* v. *Moore*, 845 S.W.2d 820 (Tex. 1993). The exemptions are not available to nonresident aliens. In evaluating the property, the appraiser must use accepted income capitalization methods applied to the average net income from the land, rather than true fair market value. There is a similar exemption for land owned by nonprofit homeowners' organizations for the benefit of their members. That land is taxed at a nominal value.

The difference in the religious, agricultural and timberland exemptions, however, is the **tax rollback** provisions. If the land changes use, such that it can no longer qualify for agricultural exemptions, the taxing authority has the right to collect up to five years' preceding taxes as if the land was not exempt, *Tex. Const., Art. 8 §1-d* and *1-d-1*. That is, the fair market evaluation of the property "rolls back" to the five previous years. Since delinquent taxes run to the owner of the real estate, the new owner of the parcel of real estate may be surprised to find he has to pay five years of back taxes (plus accrued interest) if he was not aware of the previous owner's agricultural or timberland use exemptions, *V.T.C.A., Tax Code, §23.76(a), 23.55(a), 11.201*. If the use changes, the owner has to notify the appraisal office of the change. If he does not notify the appraisal office of the change and the chief appraiser "discovers" that the eligibility is terminated, he can back-assess the property for 10 years with penalty and interest. This can have a significant impact on an unwary purchaser. Real estate brokers should be acutely aware of these provisions.

**Exempt Property.** There are certain properties that are totally exempt from ad valorem taxation because of the public policy and functions that the owners of these properties may serve as a benefit to the public generally. These include exemptions for all land owned by the state or political subdivisions of the state, all land owned by the Permanent University Fund and Texas Community Housing Development Organization, all agricultural grazing land owned by the county for the benefit of public schools, and all lands exempted by federal law. Also exempt are cemeteries; property owned by charitable organizations; property owned by youth spiritual, mental, and physical development associations, religious organizations, and schools; and historic sites. There are certain other miscellaneous exemptions for veterans' organizations, community service clubs, biomedical research corporations, and other similar qualifying organizations.

# Federal Income Taxation

In 1986, Congress passed a tax law known as the **Internal Revenue Code of 1986**, or, alternatively, as the **Tax Reform Act of 1986**. It was a sweeping change of income taxation, attempting to eliminate some inequities in the existing tax structure and to encourage simplification. The new statute did simplify income taxation to some extent, but the transition rules (because of the existing tax laws prior to 1987) created a difficult evolution into the new finalization of this tax simplification. For our purposes, this necessitates the discussion of the previous tax law, with emphasis on the 1987 changes. The new definition of "income" will be discussed first, then the special tax treatments for real estate will be discussed.

## Income

Prior to 1987, all income was categorized as "income" and there were Income certain tax-sheltered advantages to ownership of real estate. These "tax shelters" allowed real estate investors to offset their income by taking deductions for certain noncash "losses" attributable to real estate. This gave many people the perception that tax laws favored the wealthy (who are often perceived as the primary investors in real estate) and resulted in Congress's 1986 attempt to limit these "abuses." Unfortunately, the new tax laws applied to small investors as well, and the long-term impact of these changes is yet to be determined.

The 1986 tax law separates income into three categories: (1) active income, (2) passive income, and (3) portfolio income. **Active income** follows our traditional theories of income from a primary source of employment. This includes salaries and income or loss from the conduct of a trade or business in which the taxpayer materially participates. A taxpayer is deemed to be materially participating only if the taxpayer is involved in the operations of the activity on a regular, continuous, and substantial basis. It is necessary to look at the particular business activity and determine which functions are typically concerned with operations. If it is determined that the taxpayer is materially participating in those functions, the income derived would be deemed active income.

**Passive activity** is defined as any activity that involves the conduct of any trade or business in which the taxpayer does not materially participate. One of the most important defined "passive" activities is rental activity for income-producing property. Rental activity is generally deemed to be passive without regard to the level of participation by the taxpayer. There are two exceptions, however. The first is for an individual taxpayer who actively participates in real estate rental activities. In this case, passive losses can be offset against active income, so long as the passive activity loss and the deduction equivalent of that passive activity loss do not exceed $25,000 per year. The $25,000 offset is not available to corporations, estates, or trusts regardless of their level of participation. In no event, however, is a taxpayer deemed to be actively participating in real estate rental activities when his ownership interest is less than 10% during the applicable year.

The second exception (beginning in 1994) focuses on real estate brokers, salespersons, and other real estate professionals. These eligible taxpayers can deduct unlimited real estate activity losses from active income and portfolio income. Individuals are eligible if: (1) more than half of all personal services they perform during the year are for real property trades or businesses in which they "materially participate," and (2) they perform more than 750 hours of service per year in those real estate activities.

**Portfolio income** is income that is not active income or passive income. Interest, dividends, annuities, or royalties not derived from the ordinary course of business, or a gain or loss from the disposition of property producing interest, and dividends or annuities that are held for investment are some examples of portfolio income. Expenses directly allocable to the property producing this interest, dividends, annuities, or royalties can be applied against the portfolio income.

The most significant change under the Tax Reform Act of 1986 is that the passive and portfolio losses cannot offset active income, which virtually destroys the tax shelter nature of real estate investment. The special tax benefits for real estate, to the extent they still exist, are discussed in the subsequent portions of this chapter. It must be kept in perspective, however, that the effect of the special tax treatment of real estate is somewhat tempered by the limited ability of any taxpayer to offset the losses generated against his active income.

As previously stated, the tax laws provide some areas of special treatment for real estate. Since the subject of federal income taxation involves volumes of treatises at the professional level, only the fundamentals of taxation most significant to real estate will be discussed here. These are:

1. Depreciation.
2. Accelerated Cost Recovery System.
3. Capital gains tax treatment.
4. Tax-deferred exchanges.
5. Installment sales.
6. At-risk rules.
7. Homeownership benefits.

## Depreciation

**Depreciation** is generally defined as an allowance for loss of value. The federal government, through the Internal Revenue Service, recognizes the intrinsic loss of value of improvements (land may not be depreciated) and allows the taxpayer to provide for this loss of value by allowing these decreases in value to be deducted from gross income before the income is taxed. This, in effect, reduces the amount of taxes the taxpayer will pay, even though he has made no actual or "out-of-pocket" expenditures. Depreciation is often used synonymously with the term "tax shelter" because it is a deduction from gross income even though: (1) no payment is made, (2) no actual loss is suffered, and (3) depreciation is allowed in excess of the owner's equity invested. Since land cannot be depreciated, an allocation of the purchase price must be made between the improvements and land purchased. The most common allocation method used is the ratio of fair market value of the component (land or improvements) to the total value.

There are now three systems involved in the computation of depreciation: (1) MACRS, the **Modified Accelerated Cost Recovery System**, for property placed in service after 1986; (2) ACRS, the **Accelerated Cost Recovery System**, for property placed in service after 1980 but before 1987; and (3) the straight-line or declining-balance method based on salvage value and useful life if the property is placed in service before 1981.

There are specific rules for determining which depreciation method a taxpayer can use, and, in the final analysis, neither the IRS nor the courts will allow an individual to claim more depreciation than he is entitled to. Additionally, depreciation is limited to commercial (industrial and office space) and investment (residential rental) property. One's primary residence cannot be depreciated. Each taxpayer should consult his tax counsel and accountant to determine if depreciation is applicable, and, if it is, which of the depreciation methods is more advantageous for his particular needs.

The Internal Revenue Code of 1986, however, made extensive efforts to eliminate investments in tax shelters. Depreciation can no longer be deducted against "active income" if it is a "passive loss" from an activity in which the taxpayer does not materially participate. Virtually all rental activities are treated as passive activities. However, if the taxpayer "actively participates," individuals can offset up to $25,000 of nonpassive income with losses from real estate rental activities. Even this benefit, however, is reduced if the taxpayer's income for any given year exceeds $100,000.

**Straight-Line Method** The **straight-line method of depreciation** is the one type of depreciation that can always be used. The first step in determining the amount of straight-line depreciation is to establish the correct useful life of the asset. In computing the straight-line rate, one takes the basis (cost or value of the improvement) less any salvage value and divides the remainder by the number of years of economic life the taxpayer intends to use for that improvement. For instance, if a dishwasher costs $200, has a five-year life, and has no salvage value, the taxpayer is allowed 20% each year ($40) as a depreciation deduction from gross income. If a two-year life is used for the dishwasher, 50% each year ($100) can be deducted.

**Declining-Balance Method** The **declining-balance method** of depreciation can apply 200% or 150% of the straight-line rate. Assuming a property costs $30,000 and has a five-year life, the straight-line-method depreciation rate would be 20% of the cost value of the asset in the first year, or $6,000. The 200% declining-balance method, therefore, would give the taxpayer the right to deduct double the straight-line rate (40%, or $12,000); the 150% declining balance would be 30%, or $9,000. The **basis** (cost or initial value of the improvement) is reduced by the sum of depreciation claimed in years prior to the current year, so the amount to be depreciated is reduced each year. If we assume the same facts, we would come out with figures as shown in Table 21.1.

After comparing the depreciation methods, the taxpayer may find certain advantages, depending on how his personal tax structure might change over the years. The accelerated depreciation methods clearly allow a much greater amount to be deducted in the earlier years than the straight-line method; however, the straight-line method allows more to be deducted in later years and less in the first years, as shown below:

| **Methods of Depreciation** | | | |
| --- | --- | --- | --- |
| Year | Straight Line | 200% | 150% |
| 1 | $ 6,000 | $12,000 | $ 9,000 |
| 2 | 6,000 | 7,200 | 6,300 |
| 3 | 6,000 | 4,320 | 4,410 |
| 4 | 6,000 | 2,592 | 3,088 |
| 5 | 6,000 | 1,556 | 2,160 |
| Total Depreciation | $30,000 | $27,668 | $24,958 |

| Table 21.1 | The declining-balance method of depreciation. |
|---|---|

| Year | Rate | Basis Prior to Depreciation | Allowable Depreciation |
|---|---|---|---|
| **200% Rate** | | | |
| 1 | 40% | $30,000 | $12,000 |
| 2 | 40% | 18,000 | 7,200 |
| 3 | 40% | 10,800 | 4,320 |
| 4 | 40% | 6,460 | 2,592 |
| 5 | 40% | 3,888 | 1,556 |
| Total Depreciation | | | $27,668 |
| **150% Rate** | | | |
| 1 | 30% | $30,000 | $ 9,000 |
| 2 | 30% | 21,000 | 6,300 |
| 3 | 30% | 14,700 | 4,410 |
| 4 | 30% | 10,290 | 3,088 |
| 5 | 30% | 7,202 | 2,160 |
| Total Depreciation | | | $24,958 |

Although there are several depreciation classes, real estate owners are primarily concerned with the following five main classes of property:

1. 5-year property: Telephone switching equipment.

2. 7-year property: Most personal property normally associated with the building, such as furniture, fixtures and equipment, carpet, exterior lighting, exterior signage, movable wall partitions, truck bay doors, ornamental fixtures, and pictures.

3. 15-year property: Most land improvements, such as pavements, landscape sprinkler systems, fences, and excavations for lagoons.

4. 27.5-year property: Residential real estate.

5. 39-year property: Non-residential real estate.

**Recapture** One negative aspect of an accelerated depreciation method is that it may convert long-term capital gain to ordinary income when the asset is sold for a gain. This procedure is called the **recapture** of the excess depreciation. When depreciation is computed using an accelerated method, the excess amount of that depreciation over a hypothetical straight-line amount must be reported as ordinary income upon disposition of the property. It may come as quite a shock for someone using accelerated depreciation to discover that when he sells the asset, a large amount of his profits may be taxed as ordinary income because it was allocated to excess depreciation. The amount of recapture depends on the type of asset disposed of, either personal or real property, and the amount of gain realized on the disposition. As previously stated, only excess depreciation must be recaptured on the disposition of real property, but all depreciation claimed must be recaptured on the sale of personal property. Recapture on both types of property is limited to the lesser of the recapture amount or the gain.

The rules for depreciating real estate have eliminated the possibility of recapture upon the disposition of most real property placed in service after 1986. Since residential rental and nonresidential real property placed into service after 1986 are limited to straight-line depreciation, regardless of the depreciation system used, recapture is unlikely to occur. Utilizing straight-line depreciation, however, does reduce the owner's basis in the property. Therefore, when the real estate is sold, tax will have to be paid on the difference between the original basis and the depreciated basis, at the capital gains rate.

## Accelerated Cost Recovery System

In 1981, Congress passed the Economic Recovery Tax Act. The act eliminated the use of depreciation for property placed in service after December 31, 1980, by enacting another form of tax recovery for capital costs called the **Accelerated Cost Recovery System (ACRS)**. Low-income housing is permitted to be depreciated under the 200% declining-balance method, while other 15-year real estate may use the 175% declining-balance method with a switch to the straight-line method at the optimum time.

While it eliminates the flexibility that the taxpayer had under the old depreciation system, this system has some benefits for the taxpayer. The ACRS clearly and simply sets out how much can be deducted in each year, and there is very little room for error or negotiation in determining the proper deduction for the taxpayer in any given year. The ACRS eliminates the need for useful life determination on property, as all depreciable real property is written off over the applicable 15-year period.

The only variable for 15-year property is when the property is put into use. The chart below shows how the deductions are calculated under the ACRS.

It is important to note that with the ACRS, there is no salvage value, allowing the taxpayer to write off the entire cost of the investment. In addition, there are no distinctions between new and used property. All real property qualifying as 15-year utility property has the same deductions. Buildings placed into service (basically, property that has begun construction) after March 15, 1984, have an accelerated recovery period of 18 years. If the property was placed in service after May 8, 1985, and before January 1, 1987, the accelerated recovery period is 19 years.

For assets placed in service after 1986, the Tax Reform Act of 1986 provides for a **Modified Accelerated Cost Recovery System** (MACRS) that applies to all tangible property placed in service after December 31, 1986. Whereas the MACRS establishes new depreciation guidelines for certain assets, real estate is limited to two classes:

1. Nonresidential real property. This class includes any real property that is not residential rental property and is depreciated over 31.5 years. If the property is placed in service after May 12, 1993, the minimum write-off period is increased to 39 years.

### 15-Year Utility Property

| Ownership/Year 1–15 | Placed in Service after December 31, 1980 |
|:---:|:---:|
| 1 | 5% |
| 2 | 10% |
| 3 | 9% |
| 4 | 8% |
| 5 | 7% |
| 6 | 7% |
| 7 | 6% |

*Continued*

**15-Year Utility Property**

| Ownership/Year 1–15 | Placed in Service after December 31, 1980 |
| --- | --- |
| 8 | 6% |
| 9 | 6% |
| 10 | 6% |
| 11 | 6% |
| 12 | 6% |
| 13 | 6% |
| 14 | 6% |
| 15 | 6% |
| | 100% |

2.  Residential rental property. This class includes any real property that is a rental building or structure (including mobile homes) for which 80% or more of the gross rental income for the tax year is rental income from dwelling units. If any part of the building or structure is occupied by the taxpayer, the gross rental income includes the fair rental value of the part the taxpayer occupies. This property is depreciated over 27.5 years.

## Capital Gains Tax Treatment

**Capital gains tax treatment** refers to the special tax rate paid on profits from the sale of capital assets. A **capital asset** is generally defined as property that is *not* stock-in-trade (inventory), property used in trade or business of a kind subject to depreciation, and notes and accounts receivable acquired in the course of a trade or business.

There are two types of **capital gains**: long-term and short-term capital gain. Long-term capital gain is gain on the sale of a capital asset held for more than one year. A short-term capital gain is gain on the sale of a capital asset held for less than one year.

The history of capital gains has been dynamic. The Internal Revenue Code of 1986 repealed the capital gains benefit, which had a devastating impact on real estate investment and sales. Capital pains were reenacted in 1990, limiting the maximum tax rate for long-term capital gains to 28%. Under the Taxpayer Relief Act (TRA) of 1997, the maximum capital gain was lowered to 15% (5% for individuals in the 15% tax bracket).

The tax to be paid is applied to the **profit** made, which is calculated as the **sales price** less the **adjusted basis** (discussed next) the taxpayer has in the property. A confusing part of computing capital gains is determining the basis (the original cost or value) of the asset at the time of its acquisition.

Basis is generally considered to be of two types: **original basis**, which is the original cost of the asset, and **adjusted basis**, which is the original basis plus the cost of capital improvements less any allowances for depreciation. Graphically, adjusted basis may be shown as follows:

Original Basis + Capital Improvement − Depreciation= Adjusted Basis

or

OB + CI − D = AB

As an example of how capital gains may be calculated, suppose that Penny Wise acquires a building at a cost of $100,000, which is her *original basis*. After holding the property for one year, she sells it for $200,000. The amount to be taxed would be calculated by deducting the basis ($100,000) from the sales price ($200,000), which determines how much of the income ($100,000, or her profit) is to be taxed at capital gains rates.

If the building has been depreciated, the *adjusted basis* must be used. For example, Ms. Wise purchases the property for $100,000. During the course of her ownership, she adds capital improvements in the amount of $25,000 and depreciates the asset over a 39-year life, yielding a straight-line depreciation allowance of 2.56% of $100,000, or $2,560. Her adjusted basis, therefore, would be her original basis, $100,000, plus capital improvement of $25,000, minus depreciation, which in this case is $2,560. Using the formula $AB = OB + CI - D$, this would give her a taxable income of only $77,560, since the adjusted basis is subtracted from her sales price of $200,000.

## Tax-Deferred Exchanges

Most real estate transactions involve the exchange of real estate for monetary consideration. However, among sophisticated real estate investors, exchanging real property for real property has become popular for two important reasons. First, real estate trades can be accomplished without large amounts of cash by trading property you presently own for one you want. This sidesteps the intermediate step of converting real estate to cash and then converting cash back to real estate. Second, by using an exchange, you can dispose of one property and acquire another without paying income taxes on the profit in the first property at the time of the transaction. As a result, the phrase **tax-deferred exchange** is often used when talking about trading.

To illustrate, suppose that you own an apartment building (the *"exchange property"*) as an investment. The value on your accounting books is $500,000, but its market value today is $750,000. If you sell for cash, you will have to pay income taxes on the difference between the value of the property on your accounting books and the amount you receive for it. If instead of selling for cash, you find another building (the *"replacement property"*) that you want and can arrange a trade, then for income tax purposes the new building acquires the accounting book value of the old and no income taxes are due at the time of the trade. Taxes will be due, however, if and when you finally sell rather than trade. The tax deferred exchange rules apply to investment properties only. Owner-occupied dwellings are treated differently. The Internal Revenue Service permits a homeowner to sell their home and exclude all gains with the specified limits (see Chapter 14).

## Trading Up

Real estate exchanges need not involve properties of equal value. For example, if you own debt-free a small office building worth $100,000, you could trade it for a building worth $500,000 with $400,000 of mortgage debt against it. Alternatively, if the building you wanted was priced at $600,000 with $400,000 in debt against it, you could offer your building plus $100,000 in cash.

The vast majority of tax-deferred exchanges today consist of three transactions: the two conveyances and an escrow agreement with a **qualified intermediary (QI)**. The qualified intermediary can be a title company, an attorney, or in some cases, an independent company providing this service as tax advisors. The QI maintains control over the funds and the closing documents pursuant to the instructions contained in the escrow agreement. This allows the various parties to deposit documents and funds with the QI (often by mail), which makes it much more convenient. As a practical matter, the QI signs all documents relevant to the closing other than the conveyancing documents. The Internal Revenue Service rules allow the conveyancing documents to be executed by the parties to the transaction without involving the formality of the QI's execution. This prevents the QI from becoming "in the chain of title," which could further complicate the transaction.

Assume the party who wants to do the tax-deferred exchange is Seller 1, who signs a contract to convey the exchange property to Buyer 1. After executing a contract of sale, Seller 1 assigns his interest in the contract to the QI, then executes an *escrow agreement* with the QI that defines the QI's role. Seller 1 then locates the replacement property he is interested in purchasing and enters into a purchase contract to acquire that property; he then sends notice of designation of property to the QI, then assigns his interest in the contract as purchaser to the QI. In both transactions, the deed is drafted from Seller to Buyer (so the qualified intermediary owner never takes title to either tract). The QI, who has escrowed the funds from transaction #1, then uses these proceeds to pay Seller 2 to acquire the replacement property.

The key factor is that Seller 1 (taxpayer) has no control over the funds held by the qualified intermediary and cannot be deemed to be in receipt of those funds. In effect, the transaction results in Seller 1 conveying his property to the QI and the qualified intermediary conveying the exchange property to the seller.

Although trading is a complicated business, it can be very lucrative for real estate agents. Whereas an ordinary sale results in one brokerage commission, a two-party exchange results in two commissions.

The delayed exchange allows the closing to take place by giving the seller of the exchange property the right to designate a replacement property and take title after the closing. The 1984 Act specifically allows this, provided (1) the replacement property is identified within 45 days of the original closing, (2) the title to the replacement property is acquired within 180 days of the original closing, and (3) the replacement property is received before the designating party's tax return is due. These rules are strictly construed against the taxpayer. If these rules are not met the transaction will be treated as a sale for the designating party, not an exchange.

## Reverse Exchanges

What if a party signed the exchange contracts, but the sale of the exchange property is delayed and the seller has to acquire the replacement property before selling the existing property? Because of the nature of real estate contracts, this is not an uncommon occurrence. To deal with this issue, the Internal Revenue Code established a procedure to deal with this issue in 2000. The criteria requires that the qualified intermediary, pursuant to a specified arrangement between the taxpayers and the QI, become an Exchange Accommodation Title Holder. The taxpayer transfers the ownership of the Replacement Property to the Accommodation Title Holder (either paying cash or by getting a loan sufficient to pay the sales price to the seller of the replacement property) and then the Accommodation Title Holder will hold title until the exchange property can be sold. The seller, in effect, "parks" the replacement property with the Accommodation Title Holder until a buyer can be found for the exchange property. Then the same rules apply as the conveyance of the Relinquished Property must occur within 180 days after the property is parked with the Accommodation Title Holder. This has been deemed by the IRS as an "Exchange Last" reverse like-kind exchange.

## Installment Sales

One of the simplest major tax advantages of owning real estate is the **installment sale benefit**. It applies to all types of real estate, including residential property. Recent legislative changes have eliminated a number of previous requirements. Now there must be at least two payments, the first being in the year of sale. The remainder of the income is taxed as it is received over the future years. This allows the taxpayer to sell his property and report the gain over a period of years. Assume that the taxpayer sells property yielding a $100,000 total profit and will receive equal payments over a 10-year period. Under the installment sale provisions, instead of paying tax on $100,000 profit in one year (which may be taxed at a very high rate), the taxpayer is allowed to spread this profit over 10 years at $10,000 each year (which would probably be taxed at a much lower rate, depending on the taxpayer's tax bracket).

The Tax Reform Act of 1986 made significant changes in the installment sale rules. The bigger change, however, appears to be in the **Revenue Act of 1987**. The statute apparently divides the classes of sellers under the installment sale method into two basic categories: casual sellers and dealer sellers. Casual sellers are presumed to be private investors and individuals who are not **dealers** in real property. "Dealers" have generally been characterized as real estate developers and brokers engaged in buying and selling of real estate in the normal course of business.

For the casual seller of real property, the new law repeals the complex **proportional disallowance** rule, which was enacted under the Tax Reform Act of 1986. **Dealer property**, however, faces significantly different rules. The new 1987 law repeals the installment sale method altogether, forcing taxpayers who are dealers to recognize their income and pay tax on dealer sales even though the payments on the installment sale receivables may stretch out for years.

After January 1, 1988, installment sales are not recognized for dealer property.

For nondealer property, the installment method rules revert back to the same rules that were in effect before the proportional disallowance rule of the Tax Reform Act of 1986 was enacted. GEEZ! At the time, these rules created a whole new industry for accountants.

## At-Risk Rules

The Internal Revenue Code of 1986 provided special **at-risk limitations** on losses from income-producing activities with respect to property placed in service after 1986. Under the at-risk rules, the taxpayer's deductible losses from an activity for any taxable year are limited to the amount that the taxpayer has at risk in that particular activity. The initial amount at risk is generally considered to be the sum of the following items: cash contributions, the adjusted basis of the property contributed, and amounts borrowed for use in the activity for which the taxpayer has personal liability.

One major exception to the at-risk rules as they apply to real estate is that the taxpayers are not subject to these rules to the extent they use arm's-length, third-party, commercial financing secured solely by the real property. This exception applies only if there is a third-party lender and that third-party lender is not related to the taxpayer, the seller of the property or someone "related" to the seller, or a person who is paid a fee with respect to the taxpayer's investment in the property.

## Homeownership Rules

The Internal Revenue Code retains excellent tax benefits to homeowners. Home mortgage interest, with certain qualifications, and property taxes continue to be deductible. Homeowners still do not need to recognize the gain on the sale of a personal residence when "buying up" into another residence. In addition, the $125,000 exclusion of gain on a personal residence by taxpayers age 55 and over has been eliminated and replaced with a less restrictive exclusion.

**Deductibility of Interest.** Generally, some home mortgage interest payments for acquisition indebtedness and home equity indebtedness continue to be deductible from your gross income. Under the Internal Revenue Code, this interest deduction is limited to the first and second residences. The aggregate amount of acquisition indebtedness may not exceed $1,000,000 (or $500,000 for a married individual who files a separate return). The aggregate amount of home equity indebtedness may not exceed $100,000 (or $50,000 for a married individual who files a separate return). Acquisition indebtedness cannot be increased by refinancing. The total mortgage loans cannot exceed the lesser of: (1) the fair market value of the residence or (2) the purchase price of the residence.

The overall impact of these interest deductions (particularly in light of the non-deductibility of other interest payments under the new Internal Revenue Code) has created a tremendous market for loans secured by residential real estate to buy other items. For instance, if you bought a car, the interest payments on the car loan are not deductible. If, however, you use your home as security for the loan, the interest payments would generally be deductible.

**Gain on Sale of Principal Residence.** In passing the Taxpayers' Relief Act of 1997, Congress provided a large exclusion of gain on the sale of a taxpayer's principal residence. One may recall that the old rule allowed for rollovers of gains on principal residences and a onetime, $125,000 exclusion for taxpayers age 55 and older. This has all been eliminated.

The new law applies to the sale exchange of the taxpayer's residence after May 7, 1997. Under this new statute, a taxpayer can exclude $150,000 of gain from the sale of the taxpayer's principal residence. If the taxpayer is married, there is a $500,000 exclusion for married individuals filing jointly, if: (1) either spouse meets the ownership test, (2) both spouses meet the use test, and (3) neither spouse is ineligible for exclusion by virtue of sale or exchange of residence within the last two years. This exclusion is allowable each time the homeowner meets the eligibility requirements, but generally no more frequently than once every two years.

There is still a need to keep records of home improvements, however. The gain is calculated as the sales price, less the home's basis or adjusted basis, whichever is applicable. If, however, you are in a house that will never exceed the allowable gain, then there is no reason to keep a record of the home's basis and capital improvements. The IRS no longer receives notification of any home sales of $250,000 or under ($500,000 for married taxpayers), providing that the home buyer provides the escrow agent assurance that: (1) the home was a "principal residence," (2) there was no federally subsidized mortgage financing assistance, and (3) the final gain is excludable from gross income, *Internal Revenue Code, Section 6045(e)(5)*.

This new statute applies even if the homeowner has taken advantage of the old "once in a lifetime over 55" exclusion, so long as the two-year ownership requirement is met.

## ■ SUMMARY

The primary concerns in real estate taxation are ad valorem taxes and SUMMARY special tax benefits under federal income taxation.

Ad valorem taxation is assessed on real property in proportion to its value, which shall be ascertained as provided for by law. The formula for determining the tax payment is:

Assessed Value × Tax Rate = Tax Payment

The assessed value is determined by the assessor and collector of taxes; an assessed value is equal to the fair market value. The tax collector assesses the real estate according to the budget requirements for the taxing jurisdiction. The tax rate is set by the taxing authority in accordance to statutory formula.

In the event ad valorem taxes are delinquent, there is a penalty and procedure for judicial foreclosure against the property. In the event a foreclosure occurs, there is a two-year right of redemption during which the property owner can redeem his property after payment of taxes, fees, and penalties.

The advantages of federal income taxation are primarily attributable to depreciation, tax-deferred exchanges, and installment sales. Depreciation is an allowance for loss of value and can be calculated several different ways. Tax-deferred exchanges are means by which an owner may exchange property and defer the payment of taxes until the sale of the second piece of property. The installment sale benefit applies to any seller who sells his property and receives at least two installment payments, the first being paid to the seller in the year of the sale.

# APPENDIX

## SUBCHAPTER E. DECEPTIVE TRADE PRACTICES AND CONSUMER PROTECTION

### §17.42. Waivers: Public Policy

(a) Any waiver by a consumer of the provisions of this subchapter is contrary to public policy and is unenforceable and void; provided, however, that a waiver is valid and enforceable if:

(1) the waiver is in writing and is signed by the consumer

(2) the consumer is not in a significantly disparate bargaining position; and

(3) the consumer is represented by legal counsel in seeking or acquiring the goods or services.

(b) A waiver under Subsection (a) is not effective if the consumer's legal counsel was directly or indirectly identified, suggested, or selected by a defendant or an agent of the defendant.

(c) A waiver under this section must be:

(1) conspicuous and in bold face type of at least 10 points in size;

(2) identified by the heading "Waiver of Consumer Rights," or words of similar meaning; and

(3) in substantially the following form:

"I waive my rights under the Deceptive Trade Practices Consumer Protection Act, Section 17.41 et seq., Business & Commerce Code, a law that gives consumers special rights and protections. After consultation with an attorney of my own selection, I voluntarily consent to this waiver."

(d) The waiver required by Subsection (c) may be modified to waive only specified rights under this subchapter.

(e) The fact that a consumer has signed a waiver under this section is not a defense to an action brought by the attorney general under Section 17.47.

### §17.43. Cumulative Remedies

The provisions of this subchapter are not exclusive. The remedies provided in this subchapter are in addition to any other procedures or remedies provided for in any other law; provided, however, that no recovery shall be permitted under both this subchapter and another law of both damages and penalties for the same act or practice. A violation of a provision of law other than this subchapter is not in and of itself a violation of this subchapter. An act or practice that is a violation of a provision of law other than this subchapter may be made the basis of an action under this subchapter if the act or practice is proscribed by a provision of this subchapter or is declared by such other law to be actionable under this subchapter. The provisions of this subchapter do not in any way preclude other political subdivisions of this state from dealing with deceptive trade practices.

### §17.44. Construction and Application

(a) This subchapter shall be liberally construed and applied to promote its underlying purposes, which are to protect consumers against false, misleading, and deceptive business practices, unconscionable actions, and breaches of warranty and to provide efficient and economical procedures to secure such protection.

(b) Chapter 27, Property Code, prevails over this subchapter to the extent of any conflict.

### §17.45. Definitions

As used in this subchapter:

(1) "Goods" means tangible chattels or real property purchased or leased for use.

(2) "Services" means work, labor, or service purchased or leased for use, including services furnished in connection with the sale or repair of goods.

(3) "Person" means an individual, partnership, corporation, association, or other group, however organized.

(4) "Consumer" means an individual, partnership, corporation, this state, or a subdivision or agency of this state who seeks or acquires by purchase or lease, any goods or services, except that the term does not include a business consumer that has assets of $25 million or more, or that is owned or controlled by a corporation or entity with assets of $25 million or more.

(5) "Unconscionable action or course of action" means an act or practice which, to a consumer's detriment, takes advantage of the lack of knowledge, ability, experience, or capacity of the consumer to a grossly unfair degree.

(6) "Trade" and "commerce" mean the advertising, offering for sale, sale, lease, or distribution of any good or service, of any property, tangible or intangible, real, personal, or mixed, and any other article, commodity, or thing of value, wherever situated, and shall include any trade or commerce directly or indirectly affecting the people of this state.

(7) "Documentary material" includes the original or a copy of any book, record, report, memorandum, paper, communication, tabulation, map, chart, photograph, mechanical transcription, or other tangible document or recording, wherever situated.

(8) "Consumer protection division" means the consumer protection division of the attorney general's office.

(9) "Knowingly" means actual awareness, at the time of the act or practice complained of, of the falsity, deception, or unfairness of the act or practice giving rise to the consumer's claim or, in an action brought under Subdivision (2) of Subsection (a) of Section 17.50, actual awareness of the act, practice, condition, defect, or failure constituting the breach of warranty, but actual awareness may be inferred where objective manifestations indicate that a person acted with actual awareness.

(10) "Business consumer" means an individual, partnership, or corporation who seeks or acquires by purchase or lease, any goods or services for commercial or business use. The term does not include this state or a subdivision or agency of this state.

(11) "Economic damages" means compensatory damages for pecuniary loss, including costs of repair and replacement. The term does not include exemplary damages or damages for physical pain and mental anguish, loss of consortium, disfigurement, physical impairment, or loss of companionship and society.

(12) "Residence" means a building:

(A) that is a single family house, duplex, triplex, or quadruplex or a unit in a multiunit residential structure in which title to the individual units is transferred to the owners under a condominium or cooperative system; and

(B) that is occupied or to be occupied as the consumer's residence.

(13) "Intentionally" means actual awareness of the falsity, deception, or unfairness of the act or practice, or the condition, defect, or failure constituting a breach of warranty giving rise to the consumer's claim, coupled with the specific intent that the consumer act in detrimental reliance on the falsity or deception or in detrimental ignorance of the unfairness. Intention may be inferred from objective manifestations that indicate that the person acted intentionally or from facts showing that a defendant acted with flagrant disregard of prudent and fair business practices to the extent that the defendant should be treated as having acted intentionally.

### §17.46. Deceptive Trade Practices Unlawful

(a) False, misleading, or deceptive acts or practices in the conduct of any trade or commerce are hereby declared unlawful and are subject to action by the consumer protection division under Sections 17.47, 17.58, 17.60, and 17.61 of this code.

(b) Except as provided in Subsection (d) of this section, the term "false, misleading, or deceptive acts or practices" includes, but is not limited to, the following acts:

(1) passing off goods or services as those of another;

(2) causing confusion or misunderstanding as to the source, sponsorship, approval, or certification of goods or services;

(3) causing confusion or misunderstanding as to affiliation, connection, or association with, or certification by, another;

(4) using deceptive representations or designations of geographic origin in connection with goods or services;

(5) representing that goods or services have sponsorship, approval, characteristics, ingredients, uses, benefits, or quantities which they do not have or that a person has a sponsorship, approval, status, affiliation, or connection which he does not;

(6) representing that goods are original or new if they are deteriorated, reconditioned, reclaimed, used, or secondhand;

(7) representing that goods or services are of a particular standard, quality, or grade, or that goods are of a particular style or model, if they are of another;

(8) disparaging the goods, services, or business of another by false or misleading representation of facts;

(9) advertising goods or services with intent not to sell them as advertised;

(10) advertising goods or services with intent not to supply a reasonable expectable public demand, unless the advertisements disclosed a limitation of quantity;

(11) making false or misleading statements of fact concerning the reasons for, existence of, or amount of price reductions;

(12) representing that an agreement confers or involves rights, remedies, or obligations which it does not have or involve, or which are prohibited by law;

(13) knowingly making false or misleading statements of fact concerning the need for parts, replacement, or repair service;

(14) misrepresenting the authority of a salesman, representative or agent to negotiate the final terms of a consumer transaction;

(15) basing a charge for the repair of any item in whole or in part on a guaranty or warranty instead of on the value of the actual repairs made or work to be performed on the item without stating separately the charges for the work and the charge for the warranty or guaranty, if any;

(16) disconnecting, turning back, or resetting the odometer of any motor vehicle so as to reduce the number of miles indicated on the odometer gauge;

(17) advertising of any sale by fraudulently representing that a person is going out of business;

(18) advertising, selling, or distributing a card which purports to be a prescription drug identification card issued under Section 4151.152, Insurance Code, in accordance with rules adopted by the commissioner of insurance, which offers a discount on the purchase of health care goods or services from a third party provider, and which is not evidence of insurance coverage, unless:

(A) the discount is authorized under an agreement between the seller of the card and the provider of those goods and services or the discount or card is offered to members of the seller.

(B) the seller does not represent that the card provides insurance coverage of any kind.

(C) the discount is not false, misleading or deceptive.

(19) using or employing a chain referral sales plan in connection with the sale or offer to sell of goods, merchandise, or anything of value, which uses the sales technique, plan, arrangement, or agreement in which the buyer or prospective buyer is offered the opportunity to purchase merchandise or goods and in connection with the purchase receives the seller's promise or representation that the buyer shall have the right to receive compensation or consideration in any form for furnishing to the seller the names of other prospective buyers if receipt of the compensation or consideration is contingent upon the occurrence of an event subsequent to the time the buyer purchases the merchandise or goods;

(20) representing that a guarantee or warranty confers or involves rights or remedies which it does not have or involve, provided, however, that nothing in this subchapter shall be construed to expand the implied warranty of merchantability as defined in Sections 2.314 through 2.318 and Sections 2A.212 through 2A.216 of the Business & Commerce Code to involve obligations in excess of those which are appropriate to the goods;

(21) promoting a pyramid promotional scheme, as defined by Section 17.461.

(22) representing that work or services have been performed on, or parts replaced in, goods when the work or services were not performed or the parts replaced;

(23) filing suit founded upon a written contractual obligation of and signed by the defendant to pay money arising out of or based on a consumer transaction for goods, services, loans, or extensions of credit intended primarily for personal, family, household, or agricultural use in any county other than in the county in which the defendant resides at the time of the commencement of the action or in the county in which the defendant in fact signed the

contract; provided, however, that a violation of this subsection shall not occur where it is shown by the person filing such suit he neither knew or had reason to know that the county in which such suit was filed was neither the county in which the defendant resides at the commencement of the suit nor the county in which the defendant in fact signed the contract;

(24) failing to disclose information concerning goods or services which was known at the time of the transaction if such failure to disclose such information was intended to induce the consumer into a transaction into which the consumer would not have entered had the information been disclosed;

(25) using the term "corporation," "incorporated," or an abbreviation of either of those terms in the name of a business entity that is not incorporated under the laws of this state or another jurisdiction; or

(26) selling, offering to sell, or illegally promoting an annuity contract under Chapter 22, Acts of the 57th Legislature, 3rd Called Session, 1962 (Article 6228a-5, Vernon's Texas Civil Statutes), with the intent that the annuity contract will be the subject of a salary reduction agreement, as defined by that Act, if the annuity contract is not an eligible qualified investment under that Act or is not registered with the Teacher Retirement System of Texas as required by Section 8A of that Act.

(27) taking advantage of a disaster declared by the governor under Chapter 418, Government Code, by:

    (A) selling or leasing fuel, food, medicine, or another necessity at an exorbitant or excessive price; or

    (B) demanding an exorbitant or excessive price in connection with the sale or lease of fuel, food, medicine, or another necessity.

(c) (1) It is the intent of the legislature that in construing Subsection (a) of this section in suits brought under Section 17.47 of this subchapter the courts to the extent possible will be guided by Subsection (b) of this section and the interpretations given by the Federal Trade Commission and federal courts to Section 5(a)(1) of the Federal Trade Commission Act [15 U.S.C.A. Sec. 45(a)(1)].

(2) In construing this subchapter the court shall not be prohibited from considering relevant and pertinent decisions of courts in other jurisdictions.

(d) For the purposes of the relief authorized in Subdivision (1) of Subsection (a) of Section 17.50 of this subchapter, the term "false, misleading, or deceptive acts or practices" is limited to the acts enumerated in specific subdivisions of Subsection (b) of this section.

### §17.47. Restraining Orders

(a) Whenever the consumer protection division has reason to believe that any person is engaging in, has engaged in, or is about to engage in any act or practice declared to be unlawful by this subchapter, and that proceedings would be in the public interest, the division may bring an action in the name of the state against the person to restrain by temporary restraining order, temporary injunction, or permanent injunction the use of such method, act, or practice.

Nothing herein shall require the consumer protection division to notify such person that court action is or may be under consideration. Provided, however, the consumer protection division shall, at least seven days prior to instituting such court action, contact such person to inform him in general of the alleged unlawful conduct. Cessation of unlawful conduct after such prior contact shall not render such court action moot under any circumstances, and such injunctive relief shall lie even if such person has ceased such unlawful conduct after such prior contact. Such prior contact shall not be required if, in the opinion of the consumer protection division, there is good cause to believe that such person would evade service of process if prior contact were made or that such person would destroy relevant records if prior contact were made, or that such an emergency exists that immediate and irreparable injury, loss, or damage would occur as a result of such delay in obtaining a temporary restraining order.

(b) An action brought under Subsection (a) of this section which alleges a claim to relief under this section may be commenced in the district court of the county in which the person against whom it is brought resides, has his principal place of business, has done business, or in the district court of the county where the transaction occurred, or, on the consent of the parties, in a district court of Travis County. The court may issue temporary restraining orders, temporary or permanent injunctions to restrain and prevent violations of this subchapter and such injunctive relief shall be issued without bond.

(c) In addition to the request for a temporary restraining order, or permanent injunction in a proceeding brought under Subsection (a) of this section, the consumer protection division may request, and the trier of fact may award a civil penalty to be paid to the state in an amount of:

(1) not more than $20,000 per violation.

(2) if the act or practice that is the subject of the proceeding was calculated to acquire or deprive money or other property from a consumer who was 65 years of age or older when the actor practice occured, an additional amount of not more than $250,000.

(d) The court may make such additional orders or judgments as are necessary to compensate identifiable persons for actual damages or to restore money or property, real or personal, which may have been acquired by means of any unlawful act or practice. Damages may not include any damages incurred beyond a point two years prior to the institution of the action by the consumer protection division. Orders of the court may also include the appointment of a receiver or a sequestration of assets if a person who has been ordered by a court to make restitution under this section has failed to do so within three months after the order to make restitution has become final and nonappealable.

(e) Any person who violates the terms of an injunction under this section shall forfeit and pay to the state a civil penalty of not more than $10,000 per violation, not to exceed $50,000. In determining whether or not an injunction has been violated the court shall take into consideration the maintenance of procedures reasonably adapted to insure compliance with the injunction. For the purposes of this section, the district court issuing the injunction shall retain jurisdiction, and the cause shall be continued, and in these cases, the consumer protection division, or the district or county attorney with prior notice to the consumer protection division, acting in the name of the state, may petition for recovery of civil penalties under this section.

(f) An order of the court awarding civil penalties under Subsection (e) of this section applies only to violations of the injunction incurred prior to the awarding of the penalty order. Second or subsequent violations of an injunction issued under this section are subject to the same penalties set out in Subsection (e) of this section.

(g) In determining the amount of penalty imposed under Subsection (c), the trier of fact shall consider:

(1) The seriousness of the violation, including the nature, circumstances, extent and gravity of any prohibited act or practice.

(2) The history of previous violations.

(3) The amount necessary to deter future violations.

(4) The economic effect on the person against whom the penalty is to be assessed.

(5) Knowledge of the illegality of the act or practice.

(6) Any other matter that justice may require.

(h) In bringing or participating in an action under this subchapter, the consumer protection division acts in the name of the state and does not establish an attorney–client relationship with another person, including a person to whom the customer protection division requests that the court award relief.

### §17.48. Duty of District and County Attorney

(a) It is the duty of the district and county attorneys to lend to the consumer protection division any assistance requested in the commencement and prosecutions of action under this subchapter.

(b) A district or county attorney, with prior written notice to the consumer protection division, may institute and prosecute actions seeking injunctive relief under this subchapter, after complying with the prior contact provisions of Subsection (a) of Section 17.47 of this subchapter. On request, the consumer protection division shall assist the district or county attorney in any action taken under this subchapter. If an action is prosecuted by a district or county attorney alone, he shall make a full report to the consumer protection division including the final disposition of the matter. No district or county attorney may bring an action under this section against any licensed insurer or licensed insurance agent transacting business under the authority and jurisdiction of the State Board of Insurance unless first requested in writing to do so by the State Board of Insurance, the commissioner of insurance, or the consumer protection division pursuant to a request by the State Board of Insurance or commissioner of insurance.

### §17.49. Exemptions

(a) Nothing in this subchapter shall apply to the owner or employees of a regularly published newspaper, magazine, or telephone directory, or broadcast station, or billboard, wherein any advertisement in violation of this subchapter is published or disseminated, unless it is established that the owner or employees of the advertising medium have knowledge of the false, deceptive, or misleading acts or practices declared to be unlawful by this subchapter, or had a direct or substantial financial interest in the sale or distribution of the unlawfully advertised good or service. Financial interest as used in this section relates to an expectation which would be the direct result of such advertisement.

(b) Nothing in this subchapter shall apply to acts or practices authorized under specific rules or regulations promulgated by the Federal Trade Commission under Section 5(a)(1) of the Federal Trade Commission Act [15 U.S.C.A. 45(a)(1)]. The provisions of this subchapter do apply to any act or practice prohibited or not specifically authorized by a rule or regulation of the Federal Trade

Commission. An act or practice is not specifically authorized if no rule or regulation has been issued on the act or practice.

(c) Nothing in this subchapter shall apply to a claim for damages based on the rendering of a professional service, the essence of which is the providing of advice, judgment, opinion, or similar professional skill. This exemption does not apply to:

(1) an express misrepresentation of a material fact that cannot be characterized as advice, judgment, or opinion;

(2) a failure to disclose information in violation of Section 17.46(b)(23);

(3) an unconscionable action or course of action that cannot be characterized as advice, judgment, or opinion;

(4) breach of an express warranty that cannot be characterized as advice, judgment, or opinion;

(5) a violation of Section 17.46(b)(26).

(d) Subsection (c) applies to a cause of action brought against the person who provided the professional service and a cause of action brought against any entity that could be found to be vicariously liable for the person's conduct.

(e) Except as specifically provided by Subsections (b) and (h), Section 17.50, nothing in this subchapter shall apply to a cause of action for bodily injury or death or for the infliction of mental anguish.

(f) Nothing in the subchapter shall apply to a claim arising out of a written contract if:

(1) the contract relates to a transaction, a project, or a set of transactions related to the same project involving total consideration by the consumer of more than $100,000;

(2) in negotiating the contract the consumer is represented by legal counsel who is not directly or indirectly identified, suggested, or selected by the defendant or an agent of the defendant; and

(3) the contract does not involve the consumer's residence.

(g) Nothing in this subchapter shall apply to a cause of action arising from a transaction, a project, or a set of transactions relating to the same project, involving total consideration by the consumer of more than $500,000, other than a cause of action involving a consumer's residence.

(h) A person who violates Section 17.46(b)(26) is jointly and severally liable under the subdivsion for actual damages, court costs, and attorney's fees. Subject to Chapter 41, Civil Practice and Remedies Code, exemplary damages may be awarded in the event of fraud or malice.

### §17.50. Relief for Consumers

(a) A consumer may maintain an action where any of the following constitute a producing cause of economic damages or damages for mental anguish:

(1) the use or employment by any person of a false, misleading, or deceptive act or practice that is:

(A) specifically enumerated in a subdivision of Subsection (b) of Section 17.46 of this subchapter; and

(B) relied on by a consumer to the consumer's detriment;

(2) breach of an express or implied warranty;

(3) any unconscionable action or course of action by any person; or

(4) the use or employment by any person of an act or practice in violation of Article 21.21, Insurance Code.

(b) In a suit filed under this section, each consumer who prevails may obtain:

(1) the amount of economic damages found by the trier of fact. If the trier of fact finds that the conduct of the defendant was committed knowingly, the consumer may also recover damages for mental anguish, as found by the trier of fact, and the trier of fact may award not more than three times the amount of economic damages; or if the trier of fact finds the conduct was committed intentionally, the consumer may recover damages for mental anguish, as found by the trier of fact, and the trier of fact may award not more than three times the amount of damages for mental anguish and economic damages;

(2) an order enjoining such acts or failure to act;

(3) orders necessary to restore to any party to the suit any money or property, real or personal, which may have been acquired in violation of this subchapter; and

(4) any other relief which the court deems proper, including the appointment of a receiver or the revocation of a license or certificate authorizing a person to engage in business in this state if the judgment has not been satisfied within three months of the date of the final judgment. The court may not revoke or suspend a license to do business in this state or appoint a receiver to take over the affairs of a person who has failed to satisfy a judgment if the person is a licensee of or regulated by a state agency which has statutory authority to revoke or suspend a license or to appoint a receiver or trustee. Costs and fees of such receivership or other relief shall be assessed against the defendant.

(c) On a finding by the court that an action under this section was groundless in fact or law or brought in bad faith, or brought for the purpose of harassment, the court shall award to the defendant reasonable and necessary attorneys' fees and court costs.

(d) Each consumer who prevails shall be awarded court costs and reasonable and necessary attorneys' fees.

(e) In computing additional damages under Subsection (b), attorneys' fees, costs, and prejudgment interest may not be considered.

(f) A court may not award prejudgment interest applicable to:

(1) damages for future loss under this subchapter; or

(2) additional damages under Subsection (b).

(g) Chapter 41, Civil Practice and Remedies Code, does not apply to a cause of action brought under this subchapter.

(h) Notwithstanding any other provision of this subchapter, if a claimant is granted the right to bring a cause of action under this subchapter by another law, the claimant is not limited to recovery of economic damages only, but may recover any actual damages incurred by the claimant, without regard to whether the conduct of the defendant was committed intentionally. For the purpose of the recovery of damages for a cause of action described by this subsection only, a reference in this subchapter to economic damages means actual damages. In applying Subsection (b)(1) to an award of damages under this subsection, the trier of fact is authorized to award a total of not more than three times actual damages, in accordance with that subsection.

### §17.505. Notice: Inspection

(a) As a prerequisite to filing a suit seeking damages under Subdivision (1) of Subsection (b) of Section 17.50 of this subchapter against any person, a consumer shall give written notice to the person at least 60 days before filing the suit advising the person in reasonable detail of the consumer's specific complaint and the amount of economic damages, damages for mental anguish, and expenses, including attorneys' fees, if any, reasonably incurred by the consumer in asserting the claim against the defendant. During the 60-day period a written request to inspect, in a reasonable manner and at a reasonable time and place, the goods that are the subject of the consumer's action or claim may be presented to the consumer.

(b) If the giving of 60 days' written notice is rendered impracticable by reason of the necessity of filing suit in order to prevent the expiration of the statute of limitations or if the consumer's claim is asserted by way of counterclaim, the notice provided for in Subsection (a) of this section is not required, but the tender provided for by Subsection (d), Section 17.506 of this subchapter may be made within 60 days after service of the suit or counterclaim.

(c) A person against whom a suit is pending who does not receive written notice, as required by Subsection (a), may file a plea in abatement not later than the 30th day after the date the person files an original answer in the court in which the suit is pending. This subsection does not apply if Subsection (b) applies.

(d) The court shall abate the suit if the court, after a hearing, finds that the person is entitled to an abatement because notice was not provided as required by this section. A suit is automatically abated without the order of the court beginning on the 11th day after the date a plea in abatement is filed under Subsection (c) if the plea in abatement:

(1) is verified and alleges that the person against whom the suit is pending did not receive the written notice as required by Subsection (a); and

(2) is not controverted by an affidavit filed by the consumer before the 11th day after the date on which the plea in abatement is filed.

(e) An abatement under Subsection (d) continues until the 60th day after the date that written notice is served in compliance with Subsection (a).

### Sec. 17.5051. Mediation

(a) A party may, not later than the 90th day after the date of service of a pleading in which relief under this subchapter is sought, file a motion to compel mediation of the dispute in the manner provided by this section.

(b) The court shall, not later than the 30th day after the date a motion under this section is filed, sign an order setting the time and place of the mediation.

(c) If the parties do not agree on a mediator, the court shall appoint the mediator.

(d) Mediation shall be held within 30 days after the date the order is signed, unless the parties agree otherwise or the court determines that additional time, not to exceed an additional 30 days, is warranted.

(e) Except as agreed to by all parties who have appeared in the action, each party who has appeared shall participate in the mediation and, except as provided by Subsection (f), shall share the mediation fee.

(f) A party may not compel mediation under this section if the amount of economic damages claimed is less than $15,000, unless the party seeking to compel mediation agrees to pay the costs of the mediation.

(g) Except as provided in this section, Section 154.023, Civil Practice and Remedies Code, and Subchapters C and D, Chapter 154, Civil Practice and Remedies Code, apply to the appointment of a mediator and to the mediation process provided by this section.

(h) This section does not apply to an action brought by the attorney general under Section 17.47.

### Sec. 17.5052. Offers of Settlement

(a) A person who receives notice under Section 17.505 may tender an offer of settlement at any time during the period beginning on the date the notice is received and ending on the 60th day after that date.

(b) If a mediation under Section 17.5051 is not conducted, the person may tender an offer of settlement at any time during the period beginning on the date an original answer is filed and ending on the 90th day after that date.

(c) If a mediation under Section 17.5051 is conducted, a person against whom a claim under this subchapter is pending may tender an offer of settlement during the period beginning on the day after the date that the mediation ends and ending on the 20th day after that date.

(d) An offer of settlement tendered by a person against whom a claim under this subchapter is pending must include an offer to pay the following amounts of money, separately stated:

(1) an amount of money or other consideration, reduced to its cash value, as settlement of the consumer's claim for damages; and

(2) an amount of money to compensate the consumer for the consumer's reasonable and necessary attorneys' fees incurred as of the date of the offer.

(e) Unless both parts of an offer of settlement required under Subsection

(d) are accepted by the consumer not later than the 30th day after the date the offer is made, the offer is rejected.

(f) A settlement offer tendered by a person against whom a claim under this subchapter is pending that complies with this section and that has been rejected by the consumer may be filed with the court with an affidavit certifying its rejection.

(g) If the court finds that the amount tendered in the settlement offer for damages under Subsection (d)(1) is the same as, substantially the same as, or more than the damages found by the trier of fact, the consumer may not recover as damages any amount in excess of the lesser of:

(1) the amount of damages tendered in the settlement offer; or

(2) the amount of damages found by the trier of fact.

(h) If the court makes the finding described by Subsection (g), the court shall determine reasonable and necessary attorneys' fees to compensate the consumer for attorneys' fees incurred before the date and time of the rejected settlement offer. If the court finds that the amount tendered in the settlement offer to compensate the consumer for attorneys' fees under Subsection (d)(2) is the same as, substantially the same as, or more than the amount of reasonable and necessary attorneys' fees incurred by the consumer as of the date of the offer, the consumer may not recover attorneys' fees greater than the amount of fees tendered in the settlement offer.

(i) If the court finds that the offering party could not perform the offer at the time the offer was made or that the offering party substantially misrepresented the cash value of the offer, Subsections (g) and (h) do not apply.

(j) If Subsection (g) does not apply, the court shall award as damages the amount of economic damages and damages for mental anguish found by the trier of fact, subject to Sections 17.50 and 17.501. If Subsection (h) does not apply, the court shall award attorneys' fees as provided by Section 17.50(d).

(k) An offer of settlement is not an admission of engaging in an unlawful act or practice or liability under this subchapter. Except as otherwise provided by this section, an offer or a rejection of an offer may not be offered in evidence at trial for any purpose.

## §17.506. Damages: Defenses

(a) In an action brought under Section 17.50 of this subchapter, it is a defense to the award of any damages or attorneys' fees if the defendant proves that before consummation of the transaction he gave reasonable and timely written notice to the plaintiff of the defendant's reliance on:

(1) written information relating to the particular goods or service in question obtained from official government records if the written information was false or inaccurate and the defendant did not know and could not reasonably have known of the falsity or inaccuracy of the information;

(2) written information relating to the particular goods or service in question obtained from another source if the information was false or inaccurate and the defendant did not know and could not reasonably have known of the falsity or inaccuracy of the information; or

(3) written information concerning a test required or prescribed by a government agency if the information from the test was false or inaccurate and the defendant did not know and could not reasonably have known of the falsity or inaccuracy of the information.

(b) In asserting a defense under Subdivision (1), (2), or (3) of Subsection (a) of Section 17.506 above, the defendant shall prove the written information was a producing cause of the alleged damage. A finding of one producing cause does not bar recovery if other conduct of the defendant not the subject of a defensive finding under Subdivision (1), (2), or (3) of Subsection (a) of Section 17.506 above was a producing cause of damages of the plaintiff.

(c) In a suit where a defense is asserted under Subdivision (2) of Subsection (a) of Section 17.506 above, suit may be asserted against the third party supplying the written information without regard to privity where the third party knew or should have reasonably foreseen that the information would be provided to a consumer; provided no double recovery may result.

(d) In an action brought under Section 17.50 of this subchapter, it is a defense to a cause of action if the defendant proves that he received notice from the consumer advising the defendant of the nature of the consumer's specific complaint and of the amount of economic damages, damages for mental anguish, and expenses, including attorneys' fees, if any, reasonably incurred by the consumer in asserting the claim against the defendant, and that within 30 days after the day on which the defendant received the notice the defendant tendered to the consumer:

(1) the amount of economic damages and damages for mental anguish claimed; and

(2) the expenses, including attorneys' fees, if any, reasonably incurred by the consumer in asserting the claim against the defendant.

### §17.55. Promotional Material

If damages or civil penalties are assessed against the seller of goods or services for advertisements or promotional material in a suit filed under Section 17.47, 17.48, 17.50, or 17.51 of this subchapter, the seller of the goods or services has a cause of action against a third party for the amount of damages or civil penalties assessed against the seller plus attorneys' fees on a showing that:

(1) the seller received the advertisements or promotional material from the third party;

(2) the seller's only action with regard to the advertisements or promotional material was to disseminate the material; and

(3) the seller has ceased disseminating the material.

### §17.555. Indemnity

A person against whom an action has been brought under this subchapter may seek contribution or indemnity from one who, under the statute law or at common law, may have liability for the damaging event of which the consumer complains. A person seeking indemnity as provided by this section may recover all sums that he is required to pay as a result of the action, his attorney's fees reasonable in relation to the amount of work performed in maintaining his action for indemnity, and his costs.

### §17.56. Venue

Except as provided by Article 5.06 1(8), Insurance Code, an action brought which alleges a claim to relief under Section 17.50 of this subchapter shall be brought as provided by Chapter 15, Civil Practice and Remedies Code.

### §17.565. Limitation

All actions brought under this subchapter must be commenced within two years after the date on which the false, misleading, or deceptive act or practice occurred or within two years after the consumer discovered or in the exercise of reasonable diligence should have discovered the occurrence of the false, misleading, or deceptive act or practice. The period of limitation provided in this section may be extended for a period of 180 days if the plaintiff proves that failure timely to commence the action was caused by the defendant's knowingly engaging in conduct solely calculated to induce the plaintiff to refrain from or postpone the commencement of the action.

## §17.57. Subpoenas

The clerk of a district court at the request of any party to a suit pending in his court which is brought under this subchapter shall issue a subpoena for any witness or witnesses who may be represented to reside within 100 miles of the courthouse of the county in which the suit is pending or who may be found within such distance at the time of trial. The clerk shall issue a separate subpoena and a copy thereof for each witness subpoenaed. When an action is pending in Travis County on the consent of the parties a subpoena may be issued for any witness or witnesses who may be represented to reside within 100 miles of the courthouse of a county in which the suit could otherwise have been brought or who may be found within such distance at the time of the trial.

## §17.58. Voluntary Compliance

(a) In the administration of this subchapter the consumer protection division may accept assurance of voluntary compliance with respect to any act or practice which violates this subchapter from any person who is engaging in, has engaged in, or is about to engage in the act or practice. The assurance shall be in writing and shall be filed with and subject to the approval of the district court in the county in which the alleged violator resides or does business or in the district court of Travis County.

(b) The acceptance of an assurance of voluntary compliance may be conditioned on the stipulation that the person in violation of this subchapter restore to any person in interest any money or property, real or personal, which may have been acquired by means of acts or practices which violate this subchapter.

(c) An assurance of voluntary compliance shall not be considered an admission of prior violation of this subchapter. However, unless an assurance has been rescinded by agreement of the parties or voided by a court for good cause, subsequent failure to comply with the terms of an assurance is prima facie evidence of a violation of this subchapter.

(d) Matters closed by the filing of an assurance of voluntary compliance may be reopened at any time. Assurances of voluntary compliance shall in no way affect individual rights of action under this subchapter, except that the rights of individuals with regard to money or property received pursuant to a stipulation in the voluntary compliance under Subsection (b) of this section are governed by the terms of the voluntary compliance.

## §17.59. Post Judgment Relief

(a) If a money judgment entered under this subchapter is unsatisfied 30 days after it becomes final and if the prevailing party has made a good faith attempt to obtain satisfaction of the judgment, the following presumptions exist with respect to the party against whom the judgment was entered:

(1) that the defendant is insolvent or in danger of becoming insolvent; and

(2) that the defendant's property is in danger of being lost, removed, or otherwise exempted from collection on the judgment; and

(3) that the prevailing party will be materially injured unless a receiver is appointed over the defendant's business; and

(4) that there is no adequate remedy other than receivership available to the prevailing party.

(b) Subject to the provisions of Subsection (a) of this section, a prevailing party may move that the defendant show cause why a receiver should not be appointed. Upon adequate notice and hearing, the court shall appoint a receiver over the defendant's business unless the defendant proves that all of the presumptions set forth in Subsection (a) of this section are not applicable.

(c) The order appointing a receiver must clearly state whether the receiver will have general power to manage and operate the defendant's business or have power to manage only a defendant's finances. The order shall limit the duration of the receivership to such time as the judgment or judgments awarded under this subchapter are paid in full. Where there are judgments against a defendant which have been awarded to more than one plaintiff, the court shall have discretion to take any action necessary to efficiently operate a receivership in order to accomplish the purpose of collecting the judgments.

### §17.60. Reports and Examinations

Whenever the consumer protection division has reason to believe that a person is engaging in, has engaged in, or is about to engage in any act or practice declared to be unlawful by this subchapter, or when it reasonably believes it to be in the public interest to conduct an investigation to ascertain whether any person is engaging in, has engaged in, or is about to engage in any such act or practice, an authorized member of the division may:

(1) require the person to file on the prescribed forms a statement or report in writing, under oath or otherwise, as to all the facts and circumstances concerning the alleged violation and such other data and information as the consumer protection division deems necessary;

(2) examine under oath any person in connection with this alleged violation;

(3) examine any merchandise or sample of merchandise deemed necessary and proper; and

(4) pursuant to an order of the appropriate court, impound any sample of merchandise that is produced in accordance with this subchapter and retain it in the possession of the division until the completion of all proceedings in connection with which the merchandise is produced.

### §17.61. Civil Investigative Demand

(a) Whenever the consumer protection division believes that any person may be in possession, custody, or control of the original copy of any documentary material relevant to the subject matter of an investigation of a possible violation of this subchapter, an authorized agent of the division may execute in writing and serve on the person a civil investigative demand requiring the person to produce the documentary material and permit inspection and copying.

(b) Each demand shall:

(1) state the statute and section under which the alleged violation is being investigated, and the general subject matter of the investigation;

(2) describe the class or classes of documentary material to be produced with reasonable specificity so as to fairly indicate the material demanded;

(3) prescribe a return date within which the documentary material is to be produced; and

(4) identify the members of the consumer protection division to whom the documentary material is to be made available for inspection and copying.

(c) A civil investigative demand may contain a requirement or disclosure of documentary material which would be discoverable under the Texas Rules of Civil Procedure.

(d) Service of any demand may be made by:

(1) delivering a duly executed copy of the demand to the person to be served or to a partner or to any officer or agent authorized by appointment or by law to receive service of process on behalf of that person;

(2) delivering a duly executed copy of the demand to the principal place of business in the state of the person to be served;

(3) mailing by registered mail or certified mail a duly executed copy of the demand addressed to the person to be served at the principal place of business in this state, or if the person has no place of business in this state, to his principal office or place of business.

(e) Documentary material demanded pursuant to this section shall be produced for inspection and copying during normal business hours at the principal office or place of business of the person served, or at other times and places as may be agreed on by the person served and the consumer protection division.

(f) No documentary material produced pursuant to a demand under this section, unless otherwise ordered by a court for good cause shown, shall be produced for inspection or copying by, nor shall its contents be disclosed to any person other than the authorized employee of the consumer protection division without the consent of the person who produced the material. The office of the attorney general shall prescribe reasonable terms and conditions allowing the documentary material to be available for inspection and copying by the person who produced the material or any duly authorized representative of that person. The office of the attorney general may use the documentary material or copies of it as it determines necessary in the enforcement of this subchapter, including presentation before any court. Any material which contains trade secrets shall not be presented except with the approval of the court in which the action is pending after adequate notice to the person furnishing the material.

(g) At any time before the return date specified in the demand, or within 20 days after the demand has been served, whichever period is shorter, a petition to extend the return date for, or to modify or set aside the demand, stating good cause, may be filed in the district court in the county where the parties reside, or a district court of Travis County.

(h) A person on whom a demand is served under this section shall comply with the terms of the demand unless otherwise provided by a court order.

(i) Personal service of a similar investigative demand under this section may be made on any person outside of this state if the person has engaged in conduct in violation of this subchapter. Such persons shall be deemed to have submitted themselves to the jurisdiction of this state within the meaning of this section.

## §17.62. Penalties

(a) Any person who, with intent to avoid, evade, or prevent compliance, in whole or in part, with Section 17.60 or 17.61 of this subchapter, removes from any place, conceals, withholds, or destroys, mutilates, alters, or by any other means falsifies any documentary material or merchandise or sample of merchandise is guilty of a misdemeanor and on conviction is punishable by a fine of not more than $5,000 or by confinement in the county jail for not more than one year, or both.

(b) If a person fails to comply with a directive of the consumer protection division under Section 17.60 of this subchapter or with a civil investigative demand for documentary material served on him under Section 17.61 of this subchapter, or if satisfactory copying or reproduction of the material cannot be done and the person refuses to surrender the material, the consumer protection division may file in the district court in the county in which the person resides, is found, or transacts business, and serve on the person, a petition for an order of the court for enforcement of Sections 17.60 and 17.61 of this subchapter. If the person transacts business in more than one county, the petition shall be filed in the county in which the person maintains his principal place of business, or in another county agreed on by the parties to the petition.

(c) When a petition is filed in the district court in any county under this section, the court shall have jurisdiction to hear and determine the matter presented and to enter any order required to carry into effect the provisions of Sections 17.60 and 17.61 of this subchapter. Any final order entered is subject to appeal to the Texas Supreme Court. Failure to comply with any final order entered under this section is punishable by contempt.

### §17.63. Application

The provisions of this subchapter apply only to acts or practices occurring after the effective date of this subchapter, except a right of action or power granted to the attorney general under Chapter 10, Title 79, Revised Civil Statutes of Texas, 1925, as amended, prior to the effective date of this subchapter.

# Table of Cases

# Index and Glossary

**Co-owner:** In condominiums, a person, firm, corporation, partnership, association, trust, or other legal entity, or any combination thereof, who owns an apartment or apartments within the condominium project, 398

**Corporate charter:** The official document indicating the existence of the corporation as authorized by the Secretary of State, 71

**Corporation:** An artificial person or legal entity created by or under the authority of the laws of the state in which it is incorporated, 70

**Corpus:** Trust assets, the body of a trust, 76

**Council of co-owners:** All of the co-owners of a condominium project, 398

**Counteroffer,** 165

**County court:** Court whose jurisdiction is in the county in which it is situated but has a ceiling on the dollar amount that can be litigated within its jurisdiction, 6

**Court-ordered deeds,** 209

**Courts of civil appeals:** In Texas, the level of courts above the district court that only appellate jurisdiction, that is, they can only hear cases that have been previously tried in a district court, 6, 7

**Courts of equity,** 5

**Covenant against encumbrances:** A covenant in a deed that provides that such estate is at the time of the execution of such conveyance free from encumbrances, 204

**Covenant of seizin:** A covenant in a deed that provides that previous to the time of execution of said conveyance, the grantor has not conveyed the same estate, or any right, title, or interest therein, to any person other than the grantee, 204

**Covenants:** deeds, 214; subdivision restrictions, 423

**Curtesy:** The estate to which a man is entitled upon the death of his wife to the lands she seized in possession in fee during her marriage. It is a freehold estate for the term of his natural life, 51

**D**

**Dealer property:** Real property held for other than personal use, 443

**Deceptive Trade Practices—Consumer Protection Act,** 123, Appendix I

**Declaration:** *see* Master deed

**Declining-balance method of depreciation,** 437

**Deed:** Contract used to convey title to real estate, 201

**Deed of trust:** In Texas, a three-party mortgage wherein the mortgagor conveys the property in trust to a trustee as security for a debt owing the beneficiary (lender), 244

**Deed restrictions:** Private covenants affecting the use of real estate, which are enforced by the grantor, affected property owners, or subdivision developer on purely contractual theory, 423

**Deed without warranties:** *see* Bargain and sale deed

**Defeasance clause,** 244

**Delivery:** The final and absolute transfer of a deed, properly executed, to the grantee, or to some person for his use, in such manner that it cannot be recalled by the grantor, 166, 210, 212

**Department of Housing and Urban Development,** 410

**Department of Veteran Affairs,** 411

**Depreciation:** A provision in the Internal Revenue Code that allows for a deduction for the loss of value of an asset for tax purposes, 436

**Descent and distribution:** Heirship, 222

**Determinable fee:** *see* Fee on conditional limitation

**District courts:** In Texas, state courts whose jurisdiction is within a statutorily defined district that is generally larger than that of the county. Its jurisdiction is, for the most part, similar to that of county courts, but there is no dollar limit on the amount that can be litigated, 6

**Doctrine of merger:** A doctrine by which the earnest money contract in a real estate transaction is extinguished by absorption into the deed or other instruments passed at closing, 192–193; *see also under* Easements, 96

**Dominant estate:** An estate to which a servitude or easement is attached, 17, 91; *see also* Subsurface rights

**Dower:** A species of life estate that a woman is by law entitled to claim upon the death of her husband, also the lands of which he was seized and fee-issued during the marriage and any that might possibly have been inherited, 51

**Dragnet clause:** *see* Future advance clause

**Dual agency:** Agency in which the licensee represents both the buyer and the seller, 150

**Due-on-transfer clause:** A clause often found in mortgages that provides for the secured note to be accelerated to maturity if the property is conveyed, 258

**Due process of law:** Law in its regular course of administration through courts of justice, 2

**E**

**Earnest money:** A payment made by a purchaser of real estate as evidence of good faith, 187

**Easement:** A privilege, service, or convenience that one has in the property to another, 91, 93–95

**Easement appurtenant:** An easement that is attached to and belongs to a dominant estate, which passes incident

**General common elements:** *see* Common elements

**General partnerships:** *see* Partnership

**General warranty deed:** A deed in which the grantor warrants or guarantees the title to real property against defects existing before the grantor acquired title or arising during the grantor's ownership, 204

**Government National Mortgage Association,** 411

**Grantee:** One to whom a grant is made, 211

**Granting clause:** Conveyancing clause in a deed, 251

**Grantor:** The person by whom a grant is made, 211, 244

**Gross lease:** A lease of property under the terms of which the landlord pays all property charges regularly incurred through ownership. The tenant pays a fixed charge for the term of the lease, 377

**Ground lease:** Lease of land only, sometimes secured by the improvements placed on the land by the user, 378

**Guide meridians,** 57

## H

**Habendum and warranty clause:** deed, 208; deeds of trust, 252

**Habitability, warranty of:** Guarantee that premises occupied by a tenant are habitable. The definition of habitability is a fact question and is determined by the jury, 381

**Hazardous Solid Waste Amendments of 1984,** 413

**HOEPA:** The Homeowner's Equity Protection Act of 1994, 276

**Holographic will:** A will wholly in the writing of the testator, 214

**Home Equity Line of Credit Loan:** Mortgage allowing a homeowner to have a pre-approved loan that can be drawn down in increments, 265–266

**Home Mortgage Disclosure Act,** 412

**Homestead:** A legal estate that is a place of residence for a family or a single adult person that is exempt from sale by creditors except under certain specified conditions, 20

**Homestead old age tax deferral,** 433

**Houston-Galveston Area Council,** 416

**HUD-1 form,** 306

**HUD-Code Manufactured Home:** A structure transported in one or more sections which is 8 body feet or more in width and 40 body feet or more in length, 90

## I

**Implication:** Type of easement creation, 93

**In gross:** Type of easement, 91

**Incorporeal hereditaments:** Anything, the subject of property, which is inheritable and not tangible or visible, 91

**Independent contractor:** One who, exercising independent employment, contracts to do a piece of work according to his own methods and without being subject to the control of his employer except as to the result of the work, 119

**Index of grantors and grantees,** 234

**Industrialized Housing:** A residential structure designed for the use and occupancy of one or more families constructed in one or more modules built on location, 90

**Installment land contract:** An executory contract for sale of real estate, which usually lasts for a term of years. It is also known as a contract for deed, 194

**Installment sale benefits:** Provision in the Internal Revenue Code by which the profit on the sale of one's capital asset can be spread over a series of years, 442

**Installment sale contracts:** Executory contracts for the conveyance of real property, 264

**Inter vivos trust:** A trust that is established during the lifetime of the trustor, 76

**Interest:** The compensation allowed by law for the use, forbearance, or detention of money, 118, 274, 276

**Interlineations:** The act of writing between the lines of an instrument; also what is written between lines, 167

**Internal Revenue Code of 1986:** Body of laws that codify and delineate the levying, collecting, and enforcing of federal tax laws, 435

**Internal Revenue Service,** 311

**Interstate:** Transaction and proceedings that take place between and among the several states, 2

**Interstate Land Sales Full Disclosure Act,** 410

**Interval ownership condominiums:** Ownership of a condominium by exclusive fee title for a period in which the owner is entitled to possession. Unlike timesharing condominiums, the fee title only vests for a period of time and does not change from year to year, 401

**Intestate:** One who dies without leaving a will, 222

**Intrastate:** Alludes to procedures and transactions which take place entirely within the boundaries of a particular state, 2

## J

**Joint adventure:** *see* Joint venture

**Joint tenancy:** An estate held by two or more persons having one and the same interest, which includes a right of survivorship; the entire tenancy on the decease of any of the joint tenants remains to the survivors and, ultimately, fee will vest in the last survivor, 63

**Joint venture:** An association of two or more persons to carry out a single business enterprise, which is limited in its scope and duration, for a profit, 67

**Mineral interests:** An interest in the minerals in land, including the right to take minerals or the right to receive a royalty on those minerals, 16

**Minors:** In Texas, people under the age of 18, 163

**Modified Accelerated Cost Recovery System,** 436, 439

**Monopoly:** A private interest vested in one or more persons or companies consisting of the exclusive right to carry on a particular business or trade, 120

**Mortgage:** An instrument by which real property is offered to secure the payment of a debt or obligation, 242

**Mortgagee:** The lender of money, 242

**Mortgagor:** The person who executes a mortgage, usually pursuant to the borrowing of money, 264

**Mother Hubbard clause:** *see* Additional property clause

**Multiple listing:** An agreement among brokers who belong to the Multiple Listing Service that all listings will be placed on a mutually available list, that all brokers may sell any property on the list, and that the commission will be split in a predetermined fashion, 115

**Municipal court:** In Texas, a court whose territorial authority is confined to the city or community in which it is designated. It is one of the courts of lower jurisdiction, 6

**Municipal enforcement of deed restrictions,** 424

**Mutual assent:** The "meeting of the minds" in a contract, 164

**Mutual mistake of material fact,** 166

**N**

**National Flood Insurance Act,** 412

**National Historic Preservation Act,** 414

**Negotiable instrument:** An instrument signed by a maker or drawer, containing an unconditional promise to pay a certain sum of money, which can be passed freely from one person to another. This is often reflected in a promissory note or bank draft, 259

**Net lease:** One in which the tenant pays some or all of the operating expenses, giving the owner a net amount of income, 378

**Net listing:** A listing in which the owner receives a net price for the sale of his property; the broker's commission, if any, is the amount that exceeds the net figure, 115

**Nonconforming use:** A previously existing use that is inconsistent with the current zoning designation, 420

**Nonfreehold estate:** A leasehold estate, 328

**Nonoperational estates,** 51

**Nonrecourse:** Creating no personal liability, 259

**Notario Publico:** A high-ranking Mexican official, not to be confused with a "notary public," 237–238

**Notary public:** An authority appointed by the Secretary of State to take acknowledgment or proofs of written instruments, protest instruments permitted by law to be protested, administer oaths, and take depositions, as is now or may hereafter be conferred by law upon county clerks, 237

**Nothing-further certificate,** 287

**Novation:** The substitution of a new obligation for an old one, such that the previous obligor is released from liability, 267

**"Nucleus of description" theory,** 54

**O**

**Offer:** A proposal to make a contract, 164

**Offeree:** One to whom an offer is made, 164

**Offeror:** One who makes an offer, 164

**Office of Interstate Land Sales Registration,** 410

**Official Public Records of Real Property,** 233

**Old age tax deferral:** An exemption provided in Texas that prohibits the sale of a homestead for taxes if one or more of the occupants is 65 years or older, 433

**Open agency listing:** An authorization given by a property owner to a real estate agent wherein the agent is given the nonexclusive right to secure a purchaser, 115

**Option contract,** 193

**Options to purchase, in lease,** 380

**Oral earnest money contract,** 181

**Original basis:** The original cost of an asset, 440

**Original contractor:** A contractor who has the direct contractual relationship with the owner of the property or his agent, 313, 326

**Original jurisdiction:** Having jurisdiction to hear the case for the first time, before it is tried in any other court, or appealed, 6

**Ostensible authority:** Such authority as a principal, intentionally or by want of ordinary care, causes or allows a third party to believe that the agent possesses, 134, 155

**Owner's title policy,** 287; form, 289–294

**P**

**Parol evidence rule:** A rule of procedure that provides that parol or extrinsic evidence is not admissible to add to, subtract from, vary, or contradict judicial or official records or documents, or written instruments that dispose of property or are contractual in nature, and which are valid, complete, unambiguous, and unaffected by accident or mistake, 168

**Partial release fees:** Fees paid to the lender for a partial release of property, which is secured by a note, 279

**Partial releases,** 258

**Rule of Capture:** A Texas legal concept that allows the owner of the land to pump unlimited quantities of ground water from under the land, 49

**Rural homestead:** A homestead that is not in an urban area and can consist of not more than 200 acres, 36

**S**

**S corporation:** A regular Texas corporation that has elected certain tax benefits through Subchapter S of the Internal Revenue Code, 74

**Sale lease-back:** A situation where the owner of a piece of property wishes to sell the property and retain occupancy by leasing it from the buyer, 262

**Salesperson:** Defined, *see* pp. 100, 102

**Second lien:** A lien or encumbrance that ranks second, right behind the first lien, mortgage, or encumbrance, 257

**Secretary of State:** In Texas, an executive officer who performs, in addition to other functions, the maintaining of all official records for the State of Texas and companies doing business in the State of Texas, 68

**Securities and Exchange Commission:** Agency of the government that oversees and passes rules and regulations in furtherance of the Securities and Exchange Acts of 1933 and 1934, 410

**Security:** A bond, note, certificate of indebtedness, or other negotiable or transferable instrument evidencing debt or ownership, 118, 407

**Security agreement:** A form of chattel mortgage commonly used in Texas, 85

**Separate property:** In Texas, property acquired before marriage or acquired by gift, devise, or descent after marriage, 44

**Servient estate:** An estate encumbered by an easement or servitude, which is reserved for the use of another, 91

**Settlor:** One who establishes a trust, 76

**Severable improvements:** Those improvements that can be removed without material injury to the real estate, 319

**Severalty:** An estate that is held by a person in his own right without any other person being joined or connected with him, 61

**Sex Offender Registration:** Provision of the Texas Code of Criminal Procedure requiring sex offenders to register their residential address with the Texas Department of Public Safety, 137

**Shareholder:** One who owns shares in a corporation, 70

**Sheriff's deed:** Typically, a deed executed by a sheriff pursuant to a writ of execution or at a foreclosure sale, 209

**Sherman Antitrust Act:** Federal law that condemns contracts, culmination, and conspiracies in restraint of trade and monopolizing, attempts to monopolize, and combinations and conspiracies to monopolize trade, 120

**Shifting executory use:** A use that is so limited that it will be made to shift or transfer itself from one beneficiary to another upon the occurrence of a certain event after its creation. *See* Contingent remainder

**Sole control community property:** Community property that is subject to the sole control, management, or disposition of a single spouse that maintains all of its characteristics of community property, 46

**Special agency:** An agency relationship by which one is employed to conduct a particular transaction or a piece of business for his principal or authorized to perform a specific act but does not have the power to bind his principal, 136

**Special exceptions:** A use that is permitted within a certain zoning designation, but subject to control and supervision of the municipal authority, 419

**Special warranty deed:** A deed in which the grantor warrants or guarantees the title only against defects arising during his ownership of the property and not against defects existing before the time of his ownership, 208

**Specific performance:** Performance of a contract in a specific form in which it was made and according to the precise terms agreed upon, 5, 189

**Spoke annexation,** 421

**Spot zoning,** 420

**Spreading,** 281

**Springing executory use:** A use limited to arise on future event in which no preceding use is limited. It does not take effect in derogation of any interest of the grantor, and remains in the grantor in the meantime. *See* Fee on condition precedent

**Standard parallels:** 57

**State district courts:** State civil courts with no dollar-limit jurisdiction, 6

**State Property Tax Board:** 430

**Statute of frauds:** Texas statute that provides that no suit or action shall be maintained on certain classes of contracts unless there shall be a note or memorandum thereof in writing and signed by the party to be charged or by his authorized agent. Its object is to close the door to the numerous frauds and perjuries, 162

**Statutory estate:** Estate created by Texas statute or constitution, 11, 20

**Statutory retainage:** *see* Retainage

**Straight-line method of depreciation,** 437

**Subagent:** An agent appointed by one who is himself an agent, or a person employed by an agent to assist him in transacting the affairs of his principal, 136

**Subcontractor:**  A contractor who has a direct contractual relationship and works under an original contractor. He has no direct contractual relationship with the owner of the property or his agent, 313, 314

**Subject to:**  When a grantee takes title to real property "subject to" a mortgage, he is not responsible to the holder of the promissory note for the payment of any portion of the amount due, 266, 268

**Sublease:**  A lease given by a lessee to a sublessee for a part of the premises or for a period of time less than the remaining term of the lessee's original lease, 379

**Submergence:**  *see* Subsidence

**Subordination,**  378

**Subrogation:**  The substitution of one person in the place of another with reference to a lawful claim, demand, or right, 257

**Subsidence:**  When water advances to cover the previously dry land, 230

**Subsurface rights:**  Rights of the owner to use land below the surface, 16

**Superfund Amendments & Reauthorization Act of 1986,**  326, 413

**Supervening illegality:**  One of the methods to terminate an agency, 156

**Supreme Court of the United States:**  The highest court to which any cases can be appealed in the United States, 6

**Surface Mining Control and Reclamation Act,**  17

**Surface rights:**  The rights of the owner to use the surface estate of his property, 17

**T**

**Tacking,**  221

**"Taking" issue,**  420

**Tax deed:**  Deed executed at an ad valorem tax sale, 226, 433

**Tax-deferred exchange:**  Provision in tax law that allows for the exchange of "like kind" property, 441

**Tax Equity and Fiscal Responsibility Act of 1982,**  119

**Tax exemptions,**  433

**Tax-free exchange:**  *see* Tax-deferred exchange

**Tax rate:**  Rate for ad valorem taxes, expressed as dollars per hundred, set by elected officials, 431

**Tax Reform Act:**  *see* Internal Revenue Code of 1986

**Tax rollback,**  434

**Tax sales:**  Sales made pursuant to state law to satisfy a debt created by delinquent taxes, 226

**Tenancy:**  The estate of a tenant whether it be in fee, for life, for years, at will, or otherwise, 328

**Tenancy by the entireties:**  An estate created by the conveyance to husband and wife whereupon each becomes seized and possessed to the entire estate. After the death of one, the other survivor takes the whole. It may be terminated only by a joint action of husband and wife during their lives, 63

**Tenancy in common:**  An estate where property is held by several indivisible titles by entity of possession, 61, 392, 405

**Tenant:**  One who has the temporary use and occupation of real property owned by another person (called the "landlord"). The duration and terms of his tenancy usually are fixed by law or by an instrument called a lease, 221, 328

**Tenant's lien,**  309; statute, 330

**Testamentary trusts,**  76

**Testator:**  One who makes a testament or will, 214

**Texas Antiquities Code,**  414

**Texas Constitution:**  The most fundamental body of law in the State of Texas. It serves the same function for Texas as the U.S. Constitution serves for the United States, 2

**Texas Courts of Appeals:**  The Texas civil appellate court system, 6

**Texas Highway Commission,**  416

**Texas Parks and Wildlife Department,**  416

**Texas Real Estate Commission:**  The official agency in Texas for administering rules and regulations that govern real estate licensing, 99

**Texas Real Estate License Act,**  100

**Texas Residential Construction Commission Act:**  A Texas statute providing for resolution of disputes between homeowners and new home-builders, 321

**Texas Supreme Court:**  The highest court in the State of Texas to which any point of law or case can be appealed, 6

**Texas Trust Code:**  Body of laws that governs trusts generally in the State of Texas, 76

**Texas Uranium Surface Mining and Reclamation Act,**  17

**Texas Water Development Board,**  416

**Timeshare condominiums:**  Condominiums that are owned among several co-tenants who have the right, by contractual agreement with each other, to use the condominium only for a certain time period (usually from two to four weeks). This time period may change from year to year depending upon the arrangement of the co-tenants' contractual agreement, 401

**Title:**  Evidence of ownership; or in adverse possession, a regular chain of transfers from or under the sovereignty of the soil, 218

**Title commitment,**  287

them. The existing mortgages remain on the property, and the wraparound assumes an inferior position to those mortgages, 268

**Writ of attachment:**   A legal seizure of property issued by judges and clerks of the district and county courts to prevent alienation of real property pending a judicial proceeding, 312

**Writ of execution:**   A writ to put in force the judgment or decree of a court, 261

**Writ of possession:**   A writ issued by a court of competent jurisdiction commanding a sheriff to restore the premises to the true owner, 386

## Z

**Zoning:**   Exercise of police power through municipal land-use regulation, 417

**Zoning commissioners:**   Those appointed by a city council to review and enforce the city's zoning ordinance, 418